THE PORTABLE

KOBBÉ'S OPERA GUIDE

EDITED BY

THE EARL OF HAREWOOD

A PERIGEE BOOK

Perigee Books
are published by
The Berkley Publishing Group
200 Madison Avenue
New York, NY 10016

Library of Congress Cataloging-in-Publication Data

The portable Kobbé's opera guide / edited by
The Earl of Harewood.
    p. cm.
  "A Perigee Book."
  Includes index.
  ISBN 0-399-51872-X
  1. Operas—Stories, plots, etc.   I. Harewood, George Henry
Hubert Lascelles, Earl of, date.   II. Title: Kobbé's opera guide.
III. Title: Opera guide.
MT95.P7 1994   94-3880 CIP MN
782. 1' 09—dc20

Cover design by David Gatti

Printed in the United States of America
1 2 3 4 5 6 7 8 9 10

This book is printed on acid-free paper.

EDITORS' NOTE

We have not attempted to be consistent in the use of role
names. Generally, we have preferred to use whichever
version seems more natural to an English speaker, but if, in discussion of the opera in question, we have found that a character
tends to be referred to by his or her name in the original language, we have stuck to that. So, Electra is found in Strauss and
Mozart, but Orfeo in Monteverdi. In the case of Gluck's *Orfeo*,
we have used English forms of the names since the opera comes
in both Italian and French versions.

Translations of opera titles have been given in nearly all cases
unless they are either very obvious (*Tristan und Isolde*) or virtually untranslatable (*Così fan Tutte*). The English translations
of Russian, Czech and other Eastern European operas generally
appear as the main heading, with the original language
beneath.

Some more rarely performed operas have their plots sum-
marised in a brief outline rather than the more discursive treatment which has always been a mark of the Kobbé style. This
discrimination is purely for reasons of space, and does not reflect our opinion of these works.

Contents

Claudio Monteverdi
(1567–1643)

LA FAVOLA D'ORFEO
The Legend of Orpheus

OPERA in a prologue and five acts; text by Alessandro Striggio. First produced privately at the Accademia degl'Invaghiti, Mantua, February 1607; revived in 1904.

IT is fortunate that so early in the history of opera (as opposed to the longer history of music drama), there should in Monteverdi have appeared a master and that this, his first opera, should be a masterpiece. *Orfeo* opens with a clarion call, a thrice-played *toccata* in C major, still unrivalled in its way amongst operatic introductions. The Prologue consists of a five-verse recitation by Music (*soprano*) of her powers. Each verse is introduced by a *ritornello* which is played for the sixth time after the last verse. These *ritornelli* are used throughout to create appropriate atmosphere for the various scenes.

ACT I. Shepherds and Nymphs are rejoicing over the wedding of Orfeo (*soprano* or *tenor*) and Euridice (*soprano*). The two Shepherds and the Nymph have solo verses in between the choruses, and Orfeo himself sings the first of the big solos, 'Rosa del ciel'. This is followed by a stanza for Euridice, and a repeat of the choruses. The act ends with a beautiful chorus praying their happy state may bring no misfortune on the lovers.

ACT II begins with a long pastoral episode for Orfeo and the Shepherds. The mood of contentment and happiness is suddenly broken by the entrance of the Messenger (*soprano*) with the news of Euridice's death: Orfeo's seeming unclouded happiness and serenity have aroused the envy of the gods. The chorus is apprehensive of the nature of the Messenger's errand, and only Orfeo is unaware of the approach of tragedy. The Messenger's emotional and dramatic solo, 'Ahi, caso acerbo', and the few phrases of dialogue with Orfeo at the beginning, ending with his stunned 'Ohimè', produce an extraordinary intensity by the simplest means. Orfeo's lament, 'Tu se' morta, se' morta mia vita', is short and restrained, even classical, but the evocative power of the music is unsurpassed. The chorus sings an elaborate threnody and mourns the tragedies of Euridice bitten by the Serpent and of Orfeo transfixed by grief.

ACT III. In impressively solemn declamation, Orfeo is confronted by Hope (*soprano*). He resolves to seek Euridice in Hades. Charon's (*bass*) sombre refusal is followed by Orfeo's attempt by means of his power as a singer to gain admission to

1

Hades. The elaborately ornamented song is a test of virtuosity. Charon admits he has listened with intense pleasure, but yields only after Orfeo renews his plea in a simple recitative. The act ends with a madrigalesque chorus of Spirits.

ACT IV. Proserpine (*soprano*) and Pluto (*bass*), King and Queen of the Underworld, discuss Orfeo's plight, and prompted by his wife and urged by the captive spirits, the King of the Underworld agrees to release Euridice to her husband. The triumphant Orfeo's song of rejoicing is cut short as he breaks Pluto's stipulation and looks back to Euridice.

ACT V. The lamenting Orfeo, wandering on the plains of Thrace, summons nature itself, which has often benefited from his singing, to join him in his mourning. Apollo (*tenor* or *baritone*), Orfeo's father, descends from Heaven and tells his son he will be translated to divine immortality, and amongst the stars will be able to see Euridice again. Father and son ascend to Heaven singing again music full of coloratura ornament. The chorus sings its valediction in a lively 'Moresca'.

IL RITORNO D'ULISSE IN PATRIA
Ulysses's Return Home

PROLOGUE and five acts (now often three), by Claudio Monteverdi; première, Venice, 1641. Ulysses (*tenor*) on his way back from the Trojan War has incurred the enmity of Neptune (*bass*), but is protected by Minerva (*soprano*). His wife Penelope (*mezzo-soprano*) bemoans her loneliness since he left. He lands in Ithaca, lamenting that Neptune's wrath prevents him returning home. Minerva promises to help rout the suitors who are besieging Penelope. Ulysses in disguise finds his old herdsman Eumaeus (*tenor*) and then his son Telemacus (*tenor*), to whom he reveals himself. Penelope offers herself as a prize to whoever can string and draw Ulysses's bow. The suitors fail; Ulysses himself, still disguised, succeeds, transfixing all the suitors with an arrow. Penelope is not convinced of his identity until an old scar on his shoulder is revealed. Joyfully they celebrate their reunion.

L'INCORONAZIONE DI POPPEA
The Coronation of Poppaea

OPERA in a prologue and three acts by Claudio Monteverdi; text by G. F. Busenello. Première at Teatro di Giovanni e Paolo in Venice, 1642; revived in 1905.

L'INCORONAZIONE DI POPPEA is Monteverdi's last opera, written when he was seventy-five and, according to most observers, his finest achievement. The result of the collaboration between Monteverdi and the Venetian poet Francesco Busenello is a work unique in its own and indeed in succeeding centuries. The focus is on dramatic truth and real-life emotions and their expression; illicit (but passionate) love triumphs over 'right', and in the course of the action injustice is more or less manifestly done to Octavia, Seneca and Ottone.

After the overture, in a Prologue (omitted in some versions), the goddesses of Fortune and Virtue (*sopranos*) flaunt their own successes and each mocks the shortcomings of the other, until the goddess of Love (*soprano*) vaunts her pre-eminence; against her, the others are as nothing, a point of view neither seems able nor indeed anxious to refute.

ACT I. Just before dawn, outside Poppaea's house in Rome, two of Nero's guards lie asleep. Ottone (*soprano*), Poppaea's lover returning from serving abroad, sings lovingly of the house and Poppaea, until he notices the soldiers and realises he has been supplanted by the Emperor. His world is in ruins around him. The soldiers wake up and gossip about the miseries of soldiering in Rome. Suddenly they realise Nero is approaching and fall silent.

We meet Poppaea (*soprano*) and Nero (*soprano*) in one of the great love scenes of opera, the first of several in the score. She, spurred by ambition as well as love and unwilling to let him go, employs every delaying tactic known to woman, and by the time he has gone has obtained a half-promise that he will put aside the Empress Octavia to marry her. Her reiterated 'Tornerai?' has more tenderness than urgency, catching perfectly the freshness and beauty of passion, which has no regard for conventional ideas of right or wrong.

With Nero's promise very much in her mind, Poppaea expresses her feelings in an aria, 'Speranza, tu mi vai il core accarezzando' (Hope, you caress my heart). Her old nurse, Arnalta (*contralto*), tries to warn her against the snare which ambition may set for her – the Empress could seek revenge and Nero's love cool – but Poppaea believes that Love is on her side.

In her palace, Octavia (*mezzo-soprano*), the Empress, laments her humiliation and misery, in a noble utterance denouncing Nero's infidelity and calling on Jove to punish her erring spouse: 'Disprezzata regina' (Scorned Empress). Her old nurse (*mezzo-soprano*; in Leppard's version, Drusilla) tries to comfort her. Seneca (*bass*) is ushered in and gently but firmly urges the Empress to find refuge in stoicism; thus will she ensure that beneath fortune's blows she grows ever more glorious herself. Octavia objects that to promise greater glory from the

3

torments she undergoes is specious and empty comfort, and her page attacks the old philosopher for his platitudes.

Alone, Seneca has a vision of Pallas, goddess of Wisdom, who warns him that to interfere in the imperial quarrel will result in his own death. Seneca welcomes the idea, claiming to have conquered human fear. As if to reinforce his presentiment Nero tells him that he plans to set aside Octavia and marry Poppaea. Seneca warns that the heart is often a bad counsellor; he begs him to avoid arousing the resentment of the people and the Senate, and, if nothing else, to have regard for his own good name. Passions mount on both sides. Nero announces his decision to marry Poppaea and leaves Seneca in a fury.

Nero returns to Poppaea. After an extended love duet she denounces Seneca who, she says, has maintained publicly that Nero's ability to rule depends on Seneca's counsel. Nero orders one of the guards to carry a message immediately to Seneca to the effect that he must die that day. In lyrical phrases Nero reassures Poppaea that she will see what true love can do.

Ottone makes a last attempt at reconciliation with Poppaea but she spurns him and exults in now belonging to Nero. Ottone realises that, though his heart contains nothing but love for Poppaea, his pride prompts him to plot her murder. Drusilla (*soprano*), who loves Ottone, comes to bring him comfort. Ottone tries to assure her that he now loves her, but his protestations ring just short of true.

ACT II begins with one of the great scenes of the score, the death of Seneca. First, heralded by Mercury and welcomed by the old philosopher, Nero's sentence of death is communicated by Liberto, Captain of the Praetorian Guard. Seneca announces to his pupils that the time has come to prove in deed the stoic virtues he has so long preached in theory. In passionate chorus – a three-part madrigal of high and moving quality – they urge him to live, but he bids them prepare the bath in which his guiltless blood will flow away. The next scene, in which figured Virtue, Seneca and 'Un Choro di Virtù', has been lost, but Busenello and Monteverdi follow it with two scenes in direct contrast. The first, almost an intermezzo, is with Octavia's page, who tells a pretty maid that he has a strange pain in his heart; will she help him cure it? As the music flows its spirited way, it is obvious that she will. The second scene has an elated Nero carousing with his friend Lucano: 'Hor che Seneca è morto, cantiam' (Now that Seneca is dead, let us sing). The macabre situation is stressed rather than played down when Nero, left alone, sings with the utmost conviction of his love for Poppaea.

A scene between Nero and Poppaea has been lost and we next see Ottone deciding he cannot kill Poppaea. Octavia at her most domineering arrives and persuades him, not without threats to slander him to Nero, that it is his duty to kill Poppaea.

Drusilla rejoices in her love for Ottone, who enters to confide to her that he has in mind to commit a terrible crime for which he must disguise himself in her clothes. She is happy to offer garments and indeed her life's blood for him.

In her garden Poppaea opens her dialogue with Arnalta with the same words to which Nero rejoiced at the news of the death of Seneca: 'Hor che Seneca è morto'. She demands that Love shall guide her ship safe to harbour. Arnalta sings a lullaby of great beauty: 'Oblivion soave'. It has the desired effect and the goddess of Love herself descends while Poppaea sleeps and in an aria promises to watch over her as she lies defenceless. Ottone enters in disguise and with murder in his heart, but the goddess intervenes, Poppaea wakes up and she and Arnalta think they recognise Drusilla, who runs away. The goddess of Love is triumphant: having defended Poppaea, that very day she will see that she becomes Empress!

ACT III. Drusilla sings happily of her love for Ottone. She is identified by Arnalta and arrested for the attempt on Poppaea's life. She protests her innocence, and not all the threats of Nero can make her change her story. As she is about to be taken off to torture and death, Ottone appears and claims, despite Drusilla's protests, that he was responsible. A short duet between them leaves Nero in no doubt of Ottone's guilt and he pronounces sentence of banishment on him. Drusilla says she will share in his exile, and Ottone recognises the good fortune which has suddenly overtaken him in what might have proved his most evil hour. Nero announces his resolve to divorce Octavia and send her into exile.

It only remains for the lonely Octavia on the one hand and the far from lonely Poppaea and Nero on the other to meet their fates. Poppaea, announcing her re-birth, learns that it was Ottone and not Drusilla who attempted to murder her, and Nero reveals that he thinks Octavia was behind the plot. She shall be exiled and Poppaea that very day will become Empress! In grave, confident music, which only later develops into coloratura flourishes, the couple privately hymn their love.

Arnalta celebrates her own involvement in Poppaea's triumph by recalling in an aria past indignities as a servant and exulting over the prospect of future grandeur.

Octavia bids an unhappy but dignified farewell to Rome, her native land, her friends. She claims, quite inaccurately, that she is innocent, but her lament is in the great tradition started by Monteverdi himself.

The triumphant Poppaea is greeted first by Nero, who bids her ascend to the apex of sovereignty, then by the consuls and tribunes of Rome itself who hymn her coronation. There is a short intervention (often cut) by the goddess of Love and Venus, and the opera ends with the idyllic celebration by the two protagonists of their love and their triumph, 'Pur ti miro' (I behold thee).

Francesco Cavalli
(1602–1676)

LA CALISTO

PROLOGUE and three acts; première, Venice, 1651. Calisto (*soprano*) has caught the eye of Jove (*bass*) but rejects him; he takes the form of Diana (*mezzo-soprano*), with more success. Meanwhile Endymion (*counter-tenor*) is in love with the real Diana, who indignantly bans Calisto from her entourage when the nymph seeks to renew what she thinks is their mutual pleasure. Endymion and Diana pursue their passion – Diana's vow of chastity holding her back, however. Juno (*soprano*), to whom Calisto relates her experiences with 'Diana', recognises her husband's style. Jove-Diana has an embarrassing encounter with Endymion, who is eventually reunited with the real goddess. Calisto is turned into a little bear by the jealous Juno, and is received into the heavens as a star.

Henry Purcell
(1658–1695)

DIDO AND AENEAS

OPERA in a prologue (in the libretto but never set to music, or lost) and three acts; text by Nahum Tate. Première at Mr. Josias Priest's Boarding School for Girls, Chelsea, London, 1689.

THE overture has the traditional slow and quick sections, and is unmistakably tragic in feeling.

ACT I. Dido (*soprano*) with her court is attended by her lady-in-waiting, Belinda ('Shake the cloud from off your brow'). This is contrasted with the grief-laden aria for Dido, 'Ah, Belinda, I am prest with torment', a magnificent expression of sorrow, dignified and restrained as befits the Queen of Carthage, but worthy of the tragedy it foreshadows. Belinda (*soprano*) says it is the presence of the 'Trojan guest' which is the cause of the Queen's unhappiness. The chorus supports her implied suggestion, that a marriage between the two would solve Carthage's troubles. In the ensuing dialogue between Dido and Belinda, we have a taste of Purcell's extraordinary gift for compressing the most complex emotions into a few bars, and then relieving the tension and crystallising the situation in a set piece for chorus. It is introduced by a duet for Belinda and an Attendant (*mezzo-soprano*). Again, Dido's court attempts to encourage her ('The hero loves as well as you') and, after Aeneas's entrance and Dido's cold reply to his opening sentence, the chorus, then Belinda, and finally the chorus again support his suit in music of surpassing freshness. The scene ends with a Triumphing Dance, and Dido's acceptance of Aeneas (*tenor* or *high baritone*) is celebrated by the whole court to lively and simple music.

The Sorceress's (*mezzo-soprano*) cave. She invokes her evil companions to join her in plotting the destruction of Dido and of Carthage. The scene, with its laughing choruses, its reference in the strings to the horn calls of the hunt in progress, its echo chorus and its dance, proves insidious beauty can attend the course of evil just as surely as that of good.

ACT II. The Grove. Dido and Aeneas, attended by Belinda and their train, pause in the middle of the hunt. Belinda and the chorus and later the Second Woman sing of the peculiar delights of the spot they have reached, of its attractions for the goddess Diana and of how it was the scene of Actaeon's death. Meanwhile, the scene is of much activity, in the midst of which are Dido and her husband-to-be, Aeneas. The idyll comes to an end as Dido hears distant thunder, and Belinda warns the company to shelter, 'Haste, haste to town'. All leave, but Aeneas is stopped by Mercury (*soprano* or *tenor*) – the Sorceress's 'trusty elf' in disguise – who tells Aeneas that he brings Jove's command not to delay his task, of founding the new Troy on Latin soil. Aeneas, in a magnificent recitative, replies that the decision is easily reached – it is the god's command – but to reconcile himself with leaving Dido is something than which, he says, he 'with more ease could die'.

The published versions of the score make Act II end with this recitative. Benjamin Britten, in his realisation of the opera, supplied other music of Purcell's to fit the six further lines in the original libretto, as well as a dance.

ACT III. The harbour of Carthage. The Trojan fleet prepares to depart. A brisk, cynical song for a sailor (*soprano* or *tenor*), 'Come away, fellow sailors, come away', sets the mood, repeated by the chorus and followed by a hearty dance. The Sorceress and her supernatural band appear, and the First and Second Witches (*sopranos*) sing a duet, which ends with peals of highly organised demonic laughter. The Sorceress in a short solo plans the destruction of Aeneas; this is underlined by the chorus. After a dance for the Witches and Sailors, Dido and Belinda arrive, looking for Aeneas.

Dido is full of foreboding and Aeneas's first words confirm her worst fears. She taunts his attempts to explain, and, when he says he will defy the gods and stay, she will have none of a lover who had a thought of leaving her. 'Away, away', she reiterates at the end of their duet; and it is not until his departure that she admits 'Death must come when he is gone'. The chorus prepares for Dido's great farewell to life. Her aria, 'When I am laid in earth', is one of the greatest moments in all opera, an unsurpassed piece of controlled vocal writing. 'Remember me,' sings the Queen, 'but ah! forget my fate'. The sense of tragedy is increased by the chorus which follows, 'With drooping wings, ye cupids come, and scatter roses on her tomb'. It is the longest sustained number in the hour-long score, and in it Purcell shifts the emphasis of the tragedy from the particular to the universal at the same time as he provides a uniquely beautiful ending to his opera.

Purcell, a supreme writer for the voice, wrote a vast quantity of songs, many of them connected with the stage and all of the greatest beauty. It is opera's eternal loss that *Dido* should be the only true opera he left behind him; the feeling for dramatic expression, which it shows to have been his, only emphasises what was removed by his death at less than forty years of age.

George Frideric Handel
(1685–1759)

THE music of Handel's operas represents a high point of the first half of the eighteenth century, and such obstacle as there is between us and them lies in conventions which they respect and from which we were until recently largely removed. This was a period of consolidation in operatic history, and in Handel's day convention had become entrenched, with the aria, and more particularly the aria *da capo* with its obligatory repeat, reigning supreme; with an exit following each aria, itself a purely individual expression; with virtually no ensembles and no chorus, so that even an opera's final number tended to be sung by the principals together; with libretti geared to provide opportunities for 'typical' arias (expressing pity, sorrow, amorous intention, regret, despair, determination, martial ardour, etc.) rather than for character development and surprise. Castrati ruled the roost, and the music for such heroes as Julius Caesar and Tamburlaine was written for vocal virtuosi whose breath control and volume were apparently sufficient to compensate for a physique which was often obese, sometimes comic and all too frequently unmanly.

Small wonder then that the revival of interest in Handel's operas which came in the early 1920's brought with it much revision, sometimes of musical detail in the interest of musico-dramatic continuity, almost always in the *tessitura* of the voices, so as to preserve an attempt at physical verisimilitude. In a word, castrato heroes became baritones or basses. In the mid-twentieth century, during the consolidation period of the Handel revival, contrariwise a more scholarly attitude began to prevail, so that more or less strapping mezzos tackled the great heroes of antiquity, with results which were occasionally comic to look at and not always heroic vocally, but which allowed Handel's orchestration to be retained and such anomalies avoided as for instance the changing of an obbligato for flute to one for oboe, in order to cut out the solecism of matching the higher instrument to a baritone when Handel had intended it to be in double harness with a mezzo. Each solution has its snags, as has the more obviously reprehensible (but, in view of length, tempting) practice of truncating *da capo* arias, which when cut often sound either pointless or too long, sometimes paradoxically both. Performance of Handel's operas, more or less complete, with the pitch of the original voices maintained (even in an age with no castrati), is by the late twentieth century the accepted norm.

Handel himself often made changes to suit the exigencies of a new situation, altering a soprano part for tenor, importing a number from another work (and another situation) for a new prima donna, adding or subtracting as seemed to him best in each new set of circumstances. But his changes often involved recomposition, and there is a strong case to be made for his dramatic awareness within the convention, for his sheer stage craft. Most modern revivals which are sung to anything like the composer's requirements, and respect his intentions, serve to demonstrate that Handel's operas are the product of one of the medium's composers of unquestioned genius.

GIULIO CESARE
Julius Caesar

OPERA in three acts by George Frideric Handel; libretto by Nicola Haym. Première February 20, 1724, at Haymarket Theatre, London.

GIULIO CESARE is one of Handel's most completely satisfactory works for the stage. Paradoxically, few other scores contain so many numbers which have made their way with the public out of context. But Handel's arias are far more effective when surrounded by the dramatic circumstances which provide for the situation and emotion they are intended to express than without them.

ACT I. A broad plain by the Nile. During a short overture the curtain rises to show the Egyptians in chorus, greeting the victorious Romans. Julius Caesar (*contralto*[1]) enters to celebrate his triumph over his rival, Pompey, at Pharsalus ('Presti omai l'Egizia terra'). Cornelia (*contralto*) and her son Sesto (*soprano* or *tenor*) beg him show clemency in his hour of victory. At the same moment, Achilla offers Caesar the hospitality of Ptolemy (whose military help Pompey had invoked) and shows him the severed head of Pompey as proof of Ptolemy's change of heart. Caesar condemns the senseless cruelty ('Empio, dirò, tu sei, togliti') and leaves Cornelia to attempt suicide, to dismiss the proffered love of Curio (*bass*), the Roman tribune, and to lament her wretched loneliness in a beautiful slow aria ('Priva son d'ogni conforto'). Her son Sesto in his turn excitedly vows vengeance on the criminals ('Svegliatevi nel core').

Ptolemy's palace. Cleopatra (*soprano*) resolves to pit her celebrated beauty against her brother's gift of Pompey's head in a bid for Caesar's favour ('Non disperar'). Achilla (*bass*) tells Ptolemy (*contralto*[1]) of Caesar's fury at the murder of Pompey and himself offers to kill Caesar and so stabilise Ptolemy's throne if the King will grant him in reward the hand of the beautiful Cornelia. Ptolemy agrees and inveighs against Caesar ('L'empio, sleale, indegno').

Caesar's camp. The emperor in expressive recitative contemplates the monument he has raised to Pompey's memory and reflects on the transience of fame. Cleopatra enters, describing herself as Lidia, one of the Queen's women. Caesar is captivated by her beauty ('Non è si vago e bello'). Cleopatra celebrates her success ('Tutto può donna vezzosa') and then with Nireno, her confidant (*contralto*), hides to watch Cornelia movingly apostrophise the urn which contains all that she adored ('Nel tuo seno, amico sasso'). When she vows vengeance on her husband's murderer, Sesto takes the burden upon himself. Cleopatra, still calling herself Lidia, offers her help. Sesto rejoices because his dream of justice may now come true ('Cara speme'). Cleopatra exults at the prospect of victory over Ptolemy, then sings an aria ('Tu la mia stella sei'), whose melodious and lovelorn accents to some degree contradict the uncompromising nature of the sentiments of the recitative.

Ptolemy's palace. The King greets Caesar effusively, offering him entertainment but in no way deceiving the Roman, who, in a fine aria with (uniquely in Handel's operas) a horn obbligato, invokes a hinting simile ('Va tacito e nascosto') to describe the

---

[1] Sung originally by a castrato.

relationship of Egyptian king and Roman general. Caesar and the Romans leave Ptolemy and his Egyptian courtiers, and Achilla points out Cornelia to Ptolemy, who is no less struck by her beauty than is his general. When the Roman lady and Sesto advance and challenge Ptolemy to mortal combat, guards are ordered to take the youth to prison and Cornelia to the King's harem, where Achilla may visit her at the King's pleasure. Cornelia scorns Achilla's offer of freedom in return for marriage, and the act ends with a fine duet of farewell for mother and son.

ACT II. Cleopatra's palace. The Queen plans to ravish Caesar's senses with the sight of Virtue enthroned on Mount Parnassus. The orchestral *sinfonia* which accompanies his entrance and the revelation of the goddess starts a process of seduction which is fully accomplished when Cleopatra herself, in the guise of the goddess, sings the delectable 'V'adoro pupille', an aria of tender, sensual beauty. Caesar's growing passion is evident in his aria, 'Se in fiorito ameno prato'.

The garden of the harem. Cornelia sings sadly of her departed happiness ('Deh piangete, o mesti lumi') and resists the blandishments successively of Achilla and Ptolemy, who, unknown to Achilla, is his rival for her favours. Cornelia is joined by Sesto, bent on avenging his father's death, to which end Nireno contributes by offering to take him secretly to the King's presence. Cornelia urges him onward ('Cessa omai di sospirare') and Sesto proclaims his resolve in a splendid martial aria, 'L'angue offeso mai riposa'.

The scene returns to Cleopatra, who waits in the guise of Lidia for Caesar. As they are about to declare their love, Curio announces an imminent attempt by Ptolemy's soldiers on Caesar's life. Cleopatra, revealing her identity, announces she will quell the conspirators herself. She urges Caesar to flee the danger, a solution he scorns ('Al lampo dell'armi'). He rushes out and the conspirators can be heard shouting for his death. The music depicts the Queen's conflicting emotions – her desire for revenge on her enemies and her self-pity, set against her fears for the safety of the man whose love she now craves more than the political favour she once sought.

Ptolemy's harem. The King, surrounded by his favourites, including Cornelia, sings of his amorous feelings: 'Belle dee di questo core'. Sesto rushes in and attempts to stab him, but is prevented by Achilla, who brings news that Caesar has jumped from the palace window into the harbour, where he was presumably drowned. Cleopatra is now bringing her troops against Ptolemy to avenge Caesar's death. Achilla asks for the promised reward of Cornelia's hand in marriage, but is sharply turned down by Ptolemy. As the King departs for battle, Achilla mutters of revenge. Sesto in despair tries to kill himself, but

11

Cornelia again nerves him to the task in hand and the act ends with a renewal of resolve ('L'aura che spira').

ACT III. A wood near Alexandria. Achilla, with a band of soldiers, prepares to defect to Cleopatra's side in revenge for Ptolemy's treachery towards him. A Battle Symphony describes the conflict, from which Ptolemy's supporters emerge victorious. The King orders his sister to prison ('Domerò la tua fierezza'). The scene ends with her great lament, 'Piangerò la sorte mia', a beautiful *largo* aria with a vocal line of the greatest possible simplicity and containing, as contrasting middle section, a vision of herself returning as a ghost to haunt her wicked brother.

The harbourside. To *andante* music that breathes the very spirit of consolation, Caesar reappears to describe his escape from death by drowning ('Dall'ondoso periglio') and to pray for comfort in his loneliness ('Aure, deh, per pietà'). Sesto and Achilla enter, the latter mortally wounded in the battle against Ptolemy. The dying general gives Sesto the signet ring which will gain the instant obedience of his troops, who know a subterranean approach to the palace. Caesar takes charge; his determination is displayed in his comparison of his progress to that of a waterfall ('Quel torrente che cade dal monte'). Sesto feels the processes of justice are nearing completion ('La giustizia ha già sull'arco').

Cleopatra's apartments. The Queen's sad farewell to her attendant women is interrupted by the victorious arrival of Caesar to free her. Cleopatra is jubilant, and she celebrates the prospect of victory ('Da tempeste il legno infranto').

Ptolemy makes a final attempt to persuade Cornelia of his love for her, but is threatened by her with a dagger. He eventually falls dead after a duel with Sesto, whose entry saves his mother from herself avenging her murdered husband, a deed she nevertheless greets with proper enthusiasm ('Non ha più che temere').

The harbour at Alexandria. Caesar and Cleopatra's final triumph is celebrated with a march, a duet for the happy couple ('Caro! Bella! più amabile beltà') and a chorus of rejoicing.

ALCINA

THREE acts, by George Frideric Handel; première, London, 1735. Text after Ariosto. The enchantress Alcina (*soprano*) lives with her sister Morgana (*soprano*) and her general Oronte (*tenor*) on a magic island. Many knights have wooed her but have been transformed into non-human shape. Ruggiero (*mezzo-soprano*), her latest captive, has forgotten his betrothed, Bradamante (*contralto*), who, disguised as Ricciardo, has been shipwrecked on the island. Morgana discovers her and her guardian Melisso (*bass*), and is attracted to 'him'. Oronte, rebuffed by Morgana, spitefully tells Ruggiero that Alcina loves Ricciardo. Ruggiero will not believe that Ricciardo is Bradamante, until Melisso gives him a magic ring which breaks the spell and he recalls his love. Alcina in distress attempts to hold Ruggiero but is defeated when he smashes the urn containing her magic and all the knights are restored to human form.

SERSE
Xerxes

OPERA in three acts by George Frideric Handel; libretto by Nicola Minato and Silvio Stampiglia. Première April 26, 1738, revived in 1924.

THE libretto of *Serse*, with its alternating serious, even tragic, scenes and farce, allows Handel more freedom of movement and method than his previous operas. Gone is the convention that a character should exit after an aria, reduced are the number of *da capo* numbers in the score. The libretto makes *Serse* seem lighter and more varied in texture than Handel's other operas; but it was Handel who chose the libretto (an adaptation made by Stampiglia for Bononcini) and so brilliantly took advantage of its possibilities.

King Xerxes is the ancestor of the Persian King Darius III, whom Alexander the Great spectacularly defeated in 331 B.C., but his invasion of Greece figures hardly at all in the opera, apart from a mention of the destruction of the bridge of boats across the Hellespont. Instead, the opera deals with Xerxes's misfortunes in love and the absolute authority wielded by a tyrant. Xerxes (*mezzo-soprano*) and his brother Arsamenes (*mezzo-soprano*) are in love with the same girl, Romilda (*soprano*). Romilda loves Arsamenes, and Xerxes in retaliation banishes him from his kingdom. Xerxes is already betrothed to Amastris (*mezzo-soprano*), who is distressed by his infidelity but disguises herself in military uniform in order to be near him and regain his love. Atalanta (*soprano*), Romilda's sister, is also in love with Arsamenes and tries to make certain that Romilda marries Xerxes in order that she may have Arsamenes. Two comic figures play their part in the story: the servant Elviro (*baritone*) and the sisters' father, Ariodate (*bass*), the bumbling commander of Xerxes's army.

ACT I. The overture, slow, then quick, and ending with a gigue, leads straight to one of the most famous tunes ever written. Once known as 'Handel's celebrated Largo' (actually marked *larghetto*, not *largo*), this Victorian sanctification does less than justice to a glorious tune in which Xerxes whimsically apostrophises the beauties of a tree in his garden in a tune of chaste simplicity and total memorability.

Arsamenes and the grumbling Elviro arrive in time to hear the *sinfonia* which heralds the offstage singing of Arsamenes's beloved Romilda, who sings charmingly of love's victims, and not least of Xerxes, whom she has observed singing in heartfelt accents to a mere tree and who now appears to listen to and be enraptured by her singing. Romilda's second aria ('Va godendo vezzoso e bello') has two flutes in the accompaniment.

Arsamenes shall be the ambassador to declare his brother's new love, orders Xerxes, in a charming song, whose melody is taken up in a second verse with precisely opposite sentiments by Arsamenes, declaring his confidence in Romilda's love for him. Arsamenes alerts Romilda to Xerxes's intentions, a turn of events which intrigues Atalanta, herself in love with Arsamenes (arietta). Xerxes's advances to Romilda are rejected, whereupon, finding Arsamenes false to his charge, Xerxes banishes him from his kingdom. Arsamenes laments the new situation in a beautiful aria ('Meglio in voi col mio partire'), and the lovelorn Xerxes addresses Romilda in music only slightly less serious in tone, but to no avail. In an aria of touching simplicity, Romilda asserts that she is proof against temptation.

Xerxes's spurned betrothed, the foreign Princess Amastris, sings an aria of resolute character as befits her military disguise. She observes Xerxes congratulate his victorious general Ariodate whose daughter Romilda, he promises, shall marry a member of the royal family. Ariodate's simplistic philosophy is never to question, and he puts it forward in an aria of some complacency. Xerxes celebrates the strength of his new love in an extended *da capo* aria ('Più che penso').

Elviro is entrusted by Arsamenes with a letter for Romilda, an assignment he accepts with an easy show of confidence, leaving his master to lament his fate in a touching *larghetto* aria. Amastris takes a more robust view of her situation, in a grand *da capo* aria vowing vengeance on her false betrothed. Confronting Romilda, Atalanta refers to the King as 'your Xerxes', but Romilda refuses to listen to insinuations that Arsamenes may be false to her ('Se l'idol mio'). Atalanta ends the act with an extended and convincing exposition which amounts to a belief that all's fair in love as in war ('Un cenno leggiadretto').

ACT II. Elviro, disguised as a flower-seller, is on his way to deliver Arsamenes's letter to Romilda. He pauses to tell Amastris about Xerxes's passion for Romilda. Amastris inveighs against her false lover, and persuades Elviro to deliver Arsamenes's letter to Atalanta who promises to give it to Romilda. The plot thickens when, encountering the lovesick Xerxes, Atalanta gives him the letter, pretending it was written to her and that Arsamenes is only feigning to love Romilda, which, she assures the King, Arsamenes will persist in denying.

Xerxes, seizing his chance, shows the letter to Romilda, who seems to believe it was written to Atalanta but persists in rejecting the advances of the monarch. He reacts with considerable passion in a grand *da capo* aria ('Se bramate d'amar'), which is as full of pain as of spleen. Romilda alone gives way melodiously to jealousy, but Amastris takes her case even harder and only Elviro's intervention prevents her suicide. Elviro tells the unfortunate Arsamenes what he has heard from Atalanta, namely that Romilda has yielded to the importunity of Xerxes. Arsamenes's grief is all too genuine ('Quella che tutta fe').

Xerxes and Ariodate inspect the famous bridge but Arsamenes, still bewailing the shock of love betrayed, continues his lamentations, until discovered by Xerxes, who proclaims his intention not only to pardon his brother but to unite him with the woman he now knows he loves: none other than Atalanta! Arsamenes, in spite of disappointment, seems to take heart from the new situation, and continues to express to the King confidence not only in his love for Romilda but in the belief that it is requited ('Sì, la voglio'). Atalanta will have none of Xerxes's advice that she should forget Arsamenes, but Xerxes half convinces himself that there is comfort to be taken from the precarious position of the lover who does not know whether to hope or despair.

Elviro witnesses the storm which causes the bridge of boats to collapse. Xerxes and the hidden Amastris in duet bemoan the sting of jealousy, Xerxes sighing for Romilda, Amastris for Xerxes, a dramatic situation both complex and full of irony. Amastris, unobserved, watches Xerxes attempt yet again to seduce Romilda but Romilda stands firm and when Amastris in soldierly guise takes her side, the guard on Xerxes's orders intervenes. Only Romilda's standing with the King induces them to withdraw, and Amastris leaves Romilda to finish the act with a splendid celebration of the steadfast quality of her love for Arsamenes.

ACT III. Romilda and Arsamenes finally force Atalanta to admit her devious scheming, but she buoyantly looks to the future and a new love ('Nò, se tu mi sprezzi'). Xerxes takes advantage of Romilda's presumption in freeing what he thinks of as the young soldier and Romilda agrees to marry him if her father consents. Xerxes rejoices in a *da capo* aria of confident elegance, but Arsamenes turns on Romilda. She goes off, as she says, to death, leaving Arsamenes to bemoan his solitary fate in music of true poignancy ('Amor, tiranno Amor').

Xerxes obliquely tells Ariodate that his daughter shall soon be affianced to one equal in rank to the King himself. Ariodate assumes Xerxes must mean his brother Arsamenes, and rejoices at the honour. Xerxes attempts to pursue Romilda, but she confesses that Arsamenes once loved her and contrives to make him doubt her virtue. Xerxes orders the guards to kill Arsamenes. Romilda in despair seeks help from her supposed champion, Amastris, who gives her a letter for the King, before lamenting her continued love for her faithless betrothed.

Arsamenes and Romilda return to indulge in lovers' quarrelling and go off in opposite directions, only to return, still arguing to the same tune, to interrupt the ceremony which Ariodate is preparing and which promises to become their wedding. Xerxes arrives in time to hear that Ariodate's bungling misunderstanding of his instructions has resulted in his beloved Romilda marrying Arsamenes. Only the disconcerting arrival of Amastris's letter turns his fury away from Ariodate and towards his own frustration, which he vents in a magnificent virtuoso aria ('Crude furie'). It only remains for Amastris to reappear, offer Xerxes her love and prepare for an ending apparently happy for all except perhaps Atalanta.

SEMELE

OPERA in three acts by George Frideric Handel; libretto by William Congreve. First performed Covent Garden, February 10, 1744 (in oratorio form). Stage première 1925.

THE Novello vocal score (about 1878) of Handel's *Semele* carries the following introduction: 'The libretto was originally written as an opera-book by Congreve *but, being found unsuitable for the stage*, was converted by some slight alteration into an Oratorio.' What that unsuitability was and why stage performances in England had exclusively been given by amateurs until the summer of 1959 – the bicentenary year of Handel's death – remains a mystery. The music of *Semele* is so full of variety, the recitative so expressive, the orchestration so inventive, the characterisation so apt, the general level of invention so high, the action so full of credible situation and incident – in a word, the piece as a whole is so suited to the operatic stage – that one can only suppose its neglect to have been due to an act of abnegation on the part of opera companies, unless of course it is caused by sheer ignorance.

ACT I. There is an Overture, *maestoso* followed by an *allegro* of no less consequence. A stately gavotte sets the scene – the Temple of Juno at Thebes, where religious ceremonies are in progress. Semele (*soprano*), the daughter of King Cadmus (*bass*), is betrothed to Athamas (*alto*), Prince of neighbouring Boeotia, but is secretly in love with Jupiter (*tenor*), who has appeared to her in disguise. The priest (*bass*) proclaims the acceptance by Juno of a sacrifice, and the assembled people rejoice: 'Lucky omens bless our rites'. Her father and her fiancé ask Semele to delay the wedding ceremony no longer, and she begs the deity to help her in her predicament: 'Oh Jove, in pity teach me which to choose.'

Semele, in a scene occasionally omitted from performance, describes her mournful state ('The morning lark') and Athamas urges his love for her ('Hymen, haste, thy torch prepare!'). Ino, her sister (*contralto*), is afraid Semele will yield to Athamas's pleas, and seems about to admit her own passion for Athamas; Semele urges her to tell all her thoughts. Cadmus admonishes Ino ('Why dost thou thus untimely grieve?'), and her comments on the situation, together with those of Semele and Athamas, turn what seems to begin as a bass aria into a magnificent quartet. The fire on the altar dies down and this sign of godly displeasure is received with dismay by the populace: 'Avert these omens, all ye powers'. It is clear that Jupiter's displeasure has been incurred. The people are alarmed ('Cease your vows, 'tis impious to proceed') and rush out of the Temple. There is a scene for Ino and Athamas, by the end of which the latter has understood Ino's love for him. Cadmus returns with his followers, and tells of having seen Semele snatched aloft by an eagle. The others lament her disappearance, until the priests hail Cadmus and tell him that Jove's favour has lit on his family, an explanation of events which brooks no contradiction, as Semele from a cloud appears to reassure them in a beautiful aria: 'Endless pleasure, endless love Semele enjoys above'.

ACT II. A purposeful *sinfonia* leads to a scene between Juno (*contralto*) and her attendant Iris (*soprano*), who has been sent to discover Semele's whereabouts. Juno vows vengeance on Semele, while Iris tells her of the protective obstacles with which Jupiter has surrounded his new favourite; they include two dragons. In a vigorous aria ('Hence, hence, Iris hence away') Juno tells her they will together persuade Somnus, the God of sleep, to 'seal with sleep the wakeful dragons' eyes', so that she may wreak her vengeance on her rival.

Semele is asleep in her palace, surrounded by Loves and Zephyrs. She wakes and sings one of the most famous of

Handel's inspirations, 'Oh sleep, why dost thou leave me?', an air of chaste and immaculate beauty. Jupiter comes to her side and lyrically reassures her of his love: 'Lay your doubts and fears aside'. The love scene continues with Semele's florid aria ('With hope desiring'), to which the Chorus provides refrain. When Semele refers to the fact that she is mortal and Jupiter a god, Jupiter hastens to provide distraction: 'I must with speed amuse her'. He announces his intention of bringing Ino to provide company for Semele, in an Arcadian setting to which he will transport them. If his serene aria ('Where'er you walk') is any indication of the bliss that should obtain there, the sisters' lot will indeed be a fortunate one. It is one of Handel's best-known tunes.

Ino understands that she has come at Jove's express command to a hallowed spot ('But hark! the Heavenly sphere turns around'), and together she and Semele sing 'Prepare, then, ye immortal choir', leaving the final comment to the Chorus: 'Bless the glad earth with heavenly lays'.

ACT III. The Cave of Sleep. Somnus (*bass*) lies in slumber. Juno and Iris enter, to enlist Somnus's help to remove the barricade Jupiter has set up around Semele. Somnus's slow aria, 'Leave me, loathsome light' – perfect characterisation and a wonderfully beautiful piece of music – ends with the evocative line 'Oh murmur me again to peace'. But as Juno mentions Pasithea's name he springs to life: 'More sweet is that name than a soft purling stream'. Juno gives her orders: Jupiter is to be distracted by dreams of Semele, the dragons are to be soothed by Somnus's leaden rod, and Ino must sleep so that Juno may appear to Semele in her guise. In a duet ('Obey my will') the amorous Somnus, in return for the promise of Pasithea, agrees to all her demands.

Juno disguised as Ino appears to Semele, comments on her beauty and asks if this is a sign that Jupiter has already made her immortal. She holds up a magic mirror and Semele is overcome with admiration of herself. Her bravura aria ('Myself I shall adore'), with its echo effects, shows how miraculously Handel could transform a frivolous idea into music of surpassing grace and loveliness. Juno, still in Ino's shape, urges her to refuse her favours to Jupiter until he promises her immortality and himself appears, not as mortal, but in his own godly shape – Juno knows that at sight of the god, Semele will be destroyed. Semele is gullible and embraces her: 'Thus let my thanks be paid'. Juno retires as Jupiter approaches.

Jupiter tells Semele that he has had a dream in which she repulsed him, but in spite of the ardour of his aria ('Come to my arms, my lovely fair') she keeps to her resolve: 'I ever am granting, you always complain'. Jupiter solemnly swears to grant her desire, whatever it may be, and immediately Semele asks him to appear in all his godly splendour. Jupiter cannot conceal his consternation, which shows in agitated ornamentation ('Ah, take heed what you press'), but Semele, in coloratura which is no less emphatic, insists: 'No, no, I'll take no less'. In a moving recitative, Jupiter, alone, laments his oath and its inevitable consequence. Juno celebrates her forthcoming triumph ('Above measure is the pleasure'). What the libretto describes as 'a mournful symphony' accompanies Jupiter as he appears to Semele, who realises too late that the vision will scorch her to death. She dies.

At Cadmus's court, the people comment on the story they have heard Ino tell of Semele's love and death: 'Oh, terror and astonishment, Nature to each allots his proper sphere'. Ino reveals that it has been prophesied she shall marry Athamas and he rejoices conventionally at the prospect ('Despair no more shall wound me'). A *sinfonia* heralds the appearance on a cloud of Apollo (*tenor*), who announces that a phoenix will arise from Semele's ashes, and the people rejoice: 'Happy shall we be'.

THE BEGGAR'S OPERA

THREE acts; première, London, 1728. Words by Gay, traditional music (arr. Pepusch). The fence Peachum's (*bass*) daughter Polly (*soprano*) has secretly married Macheath (*tenor*), a highwayman; the Peachums plan to turn him in. Macheath invites the ladies of the town to join him in a tavern, where he is betrayed and arrested. In Newgate, the jailer Lockit's (*baritone*) pregnant daughter Lucy (*soprano*) seeks to marry Macheath. Polly appears and the women set about each other; Peachum prises her away and Lucy helps Macheath escape. Lockit berates Lucy, but then he and Peachum are tipped off as to Macheath's whereabouts. Lucy and Polly confront each other; Macheath is brought in. In the condemned cell, he laments his fate. To prevent a tragic ending, the Beggar (*spoken*) permits a reprieve, and Macheath leads a rumbustious finale, surrounded by numerous wives.

Christoph Willibald Gluck
(1714–1787)

GLUCK was a reformer, whose battle against the contemporary abuses of opera proved a turning point in the history of the art. Einstein has suggested that the normal eighteenth-century method of reform being by means of satire and parody, and Gluck being constitutionally un-fitted to this medium or that of *opera buffa*, he was obliged to become the first critical creator in opera if he was to express his thoughts on the subject; he had no other 'safety valve'. His preface to *Alceste* is one of the most famous documents in the annals of opera:

'*When I undertook to write the music for Alceste, I resolved to divest it entirely of all those abuses, introduced into it either by the mistaken vanity of singers or by the too great complaisance of composers, which have for so long disfigured Italian opera and made of the most splendid and most beautiful of spectacles the most ridiculous and wearisome. I have striven to restrict music to its true office of serving poetry by means of expression and by following the situations of the story, without interrupting the action or stifling it with a useless superfluity of ornaments; and I believed that it should do this in the same way as telling colours affect a correct and well-ordered drawing, by a well-assorted contrast of light and shade, which serves to animate the figures without altering their contours [. . .] in short, I have sought to abolish all the abuses against which good sense and reason have long cried out in vain.*

'*I have felt that the overture ought to apprise the spectators of the nature of the action that is to be represented and to form, so to speak, its argument.*'[1]

ALCESTE
Alcestis

OPERA in three acts; text by Ranieri da Calzabigi. Première at the Burg-theater, Vienna, December 26, 1767, in Italian; revised version, Paris, April 23, 1776, in French.

ACT I. A magnificently sombre overture fully vindicates Gluck's intention as set forth in the preface; here indeed is the argument of the action. The scene represents a great court in front of the palace of Admetus; at the back can be seen the temple of Apollo. The people crowd into the courtyard and mourn the illness of their King, which, the herald (*baritone*) tells them, is likely to prove fatal. The Queen (*soprano*) appears flanked by her two children and bids the crowd come with her to the temple to offer sacrifice to the gods.

In the temple of Apollo, we hear first a simple tune, which

---

[1] Extract translated by Eric Blom, from his translation of Einstein's bio-graphy of Gluck in Dent's 'Master Musicians' series.

may serve as background for a dance as well as for the entrance of Alcestis. The High Priest (*baritone*) and the chorus call upon the god to avert Admetus's fate. Alcestis adds her prayer, and a sacrifice is prepared. The High Priest, in music that grows more and more awe-inspiring, commands the people to be silent to hear the Oracle's judgment. It is more terrible than they had expected: Admetus must die, unless a friend can be found to die in his stead. The people rush from the temple in fear, leaving Alcestis and the High Priest alone. Alcestis awakes to the reality of the situation and resolves to die for her husband, without whom she cannot live. 'Non, ce n'est point un sacrifice,' she sings in an aria of noble simplicity. The High Priest tells her that her prayer is granted and she has the rest of the day to prepare herself for the advent of death.

In an aria which has become the most famous of the opera, Alcestis invokes the gods of the underworld and defies them to do their worst, what dread has she of dying for what she loves best in the world? 'Divinités du Styx' is Gluck at his most intense, justifying his own maxims as regards the situation, but with a result that is no less impressive as music than as drama.

ACT II A great hall of his palace. Admetus (*tenor*) receives the congratulations of his people, headed by Evander (*tenor*), on his apparently miraculous recovery. Dances are performed in his honour. The King enquires what brought about his recovery, and Evander tells him the condition imposed by the Oracle but does not name the victim. The King is horror-stricken and refuses to accept such a sacrifice. Alcestis joins him and shares his joy that they are reunited. But she is quite unable to hide her grief as the moment draws near when she must leave her husband and her children for ever. Admetus tries to comfort her in a *da capo* aria of great beauty, 'Bannis la crainte et les alarmes', but to no avail. The Queen avows her love, but finally admits that it is she the gods are taking in place of Admetus. Dramatically, he refuses to accept the sacrifice: 'Non, sans toi, je ne puis vivre'. Alcestis is left alone with the people, and, as they mourn for her grief, sings 'Ah, malgré moi, mon faible coeur partage vos tendres pleurs'.

ACT III. The courtyard of the palace. The people are mourning the deaths of both Alcestis and of Admetus, who has followed her. Hercules (*baritone*) arrives, rejoicing that his labours are over; but when Evander informs him of the death of his friend Admetus, and of the circumstances surrounding it, he swears to restore the King and Queen to life.

The gates of Hell. Alcestis pleads with the gods of Hell (who remain invisible) that her torment be not prolonged, that she be received at once. Admetus joins her, asking only to be reunited with her in death. The voice of Thanatos (*baritone*) announces that one of them shall offer him- or herself to Death; the choice is left to Alcestis. She will not renounce her right to die for her husband, and the choice appears to have been made, much to the grief of Admetus. Hercules appears, determined to deprive the underworld of its prey. He and Admetus defy Hell to rescue Alcestis. At the moment of their success, Apollo (*baritone*) appears, and announces to Hercules that his action has won him the right to a place amongst the gods themselves, while Admetus and Alcestis are to be restored to earth, there to serve as a universal example of the power of conjugal love.

The palace court. Apollo bids the people rejoice that the King and Queen are restored to them. Alcestis, Admetus, and Hercules take part in a trio, and the opera ends in general rejoicing.

More than perhaps any other of the operas of his maturity, *Alceste* illustrates the ideal of 'beautiful simplicity' which Gluck tells us in his preface is his aim. Berlioz's admiration for the temple scene is well known, and Ernest Newman further quotes this composer's detailed objection to the changes made in what we now know as 'Divinités du Styx' when the opera was translated from Italian, changes which ruined the beginning of the aria, according to Berlioz. Ironically, when an Italian soprano now sings this aria, she will use an Italian translation of the French translation of the original Italian, and of course employ the musical form of the French version! It should be noted that the original score included a scene in a gloomy forest near Pherae at the beginning of the second act; this is omitted in the French version, which begins with the festivities attending the recovery of Admetus. The third act, while employing much of the music of the original, is entirely altered dramatically, and, says Ernest Newman, distinctly for the worse. Du Roullet's introduction of Hercules has, according to Newman, a vulgarising effect, and only the new scene at the gates of Hell (the entire act originally took place in the courtyard of the palace, where Alcestis died, Admetus tried to commit suicide, and a happy ending was provided by the appearance of Apollo) constitutes a worthwhile addition to the score as it stood.

ORFEO ED EURIDICE
Orpheus and Eurydice

OPERA in three acts by Christoph Willibald Gluck; libretto by Ranieri da Calzabigi. First performed Vienna, October 5, 1762, in Italian; Paris, 1774, in French.

IN effect, Gluck composed *Orfeo ed Euridice* twice: for Vienna in 1762, and for Paris in 1774. Each version was written for a male hero, in Vienna for the contralto castrato Guadagni, in Paris for the tenor Legros. The 1762 version is short (about 90 minutes) and dates from *before* Gluck's conscious attempt at reforming opera with *Alceste*. The 1774 recomposition retains the old material while adding much that is new, and gives Orpheus himself bravura music ranging up to a top D. Most modern revivals which claim to be the original version in fact retain the 1762 score, recitatives and all, but slyly incorporate the most famous of the 1774 additions. The 1774 Paris version has been frequently revived, usually with some discreet transpositions. The first attempt at a compromise between the two versions was made by Berlioz (with the help of Saint-Saëns) in 1859 for Pauline Viardot. Then, the 1774 version was used, but the tenor role of Orpheus was transposed to fit a female alto voice.

ACT I. A grotto. Following a brief and solemn prelude, the curtain rises to show Orpheus (*contralto*) and friends mourning at Eurydice's tomb. During an affecting aria and chorus ('Chiamo il mio ben così') funeral honours are paid to the dead bride. A second orchestra, behind the scenes, echoes, with moving effect, the distracted husband's grief, until, in answer to his piercing cries, the God of Love (*soprano*) appears. He tells Orpheus that Zeus has taken pity on him and has allowed him to go down to Hades to persuade Pluto and his minions, solely through the power of his music, to return Eurydice to him. But, should this happen, Orpheus must on no account look back at his bride, nor explain to her why he cannot do so, until he has crossed the Styx; otherwise she will immediately die. Orpheus, confident in his power of song and in his ability to stand the test imposed by Zeus and bring his beloved Eurydice back to earth, receives the message with joy.

'Fulfil with joy the will of the gods,' sings Love, and Orpheus, having implored the aid of the deities, departs for the Nether World.

ACT II. Entrance to Hades. Orpheus is greeted with threats by the Furies. The scene, beginning with the Chorus, 'Chi mai dell'Erebo?', is a masterpiece of dramatic music. The Furies call upon Cerberus, the triple-headed dog monster that guards the entrance to the Nether World, to tear the mortal into pieces; the bark of the monster is reproduced in the score. At the scene's climax, the Furies hurl an infuriated 'No!' at Orpheus, who sings of his love for Eurydice and his grief over her death and begs to be allowed to seek her. The sweetness of his music wins the sympathy of the Furies. They allow him to enter the Valley of the Blest, a beautiful spot where the good spirits in Hades find rest, a state uniquely expressed in their slow dance with its famous flute solo. Eurydice (*soprano*) and her companions sing of their bliss in the Elysian Fields: 'E quest'asilo ameno e grato' (In this tranquil and lovely abode of the blest). Orpheus comes seeking Eurydice. His peaceful aria (with its oboe obbligato) 'Che puro ciel' (What pure light) is answered by a chorus of Happy Shades who bring Eurydice to him. Orpheus, beside himself with joy but remembering Love's warning, takes his bride by the hand and, with averted gaze, leads her away.

ACT III. Eurydice cannot understand Orpheus's reaction. He seeks to soothe her injured feelings (duet: 'Su, e con me vieni, o cara'). But his efforts are in vain; nor can he offer her any explanation. Eurydice protests in a passionate aria and duet, 'Che fiero momento', that without his love she prefers to die.

Orpheus, no longer able to resist, turns and passionately clasps Eurydice in his arms. Immediately she dies. It is then that Orpheus intones his great and famous lament, 'Che farò senza Euridice' (What is life to me without thee). It is so beautiful that Love, affected by Orpheus's grief, appears to him, touches Eurydice and restores her to life and to her husband's arms.

IPHIGÉNIE EN TAURIDE
Iphigenia in Tauris

OPERA in four acts by Christoph Willibald Gluck; words by François Guillard. Produced in the Académie de Musique, Paris, May 18, 1779.

THERE is much to support the argument that this is Gluck's greatest opera. Here he comes nearest to a complete reconciliation of his dramatic style with his lyrical. The dramatic and the sensuous meet in *Iphigénie en Tauride* to form a whole that is more consistent and more expressive than anything Gluck had previously written. Nowhere else did he achieve such homogeneity of style, with whole scenes dominated by a single idea expressed in music of the greatest power, and seldom before had he displayed such invention in the individual arias.

Iphigenia is the daughter of Agamemnon, King of Mycenae. Agamemnon was slain by his wife, Clytemnestra, who, in turn, was killed by her son, Orestes. Iphigenia is ignorant of these happenings. She has become a priestess of Diana on the Scythian island of Tauris and has not seen Orestes for many years.

ACT I. Before the atrium of the temple of Diana. To priestesses and Greek maidens, Iphigenia (*soprano*) tells of her dream that misfortune has come to her family in the distant country of her birth. She prays to be reunited with her brother ('O toi qui prolongeas mes jours'). Thoas (*bass*), King of Scythia, calls for a human sacrifice to ward off the danger that has been foretold to him ('De noirs pressentiments'). Some of his people hastily enter, bringing with them as captives Orestes (*baritone*) and Pylades (*tenor*), Greek youths who have landed on the coast. They report that Orestes constantly speaks of having committed a crime and of being pursued by Furies.

ACT II. Temple of Diana. Orestes bewails his fate ('Dieux qui me poursuivez'). Pylades sings of his undying friendship for him ('Unis de la plus tendre enfance'). Pylades is separated from Orestes, who temporarily loses his mind, in a scene which has been described as Gluck's greatest dramatic achievement ('Le calme rentre dans mon coeur'). Iphigenia questions him. Orestes, under her influence, becomes calmer, but refrains from disclosing his identity. He tells her, however, that he is from Mycenae, that Agamemnon (their father) has been slain by his wife, that Clytemnestra's son, Orestes, has slain her in revenge and is himself dead. Of the once great family only a daughter, Electra, remains. Iphigenia in a great aria laments her predicament ('O malheureuse Iphigénie').

ACT III. Iphigenia is struck with the resemblance of the stranger to her brother and, in order to save him from the sacrifice demanded by Thoas, charges him to deliver a letter to Electra. He declines to leave Pylades, nor, until Orestes affirms that he will commit suicide rather than accept freedom at the price of his friend's life, does Pylades agree to take the letter, and then only because he hopes to bring succour to Orestes.

ACT IV. All is ready for the sacrifice. Iphigenia has the knife poised for the fatal thrust, when, through an exclamation uttered by Orestes, she recognises him as her brother. The priestesses offer him obeisance as king. Thoas, however, enters and demands the sacrifice. Iphigenia declares that she will die with her brother. At that moment Pylades at the head of a rescue party enters the temple. A combat ensues in which Thoas is killed. Diana herself (*soprano*) appears, pardons Orestes and returns to the Greeks her likeness which the Scythians had stolen and over which they had built the temple.

Wolfgang Amadeus Mozart
(1756–1791)

IDOMENEO

OPERA in three acts; text by the Abbé Varesco, after a French opera by Campra and Danchet. First performed at Munich, January 29, 1781.

*I*DOMENEO, Mozart's third and greatest essay in the form of *opera seria* (his first two, *Mitridate* and *Lucio Silla*, were written respectively ten and nine years earlier) was revived only once in the composer's lifetime (for a private performance in Vienna in 1786). It was fairly frequently heard in Germany and Austria after his death but not performed in Britain until 1934, and never on the English professional stage until its production at Glyndebourne in 1951. It was not heard in America until 1947 when performed at the Berkshire Festival, Tanglewood.

Why this neglect? First, by its very nature, *Idomeneo* has never been a repertory opera, at least until the last few years. Secondly and more important, it is an example of an operatic convention whose popularity was nearing its end at the time of the first performance. A castrato was a prominent member of the original cast, and the opera was conceived during the period of vocal virtuosity associated with that breed.

The opera is not just a series of display pieces and formal movements; Mozart was at the height of his powers when it was composed, and the arias are superbly expressive, though on a more rarefied plane than the later comedies have accustomed us to. If drama consists of the interplay of motives and emotions, and tragedy of the ordering of men's destinies by a fate their own actions have provoked, *Idomeneo* is both tragic (in spite of its happy ending) and dramatic.

ACT I. Idomeneo, King of Crete (*tenor*), has taken part in the Trojan war, and it is many years since he left home. Amongst the prisoners he has sent home is Ilia (*soprano*), daughter of King Priam, who is in love with Idamante (*soprano* or *tenor*), the son of Idomeneo. The overture immediately establishes the character of an opera whose music, without exception, never relaxes its intense seriousness, underlining the dignity and stature of the characters involved. Calmly the drama unfolds. In an aria, 'Padre, germani, addio', Ilia reveals that her hatred for the conquerors of her country is as nothing to her love for Idamante. He enters at its conclusion and in veiled terms states his love for Ilia, at the same time announcing that, in honour of his father's imminent return to Crete, the Trojan prisoners are to be set free.

A chorus of rejoicing at this news precedes the entrance of Arbace to say that Idomeneo's ship has been sunk; the general consternation is given particular expression by Electra, a Greek princess (*soprano*), who, in an aria of passionate fury, fears his death will remove all obstacles to the marriage of Ilia and Idamante, with whom she is herself in love. She leaves, and, after a chorus of intercession, Idomeneo enters with his followers, whom he dismisses before explaining in an aria the nature of the vow which secured Neptune's intervention in quieting the storm: that he will sacrifice the first living creature he meets in return for deliverance from death. It is, of course, Idamante whom he sees, and their dialogue is made the more poignant because it is some time before Idomeneo recognises his son, whom he has not seen since infancy. In horror, the father orders his son from his presence, and Idamante laments his father's apparent displeasure in an aria, 'Il padre adorato ritrovo e lo perdo'. The act ends with a brilliant march and choral *ciaccona* in honour of Neptune.

ACT II. The King tells his secret to his counsellor Arbace (*tenor*), who advises that Idamante be sent with Electra to a distant country. This scene is usually omitted from modern performances and the act begins instead with the scene between Idomeneo and Ilia whose aria, 'Se il padre perdei', is touchingly beautiful. Idomeneo understands that his vow now involves not only disaster for himself and Idamante but for Ilia as well. He faces the tragedy with courage and dignity in his great aria, 'Fuor del mar ho un mar in seno', a coloratura showpiece for tenor.

A beautiful, lyrical aria for Electra, whom the prospect of requited love has turned into a happy woman, leads into a march, and thence to the famous barcarolle chorus of embarkation, 'Placido è il mar, andiamo'. Idamante and Electra take leave of Idomeneo in a superb trio, 'Pria di partir', but the music quickens and a storm breaks over the harbour, heralding Neptune's vengeance at this attempt to evade the consequences of the vow made to him. Idomeneo admits his guilt but accuses the god of injustice, and the act ends as the crowd disperses in terror.

ACT III. Ilia can think only of her love for Idamante, and her expression of it in her soliloquy 'Zeffiretti lusinghieri' is one of the most perfect moments of the opera. To her comes Idamante; he is going out to fight the monster Neptune has sent to plague the island, and he may not return. Involuntarily, she confesses her love, which leads to a duet. Idomeneo and Electra interrupt the lovers. Idomeneo still cannot bring himself to explain the exact cause of the disaster which is overtaking them all, and Idamante sadly takes his farewell in the quartet 'Andrò ramingo e solo', which shows Mozart at his noblest and most expressive; the moment in the opera when the spirit of tragedy most completely dominates the music.

The Temple of Neptune. After an introduction, the High Priest (*tenor*) exhorts the King to confess his sin to Neptune, and the people are duly horrified to hear that the sacrifice of Idamante is the price of deliverance from the god's displeasure. The priests enter to a march and Idomeneo begins the ceremony with a solemn prayer which is answered by the priests. A shout of triumph is heard outside and Arbace announces that

Idamante has killed the monster. But a moment later Idamante, who by now knows the story of his father's vow, enters and offers himself for sacrifice, and Idomeneo cannot but accept him. The ceremony is about to reach its climax when Ilia interrupts and demands to be sacrificed in Idamante's place. The whole situation is resolved by an oracular pronouncement from Neptune (*bass*), to the effect that the crime can be expiated, the vow fulfilled, if Idomeneo will renounce the throne in favour of his son. In the general rejoicing, only Electra is left with her worst fears realised; in the most furious of her violent utterances, she gives vent to her despair and rushes from the stage or, as some versions have it, falls dead or commits suicide.

All is peace and fulfilment as Idomeneo in a last recitative and aria, 'Torna la pace al core', presents Idamante to the people as their new ruler, and takes his farewell. The opera ends with the people celebrating the accession of Idamante in dance and chorus.

DIE ENTFÜHRUNG AUS DEM SERAIL
The Abduction from the Seraglio

OPERA in three acts by Wolfgang Amadeus Mozart; text by Gottlieb Stephanie from a play by Bretzner. First performed at the Burgtheater, Vienna, July 16, 1782.

*D*IE ENTFÜHRUNG is important amongst Mozart's works not least because of the ambitious and extended view he takes in it of the hitherto modest German *Singspiel*. The drama is carried on almost exclusively in speech and it is only in moments of high emotion that the characters have recourse to song – but on what a sublimated and highly expressive level is that song when it comes!

ACT I. Outside Pasha Selim's house. The overture establishes the 'Turkish' atmosphere of the piece and also includes a reference in the minor to Belmonte's aria, 'Hier soll'ich dich denn sehen, Constanze', which is heard in C major when the curtain goes up. Belmonte, a Spanish nobleman (*tenor*), believes his beloved Constanze (*soprano*), who has been carried off by pirates, is a captive in Pasha Selim's harem. Osmin (*bass*), in charge of the Pasha's harem and also, it seems, of his garden, appears singing a doleful sort of love song, 'Wer ein Liebchen hat gefunden', one of the delights of the score. He tells Belmonte it is the Pasha's house. Belmonte asks the whereabouts of Pedrillo, his servant and Osmin's rival in love for Blonde, Constanze's English maid. Osmin's surly reply is that Pedrillo should be hanged, drawn, and quartered. He chases Belmonte away, but is immediately confronted with Pedrillo (*tenor*) in person, saucier and more impudent than ever. Osmin relieves his pent-up feelings with an aria that is a virtuoso expression of rage and also, in good hands, of the comic bass's art: 'Solche hergelauf'ne Laffen'.

Belmonte returns to find Pedrillo; each is delighted at the other's news, Belmonte to hear that Constanze has remained true to him in spite of the Pasha's persuasive powers, Pedrillo that there is a boat waiting to take them all to safety if they can only spirit the women out of the harem. Belmonte sings a song of love for his absent Constanze: 'O wie ängstlich, o wie feurig'. Belmonte exits as Constanze and the Pasha land from a boat to be greeted in a chorus very much in the Turkish style. The Pasha again assures Constanze of his love and of his determination to win hers in return. She sings of the love she knew before her captivity and protests that she will be true to this memory: 'Ach, ich liebte, war so glücklich'. It is a coloratura aria, but full of sadness for her past happiness and of determination to resist temptation. She leaves the stage, and Pedrillo introduces Belmonte to the Pasha as a distinguished architect. The Pasha intimates that he will not withhold his favour from him, but after he has gone Osmin remains unimpressed and tries to bar their way. It is only after a lively trio, 'Marsch, marsch, marsch', that they outmanoeuvre him and enter the palace.

ACT II. Osmin is no match for Blonde (*soprano*) in a battle of wits, as she demonstrates in her aria, 'Durch Zärtlichkeit und Schmeicheln', and the duet which follows. He knows she will come off best and can do no more than complain at the folly of the English in allowing their women so much liberty. Constanze unburdens herself to Blonde: 'Traurigkeit ward mir zum Loose'. It is perhaps the most deeply felt number of the score, and one of Mozart's most sublime expressions of grief. Blonde retires as the Pasha tries again to woo Constanze. She is adamant and launches into one of the most considerable arias Mozart wrote for soprano voice: 'Martern aller Arten'. Laid out on concerto lines, with four solo instruments and a lengthy orchestral introduction, it is the one moment in the opera where Mozart definitely sacrifices the stage action – the Pasha and Constanze can do little more than glare at each other during the introduction. But the aria that results is musically so worthwhile that few will grumble at the large scale of the composer's inspiration.

Blonde is wondering if the empty stage means the Pasha has at last been successful when Pedrillo rushes in to tell her that Belmonte is here and a plan is afoot for their escape. Osmin is to be drugged to make way for the double elopement. Blonde's joyful song, 'Welche Wonne, welche Lust', contrasts with

Pedrillo's nervous reaction to the prospect of dealing with Osmin single-handed ('Frisch zum Kampfe'). However he soon persuades Osmin that the Muslim doctrine of teetotalism is better honoured in the breach than in the observance, and he has him tippling with the best and praising wine in one of Mozart's most exquisite inspirations, the duet 'Vivat Bacchus'. Osmin sinks into a stupor and Pedrillo is able to drag him out of the way and leave the coast clear for a reunion between Belmonte and Constanze. Belmonte in his aria, 'Wenn der Freude Thränen fliessen', is less passionate than Constanze as she begins the quartet which is to end the act. It is a noble piece in spite of the crisis which is contrived to keep it alive – the men ask to be reassured that their lovers were true during captivity – and the musical integrity is unaffected by the dramatic artifice.

ACT III. With much comic pantomime, Pedrillo organises the disposal of the ladders with the help of the captain of the ship which is to take them to freedom. Belmonte enters and is instructed to sing so that no one will notice that he, Pedrillo, is not serenading his Blonde as usual ('Ich baue ganz auf deine Stärke'). A moment later, Pedrillo is back, and ready to give the signal for escape with his enchanting serenade 'Im Mohrenland gefangen war'. Belmonte and Constanze disappear into the darkness, and Pedrillo rushes up the ladder to fetch his Blonde, unaware that his singing has woken up a guard, a mute, who dashes off to summon Osmin. This worthy arrives as the second pair of lovers is about to leave the house, and his suspicions of a double elopement are confirmed when Constanze and Belmonte are brought back by the guard. 'Ha! wie will ich triumphieren' sings Osmin, joyful that at last he has a chance to settle a hundred and one old scores with Pedrillo and a few new ones with Belmonte.

The Pasha (*spoken*), informed of the intended escape, arrives to question the prisoners. Constanze pleads her love for Belmonte as justification for the attempted escape, and her lover assures the Pasha that his father, a rich Spaniard by the name of Lostados, will pay a high ransom for his freedom. Lostados turns out to be the Pasha's greatest enemy. Belmonte and Constanze are face to face with death and perhaps torture, and their extensive duet, 'Welch' ein Geschick', reveals a serious approach to their imminent tragedy. The Pasha returns, and announces that he scorns to return evil for evil, that they are free to return to their native Spain. The happy couples return thanks in the form of a *vaudeville*, which Belmonte begins, the others singing a verse each and all joining in the refrain: 'Wer so viel Huld vergessen kann'.

Blonde cannot resist a dig at the discomfited Osmin, who is so overcome by rage that he disrupts the harmony of the ensemble with another furious outburst before rushing defeated from the stage, leaving the others to finish on a note of gratitude. They take their leave while the chorus sings the praises of the Pasha and his clemency.

LE NOZZE DI FIGARO
The Marriage of Figaro

OPERA BUFFA in four acts by Wolfgang Amadeus Mozart; text by Lorenzo da Ponte, after Beaumarchais. First performed at the Burgtheater, Vienna, May 1, 1786.

*L*E *NOZZE DI FIGARO* was Mozart's first venture with his most famous librettist, Lorenzo da Ponte. It is surprising in retrospect to note that, in spite of the brilliant libretto and even more brilliant music, *Figaro* scored only a moderate success when it was produced in Vienna, where it had to wait until the triumph in Prague before being received into popular affection. It was incidentally the success of *Figaro* in Prague which led to the commission to compose *Don Giovanni* for that city.

ACT I. An anteroom in the Count's château near Seville. The overture is extremely well known, and nothing could make a better prelude to this marriage day of feverish activity than the short *presto* movement. When the curtain rises, Figaro, the Count's valet (*baritone*), is measuring out a space on the floor ('Cinque, dieci'). The room, Figaro explains to Susanna, the Countess's maid (*soprano*), is to be theirs – 'the most convenient room in the castle, just between milord and milady'. Susanna astounds him by peremptorily refusing to accept it, but, when he remonstrates ('Se a caso, Madamà' – Supposing one evening my lady should want you), explains that while the position may make it easy for her to go to the Countess, it also makes it easy for the Count to get to her. The Countess rings, and Figaro is left alone. The light-hearted music changes as Figaro's 'Se vuol ballare' (If you are after a little amusement) shows him in a determined yet apprehensive state of mind.

He leaves, and Marcellina (*soprano*) comes in with Doctor Bartolo (*bass*), the pair of them plotting to compel Figaro to marry Marcellina as he has defaulted on a debt he owes her. Doctor Bartolo, with his legal knowledge, will ensure there is no escape for the rascal ('La vendetta' – Now for vengeance). As he goes out, Susanna enters by another door and she and Marcellina meet as they attempt to follow Bartolo; their duet as each offers the other precedence ends in Marcellina's complete discomfiture. Susanna is immediately confronted with a disconsolate Cherubino (*soprano*), who wants to enlist her help in getting the Count to reinstate him as the Countess's page. He has been dismissed because of his latest exploit with Barbarina, Antonio's niece – he is in love with every woman he meets. The page pours out his adolescent aspirations to Susanna: 'Non sò più cosa son, cosa faccio' (Is it pain, is it pleasure that fills me?).

Voices are heard outside and Cherubino has only just time to conceal himself before Count Almaviva (*baritone*) enters and starts to protest his affections for Susanna. It is not her lucky day, as the Count is followed a moment later by the music-master, Don Basilio (*tenor*); in the scramble for concealment, Cherubino nips into the chair behind which the Count takes refuge. Basilio asks Susanna about the page and the Countess – an intrigue which he says everyone is talking about. The Count emerges and demands that the gossip-mongers be found and punished. In the ensuing trio Susanna faints, but revives in time to plead the cause of the unhappy Cherubino. The Count describes how he caught him the previous day hiding in Barbarina's room. Suiting action to word, he draws the cover from the chair – and there is Cherubino again. Only the page's claim that he tried his best *not* to hear what passed between the Count and Susanna stays the penalty that he would otherwise incur.

Figaro leads a band of locals who have come to sing the Count's praises. When the song ends, the Count yields to the general entreaties, but only to the extent of giving Cherubino a commission in his regiment, effective immediately. Figaro speeds him on his way with the famous and spirited martial air 'Non più andrai' (Say goodbye now to pastime and play, lad).

ACT II. The Countess's bedroom. The Countess's (*soprano*) soliloquy, 'Porgi amor' (God of Love), is one of the most taxing entrances for any soprano. It makes us aware of her intense longing for her husband's love, and also of the reticence which her breeding makes natural to her. Susanna expounds her view of the situation to her mistress and opens the door to Figaro. His plan is that the Count shall be given an assignation with Susanna, whose place shall be taken by Cherubino, and that at the same time he shall be told in an anonymous letter that the Countess in her turn has made a rendezvous with an unknown man. Cherubino enters to be dressed for the part, but first sings a song he has just composed, the famous 'Voi che sapete' (Tell me, fair ladies). Cherubino tries on the dress to the accompaniment of a song with action, Susanna's 'Venite inginocchiatevi' (Come here and kneel before me now). A knock is heard at the door. It is the Count. Consternation. Cherubino dashes into the Countess's dressing-room and Susanna hides behind a curtain. The Count, suspecting something is being hidden from him, hears a noise and finds the dressing-room door locked. He goes off to get tools to break it down, taking his wife with him. While he is away Cherubino slips out of hiding and jumps from the window, leaving Susanna to take his place. The Count returns, and the Countess tries to explain that the page is in her dressing-room without much on because he was being fitted for a charade.

The finale is one of the greatest single movements in all Mozart's operas, unrivalled in its variety of motive, characterisation, tempo and texture. It is begun by the Count, who by now is in a towering passion: 'Esci omai, garzon malnato' (Out you come, no more concealment). The Countess's pleading seems in vain, but both are struck dumb with amazement when, at the height of the storm, Susanna emerges coolly from the dressing-room. The Count rushes in to see if Cherubino is still there but, finding he is not, can do nothing but plead for pardon. With Susanna's aid, this is obtained, but the Count's suspicions begin to take hold again. The anonymous letter? Written by Figaro, delivered by Basilio. He thinks he has found someone he can safely be angry with, but is told he must forgive everyone if he himself is to be forgiven. The moment of peace ends as Figaro bounds in to summon his master and mistress to the wedding dance which is about to begin. The Count, seeing a chance to get his own back, questions Figaro about the anonymous letter. In spite of hints from the Countess and Susanna, Figaro denies all knowledge, and has almost turned the Count's suspicions when Antonio (*bass*), the gardener, bursts in, protesting that a man has been thrown out of the window on to his flower-beds. Figaro says it was he who jumped out, but Antonio says it looked more like Cherubino. Figaro sticks to his story until the Count asks him about a paper Antonio has found near the flower-bed. Figaro, with some help from the Countess and Susanna, says it is the page's commission. Why was it left? Again with help, Figaro answers it is because the commission was unsealed. Figaro's triumph is short-lived, as Marcellina enters, with Bartolo and Basilio, to lodge formal complaint before the Count against Figaro for breach of promise. The act ends in pandemonium.

ACT III. A large hall. The Count's designs seem within reach when Susanna, who comes to borrow smelling salts for her mistress, agrees to meet him that night in the garden. Their duet, 'Crudel, perchè finora' (Oh, why are you so cruel), reveals the Count as an ardent lover, Susanna as an inattentive beloved, but the result is a masterpiece. As Susanna leaves, she meets Figaro and assures him, just too loudly, that he will win Marcellina's case against him. Sure of winning his case? repeats the Count, and launches into a superb recitative and aria, 'Vedrò mentr'io sospiro, felice un servo mio?' (Must I forgo my pleasure, whilst serf of mine rejoices?). This extraordinary piece of self-revelation takes the Count from unsuccessful lover and erring husband into something much more potent. But the balance is redressed when it is discovered, after he has given judgment for Marcellina, that the lady is in fact none other than Figaro's mother, and Bartolo, furthermore, his father. In the great sextet which follows, the Count is reduced to expressions of impotent fury.

The stage is empty for a moment, and the Countess comes in to sing the most extended and most moving of her utterances in the opera. 'Dove sono?' (I remember days long departed) consists of a lengthy recitative followed by a restrained but highly expressive aria in two sections, *andantino* and later *allegro*. Susanna enters, and the two women arrange where Susanna is to meet the Count that evening. The letter duet, 'Che soave zeffiretto' (How delightful 'tis to wander, by the breath of evening fann'd), is one of the most famous numbers in the score; the mistress dictates a letter to the Count, the maid takes it down, and the voices of both blend as they read it back together.

The wedding festivities are about to begin and a crowd of village girls presents flowers to the Countess, who is astonished a moment later, when the Count enters with Antonio, to see one of them unmasked as Cherubino. The situation is saved by Barbarina (*soprano*): 'My lord, when you kiss me and tell me you love me, you often say you will give me whatever I want. Give me Cherubino for a husband.' Figaro announces the beginning of the wedding march (a Fandango – the one Spanish element in the score).

There is a chorus in praise of the generosity and right-mindedness of the Count in having abolished the *droit de seigneur*, and the happy couples – Bartolo and Marcellina, Figaro and Susanna – receive their wedding wreaths from the Count and Countess. Susanna takes the opportunity to give the Count the letter she and her mistress have concocted for him. He opens it, pricking his fingers on the pin – a comedy which is watched all unknowingly by Figaro and commented on with some relish. The Count announces general festivity, and the act ends with a repetition of the chorus in his honour.

ACT IV. The garden, night. Barbarina, in a little half-finished cavatina, is searching for the pin which she is to return to Susanna but has lost. She tells the story to Figaro, who enters with Marcellina. He is overcome with distress at this apparent indication of his wife's unfaithfulness. Between arias for Marcellina and Basilio (often omitted), Figaro watches Barbarina hide (where she is to meet Cherubino), and tells Bartolo and Basilio to stay near at hand to witness the seduction of his wife by the Count. Figaro's recitative and aria, 'Tutto è disposto'

(Everything's ready) and 'Aprite un po' quegli occhi' (Yes, fools you are and will be, fools till your eyes are opened), is at the same time his most serious moment (the recitative is tragic in the extreme) and his most comic (the horns at the end are surely intended to be illustrative as well as musical). Susanna asks the Countess (they have exchanged clothes) to be allowed to walk a little apart from her, and sings an aria of exquisite sensibility, ostensibly to the lover she is waiting for, but in reality knowing full well that Figaro is listening to her: 'Deh vieni non tardar' (Then come, my heart's delight).

The comedy of mistaken identity begins. Cherubino attempts to flirt with the supposed Susanna, in reality the Countess. Susanna, the Count and Figaro observe, and the Count interrupts and starts to woo his wife in disguise. Figaro, who does not know about the change of clothes, invokes the gods to avenge his honour. Susanna (still dressed as the Countess) calls to him and he starts to tell her of the Count's escapade when he recognises her and talks lovingly to her as if she were the Countess, and laughs at her attempt to disguise herself from him as much as at her indignation. All is forgiven. The two convince the Count they are amorous mistress and valet. The Count summons anyone within hearing to bear witness to the unfaithfulness of his wife. All pleading is in vain, until the voice of the Countess is heard: 'Almeno io per loro perdono otterrò' (May I then for pardon at last intercede?). The Count, recognising that he is outplayed, begs forgiveness in a swelling phrase, receives it, and the opera ends in general rejoicing.

Le nozze di Figaro is an incomparable masterpiece. In the last act Mozart has achieved something remarkable in the feeling of anxiety which pervades music and situation alike. It is as though the tapestry of the comedy has been reversed and, instead of dazzling with its brilliance, it is shot through with flashes of light in the darkness; it is not so much that the garden has a thundercloud hanging over it, but that there is lightning in the air. There is always a sense of relief when Figaro's little B flat tune arrives to prove that once again we have come through the web of intrigue to the safety and happiness beyond it.

DON GIOVANNI

OPERA in two acts by Wolfgang Amadeus Mozart; text by Lorenzo da Ponte. First performed at the National Theatre, Prague, October 29, 1787.

THE two decisive factors in *Don Giovanni*'s success are, first, the unique blending of the comic and the serious as well as the speed of its dramatic and musical action; secondly, the fascinating figure of the Don himself, libertine and blasphemer, whose courage endears him to the men and his scandalous reputation to the women.

Don Giovanni was commissioned for the opera in Prague, where *Figaro* had just been a sensational success. It was performed by the same company, and many of the singers were the same as those who had sung the earlier opera when it was presented in Prague. It is set in seventeenth-century Seville.

ACT I. The overture (which Mozart supposedly wrote in three hours, the night before the première) consists of an *andante* introduction which reproduces the scene of the banquet in which the statue appears, followed by an *allegro* which characterises the impetuous, pleasure-seeking Don. Without pause, the overture links up with the song of Leporello (*bass*). Wrapped in his cloak and seated in the garden of a house in Seville, which the Don has entered secretly during the night, Leporello complains of the fate which makes him servant to such a restless and dangerous master. 'Notte e giorno faticar' (That's the life a servant leads – who cares when he sleeps or feeds?) runs his song; the music, like all that Leporello subsequently sings, is in the Italian *buffo* tradition, differing in degree of expressiveness but not in kind of expression from that of other contemporary *buffo* creations. Don Giovanni (*baritone*) rushes from the house, pursued by Donna Anna (*soprano*). There follows a trio in which the wrath of the insulted woman, the annoyance of the libertine, and the comments of the watching Leporello are expressed simultaneously. The Commendatore (*bass*) finds his daughter struggling with an unknown man, and draws his sword. In spite of the protests of Don Giovanni, who is reluctant to fight so old an opponent, a duel ensues and the Commendatore receives a mortal wound. The short, eighteen-bar trio between the Don, the dying Commendatore and Leporello contains in restricted outline but in master strokes the seeds of the serious side of the drama, just as the recitative which follows – Don Giovanni makes light of the whole affair – re-establishes the opera on a basis of comedy, only to return to seriousness with Anna's grief over the body of her father. In a duet Don Ottavio, her fiancé, tries to comfort her and swears to avenge the dead man.

The scene changes and Don Giovanni and Leporello spy a woman who appears to be inveighing against a lost lover. It is Donna Elvira (*soprano*), another of the Don's victims. When she cries with emotion, 'Ah, chi mi dice mai quel barbaro dov'è?' (Where shall I find the traitor who stole my heart away?) one feels that in spite of her anger, she is ready to forgive. She turns to find that the stranger who is attempting to console her is none other than Don Giovanni, who escapes, leaving Leporello to explain why he deserted her. Leporello's 'Catalogue Aria' – a list of his master's conquests – is one of the most famous arias in the repertory of the *basso buffo*. According to Leporello's catalogue, his master's adventures in love number 2,065 – 640 in Italy, 231 in Germany, 100 in France, 91 in Turkey, and in Spain no less than 1,003. It is small wonder that Elvira leaves the stage vowing vengeance upon her betrayer.

The countryside near Don Giovanni's palace not far from Seville. The young and pretty Zerlina (*soprano*) with Masetto (*baritone*), her fiancé, and their friends are singing and dancing in honour of their approaching marriage. Don Giovanni and Leporello join the throng. Having cast eyes upon Zerlina, the Don orders Leporello to get rid of the jealous Masetto by taking the entire gathering to his château. Masetto, while submitting to be removed, makes it clear to Don Giovanni – and to Zerlina – that he is not the fool he may look. Don Giovanni, alone with Zerlina, sings with her the famous duet 'Là ci darem la mano' (You'll lay your hand in mine, dear), which provides ample musical evidence that though the Don may be unsuccessful in each of the love affairs on which he embarks during the course of the opera, his reputation is still well deserved. Donna Elvira reappears and denounces Don Giovanni – 'Ah, fuggi il traditor!' (Be warned in time, my child) – to Zerlina, taking her off with her. Donna Anna and her fiancé Don Ottavio (*tenor*) enter, but no sooner is the Don in conversation with them than Elvira is back on the scene – a true comedy stroke. In a quartet, she again denounces Don Giovanni as a heartless deceiver, while he for his part says that she is mad; Anna and Ottavio don't know whom to believe. Elvira goes out, followed by Don Giovanni. Donna Anna is sure she recognises the voice of her father's assassin and her betrayer. Her narrative of the events of that night is a declamatory recitative followed by the aria 'Or sai chi l'onore' (You now know for certain). Its implacable vengefulness (and implacable *tessitura*) conspire to make it perhaps Mozart's most heavy and taxing music for the soprano voice. There follows, almost as an anticlimax, Ottavio's interpolated aria 'Dalla sua pace' (Mine be her burden, bravely to bear it), written for the Vienna première of the opera, when the tenor preferred not to sing 'Il mio tesoro' – but both arias are almost always included in modern performances. Don Giovanni, in the exuberant 'Fin ch'han dal vino' (Song, wine and women), gives orders for the festivity.

The garden outside Don Giovanni's palace. Zerlina begs Masetto's forgiveness in an ingratiating air, 'Batti, batti, o bel

Masetto'. Masetto's suspicions return when she seems nervous at the distant sound of the Don's voice.

Now begins the finale, one of the great masterpieces of dramatic music. Masetto overhears Don Giovanni order his retainers to spare no pains to make the evening a success, and confronts Zerlina and Don Giovanni as the latter attempts to lead her off into an alcove. The Don chides Masetto for leaving his bride-to-be alone, and takes them both into the house where the dancing is about to begin. Elvira, Anna and Ottavio appear, all of them masked. Leporello, in accordance with tradition, invites them in. After a moment of hesitation, they accept, pausing to pray heaven for aid in a remarkable trio.

The festivities are in full swing. Don Giovanni and Leporello manoeuvre to keep the still suspicious Masetto from Zerlina, but there is a diversion at the entry of the unknown maskers, who are welcomed by Don Giovanni. Masetto breaks away from Leporello, who has insisted on dancing with him and who hurries off to warn his master. Zerlina's shriek for help is heard from within. Don Giovanni rushes out, sword in hand, dragging with him the luckless Leporello, under pretext he is the guilty party. This ruse deceives no one. Anna, Elvira and Ottavio unmask and accuse the Don of murdering the Commendatore: 'Tutto, tutto già si sa' (All your guilt is now made clear). Taken aback at first, Don Giovanni soon recovers himself. He defies the threatening crowd. As a storm sweeps over the orchestra, he escapes.

ACT II. A street, with Donna Elvira's house in the background. Don Giovanni and Leporello make up their differences in a duet, 'Eh via, buffone'. This is followed by a trio for Elvira, Don Giovanni and Leporello. Elvira, leaning sadly on her balcony, gives voice to her regrets in a tune of exquisite beauty. In spite of all the circumstances she cannot hate Don Giovanni or efface his image from her heart. Meanwhile, her recreant lover changes clothes with his servant in the darkness below. While Leporello disguised as the Don attracts Donna Elvira into the garden, the Don himself mocks her with exaggerated protestations of love – 'Ah, taci, ingiusto core' (Ah, why do I remember) – which she takes at their face value.

Elvira descends, and Don Giovanni sings, to his own mandolin accompaniment, a serenade to Elvira's maid, to whom he has taken a fancy. 'Deh, vieni alla finestra' (Look down from out your window) is one of the most famous numbers of the opera. But before the Don can follow up his advantage, round the corner comes Masetto with a band of peasants seeking revenge. The still-disguised Don divides them up into parties which he dispatches, keeping Masetto with him. Having ascertained exactly what weapons Masetto has with him, the Don beats him and leaves him groaning on the ground. Zerlina hears his cries and consoles him with the graceful measures of 'Vedrai, carino, se sei buonino' (If you will promise not to mistrust me).

Elvira and Leporello (still disguised as his master) take refuge in the courtyard of a palace which turns out to be Donna Anna's. She returns home, escorted by Don Ottavio and a band of servants bearing torches. Elvira and Leporello escape, but are intercepted by Masetto and Zerlina. All take Leporello for the Don and, though Elvira pleads for him, demand his death – demands they seem reluctant to withdraw when they find out it is the servant they have caught after all. The sextet is a fine ensemble, with its variety of action and of musical sections reflecting the mood of each character. Now comes Don Ottavio's famous aria, 'Il mio tesoro intanto' (Speak for me to my lady). In spite of its rather obscure dramatic value, its musical beauty is as undeniable as its difficulty of execution. This is followed by Elvira's recitative and aria 'Mi tradi quell'alma ingrata' (All my love on him I lavished). Again its dramatic justification is slight, but in it Elvira rises to her full height.

A churchyard. Don Giovanni encounters none other than Leporello, who for his part is thankful to have got rid of Elvira. The Don is prepared to laugh the whole thing off when he hears a solemn voice issuing from the statue of the Commendatore. Leporello is ordered to invite the statue to supper, which he does in a duet, 'O statua gentilissima', his failing courage boosted by the vigorous encouragement of his master.

A room in Donna Anna's house. Ottavio enters, and she reproaches him when he hints at their forthcoming marriage; at such a time, how could she think of anything but her murdered father? Anna's 'Non mi dir' (Say no more), beautiful and famous as it is, contributes little to the dramatic development of the opera.

Don Giovanni's palace. During the brilliant introduction, he seats himself at table and sings of the pleasures of life. A stage orchestra plays airs from Vicente Martin's *Una Cosa Rara* and Sarti's *I due Litiganti*, and 'Non più andrai' from Mozart's own *Figaro* – the last-named greeted by Leporello as being a bit stale. Elvira enters, in a final plea to Don Giovanni to mend his ways. Failing, she leaves, but screams and runs back in, fleeing by another door. Leporello, sent to find out what frightened her, returns, babbling that the statue is outside. Drawing his sword, Don Giovanni goes into the corridor, but backs into the room before the statue of the Commendatore, which, with heavy footsteps echoed in the orchestra, enters. It has accepted the Don's dinner invitation. The statue asks the Don to bid him welcome and, in turn, asks him to supper. Don Giovanni accepts and gives his hand to the statue in pledge; it is seized in an icy-cold grip. A fiery pit opens. Demons seize Don Giovanni, unrepentant to the end, and drag him down to Hell.

In a contrasting epilogue, all moralise upon Don Giovanni's end and announce their plans: Zerlina and Masetto will go home to dine; Donna Anna and Don Ottavio will marry, after a year's mourning; Donna Elvira will enter a convent; and Leporello will go to the tavern to find a new – and better – master.

COSÌ FAN TUTTE

OPERA BUFFA in two acts by Wolfgang Amadeus Mozart; text by Lorenzo da Ponte. First performed at the Burgtheater, Vienna, January 26, 1790.

C*OSÌ FAN TUTTE, OSSIA LA SCUOLA DEGLI AMANTI* (All Women do Thus, or the School for Lovers) was written to a commission from the Emperor Joseph II; the story is said to have been based on a real-life incident which was the talk of Vienna at the time. The story is slight, but one of Da Ponte's neatest, and its symmetrical cast – two pairs of lovers, a third of worldly-wise cynics – and equally symmetrical construction provide Mozart with opportunities for some incomparable music. Mozart surpassed even himself in the richness and variety of his invention, in the impeccable skill with which the slenderest drama is adorned with music, in the creation of beauty. Yet, the music suggests not only the comedy which is on the surface and which remains an important part of the opera, but also the heartbreak behind the joke that goes too far and seems to take a serious turn.

The short overture has eight bars of slow introduction before the theme of the title is enunciated. Most of the rest of it is quick, until just before the end when the motto theme recurs.

ACT I. A café in eighteenth-century Naples. Three men are in the middle of a heated argument, or so one immediately assumes from Ferrando's (*tenor*) vigorous defence of Dorabella, his fiancée. There are three trios, the first with the two lovers answering the sceptical Alfonso (*baritone*), the second in the form of an accompanied solo for Alfonso, the third consisting of the lovers' jubilation at the prospect of winning the bet they make with Alfonso. It is a scene of the purest comedy and the music matches the artificiality of the mood.

Fiordiligi (*soprano*) and Dorabella's (*soprano*) garden. The sisters – paragons of faithfulness – discuss the respective merits of their young men as evinced in their portraits. The sentimental rapture at what they see is conveyed in music of exquisitely exaggerated cast, which dissolves in the middle into a cadenza in thirds on the word 'Amore'. This day-dreaming is interrupted by Don Alfonso, who makes obvious his distress at the news he is only too anxious to break to the two women: their lovers are ordered to the wars and have to leave immediately. The situation is admirably summed up in two quintets, separated by a short duet for the two officers and a military chorus. In 'Sento, oh Dio' (Courage fails me) the women are inconsolable, Don Alfonso builds up the situation, while Guglielmo (*bass*) is inclined to leave specific consolation to Ferrando and himself joins with Alfonso in a more general comment. Ferrando and Guglielmo say goodbye as soldiers march past, singing of the joys of a military existence. The sisters and their men sing a protracted and beautiful farewell, to pungent comment from Alfonso ('Di scrivermi ogni giorno': You'll write long letters often).

Their lovers departed, Fiordiligi and Dorabella show real feeling so that even Alfonso joins them in a wonderfully evocative trio, 'Soave sia il vento', as they pray for calm sea and gentle breezes for the travellers. The women leave as Alfonso muses in *secco* recitative on his plans. He grows animated at the thought of woman's changeability and launches into an accompanied tirade against the whole sex, the one inescapably bitter moment of the score.

The scene changes, and we meet the sisters' chattering maid, Despina (*soprano*). Dorabella gives vent to her feelings, in an aria of exaggeratedly tragic order, 'Smanie implacabili'. Despina advises a more moderate line; she is the female counterpart of Don Alfonso, and in her philosophy a lover's absence affords an opportunity for sport, not lamentation: 'In uomini, in soldati'. The women go out in disgust, and Alfonso enlists Despina as an ally. Enter the two officers, disguised as Albanians; Despina laughs at them but does not recognise them. The sisters return and are indignant at finding two strange men in their house and demand they leave. Alfonso embraces the Albanians as old friends of his; will the women not be kind to them – for his sake? Fiordiligi makes it clear that their protestations of love are entirely unavailing: she and her sister are each 'firm as a rock' ('Come scoglio'). Guglielmo answers for Ferrando as well as himself and is given music of such delicacy and charm – 'Non siate ritrosi' (O vision so charming) – that one cannot but be surprised that the sisters leave the room before he finishes the aria, which dissolves in laughter. Don Alfonso finally persuades his young friends that he has by no means lost the bet and that they should meet him in the garden in a few minutes. Ferrando, alone, sings of his love in a beautiful aria ('Un'aura amorosa' – Her eyes so alluring). Alfonso and Despina reassure themselves that this is only a pair of women, and there is as yet no danger of losing the bet.

The garden. Fiordiligi and Dorabella reflect on the mutability of pleasure in music of exquisite tenderness. Ferrando and Guglielmo rush in, brandishing bottles of poison which Alfonso is unable to prevent them from drinking. The Albanians sink into a coma, Alfonso and Despina rush for the doctor, and pandemonium breaks loose. Alfonso returns with the doctor (Despina in disguise), who gives the corpses the benefit of the most recent scientific discovery – mesmerism – in the form of an oversize, all-healing magnet. The corpses revive, think at first that they are in the Elysian Fields, and demand a kiss from the goddesses to set the seal on their cure. This is indignantly refused, and the act ends with the sisters defending their honour to a background of derisive exclamations from Despina and Alfonso and approving comments from the Albanians.

ACT II. Despina loses her patience with her virtuous employers, rounding off her point in an aria, 'Una donna a quindici anni'. The sisters themselves agree that there can be no harm in talking innocently with the strangers. Their minds made up, each selects the appropriate partner ('Prenderò quel brunettino' – Give me then the gentle dark one) and they are invited to an entertainment in the garden. Ferrando and Guglielmo serenade the sisters with the entrancing duet and chorus, 'Secondate aurette amiche' (Gentle zephyr, softly sighing). If this is Mozart's most hedonistically inclined opera, no other number so perfectly illustrates its prevailing characteristic. But neither Albanian seems able to pursue the advantage gained, and, in disgust, Alfonso and Despina enact the scene for them, stealing away and leaving two embarrassed couples talking animatedly about the weather. Ferrando is led off by Fiordiligi, and, after some tentative compliments, Guglielmo succeeds in giving Dorabella a heart-shaped locket, in return for which he removes the medallion (with its portrait of Ferrando) from her neck. Their duet, 'Il core vi dono' (This heart that I give you), is charmingly light in texture and sentiment.

Meanwhile, Fiordiligi is proving a harder nut to crack. She turns a deaf ear to Ferrando's advances, and he is given a magnificent aria (often omitted), 'Ah, lo veggio, quell'anima bella' (Well I knew that a maid so enchanting), in which he alternately expresses doubts and confidence as to the outcome. This is followed by Fiordiligi's great rondo, 'Per pietà, ben mio, perdona' (Ah, my love, forgive my madness), which is the showpiece of the opera. Its extensive length and range, sudden and precipitous leaps from high soprano to contralto and back again, combine to show off the singer's technique, which is mocked at the same time as it is used to express the turmoil of conflicting emotions in Fiordiligi's mind. A horn obbligato adds to the effect.

Ferrando and Guglielmo compare notes. Ferrando is furiously indignant when he hears of Dorabella's conduct and sees proof in the shape of the locket he himself has given her. Don't take it so much to heart, replies his friend, in a wonderful example of an *opera buffa* aria: 'Ladies have such variations, permutations, combinations' ('Donne mie, la fate a tanti'). Symmetry being what it is, Ferrando follows up with an aria (sometimes omitted).

Fiordiligi resolves to make a last effort to extricate herself and maybe Dorabella from an intolerable situation. She sends for a couple of old uniforms belonging to Ferrando and Guglielmo and announces her intention of going off to the wars taking her equally disguised sister. The beginning of her aria is interrupted by Ferrando, still in his Albanian disguise, who protests that she should run her sword through her heart and end his agony for ever. Resistance crumbles and Fiordiligi falls into Ferrando's arms – its emotional ambivalence makes this the opera's key scene.

Guglielmo has been watching the whole scene, and Alfonso has found it hard to keep him quiet. 'What about your fond Fiordiligi now?' asks Ferrando; 'Fior di Diavolo!' answers the discomfited Guglielmo. They are no worse than all the other women, affirms Alfonso, who makes the crestfallen lovers repeat the motto with him: 'Così fan tutte'. Despina brings the news that her mistresses intend to make their Albanian suitors happy and marry them at once.

Servants prepare the wedding under Despina's direction, and hail the bridal couples when they appear. The lovers' toast is an enchanting canon, led by Fiordiligi, which goes harmoniously on its way until it is Guglielmo's turn; he contents himself with an angry aside to the effect that nothing would please him more than that the wine should turn to poison on their lips. Alfonso brings in a notary (Despina in yet another costume) who, with much vocal disguise and a spate of pseudo-legal patter, prepares the contract, which is signed.

There is a burst of military music, which is immediately recognised by the sisters as the march to which Ferrando and Guglielmo went off to the wars. Suspicion turns to consternation when Alfonso confirms that Ferrando and Guglielmo are on their way to the house. The Albanians are bundled out, the sisters try to compose themselves, and their military lovers enter. Despina is discovered in an ante-room, Alfonso conveniently lets the marriage contracts fall where the young men cannot fail to see them, and they are told that proof of the inconstancy can be found in the next room. In a moment they reappear with bits of the Albanian costumes, singing snatches of the music that helped bring the wooing to its successful conclusion.

Everything is forgiven, the four lovers are reunited – whether in the original or Albanian combination we are not told – and the six characters sing a valedictory in praise of him who is able to take the rough with the smooth and who can fall back on reason however the world treats him.

Is *Così fan tutte* a comedy pure and simple? Maybe yes, maybe no, but if it is, like every comedy of genius, it comments profoundly and movingly and above all naturally on human life and manners during the course of its action.

LA CLEMENZA DI TITO
The Clemency of Titus

OPERA in two acts by Wolfgang Amadeus Mozart; text by Mazzolà, adapted from Metastasio. First performed at the National Theatre, Prague, September 6, 1791.

ALL his life, Mozart had a longing to write *opera seria*; his attempts began with *Mitridate*, written during his years in Italy (1770), reached their height in *Idomeneo* (1781) and culminated in *La Clemenza di Tito* (1791). Even though *opera seria* was already in 1781 an out-of-date form, it was Mozart not Gluck who was in *Idomeneo* to say the final word on the subject. *La Clemenza di Tito* is a rather different matter. Mazzolà's revised version of Metastasio's libretto, though dramatically a great improvement on its model, may not, with its conventional glorification of benevolent despotism, have been particularly congenial material for Mozart. The opera was commissioned to celebrate the coronation in Prague in 1791 of the Emperor Leopold II as King of Bohemia. Mozart had not even finished *The Magic Flute* and was engaged on the *Requiem*, yet *Tito* was written and performed within eighteen days of receipt of the commission, during part of which period the composer was travelling from Vienna to Prague. Small wonder that Mozart had to entrust the composition of the *secco* recitatives to his pupil Süssmayer! Three weeks after the première, *The Magic Flute* was brought out in Vienna; nine weeks later still, Mozart was dead. It only remains to add that the work seems to have failed at its first performance, but within a month had turned into a considerable success. It was performed in most German-speaking theatres (in German of course) before the end of the first decade of the nineteenth century, and was actually the first of Mozart's operas to be heard in London, in 1806, when it was given in Italian for Mrs. Billington's benefit.

The story is dominated by two considerations: the determination of Vitellia, the daughter of the deposed Roman Emperor, herself in love with Titus, to have revenge on him when he seems disposed to marry another; and the inclination of Titus to show clemency no matter what the provocation.

ACT I. Vitellia (*soprano*) knows of Titus's plan to marry Berenice, daughter of Agrippa I of Judaea, and she urges Sextus (*contralto*), who is madly in love with her, to fall in with her plans and lead a conspiracy against Titus. No sooner has he agreed than she hears that Berenice has been sent home and that Titus now plans to marry a Roman. Annius (*mezzo-soprano*) asks his friend Sextus to intercede with the Emperor in the matter of his (Annius's) marriage to Servilia, Sextus's sister, but Sextus is forestalled in his plan when Titus (*tenor*) tells him that he has chosen none other than Servilia to be Empress. Servilia herself (*soprano*) tells the Emperor that she is in love with Annius, and he renounces her, deciding instead to take Vitellia to wife. Vitellia has no knowledge of this change of plans, and sends Sextus off to set fire to the Capitol and murder Titus, only to hear, the moment he is gone, that she is now the destined bride of Titus. Sextus succeeds in the first part of his plan, but the conspiracy against Titus's life fails when someone else, wearing his mantle, is killed in his stead. The act ends in general confusion.

ACT II. It is known that Titus has escaped death, and moreover that the details of the plot have been revealed to him. Annius advises Sextus to throw himself on the mercy of the Emperor and to show renewed zeal in his cause. Vitellia in contrast is anxious to avoid any risk that her connection with the plot may be discovered, and she urges Sextus to fly the country. Publius (*bass*), the Captain of the Praetorian Guard, settles the matter by arriving to arrest Sextus, who is tried by the Senate and condemned to death. Titus confronts him with proof of his guilt, but when Sextus has left him, tears up the death sentence he has just signed. As Sextus and the other conspirators are about to be thrown to the wild beasts in the arena, Vitellia can bear the load of guilt no longer and confesses her share in the plot, only in her turn to be forgiven by the clement Emperor.

For years, critical opinion was agreed that the music of *La Clemenza di Tito* was written in a hurry at a time when Mozart was exhausted by illness and overwork, and is therefore of little value. Anyone hearing it again (or maybe for the first time) will find it hard to agree that it is uninspired, although certainly written against time and in an outmoded form. There is almost no dramatic impetus behind the plot of the opera, and few of the arias have powerful situations behind them. But plot was never the strong point of *opera seria*, which aimed rather at providing a dignified and apt frame for the noble music and virtuoso singing which the aristocracy wanted to hear. Mozart and Mazzolà have between them upset some of the static nature of Metastasio's original libretto but even so they have not succeeded in altering the essentially conventional nature of the entertainment; on the other hand, Mozart has succeeded in providing a very superior example of the sort of music which went with these eighteenth-century occasions – that he did not write another *Don Giovanni* is logical. He was being asked to write something entirely different.

Of the twenty-six numbers in the score, only eleven are in fact arias – which shows how much alteration was made in Metastasio's original, which made provision for no ensembles of any sort or kind. They range from a simple arietta such as that for Servilia ('S'altro che lagrime') to the great showpieces for Sextus ('Parto, parto') and Vitellia ('Non più di fiori'). These latter have elaborate instrumental obbligati, for respectively clarinet and basset horn, and Anton Stadler went specially to Prague to play them. The vocal writing is no less elaborate, and, in this combination of virtuoso styles for voice and instrument, the arias look back to 'Martern aller Arten' (or even 'Possente spirto' from Monteverdi's *Orfeo*), and forward to such different pieces as Schubert's song 'Der Hirt auf dem Felsen' and the Mad Scene in *Lucia*. The duets for Sextus and Annius and for Servilia and Annius are particularly attractive, and there is a fine trio for Vitellia, Sextus and Publius in the second act just before the arrest of Sextus. But the most notable section of the score is the finale to Act I, after the Capitol has been set on fire by Sextus. An agitated crowd off stage adds to the terror of the characters on stage, and Mozart builds up the whole ensemble antiphonally to imposing dimensions. It is genuine dramatic music, and is the only time the composer makes simultaneous use of soloists and chorus together in an extended finale.

DIE ZAUBERFLÖTE
The Magic Flute

OPERA in two acts by Wolfgang Amadeus Mozart; text by Emanuel Schikaneder. First performed at the Theater auf der Wieden, Vienna, September 30, 1791.

46

*T*HE MAGIC FLUTE's strong relationship to Freemasonry came about more by circumstance than design. Schikaneder's original plan was for a puppet show based on the oriental tale of *Lulu*, by Liebeskind. Schikaneder, a successful actor who ran a theatre company and was, like Mozart, a Freemason, had persuaded Mozart to compose the music to the show, but the project was abandoned when a rival Viennese theatre performed its own version of the tale. So the actor-writer turned his agile mind to Freemasonry, a subject much in the news at the time. As a practical man, Schikaneder saw his chance to exploit the once forbidden rites on the stage, and the ordeals of Tamino and Pamina became copies of the ceremonials of Freemasonry. He also set the opera in Egypt, where Freemasonry believes its rites to have originated. Mozart's music ennobled the libretto and lent to the whole the force of the mysterious and sacred.

Mozart was engaged on *The Magic Flute* from March until July 1791, and again in September. The first performance was given on September 30, two months before his death.

In the overture, the heavy, reiterated chords represent, it has been suggested, the knocking at the door of the lodge room, especially as they are heard again in the temple scene.

ACT I. Tamino, an Egyptian prince (*tenor*), trying to escape from a marauding serpent, falls unconscious. Three black-garbed Ladies-in-Waiting to the Queen of the Night appear and kill the serpent with their spears. In an extended trio, the Ladies (*sopranos* and *mezzo-soprano*) rejoice, commenting on the good looks of the young man they have rescued. They go, and Tamino recovers consciousness only to see dancing towards him an odd-looking man covered in feathers. It is Papageno (*baritone*), the Queen's bird-catcher. His song, 'Der Vogelfänger bin ich ja' (I am the jolly bird-catcher), is punctuated with runs on his pipe. He tells the astonished Tamino that this is the realm of the Queen of the Night and boasts that he killed the monster. The three Ladies reappear and, to punish him for lying, place a padlock on his mouth. Then they show Tamino a miniature portrait of a beautiful woman. His feelings are expressed in one of Mozart's most beautiful tenor arias, 'Dies Bildnis ist bezaubernd schön' (O loveliness beyond compare). The Ladies tell him that she is the Queen's daughter and a prisoner of Sarastro. No sooner has Tamino sworn to deliver her than the Queen herself (*soprano*) materialises to reinforce his determination with a description of her desolation and a promise that Pamina shall be his once she is free. 'O zittre nicht, mein lieber Sohn' (Be not afraid, O noble youth), she sings, and her *scena* develops into a display of coloratura fireworks, expressive also of her headstrong, passionate nature. The Ladies unlock Papageno's mouth and give him a set of chimes and Tamino a golden flute; by means of these magical instruments they will be able to escape the perils of their journey, on which they will be accompanied by three boys or Genii (*sopranos* and *mezzo-soprano*). The enchanting quintet 'Hm hm hm! Der Arme kann von Strafe sagen' ('Tis hard such punishment to suffer) introduces the 'magical' music associated later with the boys.

A richly furnished apartment in Sarastro's palace. Monostatos (*tenor*) pursues Pamina (*soprano*) with unwelcome attentions. Even in this essentially comic duet, something of Pamina's depth can be discerned. Papageno appears and scares off the Moor. Recognising Pamina by comparing her with her portrait, he assures her she will soon be rescued, and, what is more, by someone who has fallen in love with her without even seeing her – not the sort of thing, he laments, that ever happens to him. Pamina consoles him in an exquisitely simple E flat tune and assures him that love will yet be his: 'Bei Männern, welche Liebe fühlen, fehlt auch ein gutes Herze nicht' (The kindly voice of mother Nature wakes love in bird and beast and flower).

A grove in which are three Temples, dedicated to Wisdom, Reason and Nature. The three boys lead in Tamino, advising that he 'be silent, patient, persevering'. Tamino decides to enter the Temples, but at the first two he is refused admittance, and from the third emerges the Speaker (*bass*), who informs him that Sarastro, the High Priest, is no tyrant, no wicked sorcerer as the Queen had warned him, but a man of wisdom and noble character. The solemn atmosphere of their dialogue – an extraordinary example of a musical argument reinforcing words with logic – serves to awaken still further Tamino's desire for knowledge and his recitative 'O ew'ge Nacht' (O endless night) takes the form of question and answer, the answer being supplied by a hidden and encouraging chorus. He takes his flute and plays and sings to its accompaniment: 'Wie stark is nicht dein Zauberton' (O voice of magic melody). Wild animals emerge and lie at Tamino's feet, but before the end of the aria he hears Papageno's pan-pipe and rushes off to find him. Immediately Papageno enters from the opposite side leading Pamina, whom he intends to unite with Tamino. Their duet, 'Schnelle Füsse, rascher Mut' (Let us hasten, quick as thought), is punctuated with calls on the pipes and answers from the flute but becomes a trio when they are caught by Monostatos. Papageno plays his magic chimes, setting the Moor and his slaves dancing. Papageno and Pamina's rejoicing at their escape is interrupted by a flourish of trumpets and chorus of praise to Sarastro. Papageno wonders what they are going to tell him. 'Die Wahrheit!' (The truth, friend), proudly answers Pamina,

and the phrase serves to end the comedy of escape and to in-
itiate the solemnity of Sarastro's procession. She explains to
Sarastro that she was trying to escape the attentions of the
Moor. Sarastro (*bass*) assures her that he understands her predicament and that the Gods aim to provide a remedy. Monostatos drags Tamino in and denounces him to Sarastro. Instead
of the reward he expects, he is sentenced to a sound flogging.
Sarastro commands Pamina and Tamino to be brought into the
Temple, where they must prove they are worthy of the higher
happiness.

ACT II. A grove outside the Temple. After a solemn *andante*,
Sarastro informs the Priests of his plans. The Gods have
decided that Pamina shall become the wife of the noble youth
Tamino. But he must first prove, by his own initiative, that he is
worthy of admission to the Temple. Therefore, Sarastro has
taken under his protection Pamina, daughter of the Queen of
the Night, to whom is due all darkness and superstition. The
couple must go through severe ordeals in order to be worthy of
entering the Temple of Light, thus thwarting the machinations
of the Queen. Sarastro prays to Isis and Osiris that strength may
be granted to the two aspirants after the goal of wisdom ('O Isis
und Osiris').

The Porch of the Temple. The ordeals of Tamino and Papageno are about to begin. They are warned by the Priests that
they may perish in their search for the Truth, and then enjoined
to silence as the first step in their probation. No sooner are they
left alone than they are confronted by the Three Ladies who try
to persuade them to abandon their quest. But Tamino and even
(with some prompting) Papageno maintain a rigid silence. The
Priests reappear and congratulate them on having passed their
first test.

A garden. Pamina is asleep. Monostatos slinks up to her, but
a cry of 'Zurück!' causes him to start back: it is the Queen of the
Night, who flings her daughter a dagger, commanding that she
use it to kill Sarastro. In 'Der Hölle Rache kocht in meinem Herzen' (I'll have revenge, no longer can I bear it) the fires of fury
can be felt boiling in the music, with its passionate staccato
coloratura, its four top Fs, and its headlong impetus. Monostatos returns and, threatening that he will reveal the plot (to
which Pamina has never agreed to be a party), demands her
love as the price of his silence. Sarastro enters and hurls Monostatos from the defenceless Pamina, but the Moor departs promising to try if he will have better luck with the Queen of the
Night. Pamina pleads for her mother, but Sarastro assures her
that vengeance is not in his thoughts: 'In diesen heil' gen Hallen
kennt man die Rache nicht' (We know no thought of vengeance
within these temple walls). Again, the nobility of the music

expression equals, perhaps even surpasses, that of 'O Isis und Osiris'.

A Hall. Enjoined once more to keep silent, Tamino and Papageno are again left by the Priests. Papageno chatters to himself, and soon enters into a conversation with an old crone who introduces herself to him as his yet unknown sweetheart, Papagena (*soprano*). A clap of thunder and she departs, to be replaced by the three boys who appear with the flute and magic bells, carrying a table spread with food and drink. Pamina enters, overjoyed to have found Tamino. But her delight is short-lived and she suspends belief in human constancy when she can get no answer from her beloved. Her G minor aria, 'Ach, ich fühl's, es ist verschwunden' (Ah, 'tis gone, 'tis gone for ever), shows that mixture of maturity and innocence which she has consistently shown reaching its highest level of expression.

A vault. After the Priests sing a solemn *adagio* chorus of praise to Isis and Osiris, Sarastro tells Pamina and Tamino to take their last farewell of each other: 'Soll ich dich, Teurer, nicht mehr seh'n?' (And shall I never see thee more?). Meanwhile, Papageno is told he can have one wish granted but is left vaguely dissatisfied when he has drunk the wine he asks for. What is missing? 'Ein Mädchen oder Weibchen wünscht Papageno sich' ('Tis love they say, love only, that makes the world go round). The old woman returns, threatening Papageno with dire penalties if he does not swear to be true to her; when he does so, she reveals herself as the youthful Papagena. But Papageno is warned off by a Priest who pronounces him not yet worthy of her.

A garden. The three boys sing of the symbolical joys of the rising sun, whose rays drive away the fears of night and herald the reign of light and love: 'Bald prangt, den Morgen zu verkünden' (The rosy flush that greets us yonder). Not knowing she is observed, Pamina contemplates suicide ('Du also bist mein Bräutigam? Durch dich vollend' ich meinem Gram': No other way but this remains to make an end of all my pains), but is restrained and comforted by the boys in music of extraordinary tenderness. Tamino is brought in by the Priests for the last stage of his initiation. The test of fire and water is heralded by two Men in Armour, standing each side of a doorway. Tamino proclaims his resolution, but is joined by Pamina for these final ordeals. Pamina's sufferings have produced an astonishing serenity and even wisdom in her. She is not only Tamino's guide as, to the accompaniment of an *adagio* for the solo flute, they undergo successively the ordeals by fire and by water, but also in a sense Mozart's ideal woman. At the end they are welcomed into the Temple by Sarastro and the Priests.

Papageno is contemplating suicide, in a parallel trial in comic terms perhaps to those of Tamino and Pamina. The boys intervene; the *scena* ends happily with a jingle of bells, followed by an irresistible patter duet for Papageno and Papagena.

Before the Temple, Monostatos leads on the Queen and her Ladies, who are making a last bid for revenge on Sarastro. But their appearance coincides with a flood of light; the forces of night disappear before a short chorus praises the new initiates and the magic flute which was their faithful companion brings the opera to an end.

Nothing is so simple as to be absolutely clear-cut, and in life the serious and the comic are intermingled in a way that is frequently disconcerting but none the less inevitable. *The Magic Flute*, serious in its presentation of the urge towards an understanding of truth, none the less mingles the digressions of Papageno with the aspirations of Tamino and Pamina. A refusal to take the story of *The Magic Flute* seriously is to turn a blind eye to the impeccable skill of the librettist (or librettists) and also to deny to the genius of Mozart the power of discrimination and choice. His terms of reference and his plans are fascinating, but far more important is the work of art which resulted. In the case of *The Magic Flute* (and *Don Giovanni*) he succeeded in combining the two elements which make up everyday life in a way which may occasionally have been approached since his day, but which had hardly before been attempted and has never been surpassed.

Ludwig van Beethoven
(1770–1827)

FIDELIO

OPERA in two acts; text by Joseph Sonnleithner and Georg Friedrich Sonnleithner after a drama by Jean Nicolas Bouilly. Première, Theater auf der Wieden, Vienna, November 20, 1805 (in three acts).

BOUILLY's original libretto was written for the French composer Pierre Gaveaux in 1798 and was set by two other composers. For Beethoven and his audiences the French Revolution subject was as much contemporary as have been Menotti's *The Consul*, Poulenc's *La Voix humaine* and Adams's *Nixon in China* in the second half of the twentieth century.

The opera is in *Singspiel* form, with spoken dialogue between the musical numbers, and Beethoven cannot have found it easy to reconcile his predilection for high-minded, heroic themes with his chosen form's more domestic tendencies. The original version (1805), with an audience mostly made up of French troops occupying Vienna, was not a success. The 1806 revision reduced three acts to two, and the final reworking (1814) substantially revised music and text – alterations to every musical number except the March. Nonetheless, the versions of 1805 and 1806 are very far from either incompetent or negligible, as revivals in 1970, the Beethoven bicentenary year, will testify.

Confusion reigns over the four overtures. *Leonore No. 2* was played at the première in 1805, *Leonore No. 3* at the 1806 revision, and a new, less 'symphonic' prelude (the *Fidelio* overture) was composed for 1814, though, modern scholarship says, not ready until the second performance. *Leonore No. 1* (published as op. 138 and first performed eleven months after Beethoven's death) may have been meant for the 1805 production and discarded before the first night.

Before the opera begins, Florestan, who worked for the progressive Minister of State, Don Fernando, has disappeared in mysterious circumstances. Only his wife Leonore refuses to believe he is dead and has narrowed her search for him to a prison near Seville whose reactionary governor was Florestan's enemy; there she works disguised as a young man, Fidelio.

ACT I. A prison courtyard. A brisk duet between Jaquino (*tenor*), the chief gaoler Rocco's assistant, and Marzelline (*soprano*), Rocco's daughter, suggests that he is in love with her but that she prefers, as her subsequent aria confirms, Fidelio, her father's new assistant. She is joined by her father (*bass*), but the appearance of Fidelio (*soprano*) brings a change of mood to something almost mystic in a remarkable canon quartet. The theme enunciated by each character is the same but their sentiments differ, and the quartet establishes, in contrast to the two earlier numbers, the lofty aspirations of much of the rest of the opera. With Rocco's jocular, almost vulgar, aria in praise of money and young people's need for it, the *Singspiel* convention reappears (the aria was dropped for 1806, reinstated in 1814), but it wavers again with the subsequent trio. Fidelio in effect volunteers for the more taxing side of a prison gaoler's job, and Rocco praises him for his resolution; Marzelline continues her generalised adoration, and the trio is dominated by Fidelio's 'Ich habe Muth' (I have the strength).

A short rhythmically striking March bridges the scenes and proclaims the arrival of Pizarro (*baritone*), the governor. One of the dispatches he peruses warns him that Don Fernando is on his way to inspect the fortress, and he weighs in with a hefty aria presaging immediate action against Florestan. He posts a trumpeter to warn of the Minister's approach, then tosses a purse to Rocco with instructions to make away with the most dangerous of the prisoners. Rocco's reluctance grows in the course of a repetitious but effective duet, during which Pizarro determines to do the job himself. Fidelio overhears the plot and reacts in the highly dramatic 'Abscheulicher! wo eilst du hin?' (Accursed one! where do you hasten?). The grandiose aria, with its moving middle section expressing continuing hope for the success of her rescue mission, is quite outside the *Singspiel* convention.

On Fidelio's intercession and because it is the King's birthday, the prisoners are allowed into the open air and Fidelio scans their faces to see if Florestan is among them. Act II's lofty aspirations are perhaps most fully anticipated in the music of the prisoners as they grope their way towards light and hope (Prisoners' Chorus). With a great cry of 'Noch heute!' (This very day!) Leonore learns that as Rocco's assistant she will that day help him dig the grave in what may be her husband's cell. If she cannot save him, she can die with him. On Pizarro's reappearance, the prisoners are hustled back to their cells, but Rocco staves off retribution by an astute reference to the plot Pizarro wants him to be part of.

ACT II. A dungeon. An orchestral introduction of extraordinary dramatic import, all heavily weighted chords, grinding turns on the strings and an apparently endless descent into the depths, prepares us for a first sight of Florestan (*tenor*) in chains. Its arioso-recitative is a triumph of word-setting, and, if the *adagio cantabile* aria relies on recollection of things past, the quick section which follows parts company with normality as Florestan's vision of Leonore leads to hysteria. A whispered scene between Leonore and Rocco ends as Florestan recovers from his swoon and Leonore recognises her husband. She is permitted to offer him a drink and a morsel of food and his thanks for an unexpected kindness lead to a trio of extraordinary beauty and in the circumstances amazing serenity.

Pizarro enters and begins a highly dramatic quartet by making himself known to Florestan but, as he draws his dagger, Fidelio stands between him and Florestan, then reveals herself as Leonore: 'Tödt erst sein Weib!' (First, kill his wife!). A trumpet call rings out, Jaquino announces the Minister, and Pizarro's moment has gone. There is a rapturous duet ('O namenlose Freude!' – O joy beyond comparing) and a happy ending to an opera, much of whose music has presaged tragedy, is in sight.

The chorus rejoices at the freeing of the prisoners (in C major, whose brilliance is upstaged if the *Leonore No. 3* is played to cover the scene change), Don Fernando (*bass*) recognises Florestan and sets Leonore to free him from his fetters, Pizarro is arrested, and the opera, with an anticipation of the Ninth Symphony, comes to a triumphant end.

53

Carl Maria von Weber
(1786–1826)

DER FREISCHÜTZ
The Free-Shooter

OPERA in three acts; text by Johann Friedrich Kind. First produced at the Schauspielhaus, Berlin, June 18, 1821.

THE overture to *Der Freischütz* is the first in which an operatic composer unreservedly made use of melodies, rather than merely thematic material, from the opera itself.

ACT I. At the target range. Kilian (*tenor*), a peasant, has surprisingly defeated Max (*tenor*), the forester, at a prize shooting. Kilian and the villagers join in mocking Max – a clever bit of teasing in music which establishes at the very start the originality of melody, style, and character of the opera, which is set in seventeenth-century Bohemia.

The hereditary forester, Cuno (*bass*), is worried over Max's poor showing, especially since there is a competition next day which Max must win in order to marry Cuno's daughter, Agathe (*soprano*), and eventually succeed him as hereditary forester. An expressive trio for Max, Caspar (*bass*; another forester) and Cuno with Chorus ('O diese Sonne!') is followed by a short waltz. Max is in despair; life will be worthless to him without Agathe, yet he seems to have lost all his cunning as a shot, and without it he cannot win her hand. The first part of this *scena*, 'Durch die Wälder, durch die Auen' (Through the forest and o'er the meadows), is a melody of great beauty, but the music takes on a more sinister character as the threatening shadow of Samiel, the wild huntsman and a force of evil, hovers in the background. Caspar approaches Max and tells him to shoot at a high-flying eagle. Max shoots, and the bird falls at his feet. Caspar explains that he has used a charmed bullet which always hits what the marksman wills it to. Max agrees to meet Caspar in the Wolf's Glen at midnight, where they will mould bullets to enable him to win the contest. Caspar's drinking song, which precedes his tempting of Max, is forced in its hilarity and ends in grotesque laughter; Caspar has sold himself to Samiel. The act ends with a taxing aria for Caspar, in keeping with his sinister character.

ACT II. Agathe's room in Cuno's house. The music opens with a delightful duet for Agathe and her cousin Aennchen (*soprano*) and a coquettish air for the latter ('Kommt ein schlanker Bursch gegangen' – Comes a comely youth a-wooing). But Agathe has forebodings, and even her cousin is unable to cheer her up. Agathe, alone, opens the window and, as the moonlight floods the room, sings the simple and expressive prayer, 'Leise, leise, fromme Weise' (Softly sighing, day is dying). This leads into an ecstatic melody as she sees her lover approaching. It is one of the best-known tunes in all opera.

Max enters, quickly followed by Aennchen. Max says he must go after a deer he has shot in the Wolf's Glen. The women try to warn him against going, as the Glen is said to be haunted.

The Wolf's Glen. Caspar plans to turn over Max to Samiel (*spoken*) as a victim, in order to gain for himself a respite on earth. Max enters and he and Caspar (to gruesome, expressive music) mould the seven magic bullets, six of which go true to the mark, the seventh wherever Samiel wills. The ghost of Max's mother appears, to warn him away. Cadaverous animals crawl out from the rocks and spit flames and sparks. The way the music avoids the excessive but yet cunningly mixes the speaking voice and singing, the purely musical effect of Max's entrance with the atmospheric climax of the moulding of the bullets, is entirely admirable.

ACT III. After a brief introduction, with suggestions of the hunting chorus to come, Agathe sings a cavatina, 'Und ob die Wolke' (And though a cloud the sun obscure), a melody of such pure and expressive beauty that even Weber himself never surpassed it. Aennchen sings a solo (composed after the rest of the opera), and the bridesmaids enter to prepare Agathe's bridal garland.

The shooting test, attended by Prince Ottokar (*baritone*), begins with the spirited hunting chorus. Only the seventh bullet, the one which Samiel controls, remains to be fired, the others were used up during the hunt. Caspar, who expects Max to be Samiel's victim, watches from a safe place of concealment. The prince points to a flying dove and Max raises his gun. At that moment Agathe appears, accompanied by a Hermit (*bass*), and calls out to Max not to shoot, that she is the dove. But Max has already pulled the trigger; Agathe falls – but only in a swoon – and Caspar is fatally wounded. Samiel has had no power over Max, as he did not go to the Wolf's Glen of his own free will, but only after being tempted by Caspar; therefore Caspar himself is the victim. There is general uproar. Max confesses and the prince banishes him. But the Hermit, a holy man revered by the district, intervenes in a chorale-like aria and succeeds in obtaining the prince's forgiveness. The opera ends with the jubilant melody from Agathe's Act II scene.

Der Freischütz holds an important position in music and operatic development. Weber was virtually the founder of the German romantic school, which reached its peak with Wagner, its culmination perhaps with Richard Strauss. There are many similarities between *Der Freischütz* and *Tannhäuser*, but Weber is more than just Wagner's forerunner – just as Bellini has importance of his own beyond being the predecessor of Verdi. He is one of the great melodists of musical history, and perhaps no other composer of the romantic movement so completely preserved musical freshness at the same time as he introduced the literary element into music.

Otto Nicolai
(1810–1849)

DIE LUSTIGEN WEIBER VON WINDSOR
The Merry Wives of Windsor

THREE acts, based on Shakespeare; première, Berlin, 1849. Frau Fluth (*soprano*) and Frau Reich (*mezzo-soprano*) compare notes on a love-letter each has received from Falstaff (*bass*). Herr Reich (*bass*) has promised his daughter Anna (*soprano*) in marriage to Spärlich (*tenor*) although she loves Fenton (*tenor*). Frau Fluth receives Falstaff, who protests his love; they are interrupted and he hides in the linen basket as Fluth and his friends search the house. Falstaff, as planned by the women, is tipped into the river. At the inn, Fluth, unrecognised, pumps Falstaff on his relations with Frau Fluth and plots to catch him out. A charming scene follows for Anna and her three suitors. Fluth threatens his wife with exposure while Falstaff, disguised, is smuggled out by Frau Reich. In Windsor forest, amid much merriment, Falstaff as Herne the Hunter is tormented by 'fairies' before all is resolved, to a reprise of the overture's theme.

Richard Wagner
(1813–1883)

DER FLIEGENDE HOLLÄNDER
The Flying Dutchman

OPERA in three acts; text by the composer, founded on an episode in Heine's *Memoirs of Herr von Schnabelewopski*. Performed at the Hofoper, Dresden, January 2, 1843.

*T*HE FLYING DUTCHMAN is a work of wild and sombre beauty, relieved only occasionally by touches of light and grace, and has all the interest attaching to a work in which, not for the first time, a genius feels himself conscious of his greatness. Even the conventional sections – most of Eric's music and much of Daland's – are on a high level, the choral writing is superb and, in the last act, almost uniquely atmospheric, and the figures of the gloomy Dutchman and the obsessive Senta are unsurpassed in musico-dramatic terms even in the later masterpieces.

Wagner's libretto is based upon the legend of the Flying Dutchman – a sea captain who tried to double the Cape of Good Hope in the teeth of a furious gale, and swore he would accomplish his purpose even if he kept on sailing for ever. The devil, hearing the oath, condemned the captain to sail the sea until Judgment Day, without hope of release, unless he should find a woman who would love him faithfully until death. Once every seven years he is allowed ashore in search of such a woman. The opera opens just as a seven-year term has elapsed.

The overture, an eloquent and beautiful musical narrative of the whole opera, contains all the work's leading motifs, including those of the Dutchman himself, Senta's Ballad, the Sailors' Chorus, and the characteristic storm music which can be heard throughout the opera.

ACT I. A shore in Norway. A storm is raging. Daland's ship has sought shelter in a cove formed by the cliffs. The orchestra, chiefly with the wild ocean music heard in the overture, depicts the raging of the storm, and above it are heard the shouts of the sailors at work. 'Ho-jo-he! Hal-lo-jo!' As the storm abates, the sailors descend into the hold and Daland (*bass*) goes to his cabin to rest, leaving his Steersman (*tenor*) in charge of the deck. The Steersman sings a sailor song, but the phrases become more detached until at last he falls asleep.

The storm begins to rage again and it grows darker. Suddenly, the Dutchman's ship, with blood-red sails and black mast, appears. The Dutchman (*baritone*) goes on shore. He sings his dramatic recitative and aria: 'Die Frist is um' (The term is passed, and once again are ended seven long years). Daland, sighting the Dutchman, goes ashore to question him. The Dutchman, after relating a mariner's story of ill luck and disaster, asks Daland to take him to his home and allow him to marry his daughter, Senta, offering him his treasures. After a graceful duet, Daland consents that the Dutchman accompany him. The storm has subsided and the wind is fair. The crews prepare to leave port, Daland's ship disappearing as the Dutchman goes on board his vessel.

ACT II. A room in Daland's house. The music ingeniously shifts from the Norwegian Sailors' song to the Spinning

Chorus, sung by the village girls as they go about their weaving. Senta (*soprano*), leaning back in an armchair, contemplates a portrait of a man with a dark beard. She is teased by the girls and her nurse, Mary (*contralto*), for gazing so dreamily at the portrait. They ask Senta to sing the ballad of the Flying Dutchman and his unhappy fate. This masterpiece of composition, vocally and instrumentally, begins with the storm music and the strange measures of the Dutchman's motif which sound like a voice calling in distress across the sea. Senta repeats this motif, and sings in simple phrases beginning: 'A ship the restless ocean sweeps'. The orchestra depicts the surging and heaving of the ocean, as Senta's voice rings out dramatically above the accompaniment. She tells how the Dutchman can be delivered from his curse, finally proclaiming that she is the woman who will save him. The girls spring up in terror and Eric (*tenor*), a young huntsman in love with her, enters and hurries to her side. Mary and the girls go to meet the sailors off Daland's ship. Eric restrains Senta and pleads his love for her in melodious measures. He tells her his dream, in which he saw a weird vessel carrying two men, her father and a stranger. He saw Senta passionately greeting the stranger. Senta, highly excited by Eric's words, exclaims: 'He seeks for me and I for him.' Eric, full of despair and horror, rushes away.

The door opens and Daland and the Dutchman appear. Senta gives a cry and stares transfixed at the Dutchman. Daland tells her of the stranger's request and leaves them alone. The duet for Senta and the Dutchman has a broad, smoothly flowing melody and works up to a climax of considerable dramatic power. Senta gives herself unreservedly to the hero of her romantic visions, declaring she will remain faithful to him until death. Daland returns and congratulates the couple, bringing them – and us – back to reality.

ACT III. As the orchestra plays the Steersman's Song and snatches of the Norwegian Sailors' music, the scene changes to a bay outside Daland's house. His ship is anchored alongside the Dutchman's. In a vigorous chorus and dance, the men and girls call to the Dutchman's crew to join their celebrations. There is no reply. The sailors call louder and louder and begin to taunt the other crew. Suddenly the sea, which has been calm, begins to rise. Storm wind whistles through the rigging and the crew show themselves and sing a wild chorus, striking terror into the merrymakers, who flee to shrill laughter from the Dutchman's crew.

Senta enters, followed by Eric, who pleads with her to remember his love for her and the encouragement which she once gave him. Unnoticed, the Dutchman has entered and has been listening. The Dutchman, believing he has again been forsaken, rushes away to his ship, bidding Senta farewell. Senta, proclaiming her love for the Dutchman, attempts to follow him but is restrained by Eric. The Dutchman, who truly loves Senta, proclaims who he is, thinking it will terrify her, and at once puts to sea. Senta, freeing herself, dashes to a clifftop, declares herself faithful unto death, and casts herself into the sea.

Wagner intended *The Flying Dutchman* to be played in a single act – another example of his efforts to break with tradition – and at Bayreuth in 1901 his original design was adhered to, with a few cuts. But he initially agreed to a three-act version, which was performed regularly for 150 years; only comparatively recently has the one-act version been extensively performed.

TANNHÄUSER
and the Song Contest at the Wartburg

OPERA in three acts by Richard Wagner; text by the composer. Première, Dresden, October 19, 1845. Revised Opéra, Paris, 1861.

THE story of *Tannhäuser* is laid in the thirteenth century, in and near the Wartburg, where the Landgraves of the Thuringian Valley held contests between the famous minnesingers. Near this castle rises the Venusberg, whose interior was inhabited by Holda, the Goddess of Spring; in time she became identified with the Goddess of Love, whose court was filled with nymphs and sirens. She seduced the knights of the Wartburg, holding them captive to her beauty. One such knight was Tannhäuser, who, in spite of Venus's beauty, has grown weary of her charms and longs for a glimpse of the world.

The overture, as with that of *The Flying Dutchman*, is the story of the opera told in music. One of the most brilliant and effective pieces of orchestral music, it is based on four episodes of the drama: the pilgrims' chorus; the seductive Venusberg music; Tannhäuser's impassioned song in praise of Venus; and the threatening music of the Landgrave.

ACT I. The Venusberg. Tannhäuser (*tenor*) lies in the arms of Venus (*soprano*; *mezzo-soprano* in Paris version), as nymphs, satyrs and sirens dance about them. Much of the music familiar from the overture is heard during this scene, but gains in effect from the distant voices of the sirens and, of course, from the dances of the denizens of Venus's court. Tannhäuser sings his hymn to Venus, but at the same time proclaims his wish to return to the world. Venus tries to tempt him to remain with her, but he insists on leaving. She warns him of the misfortunes which await him upon earth and predicts that he will some day ask to be taken back into her realm.

Dramatic and effective as this scene is in the original score, it gains in power by the additions Wagner made for the Paris version of the opera. In this version, the overture does not come to a formal close but leads directly into the Venusberg scene. The dances are elaborated and planned on an allegorical basis, and Venus's music has been dramatically strengthened.

The scene changes from the Venusberg to the valley of the Wartburg. Tannhäuser kneels before a crucifix as a young shepherd (*soprano*) pipes a pastoral strain. The voices of the pilgrims are heard in the distance, their solemn measures interrupted by the shepherd's phrases. The chorus becomes louder and, as the pilgrims cross the scene, swells into an eloquent psalm of devotion.

Tannhäuser is deeply affected and gives way to his feelings in a lament, against which are heard the receding voices of the pilgrims. The notes of a hunting horn break in, and gradually the Landgrave (*bass*) and his hunters gather. Tannhäuser is recognised by Wolfram von Eschenbach (*baritone*), and is greeted in an expressive septet. They try to persuade Tannhäuser to return with them to the Wartburg, instead of following the pilgrims to Rome. Wolfram, in a melodious solo, tells him that Elisabeth (*soprano*; the niece of the Landgrave) has been sorrowful since Tannhäuser left the Wartburg. Tannhäuser, who has been in love with Elisabeth, is profoundly moved, and agrees to return.

ACT II. The Hall of Song, the Wartburg. The introduction depicts Elisabeth's joy at Tannhäuser's return, and when the curtain rises she rushes in and radiantly greets the scene of Tannhäuser's former triumphs ('Dich teure Halle'). Wolfram brings Tannhäuser to her, and she asks where he has been. He is evasive, but finally tells her that she attracted him back to the castle. They sing a rapidly flowing and dramatic duet. The Landgrave tells Elisabeth that he will offer her hand as prize to the man who wins the song contest. The singers enter to an effective grand march. After an address by the Landgrave, the singers draw lots to determine who shall begin. Various minnesingers sing tamely, even mundanely, of the beauty of virtuous love, to the increasing contempt of Tannhäuser who finally, no longer able to restrain himself, bursts into a reckless hymn in praise of the unholy charms of Venus, 'Dir, Göttin der Liebe, soll mein Lied ertönen' (To you, goddess of Love, shall my song resound). Horrified, the knights draw their swords as Elisabeth, in spite of Tannhäuser's betrayal of her love, throws herself protectingly before him. In short and excited phrases the men pour forth their wrath at Tannhäuser's crime. He is crushed with guilt. The septet, 'An angel has from heaven descended', reaches a magnificent climax. The voices of pilgrims are heard from the valley. The Landgrave, moved by Elisabeth's willingness to sacrifice herself for Tannhäuser, announces he will be allowed to join the pilgrimage to Rome and plead with the Pope for forgiveness.

ACT III. The Valley of the Wartburg. Elisabeth, waiting for Tannhäuser's return, prays before the crucifix, watched by Wolfram. The chorus of returning pilgrims is heard in the distance, singing the melody heard in the overture and in the first act. In vain Elisabeth looks for Tannhäuser, then sings her prayer, 'Almighty Virgin, hear my sorrow'. She rises, and slowly and sadly returns to the castle to die.

It is night. The evening star glows softly in the sky, inspiring Wolfram to sing the beautiful and tender 'Song to the Evening Star', confessing his love for Elisabeth. Tannhäuser appears, dejected and weary. In broken accents he asks Wolfram to show him the way back to the Venusberg. Wolfram persuades him to tell the story of his pilgrimage. In fierce, dramatic accents, Tannhäuser relates all that he has suffered on his way to Rome. The Pope has passed judgment: Tannhäuser can expect forgiveness only when the Pope's staff sprouts leaves. This highly impressive episode foreshadows Wagner's dramatic use of musical recitative in his later music-dramas.

Tannhäuser, having apparently lost all chance of salvation, intends to yield to the delights of the Venusberg, and Venus stretches out her arms to him in welcome. When he seems unable to resist Venus's enticing voice any longer, Wolfram invokes the memory of Elisabeth. Venus disappears. A tolling of bells and mournful voices precede a funeral procession. Tannhäuser, recognising the body of Elisabeth, falls upon her bier and dies. The pilgrims arrive with the Pope's staff, which has sprouted leaves, and the opera ends amid the hallelujahs of the pilgrims.

In 1861, Wagner remodelled *Tannhäuser* for an ill-starred production in Paris. Dissatisfied with the music for the Venusberg Ballet which followed the rise of the curtain, he rewrote it, maintaining however the original form of the overture. It was not apparently until 1872 that a reworked overture was joined to the new Venusberg music to give the opera's opening its final form. It is perhaps not surprising that there was, particularly in Vienna, something approaching a public outcry over the sensuous nature of the new music.

Evidence exists to suggest that for some years before 1861 Wagner contemplated a revised bacchanale, but it was unquestionably for Paris that he recast the scene of the Hall of Song, removing a solo for Wolfram von Eschenbach but retaining much solo music in the earlier style. For Paris, too, the orchestral introduction to Act III was shortened, and the end of the opera rewritten with Venus brought on to the stage in order to clarify dramatically her role in Tannhäuser's internal drama. One problem facing Wagner with his new version of the opera was that his Paris revision had been with French words, and not all of the new music went easily with the regular metric scheme of the German he had already written.

LOHENGRIN

OPERA in three acts by Richard Wagner; text by the composer. Première, Weimar, August 28, 1859.

WAGNER composed *Lohengrin* in less than a year. Owing to the lyric character of its story, the opera, while not at all lacking in strong dramatic situations, is characterised by a subtler and more subdued melodiousness than *Tannhäuser*; it is, in fact, more lyrical than any Wagner opera except *Parsifal*. While the score contains typical themes, they are not treated in the manner of leading motifs. On the other hand there are fascinating details of orchestration. Wagner used the brass chiefly to accompany the King and the martial choruses; the plaintive, yet spiritual high woodwind for Elsa; the English horn and bass clarinet for Ortrud; the violins, especially in high harmonic positions, to indicate the Grail and its representative, Lohengrin. Even the keys employed are distinctive. The Herald's trumpets are in C; F sharp minor, dark and threatening, is used for Ortrud; and A, the purest for strings and most ethereal in effect, announces the approach of Lohengrin and the subtle influence of the Grail.

The Prelude is based on a single theme: the beautiful and expressive one of the sanctity of the Grail. It opens with long-drawn-out high chords on violins and flutes, then on violins alone, and works up through a crescendo to a magnificent climax, after which it dies away again to the ethereal harmonies.

ACT I. A plain near the River Scheldt; tenth century. King Henry (*bass*) has summoned the Brabantians to join his army to defeat the threatened Hungarian invasion of Germany. The King has found Brabant torn by factional strife over Frederick of Telramund's claim to the ducal succession. Telramund (*baritone*) tells the King how the late Duke placed his children, Elsa (*soprano*) and Gottfried, in his care. Gottfried, the heir, has disappeared, and Telramund accuses Elsa of murdering him in order to claim the title. Telramund says he was so horrified by this that he rejected his right to marry Elsa and has instead mar-

ried Ortrud (*mezzo-soprano*), daughter of the Prince of Fries-
land. He leads her forward, and she bows to the King.

The King has no choice but to appeal to the immediate judgment of God in trial by combat between Telramund and whoever may appear as champion for Elsa. The King summons Elsa.

So far, the music has been harsh and vigorous, reflecting Telramund's excitement; but with Elsa's appearance the music is
soft, gentle and plaintive; not, however, without hope.

As violins whisper the Grail Motif, Elsa, enraptured,
describes her dream of a knight in white, sent by Heaven to
defend her cause. After a triple summons by the Herald (*baritone*), a swan is spied in the distance on the river, drawing a boat
in which stands a knight in silver armour. Elsa, not daring to
trust her senses, gazes heavenward, while Ortrud and Telramund look at each other with amazement and alarm.

The Knight (Lohengrin; *tenor*) bids farewell to the swan,
bows to the King, and approaches Elsa, betrothing himself to
her and offering to fight for her. But he warns her never to ask
where he is from or what his name is. The Warning Motif is one
of the significant themes of the opera. Elsa agrees to the conditions.

Before the combat begins, the King intones a prayer, in
which the principals and then the chorus join with noble effect.
Three Saxons for the Knight and three Brabantians for Telramund pace off the circle within which the two men are to
fight. The King strikes three blows with his sword on his shield,
and the fight begins. The Knight fells Telramund but spares his
life and bids him rise. The King leads Elsa to the Knight, while
all praise him as her champion and betrothed

ACT II. Scene i. The fortress of Antwerp, outside the knights'
palace. It is night, and skulking in the darkness are Telramund
and Ortrud, who have been banished by the King. He is
dejected; she still trusts in the power of the heathen gods she
worships. Telramund, unaware of his wife's scheming to ruin
Elsa and restore him to power, denounces Ortrud in an outburst of rage and despair, his bitterness fuelled by sounds of
revelry from inside the palace. Ortrud unfolds her plot: as
tomorrow's bridal procession reaches the steps of the minster,
Telramund will accuse the Knight of treachery and demand he
disclose his name and origin. Thus will Elsa begin to doubt.

At that moment Elsa comes out on the balcony, enraptured
by her approaching marriage. Ortrud, sending Telramund
away, calls to Elsa, who, moved by her apparent misery, descends to lead Ortrud into the palace, but not before Ortrud has
begun her persuasive work. The scene closes with a beautiful
duet, repeated by the orchestra, as Elsa and Ortrud go in.

Scene ii. In front of the minster. After a spirited chorus, the bride herself appears, followed by her ladies-in-waiting. Ortrud throws herself in her path, saying that Elsa still does not know who her Knight is, and casting doubt on his reasons for secrecy. The King, the bridegroom and the nobles enter from the palace, and Elsa shrinks from Ortrud to her champion's side. At that moment, Telramund, taking his cue from Ortrud, appears and repeats his wife's accusation. The poison has already begun to take effect. Bride and groom enter the church, but the trembling Elsa catches sight of Ortrud and goes to the altar, her feelings of love mingling with doubt and fear.

ACT III. Scene i. The bridal chamber. The wedding festivities are described in a brilliant introduction, followed by the famous Bridal Chorus. The King ceremonially embraces the couple and the procession makes its way out, leaving Elsa and her champion alone for the first time.

It should be a moment of supreme happiness for both, and, indeed, Elsa exclaims as her bridegroom takes her into his arms that words cannot express all love's hidden sweetness. When he tenderly says her name, Elsa is reminded that she cannot respond by uttering his. The Knight realises that the seeds of mistrust have been sown. Elsa begins to question him, and, in a passionate musical phrase, he begs her to trust him. But Elsa imagines she sees the swan approaching to take her Knight away from her, and she asks him the forbidden questions (the details expressed with wonderful vividness in the music). Almost at the same moment, Telramund and four of his followers burst in, intending to kill the Knight, but he fells Telramund with a single blow of his sword. The followers kneel in front of the Knight, who tells them to bear the corpse to the King.

Scene ii. The banks of the Scheldt, as in Act I. The assembled nobles and Brabantians hail the King in a brilliant march and chorus. The Knight enters, saying he has come to bid them all farewell; Elsa has been lured to break her vow, and he will now answer the forbidden questions. His narrative, 'In fernem Land' (From distant lands), is beautifully set to music familiar from the Prelude. He reveals he is from Montsalvat, the temple of the Holy Grail. The Grail gives its Knights the power to right wrong and protect the innocent, but only so long as the secret of their power remains unrevealed. The Knight says his father, Parsifal, rules as King, and that he, a Knight of the Grail, is called Lohengrin. As he proclaims his name, we hear the same measures which Elsa sang in the second part of her dream in Act I. The swan returns and is greeted by Lohengrin who sadly bids his wife farewell, handing her his horn, his sword, and his ring to give to her brother, should he return.

Suddenly a triumphant Ortrud pushes her way through the spectators. She exclaims that the swan is Elsa's brother, Gottfried, whom Ortrud changed into his present form. Had Elsa kept her vow, she explains, Gottfried would have been freed from the spell. Lohengrin falls to his knees in prayer, and a white dove descends over the boat, as the swan vanishes. In its place, Gottfried stands on the bank. Ortrud falls with a shriek, while the crowd kneels and Gottfried bows to the King. Elsa gazes at her brother in rapture, as Lohengrin is drawn away in his boat by the dove. 'My husband! My husband!' she calls, and sinks back dead. The opera ends with a repetition of the music of the second portion of Elsa's dream, followed by a superb climax with the Motif of the Grail.

TRISTAN UND ISOLDE

OPERA in three acts by Richard Wagner; text by the composer. Première, Munich, June 10, 1865.

WAGNER subjected the *Tristan* legend to a thorough re-modelling before turning it into a music-drama. He removed all unnecessary incidents and worked the main episodes into a concise, vigorous, swiftly-moving drama, showing particularly keen dramatic insight in relation to the love-potion. In the legends, the love of Tristan and Isolde is entirely the result of the love-philtre, but Wagner presents them as in love from the outset, so that the potion does no more than quicken a passion already active.

Before the opera begins, we should know that Tristan, having lost his parents in infancy, has been brought up by his Uncle Mark, King of Cornwall. He slew in combat Morold, an Irish knight, who came to Cornwall to collect the tribute that country had been paying to Ireland. Morold was betrothed to his cousin Isolde, daughter of the Irish King. Tristan, who has been dangerously wounded in the fight, places himself, without disclosing his identity, in Isolde's care, as she comes of a race skilled in magic arts. Even though she becomes aware that she is harbouring the slayer of her intended husband, Isolde not only cures Tristan of his wound but falls in love with him. Tristan too is in love, but each believes their love unrequited. Soon after his return to Cornwall, Tristan is sent to Ireland by Mark to win Isolde as Queen for the Cornish King.

The Prelude to *Tristan und Isolde* tells in music the story of the two lovers. It contains the motifs of the hero and heroine and of the Love Glance – a motif that expresses the couple's sensuous yearning – which recurs throughout the Prelude.

ACT I. The ship on which Tristan is taking Isolde to Cornwall. Isolde (*soprano*) occupies the forward deck. A Young Sailor (*tenor*) is heard singing a farewell song to his 'Irish Maid'. Brangäne (*soprano*), Isolde's attendant, replies to Isolde's question as to the ship's course and the orchestra seems to surge wildly around Isolde's outburst of impotent anger when she learns that Cornwall is near, breaking in fury as she invokes the elements to destroy the ship and all on it.

Isolde's mood is dominated by her passion for Tristan (*tenor*) and her wrath that Tristan is bearing her as bride to another. She invokes death upon the Knight but Brangäne sings his praises as Isolde asks her to send Tristan to her. Tristan refuses to leave the helm and his retainer Kurwenal (*baritone*) answers for him with a song in praise of Tristan. Isolde's anger at Kurwenal's taunts finds vent in a narrative in which she tells Brangäne of how she has come to love Tristan. Her outburst against his treachery carries the narrative to a splendid climax.

Brangäne whispers of the love-potion and takes a phial from a casket. As Kurwenal brusquely calls to her and Brangäne to prepare to go ashore, Isolde orders Kurwenal to send Tristan to her and bids Brangäne prepare the death-potion.

Kurwenal announces Tristan's approach. The motif which announces his appearance is full of tragic defiance, as if Tristan were prepared to meet his death. Isolde claims she wants to drink to their reconciliation, but in a sombrely impressive passage, he asks Isolde to slay him with the sword she once held over him.

The sailors hail the land as Isolde hands Tristan the goblet containing, as she thinks, the death draught, for which Brangäne has substituted the love-potion. He seizes it and drinks and Isolde grabs it from him. The Love Glance motif is heard as they sink into each other's arms. Brangäne separates the lovers as people crowd the deck and the act ends as Isolde's motif is heard above the general jubilation.

ACT II. A garden in King Mark's castle. The King (*bass*) and his retinue have gone hunting. With them is Melot (*tenor*), a knight who appears devoted to Tristan but is yet suspected by Brangäne, who fears the hunt is a trap. As the hunting-horns become more distant, Isolde enters and asks Brangäne if it is time to signal with a flaming torch for Tristan to join her. She laughs at Brangäne's warnings of Melot's treachery, and when Brangäne tells her that she switched the potions, Isolde says the love-potion merely intensified her passion. She will signal to Tristan by extinguishing the torch, as if she were putting out the light of her life.

Impatience leads to ecstasy as Isolde sees Tristan. They rush into each other's arms, the music awash with passion, and in a rapid exchange of phrases, they declare their love for each other. As day sinks into soft night, the music turns from urgency to rapture and the lovers commence their great duet, 'O sink hernieder, Nacht der Liebe' (Oh sink upon us, night of love). Brangäne's voice interrupts, warning that night will soon be over, and the arpeggios which accompany her warning are like the first grey streaks of dawn. But the lovers do not hear her; instead, they express their yearning for death through love: the *Liebestod*.

Brangäne calls again, but Isolde exclaims that night will protect them for ever. But with the dawn, the dream is ended. A cry from Brangäne, and Kurwenal rushes in, calling to Tristan to save himself. Surrounded by the King's followers, including the treacherous Melot, the lovers awaken to the terror of the situation. The King sings a philosophical soliloquy to the effect that nothing can explain the cause of all this trouble.

Tristan turns to Isolde. Will she follow him to the bleak land of his birth? This is too much for Melot, who draws his sword. Tristan rushes upon him but, as Melot thrusts, allows his guard to fall and is wounded.

ACT III. Tristan's castle at Kareol in Brittany. The introduction is sadly prophetic of the desolation which broods over the scene. A long, ascending phrase seems to represent the broad waste of ocean overlooked by Tristan's castle. Tristan is lying under a huge lime tree, Kurwenal by his side. A Shepherd (*tenor*) pipes a melancholy tune (solo cor anglais), then tells Kurwenal that the ship he has sent to Cornwall to bring Isolde to Kareol is not yet in sight. Eventually, Tristan to Kurwenal's great joy returns to consciousness and loses himself in sad memories of Isolde. Kurwenal tells him Isolde is coming to try to heal his wound. The ship is still not in sight and his momentary jubilation gives way to yearning. Tristan's mind wanders back to Isolde's nursing of his wound in Ireland until, in a paroxysm of anguish bordering on insanity, he curses love and sinks back apparently lifeless. But as the orchestra breathes the Isolde motif, Tristan again whispers of his love. Suddenly the Shepherd's piping takes a joyful turn. The ship is in sight! Kurwenal rushes off to meet Isolde. Tristan struggles to rise and to music of frenzied urgency tears the bandage from his wound. Isolde rushes in and Tristan, murmuring her name, dies in her arms.

A second ship arrives with King Mark and his court. Kurwenal, thinking they have come in pursuit of Isolde, attacks the newcomers, killing Melot but in turn receiving a mortal wound. Brangäne hurries in to tell Isolde she has confessed to the King that she switched the potions, but Isolde is beyond understanding. In her *Liebestod*, which reaches its climax with a stupendous crash of instrumental forces, she gazes enraptured on her dead lover until she sinks upon his corpse and dies.

DIE MEISTERSINGER VON NÜRNBERG
The Mastersingers of Nuremberg

OPERA in three acts by Richard Wagner; text by the composer. Première at the Royal Court Theatre, Munich, June 21, 1868.

NUREMBERG in the sixteenth century was a prosperous city of 30,000 inhabitants, famous for its physical beauty and its guilds. One of these was artistic, the so-called Mastersingers, who had set customs and complicated rules designed for the most part to keep out whomever the Masters did not want, but also to maintain and raise standards.

The Mastersingers is a parable of art told in terms of a simple, human love story, with touches of humour to enliven it, and interest enhanced by picturesque, historical surroundings. Wagner must have been diligent in his research, but the result is a work of such spontaneity that the method and manner of its art are of secondary importance.

Before the opera begins, we are to understand that Walther von Stolzing (*tenor*), a Franconian knight, has met and fallen in love with Eva (*soprano*), daughter of the rich, cosmopolitan goldsmith, Veit Pogner (*bass*), who is also Grand Master of the Mastersingers. Since Pogner has made the decision that Eva's hand in marriage shall be the prize in the next day's singing competition, Walther must somehow contrive to be accepted as a member of the guild, whose rules are totally outside his previous experience, and win the competition.

The Prelude gives a complete musical summary of the story; it is masterly in technical construction and rich in thematic material that is heard many times and in great variety throughout the rest of the opera.

ACT I. The Church of St. Catherine, Nuremberg. The congregation, including Eva and Magdalena (*mezzo-soprano*), is singing the final chorale of the service. Walther stands at the side, gesturing to Eva. The service at an end, Eva, in order to gain a few words with Walther, sends Magdalena back to the pew to look for a handkerchief and hymn-book. Magdalena urges Eva to go home, but when her boyfriend, David (*tenor*), Sachs's apprentice, arrives to start preparing the church for the meeting of the Mastersingers, Magdalena is only too glad of an excuse to stay. She explains to Walther that Eva is to marry the winner of tomorrow's song contest. Magdalena orders David to instruct Walther in the Masters' rules, which he does, in a long and ingeniously detailed summary. As he warns Walther: 'The Mastersingers' way/Cannot be found in just one day.'

Meanwhile, the other apprentices are putting up the marker's box, occasionally interrupting David's discourse. The Mastersingers begin to arrive, Pogner and Beckmesser (*baritone*), the town clerk, leading the way. The latter is established immediately as a suitor for Eva's hand, and, musically, as a cantankerous figure. Pogner renews his acquaintance with Walther, and is surprised to hear that the knight intends to be a candidate for the Masters' Guild. The other Masters (*tenors* and *basses*) enter, there is a roll-call and Beckmesser is chosen as marker. Pogner rises and, in a fine bass passage, offers Eva's hand in marriage to the winner of the song contest, with the proviso that Eva gives her consent.

Hans Sachs (*bass*), the cobbler, proposes an amendment: let the voice of the people be heard as well as Eva's before a decision is given. This will not only widen the basis of the competition but serve as a corrective to the rules by which the singer is judged and prevent them becoming stereotyped. The others oppose the suggestion, and Pogner proposes that the innovation be postponed for a year. Pogner introduces Walther, whose qualifications are questioned. He answers in the three verses of an aria, 'Am stillen Herd' (By silent hearth). Beckmesser, jealous of a prospective rival, enters the marker's box.

Kothner (*bass*) reads out the rules of singing established by the Masters. Walther takes his seat in the candidate's chair, Beckmesser shouts from the marker's box: 'Fanget an!' (Now begin!), and Walther, in ringing tones, repeats Beckmesser's words. His song, of the glories of spring and the gloom of winter, is both impassioned and different. It also cuts across every rule – a view reinforced by the groans and chalk-scratches coming from the marker's box. After the second stanza Beckmesser tears open the curtains and proffers his slate covered in chalk marks. Walther protests, but the Masters, apart from Sachs and Pogner, refuse to listen further.

Sachs protests that, while he found the knight's artistic method new, he did not find it formless. He says that Beckmesser's marking could hardly be considered just, as he, too, is a candidate for Eva's hand. Beckmesser chides Sachs for having delayed so long in finishing a pair of shoes for him, a remark he will come to regret.

Sachs suggests Walther finish his song, and in short, excited phrases the Masters mock Walther, whose voice soars above the hubbub while the apprentices sing and dance around the marker's box. The Masters reject Walther's song and the knight, with a proud gesture of contempt, leaves the church. Sachs, who has lingered behind, gazes thoughtfully at the singer's empty chair, then, with a humorous gesture of annoyance, turns away.

ACT II. A street in Nuremberg, with Sachs's and Pogner's houses on opposite corners. A fine summer evening. The curtain rises as David and the apprentices are putting up the shutters. Magdalena brings a hamper for David, but on learning that Walther has been rejected, snatches it away and hurries back to Pogner's house. The apprentices mock David, who loses his temper. Sachs breaks up the fight and takes the boy into his workshop.

Pogner and Eva arrive home, Pogner questioning his daughter about her role at the song contest. Her replies are discreetly evasive. Magdalena appears at the door and signals to Eva, who persuades Pogner it is too cool to remain outdoors. As they go inside, Magdalena tells Eva of Walther's failure and suggests she seek Sachs's advice.

Outside his workshop, Sachs yields to his love of the balmy midsummer night and lays down his work, lost in thought. He is distracted by thoughts of Walther's song and the conservatism of his colleagues; but the beauties of the night prove irresistible as Sachs sings a poetic monologue, 'Wie duftet doch der Flieder'.

Eva approaches Sachs and leads the conversation round to the contest. He mentions Beckmesser but she hints, referring to Sachs himself, that she might prefer a widower to a bachelor of disagreeable characteristics. While Sachs is not indifferent to Eva's charms, he sees her relationship with Walther as more appropriate. She tries to find out more about Walther's appearance before the Masters, but leaves angrily when she mistakes Sachs's comments about Walther's singing for his opinion, rather than that of the other Masters. Sachs resolves to help the young couple.

Meanwhile, Eva learns from Magdalena that Beckmesser is to serenade her. Magdalena agrees to impersonate Eva at the window. Walther arrives and Eva flies to his arms. He suggests they elope, and Eva goes into her house to prepare. The Night Watchman crosses the stage, singing a mediaeval chant. As Eva and Walther prepare to escape, Sachs deliberately opens his shutters to throw light across the street. The lovers hide in the shade of a lime tree.

Beckmesser sneaks in, lute in hand, and tunes up. Sachs, who has moved his workbench outside, begins hammering at his last and singing at the top of his voice. Beckmesser begs him to stop but the cobbler argues that he must finish the shoes that Beckmesser has said are late. Beckmesser suggests a bargain: if he may sing uninterrupted, Sachs can 'mark' his mistakes with a hammer stroke. He hardly begins before Sachs gives a resounding whack, and the hammer strokes come faster and faster as Beckmesser sings louder and louder. David, thinking

Magdalena serenaded, falls upon Beckmesser with a cudgel, neighbours rush out into the street and a *mêlée* ensues. Sachs makes an effort to restore calm; he succeeds in shoving the apprentices and journeymen out of the way, dispatches Eva into her father's arms and takes Walther with him into his shop. Quiet reigns as the Night Watchman (*bass*) reappears to sing his mediaeval call.

ACT III. Inside Sachs's workshop. The prelude, one of Wagner's masterpieces, is a musical summary of Sachs himself, showing his tender, poetic side and his good-humoured brusqueness. As the curtain rises, the cobbler is sitting in an armchair reading. David comes in, at first nervous of his master's anger, but eventually to sing his song (accidentally starting off with the tune of Beckmesser's serenade). Suddenly he realises it is Sachs's name-day. His master, gently refusing David's offer of gifts, sends him on his way. Sachs reflects on the follies of the world and its inhabitants: 'Wahn! Wahn! Überall Wahn!' (Fools, fools! All of them fools!) By the end of his monologue, Sachs has ascribed the previous night's riot to a form of midsummer madness, and determines to turn this craziness to positive advantage.

Walther enters from his room and is greeted by Sachs, who defends the Masters, saying they are, in spite of many old-fashioned notions, the conservators of much that is true and beautiful in art. Walther tells Sachs of a song he dreamt about during the night, and sings two stanzas of this Prize Song, Sachs making constructively critical comments as he takes down the words. They go to get ready for the contest.

Beckmesser enters, limping. His glance falls on the manuscript of the Prize Song, in Sachs's handwriting, no less! As the cobbler re-enters, Beckmesser accuses him of being a secret candidate for Eva's hand. Sachs denies it but allows Beckmesser to keep the song. The town clerk leaves in high spirits, confident he will win.

Eva comes to try on the shoes she is to wear at the festival. With a cry of joy (Sachs pretends to mistake it for Eva's shoe being too tight), she spies Walther as he appears. Sachs cobbles and chats away, as if he cannot see the lovers, and Walther, as if inspired, sings the third stanza of the Prize Song. Eva embraces Sachs, glorifying him in a noble phrase of love and gratitude ('O Sachs, mein Freund'). Sachs, alluding to his own love of Eva, exclaims that he will have none of poor King Mark's experience (the music quotes the King's motif from Wagner's *Tristan und Isolde*). Magdalena and David come in, and Sachs first 'baptises' the Prize Song, then promotes David to journeyman, sealing the ceremony with the customary box on the ear. Eva celebrates the inspiration of the Prize Song by leading a quintet of exalted beauty, 'Selig wie die Sonne' (Blessed as the sun). All depart for the festival.

After a tumultuous orchestral interlude, the curtain rises on a meadow on the banks of the Pegnitz. The guilds enter to appropriate music, and the apprentices start a lively dance, in which David joins. This is interrupted by the arrival of the Masters to the sturdy measures of the Mastersingers' March. Sachs rises and at sight of him the crowd bursts into the noble chorus 'Wach auf' (Awake! draws nigh the break of day), set to a poem by the real Hans Sachs. Modestly yet feelingly, Sachs gives thanks.

Beckmesser's attempt to sing Walther's poem ends, as Sachs anticipated, in utter failure and is jeered by the crowd. Infuriated, Beckmesser proclaims Sachs the author of the song. Sachs introduces Walther, who reveals the song's true beauties. All repeat the closing melody of the Prize Song in token of appreciation. Eva crowns him and Pogner advances to decorate Walther with the insignia of the Masters' Guild, which Walther impulsively rejects. Sachs saves the situation by praising the Masters and their noble purpose as conservators of German art. Walther accepts the honour and Eva takes his wreath and crowns Sachs. The opera ends with a chorus in praise of art and of Hans Sachs.

DER RING DES NIBELUNGEN
The Ring of the Nibelung

WHOLE cycle first performed at Bayreuth, Festspielhaus, August 13–17, 1876.

Wagner's vast *Ring* cycle may or may not be the greatest event inside the form loosely known as opera, but it is certainly the grandest. What is curious is that Wagner, the great musical architect, did not initially conceive it as the four-part structure we know (though he clearly always envisaged a huge canvas: modern commentators have compared it in scale with *The Oresteia*). He started work as early as 1848 and by 1850 had completed the book of what he called *Siegfrieds Tod* (Siegfried's Death), which subsequently became *Götterdämmerung* (The Twilight of the Gods) and ended originally with Brünnhilde leading Siegfried to Valhalla. He had considered immediately starting to compose *Siegfried's Death* but came to feel the need to explain the events which led up to it and in turn wrote *The Young Siegfried*, *The Valkyrie* and *The Rhine Gold*, thus creating the cycle as it were in reverse.

Composition of *The Rhine Gold* was started in 1853 and the full score of *Twilight* finished in 1874, but amazingly there occurred an interregnum of nearly twelve years (1857 to 1869) during which he had not only composed *Tristan und Isolde* (1857–9) and *Die Meistersinger* (1862–7), but attempted to cope with so severe a dip in his fortunes, considerably though not exclusively due to German political events, as to lead him at one stage to contemplate abandoning composition altogether. By summer 1856, in a letter to Liszt he was hinting at a surfeit of Teutonic heroes and villains. Even temporarily to abandon the grand design, he must have felt an overpowering need to write music of quite a different nature from what he was composing for *The Ring*; the music in *Tristan* was to come close to parting company with tonality and to pointing a way for the future not fully taken up until the time of Schoenberg's earliest experiments some fifty years later. *The Ring*, for all its invention and innovative construction, was cast from music of much less iconoclastic cut.

Wagner's studies of Teutonic and Norse myth undertaken over many years provided him with the subject matter of *The Ring*, which involves gods, demi-gods, giants, earth-dwellers and inhabitants of the underworld. The fierce competition between them for wealth and ultimate dominance constitutes the stuff of the drama, but there is room for much examination of the more human motives of the characters involved. The music is held together by a large number of motifs, sometimes with meanings and attachments as straightforward as 'the Rhine Gold', 'the Ring', 'Valhalla', 'The Giants', 'the Sword', even concepts like 'Renunciation of Love'; often with strong initial attachments but shifting connotations, as, to take an example, that of 'the Rhine', specifically descriptive of the river during the prelude to *The Rhine Gold* but later taking on wider references as when, two hours later and to its accompaniment, Erda sings of her own all-pervading wisdom. To think of them as labels or visiting cards would be not only confusing and inadequate but to do an injustice to Wagner's incredibly dexterous and fertile use of his materials, which he employs hardly ever as musical shorthand but rather as means towards the creation of musical edifices great enough to carry the burden of a colossal epic drama.

In *The Ring*, the antagonists play for great stakes but their not infrequent moral transgressions are subject to high moral laws. Both Wotan, the King of the Gods, and Alberich, ruler of the underworld Nibelungs, aspire to ultimate heights of wealth and power. In order to rob the Rhinemaidens of the Rhine Gold, Alberich renounces Love (but later in the drama fathers Hagen by an act of near-rape). From the gold he forges a Ring which will make its owner all-powerful. Wotan, by an act hard to distinguish from theft, obtains gold and Ring from Alberich, who curses the Ring. Instead of returning it to the Rhinemaidens, Wotan ransoms Freia, goddess of youth, from Fafner and Fasolt, to whom she had been promised by Wotan as fee for building Valhalla. No sooner have the giants obtained the Ring than Alberich's curse claims its first victim, Fafner killing his brother and retiring to guard Ring and treasure in the obscurity of a cave.

Wotan takes twofold precautions against the future: first, the fathering with Erda of a race of warlike Valkyries. They carry to Valhalla dead heroes who will with the Valkyries defend it in case of war with the Nibelungs. The second is more complex. The Ring can be redeemed from Fafner, restored to the Rhinemaidens, and the curse lifted from the race of the gods only through the intervention of a hero impelled by pure and unselfish motive. The gods are ruled out because they have too much to gain. Wotan therefore casts off his divinity and fathers twins, Siegmund and Sieglinde. Siegmund, to steel him for his role of hero, is subjected (like Tamino in *The Magic Flute*) to trials, but the scheme founders when he and Sieglinde fall in love.

DAS RHEINGOLD
The Rhine Gold

THE prelude sets *The Ring* on its way with a soft low E flat from the depths of the Rhine; a horn intones the Rhine motif. In lyrical music, the Rhinemaidens, Woglinde (*soprano*), Wellgunde (*soprano*) and Flosshilde (*contralto*), sing, Alberich (*baritone*) splashing lecherously around them until his eye is caught by the glint of the gold, a ring made of which he learns will invest its owner with great power – but only if he renounces love. Alberich makes such a vow and seizes the gold, thus committing the first crime in its name.

Across the Rhine can be made out Valhalla, the castle of the gods, and Fricka (*mezzo-soprano*) wakes Wotan (*bass-baritone*) who sings of its glories. Fricka reminds him he must pay for it by yielding Freia to the giants and Freia (*soprano*) appears in flight from them. Froh (*tenor*) and Donner (*baritone*), her brothers, try ineffectually to defend her against the giants' insistence, but Wotan takes courage from the appearance of Loge (*tenor*). Loge tells Wotan of Alberich's theft of the gold, cunningly inciting the curiosity of the giants as he describes his own wanderings and Alberich's renunciation of love. The giants decide to accept the gold rather than Freia but keep her as a hostage until Wotan can deliver. How to get it? 'Durch Raub!' says Loge in one of *The Ring*'s more startling moments (By theft!).

An orchestral passage takes us to the underworld of the Nibelungs, where Alberich is brutally insisting his brother Mime (*tenor*) give him the Tarn helmet he has just manufactured. Its wearer can assume any shape he chooses. To test his invisibility, Alberich pinches and punches Mime, who is alone when Wotan and Loge descend the shaft and enter the cave. Alberich forces a crowd of Nibelungs to pile up the treasure, then with a gesture of the Ring drives them off. He boasts that the Ring's power will soon allow him to threaten Valhalla, but Loge flatters him and he turns successively into a dragon, then a toad. Wotan is not slow to put his foot on the toad, Loge wrenches off the Tarn helmet and Alberich materialises writhing under Wotan's boot.

He is bound and dragged off towards the light, where it is clear his lease on power is to be brief. The gold shall be the price of his release, and Alberich with the Ring summons the Nibelungs with their hoard. When Wotan tears the Ring from his finger, he turns in his rage and, not without dignity, curses the Ring and all who henceforth possess it, until it be returned to him. Then he vanishes.

It is the moment for Freia to be ceded to the giants or for the ransom to be paid. They measure out a space the height and width of Freia, the gold is piled up, the Tarn helmet added and finally, to Wotan's fury, they demand the Ring. He seems about to refuse, but Erda (*contralto*) slowly manifests herself and majestically warns Wotan against so rash an action. He throws the Ring on the pile and Freia is free. But not so the giants from the curse, as Fafner (*bass*) quarrels with Fasolt (*bass*) over his share and beats his brother to death, dragging Ring and gold out after him. Another crime has been committed but Loge congratulates Wotan on having given up the curse-laden Ring.

The curse rests on anyone who has touched the Ring, and Wotan cannot forget that it has been through his hands. Finally, Donner ascends to the top of a rock, swings his hammer and a flash of lightning dispels the clouds so that a rainbow bridge spans the valley to Valhalla. In a magnificent peroration, Wotan greets Valhalla and leads a procession of the gods across to the castle. Wagner adds six harps to the orchestra to accompany the rainbow, but Wotan is to be denied full triumph as the Rhinemaidens, from below, beg him to restore the Ring to them, and Loge decides to defect before the gods are overcome by the disaster he predicts.

Die Walküre
The Valkyrie

IF *The Rhine Gold* was the expository first movement in the symphonic construction of *The Ring*, then *The Valkyrie* is just as plainly its slow movement, *Siegfried* the scherzo and *Twilight* the grandiose last movement in which all threads are to be pulled together and the grand design completed. Lyricism has flowered in *Rhine Gold* in such episodes as the long scene for the Rhinemaidens and the beautiful music associated, however briefly, with Freia and the idea of Eternal Youth; but it is sinewy narrative and argument, harsh dramatic collision between gods, Nibelungs and giants, or grand statements like Wotan's and Erda's with which we have been mainly concerned. This is music drama in its most epic form, but much of *The Valkyrie*, the first act in particular, is in marked contrast, full of lyrical flowering, as in the entire encounter of Siegmund and Sieglinde, or in the tenderness of the second half of the third act, when Wotan proves unable to resist the pleas of his favourite daughter Brünnhilde.

Sieglinde (*soprano*), Wotan's daughter by a human woman, has been forced into a loveless marriage with Hunding (*bass*) and has no idea of the identity of her father, whom she knows only as Wälse.

ACT I. The orchestra suggests not only a storm sweeping through the forest but the headlong flight from his enemies of the fugitive Siegmund (*tenor*). He staggers exhausted into Hunding's hut, to be found a moment later by Sieglinde. As his strength returns and she gazes at him, it becomes obvious from the music that the bond between them is so strong as to amount to love at first sight, but he protests he will bring misfortune to anyone who helps him and is about to leave when Hunding is heard approaching. Ordering her to prepare food, Hunding questions the stranger and discovers that Siegmund, whose name is as yet undisclosed, is a sworn enemy of him and his family. Hunding will respect the laws of hospitality, but in the morning, his guest, who is his foe, must be prepared to defend himself in the cause of blood feud.

Siegmund is alone. The Sword motif comes softly from the orchestra and light from the fire falls on a sword buried to the hilt in the tree round which Hunding's hut is built. From this point to the end of the act occurs what can only be described as one of Wagner's purple passages. Siegmund muses on his weaponless state and on the sympathy between him and the woman he has just met, then calls on his father – 'Wälse! Wälse!' – to help him in his hour of need. The image of the woman and the gleam from the tree link inextricably in his sub-conscious and when Sieglinde appears all becomes clear, as she tells the story of her wedding to Hunding and of the stranger who buried a sword deep in the ash trunk. Now, she has found the hero who will draw the sword and so achieve what Hunding's relations failed to do. Her words seem to release a new spirit in Siegmund, who declares he will claim both weapon and bride for himself. One side of the hut flies open and lets in the light of the full moon, which rouses Siegmund to new lyrical outpouring: 'Winterstürme wichen dem Wonnemond' (Winter storms have vanished at Spring's command). A love duet develops by the end of which Sieglinde has recognised her twin brother in Siegmund, who glories in his name and draws the promised sword from the tree before they run out together into the night.

ACT II. We leave the humans for a different world, dominated by the gods and their power struggle. The orchestra, with forward references to the Ride of the Valkyries, introduces Wotan (*bass-baritone*) and Brünnhilde (*soprano*), the latter eager, as she

shows in her war-cry 'Ho-jo-to-ho!', to accept his command to
aid Siegmund in his forthcoming fight with Hunding. But it is
not to be as sentiment might direct, and Fricka's (*mezzo-
soprano*) intervention reminds Wotan that Hunding is calling
for vengeance on a breaker of marriage vows, vows that she herself upholds. Wotan urges the sanctity of true love against the
false values of unloving vows but Fricka will have none of it,
denouncing the incestuous pair of twins, and prophesying the
end of the gods' glory now that Wotan not only casts aside
honour by whoring in cavern and on mountainside but will
stoop to abandon his wife and her honourable precepts in order
to protect the fruits of his union with an earth-woman. Wotan
reminds her of the need the gods have for a pure hero to win
back the Ring, but Fricka will not let him off the hook of the
laws of morality, nor allow him to trick her by pretending that
Siegmund is free to fight unaided when Brünnhilde will be by
his side. To uphold Siegmund means belittling his own con-
sort, and in the end he has to agree that Siegmund shall die.

The motif of Alberich's Curse punctuates the return of
Brünnhilde, who listens to her father's paroxysms of anger and
despair before he embarks on his multifaceted narrative of the
theft of the Gold, his own tricking of Alberich, the birth of the
Valkyries, and his hopes, now thwarted, that an unsullied hero
might regain the ground he – and the gods – have lost. Now, his
plans are in ruins, and rumour has it Alberich has lovelessly im-
pregnated a woman who will bear him a son and seal the fate of
the gods. At Fricka's behest, Brünnhilde must abandon Siegmund and sustain Hunding! Though it is clear from the early
part of his narration that Wotan, while initially planning a
world subject to good laws, had become embroiled in what
Ernest Newman once called a network of evil, the music in
which he expresses his rage, his hopes, his disappointments
and now, as he sees it, looming disaster, is consistently grand in
scale; the baring of his soul reveals on the one hand an unnerving tendency to believe the end justifies the means but, in
apparent contradiction, a genuine nobility. Though vast narra-
tives of past events have come to be accepted as part of
Wagner's musico-dramatic scheme, they were once deplored as
dealing mainly with events with which we are already to a
greater or lesser extent familiar.

Terror of being overtaken by Hunding and his kinsmen has
stretched Sieglinde's nerves to breaking point, and Siegmund
tells her they will rest from their flight and wait for Hunding
where she has collapsed. Brünnhilde appears to him in a foreshadowing of his death: 'Todesverkündigung'. Brünnhilde
describes the joys of Valhalla in music of the utmost solemnity,
but Siegmund rejects any possibility which would separate him

from Sieglinde. When he makes as if to kill his beloved with his drawn sword, Brünnhilde is moved to defy Wotan: she will throw her resources behind him in his fight with Hunding.

Hunding's horn calls sound nearer and nearer and Sieglinde wakes to hear his voice. As Siegmund raises his sword to fight, Wotan interposes his spear – the symbol of his power – and shatters it; Siegmund falls a defenceless victim to Hunding. Wotan commands Hunding to kneel in thanks before Fricka, but a contemptuous gesture from Wotan's spear leaves Hunding dead on the ground. Brünnhilde gathers up the splintered sword and flees with Sieglinde, while Wotan breathes threats against the disobedient Valkyrie.

ACT III opens as the eight Valkyries (*three sopranos, four mezzo-sopranos* and a *contralto*) gather on their rock with a musical scene of wild energy founded on Brünnhilde's battle cry heard at the start of Act II and now the motivating force of a great descriptive scene, the Ride of the Valkyries. Brünnhilde arrives, asking her sisters to help her hide Sieglinde, who at first seems deaf to any notion of a future without Siegmund but is eventually roused to pulsating life by reference to the child she may yet bear him, and with a stirring cry greets the future before making her escape.

As Wotan approaches, calling for her, Brünnhilde leaves her sheltering sisters and is face to face with the father whose orders she has defied. It is not he who is sentencing her, he tells her, but she herself. His will woke her to life, but now that she has rebelled against his will she has chosen another fate for herself. No more will she ride as a Valkyrie, no more – and here his heart seems on the point of breaking – may she be considered his favourite child. Instead she will lie defenceless and asleep on the Valkyrie rock, no longer divine, until claimed by the first man who wakes her.

The Valkyries are driven off by Wotan's wrath and the savagery of Brünnhilde's sentence, and it is to the sound of the bass clarinet, continuing on lower strings and taken up by cor anglais, that Wagner introduces the motif of Brünnhilde's pleading: 'War es so schmählich' (Was it so shameful). Did not Wotan himself originally favour Siegmund's cause? Was what she did so disgraceful that she herself must be plunged into disgrace? As his tone towards her softens, she pleads passionately for a mitigation of sentence: let the rock on which she sleeps be guarded by fierce flames so that only a dauntless hero may penetrate the barrier and claim her as bride.

Wotan, hedonist as well as master-strategist, has no defence against either her pleas or the inclinations of his heart, and there has been nothing in *The Ring* so far grander of scale or more touching in its examination of the human motives involved than his farewell to Brünnhilde. His last kiss is preceded by a lyrical hymn to the beauty of her eyes from which he has so often derived courage, before the orchestra meditates on the sleep which will envelop her, and Wotan with his spear invokes Loge to girdle the rock with fire.

SIEGFRIED

Sieglinde has died giving birth to Siegfried, who has been reared by Alberich's brother Mime. Mime believes the young hero he recognises in Siegfried will help him forge the broken but potentially all-powerful sword of his father (whose identity Mime knows but of which Siegfried is ignorant). With it Mime hopes Siegfried will kill Fafner, who has turned into a dragon, and regain Ring and treasure. Mime will then himself kill Siegfried and possess the Ring. Wotan, still with hopes that Siegfried may prove the hero of pure motive that Siegmund would have been, watches the development of events, as does Alberich.

ACT I. The prelude suggests Mime (*tenor*) brooding on Ring, hoard of gold and how to re-possess them. When the curtain rises, he is making a further attempt to forge the sword, with which he will attain his objective but which, every time repaired, is smashed at a single blow by the precocious Siegfried. Siegfried's music is initially hyper-active, Mime's plangent but full of venom and malice. Siegfried (*tenor*), whose horn call precedes him, torments Mime by bringing a captive bear into the cave, then shatters the latest product of Mime's work at the smithy before impatiently listening as Mime reminds him that it is to him, Mime, that he owes life and upbringing. How then, asks Siegfried, does he find his foster-father so repellent? Who indeed is his mother? Because Mime alone knows the answer to that question must be why he constantly returns, says Siegfried. Mime admits Siegfried's mother died giving birth to him, and that his father, who was killed in battle, left nothing behind him but the fragments of the sword Mime spends his time attempting to mend. Siegfried rejoices at the prospect of his father's sword reforged then runs from the cave, leaving Mime even more depressed than at the start of the act.

Wotan appears, no longer visibly a god but disguised as the Wanderer (*bass-baritone*). He wagers his head that he can correctly answer any three questions which Mime may put to him, and, in music very recognisably belonging to Wotan, comes up with the Nibelungs as the race born in the earth's deep bowels, the giants as those dwelling on the earth's back, and the gods as inhabiting the cloudy heights, each answer accompanied by appropriate and by now largely familiar motifs. The Wanderer in his turn, postulating (but not expecting) the same forfeit and castigating Mime for failing in his questioning to search for knowledge, puts three questions to Mime. 'What noble race did Wotan treat harshly and yet hold most dear?' 'The Wälsungs.' 'Name the sword with which Siegfried must strike to regain the Ring.' 'Notung,' correctly answers Mime. 'Whose hand can forge the sword?' Mime cannot answer; the Wanderer assures him only a hero who does not know fear can weld the pieces together; moreover, though he may keep his forfeit head for a while, it is through that hero that Mime will lose his life.

Mime collapses behind the anvil, where he is found by Siegfried, returning full of the confidence of youth and impatient that Mime has again failed to re-forge the sword. Mime, remembering the Wanderer's warning, asks Siegfried if he has ever known fear, which the young hero denies, while affirming he is ready to learn if that will help him face the future. Mime describes Fafner in his guise as dragon, but that only inspires Siegfried to demand the sword with which to face Fafner. Impetuously he starts to file down the pieces, then, hearing from Mime that it is called Notung and addressing it by name, he blows up the fire with the bellows and, in a scene crackling with energy and excitement, succeeds in forging it. It is the most physical scene of the entire *Ring* cycle, and Siegfried with a shout of triumph splits the anvil in two.

ACT II takes us towards dawn to the depths of the forest, near Fafner's cave. Alberich (*baritone*), lying in wait, recognises the Wanderer as Wotan, his enemy, the thief of the Ring. That his curse will bring about Fafner's downfall causes him satisfaction, but the Wanderer predicts that a young hero, guided by none other than Mime, will win the Ring, and even risks waking Fafner (*bass*) to warn him of what is in store. Mime leads Siegfried to the cave and warns of the perils to be faced when Fafner emerges, but Siegfried drives him off and is left by himself.

There follows one of the supreme lyrical episodes of the cycle, a pastoral poem to nature which marks a crucial stage in the awakening of Siegfried's sensibilities. As he lies under a lime tree and listens to the rustling of the leaves (the 'Waldweben' or Forest Murmurs as it is called in the concert hall), he reflects on his parentage, then listens to the song of the Woodbird (*soprano*) and plays on a reed in an attempt to communicate with the bird. That effort ends in fiasco and he decides to blow his horn instead (the grandest manifestation of his horn call we shall hear). This rouses Fafner from his sleep, but in fight he is no match for Siegfried and his sword, and it is not long before he is demanding who has mortally wounded him. The motive of the Curse sounds as he dies. As he pulls the sword from Fafner's body Siegfried licks the scalding blood from his hand, and instantly acquires the power to understand the bird's song, hearing first of the gold, the Tarn helmet and the Ring, which he goes into the cave to fetch.

Alberich and Mime scuttle like scavengers into the clearing in front of the cave, snarling and snapping and desisting only when Siegfried comes out of the cave with the booty Mime craves. The bird warns him first against Mime's wiles and eventually he understands that the dwarf is plotting to poison him. He gets in first and kills Mime with his sword, the motif of the Curse ringing out from the orchestra to remind us not only that it has claimed a second victim in this segment of the cycle but that the Ring is now in Siegfried's possession. But that hero's thoughts are on the present, in the form of the beauty of the forest, and on a future in which the bird seems to be promising him Brünnhilde as bride.

ACT III. Scene i sees Wotan/Wanderer musically at the height of his powers, dominant and apparently carrying all before him. But in reality he is full of fear that through Siegfried and Brünnhilde, whose partnership he sees as inevitable, the rulership of the world may pass from the gods to the human race. In his perplexity he calls, in music of power and passion, on Erda (*contralto*) for counsel, but she can give no advice and he appears to abdicate not only hope but responsibilities. Let human love supplant gods and Nibelungs; perhaps the twilight of the gods will be the dawn of a more glorious epoch.

Scene ii. The bird has guided Siegfried to the spot where Brünnhilde lies asleep, and Wotan's final attempt to hold back the inevitable, by barring the way with his spear, ends as Siegfried smashes it with a single blow. The flames which surround the sleeping maiden are now visible and Siegfried advances towards his destiny.

Scene iii is an extended duet, starting with Siegfried's first view of the sleeping Brünnhilde (*soprano*), his attempt to loosen the breastplate which covers her, and his discovery that this is no man but a woman, the first he has seen. The music swells to magnificence as she wakes, refers to her rescue of his mother, then turns to thoughts of their mutual love. For a moment of exceptional musical richness, Brünnhilde dwells on her once supernatural status ('Ewig war ich'), then Siegfried plights his troth with the curse-laden Ring, and the scene finishes with a splendid hymn to love.

GÖTTERDÄMMERUNG
The Twilight of the Gods

PROLOGUE. The three Norns (*contralto, mezzo-soprano, soprano*), daughters of Erda, discuss the progress of events and pass the golden rope of destiny from one to the other until, as they foresee the end of the gods and wonder whether Alberich is destined to supplant them, the rope breaks and they see catastrophe impending. An orchestral interlude returns us to Siegfried (*tenor*) and Brünnhilde (*soprano*) striding heroically and in an aura of requited love through the dawn, Brünnhilde preparing him for the heroic deeds he must accomplish, he leaving her with the fatal Ring as pledge. The orchestra describes Siegfried's journey down the Rhine.

ACT I. The castle of the Gibichungs, where live Gunther (*baritone*), his sister Gutrune (*soprano*), and their half-brother Hagen (*bass*), son of Alberich. Through Hagen, the product of Alberich's loveless union with Queen Grimhilde, the curse hurled by Alberich at all who possess the Ring will be worked out – with Siegfried betrayed and the rule of the gods brought to an end. Hagen excites Gunther's concupiscence with ideas of Brünnhilde as his bride, even though he stipulates that she must be won by a stronger man than Gunther. Such a man is Siegfried, a worthy mate for the unwed Gutrune. Hagen plots with a magic potion to trick Siegfried into forgetting Brünnhilde and falling in love with Gutrune, after which it will not be hard to persuade him to stand in for Gunther and win him a bride. Siegfried is greeted, drinks from the cup Gutrune offers him, and Hagen's trick starts to work. Siegfried and Gunther swear an oath of Blood Brotherhood (introduced by the Curse motif), and Siegfried goes off to win Brünnhilde for Gunther, leaving Hagen to brood alone (Hagen's Watch: 'Hier sitz ich zur Wacht': I sit here and wait).

Back at the rock to which she was once bound asleep, Brünnhilde hears from her sister Waltraute (*mezzo-soprano*) that Wotan has passed into a near-catatonic state, brooding over his splintered spear and the imminent end of the power of the gods. Only the return of the Ring to the Rhinemaidens can lift the curse. Will Brünnhilde take it on herself to cast the Ring back into the Rhine where it belongs? Brünnhilde refuses. The Ring symbolises her love for Siegfried and she will yield it to no one.

The notes of Siegfried's horn are heard, but it is apparently a stranger who braves the flames, transformed by the Tarn helmet to look like Gunther. Brünnhilde tries to defend herself but she is powerless against the intruder, who tears the Ring from her finger and subdues her – laying his sword between them as pledge to his blood-brother's honour.

ACT II. In front of the Hall of the Gibichungs, Alberich (*baritone*) appears to Hagen, who sleeps, spear in hand, against a pillar. He exacts an oath from his son that he will murder Siegfried and seize the Ring from his finger, then dematerialises. Siegfried returns from his mission boasting of his exploit. Hagen summons the Gibichung vassals to the double wedding, and in a moment Gunther is there dragging Brünnhilde by the hand. It is when she sees Siegfried standing, Ring on finger, with Gutrune, apparently oblivious to what has passed between them, that she is consumed with the idea of vengeance. She accuses Siegfried of having passed himself off as Gunther, stolen the Ring from her, and delivered his own bride to another. His defence is to swear on spear-point that he found the Ring among the dragon's treasure and has never been parted from it, and that the sword stayed between them when he found her. Hagen offers his weapon for the oath, in the knowledge that, should he swear falsely, Siegfried's death is certain at the point of that very spear. Siegfried takes his oath, and Brünnhilde, in full knowledge that he has sworn falsely, dedicates the weapon to his destruction.

Tension mounts, if that is possible, in the last scene of the act, when Hagen manipulates Brünnhilde and Gunther, the one in a state of fury and the other humiliated beyond endurance, so that they plot the murder of Siegfried in the course of a forthcoming boar hunt, intending to strike him from behind with Hagen's spear on which the oath has just been sworn.

ACT III is an extraordinary succession of melodic grace, Wagnerian narrative and high drama, followed by a peroration of unique and tragic grandeur. The hunt has taken its followers to the banks of the Rhine, where the Rhinemaidens (*sopranos, contralto*) in a scene of great lyrical beauty endeavour to coax the Ring from Siegfried. He seems on the point of handing it over but one threat too many from the Rhinemaidens causes him to change his mind: he will never give in to pressure.

The hunting party assembles, and Hagen presses on Siegfried a drinking-horn containing the antidote to the potion before getting him to relate the story of his life. Memories of Mime precede those now coming back to his mind of Brünnhilde and he relates in some detail the story of how he first penetrated the wall of flame to claim her for his bride. Gunther now knows Brünnhilde's accusation was true, and Hagen loses no time in plunging the spear into Siegfried's defenceless back. Siegfried rears himself up on his shield and relives the moment when he awakened Brünnhilde from sleep, before he falls back dead. His Funeral music is of overwhelming grandeur. In the Hall of the Gibichungs, Gutrune awaits the return of the hunt. Hagen announces Siegfried's death and when Gunther refuses to allow him to take the Ring from Siegfried's finger, kills his half-brother and adds a further death to the day's tally. Siegfried's hand with the Ring upon it raises itself threateningly from the bier, and even Hagen falls back in some consternation as Brünnhilde advances solemnly.

The rest of the drama is Brünnhilde's. Gutrune falls in a faint on Siegfried's body as Brünnhilde bids the men erect a funeral pyre and place the body on it. She apostrophises the dead hero, who at the same time betrayed her and was the most faithful of men, then, the Ring upon her finger, mounts her Valkyrie charger and rides into the flames. She will expiate the crimes of lust and greed which started with the wresting of the Rhine gold from the Rhinemaidens, and Wotan's stress will be at an end. The Rhine overflows, from Brünnhilde's finger Rhinedaughters pluck the Ring and, when Hagen tries to seize it, draw him down with them into the eternal waters. In the heavens, Valhalla is consumed in flames. It is *Götterdämmerung*, the twilight of the gods, and Brünnhilde through love – the emotion Alberich renounced to gain power – has caused a new human era to dawn in place of the old mythological one of the gods.

This is the grandest example in all Wagner of redemption through woman's heroic love. In that at least his thesis holds good today. Otherwise, the satirists are due a field day with Wagner's moral – the bastard daughter of the King of the Gods, through love of Wotan's doubly illegitimate grandson, her own nephew, purges her father's crime and rids the world of the curse which it precipitated. Or, as George Bernard Shaw would have it, we have the ultimate exposé of the Capitalist system, and only in the transcendent love of a decent woman can it have any hope of redemption.

PARSIFAL

STAGE Dedication Festival Play (Bühnenweihfestspiel) in three acts; words and music by Richard Wagner. Produced Bayreuth, July 26, 1882.

WAGNER's final opera, *Parsifal*, is drawn from three legends: *Percival le Galois, or Contes de Grail*, by Chrétien de Troyes (1190); *Parsifal*, by Wolfram von Eschenbach; and a fourteenth-century manuscript known as the *Mabinogion*.

In *Lohengrin*, the hero tells Elsa he is the son of Parsifal and one of the knights of the Holy Grail. Although *Parsifal* deals with an earlier period than *Lohengrin*, there is an element of similarity between the music of the two operas – a certain purity and spirituality breathes through them both.

Before the opera begins, Titurel and his Christian knights have been charged with the care of the Holy Grail, from which Christ drank at the Last Supper, and the Sacred Spear, with which the Roman soldier pierced Christ's side. Outside Montsalvat (Titurel's castle) in Spain lurks paganism in the form of Klingsor, a sorcerer, who has failed to gain admission to the Grail brotherhood and seeks revenge on Titurel and his knights. His method is to lure them into his magic garden, where they are seduced by Flower Maidens and the enchantress Kundry and thus enslaved by Klingsor. The elderly Titurel has been succeeded by his son, Amfortas, who, determined to destroy Klingsor, enters the garden but succumbs to Kundry's charms and drops the Sacred Spear. Klingsor seizes it and injures Amfortas, who escapes but lies gravely ill, his wound unable to heal. A voice from the Sanctuary of the Grail has foretold that the only person who can regain the Spear from Klingsor, and with its touch heal Amfortas's wound, is a 'guileless fool'. Only such an innocent will be able to resist the temptations of the garden and, through pity, become the redeemer of the knights of the Grail. The fulfilling of this prophecy forms the story of *Parsifal*, which is, in allegorical terms, the triumph of Christianity over Paganism.

The Prelude to *Parsifal* depicts the two principal themes of the opera: the religious duties and the unhappiness brought about by Amfortas's sinful forgetfulness of them.

ACT I. A forest clearing on the banks of a lake near the Castle of the Grail. It is dawn. Gurnemanz (*bass*), old but still strong, and two squires are asleep. From the castle sounds a solemn reveille, waking Gurnemanz who wakes the squires. The three of them pray. The feeling of peace is broken by two knights who have come to prepare Amfortas's bath, the King's pain having become worse. Suddenly, to furious music – a headlong four-octave descent of the strings – Kundry (*sòprano*) rushes in, hair dishevelled, eyes flashing, and thrusts a small flask into Gurnemanz's hand: it contains balsam (from Arabia, Kundry says) to soothe Amfortas's pain. This indicates Kundry's contradictory character: she has brought suffering upon Amfortas yet strives to ease it. Amfortas (*bass-baritone*) is carried in on a litter, the music's heavy, dragging rhythm expressing his physical and mental agony. Gurnemanz hands him the balsam, saying whom it is from. Kundry scorns Amfortas's offer of thanks and the procession moves on.

The squires taunt Kundry as a sorceress. Gurnemanz, defending her, says she has done some good deeds, possibly to atone for her guilt. He asks, however, why she was not there to help when Amfortas lost the Sacred Spear, to which Kundry glumly replies, 'I give no help'. One of the squires suggests that if she really wants to serve the Grail, she should help find the Spear. Gurnemanz is prompted to reminisce about how the Spear came to be captured by Klingsor and what must be done in order to regain it. He speaks of the 'guileless fool', and, as the squires repeat the words, shouts are heard from the direction of the lake; a sacred swan, its heart pierced by an arrow, falls dead at Gurnemanz's feet. Two knights bring in a young man they have seized; it is Parsifal (*tenor*), whose motif, full of wild spirit, rings out on the horns. He cheerfully admits that he killed the swan, as he would anything that flies, but he is reproved by Gurnemanz, who, to a broad, expressive melody, tells the boy that the birds are sacred. Gradually, Parsifal realises his mistake, breaks his bow and throws his arrows away.

Gurnemanz asks him about his origins; but the boy does not know who he is or what brought him to Montsalvat. He tells the old man how he grew up in the woods with his mother, Herzeleide. Kundry, who has been listening silently, tells Parsifal his mother is dead. He leaps at her, but is restrained by Gurnemanz, who says Kundry speaks the truth.

Gurnemanz, suspecting that this boy of naive yet noble bearing could be the 'guileless fool' of the prophecy, leads him to the Hall of the Grail. As the scene changes, long sustained trombone notes and approaching peals of bells are heard.

Gurnemanz and Parsifal enter the vast Hall; the old knight tells the boy to pay close attention to what he is about to see. The knights enter to a solemn processional as squires and boys cross the Hall. Amfortas is borne in, preceded by pages who carry the covered Grail. The voice of Titurel (*bass*) summons his son to perform his sacred duty – to unveil the Grail. At first, tortured by guilt, Amfortas refuses, saying he is unworthy of such a task. He begs for mercy and that his wound be healed. From the dome boys' voices chant the prophecy of the 'guileless fool' and, as if comforted by hope of ultimate redemption, Amfortas uncovers the Grail. All pray and take Communion, as Parsifal stands entranced. Amfortas becomes weaker; his wound has broken out afresh. He is carried out and the procession slowly leaves the Hall.

Gurnemanz asks Parsifal if he comprehends what he has seen. The boy shakes his head, unable to speak. Gurnemanz is angry and sends Parsifal on his way. The act comes to an end as a solo alto then unseen voices from above repeat the prophecy.

ACT II. Klingsor's castle and garden. After a turbulent and threatening prelude, Klingsor (*bass*) is seen in his tower gazing into a metal mirror in which he can see Parsifal approaching the ramparts: the 'guileless fool' will soon be in the sorcerer's power and he will have the Grail.

Klingsor summons Kundry, who appears with a terrible cry. She is ordered to seduce the approaching Parsifal, a task Kundry realises will result in her losing her last hope of salvation. The boy has scaled the castle wall, easily overcoming Klingsor's captive knights, and is standing eagerly in the magic garden. Klingsor waves his hand, and the castle vanishes. As the orchestra gives a spirited description of the combat between Parsifal and the knights, the magic garden is revealed, with Parsifal gazing in astonishment upon its brilliance.

The Flower Maidens rush in looking for their beloved knights, and Parsifal mingles with them. The Maidens, seeing he does not wish to harm them, adorn themselves with flowers and circle him, singing a caressing melody, to enchanting effect. Parsifal regards them with innocent joy. As the Maidens begin to fight over him and he is about to make his escape, Kundry's voice tenderly calls, 'Parsifal!' – the name he dreamed his mother called him. She tells him how his mother died of a broken heart after he wandered away. He must now learn to experience the same kind of love that brought him into the world.

Kundry leans over Parsifal and kisses him. In the space of the embrace, Parsifal is transformed from 'guileless fool' to conscious man. 'Amfortas! The Spear-wound!' he cries, aware now of the significance of what he saw in the Hall of the Grail and the part he must play.

Parsifal rejects Kundry's advances, offering her redemption for her sins. But she breaks out in fury and calls for help, condemning Parsifal to share her fate and wander the earth. Klingsor appears and hurls the Sacred Spear at Parsifal. As if by a superior power, the spear remains suspended over Parsifal's head, until he seizes it. He makes the sign of the Cross and Klingsor and his castle vanish, the garden crumbling to dust. Kundry collapses with a cry, as Parsifal sets off, spear in hand, telling her she will know where to find him again.

ACT III. A spring landscape near the Hall of the Grail, Good Friday morning. Gurnemanz, now very old and dressed as a hermit, hears a groaning from the undergrowth. It is Kundry, dressed in coarse penitent's clothing and now pale and gentle. Her job, she says (her only utterance in this act), is to serve.

Kundry sees a stranger approaching dressed in black armour, his visor closed, a spear in his hand. She realises it is Parsifal; but Gurnemanz takes him for an intruder and chides him for appearing so dressed on such a holy day. Parsifal thrusts the Spear into the ground and kneels before it in prayer, removing his helmet. He greets Gurnemanz, telling him of his long struggle to preserve the purity of the Spear and restore it to its rightful home. Gurnemanz, deeply moved, tells him how the Knights of the Grail have become depleted, and that Amfortas, maddened by his pain and torment, wants to die like his father, Titurel, whose funeral it is this day.

Parsifal, grief-stricken, blames himself. But Gurnemanz, transported with delight, anoints Parsifal as King of the Knights of the Grail. As his first duty, he baptises Kundry, who thus redeemed weeps passionately. Parsifal and Gurnemanz, rejoicing in the day's beauty (the 'Good Friday Music', one of Wagner's most affecting natural mood-paintings which rivals the 'Forest Murmurs' from *Siegfried*), prepare to make their way to the Hall of the Grail.

As in Act I, the scene changes slowly as the sound of bells grows closer. The Hall is filled with mourners for Titurel's death. Amfortas is on his litter in front of the Grail. The knights ask him to reveal the Grail for the last time. The only mercy is death, says Amfortas who, in despair, tears open his robe, revealing his wound and begging his knights to kill him and so rid him of his pain.

Parsifal advances and touches the wound with the Spear point. Amfortas, his wound healed, is enraptured, as Parsifal takes the Grail from its shrine and prays before it. Amfortas and the knights kneel in homage as Kundry, gazing at Parsifal in gratitude, sinks lifeless to the ground.

Johann Strauss
(1825–1899)

DIE FLEDERMAUS
The Bat

OPERA in three acts; text by Haffner and Genée, from a French vaudeville 'Le Réveillon' by Meilhac and Halévy. First performed at the Theater an der Wien, Vienna, April 5, 1874.

JOHANN Strauss the younger was already famous as a composer of Viennese dance music before he turned his hand to operetta. *Die Fledermaus* was his third, and the work as a whole – plot as well as score – is a masterpiece, the finest product of the Viennese operetta school, and a cornucopia of fresh, witty, pointed, memorable melody. The overture, a potpourri, is one of the most popular ever written. It is dominated by the famous waltz, with its lilting refrain.

ACT I. Gabriel von Eisenstein's house. We hear from outside Alfred (*tenor*) serenading Rosalinda, Eisenstein's wife (*soprano*). He is, it appears, an old flame of hers. Adele (*soprano*), the Eisensteins' maid, enters on a cadenza and proceeds to read a letter from her sister, Ida, who has been invited, as part of a ballet company, to a party given by Prince Orlofsky, a rich young Russian eccentric; if Adele can get hold of a dress she can go, too. She asks Rosalinda for time off to look after her sick aunt, but Rosalinda, distracted by Alfred's serenade and Eisenstein's five-day prison sentence due to begin that evening, tells her she cannot possibly be spared. The tearful Adele leaves, as Alfred enters and tells Rosalinda that he intends to call again that evening, when her husband will be away.

Eisenstein (*tenor*) storms in with his advocate, Dr. Blind (*tenor*), who, says Eisenstein, is to blame for his prison sentence, which is now eight days, not five. In a lively trio, Rosalinda protests her grief – perhaps a shade too much – Eisenstein rages at Blind, and the lawyer runs through a list of legal expedients he will call into play once he has a chance of appealing against the sentence.

The lawyer leaves. Adele is sent off to order supper for the master, and Rosalinda goes to look out some old clothes for him to wear to prison. Enter Dr. Falke (*baritone*), a friend of Eisenstein's, who has been secretly nursing a grievance against him ever since Carnival. It seems that Falke, dressed as a bat (hence the title), was left asleep by Eisenstein to find his way home in broad daylight and in costume. He has a plan for revenge. Why, he says, should Eisenstein not accept the invitation from Prince Orlofsky which Falke brings him, and go in disguise to the ball, giving himself up to the prison authorities next morning? Rosalinda need never know – nor need Eisenstein guess that Rosalinda is also being asked to the party, at which she will wear a mask. Eisenstein accepts the invitation with a minimum of shilly-shallying.

All is prepared. Rosalinda, Adele (who has, after all, been given the night off, in preparation for Alfred's expected visit), and Eisenstein (prepared, to his wife's astonishment, to go off to prison in evening dress) sing a delicious farewell trio. The refrain to each of Rosalinda's grief-stricken utterances glitters and sparkles as gaily as the parties they each then enjoy in anticipation. Rosalinda ends with a ringing top C, and Eisenstein bustles off.

No sooner has he gone than Alfred arrives to eat Eisenstein's supper. 'Trinke, Liebchen, trinke schnell,' sings the tenor, and Rosalinda joins in the refrain, although she cannot help noticing that Alfred is beginning to show the effects of the wine he so melodiously urges her to drink. Frank (*baritone*), the new prison governor, appears to escort Herr von Eisenstein to prison. Alfred ropes him in to sing the chorus of his song, but denies hotly that he is Eisenstein when Frank addresses him by name. The situation looks compromising, but Rosalinda carries it off with bravado: does the governor think she would be at supper as late as this with someone who is not her husband? She reconciles Frank to the delay and Alfred to his probable fate in the enchanting slow waltz refrain to her song. A farewell kiss, and Frank, who is also going to Orlofsky's party, hurries Alfred off, a brisk trio bringing the act to its end.

ACT II. The party at Prince Orlofsky's is in full swing. Although the Prince (*mezzo-soprano*) is too blasé to enjoy his parties himself, he likes them to go well – but woe betide anyone who refuses to drink with him. His song, 'Ich lade gern mir Gäste ein', a mixture of languid nonchalance and ado-lescent gaucherie, is perfect characterisation.

Eisenstein, who is introduced as Marquis Renard, feels sure he recognises one of the guests as Adele, but Orlofsky and the rest laugh at him for his curious mistake and Adele herself sings a delightful soubrette song, 'Mein Herr Marquis', in whose laughing refrain she is able to make fun of her employer to her heart's content.

Enter a masked woman, announced as a Hungarian Coun-tess. She excites Eisenstein's curiosity, and it is not long before he is showing her his chiming watch, a bait which has worked the trick on many an unsuspecting Miss. This time, though all seems to be beginning well and Eisenstein is soon timing his Countess's heart-beats, something goes wrong, and the lady ends up with the watch, which is not at all according to plan. It is one of the operetta's high points, this seduction duet, and we hear the watch chime before the singers launch into a galop, Rosalinda ending with peals of mocking coloratura.

Rosalinda will not unmask. Adele suggests the reason is that she is not a Hungarian at all. 'I will prove it,' says Rosalinda; 'the music of my native country shall speak for me.' It is a flimsy pretext for the Czardas and Frischka which follows, but once it starts the music is exhilarating enough to make us forget why it began in the first place.

The finale opens with a short section in praise of champagne, *allegro con brio*. First Orlofsky, then Adele and finally Eisenstein leads the company, which joins in the chorus after the three verses. Eisenstein and Frank (who has been introduced as the Chevalier Chagrin) toast each other, and Falke, looking round at the assembled couples, proposes in a beautiful slow waltz that they shall pledge each other in eternal brother- and sisterhood. There follows the ballet, after which Orlofsky suggests the guests should show they are no less adept at dancing themselves. The famous *Fledermaus* waltz takes the foreground for most of the time, but also serves as background for the continued flirtation of Eisenstein and Rosalinda and for much comic byplay between Eisenstein and Governor Frank. Finally, the clock strikes six, Eisenstein remembers it is high time for him to go to prison, and the act ends as he and Frank help each other from the ballroom.

ACT III. An entr'acte, part march, part waltz, introduces us to the prison, where Frosch the gaoler (a speaking part) is drunk. His inebriated gambollings are interrupted from time to time by bursts of song from cell No. 12, where Alfred is relieving the tedium of prison life with reminiscences of his serenade to Rosalinda and snatches of tunes from opera. As Frosch staggers off to make another attempt to curb this nuisance, Frank waltzes in, only a little less the worse for wear than his underling. He soon falls asleep to reminiscences of the waltz.

His is not to be the sleep of the just, for Frosch has pulled himself together sufficiently to be able to make his morning report. Nothing untoward has happened, he says, except that Herr von Eisenstein has been restive and, having asked for a lawyer, is to see Dr. Blind almost immediately. The doorbell rings and Frosch announces the two young ladies who have taken Frank's fancy at the ball – Adele and her sister. Adele asks Frank to help her start a stage career, and sings to him of her versatility ('Spiel' ich die Unschuld vom Lande': I'll play the innocent country girl). There is another ring at the door; the Marquis Renard. When he hears that the Chevalier Chagrin (whom he at first assumes to have been arrested for insobriety) is none other than the prison governor, he laughs aloud at what he thinks is a particularly good jest. Frank for his part cannot take seriously the announcement that his friend from the ball is Herr von Eisenstein; did he not himself escort that gentleman from his home to the prison, and is he not at this moment incarcerated within twenty feet of where they sit?

Frosch announces that another lady is at the door (the first two have been shown into cell No. 13, the only empty room), and Frank goes to greet her, leaving Eisenstein to waylay Blind and borrow his wig, glasses and legal paraphernalia in the hope that he may discover who it was who was arrested in his place the previous night.

Rosalinda has come to see what can be done to get Alfred out of prison, maybe with the help of the lawyer who is waiting there. Eisenstein disguised proceeds to cross-question the two, demanding the unvarnished truth, which he gets from Alfred in an agreeable tune, punctuated by his own frequent bursts of indignation. Rosalinda defends herself as the victim of a husband who is himself a monster of deceitfulness. Eventually, unable to bear the insults any longer, Eisenstein denounces (to the tune which opens the overture) their treachery, whereupon she produces the watch.

The explanation is not long in forthcoming. No sooner is the rather grandiose trio between Rosalinda, Eisenstein and Alfred over, than the rest of the company at last night's ball appears as if summoned by magic, shortly joined by Adele and Ida, who have refused to let Frosch give them their regulation bath!

Falke explains how he engineered Eisenstein's predicament as vengeance for the shabby trick played on him a year ago. Alfred and Rosalinda hastily add that their supper was also part of the joke. Eisenstein is delighted at the way things have turned out, and Rosalinda sings the only possible moral: let all join with her in praising the sovereign reconciling power of King Champagne!

Engelbert Humperdinck
(1854–1921)

HÄNSEL UND GRETEL

OPERA in three acts; text by Adelheid Wette (the composer's sister). First performed at the Hoftheater, Weimar, December 23, 1893.

ACT I. The hut of a broom-maker. Hänsel (*mezzo-soprano*) is binding brooms and Gretel (*soprano*) is knitting. The children romp, quarrel, and make up. When their mother, Gertrude (*soprano*), enters she is angry to see them idle, and trying to smack them she upsets a pitcher of milk instead. With all hope of supper vanished she sends the children out into the woods with little baskets to look for strawberries, while she herself, bemoaning their poverty, sinks exhausted upon a chair and falls asleep. A riotous song announces the approach of her husband, Peter (*baritone*), drunk as usual. She is about to reproach him when she notices that he has brought sausages, bread and butter, coffee – enough for a feast. He tells her that he has had good luck at the Fair and bids her prepare supper. When he asks for the children he is horrified to hear that they have been sent into the woods, for a wicked witch lives near the Ilsenstein who entices the children in order to bake them in her oven and devour them. Both parents rush off in search of Hänsel and Gretel.

ACT II. Near the Ilsenstein, Hänsel has filled his basket with berries and Gretel has made a wreath with which her brother crowns her. Before they realise what they are doing the children eat all the berries. Then they see that it is too dark to look for any more or to find their way home. Gretel weeps with fear and Hänsel comforts her. They grow sleepy. The Sandman (*soprano*) sprinkles sand into their eyes, but before going to sleep the children are careful not to forget their evening prayer. Fourteen guardian angels are seen descending the heavenly ladder to protect them.

ACT III. Morning. The Dew Fairy (*soprano*) sprinkles dew on the children. Suddenly they notice a little house made of cake and sugar. They start to break off little bits when a voice cries out from within and the Witch (*mezzo-soprano*) opens the door. She throws a rope around Hänsel's throat, and tells them both to come in. Frightened, they try to escape, but after binding them with a magic spell she imprisons Hänsel in a kennel, and forces Gretel to go into the house.

When she believes Hänsel to be asleep she turns her attention to the oven, then rides around the house on her broomstick. When she alights she orders Hänsel to show her his finger. But he pokes a stick through the bars and, finding it still thin, the witch orders more food for him. While she turns her back, Gretel seizes the juniper bough with which the old woman makes her spells, speaks the magic words and breaks her brother's enchantment. Then the witch tells Gretel to get into the oven and see if the honey cakes are done. But Gretel pretends to be stupid and asks her to show her how to get in. Together the children push the old witch into the oven and slam the door. The oven soon falls to pieces. The children then see a row of boys and girls standing stiffly against the house. Gretel breaks the spell for them as she had done for Hänsel. There is general rejoicing, Gertrude and Peter appear, the old witch is pulled out of the ruined oven as a gigantic honey cake and everyone on the stage joins in a hymn of thanksgiving.

Gioacchino Antonio Rossini
(1792–1868)

L'ITALIANA IN ALGERI
The Italian Girl in Algiers

Two acts; première, Venice, 1813. The Algerian Bey's wife Elvira (*soprano*) laments the loss of her husband's love. Haly (*bass*), Captain of Corsairs, is instructed to find the Bey (*bass*) an

Italian wife. The slave Lindoro (*tenor*) sings of his lost love Isabella (*contralto*), who is conveniently shipwrecked nearby and brought to the Bey. She recognises Lindoro and a Rossinian septet ensues. Isabella and Lindoro plan to escape. She gives Elvira a lesson in man-management, while Lindoro prepares to enrol the Bey in the 'pappataci', the order of model husbands. He swears to oBey the rules – which include refraining from anger at flirtatious behaviour. A boat, which the Bey thinks is part of the ceremony, is waiting to take all the Europeans home. The Bey at last realises his mistake and happily embraces Elvira as Isaballa and Lindoro sail away.

IL TURCO IN ITALIA
The Turk in Italy

TWO (now three) acts, by Gioacchino Rossini; première, Milan, 1814. Prosdocimo (*baritone*), a poet, has to produce a stage comedy. The flighty Fiorilla (*soprano*), wife of the elderly Geronio (*bass*), spots Selim (*bass*), the Turk, and invites him to coffee – upsetting Narciso (*tenor*), her lover. Selim and Fiorilla plan to elope, but Zaida (*mezzo-soprano*) recognises him as her beloved master. She and Fiorilla confront each other, to the delight of Prosdocimo. Selim proposes to Geronio that he sell him Fiorilla. Prosdocimo suggests that, at a ball that night, Zaida be disguised as Fiorilla, Geronio as Selim; Narciso also dresses as Selim. In a splendid Rossinian quintet the comedy of errors is played out. Fiorilla is unmasked, Selim returns to Turkey with Zaida, and Prosdocimo has his play.

IL BARBIERE DI SIVIGLIA
The Barber of Seville

OPERA in two acts by Gioacchino Rossini; text by Sterbini, founded on Beaumarchais's play. Première on February 20, 1816, at Teatro Argentina, Rome.

ROSSINI is a bundle of paradox, or at least of superficial contradiction. He was a man of celebrated wit and apparent worldliness, yet consumed by nerves and cursed with the thinnest of skins; he is famous two hundred years after his birth for his comedies, yet in his own time probably better known as composer of *opera seria*; he wrote prolifically and fast (thirty-nine operas in nineteen years) yet during the last twenty-nine years of his life produced no operas and, short vocal and piano pieces apart, only two full-length works, both to sacred texts.

Even his birthdate, February 29, 1792, marks him as an exception.

The contract for *Il Barbiere* was signed a mere two months before the first night, but there can be no doubt that Beaumarchais's play, already the subject of a highly successful opera by the composer Paisiello, had been in Rossini's mind for some time. He took pains to extol the virtues of Paisiello's score, but circumstances, including stage mishaps and disruptions by followers of Paisiello, conspired to make the new opera's première into a celebrated fiasco.

The subsequent history of what was to become one of opera's most enduring successes is full of changes and second thoughts. Rossini allowed the tenor's extended aria, which originally preceded the dénouement, first to be taken over by Rosina and finally transferred to become the finale of *La Cenerentola*; the mezzo-soprano role of Rosina came often to be transposed for soprano, usually with high-flying decoration; baritones cast as Dr. Bartolo at one time preferred to sing 'Manca un foglio', a straightforward aria by Pietro Romani, instead of the taxing but much superior 'A un dottor della mia sorte'; and an overture written for the earlier *Aureliano in Palmira* (and therefore thematically irrelevant to *The Barber*) was placed by the composer at the start of the score where it is paradoxically considered wholly apt to the comedy which follows.

ACT I. A square in which stands Dr. Bartolo's house; dawn. Count Almaviva (*tenor*) has fallen in love with Rosina (*mezzo-soprano*), Dr. Bartolo's ward, and his servant Fiorello (*bass*) leads a band of musicians as, with grace (but little effect), he serenades his beloved: 'Ecco ridente in cielo' (Lo, smiling in the eastern sky). He pays off the musicians and tells them to leave quietly, but his generosity provokes a hubbub. From outside the square, Figaro's (*baritone*) insistent patter starts to dominate and he dances in, singing the famous bravura air, 'Largo al factotum della città', a patter song without equal in the baritone repertory. Figaro turns out to be Dr. Bartolo's barber and immediately starts plotting with the Count to bring about an introduction to Rosina. Bartolo keeps a strict watch on his ward (whom he means himself to marry), but Rosina has noticed her unidentified suitor, and now contrives to drop from her balcony a letter asking his name. In an aria of the utmost refinement ('Se il mio nome') he somewhat disingenuously tells her it is Lindoro. The Count and Figaro improvise the next move in a brilliantly elegant duet ('All'idea di quel metallo').

A room in Dr. Bartolo's house. Rosina sings an aria suggesting that she is all sweetness and light until crossed, when she becomes the very devil: 'Una voce poco fa' (A little voice I heard just now). Meanwhile, Dr. Bartolo (*buffo bass*) makes known to Don Basilio, the singing teacher (*bass*), his suspicions about Count Almaviva; in order to run him out of town Basilio advocates a campaign of calumny which may start as a gentle breeze but will surely swell to roar like a cannon: 'La calunnia'. Figaro contrives to tell Rosina his cousin Lindoro is madly in love with her. She has already prepared a note: 'Dunque io son, tu non m'inganni?' (Am I his love, or dost thou mock me?). Bartolo crossly but accurately taxes her with having dropped a letter from the balcony, then, refusing to accept any excuse, reads her a lecture on the futility of trying to deceive him. 'A un dottor della mia sorte' is a buffo patter song on the grandest scale.

To gain admittance to Bartolo's house, the Count has at Figaro's suggestion disguised himself as a tipsy soldier, and now tries to barge his way in, claiming the right to be billeted there. He reveals himself to Rosina, then refuses to recognise the waiver which Bartolo shows him. Berta, Rosina's governess (*soprano*), and Don Basilio add their voices to the din, which attracts Figaro. Vigorous knocking at the outside door heralds the appearance of the police, to whom all at breakneck speed give what rapidly becomes a hilariously contradictory explanation of events. The officer in charge is about to arrest the Count, when that worthy shows him a piece of paper. He springs to attention. Dr. Bartolo watches thunderstruck and immobile, and all in an irresistibly comic sextet comment *staccato* on his plight before the act ends in rushing scales and general pandemonium.

ACT II. A room in Dr. Bartolo's house. Dr. Bartolo has begun to suspect that the drunken soldier was an emissary of Count Almaviva's, but his reverie is interrupted by the arrival of a music teacher, ostensibly sent by the sick Don Basilio to give Rosina her music lesson. Nothing seems to divert the newcomer from his obsequious and incessantly reiterated greeting of 'Pace e gioia sia con voi' until Dr. Bartolo explodes with irritation and brings him to the point. 'Don Alonso' succeeds in winning his confidence by producing Rosina's letter to himself and offering to persuade the girl that it was given him by a mistress of the Count's. The lesson – a grand *scena* in two parts: 'Contro un cor' and 'Cara immagine' – proceeds smoothly and at its end, Dr. Bartolo demonstrates how much better music was in his day, only to be interrupted by the arrival of Figaro. He won't be shaved today, protests Bartolo, but Figaro declines to be put off and creates a diversion during which he obtains the key of the balcony and Almaviva and Rosina contrive a word together.

At that moment, Basilio puts in an appearance, and it is all

Figaro and the Count can do to persuade him (with the aid of a purse) to admit that he has a fever and should be home in bed. 'Buona sera, mio signore' begins the delightful ensemble as they – even including Dr. Bartolo – join in sending the intruder packing, after which Figaro prepares to shave the doctor while the Count and Rosina plan their elopement. But the planning is not surreptitious enough, Dr. Bartolo gets wind of the whole affair, catches the plotters and sends them all packing.

Berta in an aria mocks the old for wanting to marry the young, the young for wanting to get married at all, and herself for sharing the symptoms, after which Bartolo manages, with the aid of the letter Almaviva felt obliged as a pledge of good faith to give him, to excite Rosina's jealousy. In her pique, she discloses the plan for the elopement and agrees to marry her guardian.

A storm blows up – a Rossini musical speciality – and as the last drops of rain fall Figaro and the Count make their appearance. The lovers are reconciled and celebrate in a delightful trio, 'Ah, qual colpo', before Figaro discovers that the escape-ladder is gone and their plot rumbled. Still, all is far from lost. When the notary appears with Don Basilio, he is easily persuaded to perform – and Don Basilio to witness – the marriage of the young couple rather than Dr. Bartolo's with his ward, and even Dr. Bartolo is reconciled to the loss of Rosina and her dowry by a gift from the Count of an equal sum. The most famous of Italian comic operas comes to an end with an *envoi*, led by Figaro, taken up by Rosina and the Count, and celebrating the triumph of love over all obstacles.

La Cenerentola
Cinderella

OPERA in two acts by Gioacchino Rossini; text by Jacopo Ferretti (founded on Etienne's French libretto for Isouard's *Cendrillon*, 1810). Première at the Teatro Valle, Rome, January 25, 1817.

THE action takes place partly in the house of Don Magnifico, the Baron, partly in the palace of the Prince.

ACT I. Cenerentola is, of course, Cinderella (Angelina, Don Magnifico's stepdaughter; *contralto*). She is making coffee for her half-sisters, singing a sad little song. The friend and counsellor of the Prince, Alidoro (*bass*), enters disguised as a beggar. The two sisters curtly dismiss him; but, to their intense annoyance, Cinderella pities him and offers him refreshment. The quarrel is interrupted by the entrance of the Prince's followers. Clorinda (*soprano*) and Thisbe (*mezzo-soprano*) feel convinced that he must fall an easy victim to their charms. They listen rather reluctantly while their father tells them at length of a dream he has had, and then go to make ready for the Prince, Don Ramiro (*tenor*), who arrives disguised as his valet, Dandini (*bass*), to find Cinderella alone.

Cinderella and the Prince fall in love at first sight and express their feelings in a duet which has all of Rossini's characteristic wit and melodiousness.

Cinderella is summoned by her sisters. The Prince, left alone, does not know what to think of his charmer. His musings are interrupted by the arrival of Dandini, masquerading as the Prince. While Dandini misquotes Latin to give himself an air, the voice of Cinderella is heard begging the Baron to allow her to go to the ball. Neither the Baron (*buffo bass*) nor her sisters will listen to her; the third daughter is dead, they tell the Prince, and Cinderella is only a servant. They leave, but Alidoro promises to help Cinderella.

The ball at the Prince's palace. The Baron has been appointed chief butler to the Prince and is busy tasting the wines. The disguised Prince has seen enough of Clorinda and Thisbe by this time to know that neither could make him happy. The girls, for their part, set about capturing Dandini, and when the arrival of a distinguished but unknown lady is announced, their jealousy is roused – but the lady looks too much like Cinderella to cause them alarm.

ACT II. Clorinda and Thisbe are no longer on friendly terms, as each believes she has made a conquest of the Prince, but Dandini is himself in love with Cinderella and asks her to marry him. Cinderella refuses and confesses her love for his 'valet'. The Prince, who overhears, proposes to her. Cinderella admits that she loves him, but before consenting to be his bride the Prince must find out who she is. She gives him a bracelet which matches another she is wearing and departs.

The Baron enters and asks Dandini whether it would be possible to speed up the wedding. Dandini has a secret; but first, if he were to marry one of the Baron's daughters, he asks, how should she be treated? The Baron tells him: thirty lackeys always at hand; sixteen horses; a dozen dukes, a coach with six footmen and 'dinners with ices' always ready. Dandini confesses that he is but a valet and that marriage with a daughter of the Baron is unthinkable.

The Baron's house. Clorinda and Thisbe scowl at Cinderella, who resembles the hateful stranger of the ball. A storm rages outside – brought about by the incantations of the philosopher, Alidoro. The Prince and Dandini seek refuge while another coach is got ready; the Baron orders Cinderella to bring the best chair forward for the Prince. Cinderella puts her hand up to cover her face, but the Prince notices the bracelet, the companion of which he holds. All the knots are gradually unravelled. The Baron, Clorinda, and Thisbe, unable to understand, order Cinderella away. The Prince grows angry and threatens them with his displeasure. The scene changes to the palace, where the intercession of the extraordinarily forgiving Cinderella results in the pardon of the Baron and his daughters, and all ends merrily.

Not the least reason for the comparative lack of popularity of Rossini's operas in the early twentieth century – only *The Barber* survived in the repertory – was the florid nature of the vocal writing. *Cenerentola* is no exception. The title role, like that of *L'Italiana*, is written for coloratura contralto. Though attempts have been made to arrange the music for a soprano (as has been done with Rosina), the opera generally has to wait for revival until a low voice with impeccable agility comes along. When it does, the unmatched ensembles for which Rossini is renowned show a modern audience the stuff a comic opera was made of in the days when every singer was a master of the bravura coloratura style, and most of them brilliant actors and actresses as well. In *Cenerentola*, it is not so much the motives of the characters which matter, nor even primarily their reactions to their own and other people's motives, but the situations these motives get them into. And situations with Rossini lead not so much to arias as to ensembles. Rossini's ability to catch hold of the verbal rhythm of a chance phrase and turn it into music (e.g. the ensemble after Alidoro's announcement of Cinderella's arrival at the ball), his dexterity with patter, his astonishing manipulation of the simplest material until it becomes a towering invention of quicksilver sound – these qualities are heard at their best in the quintet which begins 'Signore, una parola'; in the finale of Act I, which ends with the *crescendo* first heard in the overture; in the brilliantly comic duet of Dandini and Magnifico in Act II. The climax of the opera comes, not with the rondo at the end, fine though it is, but with the great E flat ensemble of stupefaction after the Prince and Dandini have taken refuge from the storm in the astonished Don Magnifico's house. This sextet is built up on a slow, *staccato* tune (marked *maestoso*: majestically) from which each singer in turn breaks away with a florid phrase, the others meanwhile keeping up the steady rhythm with a constant repetition of the tune and a maximum use of the words and particularly of the opportunities given by the rolled Italian 'r'. This is an ensemble to set beside the *Barber*'s matchless 'fredda ed immobile' as high-water marks of comedy in music.

LE COMTE ORY
Count Ory

TWO acts; première, Paris, 1828. Adèle (*soprano*) is left with-out male protection while her brother is on Crusade. The dissolute Count Ory (*tenor*) is determined to win her. With the unwitting help of his page Isolier (*mezzo-soprano*), in love with Adèle, Ory in hermit guise contrives to meet her and advises her that love will cure her melancholy, but his identity is re-vealed, to general horror. Adèle, awaiting her brother's return, feels obliged to give hospitality to a party of nuns – Ory and his friends, of course. When Isolier hears of this he is immediately suspicious, and intercepts the Count's attempts to woo Adèle, passing them on himself in the dark. Trumpets herald the Cru-saders' return; all is revealed, and Isolier helps Ory to escape.

GUILLAUME TELL
William Tell

OPERA in four acts by Gioacchino Rossini; text by V. J. Etienne de Jouy and H. L. F. Bis, based on Friedrich Schiller's play. Première, Opéra, Paris, August 3, 1829.

ROSSINI's last opera was written to fulfil the terms of an agreement with the French government. It is a noble work and must be considered, with Verdi's *Don Carlos*, as the finest example of French Grand Opera; in it Rossini demonstrates a new interest in folk music, nature and the picturesque.

Switzerland in the thirteenth century is governed by a re-pressive Austrian regime, personified by its Governor, Gesler (*bass*). Arnold (*tenor*), a young patriot, has saved the life of a Habsburg princess, and as a result they have, from the Swiss point of view unfortunately, and in spite of her nationality, fal-len in love.

The overture has four distinct movements: five solo cellos evoke, according to Berlioz, 'the calm of profound solitude'; next, a storm; then a pastoral scene, with a Swiss herdsman's *ranz des vaches*; finally, a patriotic call to arms (*allegro vivace*).

ACT I. On the shores of Lake Lucerne. At a village festivity, a triple wedding celebration presided over by Melcthal (*bass*), a fisherman (*tenor*) sings a charming song which turns into a quartet with Tell (*baritone*) and his family; Melcthal would like to see his son as one of the bridegrooms. Arnold is reluctant to reveal his love for Mathilde, but in a fine duet ('Ah, Mathilde, idole de mon âme': Ah, Mathilde, my soul's idol). Tell feels he is ambivalent when open defiance of the occupying force is demanded. In the end, there is no doubt of his love for Mathilde but equally little about his patriotism. Nonetheless, he contrives to leave, and Tell, goaded by the sound of the distant hunt in which Gesler is doubtless active, goes to look for him. The weddings proceed, a most attractive *Pas de Six* starts the dancing, but interruption comes with the precipitate arrival of Leuthold (*baritone*), who has killed an Austrian who attempted to rape his daughter. Tell volunteers to row him to safety, the Austrians headed by Rudolph (*tenor*) arrive breathing fire and slaughter and, baulked of their prey, unavailingly question the villagers before carrying off Melcthal as hostage.

ACT II. The mountains overlooking Lake Lucerne and neighbouring cantons. An Austrian hunting chorus is answered by a contrasting chorus of Swiss in devout mood. Princess Mathilde (*soprano*), separated from the hunting party, in a beautiful aria celebrates her love for Arnold ('Sombre forêt'), who himself makes an appearance. Though the obstacles to their love are clear, they pledge faith in a duet and Arnold says that, in order to be worthy of Mathilde, he will win honour fighting in the Austrian army away from Switzerland. Tell and Walter Fürst (*bass*) work on his patriotic instincts (trio: 'Quand l'Helvétie est un champ de supplices') and clinch his support by revealing the murder of his father – one of the score's grandest movements, where moreover the high notes of the tenor cast as Arnold make most effect.

The second part of the act has the gathering of the Cantons, each differently characterised in music, and, at Tell's urging, the swearing of an oath to join in casting off the Austrian yoke (the music foreshadowing Meyerbeer's *Bénédiction des Poignards*, but celebrating a better cause).

ACT III. A chapel in the grounds of the Governor's Palace. Arnold tells Mathilde he must adhere strictly to the Swiss cause, partly out of patriotism, partly out of respect for his murdered father, and she reacts with sympathy. They suspect patriotism will keep them apart for ever (this scene is usually omitted in modern performance).

The Square at Altdorf. Celebration of one hundred years of Austrian occupation has been decreed, and orders are out for the Swiss populace to genuflect to Gesler's hat symbolically displayed. A series of vividly contrasted dances follows, some with chorus, and at their end Tell refuses to bow to the Austrian symbol and is recognised as having helped Leuthold escape. Gesler orders him to shoot an apple from his son Jemmy's head. Tell addresses his son (*soprano*) in a fine aria: 'Sois immobile' (Hold yourself still). The shot succeeds but Tell has no compunction in admitting to Gesler that the second arrow he held was intended for him. When Gesler condemns both Tell and Jemmy to death, Mathilde makes a spirited intercession and demands in the Emperor's name that Jemmy be handed over to her. Tell is taken off to prison.

ACT IV. Melcthal's house. Arnold wants vengeance for his father's murder and at the same time recognises that with Tell in prison he is the natural leader of the revolt. He gazes sadly at his ruined home and pours forth his feelings in an aria ('Asile héréditaire': O home of my forefathers), famous in its own right and bristling with top C's; in Rossini's day these were sung in a 'mixed voice' and only later (notably by the French tenor Gilbert Duprez), to Rossini's distaste, by the *tenore di forza* of modern times.

A rocky shore of Lake Lucerne. A storm is rising. To Hedwige, Tell's wife (*soprano*), Mathilde restores her son Jemmy (trio: 'Je rends à votre amour un fils digne de vous': To your loving arms I return a son worthy of you). Mathilde pledges herself as surety for Tell, Jemmy lights the beacon as a signal of revolt, all pray for Tell's safety, and Leuthold announces the appearance of Tell's storm-bound boat, which he is piloting but which also contains Gesler. He lands, pushes the boat away from the shore and fires an arrow straight to Gesler's heart. The Swiss are triumphant, Arnold laments that his father did not live to see the day, and a *ranz des vaches* banishes the storm and brings back the sun.

Guillaume Tell is a long opera and by 1831 Rossini had already prepared an abridged edition in three acts. This was subsequently revised but the four-act version did not return to the Paris stage until 1856; in 1868, the Paris Opéra celebrated 500 performances of the work, which remained in the repertory until 1932. Modern practice tends towards as nearly complete a version as the audience is thought to be capable of standing, and there is little doubt that the opera's nobility and grandeur are most apparent when cuts are at a minimum.

Gaetano Donizetti
(1797–1848)

ANNA BOLENA
Anne Boleyn

Two acts, by Gaetano Donizetti; libretto by Romani. Première, Milan, 1830. In Windsor Castle the courtiers discuss the love of Henry VIII (*bass*) for Jane Seymour (*soprano*). Queen Anne (*soprano*) sadly expresses her forebodings. Henry tells Jane that he intends to marry her after exposing the Queen's unfaithfulness. Percy (*tenor*) has been recalled from exile to provide evidence. Although he still loves Anne she remains true to her marriage. The King catches her in what he purports to find a compromising situation with her page Smeaton (*contralto*). She is arrested and while waiting for trial hears from Jane of the King's marriage plans. At the trial Smeaton's 'confession' is reported. The Queen admits that she once loved Percy. She, Percy, her brother Rochefort (*bass*) and Smeaton are condemned to death. In the Tower, Anne, her reason gone, sings movingly and then in an impassioned outburst as the new Queen is acclaimed.

L'ELISIR D'AMORE
The Elixir of Love

OPERA in two acts by Gaetano Donizetti, text by Felice Romani. Première at the Teatro della Canobbiana, Milan, May 12, 1832.

Act I. The entrance to Adina's farm. Giannetta (*soprano*) and the harvesters are sheltering under a tree from the fierce noonday sun. Adina (*soprano*) is sitting apart reading. She is watched by the young peasant Nemorino (*tenor*), who loves her but laments, in a cavatina (the famous 'Quanto è bella'), that someone so beautiful and clever as she could never love a fool like him. Suddenly Adina bursts into laughter: it is, she explains, the bizarre love story she is reading. She proceeds to entertain the ensemble by recounting the legend of how Tristan won Isolde with a magic love potion that made him irresistible. 'How I wish I had the recipe,' sings Adina, as the others (including Nemorino, who is listening from the sidelines) urge her to continue the tale.

To the sound of a drum, a detachment of soldiers marches in, headed by Sergeant Belcore (*baritone*) who presents Adina with a posy of flowers and proposes marriage. In a quartet, Belcore urges her to accept; the amused Adina replies that she is in no hurry; Nemorino pleads for some of Cupid's courage; Giannetta predicts that the shrewd Adina won't be caught out.

Left alone with Adina, Nemorino tries (not for the first time) to tell her he loves her. But she says it is no use; she is as fickle as the wind. To which Nemorino replies that his feelings for her are as inexplicable yet as inevitable as the course of a river.

The village square. A trumpet announces the arrival in a splendid carriage of a travelling quack doctor, Dulcamara (*bass*), who, in a *buffo* cavatina, 'Udite, udite, o rustici' (Listen, listen, rustic ones), offers the crowd amazing cures for everything from wrinkles to toothache. Nemorino, summoning his available courage, asks Dulcamara for Queen Isolde's love potion: an elixir of love. The good doctor happens to have just the thing (actually a flask of cheap Bordeaux), which he sells to the hapless Nemorino for one zecchino, telling him it should take effect within twenty-four hours – thus allowing him plenty of time to leave town. Nemorino empties the flask in one draught and becomes, not unreasonably, quite drunk.

Adina, attracted by Nemorino's raucous singing and dancing, is astonished by his apparent indifference to her. Belcore enters and renews his offer of marriage, which Adina promptly accepts, saying they will marry within six days. Belcore receives an order that he and his troops are to leave the village the next morning. Adina, infuriated by Nemorino's apparent amusement, consents to Belcore's request to bring the marriage forward to today. This news has a temporarily sobering effect on Nemorino, who begs Adina to wait just twenty-four hours. Adina tells Belcore that the peasant is nothing more than an infatuated boy. Belcore threatens Nemorino. In a lively finale Adina invites all to her wedding banquet and she and Belcore head off to the Notary to make arrangements. Nemorino, by now thoroughly miserable, is taunted by the villagers and calls for help from Dr. Dulcamara.

ACT II. Inside Adina's farm. The banquet is in progress, although Adina has not yet signed the marriage contract. After a chorus of rejoicing, Dulcamara produces a piece of music, which he says is the latest thing from Venice: 'The Pretty Gondolier Girl and Senator Threetooth'. He and Adina sing the barcarolle, 'Io son ricco e tu sei bella' (I am rich and you are pretty), which tells how the girl rejects the senator's wealth to marry instead a young gondolier she loves.

The Notary has arrived and the opening chorus is repeated. A desperate Nemorino comes to beg Dulcamara for help. Take another dose of the elixir at once, advises Dulcamara, adding *sotto voce* that he will be gone in half an hour. The only way Nemorino can pay for another bottle, he discovers from the calculating Belcore in a lively duet, is to enlist in the sergeant's regiment, whereupon he will receive twenty scudi. Nemorino signs the paper and rushes off to find Dulcamara.

Meanwhile, Giannetta tells the village girls that Nemorino's uncle has died, leaving him a fortune. The young man, who knows nothing of this, will be the Croesus of the region and quite a catch as a husband. A quartet begins as Nemorino returns, fortified by more Bordeaux, and is immediately pounced upon by Giannetta and the girls, making him believe the potion is at last working. Adina enters with Dulcamara, and both are astonished at Nemorino's powers of attraction. Adina tries to tell Nemorino he has made a mistake in joining Belcore's regiment, but he is dragged off to dance.

In a duet, 'Quanto amore!' (Such love!), Dulcamara explains Nemorino's behaviour to Adina, and tells her about the elixir. He realises that she loves Nemorino and offers her a flask, which she refuses, saying the only elixir she needs is her eyes.

They leave, and Nemorino returns. He sings one of the greatest tenor arias of all opera, the tender romance 'Una furtiva lagrima', whose tranquil introduction, dominated by a plaintive bassoon, leads to Nemorino's discovery: he has glimpsed a furtive tear in Adina's eye as she gazed enviously at the flirting village girls; she loves him after all!

Adina tells Nemorino that she has bought him out of his contract with Belcore. Nemorino at first hands it back, saying he would rather die as a soldier, but Adina finally admits she loves him and will do so forever.

The finale begins with the phlegmatic Belcore accepting that he is losing Adina: the world is full of women, he reflects. Dulcamara reveals that, thanks to his uncle, Nemorino is a wealthy man, and that the elixir not only cures the lovesick but also makes them rich! He sells his remaining stock of Bordeaux, hops into his carriage and rides out of the village to a chorus of farewell.

MARIA STUARDA
Mary Stuart

OPERA in three acts by Gaetano Donizetti; text by Giuseppe Bardari. First performed (as *Buondelmonte*) at the Teatro San Carlo, Naples, October 18, 1834.

MARIA STUARDA, the second of the three operas Donizetti wrote involving Queen Elizabeth (*Elisabetta al Castello di Kenilworth* is the first and *Roberto Devereux* the third), is representative of the composer at his best as well as at his most typical. The opera's early history is stormy, involving censor-ship troubles in Naples and a first night with a new libretto under the title of *Buondelmonte*; rivalry between prima donnas ending in fisticuffs on the stage; and a rehabilitation in Milan for which Malibran (as Mary) was wretchedly out of voice but refused to give up the part because of the fees involved.

At the start of the opera Mary, Queen of Scots (*soprano*), has fled from her subjects and been imprisoned in Fotheringay Castle, Northamptonshire, by her cousin, Elizabeth, Queen of England. We do not meet her until Act II of Donizetti's opera, which is modelled on Schiller's play and includes the famous scene of the encounter between the two Queens, a dramatically effective falsification of history on Schiller's part.

ACT I. The Palace of Westminster, 1567. Courtiers eagerly await the arrival of Queen Elizabeth (*soprano*), rumoured to be about to unite by marriage the thrones of England and France. The Queen, however, has inclinations towards another and less exalted man, as she reveals in her graceful cavatina 'Ah, quando all'ara scorgemi'. The court and Talbot (*baritone*) urge clemency in her dealings with her cousin Mary Stuart, Cecil (*bass*) re-minds her of the untrustworthiness of her rival, while the Queen remains firm in her path of indecisiveness. When Leic-ester (*tenor*) enters, she appoints him her ambassador to France, notices his reluctance to accept, raises suspicions in the minds of the bystanders that this may be the man whom she secretly loves, and leaves the stage.

Talbot reveals to Leicester that he has been to Fotheringay and that Mary Stuart (referred to throughout the opera indis-criminately as 'Maria' and 'Stuarda') has asked by letter for Leicester's help in her predicament. Leicester, impressed again by the beauty of her portrait ('Ah, rimiro il bel sembiante') and the poignancy of her situation, longs to free her but promises Talbot not to jeopardise her safety further by any impetuous action. The Queen returns and demands to see the letter he is holding; she realises from it that Mary has at one time or an-other had designs both on the throne which she herself occupies and the man whom she at present favours. In a duet, Leicester pleads successfully that the Queen agree to visit Mary in prison at Fotheringay ('Era d'amor l'immagine', and 'Sul crin la rivale').

ACT II. The Park at Fotheringay. Mary recalls with her com-panion Hannah (*mezzo-soprano*) the soft, far-off days of her happy life at the French court ('Oh nube! che lieve per l'aria ti aggiri'). Her reminiscences turn to agitation at the approach of the Queen's hunting party and the prospect of the meeting which she has yearned for and now dreads. Leicester is first on the scene, to counsel her to adopt a submissive attitude towards

Elizabeth, to swear himself to exact vengeance if the Queen remain obdurate, and, at the end of their duet, to ask for Mary's hand in marriage.

Elizabeth appears in an atmosphere of suspicion (egged on by Cecil), mistrust (because of her doubts of Leicester's motives), and apprehension (because she and her imprisoned cousin are to meet face to face for the first time). The confrontation is preceded by one of those moments of frozen drama that are peculiar to opera, a sextet in the composer's best vein, which opens with Elizabeth's reaction to her first sight of Mary: 'E sempre la stessa, superba, orgogliosa' (Unchanged she remains, proud and haughty). Mary forces herself to kneel before her cousin and beg for forgiveness, only to hear herself accused of treachery and in effect of murdering her husband, Darnley. In furious reaction, she insults the Queen, addressing her as 'Figlia impura di Bolena' and 'bastarda'. Her cause is all too evidently lost as the Queen summons the guards, and the act ends with Elizabeth in impassioned tones condemning her rival and cousin to death.

ACT III. The Palace of Westminster Queen Elizabeth waits to sign the death warrant ('Quella vita a me funesta'). Her doubts are resolved by the appearance of Leicester, whom she suspects of an amorous involvement with her cousin, and the persistent promptings of Cecil. She signs, to start a fine trio of mutual recrimination, during which she orders Leicester to witness the execution.

At Fotheringay, Mary hears of the sentence from Cecil and refuses the services of an Anglican priest. There follows the great scene of the confession by the loyal Talbot, which, with its linked chain of expressive melodic sections, seems to look forward to the series of similarly constructed scenes in Verdi. Mary at one moment seems to see, and we and Talbot through Donizetti's trombones to perceive, the ghost of her second husband, Henry Darnley, whom the librettist makes her refer to as Arrigo ('Delle mie colpe lo squallido fantasma'). She poignantly remembers the murdered Rizzio, but, as she clears her conscience ('Quando di luce rosea'), denies all complicity in her husband's death, which she claims was the direct result of Elizabeth's jealousy of their mutual love. Schiller's play leaves this issue unresolved, but there is no doubt that Donizetti's music demands that, though she admits to complicity in the Babington plot, Mary be judged innocent of murder.

In a room next to the scene of the impending execution, Mary's supporters protest what they think of as a crime against an innocent woman. Hannah tries to stop them disturbing the last hours of her mistress, who enters, sees them for the first time since her condemnation and prays calmly and movingly to

God ('Deh! tu di un umile preghiera'). We hear the first of the three cannon shots which are to announce the moment of the execution, and Cecil brings the Queen's offer of a last wish. Mary asks that Hannah may go with her to the steps of the scaffold. She continues in a mood approaching resignation ('Di un cor che more') until the appearance of the distraught Leicester and the sound of the second cannon shot precipitate a last protest of innocence ('Ah, se un giorno da queste ritorte'). The third cannon shot sounds. Mary walks upright and dignified to her death.

LUCIA DI LAMMERMOOR

OPERA in three acts by Gaetano Donizetti; text by Salvatore Cammarano after Sir Walter Scott's novel. Première at Teatro San Carlo, Naples, September 26, 1835.

L ORD HENRY ASHTON (*baritone*), of Lammermoor in Scotland, in order to retrieve his fallen fortunes and extricate himself from a political position endangered by his former opposition to the King, has unknown to her arranged a marriage between his sister Lucy (*soprano*) and Lord Arthur Bucklaw (*tenor*). He for his part has only just become aware of an attachment which has grown up between Lucy and their neighbour Edgar of Ravenswood (*tenor*), whose family and the Ashtons are sworn enemies.

ACT I. A wood near Lammermoor. On suspicion that Edgar has been seen lurking near the castle, retainers beat the bounds but to Ashton's fury find nothing. He inveighs against Edgar (aria, 'Cruda, funesta smania': A vicious, fatal rage).

A fountain in the Park. Atmospherically introduced by the harp, Lucy, who has an assignation with Edgar, in the first of two graceful solos tells her companion Alice (*mezzo-soprano*) the legend of the fountain: 'Regnava nel silenzio' (Silence o'er all was reigning). Here an ancestress of hers was stabbed to death by her lover and has reappeared as a ghost, which the impressionable Lucy has seen. Alice begs Lucy to give up Edgar, but she affirms he is the light of her life: 'Quando, rapita in estasi' (When rapt in ecstasy).

Edgar comes to tell Lucy he leaves in the morning for a mission abroad but wants to make peace with his traditional enemies – the Ashtons have apparently in the past usurped his family's inheritance. Lucy warns him that her brother still breathes fire and slaughter at mention of his name and the duet proper ('Sulla tomba': On the tomb) starts with his fiery reiteration of his hatred for her family. Lucy is melting and conciliatory and eventually, as he puts a ring on her finger, Edgar sings of his feelings of ardent love. Their voices join in an expression of tenderness ('Verranno a te sull'aure': My sighs shall on the balmy breeze), the only time in this opera of deception and madness when there is room for such sentiments.

ACT II. Ashton's apartment. Ashton has decided that nothing but a politically expedient marriage on Lucy's part will save his fortunes and he tells her Lord Arthur Bucklaw will shortly arrive for their betrothal ceremony. He has not only intercepted and destroyed letters from Edgar but now shows her a forgery purporting to prove Edgar's unfaithfulness. Already the music suggests Lucy's mental instability and, during the long scene with her brother, he rages at her daring to oppose his wishes and she dissolves into another, less real world ('Soffriva nel pianto, languia nel dolore': My sufferings and sorrow I've borne without repining), Ashton remains adamant.

Though she now believes herself betrayed by Edgar and is moved that only she can save her brother from a traitor's death, Lucy will not take the fatal step without the family chaplain's (*bass*) advice. He advises her unequivocally to accept her brother's plans (this scene is sometimes omitted).

A hall in the Castle of Lammermoor. Wedding guests rejoice, Arthur makes his entrance, Lucy is led in like a sacrificial lamb, and the wedding contract is signed. It is the moment for Edgar's grand gesture, as he returns from his foreign duties to find his prospective bride about to be married to another. The great sextet begins ('Chi mi frena in tal momento?': What restrains me at this moment?) and intensifies as Lucy's and the other voices are added to build an edifice of sound from the tensions of the antagonists. Before the act ends with a *stretta* the chaplain enjoins that swords be returned to scabbards Edgar curses the day he fell in love with Lucy.

ACT III. Edgar's castle. Edgar is alone when Ashton comes to challenge him in an extended and impressive duet (the scene is often omitted to bring the opera more swiftly to its climax).

The great hall of Lammermoor Castle. The chaplain interrupts the wedding celebrations with news of disaster. Lucy, her mind unhinged by the sequence of events, has, on her wedding night, murdered her husband. She appears, pale and with a dagger in her hand, and there follows the Mad Scene. In her hallucination Lucy, heralded by the flute, believes she and Edgar are to be married. She is now reminded of past happiness – the love duet; now spurred to fear by memory of the ghost at the fountain; now involved in the marriage itself ('Ardon gli incensi': Incense burns). The aria traditionally finishes with a huge cadenza with the voice vying for brilliant effects with a flute; though Donizetti originally allowed for a cadenza, this was elaborated (starting in the mid-nineteenth century) until it grew to its present proportions, indeed came in many ways to dominate the opera. On the other hand, it must be said that the duet for soprano and flute is so full of virtuosity and so well known that to abandon it would demand a conductor of conviction and a soprano of monumental complacency. The expressive lyricism of the aria proper is set off by the grand scale of the cabaletta ('Spargi d'amaro pianto': Shed thou a tear of sorrow).

Finale. The Ravenswood Cemetery. Edgar still believes Lucy has betrayed him and longs for death. His recitative ('Tombe degli avi miei': Tombs of my ancestors), and aria ('Fra poco a me ricovero'), as if to balance Lucy's great scene, are on the grandest scale, and the finale, as a procession leaves Lammermoor and approaches Ravenswood, is no less impressive. The chaplain announces Lucy's death, Edgar sings despairingly of his lost love ('Tu che a dio spiegasti l'ali': Though from earth thou'st flown before me) and stabs himself.

La Fille du Régiment
The Daughter of the Regiment

Two acts; première, Paris, 1840. In a Tyrolean valley the Marquise de Birkenfeld (soprano) watches the Twenty-First Regiment of Grenadiers in battle. Sergeant Sulpice (*bass*) brings in Marie (*soprano*), a girl brought up by the soldiers of the regiment; her life has been saved by Tonio (*tenor*), whom she loves. Tonio enlists as a soldier. To general dismay, the Marquise declares that Marie is her niece and must live with her. A noble marriage is arranged for her. Tonio, promoted to captain, plans their elopement, but the Marquise admits that Marie is really her illegitimate daughter, and Marie cannot go against her wishes. Before the scandalised wedding guests she sings fondly of her childhood with the regiment; the Marquise, touched, unites her with Tonio.

La Favorite

Four acts; première, Paris, 1840. Castile, about 1340. Ferdinand (*tenor*), a novice, wishes to leave the monastery; he has fallen in love with Leonor (*mezzo-soprano*), unknown to him the mistress of King Alfonso (*baritone*). She gives him a military commission, which enables him to achieve a glorious victory. The King is admonished by Balthazar (*bass*) to relinquish his mistress, and when Ferdinand claims as his reward Leonor's hand in marriage he reluctantly assents. Leonor in a letter tells Ferdinand of her past, but Ferdinand never receives this and it is not until the wedding is nearly over that he becomes aware of the truth. Wretchedly he returns to the monastery. Leonor, now very ill, finds him and explains. As he forgives her she dies in his arms.

DON PASQUALE

OPERA in three acts by Gaetano Donizetti; text by Giovanni Ruffini and the composer. Première at the Théâtre-Italien, Paris, January 3, 1843.

THE overture is mainly concerned with Ernesto's serenade from the last act, and Norina's aria from the first. It admirably suggests the lively tone of the opera.

ACT I. Don Pasquale's room. The elderly, wealthy Don Pasquale (*bass*) is about to marry. Though determined himself to have a wife (if with no one particular in mind), he threatens to disinherit his nephew Ernesto (*tenor*) for wishing to do likewise. This disturbs Ernesto and his love, the sprightly young widow Norina (*soprano*).

When the curtain rises, Don Pasquale is impatiently waiting for Dr. Malatesta (*baritone*), who, not being able to dissuade his friend from marriage and still less able to influence him to allow his nephew to follow the dictates of his heart, pretends to acquiesce in the madcap scheme. He proposes that his 'sister' shall be the bride, and describes her in a graceful aria, 'Bella siccome un' angelo', as a timid, naïve, ingenuous girl, brought up, he says, in a convent (she is, however, none other than Norina, who is in no way related to Malatesta). At this description, Don Pasquale is quite unable to contain his delight, in spite of Malatesta's attempts to restrain him, and when he is alone, breaks into a bright cavatina, 'Ah, un foco insolito'.

Don Pasquale prepares to give his nephew a lecture on the subject of his future conduct, and tells him he intends to take a wife himself. This so arouses Ernesto's incredulity that his uncle is obliged to repeat it several times. Ernesto finally realises that this cuts him off from his own marriage. 'Sogno soave e casto' (Fond dream of love thou hast perished) he sings, in one of Donizetti's soaring inspirations, while the old uncle grumbles away in the bass. When Don Pasquale says he has already consulted Malatesta, Ernesto's last hope vanishes; there is no one now to dissuade the old fool.

Norina's room. 'Quel guardo il cavaliere' (Glances so soft and bright) begins her recitative – but she is only reading a novel aloud; her aria, 'So anch'io la virtù magica' (I know what spells a glance can dart), shows her sprightly nature. A letter is brought to her, and when Malatesta comes to tell her that Ernesto's old uncle has fallen for the scheme which shall finally make him agree to his nephew's marriage, she is anything but pleased; they have not had time to tell Ernesto about their scheme and he has written that he is furious. However, Malatesta is convinced all is going well, and he and Norina rehearse how they shall behave with Don Pasquale when finally he meets his convent-bred bride. The music is pure effervescence, with its sparkling coloratura and its gaily changing tunes.

ACT II. Ernesto's lodgings. The owner is in despair at the prospect of losing his bride and his home (Don Pasquale has told him to clear out of the house). A long horn prelude ushers in the famous recitative and aria, 'Cercherò lontana terra'.

At home, Don Pasquale receives his prospective bride and her sponsor, his friend, Malatesta. She is shy, he urges her on, and the husband-to-be watches every manoeuvre enraptured. Norina is eventually persuaded to speak to Pasquale, and assures him that she is only interested in domestic things – sewing, making clothes, and looking after the kitchen. A notary (*baritone*) has been sent for, and Malatesta dictates the terms of the marriage, the others repeating his words after him. A witness is needed, but none seems forthcoming until Ernesto rushes in proclaiming his betrayal to anyone who chooses to listen. Malatesta tries to explain the situation to him, without letting Don Pasquale know the way the wind is blowing.

The moment the contract is signed, Norina's temper changes, and she spits fire at every one of Don Pasquale's attempts at either conciliation or authority. He is confounded at the contrast, and dumb with horror when she says that Ernesto is just the person to take her out walking, something that is plainly beyond the capacity of a man of his years – or girth, for that matter. The quartet redoubles in vigour, and Norina and Ernesto have a charming lyrical aside which leaves no one in any doubt as to their mutual feelings. When Norina calls together the servants, and, finding there are only three in all, laughingly directs that more be engaged and that the wages of those at present in service be doubled, Don Pasquale can bear it no more. 'Son tradito, son tradito' (I'm a victim of collusion) he shouts in his rage, and the *stretta* of the quartet brings the act to a spirited conclusion.

ACT III. The room is the same as that of the previous scene. Servants are rushing hither and thither executing Norina's commands, and disposing of what she has ordered for the house. Don Pasquale sees her dressed up to the nines and about to go out; may he ask where? To the theatre she says – without him. Their duet works the quarrel up until Norina finds occasion to box her 'husband's' ears. As far as Don Pasquale is concerned, it is the end of his hopes and pretensions as well as his hateful marriage, and even Norina is sorry that she has had to go so far to bring the foolish old man to what is, from her and Ernesto's point of view, a reasonable frame of mind. She rushes from the room, but takes care to drop a note as she goes. It purports to be from Ernesto, and makes an assignation for that very evening in the garden. Don Pasquale reads it, and sees in it his chance of getting quit of the whole affair; he will send for Malatesta.

When he has left the room, the servants flock back into it, and comment on the happenings in the house in a charming chorus. Malatesta arrives and proceeds to give Don Pasquale the benefit of his advice. The two men confer in a famous comic duet. Its *buffo* 6/8 finish is one of the funniest pieces of music in the post-Rossinian repertory.

The garden. Ernesto sings to Norina the beautiful serenade, 'Com'è gentil'. It is immediately followed by an equally charming duet, 'Tornami a dir'. Don Pasquale and Malatesta surprise the lovers, Ernesto escapes, but Norina stays as if to brave it out. Malatesta twists everything round to everyone's satisfaction, and soon Ernesto and Norina are waiting to be married, moreover with the full approval of Don Pasquale. Suitably, Malatesta leads off the *Rondo finale* with which the work ends.

Vincenzo Bellini
(1801–1835)

LA SONNAMBULA
The Sleepwalker

OPERA in two acts; text by Felice Romani. Première at the Teatro Carcano, Milan, March 6, 1831.

ACT I. Scene i. A Swiss village green. The villagers are preparing to celebrate the marriage between Amina (*soprano*), an orphan brought up as the foster-child of Teresa (*mezzo-soprano*), the mistress of the village mill, and Elvino (*tenor*), a local landowner. Lisa (*soprano*), the proprietress of the inn, who is in love with Elvino, is jealous and not at all interested in the attentions of Alessio (*bass*). Amina with Teresa thanks her neighbours for their good wishes. She has two attractive solos:

'Come per me sereno' (How, for me brightly shining) and the
cabaletta 'Sovra il sen la man mi posa' (With this heart its joy revealing). The notary and Elvino appear, the contract is signed
and witnessed, and Elvino places a ring on Amina's finger as
they sing a flowing, expressive duet: 'Prendi, l'anel ti dono'
(Take now the ring I give you).

A stranger appears. He is on his way to the castle and wants
his horses watered and fed. But the road is bad and night is
approaching, so the young officer consents to stay at the inn.
Unbeknown to the villagers, the officer is Rodolfo (*bass*), the
lord of the castle. In a flowing cavatina, he recalls the scenes of
his youth: 'Vi ravviso' (As I view), then sings to Amina a charming cabaletta, 'Tu non sai in quei begli occhi' (Maid, those
bright eyes my heart impressing), which fails to impress Elvino.

Teresa warns all to retire, for the village is said to be haunted
by a phantom. The stranger treats the superstition lightly, and,
ushered in by Lisa, goes into the inn as the others head home.
Elvino upbraids Amina for having apparently taken pleasure
from the stranger's gallant speeches, but before they part there
are mutual concessions and forgiveness: 'Son geloso del Zefiro
errante'.

Scene ii. Rodolfo's room at the inn. Lisa shows him in, not
without a show of flirtation to which Rodolfo only partly responds. She tells him, to his annoyance, that the villagers have
discovered his identity and are on their way to offer greetings.
There is a noise outside. Lisa makes her escape, dropping her
handkerchief, which Rodolfo picks up and hangs over the bedpost. A few moments later he is amazed to see Amina, all in
white, raise his window and enter the room. He realises she is
sleep-walking; it is her somnambulism which has given rise to
the superstition of the village phantom. In her sleep Amina
speaks of her approaching marriage, of Elvino's jealousy, of
their quarrel and reconciliation. Rodolfo, not wishing to
embarrass her by his presence should she wake, extinguishes
the candles, steps out of the window and closes it after him.
Amina sinks down on the bed.

The villagers enter to greet Rodolfo. To their amusement,
they see the figure of a woman on the bed, and are about to
withdraw discreetly when Lisa, who realises what has happened, enters with a light, brings in Elvino, and points out
Amina to him. She is by now awake and Elvino mistakes her
confusion for guilt, rejecting her. Their striking duet begins
with Amina's protestations of innocence: 'D'un pensiero, e d'un
accento' (Not in thought's remotest region). Elvino's voice,
haunted by dark suspicions, joins hers, but he gives her no
comfort. The duet closes with an expressive phrase for tenor
alone, 'Questo pianto del mio cor' (With grief my heart is torn).

All save Teresa share his suspicions. Teresa takes the handkerchief hanging over the bedpost and places it around Amina's neck. Elvino turns away from her, she faints and her fostermother catches her.

ACT II. Scene i. A valley between the village and the castle. The villagers are on their way to beg Rodolfo to intercede with Elvino for Amina. Elvino meets Amina. He snatches from her finger the ring he gave her. Amina still loves him. He expresses his feelings in the air: 'Ah! perchè non posso odiarti' (Ah! Why is it I cannot hate you).

Scene ii. The village, near Teresa's mill. A slender wooden bridge spans the millwheel. Lisa has persuaded Elvino to marry her and preparations for the wedding are under way. The villagers have assembled. Rodolfo tries to tell Elvino that Amina is a somnambulist, but Elvino is incredulous.

Teresa begs the villagers to make less disturbance as Amina is asleep in the mill. When she learns Elvino intends to marry Lisa, she produces Lisa's handkerchief, which she found hanging over Rodolfo's bedpost. Elvino is convinced Lisa too has betrayed him.

Rodolfo again tells Elvino that Amina is the innocent victim of sleepwalking and at that very moment Amina, in her nightdress and lamp in hand, emerges through a window on the mill roof. She sleepwalks on to the narrow, insecure bridge and the villagers pray that she may negotiate it safely. As Amina crosses the bridge, a rotting plank breaks under her footsteps, the lamp falls into the torrent beneath, but she reaches the other side safely and descends a flight of stone steps. She kneels and prays for Elvino, then rising, speaks of the ring he has taken from her and produces the flowers given her by him on the previous day: 'Ah! non credea mirarti, si presto estinto, o fiore' (Scarcely could I believe it that so soon thou would'st wither, O flower). Gently Elvino replaces the ring upon her finger and kneels before her. 'Viva Amina!' cry the villagers. She awakens. Instead of sorrow, she sees joy all around her and Elvino with arms outstretched waiting to beg her forgiveness and lead her to the altar. The work ends with one of the showpieces of Italian opera: 'Ah! non giunge'.

NORMA

OPERA in two acts by Vincenzo Bellini; text by Felice Romani, founded on L. A. Soumet's tragedy. Première on December 26, 1831, at la Scala, Milan.

ACT I. Scene i. The sacred grove of the Druids, in Gaul, about 50 B.C. After an overture in the nature of a dramatic prelude, the high priest Oroveso (*bass*) comes with the Druids to rouse the people to war and aid them to accomplish the destruction of the Romans. The Druids are shown first in a solemn introduction (in which occurs a haunting woodwind phrase), followed by Oroveso's inflammatory pronouncement, which leads to a typical early nineteenth-century Italian march.

No sooner have they left than the Roman Pro-Consul Pollione (*tenor*) appears with his friend and centurion Flavio (*tenor*), to whom he confides that he no longer loves Norma (*soprano*), the High Priestess, although she has broken her vows of chastity for him and has borne him two sons. It is Adalgisa (*soprano*) he now loves. Pollione's cavatina, 'Meco all' altar di Venere', is interrupted by the sacred gong: the Druids are gathering for the ceremony, but he has time for a quick cabaletta before he disappears from view.

The priests and priestesses approach the altar to a march which is later used for the quick section of Norma's great and justly famous 'Casta diva', the centrepiece of the scene and indeed of the whole opera. Norma's prayer to the 'chaste goddess' is one of the most celebrated of soprano arias. Even transposed, its *fioritura* ornaments are taxing to the average soprano – but the truth is that the average soprano cannot (and never could) tackle the title role.

No one suspects Norma's intimacy with the Roman enemy. Nonetheless, she loves Pollione and seeks to avert the danger that would threaten him should Gaul rise against the Romans by prophesying that Rome will fall through its own weakness; it is not yet the will of the gods that Gaul shall go to war. She later prays to the goddess for the return of the Roman leader, who has left her.

When Norma has left, Adalgisa comes into the sacred grove and waits for Pollione, who joins her and begs her to fly with him to Rome. After some hesitation, she agrees to go with him.

Scene ii. Norma's dwelling. The priestess is sunk in deep sadness; she knows that Pollione plans to leave her and their two children, although she does not yet know her rival's identity. Adalgisa comes to unburden her heart to her superior. She confesses that she has become untrue to her faith through love – moreover, love for a Roman. Norma, thinking of her own unfaithfulness to her vows, is about to free Adalgisa from hers, when Pollione appears and for the first time Norma learns the identity of the Roman Adalgisa loves. When she learns the full truth, Adalgisa turns from Pollione; she loves Norma too well to go away with the betrayer of the high priestess. Adalgisa's impressive recitative, 'Sgombra è la sacra selva', is her only solo opportunity in the opera, but it leads to a big-scale duet with Pollione, 'Va crudele, al dio spietato'. It is followed by an extensive scene with Norma herself as she confesses her guilt, and a trio which ends the act.

ACT II. Scene i. Norma, filled with despair, is beside the cradle of her children. She feels an impulse to kill them, but motherhood triumphs over unrequited love. She will renounce her lover, and Adalgisa shall become the spouse of Pollione! Adalgisa, however, will not hear of treachery to Norma. She will go to Pollione, but only to remind him of his duty. This is the great scene for the two sopranos, 'Mira, o Norma', after the priestess has begged Adalgisa to marry Pollione and look after her children. Adalgisa's devotion is touching and beautifully shown in this duet, which contains one of Bellini's finest melodies. Norma and Adalgisa sing in thirds together in the slow section and again in the decorated quick section with which it ends.

Scene ii. A wood near the temple. Norma awaits the result of Adalgisa's plea to Pollione. She learns that she has failed and has come back to the grove to pass her life as a priestess. Norma's wrath is beyond control. She strikes the gong, and, when the warriors have gathered, joyfully proclaims her message. War against the Romans! Their determined chorus, 'Guerra!', mingles with tumult from the temple. A Roman has broken into the sacred edifice and has been captured. It is Pollione, who Norma knows has attempted to carry off Adalgisa. The penalty for his intrusion is death. But Norma, moved by love to pity and still hoping to save Pollione, submits a new victim to the enraged Gauls: a perjured virgin of the priesthood. To their amazement she admits that she is the guilty one ('Son io!'), then confesses to her father and confides her children to his care. Two great duets for Pollione and Norma form the climax of the opera and show Bellini's vocal writing at its most expressive. The first, 'In mia man alfin tu sei', takes place in private; the other, 'Qual cor tradisti', in public, with choral support.

A pyre has been built, which Norma ascends. Pollione, his love rekindled at the spectacle of her greatness of soul, joins her. In the flames he, too, will atone for their offences before God. The opera ends with a beautiful trio, 'Deh, non volerli vittime', for Norma, Pollione, Oroveso and the chorus.

With a truly great singer in the title role, *Norma*, above all Bellini's operas, flowers, gains in expressiveness and dramatic impact and the music grows to full stature as it cannot when the music is in lesser hands. Let no one imagine he has genuinely heard *Norma* without such a singer in the part. Not to have one is as dire in its consequences as a performance of *Götterdämmerung* with an inadequate Brünnhilde. The trouble as far as Bellini is concerned is that, in the twentieth century, there have been fewer great Normas than fine Brünnhildes.

I PURITANI
The Puritans

OPERA in three acts by Vincenzo Bellini; words by Count Pepoli. Produced Paris, Théâtre des Italiens, January 25, 1835.

ACT I. The English Civil War, 1649. A fortress near Plymouth, held by Lord Walton (*bass*) for Cromwell. Lord Walton's daughter, Elvira (*soprano*), is in love with Lord Arthur Talbot (*tenor*), a Cavalier and adherent of the Stuarts, but her father has promised her hand to Sir Richard Forth (*baritone*), like himself a follower of Cromwell. He relents however, and Elvira is bidden by her uncle, Sir George Walton (*bass*), to prepare for her nuptials with Arthur, for whom a safe conduct to the fortress has been provided. Sir Richard expresses his sorrow in a cavatina, 'Ah! per sempre io ti perdei' (Ah! Forever I have lost thee).

Lord Arthur makes his entrance with a grand romance ('A te o cara') in which the other voices join. It is not long before he discovers that Queen Henrietta (*soprano*), widow of Charles I, is a prisoner in the fortress and Arthur, loyal to the Stuarts, enables her to escape by draping her in Elvira's bridal veil and conducting her past the guards, as if she were his bride. They are intercepted by Sir Richard, who believes the veiled woman is the Elvira he had hoped to marry. The men draw their swords but Sir Richard discovers that the woman he supposes to be Lord Arthur's bride is not Elvira. He lets them pass. Elvira in her wedding dress sings a sparkling *polacca*, 'Son vergin vezzosa' (I am a blithesome maiden). But, when the escape is discovered, Elvira believes herself deserted and loses her reason. Those who had gathered for the nuptials now in a stirring chorus invoke maledictions upon Arthur's head.

ACT II. Another part of the fortress. The act is mainly concerned with an exhibition of Elvira's madness. Her scene, 'Qui la voce sua soave' (It was here in sweetest accents), starts with a *legato* melody of infinite pathos and beauty, one of Bellini's finest inspirations and most purely musical of all nineteenth-century mad scenes. It is followed by a cabaletta, 'Vien, diletto' (Come, dearest love) which brings the scene to a brilliant conclusion. Sir George and Sir Richard try to console Elvira, then in the famous martial duet, 'Suoni la tromba' (Sound the trumpet), announce their readiness to meet Arthur in battle and so avenge Elvira's melancholy plight.

ACT III. A grove near the fortress. Arthur, although proscribed by the victorious Puritans, seeks out Elvira. Her joy at
seeing him again temporarily clears her mind, but renewed evidence of her disturbed mental state alarms her lover. He hears
his pursuers approaching and is aware that capture means
death, but he will not leave Elvira. He is apprehended and is
about to be executed when a messenger arrives with the news of
the defeat of the Stuarts and a pardon for all prisoners. Arthur is
freed. The sudden shock of joy restores Elvira's reason and the
lovers are united. This act contains the impassioned 'Vieni fra
queste braccia' (Come to these arms) for Arthur and Elvira,
with its two top D's for the tenor. It is followed by an ensemble,
'Credeasi, misera', dominated by the tenor's part, in which
occurs a rare example of a top F written for the tenor, but of
course taken at the time in a mixed voice, not the brilliant
sound we might now (erroneously) expect.

Giuseppe Verdi
(1813–1901)

NABUCCO
Nebuchadnezzar

OPERA in four acts; text by Temistocle Solera (refused by Nicolai).
Première at la Scala, Milan, March 9, 1842.

*N*ABUCCO represents something important in Verdi's output
it was his first success, and in it he can be seen making a
serious attempt at the musical portrayal of character. It was also
the opera that established Verdi as one of the leading composers of Italy, the theme which identified him for the first time
publicly with his country's political aspirations. Its success was
huge, mainly because of its musical quality, but also to some
extent because of the vivid way in which the composer gave expression to his countrymen's aspirations towards the liberty
and self-government which had never yet been theirs. No
Italian who heard 'Va, pensiero' could fail to identify himself
with the chorus of exiles who were singing it, and it soon became one of the most popular tunes of the day.

The rather conventional overture makes effective use of
various tunes from the opera, notably the big choral themes.

ACT I. In passionate choruses, the priests and people of Jerusalem lament their defeat at the hands of Nebuchadnezzar,
King of Babylon (hereinafter, as in the opera, called 'Nabucco'),

and beg Jehovah to prevent the capture of the Temple. In an impressive solo, 'Sperate, o figli', Zaccaria (*bass*), the High Priest, exhorts them to have faith in God, but the news that Nabucco is advancing on the Temple itself throws them once more into consternation.

Ismaele (*tenor*), who brought the news of the enemy's further advance, is left alone with Fenena (*soprano*), a hostage in the hands of the Jews, whom he has loved ever since she rescued him when, as Jewish envoy in Babylon, he had been thrown into prison. They are interrupted by Abigaille (*soprano*), Fenena's supposed sister, at the head of a band of Babylonian soldiers. She threatens the two lovers with instant death, but admits to Ismaele that she loves him and will save him if he return her love. The trio which follows has the mixture of intensity and suave vocal writing which distinguishes similar moments in *Norma* (though the dramatic situation is by no means similar). Zaccaria rushes in saying the King is riding towards the Temple itself; Babylonian troops fill the Temple, and Nabucco (*baritone*) himself rides to the door. Zaccaria threatens to kill Fenena, Nabucco's daughter, if he desecrate the holy place, but Nabucco taunts the defeated Jews ('Tremin gl'insani'), and Zaccaria's attempt on Fenena's life is frustrated by Ismaele. Nabucco orders the sacking of the Temple.

ACT II. The Jews have been carried captive into Babylon, and Nabucco, away at the wars, has left Fenena as acting Regent. Abigaille, jealous of her sister's position, finds a document which proves that she is not Nabucco's daughter but merely a slave. Her fury is unbridled, but she remembers her love for Ismaele, and the first part of her great aria is smooth and expressive. The High Priest of Bel (*bass*) informs her that Fenena is setting free the Jewish prisoners; he urges her to seize power, and says he has already spread the report that Nabucco has been killed in battle. Abigaille's reaction is expressed in a cabaletta suitably vigorous and determined.

The Hebrews are gathered in a room of the palace, and, in a noble example of Verdian prayer ('Tu sul labbro'), Zaccaria invokes God's guidance. The people curse Ismaele, but Zaccaria reminds them that Fenena, for whose sake he committed the act of treachery, has become a convert to their faith.

Abdallo (*tenor*) rushes in saying that the King is dead, and Abigaille plans Fenena's death. In a moment Abigaille, surrounded by court officials, comes to demand the crown from Fenena. But Nabucco steps between them, seizes it, and places it on his own head, defying Abigaille to take it from him. Nabucco, predicting that the incident will have dire consequences, leads off an ensemble. He proclaims himself God, and commands the protesting Zaccaria and Fenena to bow down before him. There is a clap of thunder, and the crown is torn from his head by a supernatural force. When the crowd has recovered from its consternation, the King is seen to be a babbling madman. Zaccaria proclaims the punishment of heaven on the blasphemer, but Abigaille snatches up the crown crying that the glory of Babylon is not yet departed.

ACT III. Scene i. Abigaille has been installed as Regent, with the support of the priests, who demand the death of the captive Jews, amongst them Fenena. Nabucco is led into Abigaille's presence. He is enraged at finding someone else on his throne, but Abigaille taunts him into sealing the death sentence of the Jews, and, when she tells him he is a prisoner in her hands, his mood changes to one of supplication and desperation.

Scene ii. The banks of the Euphrates. The enslaved Jews sing the psalms of their lost fatherland. 'Va, pensiero' is the first of Verdi's patriotic choruses, and its poignant melody is typical of the composer's writing in this vein. Zaccaria upbraids the Jews for their defeatist attitude and tries to galvanise them into life and resistance by prophesying the imminent fall of Babylon.

ACT IV. Scene i. Nabucco in prison wakens from a nightmare to hear the crowd crying 'Death to Fenena'. He sees her being led to execution, and prays movingly to Jehovah to pardon him his sin of pride and spare her life: 'Dio di Giuda'. Abdallo appears and frees his master, who rushes out to rescue his daughter.

Scene ii. The place of execution. A funeral march is heard and Fenena has a beautiful prayer as she and the Jews prepare for death. The arrival of Nabucco and his followers arrests the sacrifice, the false idol is thrown down as if by magic, and all join in a prayer of thanksgiving to Jehovah. The rejoicing is interrupted by Abigaille, who in her remorse has taken poison and presently dies, calling on God for forgiveness. Zaccaria promises glory to his convert, Nabucco.

I LOMBARDI
The Lombards

FOUR acts; première, Milan, 1843; revised version (as *Jérusalem*), Paris, 1847. The Milanese brothers Arvino (*tenor*) and Pagano (*bass*) both loved Viclinda (*soprano*), who returned Arvino's love; years later Pagano, who was banished for attacking Arvino, has returned, ostensibly penitent but still plotting revenge. Arvino is appointed to lead a Crusade. Pagano kills their father in mistake for Arvino and, horror-struck, is cursed by all. In Antioch, the tyrant Acciano's (*bass*) son Oronte (*tenor*) loves the captive Giselda (*soprano*), Arvino's daughter. Arvino, unaware of his brother's identity, approaches Pagano (now a hermit), asking for his help. The Crusaders, led by Arvino, attack. Giselda denounces her father's violence; Oronte, however, survives, and the lovers flee. Oronte is mortally wounded and dies as the Hermit baptises him. In the Crusaders' camp the soldiers sing a great chorus of longing. Arvino and the Hermit lead the assault on Jerusalem. The Hermit is wounded and, in delirium, reveals his name. He and Giselda beg Arvino to forgive him and he dies as the Crusaders' banner unfurls on the city walls.

ATTILA

OPERA in a prologue and three acts by Giuseppe Verdi; libretto by Temistocle Solera. Première, Venice, March 17, 1846.

PROLOGUE. Scene i. Fifth century A.D. After a short prelude, the scene is a piazza in Aquileia. Attila's army of Huns has sacked the city and is celebrating victory. Their general (*bass*) appears and takes his seat on the throne. He is angry to see that, in spite of his strict orders, some of the enemy women have been saved. In an aria, Odabella (*soprano*), who leads them, proclaims the invincible spirit of the Italian women, who fought alongside their men, unlike the women who have accompanied his army. The spitfire coloratura of her music is as full of venom as that of Lady Macbeth, and Attila in admiration offers her any gift she wants – she settles for a sword, and he gives her his own. In a cabaletta, she swears to herself that with it she will exact vengeance for all that she has lost.

Ezio (*baritone*), the emissary of the Roman Emperor, is announced. In an extended duet, he offers Attila the hegemony of the world – the Emperor of the East is old, the ruler of the West a mere boy, he himself requires only that Italy be left to him. At the climax of the duet come the words 'Avrai tu l'universo, resti l'Italia a me' (You shall have the universe, Italy stays with me), and one can guess at the effect these words and the proud and challenging musical phrase must have had in *Risorgimento* Italy. Attila reacts against this apparent act of treachery; how can Italy, whose most valiant leader is a traitor, ever hope to defy him? Ezio reminds him of his defeat at Châlons and announces the defiance of Rome.

Scene ii. Foresto (*tenor*), once one of the leaders of Aquileia, has led a band of refugees out to the lagoons, where they have built a sad little group of huts, miserable now, but later to become the proud city of Venice. They salute the dawn, and

Foresto comes to greet them, still in his aria mourning his beloved Odabella, but proclaiming to the undisguised satisfaction of his followers their determination to raise from the lonely lagoon a city no less splendid than the one they have left – a compliment to Venice by Verdi's librettist, Solera, not likely to be missed by the Fenice audience in 1846.

ACT I. Scene i. A wood near Attila's camp. In heartfelt phrases over *cor anglais* and then full woodwind accompaniment, Odabella laments the death of her father. To her comes Foresto, at first, and in spite of her joy at seeing him, full of reproaches that she has betrayed him with the slayer of her family. She justifies herself and reminds him of Judith who saved Israel.

Scene ii. In Attila's tent, the conqueror lies asleep. He wakes, clearly under the influence of a dream, and tells his attendant, Uldino (*tenor*), of his vision of an old man, who warned him against continuing his march on Rome. Shaking off his forebodings, Attila calls together the priests and the army and orders that the march be resumed. A group is heard approaching, and, when it turns out to be children and virgins headed by the old man (*bass*) he saw in his dream, Attila's resolution is no longer proof against his superstitions, least of all when the old man (described in the score as Saint Leo) repeats the very words we have just heard Attila recount to Uldino. The act ends with a great ensemble in which Attila decides to bow to what is evidently the will of heaven.

ACT II. Scene i. In his camp, Ezio reads a letter from the Emperor Valentinian, commanding him to return to Rome. Such a boy to *command* him! In a beautiful aria ('Dagli immortali vertici'), he gives expression to his love of his country, then, urged by Foresto to join the forces resisting Attila, resolves to die if need be in defence of his country.

Scene ii. Attila's camp as in Act I. The troops are feasting in honour of the truce, and Attila, in spite of the warnings of the priests, entertains Ezio. The sudden extinguishing of the torches by a squall of wind appals the guests, but Attila refuses to be diverted even by so ill an omen from his purpose. When Uldino gives Attila a cup in which to pledge the guests, Odabella, who knows it is poisoned, warns Attila against drinking it. Foresto proudly acknowledges that he was responsible for the attempt on Attila's life, but, when Odabella demands his safety as the price of her warning, Attila consents to spare him, announcing at the same time that Odabella shall be his bride.

ACT III. A wood dividing Attila's camp from Ezio's. Foresto and Ezio are still determined to carry out their plan, and Foresto in a fine aria laments the faithlessness of Odabella. Ezio joins him, and they proclaim their common resolve, but even the arrival of Odabella does not quieten Foresto's suspicions of her conduct, exacerbated as they have been by the sound of what he takes – rightly – for her wedding chorus. In a beautiful trio ('Te sol quest'anima') she tries to convince him that her heart has always been his and his alone.

Attila comes to claim his bride and is astonished to find her in the arms of Foresto. He bitterly reproaches all three – the slave he was to marry, the criminal whose life he spared, the Roman with whom he has a truce – but they defy him and his threats in a lively quartet. As the Roman soldiers who have been organised by Ezio and Foresto rush in to kill Attila, Odabella stabs him to the heart: 'E tu pure, Odabella?'

MACBETH

OPERA in four acts by Giuseppe Verdi; text by Francesco Maria Piave. Première in Florence, March 14, 1847.

MACBETH represents the first time Verdi achieved a combination of the three characteristics which came to dominate his music: the theatre, patriotism, and character. The opera remained a favourite of Verdi's amongst his own works. He spent a considerable time revising it, and its comparative lack of success in his lifetime was a constant source of irritation to him. Piave, the librettist, was provided with a detailed scenario by the composer before he was allowed to put pen to paper, so that the dramatic construction is Verdi's. Faced with the difficulty of putting a long play on to the operatic stage, Verdi concentrated on three principals: Lady Macbeth, Macbeth, and the Witches – he was emphatic on this last point.

ACT I. Scene i. Scotland, 1040. After the prelude the scene is the heath. The Witches sing a fantastic chorus while waiting for Macbeth (*baritone*), and then in awesome tones prophesy his future. A messenger arrives to announce that Macbeth has been granted the title and estates of the rebel Cawdor, and Macbeth and Banquo (*bass*) meditate in a duet on the implications of the prophecy, half of which has already come true. The scene concludes with a chorus and dance for the Witches.

Scene ii. Lady Macbeth (*soprano*) reads the letter from her husband in which he tells her of the meeting with the weird band, and launches into a determined recitative. 'Vieni, t'affretta' has been described by some as an inadequate setting of the great soliloquy of Act I, but it is strikingly effective in its context. Its cabaletta, 'Or tutti, sorgete, ministri infernali', can produce an effect of tigerish ferocity.

Macbeth arrives and in a few pregnant sentences, with hardly a direct word spoken, the murder is decided upon, as the march which announces King Duncan's arrival is heard off-stage. The march is suitable accompaniment for the pantomime which goes with the King's procession – no word is spoken throughout his passage across the stage.

Macbeth, alone, sees a dagger in front of him, and with his soliloquy, in itself highly expressive, begins the great duet between the two principal characters. The murder done, Macbeth staggers down the stairs with the dagger still in his hands: 'Fatal mia donna! un murmure, com'io, non intendesti?' He describes the scene and the murmuring of the grooms in the antechamber, and the way 'Amen' stuck in his throat, and in the end it is Lady Macbeth who has to take the dagger back into the King's chamber.

Characteristically, this duet is marked to be sung 'sotto voce, e cupa', that is to say in a half voice and with dark, stifled tone. Only a few phrases, such as Macbeth's outburst of agonised horror when he catches sight of his bloodstained hands, 'Oh, vista orribile', are to be sung out, and they are specifically marked 'a voce aperta'. The original Lady Macbeth records that there were 151 rehearsals of this duet before the composer was satisfied, and that the sleep-walking scene – Verdi always maintained that these were the opera's two crucial moments – took three months before her movements and singing were judged to be satisfactory.

Banquo and Macduff (*tenor*) arrive to accompany the King on his way, and Banquo broods impressively in C minor on the horrid portents of the night, while his companion goes to rouse the King. The murder is discovered, and all gather for the magnificently sonorous and excitingly written finale, one of the most splendid in any of Verdi's earlier operas.

ACT II. Scene i. Macbeth, brooding alone (the orchestral prelude is a reminiscence of 'Fatal mia donna'), is quickly joined by Lady Macbeth, who accuses him of avoiding her. They decide that the death of Banquo is necessary to their schemes, and Lady Macbeth is left alone to sing an expressive aria, 'La luce langue', whose ferocious determination (it dates from the 1865 revised version of the opera) puts it into another class from the much tamer piece it replaces.

Scene ii. A park, where a band of assassins is waiting for Banquo. After their chorus Banquo sings his aria, a beautiful example of Verdi's writing for bass voice; at its end, the murderers fall upon him, but his son escapes.

Scene iii. The opening music of the banquet scene has a feverish, spurious gaiety which is uncannily apt in its context. The same quality is evident in the graceless, nerve-ridden brindisi, which Lady Macbeth sings to the assembled guests; the close relationship of its tune to the flowing 6/8 brindisi in *Tra-*

viata and the strong contrast of mood between the two has been pointed out by Desmond Shawe-Taylor, writing in the *New Statesman*. In between verses, Macbeth learns that Fleance, Banquo's son, has escaped. Returning to his guests, he complains that Banquo's absence detracts from the pleasure of the occasion and says he himself will sit for a moment in his place. He sees the ghost of the murdered man, and bursts into an agonised denial of his guilt, to the astonishment of the company. Lady Macbeth's remonstrances finally nerve him to face his guests again, which he does with an attempt at making light of the lapse. But the ghost reappears and Macbeth's frenzy breaks out again. The assembly draws away from him, sensing the guilt he makes little attempt to conceal. His sombre tune, 'Sangue a me', begins the finale, which is musically and dramatically no less effective than that to Act I.

ACT III. The Witches sit round their cauldron in a dark cave. Their chorus is succeeded by a ballet, written of course for Paris (1865) and interrupted in the middle by the appearance of Hecate, who tells the Witches what to do when Macbeth visits them. The dance continues and at its end Macbeth appears and demands to know his destiny. The music is extraordinarily suggestive and Verdi has perhaps nowhere else so successfully evoked the supernatural as in the scene of the apparitions, which is punctuated by the distraught comments of Macbeth himself. The King loses consciousness, and the Witches dance and sing round him before disappearing.

Lady Macbeth appears searching for her husband, and asks what he has learnt from the Witches. He tells her and reveals that he has seen foretold the line of kings which Banquo will sire. Lady Macbeth's energetic denial that this shall come to pass arouses something of Macbeth's old military spirit. Their short but vigorous duet makes a striking end to the act.

ACT IV. Scene i. We are at the turning-point in the drama, the zenith of the ambitious career of the Macbeths and the nadir of the fortunes of the Scottish people. As we might expect from the Verdi of 1847, the force opposed to Macbeth's tyranny is not only retribution but the less tragic and more immediately topical one of patriotism. 'Patria oppressa', the chorus of the Scottish exiles, is in direct line from 'Va, pensiero' in *Nabucco*, with its wailing minor second in the accompaniment, sometimes ascending, sometimes descending (it appears again in the sleep-walking scene) and its wonderfully evocative contours. The words of the chorus date from the opera's first version.

Macduff's beautiful aria completes the still moment at the centre of the dramatic action, and is succeeded by a quick movement as Duncan's son Malcolm's army crosses the stage; Malcolm (*tenor*) and Macduff sing a duet with the chorus.

Scene ii. Nothing in the score of *Macbeth* is more worthy of admiration than the sleep-walking scene, which is cast in the form of the old soprano 'mad scene', but has a freedom of movement and an expressiveness that Verdi was not to excel in a similar set piece, one is tempted to say, until Aida's arias nearly twenty-five years later. The expressive quality of the vocal writing is quite extraordinary, and the scene itself very exacting for the singer, comprising every shade of expression, and a very wide compass, from C flat at the bottom to top D flat in the last phrase of all (marked 'un fil di voce').

Scene iii. Macbeth is at bay, furious that Malcolm is marching on him with an army reinforced by English troops but confident in his knowledge that the Witches have prophesied his immunity from death at the hands of anyone 'born of woman'. He curses the low friendless state which his way of life has brought him, but leads his men defiantly to war when he hears that his wife is dead. The battle is accompanied by a fugue, which persists through the short encounter of Macbeth and Macduff and eventually gives way to a general chorus of rejoicing at the defeat of the tyrant.

Apart from the ballet, which was written specially for Paris, four pieces were inserted in 1865 in place of material which now finds no place in the revised opera: in Act II, Lady Macbeth's aria, 'La luce langue'; in Act III the final duet; in Act IV the chorus of exiles (replacing one similar in feeling and with the same words), and the whole of the battle scene (i.e. after Macbeth's aria). Originally, the opera ended with a short *scena* for Macbeth which has, on occasion, been incorporated earlier in the last act. But there is little doubt the revised ending, with its brilliantly descriptive fugue and firm, 'national' final chorus, is a vast improvement on the original.

Macbeth was the first opera in which Verdi achieved a successful portrayal of character. Macbeth himself is shown as dominated, even more than in the play, by his wife and the Witches; that is to say, his own personality plays proportionately a lesser part in determining events, and he is shown often at his worst and most susceptible, hardly ever at his best as poet or soldier. All the same, the working of remorse on his conscience is excellently shown.

Macbeth's loss – if loss it can be called – is, of course, Lady Macbeth's gain, and she dominates music and action alike. Judged purely as a role for a singing actress, it is one of the finest Verdi ever wrote, but its significance goes further than that and it is perhaps the earliest Verdian role in which a complete musical development can be traced along with the dramatic and psychological growth in a character. The progress from the aria in the first act, 'Vieni, t'affretta', through the increasingly

127

unnerving events of the intermediate scenes, to the final, long, wailing curve of the sleep-walking scene is a remarkable musical study of gradual disintegration under the influence of conscience.

RIGOLETTO

OPERA in three acts by Giuseppe Verdi; text by Francesco Maria Piave, after Victor Hugo's *Le Roi s'amuse*. Première at Teatro la Fenice, Venice, March 11, 1851.

BOTH Victor Hugo's play and the libretto of Verdi's opera ran into trouble with the censors, not surprisingly since the only character with moral fibre in a licentious court is a court jester, who moreover plots the assassination of an absolute ruler, his master. Hugo's play was proscribed after the first night and the censor caused the venue of Verdi's opera to be removed from real-life France under François I to a fictitious court of Mantua under a Duke. The essence of a closed society, where one man's word was absolute, was of course preserved, as also the elegant and light-hearted figure of the ruler-as-seducer, the Duke's music running the gamut from the throwaway brilliance of the start through the romantic fervour of his wooing of Gilda, the tenderness of his aria of regret at losing his latest love, up to the grandeur of the great quartet in the last scene. The dominating role nonetheless is that of Rigoletto, the climax one might say of Verdi's obsession with the baritone voice as protagonist. He wrote for a higher-based baritone than had Rossini, Bellini or Donizetti, and here the overall *tessitura* is perhaps higher than in any other of his scores.

ACT I. Scene i. The music associated with the curse dominates the prelude, leading into a brilliant court scene, which serves as background to the amorous activities of the Duke (*tenor*). He enters with Rigoletto in attendance. A fresh young beauty has recently caught his eye but Countess Ceprano (*mezzo-soprano*) is his immediate quarry, variety being central to his escapades: 'Questa o quella' (This one or that one). He dances a minuet with the Countess and disappears with her, heedless of comment, least of all from her husband (*bass*), who falls victim to Rigoletto's caustic tongue. Marullo (*baritone*) tells anyone who will listen that he has discovered Rigoletto has a young *innamorata*, which suggests to Ceprano a possible line of revenge. Count Monterone (*baritone*) bursts in and denounces the Duke as the seducer of his daughter. He is arrested but calls down a curse on Rigoletto's head for the mockery he has undergone at the jester's hands. Rigoletto's reaction is almost pathological – this is his Achilles heel – and the idea of the father's cursing haunts him throughout the opera.

Scene ii. A street outside Rigoletto's house, Ceprano's palace at one side of it. Memories of Monterone haunt Rigoletto, but he is confronted by the figure of Sparafucile (*bass*), who announces himself, to a subtly contrived 'nocturne' accompaniment, as a sword for hire. Rigoletto says he has no need of such services, but we are left in little doubt that he has stored up information about Sparafucile's whereabouts against possible future use. Rigoletto's soliloquy, 'Paris siamo' (How like we are!), impressively contrasts his own and his master's situations, but it is the curse which has seized his imagination and it is still on his mind when he unlocks the door to his garden and Gilda (*soprano*) runs out to meet him.

Their scene is one of great tenderness, as the music successively mirrors Rigoletto's injunction that she must never leave the garden except to go to church, his constant grief over the death of his wife, Gilda's mother, and Gilda's protestations of filial love and absolute fidelity to his wishes, the first a more accurate representation of the truth than the second. As he consigns Gilda to the care of Giovanna ('Ah, veglia, o donna': Ah, watch I pray), there are sounds outside and the Duke, with Giovanna's (*mezzo-soprano*) help, contrives to conceal himself inside the garden. Rigoletto leaves.

Gilda is a prey to worry that she has concealed from her father the attentions of a young man who followed her from church; when she turns she is confronted with none other than the young man himself, who tells her he is a student. 'È il sol dell'anima' ('Tis the Sun of the soul), he declares, and their duet celebrates young love until sounds of movement outside precipitate an impassioned farewell. Gilda's graceful aria, 'Caro nome' (Dearest name), confirms her romantic involvement. She has no sooner gone up to her room than a group of courtiers appears in the street intent on abducting Rigoletto's mistress and so avenging Ceprano. When Rigoletto returns he is blindfolded and then roped in to help in what he is assured is the capture of Countess Ceprano (Chorus: 'Zitti, zitti, moviamo a vendetta': Seize the moment for vengeance propitious). The scheme works, the courtiers are triumphant and Rigoletto, realising that Gilda has been taken, is left lamenting Monterone's fateful curse.

ACT II is set in the ducal palace, where the Duke is disconsolate – the cut of the music of 'Parmi veder le lagrime' (Art thou weeping in loneliness) leaves no doubt that, however free with his affections, he is a man with feelings. He learns from the courtiers that they have abducted Rigoletto's *innamorata*, and once he has gone, they lie in wait to torment the jester. Rigoletto is obviously on edge, searching for any clue as to Gilda's whereabouts, and only convinced she is already with the Duke when a page is turned away with obviously fabricated excuses. He rounds on the courtiers, who only then learn that it is his daughter and not his mistress they have turned over to the Duke's pleasure, and in a magnificent outburst denounces them for their cruelty: 'Cortigiani, vil razza dannata' (Oh you courtiers, vile rabble, accursed). In a moment, Gilda is in the room, the courtiers have left, and she is telling her father of the young man who followed her from church ('Tutte le feste al tempio': On every festal morning). Rigoletto consoles her ('Piangi fanciulla': Weep my daughter), then, after watching Monterone led towards prison, hurls himself into a violent pledge of vengeance, which may purge at the same time the crime against his daughter and the curse laid on him.

ACT III. Sparafucile's house, which must be split to show both outside and inside. With him lives his sister, who acts as decoy for his victims. From outside, Rigoletto and Gilda observe Sparafucile greet the Duke, who is in disguise and proceeds to sing what has become perhaps the most famous song in all opera: 'La donna è mobile' (Wayward as thistledown). Legend has it Verdi withheld it from rehearsal until the last possible moment for fear it would, even before the first night, become known all over Venice.

Meanwhile, Sparafucile has finalised his bargain with Rigoletto, who will pay half the agreed money in advance, the rest on delivery of the Duke's body. Maddalena (*contralto*), Sparafucile's sister, makes her appearance, to the discomfiture of Gilda, who still assures her father that she loves the man she now watches making advances to another woman. A great quartet develops, led by the Duke who in a soaring melody seems to be serenading not so much Maddalena as womankind in general ('Bella figlia dell'amore': Fairest daughter thou of pleasure). Maddalena responds in a quicker *staccato* melody, Gilda laments around the top of the stave while Rigoletto at the bottom mutters of vengeance. There is no more famous ensemble in nineteenth-century Italian opera.

Rigoletto sends his daughter away with instructions to disguise herself and ride to Verona, meanwhile completing his bargain with Sparafucile and reserving for himself the satisfaction of throwing the body in due course into the river. A storm blows up and during its course Maddalena, who finds the Duke attractive, proposes her brother kill Rigoletto instead and pocket the second half of his fee. But he will have none of what he sees as immorality, and when Gilda surreptitiously returns, the original bargain is still in place. In the end, Sparafucile relents and agrees to kill whoever next arrives at the inn.

Gilda overhears and, at the end of a dramatic trio, knocks on the door. The lights are extinguished, there is a half-stifled cry, more storm music and, when Rigoletto returns with the money and accepts the corpse-filled sack, he is taken aback to hear the Duke's 'La donna è mobile' coming from inside the inn. As the last top B natural dies away, he tears open the sack to find Gilda's body. She dies after a long, sad farewell to her father, who is left to lament the father's curse laid nearly three acts earlier.

IL TROVATORE
The Troubadour

OPERA in four acts by Giuseppe Verdi; text by Salvatore Cammarano from the Spanish play of the same title by Antonio Garcia Gutiérrez. Première at the Teatro Apollo, Rome, January 19, 1853.

IL TROVATORE is unsurpassed in Verdi's output for prodigality of melody, energy and sheer popular appeal. It is also notorious for incomprehensibility of plot, a reputation unfairly bestowed. It is however a fact that crucial elements of the story occur before the stage action starts, so that the prospective listener must familiarise him or herself with it beforehand; moreover, the complications of the original story are retained and compressed with results which are almost telegraphic in their terseness.

Verdi encountered the subject in early 1850, but composition was not started until autumn 1851. The legend that virtually the entire opera was composed between November 1 and 29, 1852 is probably false, but Verdi was a quick worker and nowhere in his output is there more evidence of the white heat of inspiration.

Spain is torn by civil war. Leonora (*soprano*) is lady-in-waiting to the wife of the Prince of Aragon, in whose cause Count di Luna (*baritone*) is fighting; Manrico (*tenor*), the so-called gipsy with whom she is in love, fights for the insurgents led by Prince Urgel. The mystery of Manrico's birth raises its head from time to time but is not finally resolved until the opera's last moments, when it transpires that Azucena (*mezzo-soprano*), in her overwrought attempt to avenge the murder of her mother, had thrown her own son rather than the Count's into the flames. She knows the truth and it haunts her throughout the action.

ACT I. Scene i. The guardroom of the Palace of Aliaferia. Ferrando (*bass*), captain of the guard, with a shout wakes his companions, warning them not to be asleep when the Count returns from his nightly vigil beneath the windows of Leonora's apartments, a vigil necessitated by his fear that a rival is preferred by her. Ferrando recounts, not for the first time we may imagine, the story of how a gipsy woman ('Abbietta zingara') put a spell on one of the sons of the Count di Luna, was apprehended and burnt at the stake. Her daughter contrived to make away with the boy and a little later the charred bones of a child were found. The old Count looked in vain for his son and made the surviving brother swear to continue the search.

Scene ii. The gardens of the palace. Leonora and Inez (*soprano*) wait for Leonora's unknown but favoured suitor. 'Tacea la notte placida' is one of the grandest and most effective of the arias in which Verdi in his early operas liked to introduce the leading female character. Leonora's graceful cabaletta, 'Di tale amor', is no less appealing. The ladies re-enter the palace and Count di Luna comes into the garden to be met almost immediately by (and be thoroughly disconcerted by) the sound of the troubadour preparing to serenade Leonora. 'Deserto sulla terra' he sings until Leonora, hearing his voice, comes out of the palace and, mistaking the Count for the serenader, hastens towards him. Manrico comes out of the shadows, and Leonora cannot prevent the two men drawing their swords and fighting (trio: 'Di geloso amor sprezzato').

ACT II. Scene i. The gipsy camp in Biscay. The gipsies sing the so-called Anvil Chorus, one of nineteenth-century opera's more famous numbers. Azucena, who is sitting with them, seems mesmerised by the fire (aria: 'Stride la vampa') and her mother's burning at the stake and cry for revenge. Her son Manrico asks her to tell him the story once again and she goes through the narrative ('Condotta ell'era in ceppi'), amazing him by her incoherent references to the death of her own son in the flames rather than the Count's. She reassures him, but in her turn questions him as to why he spared the life of di Luna in battle when he had him at his mercy. In the splendidly martial 'Mal raggendo all'aspro assalto', Manrico explains that a hidden force caused him to stay his hand: he could not kill his adversary. A messenger from the Prince brings an order for Manrico to go immediately to defend Castellor, adding that Leonora, believing him dead, plans to enter a nunnery. Manrico springs into action and Azucena's pleas ('Perigliarti ancor') fail to move him from his decision.

Scene ii. The cloister of a convent. Stealthily at night the Count and his followers group themselves in order to abduct Leonora. He sings of his love for her in one of the most beautiful solos of the baritone repertory: 'Il balen del suo sorriso'. It is followed by a *cabaletta alla marcia*, 'Per me ora fatale', which suggests di Luna is very much a man to be reckoned with. A chorus of nuns is heard from the convent and they are about to process to the cloister when the Count makes his move, only for Manrico and his followers to forestall him, to Leonora's infinite relief. 'E deggio! e posso crederlo' she sings, leading an impassioned finale at whose end Manrico frees Leonora and departs.

ACT III. Scene i. Di Luna's camp. He has laid siege to Castellor, where Manrico has taken Leonora, and his army sings stirringly of the pleasures of gambling. The count emerges from his tent to be confronted with a gipsy woman captured as she was prowling round the camp. She protests she is a poor wanderer ('Giorni poveri vivea'), but Ferrando claims to recognise her as the gipsy who, to avenge her mother, kidnapped the old Count's son. When she calls on Manrico for help, di Luna in his rage condemns her to be burnt at the stake.

Scene ii. A hall in Castellor. Leonora is about to become Manrico's bride, and he sings of his love in a marvellous lyrical inspiration: 'Ah sì, ben mio coll'essere'. Happiness is to be short-lived as Ruiz (*tenor*) rushes in with word that Azucena has been captured and will shortly be burnt alive. Manrico seizes his sword and launches into the vigorous cabaletta 'Di quella pira', a rousing solo crowned in many performances with the most famous unscripted top C in opera – Verdi did not write the note but he must have heard it many times and it is far from contradicting the spirit of the music.

ACT IV. Scene i. Outside a tower in the palace of Aliaferia. Manrico's sortie to rescue his mother has failed and he is a prisoner in the tower. Leonora is led in by Ruiz, and in a magnificent aria she prays for her lover in his captivity: 'D'amor sull'ali rosee'. There follows the Miserere, when, to the sound of chanting within, Leonora sings brokenly of her foreboding and Manrico of his love for her. Few nineteenth-century Italian operatic tunes are more famous, few more effective in context. Leonora caps the scene with an impassioned *stretta*, 'Tu vedrai che amore in terra'.

The Count confronts Leonora. She promises to become his if he will free Manrico. Di Luna's passion is sufficiently intense to lead him to agree. There is a solo for Leonora, 'Mira d'acerbe lagrime', followed by a duet between her and the Count, who little suspects that, Manrico once at liberty, she will take the poison hidden in her ring and escape his clutches.

Scene ii. The interior of the tower. Manrico and Azucena lie in prison. Azucena raves of the pyre on which her mother perished, and Manrico tries in long, expressive phrases to calm her spirit. In a mood between sleeping and waking, she intones a haunting melody, 'Ai nostri monti', while Manrico continues his attempt to soothe her forebodings. Leonora comes to urge him to escape, but he immediately suspects the price she has paid, suspicions confirmed as the poison starts to take effect. Leonora dies in Manrico's arms, di Luna returns to find her dead and promptly orders Manrico's execution. He drags Azucena to the window to witness her son's death, and it is a Pyrrhic victory she wins as she calls out 'He was your brother!'

La Traviata
The Fallen Woman

OPERA in three acts by Giuseppe Verdi; text by Francesco Maria Piave after Alexandre Dumas's play *La Dame aux Camélias*. Première at Teatro la Fenice, Venice, March 6, 1853.

ALEXANDRE DUMAS *fils* at the age of twenty fell in love with the brilliant courtesan Marie Duplessis, a girl from the country whose praises were sung even after her death by all who had met her. She died from tuberculosis in 1847, and Dumas published his novel, *La Dame aux Camélias*, in 1848, deriving a play from it the following year. That was not performed until 1852 but Verdi and Piave, searching for an operatic subject for the Carnival in Venice in 1853, decided on it in November 1852. Legend once had it that initial failure was because the audience could not accept a risqué story played in contemporary setting, but the fact is that in Venice it was played in the costumes of 1700 (even though Verdi's contract stipulated modern dress) and that scores continued to specify that period until well after the composer's death.

ACT I. Paris. The prelude's opening section is concerned with the music before Violetta's death, its second with her impassioned cry of 'Amami, Alfredo' in Act II. Violetta (*soprano*), who is already ill, is giving a party and Gastone (*tenor*) informs her that Alfredo (*tenor*), who is there, has fallen seriously in love with her. Alfredo leads a spirited brindisi ('Libiamo ne' lieti calici': Let us drink), and there is dancing in the next room in which Violetta is about to join when she feels faint. Alfredo remains behind and gracefully protests his love: 'Un dì felice, eterea' (One day a rapture ethereal), Violetta echoing his mood while appearing to mock. The phrase 'Di quell'amor ch'è palpito' (All that has life has its breath from you) in the course of the opera takes on something of the character of a love motif, and Violetta repeats it in her aria before the end of the act.

Alfredo and the other guests retire and Violetta is lost in contemplation, her heart touched for the first time: 'Ah, fors'è lui' (Perhaps it is he). At the end of the aria, her mood changes from introspection and she bursts into what is musically a celebration of dawning love at the same time as the words she sings deny any such possibility. It is a scene of marvellous power.

ACT II. Scene i. Violetta and Alfredo are living together in the country. He sings of his joy in his life with her ('De' miei bollenti spiriti': Wild my dream of ecstasy), but is disturbed when he discovers from the maid Annina (*soprano*) that Violetta has been selling her jewellery in order to pay the bills. He will go to Paris to raise money! Violetta receives a note from Flora (*mezzo-soprano*) to invite her to a party in Paris and smiles at the idea that she might return there. When a visitor is announced she assumes it will be her lawyer, but it turns out to be Alfredo's father, Giorgio Germont (*baritone*), come to persuade her to give up his son in order that no breath of scandal may attach to the forthcoming wedding of his daughter. His harsh tone soon softens when it is apparent she is not the gold-digger he had assumed he would find. Their scene together, cast in the loosely-knit duet form Verdi mined so productively throughout his operas, is the centrepiece of the work, and we pass through Germont's plea for his daughter's happiness ('Pura siccome un'angelo': Pure as an angel), and Violetta's attempt to put the opposite case, to reach the moment when in a tune of infinite pathos ('Ah, dite alla giovine': Ah, go tell your daughter) she ceases to resist what she now accepts is inevitable. Germont does not find it hard to love her for what she has promised to do and he assures her she will not regret it. He for his part will at some time in the future tell Alfredo that in spite of appearances her love for him never faltered.

Violetta writes Alfredo a note telling him she is going back to her old life, to be kept by Baron Douphol (*baritone*), but when he appears, she hides what she has been writing. He says he has heard from his father that he is on his way to attempt to separate them, and Violetta, as she says goodbye, seems to pour out her heart ('Amami, Alfredo'): for the soprano, one of the opera's emotional touchstones.

Alfredo is handed Violetta's letter, but he has hardly digested its contents before his father enters and in one of the most famous baritone arias, offers comfort ('Di Provenza, il mar, il suol': The sea and the earth of Provence). Alfredo nonetheless dashes off to Paris.

Scene ii. Flora's party, where festivities are in full swing. Alfredo comes in on his own, closely followed by Violetta on the arm of the Baron. 'Unlucky in love, lucky at cards' is Alfredo's comment, and he and the Baron play before supper is announced. Violetta has asked Alfredo to meet her alone, but her words only fan the flames of jealousy and he summons the other guests to insult her in front of them all. His father intervenes, the Baron issues a challenge, and Violetta recovers from a fainting fit to sing lyrically of the love for Alfredo she still holds within her heart ('Alfredo, Alfredo, di questo core': Oh, Alfred, Alfred, thou little knowest).

ACT III. Violetta lies mortally ill in bed. The slow, sad prelude echoes that of the first act, but with nothing this time to contrast with the tragedy. Violetta wakes up to read, for the hundredth time, the letter she has had from Germont telling her the Baron was wounded in the duel and that Alfredo now knows of her sacrifice and is on his way to see her. She senses the approach of death and her aria, 'Addio del passato' (Farewell to bright visions), suggests a sigh from the depths of a purified soul. Revellers can be heard below and in a moment Alfredo is in the room and holding her in his arms. 'Parigi, o cara, noi lasceremo' (We shall fly from Paris, beloved), he sings, and Violetta seems at first to believe him. But she knows she is dying ('Gran Dio! Morir si giovane': O God, to die so young), and, watched by Annina, Germont and the doctor (*bass*) and at peace with the world, she breathes her last.

La Traviata is, apart from *Stiffelio*, Verdi's solitary setting of a contemporary subject, and this is one of the rare times he abandoned the grand public events and gestures which had so far provided him with subjects and accepted something more intimate. But it represents a logical progression from the intimate scenes of *Rigoletto*, and for its unheroic, bourgeois world he had to find what amounted to a new style, an achievement the more remarkable since for much of the time he was writing it he was preoccupied with *Trovatore*, whose première took place less than two months before that of *Traviata*. Form is more flexible, vocal writing more delicate than in earlier operas, and one may wonder what nineteenth-century Italian opera rivals in subtlety this extraordinary work, which may owe much of its naturalness and the credibility of its dialogue to the original play but is transformed by Verdi's score from a comment on the life and times of its heroine into one on life itself. Not long after its première, Verdi was asked which of his operas he considered his best and is said to have replied: 'Speaking as a professional, *Rigoletto*, as an amateur, *Traviata*.'

LES VÊPRES SICILIENNES
I Vespri Siciliani – The Sicilian Vespers

OPERA in five acts by Giuseppe Verdi; text in French by Scribe and Charles Duveyrier. Première at the Opéra, Paris, June 13, 1855.

*L*ES VÊPRES SICILIENNES, as it was originally called, was commissioned for the Great Exhibition of 1855. Much as Verdi
disliked the conditions of work in Paris, he could not but find it
an honour to be asked to write music for so great an occasion in
the artistic capital of the world. In the event, he disliked the
libretto, as offending the French because of the massacre at the
end, and the Italians because of the treacherous behaviour of
the Sicilian patriots, and his relations with Scribe were even the
subject of comment in the newspapers.

The opera is concerned with the occupation of Sicily by
French troops during the thirteenth century, and the efforts of
the Sicilians to dislodge them. The overture is one of Verdi's
best, and is dominated by the long cello tune, taken from the
duet in Act III between Arrigo and de Montfort.

ACT I. A detachment of French troops is in the great square at
Palermo; a crowd of Sicilians eyes them sullenly. The French
sing of their enforced absence from their native land, the Sicilians of their hatred of their oppressors. An exchange between
de Béthune (*bass*), Robert (*baritone*), and Thibault (*tenor*) indicates that there is nothing new about the proprietary attitude
of occupying troops towards the women of the country.

Elena (*soprano*), sister of Frederick of Austria, crosses the
square. She has been praying for her brother, who was
executed by order of de Montfort, the Governor, for his
patriotic activities. A drunken soldier, struck by her beauty,
orders her to sing for the French conquerors. Somewhat to his
surprise she consents, but her song becomes a sudden and inflammatory *allegro giusto*, which whips up the courage of the
downcast Sicilians. It is a scene of considerable theatrical
power.

The Sicilians rush at the French, but the abortive rising is
quelled by the appearance of de Montfort (*baritone*), alone and
unarmed, at the door of his palace. The square clears, and
Elena, with her attendants Ninetta (*contralto*) and Danieli
(*tenor*), is left alone with de Montfort. Their quartet is mostly
unaccompanied, and at its end Arrigo (*tenor*), who has been imprisoned, rushes up to Elena with the news of his release. He
does not notice de Montfort, but, in spite of his openly expressed patriotic sentiments, is ordered by him to remain
behind. Arrigo spurns de Montfort's offer of fame in the service
of the French; he also rejects de Montfort's command to cease
associating with Elena, and rushes into her palace.

ACT II. A valley outside the city. Giovanni da Procida (*bass*),
until his banishment leader of the Sicilian patriots, has returned
secretly to stir up resistance. He salutes his beloved native land
in a recitative and aria which has become perhaps the most
famous number of the opera, 'O toi, Palermo'. In a cabaletta, he

exhorts the small band of chosen patriots to prepare with him the deliverance of Sicily.

Elena and Arrigo have been bidden to meet the exiled patriot, and he enrols Arrigo as one of the leaders of the projected revolt. Procida leaves. Arrigo declares his love to Elena and swears to avenge the death of her beloved brother. A messenger brings an invitation from de Montfort to attend a ball. Arrigo indignantly refuses it, and is immediately surrounded by soldiers and led away.

Procida learns of this new mishap, but he sees an opportunity of stirring up anti-French feeling in the betrothal festivity. He will suggest to the French that they carry off the young women, an outrage which may perhaps rouse the Sicilians from their apathy. Couples in festive attire dance a tarantella, but Procida's plan works all too well, and the French soldiers abduct some of the women.

Only a few patriots are left behind with Procida and Elena, and together in half-strangled sentences they give vent to their feelings, which are exacerbated by the sound of a complacent barcarolle being sung at sea by a boat-load of French pleasure-seekers. The two choruses combine most effectively.

ACT III. Alone in his palace, De Montfort reflects on the injustice he did years ago to the woman who became the mother of his son but escaped from him and brought up that son to hate his father as the oppressor of the Sicilians. Now, on her death-bed, she has written to him that the son he has not seen for eighteen years is no other than Arrigo, his sworn enemy. De Montfort's soliloquy 'Au sein de la puissance' (In braccio alle dovizie) gives effective expression to his indecision and agony of mind, and is in many ways more satisfactory than the big duet between de Montfort and his newly found son which immediately follows it.

Arrigo calls on his mother's memory, but accompanies his father to the great hall to watch the lengthy ballet of the seasons, which de Montfort has planned for the entertainment of his guests. This is a French ballet on a grand scale – it lasts for half an hour – and, in spite of attractive music, it holds up the dramatic action at a crucial point. On the other hand to leave it out is only half a solution, as the ball is then left as it were without its core.

Amongst the invited guests are a number of masked figures with silk ribbons fastened to their cloaks. These are the Sicilian conspirators, led by Procida and Elena. Arrigo's predicament – whether to allow his father to be murdered, or to betray his friends – is skilfully suggested by the snatched conversations he has with Elena and Procida in the midst of the general festivity. Finally, he tries to warn de Montfort that his life is in danger, but the governor refuses to leave the ball. When Procida advances upon him, Arrigo steps in between, the conspirators are arrested, and the act ends with the Sicilians cursing Arrigo's treachery.

ACT IV. The great courtyard of the fortress. Arrigo has come, armed with a pass from de Montfort, to see the prisoners. In a sombre E minor aria, 'O jour de peine' (Giorno di pianto), he reflects that his dearest friends are likely to look upon him as their worst enemy. The thought of Elena's hate is too much for him, and in an ecstasy he prays for her forgiveness. Elena appears, greeting him as a traitor, and repeating his words, 'Malheureux et non coupable' (Non son reo) after him ironically, until he admits that their enemy is his own father. Her scorn turns to pity, and later she admits in a ravishing Bellini-like cantilena that her greatest sorrow in prison was the necessity to think of the man she loves as a traitor. Their music takes on the character of a love duet, before Procida is led out of the prison by the guards. He sees Arrigo, but ascribes repentance to yet another treacherous trick.

De Montfort arrives and orders the double execution to take place immediately, in spite of the pleading of Arrigo, who demands to die with them – such an honour, says Procida, is too great for so notorious a traitor. De Montfort bids Arrigo pay no attention; let him but remember that he is his son. Procida is stupefied at this revelation, and in a few moving phrases bids farewell to the country for whose ideals he has fought. His phrases lead to a quartet (with Elena, Arrigo, de Montfort) of considerable beauty, which in its turn gives way to the execution music, with de Montfort urging that pardon will only be given if Arrigo will address him as Father. Arrigo is hesitant, Elena and Procida emphatic that death is preferable to dishonour. At last Arrigo gives in; pardon is granted and with it a general amnesty. The marriage of Elena and Arrigo is announced, and the act ends with a general ensemble.

ACT V. The gardens of de Montfort's palace, where the wedding of Elena and Arrigo is about to be celebrated. After a chorus, Elena sings her well-known *Bolero*, 'Merci, jeunes amies' (Merce, dilette amiche), a lively and appropriate display piece. Arrigo joins her and sings a charming air, 'La brise souffle au loin plus légère et plus pure' (La brezza aleggia intorno a carrezzarmi il viso), an entirely lyrical interlude in what is by no means otherwise a predominantly lyrical score.

Arrigo disappears and Elena is joined by the scheming Procida, who congratulates Elena on having provided with her wedding the opportunity for the Sicilian patriots to fall on the unarmed French, and tells her that the ringing of the bells will be the signal for the massacre. The resolute Procida defies Elena to denounce him to the French and so prevent the carrying out of his plan. Her only reply is to refuse to go through with the wedding, much to Arrigo's consternation. The impressive and extended trio for Elena, Arrigo, and Procida, one of the best numbers in the opera, dominates the finale. De Montfort enters, sweeps aside Elena's objections, the cause of which has not been revealed to him, and himself pronounces the betrothal, at the same time ordering the bells to ring out. The Sicilians rush from their hiding-places, and Procida's revenge is complete.

While it is true that *Les Vêpres Siciliennes* does not reach the heights of *Don Carlos* or *Simon Boccanegra*, there is much music of fine quality in this score. In the first act, Elena's aria and the unaccompanied quartet are brilliantly successful numbers, and in the second, 'O toi Palermo' is one of Verdi's most famous bass arias. De Montfort's monologue at the beginning of Act III is of an expressive quality worthy of Philip himself, and the choral finale after the attempted murder is most effective. The whole of the fourth act is on Verdi's highest level, the solo for Arrigo and that for Elena in the middle of their scene together being outstandingly successful, and the moment of suspense before the execution most movingly done. The fifth act can seem rather long in performance, but Arrigo's lyrical tune and the large-scale trio are first-rate.

SIMON BOCCANEGRA

OPERA in three acts and a prologue by Giuseppe Verdi; text by Francesco Maria Piave, from a play by Gutiérrez. Première at the Teatro la Fenice, Venice, March 12, 1857. Revised 1881.

*S*IMON BOCCANEGRA was unsuccessful when first performed in Venice, and indeed Verdi himself referred to this first version as 'monotonous and cold', so that it is not surprising that he chose to revise the opera over twenty years after the first performance, entrusting it to Boito, his prospective collaborator in *Otello*. In this version the opera has gradually and deservedly won its way into the international repertory, but one is bound to admit that Boito's contribution, while it included the insertion of a scene nothing short of genius, stopped short of clarifying the complications of the plot.

Genoa in the fourteenth century was ruled by a Doge, who had hitherto always been elected from the ranks of the patricians. Jacopo Fiesco (*bass*), who is in office when the story begins, has a daughter, Maria, who has fallen in love with a plebeian, Simon Boccanegra (*baritone*), and borne him a daughter. Boccanegra's seafaring exploits have won him considerable fame but not the right to treat the Doge's daughter as his equal. Their child was looked after at Pisa by an old woman while he was at sea, until one day on his return home he found her dead, and his daughter vanished. Since then, he has sought her in vain, and he does not know that she was found wandering on the sea shore by Count Grimaldi, a patrician, and brought up by him as his own child.

Prologue. Paolo (*baritone*), political leader of the plebeians, and Pietro (*bass*), an influential member of the movement, are in conversation, the former suggesting that Boccanegra should be the plebeian choice for Doge. Pietro agrees to organise the people's vote for Boccanegra in return for honour and riches for himself. Boccanegra has been called to Genoa by Paolo, and agrees to accept the position, which should win him permission to marry his beloved Maria. The people are called together, and Paolo announces that Boccanegra is to be their candidate; they unite in cursing Fiesco, in whose palace they see mysterious lights.

The whole of this section is set to music that is extraordinarily suggestive of underground movement and conspiracy under the cover of darkness, from the mysterious prelude to Paolo's cursing of the haughty patricians and his *sotto voce* working up of the crowd in fear of the nameless doings in Fiesco's palace.

The square empties, and Fiesco leaves his home, lamenting the loss of his daughter, from whose death-bed he has just come. His noble, restrained cry of grief, 'Il lacerato spirito' (Weary and worn with suffering[1]), with its moving orchestral postlude, establishes him straight away as a flesh-and-blood personality whose emotions may be subdued to his sense of position, but who is none the less anything but an insensitive, cardboard figure. He sees Boccanegra enter the square and confronts him again with an accusation of the wrong he has done Maria. It is the first of the two great duets between the adversaries, Fiesco's fury contrasting well with Boccanegra's pleading as he tells the story of the loss of the little daughter, which has robbed one of them of his only child, the other of the granddaughter he has never seen.

Fiesco tells Boccanegra that only the sight of his granddaughter can bring peace between them. He watches from a distance as the distracted man knocks on the palace door, then, finding it open, goes up, only to discover his Maria dead. Boccanegra reappears to hear the plaudits of the mob, as they

---

[1] English translation by Norman Tucker.

crowd into the square (to a most democratic-sounding march) and salute their new Doge.

ACT I. Twenty-five years have passed. Amelia (*soprano*), Boccanegra's daughter, is standing in the garden of the Grimaldi palace, near the sea. It is dawn, and she salutes the beauty of the scene and memories of her childhood in a lovely aria, 'Come in quest'ora bruna' (See how sky and ocean). She hears the voice of Gabriele Adorno (*tenor*), her lover, serenading her from a distance, and when he appears, tells him of her fears for his safety and that of Andrea (in reality, Fiesco in disguise), who she knows is plotting against the Doge. Pietro comes to announce that the Doge asks to be received by Amelia on his way back from hunting, for no other purpose, as she well knows, than that of asking her hand in marriage for his henchman, Paolo. Gabriele resolves immediately to ask the blessing of Andrea (Amelia's guardian now that Count Grimaldi has been banished from Genoa for political intrigue) on their marriage. When he does so, Fiesco tells him the story of Amelia's adoption (he has, of course, no idea of her actual identity), Gabriele swears eternal love to her, and Fiesco blesses Gabriele in his affection for Amelia and his patriotic love of Genoa.

The Doge greets Amelia, shows her the pardon he is granting to Count Grimaldi, and asks her if she is content with her life of seclusion. She answers that she has a lover, and is pursued by one she hates – Paolo. In any case she confides to the Doge that she is not Grimaldi's daughter, but an orphan, whose only clue to her identity is a locket containing the portrait of her mother. With great emotion, Boccanegra recognises it as that of Maria, and knows he has found his daughter at last. Their duet mounts in intensity, through Simon's lyrical reaction to the possibility of having found his daughter, until uncertainty gives way to proof, and he gratefully acknowledges her. Boccanegra denies any hope of Amelia to the waiting Paolo, who plots her abduction with his crony Pietro.

The finale of Act I, which plays in the Council Chamber of the Doge, dates entirely from Boito's revision, and is almost one half of the entire act. It is one of the finest scenes in all Verdi, and an extraordinary and entirely worthy anticipation of the work of the composer and librettist in *Otello*.

The Doge is surrounded by the plebeian and patrician members of his Council (the former in the majority). Their business is interrupted by sounds of rioting. The crowd is dragging Adorno to the palace; the words 'Morte ai patrizi' (Death to the nobles) can now be distinguished. In a moment, the Council has divided itself into patricians and plebeians, each group with swords drawn. Simon sends his herald to tell the crowd that he awaits them in his Council Chamber, if they wish to find him. It is a scene of breathless drama achieved by the simplest means, and the domination of Boccanegra is nowhere better shown than in his efforts to keep peace, not only in the city but within his own Council as well.

The mob rushes in, crying for vengeance on Gabriele Adorno and Andrea (or Fiesco), whom they drag into the Doge's presence. Adorno says he has slain Lorenzino, who had abducted Amelia, and that before he died, the villain admitted he was the agent of 'a man of high position'. He is about to stab Boccanegra for the crime when Amelia throws herself between the two men. Her story corroborates Gabriele's, but before she can name the offender, patrician and plebeian accuse and counter-accuse each other of the crime. Only Boccanegra's intervention prevents further bloodshed. His great plea for peace and unity, 'Piango su voi, sul placido raggio del vostro clivo' (Sadly I see the sweet bloom of spring on our native hillsides), leads to an extended ensemble, led by Amelia, who echoes the prayer that peace may return to all their hearts.

Adorno surrenders his sword to Boccanegra, who accepts it, before turning 'con forza terribile' to Paolo. He speaks with ever-increasing intensity of his determination to find the traitor who raised his hand against Amelia, and demands Paolo join with him in cursing the villain. This Paolo cannot avoid doing, and his curse is taken up by the bystanders.

ACT II. Paolo is alone, a prey to acute fear of the consequences of his action and of the curse he was obliged to deliver against himself. He rears himself like a snake to threaten the absent Doge with the most terrible and the most secret vengeance at his command – poison. Fiesco and Adorno are brought in, and he offers the former his freedom if he will kill the Doge. If he refuses, the details of the patrician plot, as well as the names of the men who lead them, shall go forthwith to the Doge himself. Fiesco refuses the offer. Paolo asks Adorno if he knows that Amelia is here in the palace, as Boccanegra's mistress?

Adorno launches into a magnificent tirade in A minor against the Doge, who once ordered his father's execution and has now ravished the girl he loves. He prays that his fears may be groundless. Amelia comes in and he confronts her with the accusation, which she denies. She attempts to persuade him to leave, but the Doge can be heard approaching, and Adorno hides, still breathing threats of revenge.

Boccanegra notices that his daughter has tears in her eyes, and tells her that he knows the reason, which she has already revealed to him: she is in love. When he hears the name of Adorno, his worst fears are realised; Adorno is a traitor and a plotter against the state. She entreats him to pardon Gabriele, with whom she would rather die than live on alone. The Doge tells her to leave him, and wonders whether it is strength or weakness which prompts him to pardon an enemy. He pours water from the jug which Paolo has poisoned, and drinks from it, reflecting on the melancholy destiny of those who wear a crown. He feels himself falling asleep, and murmurs Amelia's name while the orchestra softly adumbrates the theme of their duet in Act I.

Adorno steps from concealment; the man who murdered his father and who is now his rival is at his mercy! But Amelia steps between the two men. Boccanegra awakes and defies Adorno to kill a defenceless man. Gabriele says Boccanegra's life is forfeit in return for his father's. Boccanegra replies that his revenge is already complete since he has taken from him the thing in life that he values most, his daughter. Adorno, overcome, begs for Amelia's forgiveness and death at the Doge's hand. Boccanegra's humanity does not desert him and, in a phrase whose nobility dominates the latter part of the splendid trio, he pardons his would-be murderer.

Warlike sounds are heard outside, and Boccanegra orders Adorno to join his friends, whose rebellion has evidently started. But Adorno swears loyalty to the Doge.

ACT III. A great hall, whose window reveals a view of Genoa harbour. Fiesco's sword is returned to him and he is released. He sees Paolo with an escort of guards, and learns that he took part in the rebellion, which has been crushed, and, when captured, was immediately condemned to death by Boccanegra – but Paolo can exult in the knowledge that the Doge will follow him quickly to the grave, slain by the slow poison he has prepared for him. The strains of the wedding hymn of Gabriele and Amelia can be heard, and Paolo is conducted to the scaffold with its sound ringing in his ears, leaving Fiesco full of regret that Boccanegra's end should be brought about in so treacherous and dishonourable a manner.

A proclamation is read from the balcony, ordering that the lights be extinguished in honour of the valiant dead. The Doge himself enters the hall, already affected by the poison he has taken. The sight of the sea restores his confidence, and brings back to him memories of the life he once led as a free man on the sea he loved and understood so well. Why, asks Boccanegra, did he not find death at this early, happy stage of his career? As if in answer to his question comes an echo from the concealed Fiesco, who reveals himself as the ancient enemy long thought dead. It is the moment, not of Fiesco's revenge, but of Boccanegra's atonement, and he proudly announces that there can be peace between them now that in Amelia he has found the daughter he had lost. Fiesco's hate turns to pity for the man he knows has only a short time to live.

Boccanegra summons up strength to tell Amelia of her descent, and to appoint Adorno as his successor, before he dies in the arms of his children and surrounded by his friends and counsellors. Fiesco goes to the balcony and announces to the assembled crowd that Gabriele Adorno is their new Doge; when they shout for Boccanegra, he reveals that he is dead.

Much has been made of the complication of the original libretto, and of the difficulty Boito apparently had in tidying it up, but the truth is that very little more is needed to make the story entirely comprehensible, even easy to follow. Apart from a general concentrating of the dialogue, Boito was responsible for the finale of Act I, generally conceded to be the finest section of the opera. Verdi's revision was even more thorough. Details of the orchestration, of the vocal line, and of the harmony are altered all over the place. Entirely new is the opening scene of the prologue up to Fiesco's aria (apart from Paolo's 'L'altra magion'); the introduction to Act I, the duet for Gabriele and Fiesco, the climax of the recognition duet, and of course the Council Chamber scene; Boccanegra's short solo in Act II and Paolo's *Credo*-like soliloquy which precedes it; the opening of Act III up to the entrance of Boccanegra and to a large extent the final quartet with chorus.

Verdi's high regard for the opera is perhaps to some extent due to his love for Genoa itself. Certainly his music communicates this love as well as the city's dependence on the sea. But the most remarkable thing about the opera is its central figure, amongst Verdi's greatest creations. Never before perhaps had a composer been wholly successful in putting the unspectacular quality of statesmanship on to the stage, although quite a number had tried. Not a bar of recitative, not a note in the great solos and ensembles in which he takes part but contributes to this picture of the central figure, which is in addition perhaps the most exacting baritone part Verdi ever wrote, certainly one of the most rewarding.

UN BALLO IN MASCHERA
A Masked Ball

OPERA in three acts by Giuseppe Verdi; text by Somma, based on Scribe's libretto for Auber's opera *Gustave III, ou le Bal Masqué*. Première at Apollo Theatre, Rome, February 17, 1859.

THE first version was written for Naples in 1858; rehearsals were in progress when an Italian revolutionary, Felice Orsini, made an unsuccessful attempt on the life of Napoleon III, with the result that the performance of a work dealing with the assassination of a king was forbidden. In spite of protests and the popular slogan 'Viva Verdi!' (= Viva Vittorio Emmanuele Re D'Italia), the opera was withdrawn but mounted a year later in Rome, where Verdi accepted the unlikely setting of Boston for the assassination of an English Governor in place of the historical Swedish monarch. (Names for the 'Boston' version are given in parentheses.)

Ballo has been claimed as the best-shaped opera of Verdi's middle period, with an exquisite balance between the music's romantic and tragic elements on the one hand and its strongly ironic characteristics on the other, the latter evidenced not only in what the conspirators (particularly at the end of Act II) and Oscar have to sing, but most of all in the rounded musical picture of the tenor hero. King Gustavus III of Sweden was a liberal in politics and a lover of the arts, married but homosexual, and Verdi characterises him to the full. Nothing could be more romantic than his opening aria, the love duet, or the aria in the last act, but this monarch rejects the portentous and in the opera constantly brings the music to the boil with his exuberance, never running the risk of taking himself too seriously, as evidenced particularly in his mocking reaction to Arvidson's prophecy of doom. For Oscar, the page, Verdi seems to have taken something from the lighter world of French opera and Oscar is evidently licensed to mock pretension of any kind. The music associated with King and page brings a colour to this musical suggestion of a historical court which is unlike anything else in Verdi.

The prelude is concerned with Court, conspirators, and the love of the King for Amelia.

ACT I. Scene i. A hall in the palace. The conspirators, Ribbing (Samuele; *bass*) and Horn (Tommaso; *bass*) mutter through the opening chorus but the King (Riccardo, Count of Warwick; *tenor*) is overjoyed to notice on a list of invitations to a masked ball the name of his beloved Amelia (*soprano*), wife of his faithful secretary, Anckarstroem ('La rivedrà nell'estasi': I shall behold in ecstasy). Anckarstroem (Renato; *baritone*) warns the King of his enemies and a judge denounces a certain Mlle Arvidson for sorcery. Oscar (*soprano*) intercedes for her ('Volta la terrea': She of the stars above can read the courses) and the King decides to go in disguise to investigate whether she is genuine or not.

Scene ii. Arvidson's (Ulrica; *contralto*) abode. The sorceress conjures a spell for the crowd ('Re dall'abisso, affrettati!': Haste thee from Hell, Beelzebub!), the King arrives, and Arvidson finishes her solo in a mood of exaltation. She predicts good fortune for a young sailor (*baritone*), and the King fulfils the prophecy by slipping a note into the young man's pocket. Next, none other than Amelia is advised to cure a guilty love by gathering a herb at the foot of the public gallows (trio). The courtiers, in disguise like the King, arrive and he in a barcarolle ('Di tu se fedele') asks Arvidson to foretell his future. He will die by the hand of a friend, she predicts. The King pokes fun at the whole issue (quintet: 'È scherzo, od è follia': A jest is all 'twas meant to be) and when it is further foretold that his murderer will be the first to shake his hand and this turns out to be Anck-arstroem, he mocks the sorceress for failing to recognise him. The finale starts with a 'National Anthem' theme but ends in high spirits as the King and his page take over.

ACT II. Midnight, beside the gallows. Amelia, heavily veiled, comes to pick the magic herb and in a magnificent aria betrays her nervousness and her desperate need for reassurance ('Ma dall'arido stelo divulsa': When the leaf from the stem has been shaken). The King appears. The love duet which follows sees Amelia's initial reticence blossom into an admission of love, and is one of the most expansive and splendid in the Verdian canon. At its end, Anckarstroem, who has heard that murderers are on the King's tracks, comes to rescue him. In a short, agitated trio they discuss escape, and the finale is concerned with the unsuccessful efforts of Anckarstroem to get his disguised wife safely away, her unmasking, and the consequent rage of the one and remorse of the other. With the mocking laughter of the conspirators, this is one of Verdi's most fascinating scenes. During its course Anckarstroem makes an assignation with the leaders of the conspiracy to meet at his house next day.

ACT III. Scene i. A room in Anckarstroem's house. Anckarstroem intends to kill Amelia but yields to her plea ('Morrò, ma prima in grazia': I die, but ere my hour be come) that she may first say goodbye to their son. The King is the more guilty of the two, he decides, and in a dramatic recitative and grandiose aria, 'Eri tu' (Yes, 'twas you), inveighs against him. Anckarstroem receives the leaders of the conspiracy and agrees to make common cause with them, Amelia is forced to draw lots to decide who shall kill the King at tonight's masked ball – Anckarstroem's name emerges – and finally there is a brilliant solo for the newly-arrived Oscar which becomes a quintet of reaction to the news of that night's party.

Scene ii consists mainly of an aria for Gustavus, introspective in the recitative and full of romantic stress in the aria ('Ma se m'è forza perderti'), in which he declares his intention to send Amelia and her husband on a foreign mission.

Scene iii. The masked ball works up the tension slowly but unerringly: a dramatic recitative from the King, chorus and dancing, then Oscar's brilliant solo in reply to Anckarstroem's question about Gustavus's disguise: 'Saper vorreste' (If you'd be asking). Much of the scene is carried on over dance music and the farewell duet between the King and Amelia is particularly moving, as is the King's death. A shot rings out; Gustavus falls into the arms of Oscar, Amelia rushes to him and the dance music stops. King Gustavus dies forgiving his enemies.

LA FORZA DEL DESTINO
The Force of Destiny

OPERA in four acts by Giuseppe Verdi; text by Francesco Maria Piave, founded on a Spanish drama by the Duke of Rivas, *Don Alvaro o La Fuerza de Sino*. Première St. Petersburg, November 10, 1862.

*F*ORZA is customarily criticised for its rambling libretto, and because the destiny which is proclaimed in the title tends to be replaced in the story by the less compelling factor of co-incidence. Francis Toye is at some pains to point out that Rivas's play, *Don Alvaro*, is dominated by the principle of the blood-feud, in which facts were more important than intentions, and that to understand the original significance of the play entails an imaginative reconstruction of this outmoded Spanish attitude.

The overture is a vividly exciting affair, dominated by Leonora's aria from Act II, and the music concerned with 'fate', which begins it. Reference is also made to Alvaro's *cantabile con espressione* tune (in A minor) from the fourth act duet, and to themes from the duet between Leonora and Padre Guardiano.

ACT I. Leonora's (*soprano*) room. She says goodnight to her father and is then overcome with remorse – for she has arranged that very night to elope with her lover, Don Alvaro (*tenor*). In an aria, 'Me pellegrina ed orfana' (As wanderer and orphan), she pictures her friendless lot in a foreign country, for which even the prospect of marriage cannot console her. It is late; he surely cannot come now – but no sooner are the words spoken than he rushes in, protesting eternal love. Before they can escape, the Marchese di Calatrava (*bass*) bursts in, denouncing his daughter's seducer. Alvaro protests their innocence, and throws down his pistol in token surrender. It goes off and fatally wounds the old man, who curses Leonora as he dies.

ACT II. Leonora has been separated from Alvaro in their flight; each believes the other dead, but Don Carlo di Vargas (*baritone*), Leonora's brother, knows that they are alive and scours the land to revenge himself on the sister who has brought dishonour to his family and on what he sees as the murderer of his father.

Scene i. The inn at the village of Hornachuelos, where amongst the crowd is a mysterious student, Don Carlo in disguise. The company sings and dances until the meal is announced; Leonora appears for a moment at the door seeking shelter, but she recognises her brother and withdraws. Presently Preziosilla (*mezzo-soprano*), a gipsy, enters, telling the guests that war has broken out. She sings a song in praise of war, and proceeds to tell fortunes, incidentally informing the student that his being in disguise cannot be hidden from her.

Pilgrims can be heard outside, and all join in their prayer, not least Leonora, who prays to be delivered from her brother's vengeance. It is a splendid piece of choral writing. Don Carlo asks the muleteer (*tenor*) about the traveller he brought to the inn, and is asked in his turn, since he is so curious about others, to tell the company his own story. This he does in a ballad; he is Pereda, a young student, who has followed his friend Vargas in his quest for the murderer of his father. The murderer it appears has escaped to South America, and the sister of Vargas, whom the murderer seduced, is dead. The mayor (*bass*) says it is late, all bid each other good night, and, after a final dance, the scene comes to an end.

Scene ii. Outside the monastery of the 'Madonna degli Angeli', near Hornachuelos. Leonora has been sent here for sanctuary. In the most extended aria of the opera, she prays for forgiveness for her sin, and takes courage from the sound of the hymn coming from the church. At the beginning of the scene can be heard the 'fate' motif familiar from the overture, then, after a dramatic recitative, the aria 'Madre, pietosa Vergine' (Holy Mother, hear my prayer). Leonora rings the bell, and a window in the door opens to reveal Fra Melitone (*baritone*), who agrees to inform the Father Superior (*bass*) of her presence. He receives her kindly, and knows immediately who she is when she tells him who sent her. He warns her of the extreme loneliness of the solitary life she proposes to lead in the cave, but she is determined to go through with her plan, and he agrees to her request. He himself will bring her food daily and in case of urgent danger or the approach of death she can ring a bell to summon help; otherwise, she will never again set eyes on a human being. He tells the monks that no one is to approach the cave or make any attempt to discover the identity of the penitent.

Leonora's scene with Padre Guardiano is one of the finest in all Verdi. The expressive vocal line is enhanced by the contrasting nature of the various sections, whether it be the loose-limbed tune in which Leonora first tells of the gradual awakening of peace in her soul, or the closely knit E major duet in which Padre Guardiano immediately afterwards warns her of the danger she runs in living alone, the long sentences in which he urges her to draw closer to God, or the passionate phrases she employs to voice her thanks to the salvation she feels she has found. The finale (the short service in which the Father Superior blesses Leonora and warns the monks in future not to approach her solitary cell) is the perfect pendant to a great scene. Padre Guardiano leads them in pronouncing a curse on anyone who violates the sanctity of the cell, and then the sound of Leonora's voice floats out over the male voices of the monks in the prayer to the Virgin, 'La Vergine degli angeli'. It would be difficult to imagine music that more perfectly combines simplicity of means and beauty of effect.

ACT III. Scene i. Italy, near Velletri, where the fighting is taking place. Don Alvaro and Don Carlo di Vargas, each under assumed names and unknown to the other, have enlisted in the Spanish contingent. Alvaro sings his long recitative and aria, 'O tu che in seno agli angeli' (O sainted soul, in rest above), one of Verdi's major inspirations. Alvaro's is a tortured and lonely soul: he has deserted the woman he loves after having inadvertently killed her father, and he alternately proclaims the shame of his mixed blood and prison birth, and the glory of his noble ancestry.

In response to a cry for help, he rushes offstage, to reappear with none other than his old enemy Don Carlo, whom he has saved from death at the hands of a gang of ruffians. Having exchanged false names, they swear friendship and go off together in answer to an urgent call to arms.

Scene ii. We see a military surgeon (*tenor*) surrounded by soldiers watching the battle from a distance. The Italians and the Spaniards have won, but Don Carlo brings in Alvaro grievously wounded. When Carlo seeks to give his friend the military decoration of the order of Calatrava, he shudders at the name, but a moment later he entrusts Carlo with a small casket which contains a letter and which must be burnt unopened after his death. Carlo swears to carry out the commission. The duet, 'Solenne in quest'ora' (In this solemn hour), has become world-famous, partly, perhaps, because of the celebrity of the gramophone record made of it by Caruso and Scotti, but also because of its graceful tune and remarkably apt relationship to the situation.

Alvaro is borne away as Carlo reflects. His friend trembled at the name of Calatrava; could it be his enemy in disguise? He soliloquises on the temptation the casket presents even to a man of honour, 'Urna fatale del mio destino' (Fatal urn of my destiny), but finds a portrait inside which no oath prevents him from inspecting. It is Leonora's! The secret is out, and his newly found friend is recognised as his old enemy! At this moment a messenger tells him that Alvaro's life is saved; in an *allegro* he rejoices at the prospect of revenge.

Scene iii. A military camp near Velletri. Don Alvaro can be seen crossing the camp. Carlo calls him, and asks him if he is strong enough to fight a duel. With whom? Has he had no message lately from Don Alvaro, the Indian? Alvaro's protests and offers of friendship are in vain; Carlo insults him until he has provoked the duel he is seeking, only to be interrupted by the patrol on its way home. Alvaro, left alone, resolves to seek sanctuary in a monastery. The scene is in the splendid tradition of duets for tenor and baritone which Verdi did so incomparably.

It is dawn. Soldiers polish their equipment, pedlars offer their wares, food and drink is for sale, and Preziosilla offers to tell fortunes until the appearance of a band of recruits gives her an opportunity of leading a tarantella in an effort to dispel their gloom. Mixed up in the dance is Fra Melitone, who extricates himself and treats the company to a discourse on its several vices, the whole thing dressed up in a series of outrageous puns. The soldiers make an attempt to give him a drubbing, but Preziosilla interrupts them and sings a spirited 'Rataplan', which ends the act.

ACT IV. Scene i. The cloister of the Convent of the 'Madonna degli Angeli', where a crowd of beggars is assembling to collect the free soup which the monks dole out regularly. Fra Melitone is in charge, and his marked lack of patience and his intense annoyance at being compared unfavourably by the crowd with Padre Raffaello (in reality Alvaro in disguise) make him more than usually short with his customers. Finally, he kicks over the cauldron with what remains of the soup inside. The Father Superior, who has been watching, reproaches him gently for lack of patience. Melitone says he likes Raffaello but cannot understand his odd, haunted look – caused, says the Father Superior, by his frequent fasts and his concentration on his duty.

The monastery doorbell rings violently, and Melitone admits Don Carlo himself, asking for Padre Raffaello. Melitone says there are two of that name in the monastery, but from the description he easily knows which is meant. Alvaro comes in, Carlo discloses himself and immediately challenges him to a duel. In a magnificent duet Alvaro pleads with him to renounce his thoughts of vengeance, and believe what he now hears from the mouth of a priest, that his sister Leonora was never dishonoured, that he has nought to avenge but the misfortune which has dogged them both. Alvaro will even do what he says he has never before done, kneel at Don Carlo's feet. Carlo says this act proclaims the baseness of his birth. He strikes Alvaro across the face, branding him a coward. Alvaro proclaims that he is ready to fight him and they rush off.

Scene ii. Outside Leonora's grotto. In great long phrases of supplication she prays for peace. 'Pace, pace, mio Dio' (Peace, grant me peace, O Lord). She sees the bread which has been left for her and which serves only to prolong, as she says, a wretched life. Suddenly, the sounds of fighting can be heard, and, calling down a curse on whoever dares to profane her solitude, she returns to her cell.

In a moment, the voice of Carlo can be heard begging for absolution; he is dying, and Alvaro, distracted that he has once again the blood of a Vargas on his hands, bangs on the door of Leonora's cell and begs for help. Leonora rings the bell in her alarm but a moment later appears and is recognised by Alvaro, who tells her what has happened. She goes to her brother and a few seconds later her cry is heard as Carlo stabs her, revenge uppermost in his mind even at his last moment. Alvaro can restrain himself no longer when he sees Leonora supported by Padre Guardiano, and he curses the fate which has brought so much misery on them all. The old Father Superior in music of great nobility bids him not to curse but to prostrate himself before the might of Heaven. Leonora dies, and so expiates the curse which fell on them all with the death of her father.

DON CARLOS

OPERA in five acts by Giuseppe Verdi; text by G. Méry and C. du Locle (in French), after Schiller. Première at Opéra, Paris, March 11, 1867. Revised version (in Italian), la Scala, Milan, 1884.

*D*ON CARLOS for many years suffered from an inherent disadvantage; it was written for Paris, and at five acts was too long for non-Gallic taste. In 1882–3 Verdi and Ghislanzoni, his librettist for *Aida*, produced a shorter version, omitting the ballet music and jettisoning most of the important first act, which is hard to justify artistically. Since then, most satisfactory revivals of the opera have attempted to include the first act, whatever they may have cut later on. It is in any version a magnificent opera, weakened only by one less than first-class scene (the *auto-da-fé*) and by its excessive length.

In the 1550's Spain is nearing the end of a war with France, and a condition of peace is that the heir to the throne of Spain, Don Carlos (historically, a psychopath, but represented in Verdi as well as in Schiller's play as a brilliant young man), should marry Elisabeth de Valois, the daughter of the King of France.

ACT I. A hunt is in progress near Fontainebleau (there is no prelude to the opera) and Elisabeth (*soprano*) and her page Tebaldo (*soprano*) are separated from the main body of riders. They disappear in search of their companions and Carlos (*tenor*), who has come secretly to France, sings of the love which the sight of his bride has awakened in his heart (this romance was salvaged in a somewhat reduced version when Verdi discarded Act I in his attempt at revision). Elisabeth re-appears and Carlos offers to escort her home, saying he is a member of the staff of the Spanish envoy. She asks him about the young Spanish Prince to whom she is betrothed. She fears for her marriage if love does not enter into it. Carlos tells her she need have no fear; he shows her a portrait, which she naturally recognises as his. Their love duet, which was omitted in the 1884 version, is particularly inspired, and the delicate beauty of Elisabeth's phrase, 'De quels transports poignants et doux' (Di qual amor, di quant'ardor: Ah yes, 'tis love), as she recognises the love in her heart, is something that can ill be spared.

Tebaldo warns Elisabeth that the Spanish envoy is approach-ing to make a formal request for her hand in marriage for his master, King Philip II of Spain himself, not for Don Carlos as had originally been arranged. The two lovers are filled with consternation, but Elisabeth accedes to the prayers of the crowd, who beg her to acquiesce and so put an end to the war. The acclamations of the crowd mingle with the agonised regrets of Elisabeth and Carlos as the act ends.

ACT II. Scene i. In an effort to forget the misery of the world, Carlos has taken refuge in the Convent of San Yuste, where his grandfather, Charles V, before him, had gone to end his days, and, so it is rumoured, is still alive. Various monks are praying before the tomb of the great Emperor, and one of them pro-claims the uselessness of expecting peace in this life. The bass solo with chorus is highly impressive, the more particularly since this is the first contact we have with the influence of the Church, one of the dominating features of the opera. (In the four-act version, Don Carlos's romance occurs here.)

Carlos is overjoyed to see Rodrigo, Marquess of Posa (*bari-tone*), his greatest friend, just returned from Flanders. Carlos confides to him that he loves his stepmother. Rodrigo says he will help him and begs him to devote himself to the cause of the oppressed people of Flanders, and forget his own troubles. They swear eternal friendship, 'Dieu, tu semas dans nos âmes un rayon' (Dio, che nell'alma infondere amor: God, who has filled our hearts), to a theme which is heard frequently throughout the opera.

A procession passes by, and the King (*bass*) is seen leading his Queen by the hand. This is too much for Carlos, but he is sustained by Rodrigo. The scene ends with a reiteration of the friendship theme.

Scene ii. A garden outside the monastery. The Queen's entourage wait for their mistress, and Princess Eboli, her lady-in-waiting (*mezzo-soprano*), supported by the irrepressible Tebaldo, whiles away the time by singing the song of the veil, a Moorish love-romance. With its ambitious cadenzas and rapid coloratura, it is a fine display piece.

The Queen arrives. Posa is announced, and gives her a letter from her mother in Paris, at the same time slipping a note from Carlos into her hand. She reads the message, while Rodrigo, to a graceful dance rhythm, tells Eboli the latest news from Paris. Elisabeth thanks Rodrigo and bids him ask some favour. He will, but not for himself. In a short aria, he asks Elisabeth to use her influence with her husband to arrange an interview between the King and Carlos. Eboli, who loves Carlos, believes that he loves her. Elisabeth agrees to see her 'son', and Rodrigo manoeuvres the ladies out of hearing.

Carlos enters and greets his 'mother' formally, asking her to persuade the King to send him to Flanders. But his outward calm is not proof against contact with the person he loves, and he reproaches her for her seeming indifference, which, she tells him, is no more than the duty she owes his father. In music of melting tenderness, Carlos shows that he understands her meaning, but it is clear that love for her still dominates his thoughts.

Suddenly he falls senseless at Elisabeth's feet (the only reference in the opera to the fits which appear to have been so common with the real Don Carlos). In his delirium he once again proclaims his love for her. He revives and takes her in his arms, but she tears herself away, demanding whether he means to murder his father and then lead his mother to the altar. With a cry of grief, Carlos rushes away. Their moving duet wonderfully characterises Carlos's hopeless love for Elisabeth and the suggestive description of his delirium.

The King leaves the church to find that the Queen, contrary to his strict instructions, has been left unattended. He dismisses the offending lady-in-waiting. Elisabeth ignores the affront to herself, and does her best to console the unhappy woman in a tender aria, 'O ma chère compagne' (Non pianger, mia compagna: Do not weep, my dearest companion).

The women leave, but the King bids Posa remain. Why, he asks, has such a trusted servant of Spain never asked him for a favour – for preferment, or even an audience? Rodrigo answers that service is his reward; but there is a favour he would like to ask: a relaxation of the measures being taken against the people of Flanders. Only severity, answers the King, can cure such infidels and rebels of their heresies; and he cites the contentment and peace of the people of Spain as an example of what he hopes to bring to the Flemish. It is the peace of desolation that he brings, replies Rodrigo. Let the King beware lest history say of him: 'This man was Nero!' Let him instead build an empire founded on freedom.

The King tells him his dreams are those of youth; but let him have no fear of the throne, rather beware of the Grand Inquisitor, not only for his own sake but because the King wants him as counsellor. He confides his fear over Elisabeth and Carlos to Rodrigo, who takes this confidence in him as a sign that happier times may be at hand for all whom he loves. With a last warning to beware the Inquisition, the King dismisses Rodrigo. The duet shows Verdi's mastery in setting to music not only the clash between differing personalities but the logical arguments which take place when the personalities involved are reasoning, intelligent human beings.

ACT III. Scene i. A masked ball at the palace in Madrid (the ballet music originally occurred at this point). Carlos waits in the Queen's gardens in response to an anonymous note. He sees a figure that he thinks is Elisabeth, and pours out his heart to her. She unmasks, revealing Eboli, who accuses Carlos of loving the Queen. Posa enters and threatens Eboli, who promises to bring about their downfall. Posa persuades Carlos to give him any incriminating papers he may have in his possession. The act ends on a *fortissimo* statement in the orchestra of the theme of the oath of friendship.

Scene ii The square in Madrid. Preparations are afoot for an *auto-da-fé*, the ceremonial punishment of heretics at the stake. The people rejoice in the might of Spain as a procession of monks precedes the mournful band of victims of the Inquisition. The members of the court, headed by the Queen, enter, and the King himself comes through the door of the cathedral. He swears to wage war against the enemies of the Faith. But there is an interruption when six deputies from Flanders, led by Carlos, fling themselves at Philip's feet, protesting loyalty and begging for relief from their suffering. The King remains adamant.

Carlos asks his father to appoint him King's deputy at the head of his Flemish subjects. Philip refuses. Carlos, in desperation, draws his sword in front of the King and announces he will save Flanders. Philip orders that he be disarmed, but no one dare obey, until Rodrigo asks for the sword and gives it to the King. The procession advances, the sound of the monks singing the death-knell of the heretics can be heard, and over all a voice from heaven promises peace in the next world to the suffering.

ACT IV. Scene i. Philip's study. This first scene is one of Verdi's finest: of varied nature, but with a strong dramatic line running through it. For the first time in the opera, we see the King alone, as man rather than monarch. He sings the greatest of all Verdi bass arias, 'Elle ne m'aime pas' (Ella giammai m'amo: She has no love for me), in which he betrays his acute misery over the failure of his marriage, his loneliness not only as a king, because his state demands it, but as a man, because his wife has no love for him in her heart.

The King has summoned the Grand Inquisitor (*bass*). He is ninety, blind, but walking erect with the aid of a stick. The King explains his son has taken publicly the part of the heretic Flemish; he intends either to exact no penalty or else to punish him with nothing less than death, in which case, does he have the Church's support? The Inquisitor says that God was not afraid to give his only son that the world might be saved. The Inquisitor then tells the King that Carlos's faults are nothing to those of the Marquess of Posa. The King will not agree to sacrifice his new confidant and is castigated by the Inquisitor as a man whose heart is not wholly given to God. Refusing to make any concession, the Inquisitor departs, leaving behind him a sadder man. The duet is of unsurpassed strength: a clash between the King's logical and reasoned argument (although bigoted), and the Inquisitor's impregnable religious conviction.

Elisabeth rushes in, demanding Philip's help in finding a casket of jewels which has disappeared from her room. He asks her coldly if she is looking for the casket on his table; on his instructions she opens it to reveal a portrait of Carlos. Philip denounces her as an adulteress, and Elisabeth faints. Eboli and Rodrigo answer the King's call for help, and Philip himself expresses bitter regret at his rash and cruel suspicion. Eboli (who suggested the King look in the jewel case) is stricken with remorse, and Rodrigo realises he can rescue Carlos only by taking his place on the altar of liberty. The Queen revives and voices her loneliness and desolation. As the two men leave, Eboli throws herself at Elisabeth's feet, confessing that, through jealousy, she excited the King's suspicions, and that she has been the King's mistress. Elisabeth orders Eboli to leave her presence for ever and choose between exile and life in a nunnery. Eboli, alone, pours forth her grief at what her fatal beauty has brought about, vowing to save Carlos from death. Her aria 'O don fatal' (O don fatale: O fatal beauty) is a superb, economical piece of construction, crowning an act of almost unmatched richness.

Scene ii. Carlos's prison cell. Rodrigo, knowing that Carlos's letters from the Flemings have been found in his possession, realises his days are numbered. He bids farewell to his friend in an expressive aria, 'C'est mon jour, mon jour suprême' (Per me giunto è il dì supremo: The last day for me has dawned). A shot rings out and he falls mortally wounded by an assassin. He tells Carlos before he dies that the Queen will wait for him the following day outside the convent of San Yuste.

The King enters and attempts to return Carlos's sword to him. But his son spurns him as a murderer. A mob storms in; among them is Eboli, making a last effort to save Carlos from his folly. The people demand he be given up to them. But the Inquisitor appears and castigates the crowd.

ACT V. The cloister of San Yuste. Elisabeth sings sadly of the joys she once knew and of the sorrow she now has in parting from Carlos for ever: 'Toi qui sus le néant des grandeurs de ce monde' (Tu che le vanità conoscesti del mondo: Thou who knowest the hearts and the frailty of mortals). The wide-ranging melody shows Elisabeth in the full stature of maturity.

Carlos enters, and he and Elisabeth, in the last of their three extensive duets, recall the happiness that might have been theirs, turning their attention to the future, which holds for Carlos a career devoted to the liberal causes that Rodrigo loved so well.

Philip emerges from his hiding place, seizes Elisabeth and demands that the Grand Inquisitor, who is with him, do his duty towards Carlos. But Carlos defends himself against the guards. Suddenly a voice is heard from the tomb of Charles V: the Emperor himself appears and takes his grandson into the safety of the cloister. This ending has been much criticised as a weakened version of Schiller, where Philip hands over Carlos to the Inquisition, and some productions attempt to return to this original.

AIDA

OPERA in four acts by Giuseppe Verdi; text by Antonio Ghislanzoni from the French prose of Camille du Locle, scenario by Mariette Bey. Première at Cairo, December 24, 1871.

*A*IDA was commissioned by the Khedive of Egypt for the Italian Theatre in Cairo (not for the opening of the Suez Canal as is sometimes supposed), and written in Italian from a French prose text on an original scenario by a French Egyptologist. Taking a cue from the Triumph Scene of Act II, *Aida* has often been the subject of spectacular productions, and the scale of the voices needed to do the score justice supports this view. But a case can also be made for a sparer view of *Aida*. The prelude and the first scene (all but the finale) are concerned with soliloquies and private meetings, as is, a dance of priestesses apart, the dedication of Radames to his role as army commander in the scene which follows, and indeed the long encounter between Amneris and Aida in Act II. Act III is entirely an affair of solo, duet and trio, and the last act has Amneris in confrontation with Radames, Radames silent in face of his judges, and finally Radames entombed with Aida. Only the return of the triumphant Egyptian army in Act II Scene ii is on a truly big scale, and perhaps the end of the opening scene when the citizenry wishes its forces well. Otherwise it is individual emotions, conflicts and resolutions with which Verdi is concerned. A slimline *Aida* may be rare, but is not self-contradictory and could be revelatory.

ACT I. Scene i. The prelude puts forward Aida (*soprano*), gentle and feminine, contrasted with the implacable Egyptian priesthood of Isis. Ethiopia has recovered quickly from war with Egypt and an Ethiopian army menaces Thebes. In his aria, 'Celeste Aida', Radames (*tenor*) hopes he will be chosen to lead the Egyptian army, not least because this might facilitate his plans to marry Aida. But Princess Amneris (*mezzo-soprano*), as is plain from her entrance, is herself in love with Radames, and, in spite of feigned friendship, already jealous of her Ethiopian slave Aida (trio). On to the scene come King (*bass*) and court; first a messenger brings news that Amonasro (*baritone*), the Ethiopian king, is himself leading the enemy forces, then Radames is proclaimed Egyptian commander-in-chief. General rejoicing culminates in a cry of 'Ritorna vincitor!' (As victor now return), which, the crowd departed, is paradoxically taken up in a magnificent aria by Aida, more immediately anxious for Radames's success than concerned for Ethiopian aspirations. Her aria ends with a *cantabile* prayer ('Numi, pietà').

Scene ii is in the Temple of Vulcan, where priests chant, dancers celebrate, and Radames is invested with consecrated weaponry.

ACT II. Scene i. In Amneris's apartments, the princess, plainly languishing with love for Radames, is being prepared for the festivity which will welcome the victorious army. Amneris commiserates with Aida over the Ethiopian defeat, advancing the (fictitious) news of Radames's death as comfort. Aida's despairing reaction provides Amneris with ammunition to taunt her slave that the King's daughter is her rival. There is no greater scene for soprano and mezzo in Italian opera.

Scene ii. Before one of the gates of Thebes, King and Court assemble to greet the triumphant Egyptian army. Trumpets start the procession and soldiers with trophies march past. Finally it is Radames's turn; he asks for the prisoners to be brought before the King, and Aida recognises her father, whose

Aida VERDI

identity as king remains hidden. Radames requests they be set
at liberty, priests and populace demand death, while Aida,
Amneris, Radames and Amonasro express conflicting emotions
in a magnificent scene. The King announces a compromise: the
prisoners will be freed with Aida's father remaining as surety:
Amneris rejoices, and the King announces that her hand shall
be Radames's reward.

ACT III. From the Temple of Isis on the banks of the Nile,
priests chant as Amneris goes to pray before her nuptials with
Radames. In an aria of subtle beauty ('O patria mia, mai più ti
rivedrò': O native land, I ne'er shall see thee more), Aida wonders why Radames has asked her to meet him here and yearns
for Ethiopia. Before she can find out, her father confronts her
with a demand that, if she would outflank her rival, she must
discover from Radames the Egyptian army's route for the forthcoming battle. She recoils at the suggestion but his insistence
wears her down. The meeting with Radames is partly one of the
great love scenes of opera, partly pure seduction, as Aida lures
him to agree that they must flee together and then asks how
they will avoid the Egyptian army. No love music could be
more fragrant than Aida's, no triumph more complete than
Amonasro's when he learns the chosen route. Radames is
horror-stricken; Amneris and Ramfis (bass), the High Priest,
denounce him as a traitor but, as Amonasro and Aida flee, he
surrenders.

ACT IV. Scene i. A hall in the King's palace. Amneris, now bitterly regretting the doom her jealous denunciation will bring
upon Radames, sends for him and interrogates him. In a passage as taut as advocates making points in a courtroom, she
alternately implores Radames to exculpate himself and rages at
his refusal to do so. When he is three times silent in face of an
accusation of treason, Amneris's fury is turned on the priests in
one of the most powerful passages of writing for mezzo in all
opera.

Scene ii. Above, the Temple of Vulcan; below, a sealed dungeon. Radames is, as he thinks, doomed to perish alone, but a
voice utters his name: Aida has hidden herself to die with him.
Their farewell to life ('O terra addio') has a stillness and finality
that find echo in the almost monotone Amneris, a solitary
mourner in the temple above.

Aida can claim to be one of the nineteenth-century romantic
operas which have best stood the test of time. It is replete with
spectacle but the musical characterisation is unsurpassed; the
tunes are immediate but the writing as subtle as a string quartet;
Aida is part seductress, part faithful lover; Radames as robust as
a games captain but as unself-seeking as a biblical hero;
Amneris outwardly a power-conscious virago but inside a love-

lorn maiden. In a way, it is all things to all men – but there can have been few performances in the last hundred years without the 'house full' signs up outside.

OTELLO

OPERA in four acts by Giuseppe Verdi; text by Arrigo Boito, after Shakespeare's play. Première at la Scala, Milan, February 5, 1887.

*O*TELLO has been described as the 'perfect' opera. Verdi worked with one of Italy's foremost poets, Boito, who was in his own right a composer of rank, to produce an opera at the very height of his powers. Verdi had a hand in the construction of the libretto, although Boito must have the credit for the remarkable feat of compressing the 3,500 lines of Shakespeare's play to under 800. He cut out the Venetian scenes, and each of the four acts plays without a break with no more than a single scene change (in Act III).

ACT I. Cyprus: a quay and the sea, evening. After a *fortissimo* opening chord, the victorious Otello's ship is seen making for port through a heavy storm. Among the crowd are Iago (*baritone*) and Roderigo (*tenor*). The storm prepares us for our first encounter with Otello (*tenor*), whose opening shout of triumph, 'Esultate! L'orgoglio musulmano sepolto è in mar' (O rejoice now! The glory of the Moslems has drowned at sea), shows the warrior in all his ascendancy. He is acclaimed and proceeds to the castle. As the people start a wood fire and dance and sing 'Fuoco di gioia' (Flame of rejoicing), it transpires that Iago hates Otello because he has advanced Cassio (*tenor*) over him; we also discover that Roderigo is in love with Desdemona (*soprano*). Iago sings a drinking song and purposely makes Cassio drunk; sensitive to Roderigo's taunts, Cassio wounds Montano (*bass*) who has tried to quieten them. The tumult brings Otello to the scene. He dismisses Cassio, and Iago has scored his first triumph. Otello and Desdemona are alone. Her presence, and their long love duet, emphasise the important poetic aspect of the Moor's character. Verdi's music encompasses the sensitivity of both lovers: the mature yet impetuous Otello; the serene but passionate Desdemona.

ACT II. A hall on the ground floor of the castle. Iago, planning to make Otello jealous of Desdemona, advises Cassio to induce the Moor's wife to plead for his reinstatement. Alone, Iago sings his famous Credo ('Credo in un Dio crudel': I believe in a cruel God). Otello enters and Iago, to suggestive and fluid music, begins to arouse the Moor's suspicions, which are briefly quelled as Desdemona and Cypriot girls sing a madrigal. But his jealousy is inflamed after Desdemona asks him to pardon Cassio. In a quartet between Desdemona, Emilia (*mezzo-soprano*; her lady-in-waiting and Iago's wife), Otello and Iago, the poison begins to work. Iago takes the opportunity to steal Desdemona's handkerchief, round which so much of the rest of the plot is to turn. Alone with Iago, Otello voices his frustrations ('Ora e per sempre addio': Now and for ever, farewell). Iago pretends to calm him, but Otello hurls him to the ground, threatening to kill him should the accusations prove false. Iago describes a dream he says Cassio had, in which he talked of his love for Desdemona. He caps it all by telling Otello he has even seen in the hands of Cassio the handkerchief which Otello gave his wife when they were married. An enraged Otello pledges himself to prove Desdemona's guilt and Iago joins him in his oath: 'Sì, pel ciel marmoreo giuro' (See me swear, you heav'ns above me!).

ACT III. The great hall of the castle. The approach of the Venetian ambassadors is announced. Again Desdemona, unaware of the cause of Otello's strange actions towards her, pleads for Cassio. On her knees, she vows her constancy, but Otello's mixture of fury, irony and hysteria proves too much for her, and she rushes away. Otello soliloquises, in introspective mood ('Dio, mi potevi scagliar': Had it pleased Heaven to try me with affliction). As Iago re-enters and tells Otello Cassio is at hand, the music rises suddenly to a strident climax. Otello hides as Iago brings in Cassio, who is led to talk about Bianca – Otello, half-hearing, thinks he refers to Desdemona. During the trio, Cassio reveals the handkerchief (Iago has taken it to Cassio's quarters). As trumpets announce the ambassadors, Otello, in a few bars and with the acclamations of the crowd as background, tells Iago that Desdemona shall die in her bed that night. The ambassadors arrive and Lodovico (*bass*) announces Otello's recall to Venice and the appointment of Cassio as Governor of Cyprus. Otello strikes down Desdemona, and all join her plea for mercy. Otello, having ordered everyone to leave, is overcome by rage and emotion and falls in a swoon. The triumphant Iago stands over Otello's prostrate body: 'Ecco il Leone!', as the voices of the crowd acclaim the Moor – the Lion of Venice.

ACT IV. Desdemona's bedroom. After an orchestral introduction of great beauty, Desdemona and Emilia, who is preparing her mistress for bed, have a brief dialogue. Desdemona sings her sorrowful Willow song, 'Piangea cantando', which fades into silence as Emilia goes out, only to be recalled by Desdemona's heartrending cry, 'Ah! Emilia, Emilia, addio!' Desdemona prays before an image of the Virgin, intoning an exquisite 'Ave Maria'. This ends on a high A flat on the violins, and double basses mark Otello's entrance with a *pianissimo* bottom E, five-and-a-half octaves below. He moves to Desdemona's bed, kisses her three times, and tries to make her admit the crime he thinks she has committed; then he smothers her. A knock at the door and Emilia rushes in, crying that Cassio has killed Roderigo. Hearing Desdemona's dying gasp, Emilia screams that her mistress has been murdered. Cassio, Iago and Lodovico enter as Emilia reveals her husband's villainy. Iago escapes. Otello seizes his sword, and sings 'Nium mi tema' (Let no one fear me) before stabbing himself. The music recalls the love duet's 'Un bacio' (A kiss), as Otello dies beside his wife.

Otello's music demonstrates Verdi's skill in portraying the great Shakespearean figure. Unhurried and unrivalled in his entry and when quelling the brawl, he becomes a man of vision and introspection in the Love Duet. In Act II, the perplexed warrior is led step by musical step into Iago's trap, but then explodes into decisiveness as man of action. The same process continues in the third and fourth acts until in his last utterance Otello regains some of the nobility of the opera's opening.

FALSTAFF

OPERA in three acts by Giuseppe Verdi; text by Arrigo Boito. Première at la Scala, Milan, February 9, 1893.

IN both *Otello* and *Macbeth*, Verdi and his librettists had kept as close to Shakespeare as operatic form would allow them. But in *Falstaff*, they contrived to inject a considerable measure of the great Sir John Falstaff of *Henry IV* into the veins of the Falstaff of *The Merry Wives of Windsor*, and so the operatic adaptation is in many ways an improvement on the original.

ACT I. Scene i. A room at the Garter Inn, Windsor – the 'Giarrettiera', as the Italian has it. Dr. Caius (*tenor*) comes to complain that Falstaff (*baritone*) has beaten his servants, and that Bardolph (Bardolfo; *tenor*) and Pistol (Pistola; *bass*) made him drunk and then robbed him. Falstaff laughs and talks him out of countenance; he swears he will never get drunk again, save in the society of honest, sober people, noted for their piety. As he leaves after this grandiloquent statement, Pistol and Bardolph, beating time as they do so, sing an antiphonal 'Amen', until Falstaff stops them, complaining they sing out of time.

He looks at his bill and starts to complain that the prodigal living of his two cronies is reducing him to a state of beggary, and, what is worse, is bringing him perilously close to reducing his weight – and Falstaff, as he rightly says, without his corporation would be a shadow of his real self. The others applaud such self-revelation – 'Falstaff immenso! enorme Falstaff!' – and Falstaff proceeds to tell them that he is currently enamoured of no less than two ladies, the wives of Ford and Page. He has written two love letters, and Bardolph and Pistol are to deliver them. But they refuse; their honour will not allow them. Cursing them, Falstaff sends the notes off by a page, and rounds on the pair of them. What right have they to talk of honour, ruffians that they are? Boito has transplanted the Honour monologue, and here Verdi sets it with incomparable aptness and relish: 'L'onore! Ladri!' At its end, Falstaff picks up a broom and chases Bardolph and Pistol out of the room.

Scene ii. The garden of Ford's house, and the orchestra tells us clearly we are in the presence of the merry wives, Alice Ford (*soprano*), Meg Page (*mezzo-soprano*), and Mistress Quickly (*contralto*). With them is Anne Ford (*soprano*; Nannetta – Anne Page in Shakespeare, with a new patronym). In company with Quickly, Meg has come to show Alice Ford a letter which she has just received from Falstaff. Alice matches Meg's with one of her own, and the four read the two letters which, save for the change of address, are exactly alike. The women plan to avenge themselves upon the fat knight.

Meanwhile Ford (*baritone*) goes walking before his house with Caius, young Fenton (who is in love with Nannetta, but frowned on as a suitor by Ford), Bardolph and Pistol from whom Ford has learned that Falstaff is after his wife. He too meditates revenge, and the female quartet and the male quintet sometimes mingle, sometimes are heard on their own. Fenton (*tenor*) and Nannetta remain behind for a fleeting kiss, and sing a miniature love duet, ending with a phrase of melting beauty.

The women return, but quickly disappear when they think they are being overheard, and once again the two young lovers are alone and can indulge in their battle of kisses. The men re-appear, so do the women, and separately they put the finishing touches to their schemes of revenge. This is the famous ensemble in which Verdi combines what was previously sung separately by the men and the women.

ACT II. Scene i. The Garter Inn. Falstaff is still at table. Bardolph and Pistol beg to be forgiven for their previous infidelity, and tell Falstaff that an old woman is outside asking to be admitted to his presence. Dame Quickly comes in, and, with the orchestra, makes deep obeisance to the knight: 'Reverenza' is set characteristically to a musical representation of a curtsey. Quickly delivers her message, one from each of the ladies, to the effect that Alice will receive the knight, but that Meg's husband guards her too jealously ever to leave her alone. Alice can see him from two till three ('Dalle due alle tre') when her husband is always out. Falstaff repeats the words with evident delight. Quickly is tipped by Falstaff as he dismisses her, again with a magnificent sense of the appropriate gesture. He is left alone with thoughts of his impending success and has time for a little strutting march of self-satisfied triumph ('Va, vecchio John') before his next visitor is announced.

It is Ford, who introduces himself as Master Brook (Signor Fontana). He gives Falstaff a purse of silver as a bait, then tells him that he is in love with Mistress Ford, whose chastity he cannot conquer, and begs Falstaff to lay siege to her and so make the way easier for him. Falstaff gleefully tells him that he has a rendezvous with her that very afternoon, and that he (Master Brook) may be quite sure that he will be able eventually to attain what he so much desires. When Ford asks if Falstaff knows the husband of Alice, he hears himself described with contumelious abuse.

Falstaff goes off to change his clothes, and Ford is left alone, a prey to jealousy in its most tormenting form. His soliloquy in praise of that emotion is one of the great moments of the opera, and moreover a complete re-creation of the Elizabethan delight in the comedy of the outraged cuckold. Falstaff returns, and, after some argument as to who shall go through the door first, they go off arm in arm.

Scene ii. Ford's house. The four women get ready to give Falstaff the reception he deserves. We learn that Ford wants to marry off Nannetta to the aged pedant, Dr. Caius, while she of course wants to marry Fenton. Her mother promises to help.

As Falstaff approaches, Alice starts to play on the lute, to whose accompaniment Falstaff begins to sing her praises in extravagant terms. He sings a little song of irresistible melody: 'Quand' ero paggio del Duca di Norfolk' (When I was page to the Duke of Norfolk's grace), in which he describes his own slender and comely build when he was a boy. They are interrupted by Quickly, who announces that Ford is approaching. Falstaff is hidden behind a screen, just before Ford enters with his followers, hoping to surprise the man who has invaded his home. They begin a search of the rooms.

The women hurry Falstaff into a big washbasket, pile the soiled linen over him, and fasten it down. Scarcely has this been done when Ford comes back and hears the sound of kissing behind the screen. No longer any doubt! Falstaff is hidden there with his wife. He gathers everyone together, marches them towards the screen and knocks it down – to find behind it Nannetta and Fenton. Ford, more furious than ever, rushes out, while his wife and her friends call in the servants, who lift the basket and empty it out of the window into the Thames below. When Ford comes back, his wife leads him to the window and shows him Falstaff striking out for the shore.

ACT III. Scene i. Falstaff is sitting recovering at the Garter. His thoughts are gloomy. The world is in a sorry state, he reflects, when such a pearl of knighthood as himself can be bundled unceremoniously into a basket full of dirty linen and dropped into the water. The host appears with a bottle of wine, and Falstaff's mood alters perceptibly. The scene finishes as a panegyric in praise of wine, with the full orchestra trilling in sympathy as the wine mounts to colour his view of humanity.

Once more Quickly curtseys to him (considerably, it must be admitted, to his dismay), and offers him a rendezvous with Alice. It takes all Quickly's powers of persuasion to get him even to listen, much less to agree to a meeting-place. However, in the end he cannot resist the temptation, and settles for midnight at Herne the Hunter's Oak in Windsor forest, where he is to appear (as we learn a moment later from the concealed Alice and her friends) disguised as the black huntsman himself, who, according to legend, hanged himself from the oak, with the result that the spot is haunted by witches and sprites.

The scene ends with an ensemble as the women and Fenton arrange the details of the evening's fun, and Ford and Caius plot that Caius's betrothal to Nannetta shall be announced that very night. The women call to each other offstage and the strings offer fifteen bars of idyllic commentary as darkness falls.

Scene ii takes place by moonlight under Herne's Oak. Horn-calls and references to the love music form the basis for the prelude to Fenton's aria, which begins the act. Disguises are hastily donned, and in a moment Falstaff is heard arriving. He is wearing a brace of antlers on his head and is wrapped in a heavy cloak. Midnight strikes, echoed at each stroke by Falstaff. For a moment he is alone with Alice, but they are immediately interrupted by noises, and Alice disappears leaving Falstaff to fend for himself.

Nannetta, disguised as Queen of the Fairies, calls her followers around her, and they pirouette until she begins to sing Verdi has given them music of exquisite delicacy.

Bardolph in disguise stumbles on the recumbent figure of Falstaff (who has hidden his face so as not to see the fairies), and calls everyone to him. The merry women, Ford's entourage, and about a hundred others, all disguised and masked, unite in mystifying, taunting, and belabouring Falstaff, until the knight at last recognises Bardolph amongst his tormentors. Everyone unmasks in turn, and mocks Falstaff. He makes a valiant attempt to recapture the initiative by complaining that without his participation a joke seems to have no wit in it, and all – even

Ford – agree that his wit alone is sufficient to redeem him, in spite of his egregious faults.

Ford announces Nannetta's betrothal to Caius, and does the same to another disguised young couple whom Alice leads up to him. He bids them all unmask – to find that Bardolph has been dressed up in Nannetta's clothes and is now therefore betrothed to Caius, and that the other couple were Nannetta and Fenton in disguise. Falstaff cannot resist the temptation to turn Ford's question back on him: who is the dupe now? But Alice will not let him get away with it; he is to be placed beside Ford and Caius; if they are dupes, so is he. Ford is induced to bless his daughter and her sweetheart, and Falstaff leads the company in a final fugue: 'Tutto nel mondo è burla. L'uom è nato burlone' (Jesting is man's vocation. Wise is he who is jolly).

It would take most of a book to describe *Falstaff* in sufficient detail to do anything like justice to the kaleidoscopic variety of the score. There is a sparkle, a rapidity of utterance, a speed of movement, an economy of means in the ensemble writing that has no equal in music written since Mozart, and every bar is endowed with a refinement of expression and a restraint that it would be difficult to imagine in the composer of the operas written before *Macbeth*. The music is even more fluid than in *Otello* and rhythmic ideas are caught up, dropped, and used again with a dexterity which Shakespeare himself never excelled in his own medium. It is all as light as air, and yet out of it has been fashioned Shakespeare's Falstaff drawn appropriately in the round, speaking Italian but more English at heart than in any English musical re-creation of him.

Amilcare Ponchielli
(1834–1886)

La Gioconda

OPERA in four acts; text by Arrigo Boito (under pseudonym of Tobia Gorrio). Première at la Scala, Milan, April 8, 1876.

ACT I. Seventeenth-century Venice. The courtyard of the Doge's Palace decorated for a popular festivity. The prelude puts forward la Cieca's aria from Act I, later used to recall the indebtedness she and la Gioconda feel towards Laura. The populace sings in festive mood before leaving to watch the regatta, leaving Barnaba (*baritone*), a spy, to observe the ballad singer la Gioconda (*soprano*) lead on her blind mother, la Cieca (*contralto*). Barnaba lusts after Gioconda, who has consistently spurned him. She for her part loves Enzo Grimaldo (*tenor*), a nobleman proscribed by the Venetian authorities and now in the city in the guise of a sea captain. (To complete the amorous tangle, it should be noted that he is still in love with Laura, to whom he was betrothed until she was obliged to marry the much older Alvise, one of the heads of the State In-quisition.)

Barnaba again makes advances to Gioconda, who runs off leaving her mother a prey to Barnaba's machinations. Oppor-tunity arises when the crowd returns from the regatta with the winner and the loser, Zuane (*bass*), to whom Barnaba suggests that his defeat was caused by the witchcraft of the old blind woman sitting silently by the steps. His friends help him drag her from the church steps and only the intervention of Enzo ('Assassini!') saves her from the mob. Alvise (*bass*) comes down the great stairs of the palace with Laura (*mezzo-soprano*), who is masked and who demands justice for the old blind woman. Alvise orders her release and in her gratitude she gives Laura her most cherished possession, a rosary ('A te questo rosario').

Barnaba meanwhile has observed Laura and Enzo exchange meaningful glances and once the crowd has left, with an eye to the main chance, he taxes Enzo with his true identity ('Enzo Grimaldo, Principe di Santafior') and, in a justly famous tenor-baritone duet, explains that he will advance his own cause with Gioconda by bringing Laura to Enzo's ship so that they may elope together. Enzo departs; Barnaba summons one of his tools, Isèpo (*tenor*), the public scribe, and dictates a letter anonymously informing Alvise of the situation. Gioconda over-hears but does not know to whom the letter is addressed. Bar-naba drops it into the Lion's Mouth, the infamous method of anonymous denunciation to the state spying system: 'O monu-mento' is his soliloquy, a blueprint one might think for Iago's Credo eleven years later, also with words by Boito. The act ends with the crowd dancing, and a prayer from the church, during which Gioconda laments Enzo's unfaithfulness.

ACT II. The deck of Enzo's ship. Sailors sing and Barnaba, with his net set for Enzo and Laura, has a fisherman's ballad, 'Ah, pescator affonda l'esca'. Enzo comes on deck to sing one of the two most famous numbers of the opera, 'Cielo e mar' (O sky and sea), which testifies to his love for Laura, who, ferried by Barnaba, is quickly on the scene. Their love is expressed at first almost formally, as Enzo urges her to put fear behind her ('Deh! non turbare'). She tells him she recognised him instantly in the sailor she saw in front of the palace, and he again enjoins confi-dence ('Deh! non tremar'), until their voices combine in a passionate duet, 'Laggiù, nelle nebbie remote' (Yonder, amid the far-off mists).

Enzo leaves her to prepare their flight, and Gioconda steals on board to confront her rival in a duet that is the most dramatic number of the score: 'L'amo come il fulgor del creato' (I adore him as the light of creation), one of the gems of the mezzo-soprano repertory. Gioconda points to Alvise's armed followers approaching in a boat and is about to stab Laura when she sees la Cieca's rosary round Laura's neck. Instantly, she changes plan and bundles Laura into a boat towards safety, thwarting Barnaba of his prey and confronting Enzo when he returns. Seeing Alvise's men approaching, he impulsively sets fire to the boat.

ACT III. Scene i. A room in Alvise's palace. Alvise plans vengeance ('Sì! morir ella de'!': Yes, to die is her doom), and instructs Laura in a powerful scene to take poison before the serenade heard outside has finished. He has reckoned without Gioconda, who, to save her mother's saviour, has hidden in the palace and now exchanges a powerful sleeping draught for the poison. Laura takes it; Alvise finds the empty phial and believes his orders carried out.

Scene ii. A hall in the palace. Alvise receives his guests for whose benefit the popular Dance of the Hours is performed. Barnaba drags in la Cieca, whom he has found hiding in the house and who says she comes to pray for the recently dead. Barnaba whispers to Enzo that her prayers are for Laura, and when the passing bell is heard, Enzo leads a great ensemble, 'Già ti veggo immota e smorta' (I behold thee motionless and pallid) at whose end Laura is revealed lying apparently dead.

ACT IV. A room in a ruined palace on the Giudecca island. Two men carry the body of Laura into Gioconda's dwelling. She has bargained with Barnaba to give herself to him in return for Enzo's release from prison, and for a moment in a dramatic soliloquy – a 'terrible song' it has been called – she contemplates suicide: 'Suicidio!' Enzo enters and Gioconda excites his rage by telling him she has had Laura's body removed from the burial vault, where he will no longer find it. He threatens her with a knife when the voice of Laura, awake from her narcotic, is heard. Both Laura and Enzo pour out words of gratitude before they leave and Gioconda is once more alone. The thought of her bargain with Barnaba spurs her to flee, but the spy himself appears. He starts to work up a passion ('Ebbrezza! delirio') as she adorns herself with mock jewellery, but she seizes an opportunity and stabs herself fatally with a dagger. 'You wanted my body, you demon. My body you shall have!' she screams at him, and is dead before he can shout into her deaf ears: 'Last night your mother offended me. I suffocated her!'

La Gioconda is Ponchielli's only significant operatic success. Given the relative operatic famine in Italy after Verdi's *Aida* (1871) – his next opera would be *Otello* (1887) – this is perhaps not surprising. One may still find the over-ripe romanticism, not to say obscurity, of the book to a considerable extent compensated by the luscious tunes and skilful pacing of the score.

Arrigo Boito
(1842–1918)

MEFISTOFELE

FOUR acts; première, Milan, 1868. In the prologue Mephistopheles (*bass*) wagers that he will entice Faust (*tenor*) to evil. In Frankfurt he offers to make Faust the companion of his wanderings, upon certain conditions. Faust, rejuvenated, makes an assignation with Margherita (*soprano*), then attends the Witches' Sabbath in the Brocken. Later Margherita, imprisoned for drowning her child, has lost her reason; when Faust and Mephistopheles enter she revives a little, but then shrinks away from Faust and, praying for mercy, expires, her soul saved. Faust is next taken to the Vale of Tempe, where Helen of Troy (*soprano*) appears to him; they pledge their love. In the epilogue, Faust, once more an old man, mourns his life. Mephistopheles tempts him again, but he resists and dies clutching the Bible.

Ruggiero Leoncavallo
(1858–1919)

PAGLIACCI
The Strolling Players

OPERA in two acts; words by the composer. Première, Teatro dal Verme, Milan, May 21, 1892.

*P*AGLIACCI opens with a prologue. After an instrumental introduction, Tonio pokes his head through the curtains – 'Si puo? Signore, Signori' (By your leave, Ladies and Gentlemen) – comes out and sings. The prologue, successful even as a concert piece, indicates the story of the opera in musical phrases we shall hear again.

ACT I. The edge of the village of Montalto, in Calabria. People are celebrating the Feast of the Assumption. The opening chorus, 'Son qua' (They're here), anticipates the arrival of the players. Beppe (*tenor*), in his Harlequin costume, enters leading a donkey cart in which reclines Nedda (*soprano*). Behind her, in his Pagliaccio costume, is Canio (*tenor*), beating the drum. Tonio (*baritone*), dressed as Taddeo the clown, brings up the rear.

Canio addresses the crowd. At eleven o'clock the play will begin. They will witness the troubles of poor Pagliaccio, and the vengeance he wreaked on the treacherous Clown. Tonio attempts to help Nedda out of the cart, but is shoved aside by Canio, who lifts his wife down himself. Tonio goes off muttering threats against Canio. As the people leave, a villager suggests that Tonio will stay behind in order to woo Nedda. Canio says grimly that in the play he risks a beating, but in real life, let anyone who would try to rob him of Nedda's love beware.

Church bells ring as the villagers sing the chorus, 'Din, don, suona vespero' ('Ding, dong, the vespers bell'). Canio and Beppe go towards the village tavern. Nedda is alone. Canio's words and manner worry her but the birds are singing and Nedda recalls her childhood, 'O! che volo d'augelli' (Ah, you beautiful songbirds), which leads to her vivacious *ballatella*, 'Stridono lassù' (Forever flying through the boundless sky).

Tonio appears and protests his love for Nedda. The more passionately he pleads, the more she mocks him and the angrier he grows. He tries to kiss her, but she seizes a whip and strikes him across the face. He goes off, swearing vengeance.

Silvio (*baritone*), Nedda's lover, arrives, assuring her it is safe for them to meet as Canio is drinking at the tavern. He begs Nedda to run away with him after that night's performance. She is at first afraid but eventually agrees. After an impassioned love duet, 'E allor perchè, di', tu m'hai stregato' (Why hast thou taught me love's magic story), the lovers agree not to see each other again until they elope after the play.

Tonio has overheard Silvio and Nedda and fetches Canio from the tavern. He arrives just in time to hear Nedda call, 'Tonight, love, and forever I am yours'. Canio, dagger drawn, rushes to overtake the fugitive, but Nedda interposes herself and allows Silvio to escape. The enraged Canio demands to know his name, but Nedda refuses to give it. Canio rushes at her, but is restrained by Tonio and Beppe; Nedda's lover will be at the play – a look or gesture will betray him.

As the others leave to prepare for the performance, Canio expresses his grief over Nedda's betrayal. 'Vesti la giubba' (On with the motley) is one of the most famous arias in all opera. 'Ridi Pagliaccio' (Laugh then, Pagliaccio), sobs Canio, as he prepares for the performance. It is the old story of the clown who must laugh, and make others laugh, even though his heart is breaking.

ACT II. The theatre is prepared and the audience (including Silvio) are in their seats waiting impatiently for the performance to begin. Nedda, dressed as Columbine, goes about with a plate, collecting money, pausing to murmur a few words of warning to Silvio. She goes backstage.

A bell rings, and the curtain rises. Columbine is anxious. Her husband, Pagliaccio, is away until morning. Taddeo is at the market and she is waiting for her lover, Harlequin. A minuet provides the musical background.

A guitar is heard outside. It is Harlequin, singing a serenade, 'O Colombina, il tenero fido Arlecchin' (O Columbine, unbar to me thy lattice high). Tonio, as Taddeo, enters with a basket on his arm. He makes advances to Columbine; she summons Harlequin (Beppe), who enters and throws Taddeo out. Harlequin has brought a bottle of wine, also a sleeping potion which she is to give her husband, thus giving them the chance to run off.

Taddeo bursts in – Pagliaccio is approaching, he suspects her and is stamping with anger. Harlequin hops out of the window, telling his Columbine to pour the philtre into Pagliaccio's wine. She calls after him, just as Canio, in the character of Pagliaccio, appears in the door: 'Tonight, love, and forever I am yours!' – the same words Canio heard his wife call to her lover a few hours before. Columbine tells Pagliaccio that no one is with her, except for Taddeo who is hiding in the cupboard. His terrified voice is heard, and the audience laughs.

Suddenly Canio breaks character. He demands Nedda reveal her real lover's name. The more Nedda tries to keep up the play, the more desperate Canio becomes, insisting that he is not Pagliaccio but a real man with real feelings. The audience praises his intensity as great acting. Silvio begins to worry.

Still desperately trying to keep up appearances, Nedda sings a gavotte, 'Suvvia, così terribile' (I never knew, my dear, that you were such a tragic fellow). She stops, as Canio grabs a knife from the table and demands her lover's name. By now the audience is nervous. Nedda tries to leave the stage, but Canio catches and stabs her. She screams to Silvio who rushes to help her. Canio leaps at him and stabs him, then stands stupefied:

'La commedia è finita' (The comedy is ended), he says in a broken voice.

Pietro Mascagni
(1863–1945)

CAVALLERIA RUSTICANA
Rustic Chivalry

OPERA in one act; text by G. Menasci and G. Targioni-Tozzetti, based on a story of G. Verga. Première, May 17, 1890, at Teatro Costanzi, Rome.

*V*ERISMO in Grove's Dictionary (1954) is 'a term used to classify Italian opera of a sensational supposedly "realistic" kind, including the works of Mascagni, Leoncavallo, Puccini, Giordano etc.' Other works of reference (including the New Grove, 1980), less tendentiously, allow that the essential difference between *verismo* operas and their predecessors lies in the libretti, which deal with everyday situations as opposed to costume plays and historical episodes or legends.

But whatever definition may be preferred, the average operagoer understands from the word a distinct comment on the music, and expects something demanding first and foremost power and attack from the singer and only secondarily a smooth legato or any relevance to the art of *bel canto*. This is very far from being the whole truth, and it is the more unfortunate that the *verismo* school is often (in dictionary or history) held to have started with *Cavalleria Rusticana*, whose subject is sensational in that it deals with a story contemporary to the 1880's but whose composer at that time wrote as an instinctive successor to Bellini.

Cavalleria Rusticana is based on a compact and tense short story by Giovanni Verga, which also inspired the stage play. It is a drama of swift action and intense emotion; of passion, betrayal, and retribution. In this opera, Mascagni, at the age of twenty-six, 'found himself', and ever after was trying, not quite so successfully, to find himself again.

The prelude contains three significant passages in the development of the story: the phrase of the despairing Santuzza; the melody of the duet between Santuzza and Turiddu; and the *Siciliana*, which, as part of the prelude, is sung by Turiddu behind the curtain in the manner of a serenade to Lola: 'O Lola, ch'ai di latti' (O Lola, fair as a smiling flower).

The scene is a public square in a Sicilian village. It is Easter morning. Church bells ring, followed by a chorus which combines delight in the beauty of the day with the lilt of religious feeling. Santuzza (*soprano*) approaches Mamma Lucia's (*contralto*) house, just as she emerges. She asks for Turiddu (*tenor*), but his mother says he has gone to Francofonte to fetch wine for the trattoria. Santuzza tells her that he was seen during the night in the village. Mamma Lucia, touched by the girl's distress, asks her into her house, an offer Santuzza refuses – secretly, she is pregnant and feels excommunicated.

Mamma Lucia's questions on her son's whereabouts are interrupted by the sounds of a whip cracking and bells jingling. Alfio (*baritone*), the carter, makes an entrance (usually with horse and cart), accompanied by the villagers. He sings his cheerful song, praising a carter's life and the beauty of his wife, Lola (*mezzo-soprano*). The villagers join in the chorus, 'Il cavallo scalpita' (Gaily sound the horse's hooves). Alfio asks Mamma Lucia if she still has some of her fine old wine, but she tells him that Turiddu has gone to buy fresh supplies. Alfio says he has seen her son that very morning, not far from his own cottage. Santuzza signals to Mamma Lucia to keep silent.

Alfio leaves. A choir from the church sings the 'Regina Coeli', and the people in the square join in with the 'Allelujahs'. All kneel and led by Santuzza sing the Easter Hymn, 'Inneggiamo, il Signor non è morto' (Let us sing of the Lord now victorious).

Mamma Lucia asks Santuzza to explain Turiddu's presence in the village. 'Voi lo sapete, o mamma' (Mother, you know the story), she sings, and in one of the most impassioned numbers of the score tells the story of her betrayal. Turiddu was in love with Lola but left to go into the army, whereupon the fickle Lola married Alfio. On his return, Turiddu took up with Santuzza, made her pregnant, but went back to Lola, whom he sees when Alfio is on one of his frequent absences. Mamma Lucia pities Santuzza, who begs her to go to church and pray for her.

We see and hear Turiddu for the first time since the prelude. Santuzza upbraids him for pretending to have gone away when he is really visiting Lola. But when Turiddu admits his life would be in danger if he were caught by Alfio, Santuzza is terrified: 'Battimi, insultami, t'amo e perdono' (Beat me, insult me, I still love and forgive you').

The mood is interrupted by Lola. Her carefree song, 'Fior di giaggiolo' (O gentle flower of gold), is a key to her nature. She mocks Santuzza and goes into church. As Turiddu makes to follow her, Santuzza begs him to stay: 'No, no, Turiddu'. Turiddu repulses her and throws her to the ground. As he goes into church, she curses him.

Alfio comes on the scene, looking for Lola. Santuzza in the fewest possible words and in the white heat of suppressed passion tells him of his wife's infidelity. Alfio's outburst has the strength of genuine passion and the outcome seems no longer in doubt. Santuzza and Alfio leave.

The famous *intermezzo* recapitulates in its forty-eight bars what has gone before, and foreshadows the tragedy that impends, so justifying a century of world-wide popularity.

The congregation emerges into the sunshine. Turiddu, in high spirits because he is with Lola and because Santuzza is no longer hanging round to reproach him, invites his friends over to his mother's wineshop. Their glasses are filled and Turiddu dashes off a drinking song: 'Viva il vino spumeggiante' (Hail! The ruby wine now flowing). Alfio appears and Turiddu offers him wine, but he refuses. The women sense trouble and leave, taking Lola with them. In a brief exchange Alfio challenges Turiddu and in Sicilian fashion the two men embrace, Turiddu, in token of acceptance, biting Alfio's ear. Alfio goes off to prepare for the fight.

Turiddu calls for his mother. He tells her he is going away: 'Mamma, quel vino è generoso' (Mamma, the red wine burns me like fire), he sings, and his aria mounts in tension as in great melodic phrases and a flood of remorse he begs his mother, if he does not come back, to look after Santuzza.

He goes, as Santuzza comes in to comfort the weeping Mamma Lucia. People crowd in. All is suppressed excitement. There is a murmur of distant voices. A woman's voice is heard and repeats with a shriek: 'Hanno ammazzato compare Turiddu!' (They have murdered neighbour Turiddu). Mamma Lucia is supported by the women, but Santuzza falls in a swoon.

Umberto Giordano
(1867–1948)

ANDREA CHÉNIER

OPERA in four acts; text by Luigi Illica. Première at la Scala, Milan, on March 28, 1896.

HISTORICAL as a character though André Chénier was, Giordano's librettist, Luigi Illica, has turned his life into fiction. Chénier was a poet, dreamer, and patriot; born in Constantinople, he returned to Paris for his education, and there became a participant in the Revolution, and later its victim.

ACT I. Ballroom in a château. Preparations are in train for a big party, and Charles Gérard (*baritone*) is amongst the servants setting the room to rights. He mocks at the falsities and conventions of aristocratic life, but his words take on a more menacing character when, provoked by the sight of his old father carrying in some furniture, he launches forth into a denunciation of the masters he works for and the system which keeps them in their unearned luxury: 'Son sessant'anni' (For more than sixty years). The Countess de Coigny (*mezzo-soprano*), her daughter Madeleine (*soprano*), and Bersi, Madeleine's mulatto maid (*mezzo-soprano*), come to see that the last-minute preparations for the party are going well. Gérard comments on the beauty of the daughter of the house, with whom he is secretly in love.

The guests arrive, notable amongst them the Abbé (*tenor*) and Fléville (*baritone*), the latter of whom introduces an Italian musician, and the poet Chénier (*tenor*). After a pastoral chorus, Chénier, who has declined the Countess's request that he read a poem, agrees to recite at Madeleine's invitation.

He sings the well-known *Improvviso di Chénier*, 'Un dì, all' azzurro spazio' (One day, in the blue heaven), in which he contrasts the beauty of nature with the misery man makes around him; he denounces the selfishness of those in authority and his extremist sentiments find little favour with the guests (though the aria itself has become enormously popular since first sung).

Madeleine apologises to him for the situation her request has put them in, but the Countess quickly gets the band to strike up a gavotte. Gérard bursts in at the head of a band of beggars, announcing, butler-like, 'His Lordship, Misery!' The major-domo (*baritone*) gets them to leave, but not before Gérard has torn his coat from his back, and denounced it as a sign of slavery. The gaiety recommences and amusement goes on as if nothing has happened.

ACT II. The Café Hottot in Paris. The first phase of the Revolution is over, and at one side of the stage is an altar-like affair, on which stands a bust of Marat. Chénier sits alone at a table, and at another are Bersi and Incredibile (*tenor*), the spy. Bersi asks whether it is true that there are spies about and remarks that she herself has nothing to fear. Incredibile reads aloud from the note he is making about Bersi and about Chénier, each of whom he thinks a suspicious character.

Roucher (*bass*) goes up to Chénier with a passport which he has been influential in getting for him. He must flee at once, as he has powerful enemies. Chénier sings of his confidence in his own destiny: 'Credo a una possanza arcana' (I believe in a sovereign power). He has received several anonymous letters from a woman, whose image has been built up in his mind until she is the most beautiful creature he has ever imagined. Chénier is about to leave, when Robespierre and several other leading Revolutionaries appear, followed by a cheering crowd. Gérard is one of the leaders, and Incredibile stops him to enquire more details about the woman he is trying to find. Gérard gives him a lyrical description of the beauty of Madeleine. Roucher is approached by Bersi, who tells him that someone wishes to see Chénier.

Madeleine arrives at the meeting-place and is soon joined by Chénier. It is some moments before he recognises her and discovers that it was she who wrote the letters he has been receiving; at the same time, Incredibile looks from his hiding-place and makes up his mind that this is the woman Gérard is looking for. Madeleine asks Chénier for help in her loneliness, and he avows his love in a passionate duet. They are about to rush away together, when Gérard appears in their path, closely followed by the spy and by Roucher. Chénier shouts to his friend Roucher to take Madeleine into his charge, and he and Gérard draw their swords. Gérard falls wounded, and recognises his opponent; he murmurs to him to be on his guard – he is on Fouquier-Tinville's list as a counter-revolutionary.

Incredibile returns with police, a crowd collects and demands vengeance on the assailant of a leader of the people; but Gérard says he did not recognise his attacker.

ACT III. The Revolutionary Tribunal. Mathieu (*baritone*) tries to get the crowd to contribute money and valuables to the common fund. The response is listless, until Gérard comes in and makes an impassioned speech. Immediately, all are ready to give, not least amongst them an old woman (Madelon; *mezzo-soprano*), who says that she has already lost two sons fighting for France, but now offers the youngest. The crowd disperses singing the revolutionary song, *La Carmagnole*.

Gérard asks Incredibile whether there is news of either Chénier or Madeleine – as to the former, a newsboy can be heard crying that he is arrested, and the latter, says the spy, will not be long in coming to look for her lover. Gérard is shocked by the spy's cynicism, still more so when Incredibile urges him to write out the indictment against Chénier; it will be needed for the forthcoming session of the Tribunal.

Gérard is haunted by conscience and memory of his former patriotic enthusiasm. Can he denounce Chénier as 'an enemy of his country' ('Nemico della patria')? His revolutionary zeal, which formerly fed on such ideals as brotherly love, is now kept alive by jealousy and lust. It is an effective outburst. He impulsively signs the indictment.

Madeleine is brought in by Mathieu, and Gérard explains

that Chénier has been arrested by his orders and because of his own passion for her. She turns from him, but then offers her love in exchange for Chénier's freedom. She tells Gérard the story of her mother's horrible death, in the flames of her house as it was burned by the mob: 'La mamma morta'. The tribunal is ready to sit and the people crowd into the court.

The Tribunal is in session. Several prisoners are summarily condemned. When Chénier's turn comes, he is refused permission by the court to answer the charge. On Gérard's insistence, he is finally allowed to defend himself. He has fought for his country and his ideals with sword and with pen; let them now take his life, but leave his honour unstained: 'Sì, fui soldato' (Yes, I was a soldier). Gérard raises his voice in Chénier's defence; the indictment was false, he says. But all is in vain, and the death sentence is duly passed and acclaimed.

ACT IV In the courtyard of the Prison of St. Lazare. Chénier waits for the tumbril. Roucher is with him, and when he finishes writing, his friend asks him to read the poem he has written. 'Come un bel dì di Maggio' (just as a fine day in May time) he sings in a beautiful aria which describes his feelings as a poet in the face of death. Gérard appears at the outer gate, with Madeleine, and the gaoler lets them in. He agrees to allow Madeleine to take the place of a female prisoner condemned to death, and so to die with Chénier. Gérard leaves, determined to make a last effort in their defence, and Chénier is brought in. Their duet is on a grand scale; they exult in their love and rejoice that death will unite them for ever: 'Vicino a te' (Close at your side). In an opera in which Giordano has indulged to the full his gift for passionate, lyrical melody, it is fitting that the most lyrical and passionate moments should come in the short last act, in the shape of Chénier's aria and the great duet.

Luigi Cherubini
(1760–1842)

MÉDÉE
Medea

THREE acts; text after Euripides. Première, Paris, 1797. Jason (*tenor*) recovered the Golden Fleece from Colchis with the help of the King's daughter Medea (*soprano*), a sorceress. They returned to Thessaly but Jason eventually abandoned her and took their two sons to Corinth. There he is to marry King

Creon's daughter Glauce (*soprano*). Medea arrives and tries to reawaken his love, but in vain; she threatens a terrible retribution. Creon urges her to flee but grants her an extra day in Corinth; she asks to see her children. She orders her servant Neris (*mezzo-soprano*) to present Glauce with a sacred diadem and mantle – which she has poisoned. Medea invokes the help of the Infernal Gods, weakening as she sees her children but rehearsing her vengeful purpose until her heart is pitiless. Glauce dies; Medea, in an orgy of vengeance, kills her children and sets fire to the temple.

Daniel François Auber
(1782–1871)

Fra Diavolo

THREE acts; première, Paris, 1830. The chivalrous bandit leader Fra Diavolo (*tenor*) has a price on his head. Lorenzo (*tenor*), an officer, and his men are drinking in a Naples tavern; the daughter of the innkeeper, Zerlina (*soprano*), is Lorenzo's sweetheart. A wealthy Englishman, Lord Cockburn (*tenor*), and his wife, Lady Pamela (*mezzo-soprano*), arrive, complaining that her jewellery has been stolen. The Marquis of San Marco (in reality Fra Diavolo) is announced, and is told of the robbery. He flatters Lord Cockburn into revealing where his money is hidden. Meanwhile Lorenzo and his men have killed a number of bandits and recovered the jewellery. That night Fra Diavolo with his men Beppo and Giacomo hide in Zerlina's room in order to rob the English pair next door. He is forced to reveal himself, but in doing so compromises both Zerlina and Lady Pamela. Next day Lorenzo reproaches Zerlina who is indignant. They discover that Beppo and Giacomo are followers of Diavolo; Lorenzo orders them to give the all-clear signal and Diavolo is ambushed and shot.

Giacomo Meyerbeer
(1791–1864)

Les Huguenots

OPERA in five acts; text by A. E. Scribe after Deschamps. Première at the Opéra, Paris, February 29, 1836.

Born in Berlin, Meyerbeer, with an independent income, set out to study opera. He started in Germany, where he wrote his first works; from 1815 lived in Italy and wrote Italian operas in a post-Rossini style; and from 1825 was active in Paris, where his *Robert le Diable* followed Spontini's Paris operas, Rossini's *Guillaume Tell* and Auber's *La Muette de Portici* in establishing spectacular opera on a grand scale as a French speciality.

The background to *Les Huguenots* is political, just before the Massacre of St. Bartholomew in 1572, when feeling between Catholics and Huguenots was running murderously high. The feud came to an end only with the accession in 1589 of Henri IV (a Huguenot), who later in 1572 married the Catholic Marguerite de Valois, daughter of Catherine de' Medici and sister of François II, Charles IX and Henri III (and therefore sister-in-law of Mary Queen of Scots).

The action revolves round Marguerite's attempt to effect a dynastic and 'politically correct' marriage between the prominent Huguenot Raoul de Nangis and Valentine, daughter of a leading Catholic noble. Quite fortuitously, they are already half in love, but equally fortuitously de Nangis is led to believe – erroneously – that there exists a liaison between Valentine and de Nevers, a womanising Catholic leader.

ACT I. Touraine. Count de Nevers (*baritone*) has invited friends to a party at his château. Among them is the Huguenot Raoul de Nangis (*tenor*), who makes his entrance with considerable musical panache. Invited to toast his love in a song, Raoul obliges: 'Plus blanche que la blanche hermine'. A viola obbligato adds spice to the romance, in which he praises an unknown beauty whom he recently rescued from a group of students. Raoul's retainer, Marcel (*bass*), defies the Catholics with a stout rendition of 'Ein' feste Burg', which provokes amusement and elicits from Marcel a brisk Huguenot battle song: 'Piff, paff, pouff'. De Nevers is called away, and Raoul sees him outside in the garden with a woman he recognises, to his considerable consternation, as the lady he rescued not so long ago. He immediately assumes a liaison between them.

De Nevers rejoins his guests and Urbain (*soprano* or *mezzo-soprano*), page to Marguerite de Valois, makes his entrance with a brilliant recitative ('Nobles Seigneurs, salut!') and aria, one of the jewels of the mezzo-soprano repertory. Urbain has been instructed by his mistress to conduct Raoul, blindfolded and knowing nothing of the circumstances, to a rendezvous with an unknown lady. The Catholics are impressed that Raoul is sought after by so important a Catholic.

ACT II. In the garden of the Château de Chenonceaux, Marguerite (*soprano*) sings of the beauties of Touraine ('O beau pays de la Touraine'), following with a spectacular cabaletta ('A ce mot tout s'anime'). It was at Marguerite's behest that Valentine (*soprano*) has just visited de Nevers to ask him to release her from her engagement to him, a request which, however reluctantly, he granted. A so-called bathers' chorus and a scene for Marguerite and Urbain precede the removal of the bandage from Raoul's eyes, and his graceful compliments to the beautiful but unknown lady he sees before him (Duet: 'Beauté divine, enchanteresse'). Raoul has pledged his word, and when it is proposed that he marry the daughter of the Count de St. Bris he immediately consents, only, on recognising the woman he thinks is having an affair with de Nevers, to reject her with indignation. The Catholics sense an insult and bloodshed is narrowly averted by the intervention of Marguerite.

ACT III. Paris. The Huguenots sing a 'Rataplan' chorus, to the indignation of Catholics assembling for the marriage of de Nevers and Valentine, whose engagement has been renewed. Marcel brings a challenge from Raoul to St. Bris (*baritone*); Catholic nobles conspire to lead Raoul into an ambush and avenge the insult to St. Bris's daughter. But Valentine still loves Raoul and makes haste in an impressive duet to alert Marcel to his master's danger.

Before the duel occurs a stirring septet ('En mon bon droit j'ai confiance'), one of the score's finest numbers, and when the ambush is uncovered and Marcel summons the Huguenots to Raoul's aid, there is an effective climax in a double chorus. Excitement subsides with the arrival of Marguerite, who tells Raoul of his fatal misapprehension, but the finale employs ballet as well as chorus and military band as de Nevers conducts Valentine to their wedding.

ACT IV. In her home, where she is now the wife of de Nevers, Raoul seeks out Valentine to hear her confirm what Marguerite has told him. He hides when St. Bris, de Nevers and other noblemen enter and discuss a plan to be carried out that very night – the Eve of St. Bartholomew – to massacre the Huguenots. They join their voices in an ensemble of dedication, the so-called Bénédiction des Poignards, the blessing of the swords, and only de Nevers opts out of a plan which seems to him treacherous and dishonourable.

Valentine's decision to warn Raoul leads to the climax of the opera, the great duet for soprano and tenor in which she entreats him not to go to what she sees as certain death. They proclaim their love in one of Meyerbeer's greatest melodies: 'Tu l'as dit, oui, tu m'aimes' (Thou hast said it; aye, thou lov'st me). The voices rise slowly in succession to a high C flat, and Raoul's cadenza involves a D flat taken softly.

ACT V. Coligny, the Huguenot leader, has already been killed, Huguenots are being massacred, and Raoul, wounded,

rushes into the Hôtel de Nesle where the marriage of Marguerite de Valois and Henri IV is to be celebrated.

In a Huguenot churchyard, Marcel blesses Valentine and
Raoul, whose marriage has become a possibility with the death
of de Nevers. St. Bris and his followers approach, there is a vol-
ley of musketry and only too late does he discover that his zea-
lotry has killed his own daughter. (The opera is long and few
performances include the whole of Act V.)

L'AFRICAINE
The African Girl

FIVE acts, by Giacomo Meyerbeer; première, Paris, 1865.
Vasco da Gama (*tenor*), an explorer, awaited longingly by
his fiancée Inez (*soprano*), returns after two years' absence. He
has brought two African captives, Selika (*soprano*) and Nelusko
(*baritone*), as proof that he can find the land beyond Africa. Don
Pedro (*bass*) contrives to make these plans look futile; Vasco's
angry reaction lands him in prison.

Selika, in reality a queen, loves Vasco. She shows him the
route to the Indies. Inez arrives and to secure Vasco's release
agrees to marry Don Pedro, who is to lead the new expedition,
with Nelusko as pilot. Don Pedro's ship is wrecked and Nelusko's men kill or capture everyone on board. Selika is welcomed
home, claiming that Vasco is her husband. He seems to return
her love, but then hears Inez's voice. Selika magnanimously
arranges for Inez and Vasco to escape. She lies beneath the
poisonous mançanilla tree watching the ship carry away her
love, and Nelusko finds her dead.

Hector Berlioz
(1803–1869)

LES TROYENS
The Trojans

OPERA in five acts; text by the composer after Virgil. The work was not
produced in its entirety until twenty-one years after the composer's
death. Part II was first performed at the Théâtre-Lyrique, Paris,
November 4, 1863.

*L*ES TROYENS is Berlioz's greatest opera, and in many respects his greatest achievement. In it he unites his yearning for the classicism of Gluck, for design and form, with his own passion for what is expressive and vivid.

Berlioz's life-long enthusiasm for Virgil was second only to his love for Shakespeare; in fact, both contribute to the libretto of *Les Troyens*, the former to the narrative of the love of Dido for Aeneas as told in the first, second and fourth books of the *Aeneid*, the latter to the interpolation of the scene for Jessica and Lorenzo from *The Merchant of Venice*, which provides words for the great love duet between Dido and Aeneas in Act IV.

Les Troyens begins at the point in the Trojan war when the Trojans have lost Hector, the Greeks Achilles and Patroclus, and the Trojans have reason to believe that their enemies have had enough. The war has lasted for over nine years, and the Greeks have retired, leaving behind them the wooden horse.

PART I: *La Prise de Troie*

ACT I. Scene i. The abandoned camp of the Greeks on the wooded plain in front of Troy. The people rejoice that their ten years of confinement are over. There is talk of the wooden horse, and all rush off to see this curiosity, everyone except Cassandra (*soprano*), who prophesies the doom of Troy: 'Malheureux roi!' (Unhappy King!)[1] Even Choroebus (*baritone*), her lover, believes that her mind is deranged. He tries to console her, but she continues to predict the fall of the city and his death. She is unable to persuade him to leave Troy, but resigns herself to death on the morrow.

The character of Cassandra is splendidly depicted in the opening scene. The classical feeling of the opening aria shows Berlioz's affinity with his beloved Gluck, and the duet between Cassandra and Choroebus is full of feeling.

Scene ii. In front of the Citadel. The Trojans celebrate their deliverance from the Greeks with a procession and public games. The music is a great hymn of thanksgiving. Hector's widow Andromache and her son Astyanax, dressed in white clothes of mourning, place flowers at the foot of an altar, while Cassandra foretells for them an even greater sorrow than they have yet known.

Aeneas (*tenor*) rushes in, describing the terrible scene he has just witnessed on the seashore. The priest, Laocoön, suspecting some hidden design of the Greeks, threw a javelin into the side of the wooden horse, whereupon two serpents came up out of the sea and devoured him. All express horror and fear at this

---

[1] Translations throughout by Edward Dent.

phenomenon in a magnificent octet with chorus: 'Châtiment affroyable' (At a doom so appalling). Aeneas suggests that the disaster may have been brought upon them by Pallas, outraged at the insult to the horse, which has been dedicated to her. They should placate her by bringing the image within the walls and taking it to her temple. Cassandra, who is left alone, laments the step they are taking, which, she predicts, will lead to sure disaster.

To the sound of a march, the horse is dragged inside the city walls. In spite of the rumour that the sound of arms has been heard coming from inside the horse, the people persist in greeting its arrival with joy, and the sound of their song grows gradually in volume until it fills the whole city. Only Cassandra dissents from the rejoicing, but her suggestion that the horse should be destroyed forthwith meets with no favourable response from the crowd.

ACT II. Scene i. Aeneas's palace. His son, Ascanius (*soprano*), comes in, but seeing his father asleep, dare not wake him, and leaves the room. The ghost of Hector (*bass*) appears and marches slowly across the room. Aeneas wakes, greets the hero, and hears from him that Troy has fallen. He is instructed to take his son and the images of the gods and to take ship across the seas, there – in Italy – to found a new empire. Pantheus (*bass*), the priest, comes to Aeneas bringing the images of the Trojan gods. He tells Aeneas how, in the middle of the night, the horse opened to disgorge a troop of well-armed Greek soldiers. Priam is dead, and the town sacked and on fire. Aeneas rushes off to lead his men into battle.

Scene ii. The Temple of Vesta, where Hecuba (*mezzo-soprano*) and the Trojan women lament the fall of Troy. Cassandra announces the escape of Aeneas. For herself nothing remains, she says, since Choroebus is dead. She urges the women to take their own lives rather than fall as slaves into the hands of the Greeks, and drives out the few who are unwilling to choose death rather than dishonour, herself staying as a leader of those who are resolved to die.

The tension mounts. Some Greeks come in and demand to know where the treasure is hidden. Cassandra answers by stabbing herself. Some of the women throw themselves from the gallery of the temple, others follow her example, and as they die all cry 'Italie!'

When this first section of *Les Troyens* is played as a separate opera (under the title of *La Prise de Troie*), it is divided into three acts; the first comprises the opening chorus, Cassandra's aria and her duet with Choroebus, the second opens with the rejoicings and continues until the end of Act I proper, the third consists of Berlioz's Act II.

PART II: *Les Troyens à Carthage*

The rest of the opera takes place in Carthage. Originally, there was no prelude to the opera (which of course was designed to begin with the episodes in Troy itself), but when it was decided to give the second part alone, Berlioz composed a prelude to it, which is now printed in the vocal scores (although not in the one Berlioz prepared).

ACT III. Scene i. An amphitheatre in the garden of Dido's palace at Carthage. A festival is celebrating the progress which has been made in building the city. Dido herself (*mezzosoprano*) is greeted with a rapturous chorus, 'Gloire à Didon' (Hail, all hail to the Queen), when she takes her place on the throne. In a majestic aria ('Chers Tyriens'), she speaks of the work required to raise the city from nothing, and of what still remains to be done. The people swear to protect her and her kingdom against Iarbas, who has demanded her hand in marriage and is now daring to invade their territory.

A sort of harvest festival now takes place. Each section of national life files past the Queen, and is rewarded for its industry. Singing 'Gloire à Didon', the people march out, leaving Dido alone with her sister, Anna (*contralto*), who says that Dido is badly in need of a husband, and that Carthage needs a king just as much. Dido thinks sadly of her dead husband.

Iopas (*tenor*) comes in to tell the Queen that a foreign fleet has anchored in their harbour, driven apparently by the recent storm, and the leaders are asking to see the Queen. She agrees to receive them, then recalls her own experiences on the sea as a fugitive from Tyre. The Trojan march is heard (this time in the minor), and the survivors are led in by Ascanius, Aeneas having assumed a disguise and allowing his son to speak for the whole company. Dido welcomes them, and says that Aeneas cannot be anything but an honoured guest at her court. At that moment, her minister Narbal (*bass*) rushes in; Iarbas and his Numidian troops have advanced into their territory, even now threatening Carthage itself. Instantly Aeneas proclaims himself leader of the Trojans and offers to help repel the Queen's enemies. At the head of the army he marches out to fight the invader, leaving his son in Dido's hands.

In Berlioz's original plan, the third act ended with the great symphonic intermezzo, the *Chasse royale et orage* (Royal Hunt and Storm). In modern scores this appears at the end of the following act, where it is perhaps less happily placed, although a self-contained episode, supplying its own context.

Scene ii. A virgin forest near Carthage. Naiads cross the glade and swim in the stream. The sound of the hunt can be heard in the distance; the naiads listen anxiously, then disappear. Huntsmen cross the stage; there are signs that a storm is approaching, and one of them takes shelter under a tree. Ascanius is seen, and after him come Dido and Aeneas, the former dressed as Diana, the latter as a warrior; both take shelter. Naiads dash off, fauns and satyrs dance, and cries of 'Italie!' are heard. A tree falls struck by lightning and bursts into flames; the fauns pick up its burning branches and dance off. The scene is covered with thick clouds, the storm dies down, and peace returns. Ernest Newman has described this scene as 'the finest and most sustained piece of nature painting in all music; it is like some noble landscape of Claude come to life in sound'.

ACT IV. Dido's gardens, by the sea. Everything is decorated to celebrate Aeneas's victorious return. Narbal confides to Anna his fear that Aeneas's coming will not be for Carthage's or for Dido's good. Already she neglects affairs of state. Anna asks him if he cannot see that Dido is in love with her guest; where else could Carthage find a better king? But Narbal's forebodings are by no means quietened by this thought.

Dido comes in with her royal guest. A ballet is danced for their entertainment. At its end, Dido asks Iopas to sing; he does so, charmingly, to the accompaniment of a harp and various instruments: 'O blonde Cerès' (O Ceres, goddess fair). But Dido can find no pleasure in anything that keeps her attention from Aeneas. She asks him to continue his recital of the fate of Troy. What happened to Andromache, she asks. Though at first determined to die, in the end she submitted to love's urgings and married her captor Pyrrhus. 'O pudeur', sings Dido, 'Tout conspire à vaincre mes remords' (All conspires to vanquish my remorse).

Ascanius removes Dido's ring, and Anna comments on his likeness to Cupid. Aeneas's voice has already been heard, but now Iopas and Narbal add theirs to make up the quintet. It is one of the loveliest moments in the score, and the ensemble is built up like one of Verdi's on the individual reactions to the now apparent love of Dido for Aeneas. It is followed by a septet (Dido, Aeneas, Anna, Ascanius, Iopas, Narbal, Pantheus, and the chorus) which is no less beautiful: 'Tout n'est que paix et charme' (Night throws her veil of enchantment all around).

Dido and Aeneas are alone in the garden: 'Nuit d'ivresse et d'extase infinie' (O sweet night, night of ecstasy unending!). It is the beginning of the incomparable Shakespearean love duet, one of the finest in all opera: 'Par une telle nuit' (In such a night as this). Idea succeeds idea, and a reference to their own names brings the duet to an idyllic close. They go off with Dido leaning on Aeneas's shoulder, just as a shaft of moonlight reveals a statue of the god Mercury which comes to life and reiterates the knell of their hopes: 'Italie!'

ACT V. Scene i. The harbour at night. A young sailor, Hylas (*tenor*), sings sadly of his homeland: 'Vallon sonore' (O vale resounding). Pantheus and the Trojan chiefs direct that preparations be made for the fleet's departure, which is only delayed because of Aeneas's love for Dido; every moment wasted is likely to bring down the anger of the gods – even now the disembodied cry of 'Italie' can be heard again. Two soldiers on sentry duty grumble about having to leave the food and women of Carthage – but they break off as Aeneas approaches.

Aeneas is torn between his overwhelming love for Dido, to whom he has broken the news that he must leave, and his sense of duty and of destiny: 'Inutiles regrets. Je dois quitter Carthage' (There is no turning back; this land I must relinquish). But he thinks longingly of Dido, and cannot bear the thought of their farewell: 'Ah, quand viendra l'instant des suprêmes adieux?' (How can I ever forget how she pal'd). His initial agitation returns: 'En un dernier naufrage' (May storm and tempest rack me). Once again he hears the voices, and now sees the spectre of King Priam, followed by those of Choroebus, Cassandra and Hector; each in turn orders him to follow his destiny. His mind is made up and he orders the Trojans to their boats: 'Debout, Troyens' (Awake, awake, Trojans awake), ending with a sad, slow farewell to the absent Dido. The *scena* is one of the most magnificent in the tenor repertory.

Dido has followed Aeneas. She begs him to stay; Aeneas is almost prepared to give way until the sound of the Trojan march is heard in the distance. Then, with a cry of 'Italie', Aeneas rushes on to one of his vessels.

Scene ii. Dido's palace. Dido tries to persuade her sister Anna to go to the harbour to intercede for her. Anna says Aeneas's departure had become inevitable, if the gods were to be obeyed; but she maintains that, in spite of the gods, he still loves her. Dido says this is impossible; *her* love would compel her to disobey Jove himself. When Iopas describes the ships putting out to sea, Dido bursts out in fury, ordering the Carthaginians to pursue and destroy the traitorous Trojans. She herself has done wrong by not from the start treating the Trojans as they have finished by treating her. Why did she not serve up the body of Ascanius to Aeneas at a feast? One thing only is left her: to raise an awful pyre to the god of the underworld, and on it burn everything that was ever connected with the traitorous Aeneas.

Anna and Narbal leave her, and Dido's grief overflows: 'Ah, je vais mourir' (Now I must die). She will burn on the pyre, and perhaps from his ship Aeneas will catch sight of the flames which will signal her terrible end. She bids farewell to the great city: 'Adieu, fière cité' (Farewell, Carthage of mine, proud city that I rais'd).

Scene iii. A terrace overlooking the sea. A funeral pyre is presided over by priests of Pluto. Dido, preceded by Anna and Narbal, comes slowly in. Anna and Narbal solemnly curse the Trojans, after which Dido prepares to mount the steps of the pyre. She looks sadly at Aeneas's accoutrements on it; then, taking his sword, stands with it while she prophesies that her people will one day produce a warrior to avenge on his descendants the shame now brought by Aeneas. Then she plunges the sword into her breast. Dying, she describes a vision of Rome triumphant. The Carthaginians hurl further curses at the Trojans. But the Trojan March contradicts them, and a vision of the eternal Rome rises behind Dido's pyre.

BÉATRICE ET BÉNÉDICT

Two acts, by Hector Berlioz; première, Baden-Baden, 1862. Based on Shakespeare. Following rejoicing at the defeat of the Moors, Hero (*soprano*), daughter of the Governor of Messina, looks forward to seeing her lover Claudio (*baritone*). He arrives with Benedick (*tenor*), who immediately begins a skirmish with Beatrice (*mezzo-soprano*), and reacts furiously when teased about marriage. Gradually, however, he realises that perpetual bachelorhood may not be for him. Beatrice wonders how to suppress her growing feeling for him, and begins to welcome the tenderness she earlier despised. Although both try to conceal their mutual love, it is in vain, and two marriage contracts are signed before the opera closes with a brilliant duet.

Charles François Gounod
(1818–1893)

FAUST

OPERA in five acts; words by Barbier and Carré. Première at Théâtre Lyrique, Paris, March 19, 1859.

ORIGINALLY composed with sections of dialogue, *Faust* was reworked more than once, sung recitatives being added in 1860, Valentine's aria (written for the English baritone Charles Santley) in 1864, and an extensive ballet at the time the work reached the Opéra (1869). A brief prelude is mostly concerned with the 'Santley' aria, which was indeed derived from the prelude's melody.

ACT I. Faust's (*tenor*) study. The philosopher is alone reading, before dawn. In despair he is about to drink poison when he hears cheerful singing outside. He curses life and advancing age and calls upon Satan's help. Mephistopheles (*bass*) appears and offers him wealth and power, but Faust wants neither unless accompanied by the gift of youth. A vision of Marguerite (*soprano*) at her spinning wheel produces a rapturous response: 'A moi les plaisirs!' ('Tis pleasure I covet).

ACT II. A fair outside a city. Students, among them Wagner (*baritone*), soldiers, burghers of every age are drinking and making the most of carnival. Siebel, a village youth (*mezzo-soprano*), and Valentine, Marguerite's brother (*baritone*), make their entrance, the latter examining a medal given him by his sister Marguerite as a talisman against harm in battle. He sings the aria written for Santley. Mephistopheles sings the song of the Calf of Gold, an ironic celebration of man's worship of Mammon, before telling Siebel every flower he touches will in future wither. He picks a quarrel with Valentine by toasting Marguerite, swords are drawn but Valentine finds his powerless until he and the other soldiers extend their sword's cruciform hilts and counter the might of Mephistopheles.

He and Faust watch as there develops the famous waltz, whose grace undulates exquisitely throughout the action. Siebel is in love with Marguerite but Mephistopheles manoeuvres him away from her and Faust is at last allowed to meet his vision. In a short but telling episode he offers her his arm, only, with matching elegance, to be rejected. The waltz scintillates to the end.

ACT III. Marguerite's garden. Siebel in a charming song attempts to leave flowers in front of his beloved's house but they die as he touches them, and only when he has dipped his fingers in holy water do they remain fresh. Faust sings rapturously ('Salut! demeure chaste et pure': All hail thou dwelling, pure and lowly); the aria with its floated top C is a touchstone of the French romantic tenor repertory. Mephistopheles replaces Siebel's flowers with a casket of jewels and Marguerite, with the handsome stranger in mind, at first daydreams at her spinning wheel ('Il était un roi de Thulé'), then perceives the jewels and bursts into the brilliant Jewel Song.

There is a short interlude in the form of a quartet for Faust and Marguerite, Mephistopheles and Martha (*mezzo-soprano*), Marguerite's neighbour, before Mephistopheles invokes night and the scent of flowers to render the lovers impervious to all but their own mounting passion. Faust declares his love in an extended and justly famous duet, at whose end he and Marguerite agree to meet next day. He listens to her soliloquising into the night ('Il m'aime': He loves me!), then folds her in his arms as Mephistopheles shakes with laughter outside.

ACT IV. Scene i. Marguerite's room. Though she has been betrayed and deserted, Marguerite cannot find it in her heart to respond to Siebel's callow protestations of love ('Versez vos chagrins': When all was young); she still loves Faust.

Scene ii. A church. Marguerite kneels to pray but the voice of Mephistopheles reminds her of her sin and demons call her name. The 'Dies irae' resounds, Marguerite joins in, but Mephistopheles condemns her to eternal damnation.

Scene iii. The street in front of Marguerite's house. Soldiers return from war and sing a rousing chorus. Valentine enters the house, alerted to trouble by the obvious distress of Siebel. Mephistopheles sings a ribald serenade which stings Valentine to an attempt to avenge what he rightly takes to be an insult. A spirited trio leads to a duel, in which Faust mortally wounds his lover's brother. Marguerite throws herself on his body but with his dying breath Valentine curses her.

ACT V. The ballet which was obligatory for the Paris Opéra produced one of Gounod's most mellifluous scores, and the action involves the courtesans of antiquity who pass before Faust. A vision of Marguerite causes Faust to demand of Mephistopheles that he see her again. She is in prison, condemned to death for killing her child, and Faust tries, by recalling past happiness, to persuade her to escape with him. The reappearance of Mephistopheles banishes any idea of flight and Marguerite thinks only of the salvation she prayed for and which he interrupted in church. 'Anges purs, anges radieux' she sings in a soaring melody which brings a final cry from an angelic chorus: 'Sauvée!', as she expires.

ROMÉO ET JULIETTE

FIVE acts, by Charles François Gounod, based on Shakespeare; première, Paris, 1867. At the Capulets' ball in Verona, Tybalt (*tenor*) talks to Paris (*baritone*) of Juliet (*soprano*), Capulet's daughter. Romeo (*tenor*) and his Montague followers, deadly enemies of the Capulets, arrived masked. Romeo encounters Juliet and love is instantaneous. Later that night Romeo serenades Juliet on her balcony. The lovers are secretly married by Friar Lawrence (*bass*). In a street fight, Tybalt kills Romeo's friend Mercutio (*baritone*), and is in turn killed by Romeo; the Duke (*bass*) banishes him. Romeo comes to Juliet's room to bid her a passionate farewell. As he leaves,

Capulet comes to tell her that she must marry Paris at once. Friar Lawrence gives her a potion which will make her appear dead. In the tomb, the apparently lifeless Juliet is embraced by Romeo who takes poison. As she awakes, she sees him dying and stabs herself.

Jacques Offenbach
(1819–1880)

ORPHÉE AUX ENFERS
Orpheus in the Underworld

OPERETTA in four acts by Jacques Offenbach; text by Hector Crémieux and Halévy. Première, Bouffes-Parisiens, October 21, 1858.

OFFENBACH'S parody of the story of Orpheus originally obtained something of a *succès de scandale*; he was accused of blaspheming antiquity, of poking fun at the music of Gluck, and of satirising the government and prevailing social conditions. Since he was at the time in rather trying financial straits as manager of the Bouffes-Parisiens, success in whatever form it came was by no means unwelcome. Within eighteen months of the first night, the Emperor Napoleon III ordered a Command Performance of *Orpheus* and congratulated Offenbach afterwards. The original *opéra-bouffe* was in two acts and designed by Offenbach's friend, the painter Gustave Doré, but in 1874, when his fortunes were again at a low ebb, he re-wrote and greatly expanded *Orpheus*, adding ballets and transformation scenes and making the whole thing into a four-act operetta on a grand scale. This is what is mostly played today.

The overture, in fact, was not by Offenbach, but compiled by a certain Carl Binder for the first performance in Vienna; he made use of the overture which Offenbach wrote (an introduction, minuet, and embryonic canon) and added to it the famous violin solo and the Can-Can.

ACT I. First tableau. Shepherds and shepherdesses rusticise, Public Opinion (*mezzo-soprano*) introduces the plot, Councillors process with a pomposity worthy of the Mastersingers, and Eurydice (*soprano*) sings lightly and prettily of the extramarital love she feels in her heart, while the flutes bill and coo around the vocal line: 'La femme dont le coeur rêve, n'a pas de sommeil'. It appears that she and Orpheus (*tenor*) have each lost their hearts to someone else, and neither intends to renounce

the new-found love in favour of connubial bliss. They quarrel
and it transpires that Eurydice has a morbid dislike of Orpheus
as an artist, hating his fiddle-playing above everything. This is
the crowning insult. Orpheus announces he will play for her
his latest violin concerto (lasting one and a quarter hours, he
says), and the famous violin tune starts. The duet which it
initiates is charming, and it is not long before the fiddle tune
influences the vocal parts.

Eurydice's lover is Pluto (*tenor*), god of the Underworld, who
appears on earth in the guise of a shepherd and bee-keeper
under the name of Aristaeus. He charms Eurydice with a Chanson Pastorale, but admits to her that love for him involves trans-
porting her to the underworld. She says goodbye to life most
attractively, and leaves a note behind for Orpheus, telling him
that she is dead. This he finds, but his discreet rejoicings are
broken in upon by Public Opinion, who threatens him with
scandal if he does not follow his wife to Hades. They start off on
their journey, Orpheus complaining at the way he is treated,
Public Opinion urging him on in a delightful *marziale*
duettino.

ACT II. Mount Olympus, where the gods are sleeping peacefully. They introduce themselves one by one, Cupid (*soprano*)
being followed by Venus (*soprano*), a wordless chorus dividing
their verses. Jupiter (*baritone*) is woken up by Diana's horn.
Diana (*soprano*) is unhappy, and admits it is because she could
not that morning any longer find Actaeon on earth in his accustomed place. Jupiter reveals that he took it upon himself to
change Actaeon into a stag, as he was worried that Diana
seemed to be compromising herself rather badly with him. All
the gods complain about Jupiter's high-handed, tyrannical
ways, but they are interrupted when Mercury (*tenor*) brings
news that Eurydice is in hell and that Pluto is on his way to see
them. Pluto makes his entrance and is rebuked by Jupiter for
having carried off the delightful Eurydice. He defends himself,
and soon the gods join in chorus to announce that they are re-
belling against the intolerable domination of Jupiter – to say
nothing of the monotony of their eternal diet of nectar and
ambrosia. In turn, Minerva, Cupid, Venus, and Diana remind
Jupiter of the disguises he has in the past assumed for his
earthly amours, and, in charming and witty 'Couplets', they
mock him for his obvious interest in the case of Eurydice. Pluto
adds insult to injury by saying that in his view the disguises
were necessary because Jupiter was so villainously ugly that he
would have got nowhere with the girls without them.

At this juncture, Orpheus and Public Opinion are
announced, and Jupiter exhorts the gods to be on their best behaviour. Pluto leads off the finale and continues to deny that he

has had anything to do with hiding Eurydice. Orpheus starts to ask for Eurydice back, but he has only got as far as the first phrase of 'J'ai perdu mon Eurydice' when the gods and goddesses take up the tune and sing it for him; his demands are obviously granted in advance, since the appeal of his song has penetrated even to Mount Olympus. Much to Orpheus's dismay, Jupiter orders Pluto to return Eurydice to her husband, and says that he will himself come down to Hades to look for her. Won't he take them too, please, ask the other gods and goddesses, and, when he grants their request, they all join in a hymn of praise which soon becomes a jolly gallop tune.

ACT III. A sparkling *allegretto* entr'acte introduces the scene in the underworld. Eurydice is being looked after by John Styx (*baritone* or *tenor*), a complete fool on earth and now charged with prison duties in Hades. In a song with an enchantingly silly melody, he explains that he was once king of Beotia: 'Quand j'étais roi de Béotie'. Once he is out of the way, Jupiter comes looking for Eurydice, in whom he is considerably interested. A Tribunal sits to discover the truth, but it is Cupid who comes to Jupiter's aid, preceded by a group of some twenty tiny policemen, singing a very agreeable tune in chorus. This is followed by a wide-ranging and highly attractive slow waltz sung by Cupid himself, who advises Jupiter to disguise himself as a fly. This he does, and imitates its buzzing. Eurydice quickly takes a liking to the fly ('Bel insecte à l'aile dorée'), and they sing and buzz a duet together. At the end, Jupiter in his own voice rejoices at the capture that he seems to have made, and he eventually admits his identity. The scene ends as John Styx repeats his song and is imitated by Pluto.

ACT IV. A splendid *Choeur infernal* opens the scene. Eurydice has by now been turned by Jupiter into a Bacchante, and she is persuaded by Cupid to sing a Bacchic Hymn for their delight. Jupiter proposes a minuet, and all comment on his admirable dancing of it. Then begins the famous Can-Can tune, the best-known piece in the opera. Jupiter is about to go off with Eurydice when Pluto stops him, just at the moment when they can hear the sound of Orpheus's fiddle playing 'J'ai perdu mon Eurydice' for all it is worth. He is warned that he must walk in front of his wife, and that even to glance back at her will lead to a revocation of his permission to take her back with him to earth. Public Opinion urges him to obey the god's injunction, but Jupiter has an unexpected card up his sleeve; he hurls a thunderbolt and so shocks Orpheus that he involuntarily looks round, and thus forfeits his right to his bride. Everyone is delighted, Eurydice stays on as a Bacchante, and all join in a final version of the Can-Can to express their pleasure at the turn events have taken.

LA BELLE HÉLÈNE
The Fair Helen

OPERETTA in three acts by Jacques Offenbach; libretto by Meilhac and Halévy. Première December 17, 1864, at Théâtre des Variétés, Paris.

ACT I. After an introduction consisting of the March of the Kings, and Paris's song played on the oboe, we are in front of the temple. A chorus pays mock homage to Jupiter during a festivity in honour of Venus. Helen (*mezzo-soprano*) leads the women in their devotions. She sings a mellifluous air in 6/8 ('Amours divins'), then reveals to Calchas (*bass*), the High Priest, that she is obsessed with the promise Venus has made to Paris, that he shall win the most beautiful woman in the world. This is clearly a delicate situation for her, as who else can lay claim to such a title? To a comic march there enters Orestes (*soprano*), precocious son of Agamemnon, with Leoena and Parthoenis, two courtesans. He has a skittish song, in whose refrain Calchas joins. Calchas is embarrassed at Orestes's insistence on bringing the two ladies into the temple and Orestes accommodatingly leaves, singing his refrain as he goes.

Enter a shepherd (*tenor*) asking peremptorily whether a message has yet come from Venus. Even as he speaks the messenger-dove arrives, a little out of breath, and Calchas reads Venus's command – that the shepherd shall win the most beautiful woman in the world, clearly Helen. Calchas realises it is Paris, agrees obsequiously to help, and asks rather knowingly for a first-hand impression of Venus. This Paris gives him in his famous song ('Au mont Ida').

To the accompaniment of a very graceful piece of music, Helen and the women process from the temple, and Helen interrogates Calchas about the handsome young shepherd. Calchas leaves them together, but they have time for only a few words before the Kings of Greece enter in procession. The two Ajaxes, King of Salamis (*tenor*) and King of Locris (*baritone*), followed by Achilles (*tenor*), announce themselves and their attributes in comic fashion. Next it is the turn of Menelaus (*tenor*), hymning his expectation of imminent cuckoldry, and finally of Agamemnon (*baritone*), King of Kings. The whole episode is Offenbach at his best; memorable and devastatingly comic. A game of charades is proposed; the winner will receive his prize from Helen herself. The Kings are bad at the competition, which is won by Paris, still disguised as a shepherd. He announces his identity and, amidst general acclamation ('C'est l'homme à la pomme'), Helen crowns him victor, and invites him to supper. On the side Calchas agrees to try to arrange for Menelaus to be absent. There is a clap of thunder, and Calchas takes the opportunity of announcing a decree from Jupiter: Menelaus must go to Crete ('What the devil to do?' is his aside). The finale gets under way as they all, led by Helen, admonish Menelaus 'Pars pour la Crète'.

ACT II. An entr'acte based on the ripe waltz tune of the act's finale takes us to Helen's apartments, where she sits, surrounded by her women. Helen for once seems virtuously inclined and chooses a sober dress; let fate not have it *all* its own way. A message comes from Paris, asking Helen to receive him. She tries to refuse, but sighs: 'Pourquoi, ô déesse, as-tu toujours choisi notre famille pour faire tes expériences?' In a song that is a gem of wit and beauty, Helen laments (if that is the right word) her fatal gift.

Paris comes in unannounced, finds her determinedly resistant to love and to threats, and bids her beware of trickery. The music announces the gambling-game of Goose (Snakes and Ladders) – more party games! The Kings bet, Calchas is caught cheating and treated in an ensemble as if he were a welshing bookmaker.

Helen sends for Calchas and asks him if he will through prayer cause her to dream a rendezvous with Paris. She sleeps, Paris enters disguised as a slave, sends Calchas packing, and is alone with Helen. Orestes and the girls can be heard singing outside and soon Helen wakes up. She takes the reality of Paris for the dream she so much wanted, and their extended love duet ('Oui, c'est un rêve') is interrupted by the unexpected arrival of Menelaus, who raises the alarm and summons the Kings, having supper next door.

Orestes with his perpetual song arrives first, but the others are not far behind. Menelaus asks what sort of a show they have made of looking after his honour in his absence. Paris vocalises, but Menelaus is more taken aback by the suggestion, quickly seized on by Helen, that he is really the most to blame; it is customary for husbands to send warning of their return, is the burden of Helen's delightful song! Agamemnon tries to send Paris away – but, Paris rejoins, in that case he will have to return later. To the tune of the waltz of the entr'acte, now with a mocking onomatopoeic verbal accompaniment, they urge him on his way.

ACT III. The seaside resort of Nauplia. The entr'acte makes use of Orestes's tune and the curtain goes up to show the Spartans in holiday mood, singing the praises of Venus. Orestes is inclined to think that Menelaus's insistence on the departure of Paris has offended Venus, who seems to have taken revenge on the women of Greece by making them more susceptible than usual to the dictates of the heart. The Kings complain about the crowd now to be found at the seaside – there is no room for decent bathing any more.

Enter Helen and Menelaus quarrelling. Why had Helen said, 'Oh, then it *wasn't* a dream'? Helen explains that Venus had a hand in it, and Paris *is* very attractive. Agamemnon is dissatisfied – Greece is in a sorry moral state due to Venus's displeasure at Paris's departure. It's all Menelaus's fault; if his behaviour could pass as exemplary for a man, it is nothing short of idiotic for a King. In a famous trio, satirising at the same time patriotic moments in *Guillaume Tell* and *La Muette de Portici*, Agamemnon and Calchas try to persuade Menelaus to give up Helen to Paris – in order to save Greece from moral chaos!

Menelaus has had what he thinks is a better idea. He has invited the High Priest of Venus from Cythera to exorcise their troubles, and at that moment he appears in a great ship accompanied by his retinue. The Greeks welcome him and pray for help in their predicament. Of course, it is Paris all the time and he chides them for their melancholy reception – Venus's cult is a bright and breezy affair – and breaks into a *Tyrolienne*, complete with yodelling effects. The High Priest promises them pardon in Venus's name, provided Menelaus allows Helen to embark forthwith for Cythera to make sacrifice to Venus. Helen appears, agrees after some persuasion to go, and embarks, whereupon Paris reveals himself: Menelaus will not see Helen again – but the implied threat is lost in the final chorus of good wishes for the voyage to Cythera.

LES CONTES D'HOFFMANN
The Tales of Hoffmann

OPERA in three acts by Jacques Offenbach; text by Barbier and Carré, after F. T. A. Hoffmann. Première Opéra-Comique, Paris, February 10, 1881. The Venetian act was not included in the première. It is customary for the incarnations of Hoffmann's evil genius (Lindorf, Coppelius, Dapertutto and Dr. Miracle) to be undertaken by the same singer, as are, exceptionally, the four soprano roles. Andrès, Cochenille, Frantz and Pittichinaccio are usually taken by the same character tenor.

OFFENBACH died during rehearsals of *Hoffmann*, and Ernest Guiraud orchestrated the piece for its Opéra-Comique première, 'tidying' it up and dropping the Giulietta act in the process (in order to retain the barcarolle, he set the Antonia act in Venice!). A dozen years after the first performance Giulietta was brought back, but out of sequence, before Antonia rather than after as Offenbach and his librettists had intended. The episodes of Hoffmann's three loves have little intrinsically in common, and the invention of an evil genius appearing in different disguises to remove the ladies from Hoffmann's grasp (or save his poetic genius from them?) provides continuity rather than a powerful dramatic clash. Editors therefore have seized on the fact that there is no genuinely final version and have cut, added and generally reworked the opera for almost every revival. These days, in any remotely 'authentic' performance, the order is as given hereafter and the opera is in *opéra-comique* form, with a considerable quantity of spoken dialogue.

Prologue. Luther's Tavern in Nuremberg, next door to the opera house, where a performance of *Don Giovanni* is in progress. A drinking chorus can be heard offstage. Lindorf (*bass*) comes in with Andrès (*tenor*), the servant of the prima donna Stella (*soprano*), who is singing in *Don Giovanni*. Lindorf obtains from him a letter his mistress has written to Hoffmann, making an assignation for that evening and enclosing the key of her room. Lindorf in an aria exults over his prospective victim. A crowd of students enter the tavern and immediately start to celebrate the prospect of the beer which Luther (*bass*) brings them.

Hoffmann (*tenor*) comes in with Nicklausse (*mezzo-soprano*). Hoffmann seems out of humour, and it appears that he is haunted by the sight of Stella, with whom he was once in love. He is prevailed upon to sing a song to the assembled company, and strikes up the Legend of Kleinzach ('Il était une fois à la cour d'Eisenbach': Now long ago there lived at the court of Eisenbach[1]). With the chorus echoing his phrases, he goes briskly through the description of the little dwarf, but suddenly falls into a reverie and starts to rhapsodise on the features of his lady-love. He recovers himself and finishes the song he began.

Hoffmann and the students complain about the quality of Luther's beer, and a punch bowl is brought and duly greeted in song. Hoffmann is not pleased to see Lindorf, whom he refers to as haunting his steps and bringing him bad luck. He offers to tell the story of the three great loves of his life, and, in spite of Luther's warning that the curtain is going up on the second act of *Don Giovanni*, all announce their intention of staying behind to listen. The first, says Hoffmann, was called Olympia.

ACT I (Olympia) is introduced by a mocking minuet. Spalanzani (*tenor*) is in his room, waiting for the arrival of guests who have been invited to see his performing doll, Olympia. Spalanzani mutters about the fortune he hopes to make from his invention, which will recoup him for the loss he suffered when Elias the banker went broke. If only his rival Coppelius does not try to claim a share of the proceeds!

---

[1] English translations throughout by Edmund Tracey.

Hoffmann appears, and is immediately impressed by Olympia (*soprano*), whom he takes for Spalanzani's daughter. He sings ardently to her of his love. His aria, 'Ah, vivre deux' (To live as one), is one of the loveliest expressions of his romantic spirit which is to be found in the whole opera. Nicklausse comments tartly on the improbable nature of the new object of his master's affections – a mechanical doll indeed!

Dr. Coppelius (*baritone*) comes in and tries to interest Hoffmann in his own invention: eyes and spectacles to suit every requirement. 'J'ai des yeux' (If we were one) he sings as he shows off his wares. The pair he sells to Hoffmann seem to increase his delight in beholding Olympia. Spalanzani sees Coppelius, and is forced to acknowledge the latter's share in Olympia; he supplied her eyes, in consideration of which Spalanzani makes him out a bond for five hundred crowns – drawn on Elias's bank.

The guests start to arrive. Spalanzani produces Olympia, whom he describes as his daughter, for their admiration, and accompanies her on the harp while she sings her famous Doll's song to the assembled company: 'Les oiseaux dans la charmille' (Songbirds in the grove of Eden). The others go in to supper, leaving Hoffmann and Olympia alone. He sings to her, but she goes quickly to her room; he follows.

Coppelius returns having found out that he has been cheated by his rival. The dance begins again, and Hoffmann waltzes with Olympia, going faster and faster. Spalanzani finally manages to stop her and she breaks out into coloratura gyrations over the top of the chorus. Olympia is put away in her room, and all bend over to see what damage has been done to the exhausted Hoffmann. Suddenly, the noise of smashing machinery is heard. Coppelius emerges from Olympia's room, laughing with triumph, and Hoffmann is left disillusioned at the discovery that his beloved was only a doll.

ACT II (Antonia). Munich; a room in Crespel's (*baritone*) house. Antonia (*soprano*), his daughter, sits singing: 'Elle a fui, la tourterelle' (Poor young dove, vanished for ever). Crespel is distressed to find his daughter in a fainting condition. She has broken her promise not to sing, but she says it was the sight of her mother's portrait that prompted her to it. Crespel has already seen signs of the consumption which carried away her mother, and he blames her overwrought condition on Hoffmann, to escape whose attentions he has brought her to Munich. Crespel shouts for his deaf old servant Frantz (*tenor*), to whom he gives orders that no one is to be admitted to the house on any pretext whatsoever. Frantz soon falls asleep in a chair, from which Hoffmann, who comes through the door with Nicklausse, at last manages to rouse him.

Hoffmann looks at the song which is lying open on the harpsichord, and has just begun to sing it when Antonia appears. After an impassioned duet, Antonia hears her father coming, and Hoffmann hides as she leaves the room. No sooner has Frantz told Crespel that Dr. Miracle (*baritone*) is at the door, than the doctor enters. Hoffmann from hiding sees Miracle's preparations to treat Antonia, and recognises that he is evil; Crespel is in despair at not being able to get rid of the man who, he is certain, killed his wife and means to kill his daughter as well. Crespel begs Miracle to leave her alone, but he insists that he can cure Antonia. A fine trio for male voices develops in the course of the action.

Hoffmann is joined by Antonia, whom he tries to persuade to renounce her singing for the sake of her health and her love. She agrees, but no sooner is Hoffmann safely out of the way than Dr. Miracle is back, pouring temptation into her ear. Before long, Antonia hears the voice of her mother (*mezzo-soprano*) calling upon her to sing. Miracle says that he is only there to cause her to give effect to her mother's dearest wish. During a splendid trio Miracle seizes a violin from the walls and plays wildly on it. Antonia's voice rises higher and higher until she falls dying to the ground. Miracle disappears, and Crespel rushes in to hear his daughter's last words. When Hoffmann comes in, Crespel blames him for Antonia's death. Hoffmann wants to call a doctor, but, in answer to his summons, it is Miracle who comes.

ACT III (Giulietta). Venice. The gallery of a palace overlooking the Grand Canal. The guests of Giulietta (*soprano*), a courtesan, are grouped around. Nicklausse and Giulietta in a gondola sing the famous barcarolle, 'Belle nuit, ô nuit d'amour' (Burning night, oh night of love), one of the world's most popular operatic tunes.

Hoffmann objects to its melancholy strains, and responds with a lively drinking song, whose refrain is taken up by the chorus. Giulietta introduces her guests and invites them to a game of cards. Hoffmann swears to Nicklausse that he will not succumb to her charms – may his soul be forfeit to the devil if he does!

As Hoffmann leaves, Dapertutto (*baritone*) produces a great diamond, with which, he says, he will persuade Giulietta to capture Hoffmann's soul for him as she has done with that of Schlemil (*bass*), her lover. They have only to look into his magic mirror, and their souls stay with their reflections. He is given a powerful aria, 'Scintille diamant' (Flashing diamond).

Giulietta agrees to do Dapertutto's command, and upbraids Hoffmann for wishing to leave just because he has lost his money gambling. Hoffmann, unable to resist her, sings of the passion which overwhelms him in her presence: 'O Dieu de quelle ivresse' (What haunting dreams of rapture).

There is an ecstatic duet for them, 'Si ta présence m'est ravie' (If they should ever make me leave you), during which she obtains the reflection which Dapertutto covets. Then, Schlemil rushes in and denounces Giulietta's unfaithfulness. Hoffmann discovers that he has no reflection when he looks into a mirror, but still he will not leave Giulietta, whom he loves madly, he says. A septet begins, in which Hoffmann declares his love, Dapertutto and Pittichinaccio (*tenor*) their contempt for the poet; Giulietta admits that she found the diamond irresistible, Schlemil anticipates revenge, and Nicklausse and the chorus look with pity at Hoffmann's predicament.

Giulietta suggests an excursion on the canal, but Hoffmann and Schlemil fight, the former, using Dapertutto's sword, succeeding in killing his rival and removing from a chain round his neck the key of Giulietta's room. The sound of the barcarolle can be heard, but, when Hoffmann rushes out to find his Giulietta, it is to see her float away in the gondola, in the arms of Pittichinaccio.

Epilogue. There is an intermezzo based on the barcarolle, and we are back in Luther's tavern. Hoffmann's story is finished; so too is *Don Giovanni*. Stella is doubtless, as Nicklausse observes, the personification of the three types of womanhood that Hoffmann has idealised in his stories. But Hoffmann is too drunk to care – Lindorf is perfectly confident on that score – and, as the students eddy round him singing the drinking song from the prologue, the Muse of Poetry appears by his side claiming him for her own. Hoffmann seems to be in a stupor. As Lindorf leads Stella from the room, she turns and throws a flower from her bouquet to him. He looks blankly in her direction. There is no doubt that he is dead drunk.

Camille Saint-Saëns
(1835–1921)

SAMSON ET DALILA

OPERA in three acts; text by Ferdinand Lemaire. Première at Weimar (at Liszt's instigation), December 2, 1877.

SAINT-SAËNS was a composer (and pianist) of erudition and sensibility, with a wealth of chamber and symphonic music to his credit, and it is in some ways surprising that his most

famous opera should be noted for its sensuous melody, Delilah's solos and the last-act Bacchanale in their own way quite
outstanding. It is a powerful work, full of contrast, and remains
a sure-fire hit given a mezzo-soprano with a fine voice and physique to match, and a tenor as heroic an actor as he is in voice.

ACT I. Gaza. The Hebrews are forced by the Philistines to
work (fugue: 'Nous avons vu nos cités renversées': We have
seen our cities overthrown). Only Samson (*tenor*) has faith in
God's promise of liberty and addresses his compatriots in stirring terms: 'Arrêtez, o mes frères' and 'L'as-tu donc oublié?'
(Hold your ranks, my brethren; Had you then forgotten). His
third outburst induces in the Hebrews a new spirit of defiance
and attracts the attention of Abimelech (*bass*), the satrap, who
comes in with guards and pours scorn on the God who so sig-
nally fails his people in their plight. Samson slays Abimelech
and then, as Israel's champion, sets out to complete the work of
liberation ('Israël! romps ta chaîne!': Israel, break your bonds).

Dagon's High Priest may rage ('Maudite à jamais soit la race':
Cursed forever be the race) but he cannot rouse the Philistines
to effective resistance, and the Hebrews are left masters of the
centre of Gaza. They sing God's praises and a group of Philistine girls, Delilah (*mezzo-soprano*) at their head, appears to pay
tribute to the victorious Samson: 'Je viens célébrer la victoire' (I
come to celebrate your victory). An old Hebrew (*bass*) solemnly
warns Samson against the wiles of Delilah, but his old love for
her has revived and his prayer for strength to resist is doomed
to failure from the start. To a seductive tune, the girls dance,
and Delilah, in spite of the reiterated warning of the old Hebrew, completes her ensnarement of Samson in the languorous
aria 'Printemps qui commence' (O spring that is coming).

ACT II. The Valley of Sorek. A rich orchestral introduction
paints a dark picture as the seductress waits for her victim and
in an aria invokes love to further her revenge: 'Amour, viens
aider ma faiblesse' (Love, come to aid my frailty). Here we have
a new mixture, steely determination added to the voluptuous
quality already apparent in 'Printemps qui commence' – a
potent combination indeed!

To her comes the High Priest of Dagon (*baritone*). The
Hebrews have overrun the town, he tells her, Philistine soldiers
fleeing before Samson, who is rumoured to have renounced the
love he once had for her. He offers her money if she will deliver
Samson to him, but she is confident he is still her slave and she
will trap him for her own reasons of vengeance. Their duet ends
with a ferocious joint declaration of hate and revenge.

To an orchestral background which foreshadows the accompaniment to her forthcoming aria, Delilah wonders if Samson's
infatuation will bring him to her. When he arrives, it is plain

that the struggle between infatuation and duty has ended in victory for the former; a love scene develops, culminating in Delilah's 'Mon coeur s'ouvre à ta voix' (Softly awakes my heart), than which opera contains no more seductive a melody. Samson joins in the second verse, then, after protesting his love, somehow summons up reserves of resistance and refuses to tell her the secret of his strength. She rushes into her house, and after a moment of indecision Samson goes after her. Delilah's cry followed by Samson's howl of anguish summons the Philistines, who burst into the house.

ACT III. Scene i. A prison in Gaza. If Act II is Delilah's, Act III is unquestionably Samson's. The orchestra suggests the grinding of the mill, which the blinded giant must push on its punishing round, and his voice mingles with the plaints of captive Hebrews who blame him for their plight as he gives magnificent expression to his despair and repentance ('Vois ma misère, hélas': See my despair, alas).

Scene ii. Philistines drag him to the celebration of their triumph in the Temple of Dagon; the singing is reminiscent of the first act's elegant greeting to spring. The Bacchanale which follows initially contains pastiche eastern music of a distinctly elegant cast, then a wonderfully sumptuous passage before it degenerates into orgy. Samson, led in by a child, is mocked for his love for Delilah by all and sundry, including the false temptress herself, who does not scruple to reveal that hatred, not love, prompted her to seduce him. Samson's rage strikes fear into nobody, and as libations are poured the High Priest with Delilah leads a spirited chorus of praise for Dagon ('Gloire à Dagon': Praise be to Dagon). Samson prays for strength, then quietly asks the child to lead him between the two pillars which support the Temple. While the intoxication of the feast seizes everybody, he clasps the pillars, then, with a terrible crash, pulls them down and buries the Philistines and himself in one last gesture of defiance.

Léo Delibes
(1836–1891)

LAKMÉ

THREE acts; première, Paris, 1883. In the garden of an Indian temple, Lakmé (*soprano*), daughter of the fanatical Brahmin priest Nilakantha (*bass-baritone*), and her companions sing to the gods. Two English officers, Gérald (*tenor*) and Frédéric (*baritone*), with their party, enter the garden; when Gérald sees Lakmé he falls in love with her, but leaves before Nilakantha enters crying vengeance. The priest and his daughter come to the festival, which the English party also attend. Gérald is told that his regiment leaves before dawn. Nilakantha asks Lakmé to sing (the Bell Song) to flush out his enemy. She faints on seeing Gérald and Nilakantha plots to destroy him. During the procession Gérald is stabbed but not badly hurt. Lakmé takes him to her hut. Frédéric tracks him there and reminds him of his duty. Sensing that he will leave, Lakmé eats a poisoned leaf and dies as they swear eternal love.

Georges Bizet
(1838–1875)

Les Pêcheurs de Perles
The Pearl Fishers

OPERA in three acts; text by Carré and Cormon. Première at the Théâtre-Lyrique, Paris, on September 30, 1863.

A CT I. Ceylon. The seashore. The fishermen are holding fête preparatory to choosing a chief. They sing and dance, and eventually select Zurga (*baritone*) as king; he accepts their confidence. Nadir (*tenor*) appears, is greeted after his long absence, and describes his adventures in the jungle. There is a fond reunion between Zurga and Nadir. They were formerly friends, but recall their rivalry for the hand of the beautiful priestess, Leïla (*soprano*), whom they had seen together in the Brahmin temple of Candy. Their love for her brought enmity between them, but they recall that the oath of friendship which they swore has never since been broken. Their duet, 'Au fond du temple saint' (In the depths of the temple), is an example of Bizet's melodic inspiration at its finest. Its theme is used throughout the opera as a friendship motto.

A boat has arrived, bearing the unknown virgin whose duty is to pray during the time the fishermen are at sea, so as to ward off evil spirits. Zurga tells Nadir that she is veiled and must not be approached or seen by anyone during the time of her vigil. She is brought in by the old priest Nourabad (*bass*), and welcomed by the fisherfolk. Zurga swears her in as the inviolate virgin protectress of the fishermen, and threatens her with death if she prove false to her oath.

Leïla and Nadir recognise each other, and he stands watching as if in a dream as she ascends the cliff. In an aria of great beauty he reflects on his love, which has never been dimmed by the passing of time: 'Je crois entendre encore' (I hear as in a dream). This is the best known section of the score, not least in its Italian translation, 'Mi par d'udir ancora', and it is concerned, like the duet for tenor and baritone, like the love duet, with a kind of erotic hypnosis, gentle and seductive, musically elusive and yet compelling, with which Bizet ensnares his young lovers and impregnates his score – hence one of the secrets of its attraction. Leïla reappears, and sings an invocation to Brahma, echoed by the chorus, before she is left alone on her rock for her vigil. Before the end of the act, Nadir, gazing up at Leïla, sings ardently of his love for her and swears to protect her from danger.

ACT II. A ruined temple. The high priest, Nourabad, warns Leïla on pain of death to be faithful to her religious vows. She will be alone but well guarded. Leïla tells him he need have no fear; she never breaks her promise. The necklace she wears was given her by a fugitive, whose hiding-place she refused to reveal although the daggers of his pursuers were pointed at her heart.

Nourabad leaves her, and she sings of the love which fills her heart: 'Comme autrefois dans la nuit sombre' (As once upon a time in the dark of the night). Suddenly, not far away, she hears the voice of Nadir singing a serenade: 'De mon amie fleur endormie' (Beloved friend, folded flower). A moment later he is with her, and a passionate duet develops: 'Ton coeur n'a pas compris le mien' (In your heart you have not understood what I feel). Leïla begs Nadir to leave her, and they agree to meet again the next day; but Nourabad has seen Nadir leave, and he calls down anathema on both their heads, while the chorus mutter that they can see a storm arising. Nadir is captured by the guards, Nourabad accuses the lovers of sacrilege, the crowd take up his cry for vengeance. Zurga claims the right, as chief and therefore judge, to settle the case himself, and he inclines to be merciful for the sake of his friend. But Nourabad tears the veil from Leïla's head, and Zurga, recognising Leïla, swears to be revenged on Nadir for his treachery. Leïla and Nadir pray to Brahma for help, while the crowd call on him to avenge the sacrilege.

ACT III. Scene i. Zurga's tent. The chief contrasts his own restless state of mind with the abated storm, which for a time threatened destruction of the fishing fleet. He laments the breaking of his friendship with Nadir: 'O Nadir, tendre ami de mon coeur' (Oh Nadir, faithful friend of mine). It is a fine lyrical *scena* of considerable power. Leïla appears before him, and expresses her willingness to die, but pleads for Nadir. Zurga eventually gives in to jealousy at the idea of losing Leïla to Nadir, and is cursed by Leïla for his jealous cruelty. Just before leaving him, she asks that a last favour may be granted her; she has a necklace which she would like to have sent to her mother far away. This she puts into Zurga's hands.

Scene ii. The place of execution, where a funeral pyre has been erected. There are savage dances and choruses, the sopranos reiterating 'Brahma!', before Nourabad leads Leïla out into the middle of the populace. Just as the guilty lovers are to meet death, a distant glow is seen. Zurga dashes in crying that the camp is on fire, and the people rush out to fight the flames. Zurga tells Leïla and Nadir that it was he who set fire to the camp; the necklace she gave him was once his, and he the fugitive she saved from death long ago. He unfastens their chains and bids them flee; there is a solemn trio 'O lumière sainte' (Oh light of heaven), composed by Godard and frequently still performed in an attempt to strengthen Bizet's ending. Zurga impedes their pursuers, but is denounced by Nourabad, who had stayed behind in hiding when the others left. The music of 'Au fond du temple saint' is heard in the orchestra, and the top line is sung by Leïla and Nadir in octaves as they appear safe on the top of the rock.

CARMEN

OPERA in four acts by Georges Bizet; words by Henri Meilhac and Ludovic Halévy, based on the novel by Prosper Mérimée. Première at Opéra-Comique, Paris, March 3, 1875.

CARMEN is an *opéra-comique* with a tragic ending, and a substantial portion of the action is carried on in dialogue. For Vienna in 1875, some (but not all) of the dialogue was set as recitative by Bizet's pupil and colleague, Ernest Guiraud, and this version was for some eighty years adopted in most large non-French opera houses (and in a few, is still used). But *Carmen* is a better work with the dialogue Bizet intended, so that his brilliantly inventive, subtly-scored genre music recreates the world he aimed at so precisely, a world of sophisticated gestures on a small scale rather than grand arias, large ensembles, rumbustious finales. Even so, in any version and in theatres large or small the opera has for well over a century been probably the most popular in the repertory, and is almost invariably revealed as a masterpiece of virtual perfection and unerring design.

The opera was not initially a success (nor yet quite the failure legend would have it – forty-five performances in its first year), and this was mainly due to its low-life theme and violent conclusion offending against the traditionally family atmosphere of the Opéra-Comique. By 1883, after successes abroad, *Carmen* returned in triumph to Paris, and by the end of the year had clocked up its hundredth performance.

ACT I. A square in Seville, containing cigarette factory and guard-house; about 1830. The prelude introduces the music of the *corrida*, then Escamillo, the bullfighter, finally the brooding, apprehensive motif of fate and Carmen's obsession with it.

The atmosphere is heat-laden as townsfolk idly watch the world go by. Corporal Moralès (*baritone*) tries to pick up Micaëla (*soprano*), who is looking for Don José and will return later, but the action proper starts with a march heralding the relief guard, children parody the soldiers' drill. Corporal José (*tenor*) tells Lieutenant Zuniga (*bass*) that the girls from the cigarette factory tend to be pretty but that he has eyes for no one but Micaëla, his foster-sister. A bell rings; the male crowd voyeuristically anticipates the arrival of the girls, who emerge to sing melodiously of the factory's produce. Electricity is in the music as the gipsy Carmen (*mezzo-soprano*) darts out of the factory to become the cynosure of all eyes but proof against any advances. She sings a sultry *habanera*. A musical reference to the fate motif brings Carmen face to face with José, who seems not to notice her. She chucks a flower at him and runs into the factory, leaving him to pick it up as Micaëla returns. Micaëla brings José money and news of his mother ('Parle-moi de ma mère': Tell me about my mother), and they sing an extended duet full of charm but devoid of passion.

Shouts from the factory suggest someone has been stabbed – by Carmen, cries one faction. Zuniga tries to get sense from the hubbub, then sends José to sort it out inside. He brings Carmen out, but she answers Zuniga's questions only with humming and singing so that José is instructed to tie her hands. Zuniga makes out a warrant while Carmen urges José to let her go – because, she says, he is in love with her ('Près des remparts de Séville': Close by the walls of Seville). She is right, as is immediately clear when he joins his voice to hers, loosens the knots and lets her give him a shove and run off to freedom, the crowd frustrating the soldiers' pursuit.

ACT II. Lillas Pastia's tavern. The prelude (or entr'acte as it is called) anticipates Don José's entrance song of a little later. A crowd is drinking and smoking, soldiers as well as gipsies like Carmen, Frasquita and Mercédès (*sopranos*), who form a trio to sing a Chanson Bohémienne ('Les tringles des sistres tintaient': The strings of the guitar were throbbing). There follows the entry of Escamillo (*baritone*), the matador, attended by an admiring crowd (Toreador's song). He is obviously attracted to Carmen, but she brushes him off, at least for the moment, and, when he has gone, she does the same to Zuniga, all for love of José, who is due that day out of gaol.

The inn shut, smugglers in the persons of Dancairo (*tenor* or *baritone*) and Remendado (*tenor*) emerge as it were from the woodwork, and in a quintet of outstanding brilliance plan the immediate future. Frasquita and Mercédès will of course join that night's foray, but Carmen says she has unfinished business: she is in love and they must go without her. The sound of José's voice is heard outside (singing the melody of the entr'acte), and Carmen sets about seducing him with a dance, interrupted when José hears the bugle sound 'retreat'. He must obey what amounts to an order and Carmen rounds on him, silenced only when he pours out his feelings in the so-called Flower Song ('La fleur que tu m'avais jetée': See here the flower that you threw me), a declaration of love wrung from the very heart. Carmen returns to the attack ('Là-bas dans la montagne') and Don José is already almost in the net when Zuniga barges his way in, to be defied by José and disarmed by smugglers attracted by the noise of a fight. Don José has drawn his sword against a superior officer and has no option but to join the smugglers' band.

ACT III. A rocky spot on the frontier. An entr'acte of ethereal beauty, all wind and strings, has little relevance to the action which involves the smugglers preparing to reconnoitre their route. José cannot easily accept that he is a deserter; Carmen hints at their affair winding down. Frasquita and Mercédès spread the cards and Carmen joins them to read her fortune. She foresees death and her fatalistic creed means she cannot evade it: 'En vain pour éviter' (Useless to try to avoid). The smugglers prepare to move off, the three girls, in a passage of high swagger and to José's jealous indignation, promising to take care of the guards.

José is left on watch, but is out of sight when Micaëla, led by a guide, comes to look for him. Her aria ('Je dis que rien ne m'épouvante': I try not to own that I tremble) is a beautiful lyrical invention, but Micaëla hides when José takes an unsuccessful shot at a stranger. Escamillo has come looking for a girl he admits he fancies, and it is not long before he squares up to José, the dragoon Carmen (he has heard) once loved. As Escamillo slips and looks likely to lose, their fight is interrupted by the returning smugglers. Escamillo and Carmen exchange glances, and he invites the whole band to the *corrida* in Seville. Micaëla is discovered and Carmen advises José to comply with her plea to go to his dying mother. José's frantic 'Dût-il m'en coûter la vie' (Even if it cost me my life) is one of the score's most dramatic incidents, but the act ends with a reiteration of Escamillo's song.

ACT IV. Outside the bullring in Seville. The entr'acte is a Spanish dance. Crowd animation precedes the entry of the various elements of the quadrilla (to the music of the prelude to Act I), and eventually the crowd hails Escamillo himself. He embraces Carmen ('Si tu m'aimes, Carmen': If you love me, Carmen), and she is warned by Frasquita and Mercédès that José is lurking in the crowd. She confronts him alone but will not listen as his pleas turn to threats. To the sound of applause for the victorious Escamillo, she hurls at José the ring he once gave her. He stabs her and surrenders as the crowd starts to leave the arena.

Alexis Emmanuel Chabrier
(1841–1894)

L'ÉTOILE
The Star

THREE acts; première, Paris, 1877. King Ouf (*tenor*) wants a public execution to celebrate his birthday. Siroco (*bass*), the Court Astronomer, is told he must die soon after the King. Hérisson (*tenor*) and his wife Aloès (*soprano*) bring in Princess Laoula (*soprano*), the King's fiancée. The pedlar Lazuli (*mezzo-soprano*) is in love with Laoula; believing she is Hérisson's wife, he insults the King and is arrested, but the stars reveal that the King's death will follow his and he is pardoned. Great efforts are made to keep him safe from Hérisson, and he is allowed to go off with Laoula. She brings the sad news that he has been shot. The King and Siroco await death, fortified by strong drink, but Lazuli has escaped after all, and in his relief the King pardons him and blesses his marriage to Laoula.

LE ROI MALGRÉ LUI
King in Spite of Himself

OPÉRA-COMIQUE in three acts by Emmanuel Chabrier; libretto by Emile de Najac and Paul Burani. Première, May 18, 1887, Opéra-Comique, Paris.

Written in only nine months, *Le Roi malgré lui*, in spite of a clumsy libretto, is often considered Chabrier's masterpiece – full of wit and erudition, of tender lyricism and comedy.

ACT I. A castle, near Cracow. Henri de Valois (*baritone*), King of Poland, is bored with position and surroundings; nothing, he thinks, would please him better than to be rid of both. The French nobles of his court (including the Comte de Nangis; *tenor*) are whiling away the tedium of life in a city far from home. The King enters and is told that his life is in danger. In a beautiful romance he hymns the praises of his longed-for native land. He is depressed at his awkward position: his French advisers fear he will rush off to France; his Polish subjects, led by Count Laski (*bass*), dread his staying in Poland. The King decides to go incognito (even though the Poles do not know him by sight) amongst his subjects to discover their views.

Enter the Duke of Fritelli (*buffo baritone*), an Italian attached to the Court but married to a Pole, niece to Count Laski. He is a recognised figure of fun but, when asked, gives the King an account of the Polish character in a remarkable and brilliantly characterised Mazurka ('Le Polonais est triste et grave': Your average Pole is sad and serious). The King, preferring to talk of women, tells him of a recent adventure with a masked Venetian in her native city. The Duke goes to fetch his wife, whom the King wishes presented, and the King discovers from Nangis that he is in love with Minka (*soprano*), a serf in the household of Count Laski. She regularly passes on information of her master's plots against the King. With that, the King tells Nangis that they will go in disguise to Cracow to spy out the land.

The King and his attendants leave, and Nangis rescues Minka from a soldier who attacks her with a whip. In tender music they celebrate their mutual love. Minka reveals that there is to be a ball that night at Count Laski's. Nangis goes to the King, but not before agreeing to meet Minka in the park later on – she will sing, so he will be able to find her in the dark. Minka hides at the approach of the Duke and Duchess of Fritelli.

Alexina (the Duchess; *soprano*) tells her husband, who is also in the plot, that the Polish opponents of Henri de Valois will meet that night at her uncle's house. She spurns her husband's advances and starts to tell him of an adventure she had in Venice, when Fritelli realises it is essentially the same tale he has just heard from the King: *she* was the masked Italian! News comes that the King is too busy to see the Duchess. An overjoyed Fritelli announces to her his convinced adherence to the plot to drive out the foreign ruler.

They leave. Minka is about to tell Nangis of the plot when the King himself comes in. He dismisses Nangis, and Minka, taking him for a member of the King's entourage, in a charmingly

lyrical duet tells him about the plot, her love for Nangis, and
reveals that Fritelli is a conspirator. Immediately the King confronts the Italian, then pardons him on condition that Fritelli
takes him to the ball. The King looks for a pretext for a French-
man to present himself as a prospective conspirator; he
pretends to lose his temper with Nangis and sentences him to
immediate imprisonment. After a fine ensemble of perplexity à
la Rossini ('Qu'a-t-il fait? En effet qu'a-t-il pu commettre?':
What's he done? My goodness, what could we have done?), the
King departs as Nangis is led off by the guards.

Fritelli starts to explain to his wife why the King can't receive
her when he appears unannounced. Each recognises the other,
but neither has an inkling of the other's identity. Fritelli is made
to introduce the King as Nangis who, because of his unjust
treatment, wants to join the conspirators. The trio, 'Quelle surprise, ma beauté de Venise' (What a surprise, my Venetian
beauty), makes a brilliant effect, but is interrupted by Minka's
voice from the park. The night watch goes by, challenges and
recognises Fritelli, and the King brings the act to a close: 'Con-
spirons tous trois contre Henri de Valois' (Let us plot all three,
against Henri de Valois).

ACT II. The great hall of Count Laski's Palace. The ball has
begun. The music – the well-known Fête Polonaise – is a choral
dance which culminates in a glitteringly orchestrated waltz
sequence. The conspirators gather, and Alexina introduces the
Comte de Nangis (the King in disguise). There is a complication when Minka overhears the introduction and knows
some deception is afoot. The conspirators swear to do all possible to remove the King from Poland and Fritelli is charged
with abducting his master and placing him in a closed carriage
bound for the border. When most have gone, the disguised
King tells Fritelli he has a more subtle plan to effect the removal
of Henri de Valois – who was, Alexina points out, Fritelli's
greatest friend. 'Rien n'est aussi près de la haine que l'amitié'
(Nothing is closer to hatred than friendship) is the burden of a
witty and exquisite quartet, in which Alexina and the King are
joined by Fritelli and Laski.

After an interlude, which includes an exceptionally brilliant
solo for Minka (*Chanson tzigane*), the King enters with Alexina,
who is still ignorant of his identity but knows him as the man
who jilted her in Venice; their duet turns to a barcarolle reminiscence of their rapturous experience. Alexina is clearly in
love, and, when she leaves, the King unsuccessfully asks Fritelli
whose wife she may be, but has the last word when he says he
will get Laski to release him from his promise because he is in
love with a Pole!

Fritelli asks Minka to tell the Count that the King is at the ball in disguise, then decides to tell Laski himself. Alone, Minka sings to attract Nangis and quickly tells him of the King's supposed presence at the ball. The news passes round and Laski has the doors shut and guarded. When Nangis does not remove his mask, Laski assumes he is the King and an ensemble begins culminating in Nangis's spritely song (prompted by the real King), 'Je suis Roi' (I am the King). The Poles demand his signature to an act of abdication, the King orders him to sign, but, prompted by Minka, he refuses. His captors deliberate how to get rid of him. When death is voted as an alternative to abdication, the real King proposes himself as the true victim – much to everyone's consternation.

When the conspirators draw lots for the man to deal the fatal blow, each writes 'Nangis' on the paper, but when the King makes as if to enter and deal a death blow to himself, Minka appears and admits she helped Nangis escape. The conspirators realise that vengeance may soon overtake them, and, the King promising to keep his oath, they agree to leave the house.

ACT III. The hall of an inn on the Polish frontier. It is full of decorations, most bearing the letter H. A crowd acclaims the prospect of a new King, but Fritelli, looking at the decorations, has to explain the new King is Archduke Ernest, not Henri de Valois! Fritelli learns that a distinguished-looking traveller arrived the night before and is in room eight: it must be Archduke Ernest – but it is a grinning Henri de Valois who comes through the door. The coachman deposited him here. Will the Duke please order him a carriage to take him further? Also, will he convey his infinite regrets to Count Laski's charming niece that he had to leave without saying goodbye? The Duke, more confused than angry, goes off to do the King's bidding, as Alexina and Minka, who have arrived in another carriage, mellifluously lament the departure of the men they love – fine sentiments, inextricably confused names.

Fritelli returns and announces that the King and Nangis have left for France. He then berates Alexina for her indiscretions, 'Je suis du pays des gondoles'. Explaining he is on an errand for the Archduke, he enters room number eight, while Alexina prepares to salute the new King, only to see her lover come out.

All is explained: his identity as King and hers as the Duke's wife, but Minka rushes in, crying that Count Laski is there to take her back to Cracow and the King will be slain. Henri consents to leave, saying he has kept his word: Minka believes he has killed her lover and runs after him, vowing revenge; and Laski is told 'Le roi n'est plus' (The King is dead!). But there has been a change: the Polish nobles, impressed by Henri's renunciation of the throne, have decided to withdraw their opposition. He must be stopped before it is too late!

Nangis appears to explain the deception to Minka (who has had an aria of despair) and claim her in a love duet. The march of the King's guard is heard and Henri returns in triumph, the opera ending with a general acclamation for 'Le roi malgré lui'.

Jules Massenet
(1842–1912)

MANON

OPERA in five acts; text by Meilhac and Gille, based on the story by the Abbé Prévost. Première, Opéra-Comique, Paris, January 19, 1884.

ACT I. The inn at Amiens; 1721. The busy scene echoes the general glitter and bustle of the prelude. Guillot (*tenor*), an old roué, and de Brétigny (*baritone*) are waiting impatiently to dine with three lively ladies of the town. Lescaut (*baritone*) has taken time off from gambling to meet his cousin (in the novel, his sister), on her way to a convent. The stagecoach arrives and Manon (*soprano*) appears, heralded by a naïve tune on the clarinet which becomes her first song. 'Je suis encore tout étourdie' (I think my head is surely reeling[1]), in which she celebrates the joys and surprises of her first experience of travel. Guillot, dazzled by the sight of Manon, suggests to her that his carriage is at her disposal. He is rebuffed by Lescaut, who lectures Manon as to her future conduct: 'Ne bronchez pas' (Now don't you stir).

Manon is alone and a little sad that the brilliance of the outside world seems to be forbidden her: 'Voyons, Manon, plus de chimères' (No use, Manon, no use in dreaming). The aria breathes the spirit of innocence, albeit of innocence ready to be awakened. The Chevalier des Grieux (*tenor*) has come to catch the stagecoach home. He, too, is overcome by the sight of Manon. As their duet develops, we watch young love grow until it sweeps both celebrants along to realisation that fate could remove Manon to the convent; they belong together, and a solution to their immediate problem is at hand in the shape of Guillot's carriage. 'Enchanteresse! Au charme vainqueur! Manon, vous êtes la maîtresse de mon coeur!' (You are a goddess, a being apart. Manon, I worship you as ruler of my heart), sings des Grieux; and after a little encouragement from Manon, 'Nous vivrons à Paris, tous les deux' (Live with me, be my love).

---

[1] Edmund Tracey's translation throughout.

211

Most performances end the act there, as permitted in the revised score of 1895, but originally Lescaut, having lost at cards, comes out to find Manon gone and to blame Guillot, who in his turn understands he has been duped and vows revenge.

ACT II. The lodgings of Manon and des Grieux in the Rue Vivienne, in Paris. A constantly reiterated theme heralds a first sight of the lovers happily together, she interrupting his writing, he gently chiding and then getting her to read aloud the letter explaining her to his father: 'On l'appelle Manon' (So her name is Manon). Manon feels their love is enough but des Grieux says he wants to marry her.

Lescaut and Monsieur de Brétigny (who is disguised as a soldier in Lescaut's regiment) come in. Clearly Lescaut smells more profit for himself in a liaison between Manon and a wealthy nobleman than in her relationship with des Grieux. When he demands if des Grieux intends to marry the girl, des Grieux shows him the letter. Meanwhile, de Brétigny tells Manon that the Chevalier's father has arranged to have his son carried off that very night. Her threats to alert des Grieux would be useless, warns de Brétigny, who then offers Manon wealth and luxury. From the music there can be little doubt of the genuine nature of de Brétigny's feelings for Manon, and, though she protests that she loves des Grieux, in the face of threats she is somehow incapable of translating words into action.

After a lively quartet, Lescaut and de Brétigny leave. When des Grieux goes to send his letter, Manon sings sadly and touchingly to the table, which she takes as a symbol of her domestic life with des Grieux. He returns to tell her of a daydream, in which he saw a veritable paradise, which lacked only one thing: Manon! Des Grieux's dream of Manon is an example of the delicate side of Massenet's art at its best – sensitive, expressive and full of style.

There is a disturbance outside; Manon knows that the men are coming to snatch her love away. He is overpowered and she is left with a heartfelt exclamation of 'Mon pauvre Chevalier!'

ACT III. Scene i. A graceful minuet takes us to a popular fête in the Cours la Reine in Paris. Lescaut finds the chance for an eloquent expression of his gambler's happy-go-lucky philosophy: 'A quoi bon l'économie' (Where's the fun in living cheaply). Guillot appears and is discovered by de Brétigny, who admits (to Guillot's ill-concealed glee) that he recently refused Manon's caprice to have at her house the Ballet of the Opéra.

Manon appears. She is at the height of her worldly success, admired by all and inclined to bask in her popularity and fame: 'Je marche sur tous les chemins' (I rule as queen of the land). Her bravura *arioso* is succeeded by the famous gavotte: 'Obéissons quand leur voix appelle' (Venus is calling, I must obey her).

Manon overhears a conversation between de Brétigny and the Comte des Grieux (*bass*): his son is to take holy orders at Saint Sulpice. She carefully asks the old man (she is unsure if he knows her) if des Grieux has recovered from his recent affair. He makes it plain the affair is over and his son is quite recovered. It is a passage of delicacy and economy and a perfect example of Massenet's conversational style and of his ability to advance drama in a set-piece.

The Ballet arrives and performs a four-movement pastiche, together with a Préambule, during which Manon broods over her lost love. She makes up her mind and asks Lescaut for her chair to take her to Saint Sulpice. Guillot is left with the bill and a mere nod of indifference from the preoccupied Manon.

Scene II. Saint Sulpice. A chorus of devout ladies enthuses over the maiden sermon of the new Abbé des Grieux, who comes in with his father. Nothing he can say seems to shake his son's resolve to take holy orders. The Comte leaves, and the Chevalier launches into an impassioned wrestling with his past and his conscience: 'Ah, fuyez douce image' (Ah, farewell dream of love), one of Massenet's grandest and most effective arias.

No sooner has he gone to take part in the service than Manon appears, asks to see him and sails into a dramatic and heartfelt *arioso* prayer to God for a restoration to her of the love of des Grieux. In a moment, he is at her side, denying her pleas albeit with a note of mounting hysteria, until Manon plays her last card: 'N'est-ce plus ma main que cette main presse?' (Don't you feel my hand on your own hand pressing?). As the melody winds its tendrils around his very heart, des Grieux finds his resolve crumbling into an avowal of eternal love.

ACT IV. A fashionable gambling house at the Hôtel Transylvanie. Lescaut with Poussette, Javotte and Rosette (*sopranos*) are at the tables. Guillot sings a risqué song about the Regent and his mistress. Manon arrives with des Grieux, whom she urges to play until she wrings from him an avowal of love more complete if possible than any that has gone before. Twice comes the phrase of total surrender before Manon, apparently in an ecstasy of pleasure, sings 'A nous les amours et les roses!' (A lifetime of love and of roses!), the most frivolous of her musical utterances, in whose refrain the three *filles de joie* join. Lescaut has meanwhile been cleaned out, but Guillot challenges des Grieux, who wins and attempts a repetition of his love-song. Guillot accuses his opponent of cheating. He leaves, but des Grieux refuses to escape, as Manon urges him, as it would be an admission of guilt. The lovers are arrested: des Grieux to prison and a quick release; Manon to trial and certain transportation as a condemned lady of easy virtue.

ACT V. The road to Le Havre. Des Grieux has plotted with Lescaut to effect Manon's escape as she is led towards the ship and transportation. But Lescaut reveals his men have fled. The party approaches; Lescaut bribes the sergeant and Manon appears, exhausted. She and des Grieux remember past happiness; she asks him for forgiveness, before dying with a half-smile and a quote from the first meeting: 'Et c'est là l'histoire de Manon Lescaut' (Now you know the story of Manon Lescaut).

History has tended to put forward *Manon* as Massenet's *chef d'oeuvre*, and it is certainly his most-performed work. If for nothing else, his portrayal of his heroine would proclaim him an operatic master. Manon's solos plot her development, and we see her awakening from child to young woman; the gradual development from the disingenuous 'On l'appelle Manon' and the heartrending 'Adieu, notre petite table' through the proud confidence of Act III's entrance and the touchingly vulnerable scene with des Grieux *père* to the impassioned and wholly sincere *arioso* at Saint Sulpice and the calculating but irresistible 'N'est-ce plus ma main' which closes that scene. At her death the various strands of Manon's musical character – the genuinely simple, the passionate, the sincere, the mundane – are combined. This is a multi-faceted and fascinating musical portrait and his celebration of an aspect of the eternal feminine inspired Massenet to write what is, with *Carmen*, the greatest example of the genre created for the Opéra-Comique and its audience.

WERTHER

OPERA in four acts by Jules Massenet; text by Edouard Blau, Paul Milliet and Georges Hartmann, after Goethe's novel. Première (in German) at the Vienna Opera, February 16, 1892; first performed Opéra-Comique, Paris, January 16, 1893.

A CT I. After a prelude consisting of the music associated with the more forceful as well as the idyllic side of Werther's character, the scene is the garden outside the Magistrate's house in Frankfurt, about 1780. The owner (*bass*) is rehearsing his children in a Christmas song; they sing it badly, but his comment – that they would not dare sing like that if their sister Charlotte were there – has the effect simultaneously of introducing Charlotte (*mezzo-soprano*) and improving the singing. Two friends of the Magistrate, Johann (*bass*) and Schmidt (*tenor*), remind him of his promise to meet them later that night. Sophie (*soprano*), Charlotte's younger sister, has come in and mention is made of the dreamer Werther and the practical Albert; the last-named will make, says Schmidt, a model husband for Charlotte. Schmidt and Johann go off singing 'Vivat Bacchus', and everyone else goes into the house.

Werther (*tenor*) appears, expressing his pleasure in the country atmosphere in a graceful recitative and aria, 'O nature pleine de grâce' (Mother nature, great is your bounty[1]). Charlotte, dressed for that evening's dance, comes out of the house with the children and takes advantage of the lateness of her escort to cut them their bread and butter. Charlotte says good-night to the children, who, the Magistrate says, have been in her charge since their mother's death. Werther is enraptured at the family scene: 'O spectacle idéal' (O sweet vision, ideal of love).

Most successful is the way Massenet in a few minutes of music suggests the passage of time while Charlotte and Werther are at the ball: a few sentences for the Magistrate alone and then with Sophie, an empty stage before the entry of Albert (*baritone*), his recognition by Sophie followed by his aria – and night has fallen completely, the moon risen, and the scene is set for the return of the principals.

The music of the 'Clair de lune' (Moonlight) is heard in the orchestra as Charlotte and Werther come into the garden. Their mutual attraction is obvious and Werther declares his love before Massenet interrupts the duet with an effect that is as simple as it is telling: the Magistrate calls out that Albert is back – the idyll is shattered, and we have taken a turn towards tragedy. The 'Clair de lune' duet shows many of Massenet's qualities at their best – the elegant simplicity of the vocal line, the economical role of the orchestra, the shapely, rewarding contours of the tunes, the evocative atmosphere of the whole. It is not undramatic but it is still the world of understatement, of the small gesture as opposed to the large, the world which Massenet knew and interpreted best. A few hasty sentences explain that Albert is the fiancé Charlotte's mother wished for her, and the curtain falls on Werther's desperate cry, 'Un autre! son époux!' (She'll be another's wife!)

ACT II. In front of the church. Johann and Schmidt are drinking at the inn. Inside the church the golden wedding of the village pastor is being celebrated. Charlotte and Albert appear, apparently full of happiness after three months of marriage, and go into the church. Werther, who catches sight of them, soliloquises in music of more vigorous character than we have previously heard from him as he laments that marriage with Charlotte is an impossibility for him: 'J'aurais sur ma poitrine' (These

---

[1] Translation by Norman Tucker throughout.

arms would now be holding). Albert comes out of the church, and talks to his friend, who, he thinks, is, or has been, in love with Charlotte. After a painful admission, Werther affirms his loyalty to both: 'Mais, comme après l'orage' (But, as when storms are over). Sophie, in a little song 'Le gai soleil' (Look at the sun), sings of the happiness in her heart. Werther resolves to leave, but the sight of Charlotte is too much for him and he renews his protestations of love. She begs him to go and at all events to stay away until Christmas time. Werther is overcome and prays at the same time for strength to stay away and for the happiness which his return could bring him: 'Lorsque l'enfant revient d'un voyage' (When any son returns to his home). He tells Sophie he is going away, never to return. She tells her sister and brother-in-law of this, and Albert comments darkly that this can mean only that Werther is still in love with Charlotte.

ACT III. It is Christmas. Charlotte, at home, realises that she returns Werther's love; merely to re-read the letters he has written her is enough to bring her to the verge of hysteria. Her sister's efforts to cheer her up are in vain, and when Sophie refers to Werther, Charlotte's reserve breaks down and she collapses in floods of tears: 'Va! laisse couler mes larmes' (There! Now let my tears flow freely!). Left alone, she prays for strength: 'Ah! mon courage m'abandonne' (Ah! I am losing all my courage). Her reading of the letters, the 'Air des larmes', and her prayer for strength together make up a scene which is hardly less powerful and convincing than Tatiana's 'Letter scene' in *Eugene Onegin*. In a moment Charlotte becomes a real and believable person, not the prig we have known up to now.

Suddenly, Werther himself appears; reason had urged him to stay away but instinct proved too strong; he is here on the appointed day of Christmas. They look together at the books they used to read and Charlotte reminds Werther that he was translating Ossian before he went away. The sight of the book awakens memories, and from it he sings a song of tragic love: 'Pourquoi me réveiller?' (Awaken me no more). This aria has become enormously popular, and in it for the first time in Charlotte's presence Werther uses the directness of musical expression which has hitherto been reserved for soliloquies.

When Charlotte's voice betrays her feelings, Werther abandons restraint and embraces her. From the beginning of Act III, there is a straightforwardness and a decisiveness that contrasts with the frustration, the continual second thoughts of the first two acts. Werther draws back and Charlotte rushes from the room, locking the door behind her. Albert comes in and connects his wife's agitation with Werther's return, of which he has already learned. Just then the servant brings a message from Werther: 'I am going on a long journey, will you lend me your pistols?' Albert tells Charlotte to give them to the servant; she fully understands the significance of the message.

ACT IV. The scene changes to Werther's apartment (Acts III and IV are played without an interval). Charlotte comes in to find Werther dying. He prevents her going for help, and is contented when she tells him she has loved him from the moment they first met. As he dies, the voices of children celebrating Christmas can be heard outside his room.

THAÏS

OPERA in three acts by Jules Massenet; text by Louis Gallet after the novel by Anatole France. Première March 16, 1894, at Opéra, Paris.

D'INDY, not only a sharp critic but a rival composer, wrote of the 'discreet and semi-religious eroticism' of Massenet's music and it was *Thaïs* he had in mind. But the central relationship between Thaïs, courtesan turned nun, and Athanaël, the monk drawn irresistibly to the world of the flesh he thought he despised, is a stronger one than d'Indy's *bon mot* suggests. Anatole France, in the novel on which *Thaïs* is founded, mocks more than he pities Paphnuce/Athanaël, but the figure Massenet and his librettists have created is pivotal to the opera, and the pull between his urge to denounce sin and the irresistible attraction Thaïs has for him provides a powerful basis for musical drama.

ACT I. Scene i. A Cenobite establishment on the banks of the Nile; late fourth century. Athanaël (*baritone*) returns from Alexandria scandalised by the sensation caused there by the activities of the shameless courtesan and dancer, Thaïs (*soprano*). Before joining the Cenobites he knew her ('Hélas! enfant encore') and once as a young man hesitated in front of her door. Now, a man of God, he must save her soul. Palémon (*bass*) advises against any such action, but once asleep Athanaël has a vision of Thaïs in the theatre and wakes to proclaim his mission.

Scene ii. A terrace with a view of Alexandria. A grandiose orchestral introduction leads to Athanaël's majestic apostrophising of the city of his birth ('Voilà donc la terrible cité': See before me the city of sin). He greets his friend Nicias (*tenor*), a young Alexandrian who has purchased the love of Thaïs for a week, of which there is still one day to run. Nicias will clothe and bathe Athanaël so that he may be introduced to the high priestess of Venus whom he plans to save. Graceful music depicts the adorning of Athanaël, supervised by Crobyle and Myrtale (*soprano* and *mezzo-soprano*), the meeting of Thaïs and Athanaël, and the act's finale as Athanaël goes off to wait outside her house. Her 'Qui te fait si sévère?' (What makes you so harsh?) is one of the score's most attractive moments.

ACT II. Scene i. Thaïs's house. Thaïs's mood of introspection as she contemplates herself in a mirror turns to something closer to a celebration of her beauty as she demands reassurance ('Dis-moi que je suis belle': Tell me that I am beautiful). Reassurance is not what Athanaël plans to provide in his forceful attempt to convert her. He argues that the word 'Amour' has connotations beyond the physical and her hysterical outburst suggests the breaking down of barriers.

Scene ii is preceded by an interlude, the so-called 'Méditation', which consists of a violin solo over harp and eventually full orchestra and chorus, and is the score's most famous number. Thaïs in a rough woollen dress is prepared to forsake the past and follow Athanaël. She must destroy her possessions, he says, but she begs to be allowed to keep a little statue of Eros: 'L'amour est une vertu rare' (Love is no common virtue) – an aria graceful and chaste beside the bravura of the Air du Miroir. But Athanaël dashes it to the ground. Here occurs the ballet, a divertissement in seven movements danced for Nicias and his friends, at whose end Thaïs's house disappears in flames (the ballet is often cut in modern performance though once *de rigueur* for the Opéra).

ACT III. Scene i. The oasis. This scene was added during the opera's first run, and orchestrally it is full of the shimmering heat and destructive sun which beat down on Thaïs and Athanaël as they make their way towards the nunnery Albine (*mezzo-soprano*) has established far from the contamination of civilisation. Thaïs is at the end of her strength and, in an extended duet, she pleads her exhaustion; he goads her forward, until the extent of her plight moves him to fetch water from a well and she sings: 'O messager de Dieu' (O messenger of God). Their voices join in the scene's culmination, a duet of exquisite tenderness: 'Baigne d'eau mes mains et mes lèvres' (Bathe my hands with water and my lips). Thaïs is consigned to Albine for the rest of her earthly life, and only then does Athanaël know the unbearable agony of saying goodbye.

Scene ii. With the Cenobites once more, Athanaël confesses that since he returned from his conversion of Thaïs, he has not known a moment's peace. As he sleeps, a vision of the courtesan invades his mind; he is convinced she is about to die and he must go to her.

Scene iii. Arrived at the huts of Albine's nunnery, Athanaël's vision is confirmed, and Thaïs's pious thoughts as she dies ('Te souvient-il du lumineux voyage?': Do you recall the unforgettable journey?) are contrasted with the powerless rage of Atha-naël. The Méditation returns to haunt the monk in his despair.

DON QUICHOTTE

Five acts, by Jules Massenet, text after Cervantes; première, Paris, 1910. Dulcinea (*contralto*) is being wooed by her four admirers. Don Quixote (*bass*) and Sancho Panza (*baritone*) appear, and the Don serenades his love, promising to recover a necklace she lost to a bandit. He tilts at the windmills which he thinks are giants, and is caught in the sails. The bandits capture him and Sancho but, touched by the Don's chivalrous creed, return the jewellery. Dulcinea's gratitude prompts him to ask for her hand. She tries to let him down lightly, turning on her admirers, who are mocking him. In a moving final scene the old man, who fought only for good, gently expires watched over by the faithful Sancho.

Mikhail Ivanovich Glinka
(1804–1857)

A LIFE FOR THE TSAR[1]
Ivan Susanin

OPERA in four acts and an epilogue; text by G. F. Rozen. Première December 9, 1836, St. Petersburg.

Act i. A village street at Domnin; 1613. The peasants sing a patriotic song to celebrate the imminent return of Sobinin (*tenor*) from the wars. In a cavatina Antonida (*soprano*), his fian-cée, pours out her happiness at the prospect of seeing him again. Susanin (*bass*), her father, brings news that a Polish army is advancing on Moscow. Fears lessen when Sobinin himself appears and tells them that the Poles have in fact been repulsed. He is anxious that his marriage with Antonida should im-mediately be celebrated, but Susanin, full of forebodings at the state of the country, will not bless their union until a Tsar has

---

[1] Glinka originally called his opera *Ivan Susanin* and changed it only after prompting from the Imperial Court to *A Life for the Tsar*. In Soviet Russia (though not invariably outside) the original title was used.

been elected. Sobinin finds this objection easy to overcome; a Tsar has in fact just been chosen, and it is none other than their own landlord, Romanoff. Susanin withdraws his objections, and, amidst general rejoicing, agrees to the wedding.

ACT II. The Polish headquarters. A magnificent ball is in progress, and the Poles are full of confidence that their forthcoming campaign against the Russians will be crowned with success. A series of dances follows, including a Cracoviak and two Mazurkas. A messenger tells the Polish commander (*baritone*) of the Polish defeat and of the election of Romanoff as Tsar of Russia. The Poles plan to capture the young Tsar at the monastery where he is living.

ACT III. Susanin's house. Vanja, Susanin's adopted son (*contralto*), sings a song, and Susanin joins in to comment on Russia's present happy state. He goes on to say that he hears rumours that the Poles are planning to abduct the Tsar. Vanja and Susanin look forward to the day when the boy will be old enough to take his place amongst Russia's soldiers. Peasants congratulate Antonida and Sobinin on their wedding, and a quartet follows for Antonida, Vanja, Sobinin, and Susanin.

The rejoicing is interrupted by Polish troops, who try to force Susanin to tell them the way to the Tsar's monastery. Susanin at first refuses, but then manages to convey to Vanja that he must ride ahead to warn the Tsar while Susanin himself leads the Poles out of their way. He goes off with them much to the despair of Antonida. She tells Sobinin of the disaster which has come upon them; he does his best to console her, and gathers a band of peasants with whom he goes off in an attempt to rescue Susanin.

ACT IV. Scene i. A forest, at night. Sobinin's men are disheartened by the intense cold, but in a vigorous aria he restores their confidence. Glinka composed an alternative version for this scene, and set it in the forest near the monastery. Vanja, who has ridden his horse to death, rushes in, knocks at the monastery doors and convinces the servants of the danger which threatens the Tsar's life.

Scene ii. Another part of the forest. The Poles accuse Susanin of having lost the way. He denies it, and they light a fire before settling down to rest for the night. Susanin is left alone, and in a famous scene he makes up his mind that it is his duty to give his life for his country. A storm blows up, the Poles awake, and, as day dawns, Susanin tells them that he has deliberately led them astray into the wildest part of the forest; the Tsar is safe and beyond their reach. They kill him.

Epilogue. A street in Moscow. Everyone sings the praises of the Tsar. Antonida, Vanja and Sobinin arrive. The news of Susanin's death has reached the crowd, which shares the grief of his dependants. The scene changes to a square in front of the Kremlin; the Tsar's procession enters the capital.

RUSSLAN AND LYUDMILA

FIVE acts, by Mikhail Glinka; première, St. Petersburg, 1842. Text after Pushkin. The Grand Duke of Kiev (*bass*) is entertaining the suitors of his daughter Lyudmila (*soprano*): Russlan (*baritone*), a knight, Ratmir (*contralto*), a poet, and Farlaf (*bass*), a warrior. At a sudden thunderclap Lyudmila disappears. Russlan discovers from Finn (*tenor*), the wizard, that she has been abducted by the dwarf Tchernomor. Farlaf seeks the advice of Naina (*mezzo-soprano*), a wicked fairy. Russlan subdues a gigantic head and finds a magic sword. He is lured by the sirens of Naina's palace, but Finn rescues him. He defeats Tchernomor but cannot waken Lyudmila from her trance until Finn gives him a magic ring and she is restored to consciousness.

Aleksandr Porfyrevich Borodin
(1834–1887)

PRINCE IGOR

OPERA in a prologue and four acts; text by the composer after a play by V. V. Stassov; completed by Rimsky-Korsakov and Glazunov. Première November 4, 1890, at St. Petersburg.

BORODIN, who divided his life between science and music, worked on *Prince Igor* piece by piece. It remained unfinished at his death, but was completed by Rimsky-Korsakov and his pupil Glazunov and received its first performance three years after Borodin's death.

The overture (orchestrated by Glazunov) includes music which precedes Igor's great aria in Act II, themes later associated with Khan Kontchak and Kontchakovna, and reaches a climax with the themes of Igor's aria.

PROLOGUE. The marketplace of Poutivl; 1185. There has been a solar eclipse, regarded by Prince Igor's people as an evil omen. They implore the Prince (*baritone*) to postpone his departure to pursue the Polovtsi, a Tartar tribe, formerly driven to the plains of the Don by Igor's father, Prince Sviatoslav of Kiev. But Igor and his son Vladimir (*tenor*) set off.

221

ACT I. Scene i. The house of Prince Vladimir Galitzky (*bass*), brother of Igor's wife, Yaroslavna (*soprano*). He has been appointed to govern Poutivl and watch over Princess Yaroslavna, and is popular on account of his easy-going, profligate ways. In an incisive, vigorous aria, which perfectly sets off his irresponsible character, he makes it clear that he is a man of mettle, and one to be reckoned with.

Some young girls appeal for Galitzky's help and protection against his hangers-on, who have abducted one of them. He refuses. Skoula (*bass*) and Eroshka (*tenor*), a pair of drunken *Gudok* players who have deserted from Igor's army, try to stir up the mob against their absent chief and in praise of Galitzky, whom they want as prince.

Scene ii. Yaroslavna's room. After a beautiful, warm *arioso* passage for Yaroslavna alone, she is approached by the girls who have failed to enlist Galitzky's support. She proves more than a match for her brother, who has come in, and compels him to agree to give up the girl who was abducted.

Meanwhile, disasters have befallen Igor: he has been defeated; he and the young Prince are prisoners, and the enemy is marching on Poutivl. The alarm is sounded, but the act ends on a note of defiance, the loyal boyars swearing to defend Yaroslavna, their Princess.

ACT II. The Polovtsi camp. In this and the next act, Borodin successfully gives his music something of an oriental colour. Khan Kontchak (*bass*) sings music that is totally different from Galitzky's (although the two roles are often, valuably, sung by one and the same singer), and Kontchakovna, his daughter (*mezzo-soprano*), obviously inhabits a different world from Yaroslavna. This difference is immediately apparent in the opening scene, when the young Polovtsian maidens sing their languorous song to their mistress. They dance for her, but it is dusk, and she puts an end to their activities, herself singing a beautiful nocturne whose languishing, chromatic melody speaks longingly of love: 'Now the daylight dies'.

Kontchakovna bids her women give water to a newly-arrived group of Russian prisoners, who thank her and move on towards captivity, followed by the Polovtsian guards. Prince Vladimir, Igor's son, is in love with the Khan's daughter, and he expresses his feelings in an aria of exquisite beauty, 'Daylight is fading away'. This is followed by a passionate love duet.

Kontchakovna tells Vladimir she is confident her father will not oppose their marriage, but Vladimir is sure Igor will not even consider giving his approval to a match with the daughter of his enemy. They leave as Igor approaches, filled with longing for his homeland, and walks through the camp where he is held prisoner. In a magnificent aria, he sings desperately of his past happiness and present misery, and longs for freedom to re-establish his glory and to ensure the safety of his people.

The Tartar traitor Ovlour (*tenor*) approaches and, in music of insinuating character, offers to help Igor escape. He refuses: honour prevents him taking such a course, however strong the temptation.

Hardly has Ovlour gone than Khan Kontchak himself appears before Igor, whom he regards as an honoured guest, not a prisoner. In a great bass *scena*, the Khan offers the Prince anything he may desire to make his captivity less irksome. Igor answers that nothing irks him, only his loss of liberty. Even liberty the Khan will restore him, if he will pledge his word not to make war on him again. Why should they not unite? To-gether the world would be at their feet. But Igor admits that if he were given his freedom, his first action would be to raise an army and march against the Tartars who threaten the peace of his land. The Khan appears to like his guest's frankness, and gives orders that the dancing slaves perform for their entertain-ment.

Now begin the famous Polovtsian Dances, known from fre-quent performance with or without the chorus (which is in reality an integral part of them), in the concert hall, and as a separate ballet. They range from soft enticing melody to harsh vigour, with more than a touch of the barbaric, and make a thrilling finale to an act whose varied musical splendours con-stitute perhaps Borodin's most enduring memorial.

ACT III. The Prelude, a savage Polovtsian march, continues, augmented by the chorus, to accompany the entrance of Khan Gzak (*bass*) and his warriors. Like Kontchak they have triumphed over their Russian foes and have brought in a crowd of prisoners. We see the primitive side of Kontchak's character in the vigorous and triumphant aria in which he welcomes his brothers-in-arms and rejoices in the slaughter and devastation they have left behind them. The two Khans go off to make new plans for their campaigns against the Russians. Left alone, the Russian prisoners lament the state into which their country has fallen. Is it not Igor's responsibility to escape and lead his countrymen to revenge and freedom? Igor is persuaded that he must sacrifice honour to duty.

The Polovtsi guards are drunk. It is Ovlour's chance. He arranges to meet Igor and Vladimir with the horses he has wait-ing on the other side of the river. But they reckon without Kont-chakovna, who has had word of the escape attempt and pleads with Vladimir to take her with them. In a fine trio, Igor opposes Kontchakovna's suggestion. The Khan's daughter has recourse to a desperate expedient and rouses the camp. Igor escapes, but Vladimir is left behind in the hands of the Polovtsi, who demand his death. Kontchak arrives and admits his admiration for Igor; in his position, he would have done the same. In a couple of phrases, he shows both sides of his simple yet complex nature; let them hang the guards who should have prevented the escape, but spare Vladimir to live amongst them as Kontchakovna's husband, and their ally. The act ends with a chorus of praise to Kontchak.

ACT IV. The city walls and public square of Poutivl. In an extensive *scena*, Yaroslavna laments her lost happiness. Some peasants pass by and express their own woes.

But the tide is due to turn for the Russians. Yaroslavna spies two horsemen riding furiously towards the city. One is dressed as a prince, the other a Polovtsian. Dare she hope her husband has returned? She recognises Igor, and in a moment they are in each other's arms. After a rapturous duet they go off towards the citadel, just as Eroshka and Skoula come into sight, slightly drunk and giving vent to disloyal sentiments on the subject of their rightful prince. Igor is the cause of all their woes, they sing. Suddenly they see the subject of their conversation standing in front of them. What now – exile or death? Borodin was much too fond of his drunken rascals to let them finish the opera with anything but a flourish. So Eroshka and Skoula announce the return of Igor to his unsuspecting subjects. They are allowed to participate in the finale (marked *allegro marziale*), in which the return of Igor and the imminent fall of Galitzky are jointly celebrated.

Modest Petrovich Moussorgsky
(1839–1881)

BORIS GODOUNOV

OPERA in a prologue and four acts; text from Pushkin's play of the same name and Karamazin's *History of the Russian State*. There have been no fewer than four main versions of *Boris*:

(A) Composed and orchestrated between October 1868 and December 1869, consisting of seven scenes: Courtyard of Novodevichy Monastery; Coronation; Pimen's Cell; The Inn; The Tsar's Apartments; Before the Cathedral of St. Basil, Moscow (including the Simpleton); Death of Boris. This version was rejected by the committee of the Imperial theatres.

(B) Moussorgsky immediately started on a second version, finished by June 1872. This was also rejected, but the inn scene and the two scenes of the Polish act were performed publicly in February 1873 at the Marinsky Theatre. As a result of the success of this performance, the entire opera (with cuts) was performed on January 27/February 8, 1874, to public acclaim but critical scorn. By 1882 it was dropped from the repertory.

(C) In 1896 (fifteen years after the composer's death) Rimsky-Korsakov revised and re-scored the work, making a large number of cuts and composing some new passages to bridge the gaps caused by the cuts. This was performed the same year.

(D) In 1906–8, Rimsky-Korsakov worked on another edition, re-storing previous cuts but retaining his own additions to the score. It is in something like (D) that the opera has most often been performed.

*B*ORIS GODOUNOV is based on one of the most curious episodes of Russian history in the sixteenth and seventeenth centuries. Boris, the brother-in-law and chief minister of Tsar Fyodor, son of Ivan the Terrible, has had assassinated young Dimitri, the Tsar's half-brother and heir. On the death of Fyodor, Boris himself ascends the throne. At about the same time, a young monk, Grigory, escapes from his monastery and goes to Poland where he poses as the dead Tsarevich Dimitri. The pretender marries Marina, daughter of the Voyevode of Sandomir, raises a Polish army and marches against Russia. They hear of the death of Boris, and the false Dimitri, taking advantage of the circumstances, in turn usurps power.

As a matter of historical fact, Boris's son Fyodor was murdered and his daughter Xenia taken by Dimitri as his mistress (Dvořák's opera *Dmitrij* deals with these events). Dimitri was soon deposed and killed by Shouisky, who reigned in his stead. History has acquitted Boris of the crime of murdering Dimitri (although for the purposes of the opera it must of course be accepted as true), but Shouisky goes down as an ambitious and cruel Tsar. Marina seems to have been all that is implied in the opera; after the death of Dimitri she became the wife of yet another pretender to the throne, whom she claimed to recognise as her lost husband.

PROLOGUE. Scene i. The courtyard of the Monastery of Novo-devichy, near Moscow; 1598. The confused crowd is ordered by a police officer to keep up a prayer for guidance, interrupted by the appearance of Tchelkalov (*baritone*), the secretary of the Douma, who informs them that Boris has not yet accepted the crown.

Scene ii. The courtyard of the Kremlin. Bells peal, a procession of boyars and guards crosses the stage before Prince Shouisky (*tenor*) cries, 'Long life to thee, Tsar Boris Feodorovich', and the people break into praise of the new Tsar. Boris (*bass*) himself appears, and, in introspective mood, prays for the guidance of Tsar Fyodor to justify the people's confidence in the reign that is just beginning. After prayer, the people from beggar to prince shall feast as his guests. The people acclaim their new Tsar.

ACT I. Scene i. Five years later. Famine and plague are rife and the people have abandoned law and order and take to pillage. Boris is blamed – in spite of his effort to rule wisely and well. In a cell in the monastery of Chudov the old monk, Pimen (*bass*), is engaged on his chronicle of the history of Russia. He is satisfied he has reached the end of his labours. Chanting is heard; suddenly Grigory (*tenor*), Pimen's young companion in his cell, wakes up. For the third time he has had a nightmare that he has fallen from a high tower in Moscow (the reference is to a version of Dimitri's murder; he is thought to have been thrown from a high tower).

Pimen tries to comfort him, but Grigory continues to lament that his whole life has been spent in monastic seclusion. Pimen reminds him that many of Russia's most famous warriors turned to a solitary existence to end their days in peace, not least of them war-like Ivan himself, who died in this very cell. The last Tsar, Fyodor, was a man of peace, but now God has sent to Russia the fierce Tsar Boris, a regicide. At this, Grigory asks Pimen how old Fyodor's brother, Dimitri, would have been had he lived. Pimen replies he would have been about Grigory's age, nearly twenty.

The matins bell is heard. Pimen, as he leaves, expresses hope that Grigory will carry on his work as chronicler. Grigory vows that Boris shall not escape the judgment of heaven for his crime.

Scene ii. An inn on the Lithuanian border of Russia. The hostess's (*mezzo-soprano*) little song is interrupted by the sound of singing from outside. In stagger two drunk and disreputable monks, Varlaam (*bass*) and Missail (*tenor*). With them is Grigory, who has fled from the monastery, and is on his way to Lithuania and freedom, pursued by the police.

Varlaam launches into a ferocious song about his achievements as a soldier in Ivan the Terrible's army at the battle of Kazan. Meanwhile, Grigory discovers from the hostess the safest route to the Lithuanian border.

Suddenly the police arrive. They question Grigory, who seems harmless enough, then turn their attention to the vagabond monks. The captain (*bass*) orders Varlaam to read a warrant they carry, but he pleads lack of practice. Grigory, who is instructed to read it aloud, substitutes a description of Varlaam. The police round on the old monk, who, with much difficulty, deciphers the paper. As all realise that Grigory is their man, he escapes through the window.

ACT II. The Tsar's apartments in the Kremlin. The Tsarevich Fyodor (*mezzo-soprano*) is studying a map of the Russian empire, while his sister Xenia (*soprano*) sings a sad song. The

Nurse (*contralto*) tries to comfort her, then sings a song about a gnat. Fyodor leads a clapping game, at the climax of which the Tsar himself appears, to the terror of the Nurse. Boris comforts his daughter and bids his son take his lessons seriously; the time may soon come when he will be called on to rule over the countries he sees outlined on his map.

Boris pours out his agony of mind, the doubts and torments which his rule of Russia has brought him, the enemies who conspire against him, the remorse which fills his soul when he recalls the murdered Dimitri. This great monologue ('I have attained the highest power') rises in intensity, then falls away as Boris himself sinks under the weight of conscience.

He hears a noise outside and sends Fyodor to investigate. The boyar-in-waiting comes to ask for an audience on behalf of Prince Shouisky. The boyar warns that disaffected nobles have been in touch with the Poles, and that Shouisky himself is in league with them. Fyodor returns and tells his father in a charming song that the noise was an escaped parrot.

Shouisky comes in. Boris accuses him of hypocrisy and treason. Shouisky denies the accusations, but tacitly admits his correspondence with the rebels. He brings grave news: a pretender in Poland has been publicly acknowledged by the King, and privately by the Pope. He assures the Tsar his throne is inviolate, but warns him that the Russian people might join the pretender's cause were he to cross the border claiming to be the lost Tsarevich, Dimitri.

The Tsar dismisses his son and orders Shouisky to confirm that the body buried at Uglich was Dimitri's. Shouisky makes as if to soothe his fears: while the bodies of the prince and the men killed by the crowd as his murderers lay on the cathedral steps, the others began to putrefy, but Dimitri's was as fresh as when he was killed.

Boris, exhausted, signals to Shouisky to leave him. He feels that he is suffocating, as much with terror and remorse as from lack of air. Boris takes the figures on a chiming clock for an apparition of the murdered child. His hysteria verges on madness, and he sinks sobbing to the floor, praying to God for forgiveness.

ACT III. Scene i. The Polish Act. The apartments of Marina Mnishek (*soprano*), daughter of the Voyevode of Sandomir. The girls sing but she dismisses them and sings an air *alla mazurka*, in which she gives vent to her ambitions concerning the pretender Dimitri, through whom she hopes to ascend the throne of Russia. She is interrupted by Rangoni (*bass*), a Jesuit, who exhorts her to remember her duty when she becomes ruler: she must convert the heretic Russians to the true religion.

Scene ii. A fountain in the garden of Mnishek at Sandomir. Dimitri sings ardently of his love for Marina. Rangoni sidles into view, and tells him that he will lead him to Marina, who loves him. In return he asks for nothing more than to be allowed to watch over his spiritual welfare.

During a polonaise, the nobles pay court to Marina and plan their march on Moscow. Marina comes out to find Dimitri full of tender phrases, and it takes all her haughtiness to provoke him into declaring an immediate intention to lead an army on Moscow. Marina, her wish fulfilled, begins to fawn on him, in the famous love duet. At the moment of their embrace the orchestra runs down Rangoni's chromatic scale to show the triumph is neither Marina's nor Dimitri's, but his and his Church's.

ACT IV. Moussorgsky (in version B) placed the scene of Boris's death before the so-called revolutionary scene, thus implicitly making the Russian people the real protagonists of his drama. But in (C) and (D), Rimsky-Korsakov reversed the order, finishing the opera with the death of Boris, preceded by the revolutionary scene.

Thus in Moussorgsky's latest version (B), the first scene of Act IV is set in the Granovitaya Palace in the Kremlin, where the Douma is discussing measures necessary to repel the threatened invasion. Shouisky tells them that the previous day he saw the Tsar muttering to himself and seemingly warding off some spectre, crying, 'Away, away!'

At this moment, Boris's voice is heard outside, uttering the same words. Shouisky brings him to his senses, and he takes his seat on the throne. Shouisky says that a holy man of great age wishes to speak to the Tsar. It is Pimen, telling a strange story of a blind shepherd who was told in a dream to go to the tomb of the Tsarevich Dimitri and pray. He did so, and his sight was restored. Boris, overcome with horror, falls into the arms of the boyars. He realises he is dying and sends for his son.

Boris orders they be left alone. He tells Fyodor that he is lawful heir to the throne of Russia. Let him beware of the nobles and their plots, let him care for the people and for his sister, Xenia. There is the tolling of a bell and chanting of monks praying for the repose of the Tsar's soul. The boyars return. Boris, with a last cry, 'While I have breath I still am Tsar', falls dying in their midst.

Scene ii. A clearing in the forest of Kromy.[1] Dimitri and his troops have marched into Russia and the country is in chaos. A

---

[1] This scene replaces one which would come at the beginning of Act IV, set in Moscow, outside the Cathedral of St. Basil. The crowd does not

mob is baiting a landowner and children mock a Simpleton (*tenor*), who sings a pathetic song, and steal the few pence he has collected. Varlaam and Missail chant the praises of Dimitri, and, when two Jesuits (*basses*) appear, denounce them to the crowd, which prepares to lynch them.

A procession heralds the approach of Dimitri and his troops. He releases the boyar and Jesuits, and bids the people follow him to Moscow. The stage is empty except for the Simpleton, who has taken no part in welcoming the new Tsar. He bewails the fate of Russia: 'Woe and sorrow always, lament, Russian folk, poor hungry folk'.

KHOVANSHCHINA
The Khovansky Rising

OPERA in five acts by Modest Moussorgsky; text by the composer and V. V. Stassov. Première February 21, 1886, at St. Petersburg. Completed and orchestrated by Rimsky-Korsakov.

MOUSSORGSKY'S aim was to picture the struggle between the old and the new in Russian life at the time of the assumption of power by Peter the Great. On the one hand are the reactionary Princes Khovansky with their Streltsy followers who engage in political strife with the Regent (Golitsin's party); on the other, the Old Believers under Dositheus, who had refused to accept the reforms imposed as long before as 1654. The 'new' regime of Peter the Great was victorious in its struggle against both the Streltsy and the Old Believers, and it is with the outcome of this clash that *Khovanshchina* is concerned.

Moussorgsky, although he began the opera as early as 1872, did not live to finish it himself, the necessary work of scoring and piecing together being done by Rimsky-Korsakov, who also effected a number of changes in his 1883 edition. A more faithful edition by Shostakovich appeared in 1959.

---

believe that Dimitri is dead and wonders whether the Tsar's anxiety over Grigory and his claim to be the Tsarevich suggests he is of the same mind. A Simpleton turns to Boris as he leaves the Cathedral, and begs him in retribution to kill the ragamuffins who stole from him 'as he killed Dimitri'. Boris, unnerved, asks the Simpleton to pray for him. 'No one can pray for Tsar Herod' is his reply. The scene is so effective that many modern productions have included it as well as the Kromy Forest scene, but this involves the solecism of having the Simpleton appear twice in two geographically distant places.

ACT I. There is a beautiful prelude beginning *andante tranquillo*. The Red Square in Moscow at sunrise. Kouzka (*tenor*), a musketeer,[1] lies half asleep on guard. A passing patrol sees him and from their conversation it appears that the Streltsy were busy during the night 'making short work' of their opponents in the city. The Scrivener (public letter writer; *tenor*) arrives and is soon engaged by the Boyar Shaklovity (*baritone*) who dictates a letter to the Tsar and his council warning them of the plots of Prince Ivan Khovansky, who, aided by the Old Believers, would become Tsar. The letter must be anonymous and the Scrivener must forget that he wrote it. A mob arrives and forces the Scrivener to read them the proclamation the Streltsy have stuck on the pillar in the middle of the square. The chorus splendidly announces the arrival of Prince Khovansky (*bass*) and the Scrivener flees. The Prince tells the people that treason is rife in Russia and that he is determined to crush the enemies of the Tsars. The people end with an invocation of the 'White Swan'. With the assent of the people he orders the Streltsy to patrol the city.

The procession and the crowd leave and Emma, a young German girl (*soprano*), enters followed by the Prince's son, Andrew Khovansky (*tenor*), who attempts to kiss her. Emma's alarm is allayed by the arrival of Martha (*mezzo-soprano*), whom Andrew Khovansky has loved and left. Martha upbraids Andrew and bids him repent. The angry youth answers by attacking her with a dagger. Martha successfully parries the blow.

The arrival of Andrew's father and his Streltsy puts an end to the quarrel. The old Prince likes Emma's looks and orders his guards to take charge of her. His son would rather kill the girl than see her in the hands of the Streltsy, and would do so but for Dositheus (*bass*), who arrives in time to arrest Andrew's blow. The chief of the Old Believers restores peace. Martha takes Emma in her care and departs with her. Prince Khovansky and his Streltsy return to the Kremlin, while Dositheus and the Old Believers fall to prayer.

ACT II. An apartment in the house of Prince Golitsin (*tenor*), councillor and one-time lover of the Tsarevna. The Prince is reading a love-letter from the Tsarevna. His uneasy conscience tells him, however, not to trust to the favour of the ruler. Varsonofiev (*baritone*) announces a Lutheran Pastor (*baritone*) who complains of the ill-treatment of Emma by the Khovanskys, a private quarrel in which Golitsin says he cannot intervene. He

---

[1] Or *Streltsy*, a band of ill-disciplined troops, who had originally put the Empress Sophia on the throne, but were later led by Prince Ivan Khovansky. Many of them were 'Old Believers'.

has invited Martha to his house to cast his horoscope. A bowl of water is brought, and Martha in her so-called 'Divination', a celebrated and impressive passage, tells of the disgrace and poverty that will be Prince Golitsin's portion in the time that is coming. He dismisses her and gives orders that she must be secretly drowned. Alone, he broods on his past services to Russia. His musing is interrupted by the arrival of Old Prince Khovansky, who has come to complain of Golitsin's interference in his capacity as adviser to the Tsarevna. Angry words pass between them until Dositheus appears and advises that differences be reconciled and a return made to government based on the ancient books and customs. The song of the Old Believers heard in the distance angers Golitsin, while Khovansky sees in them the saviours of Russia. Martha rushes in to ask Golitsin's protection against his servant who attempted to drown her. The attempt was foiled by the arrival of the Petrovtsy, the bodyguard of Peter the Great. The presence of the Tsar's troops in Moscow, unsuspected hitherto, alarms the Princes. The Boyar Shaklovity comes to tell them that the Khovanskys have been denounced to Tsar Peter as traitors.

ACT III. The Streltsy quarter, near the home of Prince Andrew Khovansky. Martha, to a beautiful tune, sings of her past love. She is overheard by Susanna (*soprano*) who accuses her of irredeemable sin. Dositheus appears and comforts Martha. As they retire, Shaklovity comes in and, in an aria of almost prophetic dedication, expresses the hope that Russia may be freed from a government which oppresses her. The chorus of the Streltsy approaches and Shaklovity conceals himself. They arrive singing a drinking song and urging one another to repay theft or gossip of neighbours by ravage and destruction. Their womenfolk now enter and revile them. The uproar is stilled by the arrival of the Scrivener. He has seen foreign mercenaries attack women and children on the outskirts of the Streltsy's own quarters. The Streltsy call in alarm to Prince Khovansky, but the Prince advises submission to the will of Tsar Peter.

ACT IV. Scene i. The residence of Prince Ivan Khovansky, where takes place one of the tautest, most gripping episodes of the entire epic. As the Prince listens to the singing of his serving girls, Varsonofiev warns him of the danger which threatens him. Khovansky ignores the warning and orders his Persian slaves to dance for him. As the dancing ends the Boyar Shaklovity enters to invite Khovansky to the Tsarevna's council. Khovansky at first refuses to go but later makes ready to accompany him. As he leaves the room he is stabbed in the back by Shaklovity.

Scene ii. The square in front of the Church of Saint Basil in Moscow. To the sound of impressively solemn music (in concerts, often known as 'Entr'acte, Act IV'), the people watch the departure of Prince Golitsin in a carriage guarded by troopers. He has been condemned to exile. Dositheus enters lamenting the fall of the two great nobles, Khovansky and Golitsin. After a short dialogue with Martha he leaves her alone to face Prince Andrew Khovansky, who angrily demands news of Emma. Emma, answers Martha, is now safe and perhaps wedded to the man she loved, from whom she had been separated by Andrew. He threatens Martha with the death of a sorceress at the hands of the Streltsy. Martha defies him and Andrew calls the Streltsy. They come, but not in answer to his call – a mournful procession, carrying blocks on which their heads soon must fall. Andrew is taken to a secret refuge by Martha. The crowd asks for the death of the Streltsy, but the herald of the Tsar's guards comes to announce that they have been pardoned. (As a matter of historical fact, the Streltsy were not pardoned but put to death with the cruellest tortures.)

ACT V. A pine wood near Moscow. The Old Believers have come to their hermitage for the last time. Their cause is lost; the quarrels of princes have brought about their ruin. Rather than yield to the soldiers who surround their retreat they will perish together. Dositheus sings a beautiful prayer in which he says that the world shall see how men can die for its salvation. The Old Believers, amongst whom are Martha and Andrew, build a funeral pyre which they ascend carrying a lighted taper. As the flames overpower them the troops sent to arrest them arrive and fall back horror-stricken at the sight of the smoking pyre.

Peter Ilitsch Tchaikovsky
(1840–1893)

EUGENE ONEGIN
Yevgeny Onyegin

OPERA in three acts; text by the composer and K. S. Shilovsky, after Pushkin. Première Imperial College of Music, Little Theatre, Moscow, March 29, 1879.

T HE idea of setting Pushkin's poem *Yevgeny Onyegin* as an opera seems to have been suggested to Tchaikovsky in 1877, by which date he had already written four operas. After a short hesitation, he accepted the subject, and with it the risk of being accused of misrepresenting a classic – for Pushkin's poem was already looked upon in Russia as being in that class. He seems to have set the Letter scene straight away, and at the time he wrote that he loved Tatiana and was terribly indignant with Onegin, who seemed to him a cold, heartless coxcomb. It was during the course of work on his opera that he himself received a passionate avowal of love from a girl who had apparently made his acquaintance while he was teaching at the Conservatory in Moscow; his determination not to emulate Onegin was so strong that he took the fatal decision to embark on a loveless marriage.

ACT I. Scene i. Madame Larina's (*mezzo-soprano*) garden. She is sitting with Filipievna (*mezzo-soprano*) making jam, and through the open window of the house can be heard the voices of Tatiana (*soprano*) and Olga (*contralto*) as they practise a duet. The two older women listen to the first stanza in silence but start to talk (like all country house audiences, big or small) during the second, and the duet of necessity becomes a quartet. Outside the garden can be heard the sound of a chorus of reapers coming nearer. They present Madame Larina with a decorated sheaf, singing an attractive folk-tune, followed by a rapid choral dance.

Tatiana timidly says that these country songs transport her in imagination to far-off regions, but Olga says they do nothing but make her want to dance too. In a little song she gives expression to her light-hearted philosophy. Madame Larina and Filipievna notice that Tatiana looks pale, but she says she is only absorbed in her book, with its tale of lovers' troubles. A carriage is heard on the drive; Lenski must be here – and is it not Onegin with him? Tatiana's imagination flies ahead of her and she tries to get away, but is restrained.

Madame Larina greets her guests, but leaves her daughters to entertain them. A quartet begins, the men and the women conversing separately. Finally, Lenski (*tenor*) goes towards Olga, Onegin (*baritone*) to Tatiana, and the first pair talk of their mutual pleasure in meeting – they are engaged and have not seen each other since yesterday – and the second of the pleasures, or otherwise, of existence in the country. Before the scene ends a short passage gives Filipievna the chance to speculate if Tatiana is interested in Onegin.

Scene ii. Tatiana's bedroom. Filipievna is saying good night to her charge. Tatiana cannot get to sleep and asks Filipievna to tell her a story – about her own early life, and her marriage. Tatiana's thoughts soon wander and the gradually mounting tension in the orchestra shows the way her feelings are rising. Filipievna asks her if she is ill; no, but she is in love, Tatiana tells her – and Filipievna must keep it a secret.

The moment she is alone, the violence of her emotion is released. She starts to write and the orchestra with a wealth of detail supplies what she does not say aloud. Snatches of recitative are interspersed with the letter-writing, and the music is now lyrical and reflective, now impassioned and almost declamatory, the contrasting moods being bound together by the commentary of the orchestra. Could she love another, she asks herself? Never! Everything she has ever done has been done for him.

Each stage of the fateful letter which is to change Tatiana's life is expressed in the music until finally it is finished and nothing is left but to send it. Day is dawning, the sound of a shepherd's pipes can be heard, and Filipievna comes to waken Tatiana. She is sent to deliver the note to Onegin, and the curtain falls as the orchestra recapitulates Tatiana's longing.

Scene iii takes place in a different part of the garden. Girls sing a graceful, folk-like chorus as they gather berries, and Tatiana arrives in a state of considerable emotion; she has seen Onegin making his way towards her. Onegin in his aria expresses himself calmly and collectedly. She has written frankly to him, he will answer her no less frankly. He is not cruel, but discouraging within the code of manners. Love and marriage are not for him; he loves her like a brother, no more. The chorus is heard again as Onegin gently leads the humiliated Tatiana from the scene.

ACT II. Scene i. A ball is in progress at Madame Larina's house in honour of Tatiana's birthday. The guests are engaged in an old-fashioned waltz. Onegin is dancing with Tatiana, a combination which gives rise to some ill-natured gossip amongst the more senior element of the neighbours, who look upon Onegin with anything but favour. He is bored and directs his spite against Lenski, who insisted he should come, by stealing a dance from Olga that she had promised to her fiancé. Lenski's remonstration is in vain, and Olga defends her behaviour when he reproaches her with it, giving the Cotillon as well to the persistent and – says Lenski – flirtatious Onegin.

There is a diversion as Triquet (*tenor*), the old French tutor, consents to sing a song, which he dedicates to Tatiana. It is a charming piece of pastiche. The Cotillon begins with a Mazurka, and Onegin and Olga dance, watched angrily by Lenski. Onegin provokes him by asking why he does not join in, and a quarrel slowly works up until Lenski challenges his erstwhile friend to give him satisfaction for his behaviour. Madame Larina is in a great state that this sort of thing should happen in her house. In music of melting tenderness, Lenski recalls the happiness he has known in this house which he has now made the scene of a quarrel and a scandal. In the ensemble which follows, Onegin bitterly regrets his provocative and thoughtless behaviour, and everyone else, including by now Tatiana, is filled with consternation at the prospect of the duel. Onegin makes up his mind that the affair has gone too far for there to be any possibility of reconciliation, and he and Lenski insult each other, rush together and are separated as the scene ends.

Scene ii. Early next morning, near a mill on the banks of a stream. The melancholy prelude anticipates Lenski's great scene of farewell to life and all he has loved. He and his second, Zaretski (*bass*), exchange a few words and he is then left alone. He sings of his past, his carefree youth, and contrasts it with his present state, when he cares little whether as a result of the duel he is left alive or dead; the loss of Olga will be his one regret. It is a fine lyrical outpouring, supreme amongst tenor scenes in Russian opera, and unbearably pathetic in its context.

Onegin arrives and introduces his servant as his second. The two seconds go off to discuss the conditions of the duel, and Lenski and Onegin stand apart without looking at one another and sing a canon, whose form exactly expresses the relationship – the thoughts of the two men are similar but divided by form and come together only as they regret that etiquette precludes a reconciliation at this late hour. The bleak tune has just that deadpan nervousness which the situation might be expected to produce, and the repetition of the word 'No' at the end has a chilling finality. The opponents measure up, and Lenski is killed. Students of irony will remember that Pushkin himself was killed in a duel only six years after writing *Yevgeny Onyegin*.

ACT III. Scene i. Some years have passed and the end of the story takes place in St. Petersburg. A ball is in progress in a fashionable house – the contrast with the country dance at Madame Larina's cannot be over-emphasised. As the curtain rises, a Polonaise begins. Onegin is there, just returned at the age of twenty-six to civilisation after the years he has spent in the wilderness to atone for the death of the friend he killed. An Ecossaise begins but the tempo changes to a slow waltz in D flat as Prince Gremin, a retired general (*bass*), and his wife – Tatiana, no less – come into the ballroom. The Prince goes to talk to his kinsman, Onegin, who questions him as to the identity of the lady with whom he has come to the ball, while Tatiana asks those nearest her who it is her husband is talking to. The beauty of the waltz theme and the skill with which Tchaikovsky uses it as a background for conversation are equally notable here.

In an aria Gremin tells Onegin of the love and beauty Tatiana has brought into his life since their marriage two years ago. The aria has the important effect of maintaining Gremin as no lay figure but a thinking, feeling person, part of Tatiana's background it is true, but real enough to make her loyalty entirely plausible. Gremin introduces his cousin to his wife, and Tatiana asks to be taken home, leaving Onegin to vent his feelings in an impassioned aria, whose final section is the same (a minor third lower) as the opening section to Tatiana's Letter scene. The scene ends with a repeat of the Ecossaise.

Scene ii. A reception room in Prince Gremin's house. Tatiana has had Onegin's letter and there is no doubt that he is now hopelessly in love with her, to such an extent that words fail him at his entrance and he sinks on his knees at Tatiana's feet. Tatiana recalls their former meetings – the letter, and his lecture to her on the subject of maidenly reticence. She contrives to make some show of indignation at his return; is he only looking for the notoriety of having his name coupled with that of a woman prominent in society? But he is so obviously sincere and in earnest that she cannot restrain her tears for long. For a moment they recall the happiness that could have been theirs long ago, but which, through fate's decree, is now out of their reach. They must part, says Tatiana, since she is Gremin's wife. But Onegin urges his love once more, and, although she admits she loves him, she admonishes Onegin to remember the path of honour and leave her. She prays for courage and suddenly finds the strength to go, leaving Onegin distraught behind her.

MAZEPPA

THREE acts, by Peter Ilitsch Tchaikovsky; première, Moscow, 1884. Maria (*soprano*), daughter of Kochubey (*bass*), loves her father's contemporary Mazeppa (*baritone*), a Cossack leader. Andrei (*tenor*) loves her hopelessly. When Mazeppa asks for Maria's hand, Kochubey demands that she leave. Maria is torn, but goes with Mazeppa. Kochubey plans revenge and Andrei offers to reveal to the Tsar Mazeppa's treachery. The Tsar, disbelieving, hands Kochubey over to Mazeppa, who is planning to set up an independent state. Maria affirms that she would choose Mazeppa's life above all others, but is horrified to find that her father is to be executed. Mazeppa's venture fails and he mortally wounds Andrei. Maria has lost her reason, and Mazeppa abandons her. Alone with Andrei, she cradles him until he dies.

THE QUEEN OF SPADES
Pikovaya Dama/Pique Dame

OPERA in three acts by Peter Ilitsch Tchaikovsky; text by Modest Tchaikovsky (the composer's brother). Première, St. Petersburg, December 19, 1890.

ACT I. A short prelude leads to Scene i, the Summer Garden, St. Petersburg. It is spring and children are playing while nurses and governesses chat. Sourin (*bass*) and Tchekalinsky (*tenor*) discuss Herman's gambling propensities; last night he was at his usual habit of watching the players, silent and never risking a throw.

Herman (*tenor*) arrives with his friend Count Tomsky (*baritone*). Herman explains his sorrowful mood by saying that he is in love, but does not even know the lady's name (*arioso*). Tomsky suggests that he find out then begin to woo her in earnest, but Herman is afraid she is socially beyond his reach.

Tomsky greets Prince Yeletsky (*baritone*), who has just become engaged. His rejoicings contrast with Herman's despair, especially when the Prince points out his Lisa: Herman recognises her as his own beloved. Lisa (*soprano*) and her grandmother, the Countess (*mezzo-soprano*), notice Herman's ardent looks, but are unaware of his identity. After a short quintet, Tomsky greets the Countess, who asks Herman's name, and Yeletsky goes towards Lisa.

The Countess and Lisa leave; the others speculate on the Countess's past. She was a great gambler, it seems, who has now renounced cards. In a ballad, Tomsky tells her history. As a young beauty the Countess was wooed by the Count Saint-Germain; but she preferred gambling to love. One day she lost everything at the tables; the Count offered to reveal the secret of 'Three cards', should she but grant him one rendezvous. She agreed, and next morning was back at the tables, where nothing could stop her winning run. She supposedly passed the secret to her husband, and years later to a young gallant who had taken her fancy, but in a dream she had been warned that she would die when next anyone tried to win the secret from her.

A storm is brewing, and all take shelter except Herman, who stays trance-like, brooding on the story – what use would the secret be to him with Lisa beyond his reach? – and expresses his determination to win Lisa from the Prince.

Scene ii. Lisa's room. Lisa is sitting at the harpsichord, surrounded by girls of her own age. She and Pauline (*contralto*) sing an old-fashioned duet, after which Lisa asks Pauline to sing alone, and she follows her romance with a lively peasant song; the governess comes in to ask for a little less noise.

Lisa sees her friends to the door, and tries to fob off Pauline's enquiries about her gloomy look. Alone, she gives vent to her feelings in a beautiful aria. Is this marriage to which she is contracted the fulfilment of her dreams? Nobody could have better qualifications than the Prince, and yet her heart is full of foreboding.

Suddenly Herman appears at the window. He persuades Lisa

to stay and listen to him for a moment. In music of passionate tenderness, he declares his love, and it is immediately evident that Lisa is far from indifferent to what he says. They are interrupted by a knocking at the door; it is the Countess, checking if Lisa is asleep. Herman hides, Lisa calms the Countess's fears, while Herman softly echoes the refrain of Tomsky's ballad; can it be true that she will die when a third man 'impelled by despair' demands to know the secret? When they are alone, Lisa sinks into Herman's arms.

ACT II. Scene i. A large reception room. A masked ball is taking place at the house of a rich dignitary. The guests go into the garden to see a firework display, and Tchekalinsky and Sourin plan to play a trick on Herman, who, they say, is obsessed by the idea of the Countess's 'three cards'. The Prince sings a noble and touchingly chivalrous aria to Lisa, and they go off together. Herman appears reading a note from Lisa: 'After the performance wait for me in my room. I must speak with you.' Did he but know the secret of the 'three cards', he could be wealthy and aspire to Lisa's hand. As if to echo his thoughts, he hears Tchekalinsky and Sourin whisper: 'Are you then that third man? . . . three cards?' Herman wonders whether he is hearing the voice of a ghost. There follows a masque, *The Faithful Shepherdess*, based on the story of Daphnis, Chloë, and Plutus – the last two played by Pauline and Tomsky.

Herman waits for Lisa, who gives him a key and tells him to enter the house through her grandmother's room – the old woman will still be playing cards at midnight – and then use the key to open a secret door behind the Countess's portrait, which leads to her apartments. Herman says he will come that very night; Lisa is submissive to his desires. The Empress herself arrives and the guests welcome her.

Scene ii. The Countess's bedroom. Herman hides as the Countess, preceded by maids and attendants, comes in. She prepares for bed and reminisces of 'the old days' when people really could dance and when she sang before the King. Suddenly aware that the room is still full of curious servants, the Countess sends them packing.

Alone, she catches sight of Herman, and mouths incoherently as if she had lost the power of speech. Herman begs her not to be frightened; he wants nothing but the secret of the 'three cards'. In desperation Herman draws his pistol, and the Countess dies of shock. With a despairing cry that he can now never know the secret, he turns to find Lisa entering the room, alarmed by the noise. She is horrified by the sight which meets her eyes, and no less horrified to learn that it was for love of gambling, not for her sake, that he came here at midnight! She bids him leave.

ACT III. Scene i. Herman's quarters in the barracks. Drums and trumpets suggest a funeral march. Herman sits reading a letter from Lisa, in which she apparently forgives him, understanding that he did not intend to kill her grandmother, and makes an appointment for midnight by the canal. Herman is overcome by conscience, and obsessed by memories of the Countess's funeral. Suddenly, the door opens, the candle is blown out, and the ghost of the Countess appears. She tells Herman that he must marry Lisa, and that the secret of the three cards shall be his: 'Three! Seven! Ace!' He mutters the formula to himself.

Scene ii. By the canal. Lisa waits for Herman. Her nerves are worn with sorrow as she sings 'It is near to midnight', a particularly fine aria. Her fears are quieted when Herman appears, and sings to her of their future together. But he tells her they must leave for the gaming house. Lisa thinks he is mad, but he blurts out his obsession, and, deaf to her pleading, pushes her aside and goes his way. Lisa throws herself into the canal.

Scene iii. The gambling house. Tomsky greets the Prince with surprise, since he is no longer an habitual gambler. Yeletsky admits that he has come to take his revenge: unlucky in love, lucky at cards. Tomsky is persuaded to sing for their entertainment, which he does to a lively tune. Herman enters, and asks who will play with him. Tchekalinsky accepts, and Herman stakes hugely and wins twice, on the three and seven. He rejoices in his fortune: 'What is our life? A game!', then challenges anyone to stake once more. The Prince offers to play, and Herman reluctantly agrees, turning up a card, announcing an ace without even looking at it. But the Prince calmly rejoins: 'No, 'tis your Queen of Spades'. With a wild cry, Herman sees the ghost of the Countess. Gibbering with fear and rage he stabs himself, and with his dying breath asks for the Prince's pardon for what he has done to him. A prayer goes up for his soul, and Herman dies.

Nikolai Andreevich Rimsky-Korsakov
(1844–1908)

THE SNOW MAIDEN
Snegurochka

Pᴿᴼᴸᴼᴳᵁᴱ and four acts; première, St. Petersburg, 1882. Spring (*mezzo-soprano*) and Winter have a daughter,

Snegurochka (*soprano*), now sixteen; she would die if the sun-god Yarilo should glimpse her. She suffers unrequited love for Lehl (*alto*), but is loved by Misgir (*baritone*), to the desolation of his bride Coupava (*soprano*). The Tsar, impressed by Snegurochka's beauty, promises a reward to anyone who wins her love. Lehl again spurns her and chooses Coupava. Misgir urges his suit but is rejected. After an appeal to her mother Snegurochka finally returns his love, but the sun-god has warmed her heart; she melts away, and Misgir kills himself. The Tsar sees the tragedy as a sign that Yarilo will now bless them, and all invoke the god.

LE COQ D'OR
Zolotoy Pyetushok/The Golden Cockerel

OPERA in three acts by Nikolai Rimsky-Korsakov; text by V. Bielsky after Pushkin. Première, Moscow, October 7, 1909.

*L*E COQ D'OR was Rimsky-Korsakov's last opera. It was censored and not performed until after the composer's death. The story is taken from Pushkin. It is quite possible to fill it with symbolical meaning, although the librettist, Bielsky, preferred to think of it as dealing with human passions and weaknesses in their essence and quite apart from any particular context.

PROLOGUE. After a short prelude, the thin, *staccato* sound of the xylophone heralds the appearance of the Astrologer (*tenor*) before the curtain. He says he will conjure up a tale from long ago; though it is only a fairy story, its moral is excellent. The Astrologer's music is instrumental rather than vocal in character and its *tessitura* abnormally high.

ACT I. The court of King Dodon (*bass*). The King is seated with his ministers and advisers and his two sons, Guidon (*tenor*) and Afron (*baritone*). He complains that his neighbours treat him unfairly; when he was young and vigorous, he used to go out to attack them; now that he is old, they are inclined to invade him, in spite of the fact that he finds it more and more troublesome to engage in warfare. What advice can his councillors give him? Guidon, his elder son, recommends that the King withdraw his army inside his kingdom, and there, supplied with a vast stock of provisions, think out the whole problem.

All applaud the suggestion, except old General Polkan (*bass*), the King's chief minister, who finds the whole notion futile. Afron spurns his brother's plan, and advises that the army be disbanded and sent home; once the enemy is past them, they may re-unite and fall upon him from the rear and destroy him. Dodon is delighted, but Polkan demolishes Afron's proposal as quickly as he had Guidon's. There seems no reasonable and practical solution.

Suddenly the Astrologer appears. In music of characteristic cast, he offers the King a magic golden cockerel (*soprano*), which has only to be placed so that it has a view of the surrounding country, and it will crow to give warning of any danger. When it is quiet, the King may rest peacefully and take his ease. Dodon rejoices, and offers the Astrologer any reward he likes to name, but the old man merely asks for the King's promise in writing so as to take advantage of his offer in future. This request is refused, the King saying in effect that his word is his bond.

The cock bids the King take his ease heedless of danger. Dodon, delighted, will indulge his pleasures from now on. He begins to feel sleepy, and the royal nurse, Amelfa (*contralto*), has his bed brought in. He lies down, eats sweetmeats, and plays with his parrot, which sings to him (in the orchestra). As he goes to sleep the orchestra begins the slumber scene (as it is known in the orchestral suite), in which the woodwind quietly repeat the cockerel's assurance that he can rest undisturbed while the cellos play a gentle lullaby. Even Amelfa falls asleep.

But the King has not slept for long before he is aroused by the warning cry of the cockerel, which is echoed by the instruments of the orchestra. Polkan manages to wake his master, who gives orders for a general mobilisation of the army. It gets under way to the sound of a march. Soon all is quiet, and Dodon is allowed by his watchful bird to return to his slumbers. He cannot recapture nor remember an amorous dream he was enjoying. Amelfa tries to help him and makes one or two suggestions, finally hitting upon the right one. All go to sleep once more, only to be awakened by an even more urgent summons from the cockerel. The crowd rushes around, and this time Polkan warns the King that he is in danger himself, and that he must lead his army to victory. With much grumbling, Dodon prepares to don his armour. In the end, he is sufficiently, if awkwardly, arrayed to go off to the wars, which he does to the acclamation of the crowd.

ACT II. A narrow pass. The war goes badly, and the moonlight reveals the bodies of the soldiers and the King's two sons. The march of the preceding act is now oppressed with gloom, and Dodon bursts into lamentation when he finds the bodies of his slain sons. The mists which have shrouded the pass lift, and reveal a tent. General consternation. Could it belong to the enemy general? Reluctantly the soldiers fire on the tent. But its only effect is that a beautiful young woman (*soprano*) emerges. All but Dodon and Polkan flee. The young woman sings the praises of the sun, which gives life and beauty to her native land. This is the famous 'Hymn to the Sun', whose sensuously beautiful melody has made it one of Rimsky-Korsakov's most popular vocal compositions.

The girl reveals that she is the Queen of Shemakha, come to subdue Dodon, not by force of arms but by her own physical beauty. Dodon is shyer than Polkan, but eventually Polkan's bluntness goes too far and she asks for him to be sent away. Dodon promptly complies, but Polkan watches from behind the Queen's tent (the bodies of the soldiers have by now been cleared away, and the scene is bathed in sunlight).

The Queen proceeds to seduce Dodon. Even an orchestral reference to the cockerel's warning makes not the slightest difference to the King. The Queen tells him he must sing for her, and he starts an incredibly primitive-sounding melody, much to her glee. The Queen tries new tactics. At home everyone obeys her slightest whim, and her caprice rules her kingdom; oh, for contradiction, even domination! Timidly Dodon offers himself as dominator, and she asks him to dance for her. She rigs him up with a fan and scarf in place of his cumbersome armour, and has her slaves play a slow melody to accompany him. She joins him and mocks his efforts, which land him, as the music gets quicker, on some cushions in a state of collapse.

By now, the King is completely under the Queen's spell. He repeats his offer of his hand, his possessions, his throne, his kingdom. She accepts with the proviso that Polkan shall forthwith be whipped; Dodon offers to go further and behead him. Preparations are immediately put in hand for a return to Dodon's kingdom, and, while the Queen's slaves mock at her newest capture, Dodon's army lines up to escort their monarch and his bride to their capital. The act ends with the grotesque procession.

ACT III. Dodon's capital. The crowd is wondering if and when he will return. Rumours are that he has won a great victory, but lost his two sons, and is escorting home as his bride a young queen whom he rescued from a dragon. All must be well, argue the people, since the cockerel is quiet. Then the cry goes up that the procession is at hand. It files through the crowd, and eventually the King and his bride appear, riding in their gilded chariot, and acclaimed by the crowd.

Suddenly, proceedings are interrupted by the appearance of the Astrologer. He has come to claim his reward from the King;

it shall be the princess who rides by the King's side! The King angrily refuses, but the Astrologer persists, emphasising his determination to risk marriage even at his age with a sustained top E (Rimsky-Korsakov, in his preface to the score, underlines the fact that the role of the Astrologer requires a tenor with a highly developed falsetto voice). The King orders his guards to remove the old man, and when he seems still anxious to continue the dispute, Dodon strikes him with his sceptre, and kills him. The sky darkens, thunder is heard, and Dodon has the grace to appear embarrassed at the turn events have taken; such a bad omen on one's wedding day! The Queen laughs at the whole episode, but, when Dodon tries to embrace her, repulses him in disgust. The cockerel suddenly comes to life, utters a piercing cry, flies over the head of the crowd and pecks the King on the head. He falls dead, and the crowd loyally breaks into lamentation for him. The sky becomes completely dark, and when light returns, both Queen and cockerel have disappeared.

In the epilogue, the resuscitated Astrologer announces that the story is only a fairy tale and that in Dodon's kingdom only the Queen and he himself were mortals.

Bedřich Smetana
(1824–1884)

THE BARTERED BRIDE
Prodaná Nevěsta

OPERA in three acts; text by Karel Sabina. Première, Prague National Theatre, May 30, 1866; some alterations were made to the work in 1869 and the final version produced in 1870.

*T*HE BARTERED BRIDE is so much of a national institution inside Czechoslovakia, and has more recently been accepted by the outside world as so typical of the very best type of 'folk opera', that it is surprising to remember that Smetana was looked upon during his lifetime as insufficiently nationalist in feeling, and his other operas as too strongly under the influence of Wagner.

The Overture, written before the rest of the opera, is immensely and justifiably popular as a concert piece.

ACT I. Spring in a Bohemian village. The villagers are rejoicing at the prospect of the dancing to celebrate the holidays. Only Mařenka (*soprano*) and Jeník (*tenor*) seem subdued –

caused, we hear, by the fact that Mařenka has just learned that her parents plan a rich marriage for her, in spite of her loving the handsome but impecunious Jenik. The villagers go off to dance, and Mařenka tells Jenik that her heart would break were he to desert her; her love is his, even though she knows so little of his background. Their love duet leaves little doubt of their mutual affection; the lyrical main section is heard fairly frequently during the course of the opera as a love motif.

They leave. Mařenka's parents come in with Kečal (*bass*), the marriage broker. He has the gift of the gab, and it is some time before either of his listeners can get a word in. When they do, it is clear that they are prepared to accept his suggestion that Mařenka shall marry the son of Tobias Micha (*bass*), a rich neighbour. Krušina (*baritone*) thinks the contract should be taken up forthwith; he himself knows Micha, but he cannot so much as remember the names of his two sons. Kečal protests that there is only one; the other, by Micha's first marriage, disappeared from home years ago and is now presumed dead. In spite of Kečal's enthusiastic description of the prospective bridegroom, Ludmila (*mezzo-soprano*) still thinks the final decision should be left in Mařenka's hands.

The trio becomes a quartet when Mařenka herself appears on the scene and announces her engagement to Jenik. Kečal refuses to take such objections seriously, Krušina is furious that his permission has not already been asked, and even Ludmila thinks Mařenka might have handled the whole affair with a little more tact. Mařenka knocks the contract out of Kečal's hand, and leaves her parents wishing that Kečal had brought the bridegroom along with him; a sight of him might have caused her to change her mind. The act ends with a spirited polka.

ACT II. The inside of the inn. The men sing the praises of beer. Kečal is looking for Jenik, who seems sunk in reflection. Both, however, join in the chorus, Kečal vaunting money as the most desirable of possessions, Jenik preferring love. All dance a brilliant and energetic Furiant, then leave.

Vašek (*tenor*) comes shyly in, stammering out that he has been sent off by his mother to woo his prospective bride. He is an enchantingly silly figure, with his stutter and his transparent guilelessness. It does not take long before Mařenka, who comes in to find him alone, realises that this is the bridegroom who has been picked out for her. She is horrified, and proceeds to tell him that she, like all the other village girls, is really sorry that so handsome a lad is contracted to Mařenka, a flighty girl who will lead him an awful dance once they are married. She paints a much brighter prospect for him with another girl, prettier than Mařenka and already very much attracted to him from a distance. He eventually agrees to give up Mařenka, and tries to kiss the pretty girl in front of him.

Kečal does not intend to lose the sizeable commission if he brings off Mařenka's betrothal to the son of Tobias Micha. Accordingly, he is prepared to invest a proportion of it in buying off the tiresome suitor whom Mařenka appears to favour. He takes Jenik to the inn for a drink, and talks the matter over. However, even the brilliant and lively tune of their duet, which Jenik repeats after him, is not enough to persuade the young man to give up his sweetheart, and Kečal is eventually reduced to offering him a substantial sum of money if he will renounce his claim. Jenik takes some persuading, but finally agrees to do so – but only in favour of the eldest son of Tobias Micha, the money to be paid to him and to be reclaimable under no circumstances whatsoever.

Kečal goes off. Jenik knows quite well that the eldest son of Micha, presumed dead, is none other than himself. He has acquired a marriage contract to his beloved and a dowry from his cheese-paring stepmother at the same time! The plan must succeed! We can have no doubts as to the sincerity of Jenik's love for Mařenka after the beautiful love song which he sings the moment Kečal's back is turned.

Kečal brings in Krušina and the villagers to celebrate his successful handling of what turned out to be by no means a simple affair. The finale uses the material already heard in the overture. Kečal calls for silence. In legal language, he reads the document out; it is to the effect that Jenik has agreed to renounce Mařenka. Krušina and Kečal are delighted, so apparently is Jenik, but the villagers cannot quite understand the position until Kečal adds that the whole thing is in consideration of the sum of three hundred gulden. Then popular fury knows no bounds; even Krušina is shocked that Jenik should abandon Mařenka for money, and Jenik signs amidst general demonstration of hostility.

ACT III has the same setting as Act I. Vašek is in stuttering despair that he cannot find the attractive girl who gave him such good advice. His genuinely comic aria is marked *lamentoso*. His thoughts are interrupted by the arrival of a circus troupe, headed by a redoubtable Ringmaster (*tenor*) and heralded by the so-called March of the Comedians. The Ringmaster announces that the attractions include the great dancer, Esmeralda (*soprano*), and a real, live, American bear. To the accompaniment of the delightfully varied and tuneful Dance of the Comedians, the clowns and dancers go through their paces, watched by an admiring throng.

When all have gone their way, only Vašek is left behind admiring the beautiful Esmeralda. One of the clowns tells the

Ringmaster that the man who usually plays the bear is much too drunk to go through with his role, and that no substitute can be found. Esmeralda suggests that the dimwit who has been gawping at her for some minutes would be just the right build. The Ringmaster asks Vašek if he would like to dance with the beautiful girl, Esmeralda assures him that she will teach him how, and the agreement is completed. He will make his début that night – all this to an enchanting dance tune sung by the two circus professionals, but made into some kind of trio by the prancing if silent Vašek.

Vašek's parents come in. Hata (*mezzo-soprano*) wants him to meet his future bride, but he is unwilling when he hears that it is Krušina's Mařenka who is his destined spouse. He escapes, and a moment later in comes Mařenka, furious and mortified at the news that Jenik has sold her love for money.

Vašek reappears and is overjoyed to hear that the girl who stands before him, whom he found so attractive, is Mařenka after all. But poor Mařenka asks for time in which to make up her mind, and the parents of the prospective bride and bridegroom join with Kečal in exhorting her to give the matter serious thought. This sextet (Mařenka joins them just before it finishes) is a lovely, contemplative piece. The mood is continued when Mařenka is left alone to lament in an aria her unhappy position. Everything around her seems dead, she sings, but her misery gives way to melancholy when she reflects that it is she who has changed, and not the spring, which is as lovely as ever.

Jenik comes in, apparently in the best of spirits. Mařenka is furious with him, and even more so when he seems to treat the whole affair as an excellent joke. The argument is by no means over when Kečal tells Jenik he can have his money as soon as Mařenka has signed the contract. Jenik urges her to do so, which naturally only increases her fury.

The villagers assemble to see the betrothal of Mařenka and (as Jenik insists the description shall run) 'the son of Tobias Micha'. Everyone congratulates Mařenka on the match, nobody louder than Jenik, who has no sooner opened his mouth than he is recognised by Hata and Micha as the long-lost son of the latter. He asks Mařenka whether she will have him or Vašek, and her triumphant answer leaves Kečal babbling with fury at having been outwitted.

Two small boys rush in shouting that the bear is loose! He shambles in, but it is not long before the voice of Vašek can be heard inside the skin saying that nobody need be frightened, as the bear is only him. Hata takes him off, and the rest of the company rejoice at the betrothal of the bartered bride and her faithful lover.

DALIBOR

OPERA in three acts by Bedřich Smetana; German text by J. Wenzig, Czech translation by Spindler. Première at Prague, May 16, 1868.

THE fifteenth-century legend of *Dalibor* symbolised Czech aspirations long before Smetana took it as a subject for an opera. It is hard to believe that his librettist's treatment of the story owed nothing to *Fidelio* and that dramatic resemblances between the two are pure coincidence. After Czech independence in 1919, the opera took on new significance for the Czech people, and it has since then been looked on, with *The Bartered Bride*, as a national institution.

ACT I. There is no extensive overture, and the curtain rises after fifteen bars of music on the judgment hall of King Vladislav's (*baritone*) palace in Prague. Dalibor, a knight (*tenor*), has been engaged in strife with the Burgrave of Ploskovice; his friend Zdeněk was captured and put to death, and, in revenge, Dalibor has killed the Burgrave. For this he is coming up for judgment in front of the King. The people, amongst them Jitka (*soprano*), an orphan whom Dalibor has befriended, are waiting for the assembly of the court; they praise Dalibor as their friend and protector. The King enters with his judges, and rehearses the charges against Dalibor. He calls Milada (*soprano*), the sister of the dead Burgrave, to substantiate her accusations.

Amidst expressions of sympathy for her bereavement, she tells the dramatic story of Dalibor's entry into the castle, and of how he killed her brother. The King assures her Dalibor will pay for his crime with his life, and he orders that the accused be brought in. As he enters, murmurs of admiration are heard on all sides, and even Milada is compelled to comment on his fearless, noble appearance. Dalibor does not deny his action; only, it was not murder but vengeance for murder. In an aria he tells of his love for his friend and of his violin playing (the solo violin is throughout associated with Zdeněk). Zdeněk was captured in battle, and when Dalibor asked what ransom was required to redeem him, he was sent his head on the end of a lance. Milada begins to feel pity for her former foe. Dalibor defies the King; he has committed no crime, only revenged the murder of his friend. If now his life is spared, he will continue to exact vengeance; not the King himself shall stand in his way!

The verdict of the court is imprisonment for life; Dalibor invokes the free spirit of Zdeněk – did he hear the sentence? Dalibor is led away, and Milada pleads for his life. But the judges say he has openly threatened the King; even when Milada protests that she herself, whom he has most wronged, is prepared to forgive him, they are unimpressed. Milada, thinking she is alone, admits to herself that she is in love with Dalibor. Jitka overhears her and begs her to exert herself to free Dalibor. In a vigorous concluding duet, they agree together to free him from prison.

ACT II. Scene i. A street below the castle in which Dalibor is imprisoned. Jitka and Vítek (*tenor*), Dalibor's page, greet each other eagerly in a charming duet. They discuss Dalibor's plight and Jitka reveals that Milada is already inside the prison disguised as a boy. Dalibor will soon be out, and victory and freedom will be theirs. The music has an exuberance that is positively Weberian in character.

Scene ii. The house of Beneš (*bass*), the gaoler, inside the castle. Night is falling and sentries patrol up and down. Budivoj (*baritone*) warns Beneš that there is a danger of a rising in favour of Dalibor. Budivoj looks at Milada who is standing nearby in disguise, and enquires who it is; Beneš tells him it is his new assistant. In music of sombre character, Beneš reflects on the gloomy nature of his calling.

Milada comes to tell Beneš that his meal is ready. The gaoler refers most sympathetically to Dalibor, who, he says, has asked for a fiddle to play in his dungeon. He tells Milada to take the instrument down to the prisoner. Milada, left alone, rejoices at the prospect of seeing Dalibor for the first time face to face. Beneš returns and gives Milada instructions on how to find the appropriate dungeon.

Scene iii. Dalibor's cell. Dalibor has a vision of Zdeněk, who appears to him and plays his violin; when he has gone, Dalibor invokes his reappearance in a beautiful aria. Presently Milada brings him the instrument he has asked for. She admits that she was his accuser at his trial, and that she hated him. Will he pardon her for what she has done to him; ever since the trial she has loved him from afar. The whole scene is one of extraordinary power, and the lyrical duet itself of haunting beauty: one of the most remarkable duets in all opera.

ACT III. Scene i. The throne room of the King. He is surrounded by his councillors. Budivoj and Beneš appear in front of him, the former saying that he has news of a rising in Dalibor's favour. Beneš tells his story: he had an apprentice, who suddenly disappeared, leaving behind him some money and a note of thanks. But at least Beneš was in time to prevent Dalibor's escape – the lad had certainly something to do with the preparations he discovered for freeing the prisoner. Beneš pleads for leniency for himself. The King, in spite of misgivings as to the justice of his action (voiced in a beautiful aria), finally accepts the judgment of his Council that Dalibor be condemned to instant death.

Scene ii. Plans are afoot for Dalibor's escape, and he stands in his cell, free of fetters and rejoicing in a brilliant aria as he thinks of the freedom he can bring to his people. But Budivoj rushes in with his guards, secures his prisoner and informs him of the court's decision that he shall die. Dalibor muses on his coming death in music of poignant sadness.

Scene iii. During a march interlude, the scene changes to an open square in front of the castle. Milada, clad for battle with Jitka, Vítek, and their armed supporters, waits for the signal. They hear the tolling of a bell and the sound of a chorus of monks, and Milada is afraid that Dalibor is being done to death inside the prison while they wait for his signal to attack it. They prepare to assault the castle.

Women comment on what they can see, and presently Dalibor comes out of the castle carrying Milada, who is wounded. She dies in his arms, and, when Budivoj appears with troops, Dalibor stabs himself and dies with his beloved.

Antonín Dvořák
(1841–1904)

RUSALKA
The Water Nymph

OPERA in three acts; libretto by S. J. Kvapil. Première, March 31, 1901, National Theatre, Prague.

IN 1899, six months after finishing his comedy *Čert a Káče* (Kate and the Devil), Dvořák let it be known that he was looking for a new libretto. The thirty-one-year-old poet and dramatist, Jaroslav Kvapil, responded with one already written and Dvořák set *Rusalka* without asking for changes. The origins of the story lie in the French *Melusine*, Hans Christian Andersen's *Little Mermaid*, Friedrich de la Motte Fouqué's *Undine*, and Gerhardt Hauptmann's *The Sunken Bell*, and the resulting story and score are far from the kind of subject which was popular in Prague in the 1890's, when the tendency was for younger composers to turn to *verismo* rather than fairy story and folk lore.

ACT I. The short and beautiful prelude admirably suggests the poetical, twilit atmosphere of the opera, its tenderness and yearning.

A clearing on the shore of the lake; in the background, a cottage. The good-natured old Spirit of the Lake (*bass*) is tempted out of the lake depths, where he has his abode, by the spirited singing of the Wood Nymphs. When they have gone, Rusalka (*soprano*), heralded by the harp, rises from the water and sadly asks her father for advice. The music has a warmth and tenderness that is Dvořák at his finest as she tells him in an aria that she has fallen in love with a handsome young prince (*tenor*) and wants to become human in order to know the bliss of union with him. Her confession fills her father with sadness, but he advises her to visit the old Witch who lives nearby. When she is alone Rusalka confides to the moon the secret of her longing – this passage ('O silver moon') is justly famous as one of the most touching and yet chaste of operatic love songs.

Rusalka calls to Ježibaba (*mezzo-soprano*), the Witch, and in a passionate *scena* begs for her help. Ježibaba will grant her human attributes, but she will not be able to speak and, if he prove false to her, both she and her lover will be damned for ever. Together Rusalka and Ježibaba cast the spell; Rusalka's decision is irrevocably taken.

The sound of horns and of a huntsman's (*baritone*) song in the distance – rapt, intense, lyrical music – set the scene for the Prince's entrance. He is in pursuit of a white doe, but feels a mysterious attraction when he is by the shores of the lake. He suspects magic but sends his companions back to the palace saying he wants to stay alone with whatever power rules the place. Rusalka comes into sight. The Prince is enchanted at her appearance and sings her praises in music of the utmost tenderness (derived from the huntsman's distant song). Her sisters and the Spirit of the Lake are filled with alarm but without a word – in the Prince's presence she is dumb – Rusalka clings to him. He is enraptured – the music becomes a kind of one-handed love duet – and flinging his cloak round her, takes Rusalka off towards his palace.

ACT II. The palace grounds. The palace is full of guests invited to the wedding of the Prince and the mysterious Rusalka. In a charming scene, a forester (*baritone* or *tenor*) and a boy (*mezzo-soprano*) from the palace kitchen exchange the latest news – the kitchen boy is frankly scared by Rusalka; the forester suspects witchcraft. There is more gossip: the Prince is said already to have begun to tire of his silent beauty and his eyes have turned towards a foreign Princess. They hurry out as the Prince and Rusalka are seen approaching. That she has given him so little sign of her love has begun to baffle him. When the foreign Princess (*soprano*) comes by, the Prince sends Rusalka into the palace to dress for the Ball and he himself goes off with the Princess, who clearly takes it as a personal slight that the Prince is to marry Rusalka.

A brilliant scene follows as the Ball begins. It is temporarily interrupted by the melodious lament of the Spirit of the Lake, who expresses his despair at the downfall of his favourite daughter. He continues to mourn while the chorus sings the beautiful 'White flowers are blooming by the way'. Rusalka runs to him and is now able to give passionate voice to her misery that the Prince has all evening paid court to the foreign Princess. Before long the Prince leads his new lady-love away from the dancing and their fiery duet contains all the warmth that the Prince had missed in Rusalka. They embrace, but Rusalka throws herself into her bridegroom's arms, and the Spirit of the Lake proclaims that the Prince will now never be free of her. The Prince implores the foreign Princess's help, but she turns proudly away from him.

ACT III. A glade by the side of the Lake, as in Act I. Evening. Rusalka is now the victim of her lover's infidelity and condemned to wander for ever as a will-o'-the-wisp. In a grandiose aria, with insidiously beautiful orchestral accompaniment, she longs for death, but Ježibaba comes out of her hut to say that only the shedding of human blood can now redeem her from the curse which hangs over her. Rusalka sings touchingly and resignedly of her fate and sinks alone into the waters.

The forester and the kitchen boy come to ask the Witch to help the Prince, who is, they fear, under supernatural influence. Neither dares knock at the door. When Ježibaba answers to the cries of her name, she makes short work of their plea to help restore the confidence of the Prince, and between them she and the Spirit of the Lake put the timid pair to flight.

The Wood Nymphs gather at the side of the lake and sing and dance to music of graceful character – the first Nymph has a particularly appealing solo, 'Golden is my Hair' – until stopped by the Spirit of the Lake, who reminds them of Rusalka's melancholy fate. The Prince staggers out of the wood, muttering about the snow-white doe, which first led him here to Rusalka. He recognises the place and, to the music in which he addressed her at their first meeting, calls on Rusalka to come back, in magically tender phrases. Rusalka is returned to him. The Prince begs her if she is a ghost to take his life too, and he asks her forgiveness for his cruelty towards her. Tenderly she reproaches him for having lied to her; she was not able to give him the passion he craved, and now, if she were to embrace him, he would die at her caress. In ecstatic phrases he begs for the kiss which will end his life, and he dies in her arms. Even the Spirit of the Lake's pronouncement that Rusalka's fate will not be mitigated by her lover's sacrifice cannot mar the apotheosis of Rusalka and the Prince through the love that finally they share.

In 1983 for English National Opera, David Pountney staged

the opera as a young girl's dream of adolescence and awakening. The Spirit of the Lake was Rusalka's grandfather, the Wood Nymphs her sisters, the Prince an older man in whose presence the young girl is tongue-tied, and the foreign Princess a sophisticated threat to first love. The Witch became that Victorian source of comfort and enlightenment as well as of alarm, a black-bombazined and beetle-browed governess. The psychoanalysts Freud and Jung, the painters Magritte and Delvaux, the writer Apollinaire, bulk larger in this production than Hans Christian Andersen or de la Motte Fouqué, and there was protest at the lack of romantic trappings.

Richard Strauss
(1864–1949)

SALOME

OPERA in one act; words after Oscar Wilde's stage poem of the same name, translated into German by Hedwig Lachmann. Première in Dresden, December 9, 1905.

THE action takes place in Galilee on the moonlit terrace of Herod's palace, off the banquet hall, where the Tetrarch (*tenor*) is giving a dinner, the noisy proceedings of which are commented on by two soldiers as the opera begins. But the captain of the guard, Narraboth (*tenor*), a Syrian, has eyes only for Salome (*soprano*), who, he says, looks pale. A Page (*alto*) of Herodias warns Narraboth of the dangers of paying too close attention to the young Princess.

Suddenly, from the depths of an old cistern, comes the voice of Jokanaan (John the Baptist; *baritone*). He has been imprisoned by Herod, who fears him and has forbidden anyone to go near him.

Salome runs on to the terrace. She has escaped from the banquet, from her stepfather's lascivious looks and from the noisy disputations of his guests, who include envoys from Rome and zealots from Jerusalem. But these thoughts vanish as Salome hears the voice of Jokanaan. She refuses to return to the table (Herod has dispatched a slave to summon her back) and demands to see the Prophet. The soldiers refuse, so Salome persuades Narraboth, who cannot resist her blandishments, to have the lid of the cistern raised and the Prophet brought forth. The strange, gloomy figure of Jokanaan, noble in the rags of captivity, emerges to extended orchestral music.

The sight stirs Salome, and there is a lengthy scene between them. As soon as he appears, Jokanaan denounces Herod and Herodias (the latter has killed her husband in order to marry the Tetrarch), proclaiming, 'Wo ist er, dessen Sündenbecher jetzt voll ist?' (Where is he, he whose sins are now without number?[1]). Salome is fascinated and he turns on her ('Wer ist dies Weib, das mich ansieht?': Who is this girl who's so curious?), and rages at her as the daughter of an iniquitous mother. Salome tells him in music of rising intensity of her desire for his body ('Jokanaan, ich bin verliebt in deinen Leib': Jokanaan, your body wakens my desire'), his hair ('In dein Haar bin ich verliebt': I'm enamoured of your hair) and his mouth ('Deinen Mund begehre ich': 'Tis your mouth that I desire).

All of Salome's seductive powers are brought into play, but with the sole result that the Prophet bids her do penance. This only drives her further. Nothing will dissuade her; not even Narraboth who, appalled by her actions, kills himself with his sword; Salome does not even notice. The Prophet warns her to seek the only one in whom she can find redemption, the Saviour of Galilee: 'Es lebt nur Einer, der dich retten kann' (There lives but one man who can save you now). But still Salome will not listen, and begs to kiss Jokanaan on the mouth. Revolted, the Prophet curses Salome ('Daughter of Sodom') and returns to the cistern.

After an orchestral interlude, Herod, Herodias (*mezzo-soprano*) and their guests come on to the terrace. The Tetrarch has come in search of Salome. The superstitious Herod veers between lucidity and a condition bordering on madness – not helped when he slips in Narraboth's blood, then spies the body. He has hallucinations that a wind is blowing round his head and that he can hear the beating of vast wings. Herodias says she feels and hears nothing and demands they go back inside. But Herod is determined to remain where he is.

In a scene which is an amazing depiction of neurasthenia and eroticism, Herod asks Salome to share his wine and eat fruit with him; she says she is neither thirsty nor hungry. He then asks her to sit beside him on her mother's throne; she says she is not tired. Herod's entreaties, Salome's indifference and Herodias's scorn are interrupted by the voice of Jokanaan. Herodias says the Prophet insults her, and asks Herod to give him up to the Jews, who have been clamouring for him. Herod refuses, insisting that the Prophet is a holy man who has seen God. This starts an intense theological argument among the Jews, who dispute in a fugal quintet. No sooner is it finished than two

---

[1] Translations throughout by Tom Hammond.

Nazarenes (*tenor*, *bass*) proclaim their conviction that the Messiah is among them; he has even raised the dead from their graves. Herod is filled with misgivings, which are not dispelled by Jokanaan's continuing predictions of doom.

It is almost as much because of his dread of the future as for longing for her that Herod suddenly asks Salome to dance for him. She refuses, until Herod swears to grant her any request she may make of him. Salome performs the Dance of the Seven Veils (its self-contained music is often performed as a concert piece), which can be an exacting undertaking for any *prima donna* who has still the most taxing part of her vocal assignment to come. It has been performed by a dancer (for example, at the opera's first performance), but in the latter half of this century, a performance where a dancer, not a singer, casts her veils is something of a rarity.

Herod asks Salome what her reward shall be. She demands the head of Jokanaan, brought to her on a silver charger. Herod is shocked, while Herodias congratulates her daughter. Salome refuses the Tetrarch's compromise offers – precious stones, his white peacocks, the Mantle of the High Priest, even the Veil of the Temple – and will not release him from his oath. Finally, almost faint with weariness and fear, Herod gives in, saying that Salome is, indeed, her mother's child.

The executioner descends into the cistern, while Salome hovers impatiently, to the eerie sound of a pinched B flat on a solo double-bass (said by the composer to represent not the execution but the excited, tense state of Salome as she waits for her prey). The executioner delivers Jokanaan's head. Salome, in ecstasy, seizes the head, and, in a long monologue, pours out her feelings of revenge and lust as if Jokanaan were still living. Herod, quivering with fear, demands the torches be extinguished and his retinue go in to the palace. A cloud covers the moon. As it lifts, Salome is seen kissing the mouth of Jokanaan. Herod commands his guards, 'Kill that woman!' They crush her beneath their shields.

Salome was Strauss's third opera but his first great success, and there is no questioning its continued vitality. What could be more evocative and suggestive of what is to come than the opening music, which so unerringly sets the scene? Strauss's vivid characterisations are equally notable: the extraordinary portrayal of obsessive lust in the music of Herod, decadence and fear in every bar he sings. But the best character study is Salome herself. Each and every change of this emotionally unstable character is reflected in the music, and her final scene with the head of Jokanaan transcends the dramatic implications of the words, and is written, through her eyes as it were, as a sort of psychopathic *Liebestod*.

ELEKTRA

OPERA in one act by Richard Strauss; text by Hugo von Hofmannsthal, after Sophocles. Première Dresden, January 25, 1909.

BEYOND the fact that Agamemnon was murdered by his wife, Clytemnestra, and her paramour Aegisthus, it is not essential to know the details of the Greek story, but it is nevertheless against this background that even Hofmannsthal and Strauss, with all their changes of emphasis, have laid their opera. Agamemnon and Menelaus, the sons of King Atreus, married the sisters Clytemnestra and Helen. The latter was carried off by Paris, son of Priam, King of Troy, and it was to procure her return to her husband and to avenge the insult to Greece that the Trojan war began. On their way to Troy, the Greek fleet touched at Aulis and was caught there by the adverse winds, the goddess Artemis being angry with Agamemnon, who had killed one of her sacred hinds. To appease the goddess and to ensure that the fleet reached Troy in safety, Agamemnon sent for his daughter Iphigenia and sacrificed her. The war over, Menelaus and Helen were driven by storms to Egypt, where they stayed for some years, and Agamemnon returned to Mycenae. Here he found that Clytemnestra had installed Aegisthus as her lover. With the excuse of the sacrifice of her daughter to salve her conscience Clytemnestra murdered Agamemnon in his bath. Three children survived their father: Electra, who was reduced to menial status, Chrysothemis, and Orestes, who was sent away to safety, according to some versions by a faithful slave, to others by Electra. Eventually, Orestes returns, gives out that he is dead, gains admittance to the palace, and slays the guilty Clytemnestra and her lover.

The opera is in one long act. There is no prelude, just a *fortissimo* statement of Agamemnon's theme, which dominates the opera as surely as any of its main characters. The curtain rises on the inner court of the palace of Mycenae. The servants are drawing water from a well. They discuss the unpredictable Electra, who howls like the dogs with whom her mother and stepfather have condemned her to live and eat. Some hate her, others pity her, only the fifth maid (*soprano*) reveres and loves her. For her defence of Electra, she is set upon by the others, and when they have gone inside, the fifth maid can be heard crying out that she is being beaten.

The scene is empty before Electra (*soprano*) comes from the house alone. In a great monologue ('Allein! Weh, ganz allein!': Alone! Alas, quite alone!) she rehearses the story of her father's murder, calls on his name, and looks forward to the time when his death will be avenged by herself and Orestes. When this is accomplished she will dance in triumph round the corpses of her enemies. Electra is interrupted by Chrysothemis (*soprano*). Hofmannsthal designs her as a weaker and more human contrast to the implacable Electra, and she is little inclined to join her sister in the schemes for revenge which are constantly being urged upon her. Instead, she issues a warning that further horrors are in store for Electra. Poor Chrysothemis feels the fires of love frustrated within her ('Ich hab's wie Feuer in der Brust': There's a storm of fire within my breast) and longs to escape from her hateful prison, to which she is doomed by the fear which her sister's weird hatred inspires in Clytemnestra. The ordeal to which both are subjected is leaving its mark on them, she says.

Noises are heard within of running footsteps, torches can be seen, and Chrysothemis says she will not stay to meet Clytemnestra who must surely be coming out. Electra, however, is determined to speak to her mother.

Clytemnestra (*mezzo-soprano*) is bloated and decayed, and sleepless nights and debauched days have left her looking as though it were an effort to keep her eyes open. She leans on the arm of her Confidante (*soprano*). Her first words are to mourn the evil workings of fate which have given her such a child, but presently she comes down to the courtyard, and is left alone with the daughter she hates and fears so much.

She is tormented by dreams; Electra is wise, and alone can help her find a remedy. She describes her sleepless nights; is there not some sacrifice she can make to the gods to alleviate the torture she suffers? Electra answers her insinuatingly, and ambiguously. Yes, there is a victim, who is unconsecrated and roams free; it is a woman, married, who can be killed at any time of day or night, with an axe, by a man, a stranger, but of their kin. Clytemnestra becomes impatient, and Electra asks whether her mother means to call her brother back from exile. Clytemnestra is uneasy at mention of him, and Electra accuses her of sending money to bribe those who are looking after him to kill him. Clytemnestra says she fears nobody. She will find means of dragging from Electra the secret of whose blood must flow to cause her nightmares to abate. Electra springs at her; it is *her* blood that is required. *She* is the victim the gods have marked down. Electra describes the chase which will end with Clytemnestra's death.

At this moment the Confidante runs out of the palace and whispers in Clytemnestra's ear. A look of triumph comes into the Queen's face, and she goes into the palace, leaving a puzzled Electra alone in the courtyard. Chrysothemis rushes out, crying the dread news that Orestes is dead. She says that two strangers, one old, the other young, brought the news; Orestes was dragged to death by his own horses. A servant comes out of the palace, demanding a horse as quickly as possible so that he may carry the news to Aegisthus.

Electra demands that Chrysothemis shall help her in her self-appointed task; alone she cannot slay Clytemnestra and Aegisthus but with her sister's help she would be able to accomplish the deed. She flatters Chrysothemis that she is strong, and she promises that she will henceforth look after her as if she were her slave. She holds Chrysothemis fast, but when her sister eventually frees herself, she hurls a curse after her.

Electra begins to dig like an animal at the side of the courtyard. She looks up twice, and then sees someone standing by the gate. He asks her if she works in the palace. She answers bitterly that she does. He tells her that he has business with the Queen; he and another have brought news of Orestes's death. Electra's grief at the news is overwhelming; must she look upon him who lives, while someone a thousand times as good as he lies dead? The stranger (*baritone*) asks her if she is of the royal house that she takes Orestes's death as so personal a matter. She reveals her name, and the stranger exclaims in astonishment. He reveals that Orestes is not dead, and, a moment later, servants come in and kiss his hand. Who is he, demands Electra? Everyone knows him, he replies, except his own sister.

The Recognition Scene is the emotional climax of the opera. Electra's ferocity drops from her to be replaced by tenderness, and the unremitting tension of the music gives way to lyricism: 'Orest! Orest! Orest!'

Electra will not allow her brother to embrace her. She contrasts her former beauty with her present state. Together they exult in the prospect of the righteous revenge they will exact.

The last stage of the drama begins when the Confidante leads Orestes and the tutor (*bass*) inside. Electra is alone, in horrible excitement, waiting for the sounds which will tell her that the first part of the revenge is over. A shriek tells her that Orestes has killed Clytemnestra. By now the palace is aroused, but Electra bars the entrance with her body.

To an appropriately jaunty tune, Aegisthus (*tenor*) saunters into the courtyard, and Electra offers to light him into the palace. Aegisthus wonders at the change that has come over Electra, who is circling round him in a strange sort of dance. Aegisthus enters the palace, but re-appears a moment later at a window, yelling for help.

Women rush out of the palace, amongst them Chrysothemis, who has discovered that Orestes is back. Their rejoicings are very different in character, and Electra breaks away from her sister, throwing back her head like a maenad, and dancing about like a demented creature. Her thirst for vengeance is satisfied, and her dance increases to frenzy. Suddenly she collapses dead upon the ground. With a last cry of 'Orest!' Chrysothemis rushes to the door of the palace, and bangs on it. The orchestra continues to hammer out Agamemnon's motif.

DER ROSENKAVALIER
The Knight of the Rose

OPERA in three acts by Richard Strauss; text by Hugo von Hofmannsthal. Première January 26, 1911, in Dresden.

I T was Hofmannsthal, the modifier of Sophocles's text for Strauss's fourth opera, *Elektra* – his second success – who suggested the subject of *Der Rosenkavalier*, a comedy to be set in Vienna in Maria Theresa's time. The opera was a success from the start, and has been played more often than any other German opera written in the twentieth century.

It can be claimed as a masterpiece, or alternatively as an edifice of pastiche and paradox – an evocation of an unrealistic, fairy-story Vienna of long ago, where wit and elegance redeemed anything and all could be forgiven provided it were done with style. The result may be magical, but no more realistic than *Die Fledermaus*. The means Strauss and Hofmannsthal employed are undeniably attractive but either anachronistic, like the ubiquitous and seductive waltzes, which perfectly suggest a period atmosphere of which they were never part, or else invented, like the plausible but unhistorical presentation of a rose to an engaged girl.

The marvel is that one of the fine fruits of the collaboration of Strauss and Hofmannsthal is a fast-moving musical conversation, an outstanding example of speech heightened by music, and that on this basis grow moments of genuine pathos which give the opera memorability, like the 32-year-old Marschallin's reflections on the passing of youth, and set-pieces such as Ochs's waltz, the Presentation of the Rose, or, best of all, the great third-act trio, which provides a splendid and cathartic musical summary of the drama's emotional threads.

ACT I. The bedroom of the Feldmarschallin (*soprano*). The prelude is explicitly intended to represent the love-making which takes place before the curtain rises. The first seven notes, rampant and assertive, are associated with Octavian (*soprano* or *mezzo-soprano*), the Marschallin's music (after a climax) comes a little later and is both passionate and contemplative. Octa-

vian, a youth of seventeen and certainly not the first of the Marschallin's lovers, is as keen to prolong the moment as she is
loath to let him go – it is a scene of great tenderness, with a little
jealousy mixed in – but he hides when chocolate is brought in
and both take alarm when they think the Feldmarschall himself
is on his way up. Octavian scampers out, but it is only one of
the Marschallin's relatives, the country-bred Baron Ochs von
Lerchenau (*bass*), insisting in spite of the servants' protestations
on seeing her. Octavian returns in a maid's uniform and the
Baron is almost diverted from making appropriate obeisance to
his cousin by the presence of the pretty 'Mariandel'. He tries to
make an assignation for later and comes only reluctantly to the
point: will the Princess do him the honour of naming a Knight
of the Rose to go on his behalf to his fiancée, Sophie von Faninal? He also needs a notary. A chance remark sets him off on his
favourite subject: love-making, his monologue consisting
partly of reminiscence, partly of pure fancy – if only like Jupiter
he could take on disguises for his amours!

The morning levée begins, and aspirants to the Princess's
favour mingle with her notary, chef and hairdresser. An Italian
tenor demonstrates his art in a pastiche aria of considerable
charm, the Marschallin rejects the attempts of two Italian scan-
dalmongers, Valzacchi (*tenor*) and Annina (*mezzo-soprano*), to
interest her in a gossip sheet, and finally Ochs erupts at the
attorney's suggestion that a dowry is due from him to the bride,
not the other way round. The Baron and his down-at-heel
retinue depart, leaving the Marschallin prey to autumnal
thoughts. Was she not herself just such a girl as this poor unsuspecting creature whom Ochs, with all his crudity, plans to
marry? Even the return of Octavian, booted and spurred and
full of chivalrous talk, only reminds her he will soon find a
younger woman. Her reflections on the passage of time are full
of melancholy, and Octavian takes an almost formal leave,
without even a kiss. The Marschallin sends her little black page
after him with the silver rose; Count Octavian, she tells him in
an exquisitely poised phrase, will know what to do with it.

ACT II. The grand Salon in Herr von Faninal's (*baritone*)
house. Sophie (*soprano*) and her duenna (*soprano*) are to await
her bridegroom, etiquette demanding that Faninal be absent
when the bearer of the silver rose arrives. His entrance triggers
what is perhaps Strauss's most magical set-piece, the Presentation of the Rose, with a glistening, ice-cold orchestral texture to support Sophie's soaring vocal rapture, itself a perfect
example of the composer's idiomatic writing for soprano voice.
The young people engage in polite conversation whose increasingly intimate tone is interrupted by the Baron's entrance.
His total lack of manners repels Sophie, Octavian boils with

rage and only Ochs's humming of his favourite waltz tune shows a less disagreeable side to his make-up.

Ochs goes into an adjoining room to sign the marriage contract, and the outraged Sophie sinks gratefully into Octavian's arms. Cries from Valzacchi and Annina, anxious to ingratiate themselves with Ochs, bring him in, but he refuses to take seriously Octavian's assertion of Sophie's antipathy. Eventually, Octavian's taunts force him to draw his sword. In the encounter, Octavian lightly pinks the Baron, whose outrage creates commotion, stilled only when recovery sets in after another draught of Faninal's good wine.

Octavian is determined to win Sophie and makes use of the two intriguers. To the Baron, alone on the sofa and humming his favourite waltz tune, comes Annina to hand him a note purporting to be from the Marschallin's chambermaid and promising him a rendezvous. Delighted with his new conquest, he allows the end of the act to be dominated by his famous waltz.

ACT III. An inn near Vienna, where, after a brilliant orchestral *fugato*, Annina and Valzacchi, now in the service of both Octavian and Ochs but inclined to favour the former because he pays them better, prepare a room full of surprises for the Baron's assignation. Between him and Octavian, dressed as Mariandel, develops a rude scene of courtship mostly to the accompaniment of a chain of waltzes, to one of which Octavian sings 'Nein, nein, ich trink' kein Wein!' (No, no, I don't drink wine!), a tune which will later assume significance. Even the resemblance of Mariandel to Octavian does not put the Baron off, but he is soon to discover he is the victim of an elaborate practical joke. First, figures appear at the 'blind' windows, then a disguised Annina insists she is his deserted wife, children claim they are his, a policeman (*bass*) called to defend the Baron against his tormentors turns out to be strict about young women apparently brought to an inn for seduction. When Faninal puts in an appearance, Ochs, who has in desperation described Mariandel as his fiancée, is driven to say he has never seen him before, and the arrival of the Marschallin – summoned by one of Ochs's servants – puts the lid on an evening which for Ochs is fraught with disaster.

She quickly takes in the situation. The Police Commissary was once her husband's orderly and it is easy to persuade him that the whole matter was just a joke and nothing more. Sophie is heartbroken at the idea that the 'joke' may have included Octavian and herself, but the Marschallin takes things in hand, sends Ochs packing and pushes Octavian and Sophie together.

The last section of the opera removes something of the impression of musical bustle which has dominated the rest of the act, containing as it does the great trio for the Marschallin,

Sophie and Octavian (based paradoxically on the inconsequen-
tial little tune of 'Nein, nein, ich trink' kein Wein'). Then, with
Octavian forgiven, the lovers are left alone to sing an extended
duet set to the simplest of tunes and punctuated by an orchestral snatch from the Presentation of the Rose. Sophie and Octavian go hand in hand to the waiting carriage. But it is not quite
the end of the opera. Mahomet, the little page, comes to look for
Sophie's handkerchief, finds it, and runs out as the curtain falls.

ARIADNE AUF NAXOS
Ariadne on Naxos

IN its original form, opera in one act by Richard Strauss; text by Hugo
von Hofmannsthal. First heard at Stuttgart October 25, 1912; revised,
with a prologue and one act, première in Vienna, October 4, 1916.

ONE of the first things to strike anyone who reads the correspondence of Strauss and Hofmannsthal is the considerable difference there often is between their first thoughts on the
subject of one of their operatic collaborations, and their last.
Thus the strange evolution of *Ariadne*. Originally conceived as
an opera lasting half an hour, and designed as a thank-offering
to Max Reinhardt, who produced *Rosenkavalier* in Dresden, it
was intended to form the musical divertissement in Molière's *Le
Bourgeois Gentilhomme*, taking the place of the Turkish ballet
called for by Monsieur Jourdain. In the end the opera became a
much more extensive affair lasting about three times as long as
projected. Unfortunately, the combination of a theatrical with
an operatic company proved beyond the means of most
theatres, and the work as it stood was declared impracticable.
Strauss revised it and substituted a musical prelude (lasting
about thirty-five minutes) for the Molière play, making some
alterations in the body of the opera itself.

The theme of *Le Bourgeois Gentilhomme* is that Monsieur
Jourdain, the bourgeois who is determined to become a gentleman by sheer concentrated hard work and who means to learn
to dance, sing, fence, compose, philosophise, is at the same
time laying siege to the affections of a certain Marquise Dori-
mène. She for her part is in love with the shady Count Dorante,
who has undertaken to bring her to the lavish dinner party
which is given in their honour by Jourdain. The play is gar-
nished with some delightful incidental music by Strauss, and
the three principal characters remain at the side of the stage
while the opera is performed for their benefit.

Prologue (in the revised version). At the house of a Viennese
nouveau riche (not in Paris, as in the Molière). Much preparation

is under way for the first performance of a serious opera which has been specially commissioned by the owner of the house. There is consternation when the Major-Domo (*spoken*) announces that after the opera there will be a Harlequinade entertainment; moreover, the two shows must not overrun their allotted span of time, as the fireworks will begin precisely at nine o'clock! Worse is to come, as a little later the Major-Domo comes in to inform the two troupes that his master has changed his mind, and now both entertainments will be played simultaneously, the serious opera being punctuated by intervals of dancing from the comedians.

The dominating figure of the prologue is the composer (a 'trouser-role' for soprano or, less suitably, mezzo-soprano), a creation of the second version and a touching figure which has found admirable exponents almost every time the opera has been performed. He extemporises an aria which he intends for the tenor (this is derived from a little song heard during the course of the play in the first version), he languishes at the idea of his masterpiece being combined with a common dancing show, he tries to explain to Zerbinetta (*soprano*), the star of the comedians, that Ariadne prefers death to the embraces of any man other than her beloved, and, proving unsuccessful in this, he indulges in a duet with Zerbinetta in which he comes perilously close to declaring that he loves her. There is some trouble with both tenor and *prima donna*, after which the composer brings the prologue to a suitable end by declaring his conviction in the power of music, the most sacred of the arts.

After an interval, the curtain rises on the opera itself. On Naxos, Ariadne (*soprano*) sleeps in her cave, watched by Naiad (*soprano*), Dryad (*contralto*) and Echo (*soprano*). In a trio (of the type made familiar by Wagner's Rhinemaidens), these creatures express a certain sympathy with Ariadne's sorrow, to which however they have become accustomed.

A great *scena* begins for Ariadne. She sings as if in a dream, and takes no notice when the Harlequinade quartet and Zerbinetta comment on her distress and try to think of means of comforting her. Ariadne welcomes the idea of death, and not even a determined effort by Harlequin to cure her of her madness – for he thinks it must surely be that which is wrong with her – can stop her for long. 'Es gibt ein Reich, wo alles rein ist; es hat auch einen Namen: Totenreich' (There is a land where all is purity: it also has a name – Death's domain)[1] she continues, and at mention of death's messenger, Hermes, her monologue becomes more urgent. The last section of the monologue,

---

[1] English translations by Tom Hammond.

where Ariadne rejoices in the idea of the deliverance death will bring to her, is ecstatic in import, and (from the singer's point of view) Wagnerian in weight.

The four comedians make another attempt to cheer up the melancholy Ariadne, but eventually, Zerbinetta bids them leave her to see what she can do on her own. Her *scena* is surely the most taxing ever written for coloratura soprano. After a recitative, 'Grossmächtige Prinzessin' (Most gracious sovereign lady), she appeals to Ariadne as woman to woman. Ariadne is not the first to be abandoned by her lover, and will not be the last. Zerbinetta expounds her own fickle philosophy, and is quite unconcerned when Ariadne disappears inside her cave. She goes into details of her amorous career in an *allegretto scherzando* ('So war es mit Pagliazzo': 'Twas so with poor Pagliazzo) at which point the vocal writing parts company with what is normally considered advisable to write for a singer and becomes a fantastic display of vocal fireworks.

The section of the opera which begins at her recitative is entirely Zerbinetta's. She is pursued by the four comedians, each of whom seems amorously inclined. Zerbinetta encourages and eludes them all, until only Scaramuccio (*tenor*), Brighella (*tenor*), and Truffaldino (*bass*) are left on the stage. Much to their annoyance, Zerbinetta is immediately heard conversing tenderly with Harlequin (*baritone*), whom they had thought safely out of the way. They rush out to see what they can do about it.

The three attendant nymphs return, full of the sight they have just seen. A youthful god is coming, Bacchus (*tenor*), fresh from the embraces of Circe, but eager for new adventure. They call to Ariadne, who emerges from the cave in time to hear Bacchus offstage calling for Circe. The nymphs beg him to continue singing, and Ariadne hails him as the longed-for messenger of death. The opera ends with an extended love duet, Wagnerian in its length and weight if not in its character. In Bacchus's arms, Ariadne finds consolation, and Strauss even allows Zerbinetta to pop in for a moment to comment that all has turned out exactly as she would have expected. Bacchus and Ariadne go together into the cave.

DIE FRAU OHNE SCHATTEN
The Woman without a Shadow

OPERA in three acts by Richard Strauss; text by Hugo von Hofmannsthal. Première in Vienna, October 10, 1919.

THE Emperor of the South Eastern Islands (*tenor*) is married to a supernatural being, the daughter of Keikobad, King of the Spirits. She emerged from a white gazelle which he shot while out hunting. Their love is mutual and ardent, but their marriage is childless; in token of her barren state, the Empress (*soprano*) throws no shadow. This is the main theme of the story; to make love complete, the woman must bear children, and of this the shadow is the outward sign.

ACT I. Scene i. The imperial gardens. To the Nurse (*mezzo-soprano*), who crouches in the gloom, appears a messenger (*baritone*). After reassuring himself that the Empress still throws no shadow, he tells the Nurse that he is from Keikobad and has come to inform her that the Empress may stay only another three days on earth. She must then go back to Keikobad, and the Emperor will be turned into stone.

As the messenger disappears the Emperor comes from the house. He recounts the story of how he first saw and won his wife. He tells the Nurse that he is going hunting for three days, and refers to his favourite falcon which he has not seen since the day he met his wife. The Emperor leaves, day dawns, and the Empress comes from her chamber. She too talks of her love, but then catches sight of the falcon (*soprano*), whose voice is heard to say: 'The woman throws no shadow, the Emperor must turn to stone.' The Empress understands that the only way to save him is to acquire a shadow, and she begs the Nurse to help her find one.

Scene ii. The orchestra represents their journey to earth. In the hut of the dyer, Barak (*bass-baritone*), his three deformed brothers (*basses, tenor*) are fighting. In the scene which ensues, the contrasting characters of Barak and his wife (*soprano*) are made apparent. She nags and complains, he is patient and full of natural goodness. But he upbraids her for not having given him a child in the two and a half years of their marriage. He goes off to take his goods to market.

The Empress and her Nurse come in, dressed simply as peasants. The Nurse is immediately aware that in the dyer's wife she has found a good subject for her black arts. She praises her for her beauty, and asks if she does not know that she could sell her shadow and get for it all the luxuries and riches she has always desired. The Nurse tempts her with visions, which she summons to aid her in achieving her object.

The dyer's wife agrees to exchange her own prospect of motherhood for the promise of riches. She will deny her bed to her husband. The Empress and the Nurse say that they will be back next day. When she is alone, the woman has another vision. This time she hears the voices of her unborn children coming from the flames of the fire. She is terrified.

Barak enters to find his bed separated from his wife's. He is sad, but optimistic that this is only a temporary state of affairs. As they lie down, the voices of nightwatchmen can be heard coming from outside.

ACT II. In his introduction to the published libretto, Hofmannsthal says: 'The trials continue; all four must be cleansed – the dyer and his wife, the Emperor and the daughter of the spirits. The one pair is too much of the earth earthy, the other too full of pride and remote from the earth.'

Scene i. In Barak's hut, the struggle to obtain the shadow continues. The Nurse tempts the woman with the apparition of a handsome youth, who appears each time the dyer is out of the hut. The woman believes she hates her husband and thinks it would be simple to deceive him, and yet does not quite dare to do so. Barak feels the change in her reaction to him, and grows sad. He invites some beggar children to share in their meal.

Scene ii. The Emperor's falcon house in the forest. The Emperor has followed his bird. In the house he sees his wife, from whom he has had a letter to the effect that she has been alone and seen no one during his absence hunting. He senses immediately that she has been in contact with the things of the earth.

Scene iii. Barak's hut. It is the third day and the Nurse continues her efforts to gain the shadow of the dyer's wife for the Empress. The Nurse and the dyer's wife go out of the hut together, leaving the Empress and Barak. She is beginning to feel sympathy towards Barak, and regrets what she is causing to happen to him and his wife.

Scene iv. The Empress's bedroom in the falcon house. She is in restless sleep, and the Nurse lies at the foot of the bed. The Empress has a vision of her husband wandering through tomb-like caves, and hears the voice of the falcon: 'The woman throws no shadow; the Emperor must turn to stone.' She is much moved by this, but also touched by Barak's distress, which she is fully aware is caused by her actions.

Scene v. Barak's hut. The Nurse makes her final attempt to win the woman's shadow. Although it is midday, it is growing dark, a storm is brewing, and Barak's brothers are howling in terror. The Nurse senses that there are supernatural powers at work over which she has no control, but assures the Empress of their ultimate attainment of their object. The Empress is appalled by the sufferings of men, but grateful that fate has led her to meet Barak, whose integrity has convinced her of the dignity of humanity. The climax of the scene comes when the woman tells Barak that she has been unfaithful to him and sold her shadow and her unborn children with it. To prove the truth of her words, the brothers light a fire and it is seen that she throws no shadow. Barak threatens to kill her, and a sword appears in his hand. The Empress refuses to take the shadow at such a price, but the woman, overcome by remorse when she sees the result of her admission, tells Barak that she has not done what she has confessed, but has only wished to do it.

As the Nurse tears the Empress from the scene, the earth opens and swallows up Barak and his hut.

ACT III. Scene i. A subterranean vault, divided by a thick wall. On one side is Barak, on the other his wife, each unconscious of the presence of the other. In a famous passage, she wrestles with her conscience ('Schweigt doch, ihr Stimmen': Be silent, you voices); he tries to find consolation and peace for the two of them ('Mir anvertraut, dass ich sie hege': Entrusted to me, I'll cherish you).

Scene ii. The vault disappears, and the Empress and her Nurse enter in a boat. Trombone calls summon the Empress to the judgment hall where her father Keikobad presides. The Nurse wants to prevent her from entering, for she fears Keikobad's anger more than death; her purpose now is to persuade the Empress to return to earth to continue her search for the shadow. But the Empress is determined to enter where she knows her husband is being judged. She bids the Nurse farewell for ever; the Nurse does not understand men and their struggles and the price they pay for their guilt. She herself has learned to love them and to understand them in their misery. She enters the Temple. The voices of Barak and his wife are heard calling for each other.

The Empress demands to know her place in the scheme of the universe. A voice from above tells her to drink of the Water of Life and the shadow of the woman will be hers and she will be human. But the voices of Barak and his wife are again heard, and the Empress refuses to drink and be guilty of the crime of their undoing. She feels she belongs to the human race, and yet she refuses to yield to the temptation, which would involve the destruction of innocent beings. She demands to see her father, her judge. The alcove is illuminated, and the Emperor appears, turned to stone except for his eyes, which can be seen pleading with her for life. Her anguish is increased when she hears a voice call: 'The woman throws no shadow, the Emperor must turn to stone.' She is again urged to drink of the Water of Life, to gain the shadow and save her husband. It is her moment of supreme trial, and she falls to the ground in the agony of her inner struggle. Finally, a cry breaks from her lips: 'I will not.'

Scene iii. As soon as this cry is heard, the water disappears, and the Temple is brightly lit from above. The Empress rises to her feet and it can be seen that she throws a shadow. The Emperor descends from his alcove, the voices of their unborn children are heard singing from above, and in their happiness the Emperor and Empress embrace and fall on their knees to give thanks for deliverance from their trial.

Scene iv. A beautiful landscape, with a waterfall in the middle. The Emperor and Empress stand beside it. Below it can be seen the figures of Barak and his wife, who have found each other. The voices of unborn children complete the happiness of each couple.

INTERMEZZO

Two acts; première, Dresden, 1924. The opera is based on incidents in the composer's private life. Robert Storch (*baritone*), a composer, and his wife Christine (*soprano*) are packing, she thoroughly bad-tempered with everyone. She meets a young man, Baron Lummer (*tenor*); she fawns on him and asks him to visit her. He, in need of money, requests a large sum. She opens a letter to her husband which indicates that he is having an affair, and in a rage telegraphs that she is leaving him. At a card party Storch receives the telegram with distress. He has no idea who the letter-writer is, but his friend Stroh (*tenor*) realises that it was meant for him. Stroh goes to see Christine to explain. She is excited at Robert's return, but acts coldly; he gives her a piece of his mind, and pretends to be jealous of the Baron. He finds the request for the money a great joke, and the two are reconciled.

ARABELLA

OPERA in three acts by Richard Strauss; text by Hugo von Hofmannsthal. Première Dresden, July 1, 1933.

ACT I. A salon in a hotel in Vienna; 1860. We soon learn that the fortunes of the Waldner family are low. Graf Waldner (*bass*) is a gambler and has been losing heavily, and the only hope seems to lie in matching the beautiful Arabella (*soprano*) with a rich suitor. Zdenka (*soprano*), the younger child, has been brought up as a boy, as they cannot possibly afford to have two daughters coming out near the same time.

Adelaide (*mezzo-soprano*) is having her fortune told, and Zdenka, dressed in boy's clothes, is making excuses for her parents to the tradesmen who call to talk about their unpaid bills. Zdenka is left alone, and shortly afterwards a young officer, Matteo (*tenor*), who is desperately in love with Arabella, comes in. He asks for news of his beloved from Zdenka whom, like everyone else, he believes to be her brother (and therefore Zdenko). Arabella has not looked at him for days, and if it were not for the wonderful letter she wrote him a day or two ago, he would be in complete despair. He threatens to go away or kill himself if Arabella continues to ignore him. When he has gone, Zdenka reveals her perturbation; she is in love with Matteo herself and it is *she* who wrote him the letter.

Arabella comes in. As usual she has presents from her three noble suitors, and from Matteo as well, but she has no real interest in any of them, and Zdenka's pleading for Matteo affects her little. One day the right man will come along, and she will know him straight away ('Aber der Richtige, wenn's einen gibt für mich': The one who's right for me, if there is one for me in all this world[1]).

The two voices join in a charming and typically Straussian duet, whose theme is frequently heard in the course of the opera. Arabella is confident in the future, even though it is the end of Carnival and she should decide which suitor she will accept before the night is over.

Graf Elemer (*tenor*), one of the three suitors, comes to take Arabella for a sleigh-ride; she says she will be ready in half an hour. When Elemer has gone, Arabella asks Zdenka if she has noticed the attractive stranger whom she has seen during the past day or two from her room. No sooner has she spoken than he appears again in the street but goes away without so much as looking up at the window.

The parents come back. The Count is depressed that he finds only bills waiting for him, and no word from any of his regimental cronies, to all of whom he has written for help in his financial embarrassment. There was one in particular, a Croatian, rich and eccentric, Mandryka by name, who, he thought, would never fail him. Adelaide tells him she has dreamed all will go well. A servant announces that there is a gentleman to see Graf Waldner. It turns out to be Mandryka (*baritone*), nephew and heir of the Count's old comrade, now dead. He has fallen in love with the photograph of Arabella which Waldner sent with his letter, and in a strange mixture of formality and open-heartedness (a musical purple passage) asks for her hand in marriage. To pay for his journey to Vienna he says he sold some woods, and he offers Waldner a couple of thousand-gülden notes. The latter can hardly believe his senses, and when Mandryka has gone, he imitates his tone of voice: 'Teschek, bedien' dich' (Please, help yourself!).

There is a short scene between Zdenka and Matteo, in which she tells him he may have Arabella's letter at that night's Fiaker-

---

[1] English translations by John Gutman.

ball (a ball to which everyone goes in costume: a 'Fiaker' was a two-horse cab). He leaves, and Arabella comes in ready for her drive with Elemer. But the idea of the romantic stranger is much more attractive to her, and even the horrid thought that he may be already married does not dampen her enthusiasm.

ACT II. A ballroom. Arabella, very much the queen of the ball, is introduced by her parents to Mandryka. Arabella recognises the stranger she has seen from her window. She is left alone with him, and sits down, refusing a dance to each of her other suitors in turn. He is a widower and his flowery language astonishes her, but she is completely fascinated and convinced that she has found the right man in him: 'Und du wirst mein Gebieter sein' (My lord and master you shall be). Their love duet is impassioned enough to suggest to us that she is right. During its course, Mandryka conveys the information that in his country a glass of water is given by the girl to her prospective fiancé in token of engagement.

She asks to be allowed an hour at the ball to say goodbye to the things which have made up her girlhood. At that moment, the rest of the guests crowd around her, and the Fiakermilli (*soprano*) – a pretty girl dolled up to the nines – curtsies and brings her a bouquet. She sings a brilliant coloratura polka song for Arabella's entertainment, after which Arabella goes off to dance with Graf Dominik (*baritone*).

Waldner is delighted at the news of Arabella's engagement. Matteo, however, is heart-broken, not at the news (which he has not heard), but because Arabella has not looked in his direction all evening. Zdenka does her best to reassure him. Mandryka orders champagne for everyone. Arabella bids farewell to her three suitors, and goes off again to dance.

Zdenka gives Matteo a letter, which she says is from Arabella. It contains the key of Arabella's room, according to Zdenka, and she insists that if the unbelieving Matteo come to that room in a quarter of an hour, he will receive everything that he most longs for. Mandryka overhears the conversation and cannot believe his ears. His worst suspicions are justified when he cannot find his fiancée. In desperation, Mandryka flirts with the Fiakermilli. A note from Arabella is handed to him: she has gone home but will be his tomorrow. Arabella's parents notice her absence, and they go off with Mandryka to find her.

ACT III. A lounge in the hotel, with staircase leading upstairs. Night. After a short prelude, Matteo is seen about to come down the stairs. He hides when he hears a bell. Arabella comes in and sings of the happiness which she and Mandryka will enjoy amidst his fields and forests. Matteo reappears and is astonished to see Arabella in the hall. She can make no sense at all of his ardour and his insinuations, and he for his part cannot understand her coldness and apparent heartlessness.

Arabella's parents arrive with Mandryka, who immediately recognises Matteo as the man he saw receive the key at the ball. He remains unpersuaded by Arabella's protestations of innocence, tempers rise, and a duel between Mandryka and Matteo is only prevented by the sudden appearance of Zdenka, in a negligée and with her hair down. She rushes down the stairs, and says that she only wants to say goodbye before throwing herself into the Danube. Arabella says she will stand by her whatever her trouble, and Zdenka eventually stammers out that it was she who sent the note to Matteo, and the key inside it was to her room, not Arabella's. The room was dark, and Matteo could not have known that it was not Arabella.

Mandryka tries to put his shame and sorrow into words, but Arabella turns to Zdenka without a glance in his direction and thanks her for teaching her to follow the dictates of her heart. Prompted by Arabella and Mandryka – Arabella bears no malice – Waldner agrees to give Zdenka's hand to Matteo, and the crowd, which has been attracted by the noise, begins to disperse. Arabella tells Mandryka that there must be no attempt at explanation until morning; she would however be grateful if one of his servants could fetch her a glass of clear, cold water. She would find it refreshing after the tumult of the evening's events. She goes slowly up the stairs without another word.

Mandryka waits dejectedly below, when at the top of the stairs appears Arabella. Holding the glass of water in her hand she makes her way slowly down and offers it to him. The opera ends with their love duet: 'Das war sehr gut, Mandryka' (I'm very glad, Mandryka).

CAPRICCIO

OPERA in one act by Richard Strauss; text by Clemens Krauss. Première, Munich, October 28, 1942.

*C*APRICCIO was Strauss's last opera and the subject is opera itself – the theme 'Prima le parole, dopo la musica' led by Olivier, a poet, and Flamand, a musician, rivals in love as well as art.

The action is set in about 1775, in the salon of a château near Paris where plans are afoot to celebrate the birthday of the young widowed Countess Madeleine (*soprano*). Flamand (*tenor*) has written a string sextet for the occasion, and he and Olivier (*baritone*) are listening to the music, on whose qualities the theatre director La Roche (*bass*) seems already to have passed judgment by falling asleep in an armchair. He wakes to join in the discussion and they point out that this is the man in whose hands lies the fate of composers. La Roche believes in entertainment – splendid decor, top notes, beautiful women. He is for Italian opera and he cannot resist mentioning that even highbrow creative artists have their foibles: Olivier did not seem to disdain the talent – or the beauty – of the famous Clairon (*contralto*), who by happy chance is not only the subject of the Count's admiration but will arrive soon at the château to play opposite the Count in Olivier's play.

The Count (*baritone*) and Countess (they are brother and sister) come in from next door and the others quickly disappear. The Count clearly favours the poetic muse, perhaps because of his interest in Clairon. The countess equally obviously inclines towards music – but by no means to the exclusion of words. The Count is in no doubt about his sister's interest in the two artists and wonders aloud which she will eventually choose.

Re-enter La Roche, Flamand and Olivier; the first announces that all is ready for the rehearsal of the birthday entertainment, which will consist of the new music by Flamand, Olivier's drama and finally an *azione teatrale* by his entire company. All discussion stops with the entrance of Clairon, who dominates proceedings as she greets the Countess and then enquires from Olivier if he has yet finished the play.

He has, and Clairon and the Count read the scene, which culminates in the Count's declamation of a sonnet.[1] He is congratulated and La Roche takes them all off into the theatre, leaving Flamand and Olivier with the Countess.

Olivier criticises the way the Count reads the sonnet and recites it to the Countess as a personal utterance. Flamand goes to the harpsichord and begins to improvise and eventually leaves the room with Olivier's manuscript. It is Olivier's chance to declare his love, which he does delicately and gently. Flamand returns to sing the sonnet he has just set ('Kein Andres, das mir so im Herzen loht': Naught else there is that flames so in my heart) and the Countess and Olivier join their voices to his to make a trio of extraordinary beauty. Flamand and Olivier seem likely to quarrel about the true authorship of the sonnet, but the Countess decides the issue quite neatly: it is now hers!

La Roche takes Olivier away to rehearsal and Flamand in his turn is able to declare his love. He presses Madeleine to decide between him and Olivier, and she promises that he shall hear her answer next morning at eleven o'clock.

The sounds of rehearsal can be heard from next door (where

---

[1] A translation of a sonnet by Ronsard.

the Prompter, to general amusement, is found to have fallen asleep) and the Countess orders refreshment to be brought in. She and the Count exchange thoughts on the progress of their affairs of the heart. He must not be too easily carried away by his feelings for Clairon, she advises him, only to have to admit that for her own part she is still undecided between poet and composer, but has already started to wonder whether an opera might not be the collaborative outcome of their interest in her.

Rehearsal is over, and refreshments served while La Roche introduces a dancer for their delectation (*Passepied, Gigue, Gavotte*). During the course of the *Gigue*, Olivier tries unsuccessfully to make up to Clairon, and after the dancing is over the Count comments to Flamand that the dance is an aspect of art where his own contribution is entirely secondary. On the contrary, says Flamand; without music, it would never occur to anyone even to lift a foot.

A fugue ensues, described as 'discussion on the theme "Words on Music"'. Music goes deeper than words; words express thought with greater clarity; music is the art of the sublime; in the theatre, words and music must work together. The Count, Clairon and Olivier are against opera, but the director has a passion for *bel canto*, and at this point introduces two Italian singers (*soprano, tenor*) who entertain the company with a duet in the Italian style.

The Count offers to take Clairon back to Paris, but the director now takes the opportunity of announcing the form the entertainment will take for the Countess's birthday. The first part of the act of homage will consist of a sublime allegory: 'The Birth of Pallas Athene'. This revelation and the details of the action provoke a torrent of abuse and disbelief and the assembled company expresses its feelings in the first part of a great octet, subtitled 'Laughing Ensemble'.

The Countess tries to mend matters and asks La Roche for an exposition of the second part of the play. This, he says, shall be heroic and highly dramatic: 'The Fall of Carthage'. Olivier and Flamand begin to attack him, and the second part of the octet ensues (titled 'Dispute'). But La Roche launches into a most effective defence of the eternal art of Theatre itself. He proclaims himself the friend of comedy, a guardian angel of artists, the patron of serious art.

La Roche's declaration has won the day and all congratulate him. The Countess demands a collaboration between Flamand and Olivier, to the dismay of her brother who realises that she has commissioned an opera. In spite of his reservations, they start to discuss a subject – *Ariadne*? *Daphne*? No, says the Count; choose a theme which describes everyday life; write about today's events as all have lived them! The idea is taken up and in the end La Roche sweeps off poet and musician, actress and her admirer, and the Countess retires to her room, leaving the salon to the care of eight servants, who enter and comment in an extended chorus on the events of the day. No sooner have they left than a voice comes from the darkness: 'Herr Direktor!' It is Monsieur Taupe (*tenor*), the prompter, who has fallen asleep and now wonders how on earth he is to get home. The major-domo (*bass*) is almost ready to take him at his own valuation – without him the theatre could not function at all – and offers help in his predicament.

Moonlight floods the salon. The Countess comes in, followed by the major-domo, who gives her two messages: that her brother will not be home for supper that evening; and that the poet Olivier will call on her to learn how the opera should end – tomorrow, at eleven. The great final scene, one of Strauss's most splendid perorations and a hymn in praise of the beauty of the high female voice, leaves one in no doubt as to which side engages the composer's sympathy in the argument between words and music. The Countess comes to understand that these two men are as inextricably bound up in the art that between them they can produce as they are as rivals for her hand. She sings two verses of the sonnet, looks at herself in the mirror and realises that she cannot make the choice which will give the opera an ending. Either alternative seems trivial.

The major-domo solves the problem by announcing that supper is served.

Hans Pfitzner
(1869–1949)

PALESTRINA

Opera in three acts; text by the composer. Première Munich, June 12, 1917.

Act i. 1563. A solemn prelude leads straight into the action which is laid in a room in Giovanni Pierluigi Palestrina's house in Rome. Silla (*mezzo-soprano*), Palestrina's pupil, is trying over one of his own compositions on the viol (in the last bars of the prelude, this is suggested in the orchestra by two solo violas). Ighino (*soprano*) comes in, looking sad. He is worried that his father looks unhappy. Silla says he sees little wrong with his master, but Ighino pours out his feelings: fame has brought his father little; he has been desperately lonely ever since the loss of his wife, and has written nothing. His life in fact seemed to come to an end with her death.

Palestrina (*tenor*) comes in with Cardinal Borromeo (*baritone*), and the two boys leave. The Cardinal is astonished at the music he heard when they came in (Silla was practising his song again), and he asks Palestrina whether he likes that kind of thing. It is perhaps the new music, the music of the future, replies the master wearily. Borromeo is impatient with Palestrina's attitude. He reveals the reason for his secret visit: the Council of Trent, which has been sitting these eighteen years, is now coming to an end. Pope Pius IV (*bass*) was originally not content with reforming the abuses of church music, but wished to return to Gregorian chant and consign to the flames all other sacred music. Only he – Borromeo – resisted this reactionary view, but he had an ally in the Emperor, who opposed so drastic a change. The case is now won, but can be proved only if a Mass is written by a contemporary composer of such calibre as to convince the Pope and his Council. Such a work would be a model for future composers, and would secure the future of church music. It is Palestrina's task to write it!

But Palestrina declines, insisting that even an artist's powers can grow old. Borromeo's anger overflows, and in the end he accuses the composer of blasphemy. He leaves the room in ungovernable fury. Palestrina is moved by what he has seen and heard: there goes my last friend, is his comment. As he muses he is surrounded by a vision of the composers of the past. They encourage him, and tell him that his ultimate duty is not yet accomplished.

As Palestrina's resistance is slowly overcome, the composers gradually disappear, but immediately he starts to hear the voices of angels, which dictate his Mass to him. At the height of his inspiration, Palestrina sees the ghost of his wife, Lucretia (*contralto*), bringing a message of peace, the peace for which he has longed ever since her death. This scene of the dictation of the Mass is the crux of the opera. It is perhaps sufficient praise to say that it succeeds in giving an impression of the artist's exaltation at the moment of creation.

It is dawn, the angel voices die away, the bells of Rome can be heard in the distance, and Palestrina sinks down exhausted. The floor of the room is covered with music-paper, and, when Silla and Ighino come for their morning lesson, they are overjoyed to see that the master has spent the night working. They realise that an entire Mass has been written in a single night. Silla wonders whether anything written so quickly can possibly add to the master's fame.

ACT II. The agitated prelude is in direct contrast to what preceded the first act. In the great hall in the palace of Cardinal

Madruscht (*bass*) at Trent, preparations are almost complete for renewal of the conference. Cardinal Novagerio (*tenor*) makes fun of the farce which always attends the Spanish delegate's efforts to obtain his rightful precedence, and a little later takes the opportunity of warning the servants, who are all of different nationalities, that they will be severely punished if they again start to quarrel in the streets.

Borromeo arrives, and has a fairly lengthy political discussion with Novagerio. Novagerio congratulates Borromeo on the way he has managed the question of church music, but Borromeo reveals that he has been unsuccessful in getting Palestrina to write the Mass he needs. He has had him thrown into prison, but doubts whether the work can be ready in time, even if gaol were to break Palestrina's self-imposed silence. Novagerio suggests to Borromeo's horror that there are ways to force men to bend to the will of their masters.

The other delegates begin to arrive, the Italians suspicious of the Germans, the Spaniards commenting on the Italians who, they say, swarm over the place like ants. The master of ceremonies, Bishop Ercole Severolus (*bass-baritone*), announces that the conference is about to begin and the delegates take their places. They are addressed by Morone (*baritone*), the papal legate, who prays that wisdom may attend their deliberations and inform their decisions. He calls down a malediction on all heretics, in which the entire conference joins, apart from the liberal-minded but boorish Bishop of Budoja (*tenor*), who makes the mistake of praying that they may be enlightened rather than destroyed.

Discussion begins on the subject of the musical side of the church service. The Pope's approval is dependent on a work being written which satisfies ritual considerations. Borromeo announces that such a Mass is being written, and that Palestrina is the composer. The business of the conference proceeds, but points of order seem to be preferred for discussion to points of doctrine. The Spanish envoy's (*baritone*) quarrelsome attitude brings down upon him the objections of a number of delegates based on precedence and the exalted position he has claimed as his by right. The meeting degenerates into nationalist quarrelling and Morone ends the session. He calls the delegates for the afternoon, but warns them that the co-operation of them all, and not least of the Spanish envoy, will be needed if this last session is to accomplish the task set before it.

As soon as the delegates have gone, the Spanish servants gather and mutter that their delegate has been insulted, and it is not long before a free fight develops between the servants. Madruscht appears with soldiers at his back; seeing the disorder, he commands them to open fire and bids them to take any survivors they can catch to the torture chambers. No one shall thus defile the Church's Council with unseemly conduct.

ACT III. Palestrina's room as in Act I. The composer is sitting in his chair. Five singers from the chapel stand round him, and Ighino is kneeling by his side. The singers express concern for Palestrina's condition, and when he wakes from his trance, he does not seem to recognise them, though they are from his own choir. He asks Ighino why they are waiting and gazing at him. His son tells him that at that very moment his Mass is being sung at the Pope's Palace. He seems not to grasp the significance of this, but refers to being asked some question about it in prison. The others remind him that they gathered together the pages of the Mass he wrote and that they were subsequently taken away from them.

Suddenly the people can be heard crying: 'Long life to Palestrina, saviour of music!' People crowd into the room, asking for the master, Palestrina, and saying that the Pope has called the new Mass Palestrina's best work and is himself coming to congratulate him! The Holy Father makes his entrance, followed by his Cardinals, amongst them Borromeo, and tells Palestrina of the enormous impression his Mass has made on them all. He must remain in his service until the end of his life.

The Pope leaves, blessing Palestrina and his singers. The Cardinals follow the Pope, all, that is, except Borromeo, who makes a sign to the singers to leave him alone with Palestrina. They look at each other for a moment, then with a cry Borromeo falls on his knees in front of the composer, who puts his hands gently on the Cardinal's head. Palestrina raises the Cardinal to his feet and they stay for a moment in an embrace, before the Cardinal goes quickly from the room.

Ighino, who has watched the scene from concealment, rushes out to ask his father if he is not the happiest man in the world. Maybe, says his father, but he is old and shows his happiness less demonstratively than Ighino. Where is Silla, he asks. He guesses he has gone to Florence, and Ighino confirms his impression. There is more acclamation for Palestrina from outside, and he bids his son laugh and dance and sing if he wants to. He himself remains alone in his room. He goes quietly towards the portrait of his wife, then walks to his organ and plays softly, to the sounds of the shouts of the crowd.

Arnold Schoenberg
(1874–1951)

MOSES UND ARON
Moses and Aaron

OPERA in three acts; text by the composer. Première in concert, March 12, 1954, NWDR Hamburg; stage, Zürich, June 6, 1957.

SCHOENBERG started work on the music of his last and only full-length opera in 1931 and the second act was finished in Barcelona in 1932. He never finished Act III, but, as it remains, the opera has always been considered a performable piece.

The text is the composer's own and represents his religious and philosophical thoughts. The drama lies in the conflict between Moses the thinker and Aaron the man of action; Aaron's every attempt to give practical expression to Moses's thoughts results in compromise and a debasing of ideals.

ACT I. The Calling of Moses. There is no prelude, but soft, slow chords introduce Moses (*spoken*) at prayer. The six solo voices in the orchestra and a spoken semi-chorus answer him from the Burning Bush. He is called to lead the Israelites out of Egyptian bondage, and to his protest that he is old and unable to convince the unbelieving people, the answer comes that Aaron his brother will be his mouthpiece.

Moses meets Aaron (*tenor*) in the Wasteland. *Grazioso* music of almost chamber music delicacy introduces the second scene. Though Aaron immediately understands the part he must play in fulfilling the destiny of the Israelites, it is apparent that he and Moses approach their task from opposite points of view. Moses, the thinker bound by doctrine, cannot see God in any other way than as a pure thought, whereas Aaron, the single-minded realist, needs an image in order himself to believe and to persuade the people to believe.

Moses and Aaron bring God's message to the people. Three young Israelites have seen Aaron in a state of religious exaltation, but others, particularly the priests, are less inclined to believe that a new God will deliver them from Pharaoh. When the people demand a God they can understand if they are to follow him, Moses feels that he has failed in the task for which he was chosen, but Aaron snatches his rod and rouses the people to a state of religious mania with his miracles. The people express their fervour in a march, Aaron celebrates his moral victory in a big aria – the victory which has at the same time won over the people and betrayed Moses's ideals – and, to the tune of the march, the Israelites prepare to set out on their journey through the desert.

ACT II. Between the acts, there is an interlude.

Aaron and the Seventy Elders before the Mountain of Revelation. The Israelites are encamped below Mount Sinai and now even the Elders grumble at Moses's continued absence: 'Forty days now, yet we're still waiting.' Aaron tries to pacify them, but the sound of a mob can be heard approaching and in a moment the angry people burst on to the scene. When they threaten to vent their rage on the priesthood as well as on Moses, Aaron promises to give the gods comprehensible form. He sends for gold and the people rejoice in chorus.

The Golden Calf and the Altar. *The Dance before the Golden Calf* is the climax of the opera, as vast a conception musically as it is complicated visually. Animals of all sorts are brought in, decorated and finally sacrificed, all this to the accompaniment of the orchestra alone in music of the richest texture. The music dies down in a lyrical episode as a sick woman (*contralto*) is carried to the image and healed the moment she touches it. Beggars bring their last possessions, old men sacrifice themselves in front of the calf, and the tension mounts again as, to the sound of trombones, the tribal leaders gallop in to worship the calf. The rejoicing soon turns to ecstasy, ecstasy to a savage frenzy as four naked virgins (in a contrasting and delicately beautiful vocal quartet; *sopranos* and *contraltos*) offer themselves for sacrifice upon the altar. Destruction and suicide are followed by an orgy of rape until gradually the people pass into exhaustion and sleep. The music dies down, the fires are extinguished and the stage is in almost complete darkness when a man cries: 'Moses is descending from the mountain.'

Moses appears, the tablets of the laws in his hands, and commands: 'Begone, thou image of impotence.' The people are terrified as the Golden Calf disintegrates, and they leave Moses alone with Aaron.

Moses and Aaron. In answer to Moses's angry question, Aaron explains that his actions were the logical outcome of Moses's idea; as Moses's mouthpiece he must interpret his ideas in terms which the people can understand. Moses in his fury smashes the tablets of stone, which he sees in their turn as no more than images. Moses unswervingly reiterates his faith, and Aaron in music of florid cast defends the integrity of the people. In the background, led by a pillar of fire, the children of Israel can be heard and seen as they resume their march to the promised land. Moses is left alone and in despair. 'O Wort, du Wort, das mir fehlt' (O word, thou word that I lack) is his moving last utterance.

Alban Berg
(1885–1935)

WOZZECK

OPERA in three acts and fifteen scenes; text adapted by the composer from Büchner's drama of the same name. Première, Berlin Staatsoper, December 14, 1925.

CONCEIVED in 1914, when Berg saw a performance of *Woz-zek*, the stylistically prophetic play by Georg Büchner (1813-1837), *Wozzeck's* composition was interrupted by the First World War, in which Berg served. The music was completed in 1921, and in 1923 Universal Edition undertook to publish the opera.

Wozzeck is in three acts, each of five scenes. The music is continuous and often Berg provides no more than a few seconds of interlude music during which the scene change must be made. The setting is Germany, c.1830.

ACT I. Scene i. The Captain's room. It is morning, and the Captain (*tenor*) is being shaved by Wozzeck (*baritone*), his soldier-servant. The Captain, a garrulous, digressive individual, moralises to the bewildered Wozzeck: if he hurries so much, what will he do with the ten minutes he saves? His observation that Wozzeck is a good fellow, but without moral sense – witness the fact that he is unmarried but has a child – finally breaks through Wozzeck's preoccupation. Did not the Lord God say 'Suffer little children to come unto me', asks Wozzeck. The Captain's voice rises to a top C in his astonishment at this answer, and Wozzeck explains that only the rich can afford conventional morality. Wozzeck thinks too much, muses the Captain, and he dismisses him with the admonition that he is not to hurry so dreadfully.

Scene ii. Wozzeck and Andres (*tenor*) are cutting sticks at sundown in a field near the town. Andres sings to himself, but Wozzeck imagines every sort of thing, babbles of the intrigues of the Freemasons, thinks the ground is going to open under his feet, and is convinced the whole world is on fire when the setting sun colours the horizon red. The short scene contains some of Berg's most dazzling orchestral invention.

Scene iii. Marie's room; evening. Marie (*soprano*) is watching a band going back to barracks. The Drum-Major (*tenor*) waves to her, and she sings happily to the band's march, so happily in fact that her neighbour Margret (*contralto*) cannot resist a malicious comment about her lively interest in soldiers. After an exchange of abuse Marie slams the window and shuts out the sound of the band. She sings a lyrical cradle song to her child, before there is a knock at the window, and Wozzeck himself is seen standing there. He is late and has not even time to look at the child which Marie holds up to him. His confused talk worries her and, after he is gone, she rushes out of the door.

Scene iv (the Passacaglia). The Doctor's study, next day. Wozzeck, in return for a small pittance, is prepared to act as a guinea-pig for the doctor's dietetic experiments. The Doctor (*bass*) complains that Wozzeck does not follow all his instructions, and his scientific talk further confuses the unhappy man, whose outburst causes the Doctor to suggest that he may well end up in a lunatic asylum. The Doctor is ecstatic about the fame which will result when his new theories are published, and the scene ends as he re-examines Wozzeck's tongue.

Scene v. The street in front of Marie's house, where the Drum-Major is posturing to her evident admiration. Marie repulses him when he tries to embrace her, but the second time does not resist him, and, with the exclamation 'What does it matter? It's all the same', takes him into her house.

Act II. Scene i. In her room, Marie is admiring herself and her new earrings in a bit of broken mirror. Wozzeck comes in, and asks what it is that she is trying to hide. She says she found the earrings, and he observes that he has never had the luck to find things like that in pairs. He looks at the sleeping child, and reflects that life is nothing but work, and that even in sleep man sweats. He gives Marie the money he has earned from the Captain and the Doctor and goes out, leaving her to reflect sadly on her infidelity.

Scene ii. In the street. The Doctor is stopped by his friend the Captain, on whom he revenges himself by giving him details of various fatal cases he has recently seen, ending with a warning that the Captain's own flushed condition may easily be a symptom of an impending apoplectic fit, from which death, or at least paralysis, is likely to result.

They are interrupted when Wozzeck comes rapidly down the street – he cuts through the world like one of his own razor blades, says the Captain in a depressed way. He and the Doctor proceed to torment Wozzeck with innuendo about Marie and the Drum-Major, even imitating a military march. The seriousness with which Wozzeck takes their insinuations quite shocks his tormentors, and he bursts out with a *fortissimo* imprecation at the impossibility of finding satisfaction in life.

Scene iii. The street in front of Marie's house. Marie is standing in front of her house when Wozzeck comes up to her. She is as beautiful as sin, he says – but how can sin be beautiful? Did *he* stand there? Marie replies that she cannot control who walks in the street, and, when Wozzeck looks as though he will strike her: 'Better a knife blade in my heart than lay a hand on me . . . My father would never dare when I was little.' Wozzeck repeats her words.

Scene iv. A beer-garden, where dancing is in progress to a slow Ländler played on the stage by a Heurige orchestra. There is general dancing, and a couple of exceedingly drunk workmen (*baritone, bass*) sing in a maudlin way of the effect of brandy on the soul. Wozzeck comes in and sees Marie dancing with the Drum-Major; his jealousy grows until he is about to separate them, when the dance stops. The soldiers, with Andres as soloist, begin a lusty hunting song. The first workman climbs on to a table and starts a most effective discourse in a style traditionally associated with the very drunk.

An Idiot (*tenor*) appears, wanders over to Wozzeck, and observes 'Lustig, lustig . . . aber es riecht . . . ich riech Blut' (Joyful, joyful . . . and yet it reeks . . . it reeks . . . of blood). The tiny scene in which the Idiot appears, to a mainly accordion accompaniment, has an extraordinary fascination and significance. As the dancing begins again Wozzeck's imagination is obsessed with the idea of blood.

Scene v. Wozzeck's barrack room at night. The sound of snoring can be heard from the sleeping occupants of the room (the chorus in five parts hum wordlessly with half-open mouths), and Wozzeck complains to Andres that he cannot sleep for memories of the dance hall. The Drum-Major staggers into the room, proclaiming his conquest at the top of his voice and demanding that Wozzeck drink with him. The latter turns away and whistles to himself, whereupon the Drum-Major yanks him from where he stands; they fight for a moment, Wozzeck is knocked to the ground, and the Drum-Major shakes him. He goes out, leaving Wozzeck staring in front of him. 'He bleeds,' exclaims Andres. The suggestion of blood seems to Wozzeck like fate's prompting: 'One time after another.'

ACT III. Scene i. Marie's room at night. The solo viola gives out the theme. Marie is reading the story of Mary Magdalen in the Bible, and cannot help comparing what she reads with her own life. She ends with a cry for mercy: 'Saviour . . . as Thou hadst mercy on her, have mercy now on me, Lord!' The scene is one of haunting beauty.

Scene ii. A pond in the wood, later that night. Wozzeck appears with Marie, whom he prevents from going home as she wishes. He reflects on how long they have known each other, and, when Marie sees the moon rise, draws a knife and cuts her throat, then bends over her: 'Dead!' The interlude consists of two long *crescendi* on B natural, beginning with a *ppp* solo horn, and continuing through the whole orchestra until, after a percussive rhythm, the second *crescendo* takes in the percussion as well. Straightaway the curtain rises on Scene iii. An inn, with the hammering of a quick polka on an out-of-tune piano. Wozzeck is amongst the dancers. He takes Margret for partner, and leads her to a table, where he tries to make love to her. She sings a short song, but stops when she sees blood on Wozzeck's hand. He says he has cut his arm, then pushes through the dancers and rushes from the room.

Scene iv. The pond. Wozzeck searches for the knife, which he dropped after the murder. He finds it, pauses for a moment to look at the body of Marie, then throws the knife into the water and watches it sink. The whole world seems to him bathed in blood; he sees spots on his hands and his clothes; he walks hopelessly into the water to wash it off, and disappears. The Doctor and the Captain comment on the sound they hear – the sound of a man drowning, hazards the Doctor.

The great D minor interlude forms the climax of the opera, and at the same time a lament for Wozzeck himself, the opera's hero. Reference is made to music from earlier scenes, and the themes most closely connected with Wozzeck himself are heard in ennobled form.

Scene v. The street outside Marie's house. Children are playing. Apart and playing by himself is Marie's child (*treble*). Other children come running in, and one of them says that Marie has been found dead. The child cannot take in what he is being told, and as the opera ends goes on playing his game: 'Hopp-hopp, hopp-hopp, hopp-hopp.'

LULU

OPERA in three acts by Alban Berg; text adapted by the composer from Wedekind's *Erdgeist* and *Die Büchse der Pandora*. Première in the unfinished (two-act) form, Zürich, June 2, 1937. Three-act version, completed by Friedrich Cerha, first performed Opéra, Paris, 1979.

*L*ULU, Berg's second and last opera, is written throughout in the dodecaphonic system. When the composer died, he had finished Acts I and II, and part of Act III. In addition, he had sketched, in more or less elaborate form, the whole of the rest of the work, setting all the words, apart from some lines in the ensemble. Efforts were made after Berg's death to have the opera finished by one of his contemporaries sympathetic to his music. When initial attempts failed, the composer's widow gradually imposed an embargo on any work on her late husband's opera. The two acts were performed and most commentators accepted *Lulu* as one of the great operatic masterpieces of the twentieth century, even without its third act. Universal Edition eventually allowed Friedrich Cerha, the Viennese composer, to complete the work.

Prologue. An animal-tamer (*bass*), accompanied by the clown, steps in front of the curtain and introduces his troupe, amongst whom is Lulu, dressed in Pierrot's costume.

ACT I. Scene i. A painter's studio, where Lulu (*soprano*), dressed as Pierrot, is being painted. Dr. Schön (*baritone*), a newspaper editor, watches the proceedings. Schön's son, Alwa (*tenor*), enters and takes his father off to his dress rehearsal, leaving Lulu and the Painter (*tenor*) alone. The latter tries to embrace Lulu, chasing her vigorously round the room, and kisses her hands just before the sound of her husband's knocking is heard. He breaks in, only to collapse at their feet with the shock of finding them in a compromising position. They realise he is dead and Lulu comments, with more interest than regret, on his death (*canzonetta* introduced by saxophone solo). There is a duet for Lulu and the Painter, in which his questions about her beliefs receive the unvaried answer 'I don't know', and the Painter sings an *arioso* when Lulu leaves him alone while she goes to change her clothes.

An interlude leads to Scene ii, an elegant room in which hangs Lulu's portrait as Pierrot. The Painter, who is now her husband, comes in with the mail, and Lulu reads with amazement a notice of the engagement of Dr. Schön. After a light-hearted *duettino* the studio bell rings. The Painter looks out and says it is a beggar. He goes off to his studio to work, and Lulu lets in the 'beggar', who turns out to be Schigolch (*bass*), who is supposed to be her father, but in reality may be a former lover. He expresses admiration for her present surroundings; she has gone a long way since he last saw her.

As he leaves, Schön enters (Sonata movement begins), recognises Schigolch with some surprise, and then proceeds to tell Lulu that she must stop coming to see him now that he is engaged. She retorts that she belongs to him (the slow beginning of the coda of the sonata's exposition has something of the significance of a love theme); he rescued her from the streets as a child, and anyhow her husband is blind to anything she does.

The Painter enters, Lulu leaves, and Schön first urges him to watch Lulu more carefully, then, as the music gains in urgency, gradually reveals something of her past to him. The Painter makes as if to go out and talk to Lulu, but presently groans are heard and Lulu and Dr. Schön force open a locked door (rhythmical canon of percussion) to find the Painter lying dead.

The bell rings and Alwa comes in full of excitement at the news that revolution has broken out in Paris. Schön fears that the scandal which will inevitably follow discovery of the

Painter's suicide will endanger his own engagement, but, editor-wise, hopes the sensation of the news from France may serve to cover it up. The curtain falls to Lulu's words, sung to her motive: 'You will marry me after all.'

Scene iii follows an extended interlude, in which the love theme is developed. Lulu's dressing-room in a theatre. Alwa waits for Lulu to come off the stage, and reminds her how, as a young man, he wanted to induce his father to marry her after his mother's death. Lulu replies that she knows perfectly well that Dr. Schön put her on the stage so that somebody rich should fall in love with her and take her off his hands.

She goes out for the next part of her act, and Alwa observes that her life history would make a splendid story for an opera. A Prince (*tenor*), who intends to marry her, enters and launches into extravagant praise of Lulu. There is a noise offstage, and Lulu is carried in after fainting during her act – an accident caused, Lulu explicitly says, because she had to dance in front of Schön's prospective bride.

Lulu and Schön are left alone (development section of the Sonata) and a scene ensues between them. In despair, he tries to tear himself away, but she shows herself the stronger (recapitulation of the Sonata) and forces him to write, to her dictation, a letter to his fiancée, breaking off the engagement. The curtain falls as Schön exclaims 'Now comes my execution' (love music). Lulu prepares to continue the act which was interrupted by her fainting fit.

ACT II. Scene i. A palatial hall decorated in the German Renaissance style. Gräfin Geschwitz (*mezzo-soprano*) is paying a call on Lulu, to whom she is obviously very much attracted. Schön, who is now Lulu's husband, is jealous to the verge of madness. He looks behind the curtains, a loaded revolver in his hand, as if he expected to find some lover there. Lulu returns and she and Schön leave the stage together.

Geschwitz sneaks back into the room and conceals herself, just before Schigolch, an Athlete (*bass*) and a Schoolboy (*contralto*) come in (the last-named a 'Hosenrolle', or travesty part). The boy is in love with Lulu and Schigolch has acted as go-between. They are drinking and smoking when Lulu comes in, but all hide when Alwa is announced. Alwa with rising excitement declares his love for Lulu. She counters that it was she who was responsible years ago for poisoning his mother. Dr. Schön watches the scene from a hiding-place, and notices the Athlete, who is also hiding. Schön leads Alwa, who is no longer in control of himself, from the room, and returns to launch a tirade against Lulu, offering her the revolver and telling her to use it against herself.

Next he finds Geschwitz and drags her from the room, all the time continuing to urge Lulu to commit suicide. Here follows Lulu's song, in which she justifies herself and says she has never tried to seem other than she is. Schön again attempts to force the revolver against Lulu, there is a cry from the boy, and Lulu fires five shots into Schön's body.

Lulu is horrified by what she has done; Schön was her only love. Alwa returns, and Schön's last words to him are in the nature of a demand for vengeance. Lulu in an arietta pleads to Alwa for mercy, but the curtain falls as the police appear.

The exciting Interlude between the scenes is designed to accompany a silent and largely symbolical film, showing what happens to Lulu in the time which intervenes. It involves a court scene, during whose course Lulu is condemned for the murder of Schön; her entry into hospital after she has contracted cholera; and the means of escape through the intervention of Geschwitz.

Scene ii. As before, the room however looking dirty and ill kept. Geschwitz, Alwa and the Athlete (dressed as a footman) are talking. Lulu has had cholera, from which Geschwitz has also only just recovered, and is to be rescued from the prison hospital where Geschwitz will take her place; Lulu is to marry the Athlete. Schigolch takes Geschwitz off to put the plan into execution – we hear that Geschwitz in her passion for Lulu purposely contracted cholera to make the plan of escape possible.

No sooner are Alwa and the Athlete alone than the Schoolboy appears with a plan for Lulu's escape. They try to convince him that she is dead, and hustle him out of the room just before she comes in, supported by Schigolch. She looks so pale and emaciated that the Athlete shouts abuse at her, and leaves. Schigolch goes off to collect the tickets for Paris, and Alwa and Lulu are alone. After a passionate love duet, they leave for Paris.

ACT III. Scene i. A salon in a Casino in Paris, obviously frequented by characters of the demi-monde. The Athlete proposes a toast to Lulu, and the company, as it moves into the gaming room, talks about the rise in the value of some railway shares in which they have all invested. The Marquis (*tenor*), an elegant white-slave trafficker who knows of Lulu's past, suggests that she should enter a brothel in Cairo; if she declines his suggestion, he threatens to expose her to the police. Lulu offers to pay, and the company returns in great heart from their gambling, everyone having won. The Athlete now threatens Lulu if she does not pay him too, and at this juncture the page brings the banker a telegram with news of the collapse of the railway shares. Even Schigolch asks Lulu for money and when she tells him of the Athlete's threats, Schigolch proposes to lure him to his hotel room and dispose of him. The Marquis leaves to inform the police and Lulu persuades Countess Geschwitz to go with the Athlete to Schigolch's hotel. The banker's announcement and insistence on payment in cash means that almost everyone present is bankrupt. Lulu escapes, having exchanged clothes with the page.

Scene ii. An attic in a London slum. Lulu is now on the streets and with her earnings keeps Alwa and Schigolch. Her first client is a professor (*tenor*), whose overcoat pockets Schigolch searches while Lulu is in her room with him. It does not take long, and Geschwitz appears from Paris having saved Lulu's Pierrot portrait which she shows them. Lulu is back on the streets and Schigolch hides as a second client, the negro (*tenor*), is brought into the room. He argues with Lulu about money and Alwa, who tries to help, is struck dead before the negro leaves.

Lulu's last pick-up is Jack the Ripper (*baritone*). Geschwitz makes up her mind to return to Germany as a fighter for women's rights. Jack murders Lulu and, when Geschwitz tries to come to her aid, kills her as well. He washes his hands and leaves as Geschwitz dies.

Carl Orff
(1895–1982)

DIE KLUGE
The Clever Girl

ONE act; première, Frankfurt, 1943. The Peasant (*bass*) is unjustly imprisoned. The King (*baritone*) promises the Daughter (*soprano*) he will free her father if she can solve three riddles, which she does easily. The King marries her. Two men seek justice and the Queen tells one of them to follow her advice. When he gives the King an impertinent response the King, recognising his wife's hand, banishes her, telling her she may take a chest of his possessions. She gives him a sleeping draught and he awakes to find himself in the chest – he himself was what she wanted most! The King is full of admiration for her cleverness and all ends happily.

Paul Hindemith
(1895–1963)

MATHIS DER MALER
Mathias the Painter

OPERA in seven scenes; text by the composer. Première, May 28, 1938, Zürich Stadttheater.

HINDEMITH was a native of Mainz, and for his eighth opera he took as his central figure the early sixteenth-century painter, Mathias Grünewald, who spent much of his life in the service of the Archbishop of Mainz, and who is famous for the great altarpiece of Isenheim. The story takes place against a background of the Reformation and of the Peasants' War in Germany. It is divided into seven scenes, and it is customary to have an interval after the fourth scene.

The prelude to the opera bears the subtitle of 'Engelkonzert' (Concert of Angels) and is inspired by part of the Isenheim polyptych. It is well known as the first movement of the symphony Hindemith arranged from the music of his opera.

Scene i. The courtyard of St. Anthony's monastery at Mainz, where Mathis (*baritone*) is painting a fresco. In an introspective monologue, his rejoicing at the coming of spring cannot be separated from his doubts as to whether he is worthily fulfilling his mission as a painter. Schwalb (*tenor*), leader of the peasants, and his daughter Regina (*soprano*) arrive, seeking sanctuary from the pursuing troops of the Fürstenbund. Mathis extends his help, and takes pity on Regina. He gives her a ribbon with which she binds her hair, and their conversation is interrupted by the return of Schwalb, refreshed and with his wounds bound up. He expresses astonishment that Mathis paints instead of taking part in the struggle for freedom.

Regina rushes in to warn her father that their pursuers are in sight, and Mathis gives them his horse, telling Schwalb that he can count on his help. Mathis admits to Sylvester (*tenor*), an officer, that he has helped the rebel leader to escape, and claims his right to answer for his actions to no one but the Cardinal-Archbishop (*tenor*).

Scene ii. The hall in the Martinsburg, the Cardinal-Archbishop's palace in Mainz. The rival factions of Papists and Lutherans dispute while waiting for the arrival of the Archbishop. Pommersfelden (*bass*) stands with the Papists, Capito (*tenor*) with the Lutherans, amongst whom are Riedinger (*bass*) and his daughter, Ursula (*soprano*). Peace comes momentarily with the

Archbishop's entrance, and all leave the hall except Pommersfelden, Capito, Riedinger and his daughter. Mathis comes in
after his year of absence to be greeted with an expansive phrase
from Ursula, who is in love with him. A quartet ensues in which
Mathis and Ursula sing of their pleasure in seeing each other
again, while the Cardinal promises Riedinger that the order to
burn Lutheran books shall not be executed in Mainz. Pommersfelden objects that the order is from Rome itself, and the
Cardinal reluctantly agrees that it must be carried out.

There is some dispute about the suitability or otherwise of
Mathis's representation of the saints in his pictures, which
turns before long to a discussion of the empty state of the Cardinal's treasury. Sylvester enters and accuses Mathis before the
Cardinal of having helped Schwalb's escape. Mathis admits the
accusation but pleads strongly for the peasants' cause, and begs
the Cardinal not to furnish the Fürstenbund with the money
they have just asked for, but instead to support the juster cause
of the rebels; in return, he will serve his patron without payment for the rest of his life. The Cardinal replies that his official
conduct is bound by treaties; only where art is concerned has
he a free hand. Let Mathis not interfere with what he does not
understand. Mathis defies his patron and his prince, and the
differing points of view of the Cardinal, Mathis, Pommersfelden, Capito, and the warlike Sylvester are combined in a
noble quintet. Mathis receives permission to withdraw from
the Cardinal's service.

Scene iii. A room in Riedinger's house. Riedinger and his
friends attempt to hide their treasured possessions, but soldiers
assisted by Capito carry them off. Capito appeases the wrath of
the Lutherans by showing them a letter purporting to have
come from Luther to the Cardinal in which he urges him
strongly to give a lead to the clergy by renouncing his celibacy.
Capito's scheme is to persuade the Cardinal, who is in urgent
need of money, to make a rich marriage – and with whom more
suitable than Riedinger's daughter, Ursula, who at that moment
comes into the room. Riedinger himself hints at what is
planned for her before he leaves Ursula, to join his fellow-
Lutherans as their books are burnt in the market-place, a scene
that is suggested by the chorus in the background.

Mathis comes to bid Ursula farewell. She welcomes him exultantly, and tells him how much she has missed him during
his year of leave from the Cardinal's service. He answers that he
must leave her and his work to join in the struggle for freedom;
only through contact with misery can he recover his own soul.
They protest their undying love for each other, but their duet
ends with the cry: 'The love, the unity in which we have lived,
gives way to suffering.' Mathis embraces Ursula and goes out.

Ursula tells Riedinger she will accept the sacrifice demanded of her by her faith. Riedinger rejoices.

Scene iv. The rebellious peasants have seized a war-ravaged village and are terrorising the local nobility. They drag in Count von Helfenstein and his wife, and kill the Count almost before her eyes. Mathis tries to defend the Countess (*contralto*) but is knocked down. Only the advent of Schwalb saves him from further injury. The peasants' leader calls them all to arms to fight the Fürstenbund army, but they are already downhearted at the prospect of meeting trained troops, and soon come back in disorder. Schwalb himself is killed. Mathis only escapes with his life through the Countess's intervention, and he comes to understand his own complete failure as a man of action. He takes Regina away with him to look for shelter.

ACT II. Scene v. The Cardinal's study in the Martinsburg in Mainz. Capito has been trying to persuade the Cardinal to renounce his oath of celibacy and marry; but Albrecht resents Capito's attempt to interfere. Capito then introduces Ursula as the prospective bride. The Cardinal is astonished to see her. In music of ever-increasing fervour she explains to him that she is willing to submit to marriage for the sake of the cause she loves.

The Cardinal calls Capito and Riedinger into the room and tells them that Ursula's example has shown him that he too must stand by what he has been taught. He dismisses Capito from his post, saying he will lead a simpler life in the future; and he gives permission to the Lutherans to declare themselves openly. There is an impressive quartet between the Cardinal, Ursula, Capito, and Riedinger, and at its end Ursula asks the Cardinal to bless her before she goes out again into the world. He consents, and Ursula departs.

Scene vi. In the Odenwald, Mathis and Regina pause during their flight. Regina says she still dreams she is pursued by the image of her dead father. Mathis tries to calm her by describing to her his vision of the Concert of Angels, accompanied in the orchestra by the music we originally heard in the prelude. Together they sing the chorale ('Es sungen drei Engel'), also heard in the prelude, until Regina falls asleep and Mathis despairingly contrasts his present spiritual misery with the comparative state of grace in which he painted the picture he has just described.

In the manner of the Temptation of St. Anthony, Mathis is tempted successively by Luxury, wearing the face of the Countess; by wealth (Pommersfelden); a beggar, a courtesan, and a martyr (Ursula); scholarship (Capito); and a knight in shining armour (Schwalb). The music works up to a climax when the demons appear to torment the Saint. There is a great ensemble, at whose end the Cardinal, in the guise of St. Paul, comes to comfort and advise St. Anthony (part of the Isenheim altar depicts the Conversation between St. Paul and St. Anthony). St. Anthony asks what he has done that he should have reached his present state of uncertainty. St. Paul tells him that he has been untrue to himself. In throwing in his lot with the people, he has denied the gifts he had from God, and has in fact withdrawn from the people he tried to help. Let him return to his art, denying himself but dedicating his work to God. In so doing he will become part of the people. At the end of the vision, in which the composer speaks his mind on the subject of the artist, the two voices join together in a paean of praise, ending with a magnificent 'Alleluia'. It is the crucial scene of the opera.

Scene vii. Mathis's studio in Mainz. Mathis is lying asleep, exhausted with his work, and Ursula watches alone by the side of the dying Regina. Regina wakes and raves about the memory of her dead father, whose face she can see in Mathis's painting of the Crucifixion. She asks Ursula to give Mathis the ribbon which she originally received from him at their first meeting, and Ursula recognises it as one she herself had given Mathis. Regina sings a couple of sentences of the chorale, before dying with Mathis by her side.

The interlude, marked 'Very slowly', is entitled 'Entombment' (it serves as the slow movement of the symphony). At its end, the curtain rises to show the studio empty except for a table, on which lie several objects. The Cardinal comes to say farewell to Mathis, embracing him for the last time. Mathis himself takes a case and puts away materially and symbolically the things which have represented the main efforts of his life. It is in this spirit of utter humility that the opera ends.

Viktor Ullmann
(1898–1944)

DER KAISER VON ATLANTIS
The Emperor of Atlantis

FOUR scenes, written for Terezín concentration camp, 1944, but banned by the Nazi authorities once they understood that the Emperor was really Hitler. Death (*bass*) in disgust at present-day motorised warfare takes a holiday and no one can die. Pierrot (*tenor*) longs to. The Drummer (*mezzo-soprano*) proclaims total war, parodying *Deutschland über alles*. The Emperor (*baritone*) hears the same report from everywhere: no one is able to die! A Soldier (*tenor*) and Girl (*soprano*) meet and make love. In his study the Emperor is beside himself at the horrible turn of events. He pulls the sheet off the mirror and finds behind it Death, who consents to return only if the Emperor will be his first victim. After an impressive farewell the Emperor is led through the mirror. The chorale *Ein' feste Burg* makes a grand, cathartic ending.

Kurt Weill
(1900–1950)

AUFSTIEG UND FALL DER STADT MAHAGONNY
Rise and Fall of the City of Mahagonny

OPERA in three acts; libretto by Bertolt Brecht. Première, Leipzig, March 9, 1930.

WHATEVER else it may be, *The Rise and Fall of the City of Mahagonny* is an opera, written for opera singers (it was not until the Berlin production that Lotte Lenya, the composer's wife, took over the role of Jenny), and designed in what can only be described as the operatic convention. After his collaboration with Brecht came to an end, Weill never again found a librettist to inspire him to that unique mixture of ragtime, operetta, pop and counterpoint that has come, in the minds of most listeners, to be identified with the singing of Lotte Lenya and with the Berlin of the Weimar Republic.

ACT I. Scene i. A desolate part of America. As the music dashes energetically into action, a battered truck arrives, bearing Leokadja Begbick (*contralto*), Trinity Moses (*baritone*) and Fatty the book-keeper (*tenor*), all on the run from the police. If they can't go any further, why not stay here and found a new city, where no one has to work and where there are prize fights every third day – so explains Leokadja in an extended *arioso* ('Sie soll sein wie ein Netz' – it is to be like a net, which is put out to catch edible birds).

And so the city is founded and called Mahagonny, and the first sharks move in. Enter Jenny (*soprano*), the mulatto from Cuba, and six other girls, who sit on their suitcases and introduce themselves in the famous *Alabama-song*, written originally in Brecht's peculiar pidgin-English and set to one of Weill's most haunting tunes.

291

The news of the founding of a city of pleasure reaches the big cities, where the inhabitants hymn their misery while Fatty and Moses cry the praises of Mahagonny. In the next few days, all the malcontents of the continent move to Mahagonny, notably the lumberjacks Jim, Jake, Pennybank Bill (*baritone*) and Alaska Wolf Joe (*bass*), who sing a quick fox-trot in anticipation of the pleasures to come.

The hero of the story is Jim Mahoney (*tenor*), and he and the others are greeted by Mrs. Begbick, Trinity Moses losing no time in proffering pictures of the available girls. Jenny and the six girls are produced, and Jake (*tenor*) offers $30 for Jenny, who protests in a song: 'Ach, bedenken Sie, Herr Jakob Schmidt' – just think how little you get for $30. Jim says perhaps he'll take her, and when the others have gone, he and Jenny exchange to a wistful tune such vital information as whether Jenny shall comb her hair forward or back, shall or shan't wear underwear under her skirt.

Disillusion has set in and, says Mrs. Begbick, people are starting to leave town. Fatty counters with the news that the police are catching up with Begbick. Jim comes in, planning to leave because he has just seen a notice 'Forbidden'! Jake, Bill and Joe sing the praises of the city with its everlasting freedom, but Jim's blues come straight from the purposelessness of it all.

In front of the inn, which is known as 'Nothing barred', the men drink and listen to the strains of 'The Maiden's Prayer' – eternal art, thinks Jake. Jim's mock ballad of the sufferings he underwent in Alaska in order eventually to reach a haven of rest complains of the inadequacy of what he has found, and it takes a concerted effort to prevent him carving up everything in sight with his famous knife.

The loudspeaker announces a 'typhoon', and a *fugato* introduces an impressive set piece of lamentation.

Scene ii. 'The Night of the Hurricane'. The men sing determinedly in chorus, Jake laments and Jenny sadly repeats the Alabama-song. Jim mockingly expounds his philosophy: what sort of horror is a hurricane when compared to man? We learn that the hurricane is heading straight for Mahagonny and that the police who were pursuing Mrs. Begbick have been killed. Jim leads what is perhaps the best (as well as the best-known) of the songs: 'Denn wie man sich bettet, so liegt man' (As you make your bed, you must lie there).

ACT II. Radio announcements say 'the hurricane has been diverted past Mahagonny and continues on its way'! The citizens rejoice. From now on the motto is 'nothing barred'. First, gluttony. To a slow parodistic waltz (zither and accordion), Jake sits down to dine and eats three entire calves, expiring as he asks for more.

Next, love. A girl and a man are with Mrs. Begbick, who admonishes the man to spit out his gum, wash his hands and behave decently. The lights go out, the chorus sings the Mandalay-song and urges him to get on with it, but when the lights go up, Jenny and Jim are seen sitting a little way apart, he smoking, she making up. They sing tenderly about two cranes flying in the sky, a duet in which Brecht's lyrical invention is matched by Weill's to form one of the most purely 'operatic' numbers in the whole score.

Next, prize fights. Trinity Moses and Alaska Wolf Joe are matched to the astonishment of the men, who predict a walk-over for Trinity Moses. Jim puts his money on Joe, who duly fulfils expectations and is knocked out. 'Dead!' says the referee. The crowd laughs, and the men come forward with a reminder that here nothing's barred, that we may now expect the boozing as well.

Jim, Bill and Jenny are playing billiards, and Jim invites everyone to drink with him. Jim finds he has run out of money and asks Jenny to help him. They make a boat out of the billiard table, and Jim, Bill and Jenny climb on it, until Jim announces that they have arrived back in Alaska. Trinity Moses and the widow Begbick demand payment, but Jim has nothing left. He has committed the ultimate capitalist crime of running out of money, and is bound and led away. The act ends with Jim alone in the forest, tied to a tree and longing in an impressive *scena* for the night to continue and for the day never to arrive.

ACT III. Jim is to be tried in what passes for a Court of Justice in Mahagonny – the widow Begbick sits as judge, Fatty is defence counsel and Trinity Moses prosecutes. One Toby Higgins (*tenor*) is being tried for murder, and can be seen bargaining in mime with the judge. Apparently he offers a big enough bribe because defending counsel is allowed to ask for the injured party to be produced, and nobody coming forward the case goes by default.

Jim asks his friend Bill to let him have $100 so that his case can be conducted decently, but he refuses. The prosecution starts its case: Jim is accused of the seduction of Jenny, of singing cheerfully during the approach of the 'typhoon', of corrupting the entire city, of sending his friend to certain death in a prize fight merely to win his bet, of not being able to pay for the whisky which he drank and the curtain rod he broke. Each time the question is, 'Who is the injured party?'

The men demand Jim's acquittal on the grounds that his behaviour during the typhoon injured nobody, that it certainly wasn't he who killed Alaska Wolf Joe, but as he is undoubtedly guilty of the last charge, he is sentenced on all five, and the penalty becomes increasingly stiff, ending with death for the

293

failure to pay for the whisky. The verdict is universally applauded.

People are sitting around in a bar reading a newspaper and displaying the disillusion which has once again overtaken Mahagonny. The loudspeaker announces the impending execution of Jim Mahoney. A tender farewell between Jenny and Jim, who consigns her to his best friend Bill, precedes his walk to the place of execution. Jim is seated on the electric chair but asks whether they do not know that there is a God. During his execution the others act out the coming of God to Mahagonny, Trinity Moses taking the chief role.

The loudspeaker announces that giant processions took place in protest against the tremendously high cost of living, and that these heralded the end of the 'City of Nets'. During the march-finale which is dominated by 'Denn wie man sich bettet, so liegt man' and the Alabama-song, the processions appear, each of them carrying an appropriate banner, and the opera ends with the line 'Können uns und euch und niemand helfen!' (We can't help ourselves or you or anyone).

STREET SCENE

OPERA in two acts by Kurt Weill; libretto in English by Elmer Rice and Langston Hughes (based on Elmer Rice's play). Première December 16, 1946, Philadelphia.

KURT WEILL and his wife Lotte Lenya went to America in 1935 and, once naturalised, Weill lost few opportunities of emphasising his identification not only as an anti-Nazi but as an American, moreover one who as a former Berliner had constantly fantasised about America and incorporated his fantasies in his music. It is easy with hindsight to see that Weill, from the moment he arrived in the U.S.A., had been inching his way towards writing an American opera. By late 1945 he was in discussion with Elmer Rice, and the new work was ready for performance a year later. It was critically panned in Philadelphia but had considerable success in New York, though its total of 148 performances on Broadway was considered a disappointment.

ACT I. New York, 1946. An evening in June. It is indescribably hot and neighbourhood talk is of little else. A slow-moving but highly effective ensemble gives way to a blues sung by Henry (*baritone*), the Janitor. Mrs. Jones (*mezzo-soprano*) leads a trio of neighbours gossiping about the man they have seen Anna Maurrant (*soprano*) with more than once recently. Mrs. Maurrant's return pushes the gossip in another direction and we discover in quick succession that Mrs. Maurrant thinks she and her daughter do not always have the same tastes as her husband; that the neighbourhood, while full of foreigners, harbours considerable xenophobic sentiment; that Sam Kaplan (*tenor*) is more than a little interested in Rose Maurrant (*soprano*). But the most urgent topic is Mrs. Buchanan's pregnancy, and in slow 6/8 her husband emphasises how difficult having a baby can be, particularly for the husband.

We meet for the first time the cross-grained Frank Maurrant (*bass-baritone*). Rose staying out late is a particular bone of contention, and he is quite happy to blame it on his wife. 'Somehow I never could believe that life was meant to be all dull and grey' she sings, and her substantial aria tells us about her early optimism, and the hope she still somehow manages to cling to. Steve Sankey (*spoken*), the Milk Company Collector, strolls by and goes off to the drugstore. Mrs. Maurrant says she must look for her son Willie (*treble*), and the field is clear for the gossips: 'Get a load of that!' What will happen to Sankey when Maurrant hears his wife is carrying on? But life on the Street is not all gossip and Lippo Fiorentino (*tenor*), the Ice Cream Salesman, leads a substantial Ice Cream Septet.

Kaplan (*tenor*) and Maurrant, traditionalist and liberal, disagree vigorously on the handling of children and Maurrant rams home his point of view in an aria, 'Let things be like they always was'. Children march in followed by girls coming from graduation to one of the score's most obviously popular numbers: 'Wrapped in a ribbon and tied in a bow'.

Mrs. Maurrant dances for a moment with Lippo Fiorentino, Sankey passes by on his way home (Maurrant wonders why he's hanging around), and Willie Maurrant has apparently been fighting with another boy who has been rude about his mother. When the Maurrants leave, gossip breaks out again, but Sam explodes with indignation and eventually, alone, embarks on his big *arioso*, 'Lonely house, lonely me!' He goes into the house as Rose comes in with Harry Easter (*baritone*), manager of her office, who contrives to sneak a kiss and is attempting to entice her away from the neighbourhood: 'Wouldn't you like to be on Broadway?' Rose is obviously tempted, but at the moment more worried by the notion that the neighbours might see her with a stranger and tell her father. Easter has a wife and Rose doesn't figure on being a mistress, as she makes very clear in 'What good would the Moon be, Unless the right one shared its beams?' Maurrant nearly catches them saying goodnight and provokes an element of rebellion in her before she reverts to a reprise of 'What good would the Moon be'.

When Mr. Buchanan (*tenor*) rushes from the house Rose says she will telephone the doctor. The arrival of Dick and Mae brings a complete change of mood in the most obviously Broadway-style number in the score, 'Moonfaced, starry-eyed', designated Song, Scene and Dance, and ending with a Blues on the trumpet. But the act is not over and Vincent Jones makes a pass at Rose and then fells the unfortunate Sam who answers her cry for help.

He is obviously not seriously hurt and Rose asks him, rather shyly, if he thinks it's true what they are saying about her mother. His awkwardness seems to confirm her fears but their duet not only makes a fine ending to the act but an emblem for their love. The curtain falls to a reminiscence of Henry's Blues from the beginning of the act.

ACT II. Daybreak, the next morning. During a game for the children, 'One, Two, Three, for Superman, come and catch me if you can', a scrap breaks out which Sam Kaplan finally climbs out of the window to break up. Mrs. Buchanan has had a baby girl but she and her family are to be evicted that day because they are behind with the rent. Rose attempts to get her father to be gentler with her mother but to little avail. An impassioned trio follows, full of expostulation from all three participants and, when his wife asks when he'll be back, he rounds on her: 'In case somebody came calling, huh?' Rose tries to comfort her mother, then makes an effort to tidy Willie before he goes off to school. He'll have none of it until his mother intervenes and rubs him up the right way: 'A boy like you'.

Shirley Kaplan (*spoken*) gently tries to warn Rose off Sam, but when Sam comes out, the two young people fantasise of lilac bushes and a happier future: 'We'll go away together'. For a moment it is a dream of happiness but they are interrupted by the reappearance of Easter, who offers Rose a lift to the office funeral. In the end she walks off with Easter and leaves the coast clear for Sankey to reappear and go into the house with Mrs. Maurrant. Sam has noticed all this but is distracted by the appearance of the Marshal whose job is to supervise the eviction of the Buchanans. When Maurrant reappears, Sam cannot block his way and he goes menacingly upstairs. There is a scream of terror, then shots and a moment later Maurrant reappears and disappears down the cellar steps. The crowd erupts in general hubbub before the Marshal regains control of them and Rose reappears. There is a threnody for the tragedy, during which Sam gives particular voice to what everyone feels, then Rose makes an attempt to talk to her mother as she is carried out on a stretcher. It is the end of the scene and in many ways the most impressive number in the score.

An interlude takes us to mid-afternoon the same day. The eviction of the Buchanans is over but some of their furniture is still on the sidewalk. Two Nursemaids go by with a pram and stop under the Maurrant windows to sing a satirical lullaby.

Maurrant is recaptured but the police let him have a word with his daughter. It is his moment of truth: 'I loved her too'. He is asking understanding, not mercy, and Rose and the neighbours seem prepared to accord him that. In the end the police lead him away and Sam is left attempting to console Rose. She says she will go away, alone, and no argument Sam can advance will dissuade her, not even a reference to the lilac bush. They say goodbye and she starts to leave, Mrs. Jones not missing the opportunity for an acid comment, before the neighbours go back to moaning about the heat.

Street Scene works at almost every level: it strikes a blow for Weill's instinctive feeling for popular contact; it is in no sense a betrayal of his former work; though rather long and certainly downbeat in content, it is unmistakably a Broadway show; and it is no less obviously an opera.

Bernd Alois Zimmermann
(1918–1971)

DIE SOLDATEN
The Soldiers

FOUR acts; première, Cologne, 1965. The composer wanted to depict 'the simultaneous occurrence of past, present and future', and the opera consists of many short scenes. Marie (*high soprano*), daughter of Wesener (*bass*), a merchant of Lille, is in love with Stolzius (*high baritone*). She is courted by Baron Desportes (*high tenor*), a French officer, and is not immune to his charm. Stolzius is teased by the soldiers about Marie's behaviour. He writes her a reproachful letter, which is the trigger for Desportes to seduce her. Stolzius, seeking vengeance, becames batman to Major Mary (*baritone*) – with whom Marie has taken up since Desportes left town. The stages of Marie's downfall are now shown simultaneously on several stage levels and three screens. After being raped by Desportes's gamekeeper she becomes a common prostitute. Stolzius poisons Desportes and himself dies. Marie, now a wretched beggar, accosts her father, but he does not recognise her. The work ends with the relentless marching of soldiers, symbolising the power which is responsible for the misery of others.

Györgi Ligeti
(b. 1923)

LE GRAND MACABRE

OPERA in two acts (four scenes); libretto by Michael Meschke and the composer after Michel de Ghelderode's 'La Ballade du Grand Macabre'. Première Stockholm, April 12, 1978.

L E GRAND MACABRE is an individual work, bizarre for much of the time, often jocular, always imaginative, and so far from narrative-opera that no one of its several productions in the first five years of its life closely resembled any other.

The prelude is written for twelve tuned motor-horns, precisely notated, less precise in intonation, but producing an effect that combines rhythmical, even melodic, interest with the sheer quirkiness that somehow typifies one aspect of Ligeti's vision.

ACT I. Scene i. Breughelland. It is a mixture of the *Dies Irae* and the praises of his own country which Piet the Pot (*buffo tenor*) sings, while an epicene amorous pair, Clitoria (*soprano*) and Spermando (*mezzo-soprano*), search for a place where they can make eternal love. Piet is sometimes tipsy, sometimes drunk (say the stage directions). Clitoria and Spermando sing a duet in a land of unending 'O altitudo!' and have found, if the gentle strains of the music are to be believed, the secret of suspended, but continually erotic, animation (Clitoria climaxes on a top D). As Piet watches them in amazement and delight, Nekrotzar (*baritone*) can be heard prophesying death, and indeed grandiloquently claiming to be no less a person than Death himself. It is, he says, his task to bring the world to an end. The music of Piet and Nekrotzar cavorts until it almost gets out of hand, and in the end Piet, in spite of his efforts at evasion, is conscripted to help Nekrotzar in what he conceives to be his mission. Piet collects scythe, hat, cloak, from the tomb which Clitoria and Spermando have appropriated for love-making, and hears Nekrotzar's proclamation of doom as Nekrotzar rides off on his back.

Motor-horns take us in a short interlude to Scene ii. Astradamors (*bass*), the astrologer, is fortunate, as a masochist, in that his nymphomaniac wife Mescalina (*mezzo-soprano*) is a sadist. She is seen whip in hand at curtain rise and their love play is extensive and explicit, she in leather, he at first in female clothing. Astradamors goes to his telescope only to discover elements of the skyscape just as alarming, it would appear, as what has been going on on earth. Mescalina falls asleep totally drunk, and implores Venus (*soprano*) to send her down a lover a bit more active than her husband.

It is not long before her prayer is answered as Nekrotzar comes in with Piet, and he turns out to be not at all backward in responding to her appeal. His love-making is so vigorous that she expires. Astradamors, who does not conceal his delight to be rid of her, joins Nekrotzar and Piet in their journey to the Prince's Palace.

ACT II. Scene iii. In contrast to Act I, Act II starts with tuned and tinkling electric bells, which bring us to Prince Go-Go's Palace. The Prince (*soprano*) at first seems scared of anything, but in the course of the action turns out to be not without his effective moments. Two politicians (*spoken*) are trading insults and the Prince does not seem disposed to intervene. At one point he is lifted against his will on to a rocking horse for his riding lesson, and later he is required to memorise a speech. Eventually, the Ministers in dudgeon offer to resign and the Prince, to their astonishment, accepts.

The Chief of the Secret Police (*soprano*), disguised as a brightly-coloured bird (so say the stage directions) comes in, all brilliant coloratura, staccatos, high notes, two-octave jumps, to bring news of serious public disturbances and the approach of a procession. This galvanises the Prince to action and he makes a speech to produce quiet among the people.

The peace turns out to be short-lived, as the imminent arrival of Nekrotzar, with Piet and Astradamors, will produce little short of panic. The Chief of Police starts to expostulate in even greater flights of coloratura, and, after reading a dispatch, he warns of some terrible coming. When Astradamors appears, he is jovial, it must be admitted, rather than terrible.

Here in the published score (but in Stockholm at the première it preceded Act II) comes a large-scale instrumental number based on the theme from the finale of Beethoven's *Eroica* (on timpani and lower strings) with four solo instruments (violin, piccolo, E flat clarinet, bassoon; in Stockholm, on stage) playing variations above it. During its very attractive course, Nekrotzar, still riding on Piet's back, enters in procession. Nothing apparently can stop his prophecies of doom, but Piet and Astradamors unwittingly cause a diversion by filling him up with drink, which he takes at first absent-mindedly from them. Eventually, after a lengthy and in the end almost ritualistic carousal, Nekrotzar starts to wax almost lyrical, so that, with Prince Go-Go joining in, when it comes to it, he has just enough control of speech to utter the words that should, as midnight strikes, bring the world to an end.

Scene iv. The music at first is as dimly lit as the scene, but briefly accelerates before the trombones apparently run out of steam and we are in calmer waters, back in Breughelland, with Piet and Astradamors hovering just above the ground, dreaming that they are in heaven. They leave the scene but Prince Go-Go seems to have survived as well, nervous when he finds himself apparently alone, and, it would seem, with some reason when three cut-throats set about him. He is rescued by Nekrotzar, thoroughly hung-over from the night before and amazed to find any survivors of the apocalypse. When Nekrotzar tries to get back into the tomb from which he emerged in the first place, Mescalina jumps out of it and starts chasing him. Prince Go-Go tries to assert his authority, and it is not long before the two Ministers, as well as Piet and Astradamors, come on to the scene. Piet, Astradamors and Prince Go-Go drink, and there ensues a quiet and very beautiful musical section marked *andante calmo* during which Nekrotzar starts to shrivel up and collapse, until by the end of this mirror canon, he has entirely disappeared.

At this point, the two lovers emerge from the tomb, quite ignorant of what has been going on. Their mood, post-coital and serene, starts to affect everyone and in a final *passacaglia* they decide that there is nothing to fear in death.

Le Grand Macabre (how translate the title? *The Great Horseman of the Apocalypse*?) is, it has been said, an opera for a time without answers, an opera whose subject is sex and death, and in which the only victim of the holocaust is the bringer of death himself. The composer called it an 'anti-anti-opera'.

Hans Werner Henze
(b. 1926)

HENZE was the first to come to international attention of the musicians associated with Darmstadt, where after 1945 a centre grew up for German composers whose interests lay in the currents of contemporary music banned as decadent by the Nazi regime. He was a pupil of Wolfgang Fortner's and rapidly became the leading German composer of his generation. In 1988, he inspired and to a large degree directed a major operatic enterprise, the Munich *Biennale*, at which new works for smallish forces were given their premières. Henze himself contacted and commissioned composers, and was the inspiration behind many of the new works: the composer as Maecenas!

BOULEVARD SOLITUDE

OPERA in seven scenes, text by Grete Weil, after the play by Walter Jockisch, which in its turn is a modern version of *Manon Lescaut*. Première, February 17, 1952, in Hanover.

Henze's first opera (1950–1), a modern version of the Manon story, secured an immediate success with the critics and before long with the public as well. Henze's style is eclectic, and this thoroughly attractive little work – small in pretensions and length (less than two hours including interval), considerably greater in achievement – invokes some jazz and popular elements as well as Stravinsky and Berg.

Scene i. The crowded waiting room of a large French railway station; the music at first entirely timpani and percussion. When the departure of a train is announced, Francis (*baritone*) claps his friend Armand (*lyric tenor*) on the shoulder and leaves. Manon (*soprano*) comes in with her brother, Lescaut (*baritone*), who steers her in the direction of Armand's table and then leaves her to go and drink at the bar. Armand launches into a sad account of the loneliness of student life in Paris and the unattainability of the sort of woman he dreams of. Manon joins in and the two get up and leave together; the pick-up is completed.

Scene ii. A small attic room in Paris. Armand and Manon lie in bed in the morning and sing a wistful song. Manon chatters gaily of a hat which has taken her fancy and announces her intention of buying it. No, protests Armand; since he stopped his studies, his father has cut off his allowance and they have no money. He gets up to dress and goes off in search of his friend Francis. While he is out of the room, Lescaut comes in. He has found her a new admirer, old and fat but rich as well. Armand comes back and Manon embraces him tenderly as he goes out. Lescaut in a wild song sardonically compliments his sister on her cruelty to Armand – the more brutally she treats her lovers, the higher will she rise – then leaves, giving her five minutes to make up her mind.

Scene iii. An elegant boudoir in the house of Lilaque *père* (*high tenor buffo*). Manon sings an aria as she writes to Armand, reassuring him that she is happy and treated with every consideration by the generous Monsieur Lilaque. The only flaw in her existence is that Armand cannot visit her, and that could easily be remedied as every day at five in her own little carriage she drives in the Bois de Boulogne. At this point she is interrupted by Lescaut who is furious that she prefers to write to her lover instead of looking after Lilaque and proceeds to tear the letter up. When Manon protests, he retorts that she is his source of income and he needs more money at once. He notices a strongbox, forces it and in spite of Manon's protests steals the money it contains. Lilaque enters, greets Manon tenderly and Lescaut with courtesy, at once offering to leave brother and sister alone to finish their talk. However, as he is about to leave the room he notices the broken safe and his good humour turns to rage as he throws the two out.

Scene iv. A university library. Armand and Francis, with other students, are studying the poems of Catullus. Armand can think only of Manon, and when Francis tells him that she and Lescaut have been chucked out of Lilaque's house for theft, Armand protests that he would believe anything of Lescaut but that Manon could commit no crime. Manon enters and sits by Armand. They join in reading a love poem which all too aptly fits their own situation and which gradually becomes an impassioned love duet.

Scene v. A dive. The reconciliation has not lasted long, Armand has taken to drugs, and while he sings of the forgetfulness he buys, everyone else dances to music that recalls *Wozzeck* with overtones of Gershwin. Lescaut comes in with Lilaque's son (*baritone*) – Manon's latest 'suitor' – and they sit at the bar. Lescaut asks Armand where Manon is, but Armand's only interest is in more cocaine.

Manon enters and joins her brother and Lilaque *fils*. Stimulated by the drug, Armand starts to rave and tries to stop Lilaque from touching Manon. Lescaut orders him off and Manon tries to soothe him with promises for the future. Lilaque finally loses patience and goes off with Manon and her brother. A beautiful girl comes in and gives Armand a letter. As he reads it, Manon's voice is heard telling him to come and see her the following night as Lilaque will be away.

Scene vi. After a striking interlude, a room in the apartment of Lilaque *fils*. It is early morning and Manon and Armand are together. Manon gaily remarks on the change in her fortunes from the grimy railway station and the little attic to her present luxury, but Armand reminds her that once they were alone together, a point of view Manon cannot understand. Lescaut hurries in and tells Armand he must be off in case the servants see him. As he is about to take Armand out, he notices an abstract painting on the wall, rips it from its frame and hides it under his coat. At this point they hear the voice of Lilaque *père* who has been called by a suspicious servant. Manon quickly hides the two men behind a curtain and goes out in an attempt to prevent the old man from coming in. He is delighted to see her again and insists she see his modern paintings, said by psychiatrists to be most beneficial to the subconscious. The moment he sees

the picture has gone he starts to raise the roof with his accusations. Lilaque shouts to the servant to call the police and himself bars the door. Lescaut shoots him dead, pressing the gun
into Manon's hand as he escapes. Lilaque *fils* enters and sees
Manon and Armand standing over his father's body.

Scene vii. An intermezzo introduces the last scene, outside a
prison on a grey winter's day. Armand waits to catch a last
glimpse of Manon as she is taken off to prison and sings an aria
of hopelessness. The police herd Manon and some other
prisoners away before she and Armand can exchange a word.
From this point the action becomes a symbolical pantomime,
involving people from the railway station, police, singing
children, and Lilaque *fils* following the corpse of his father on a
barrow.

KÖNIG HIRSCH
Il Re Cervo/King Stag

OPERA in three acts by Hans Werner Henze; text by Heinz von Cramer
after the story by Carlo Gozzi. Première (as *König Hirsch*), Berlin Städ-
tische Oper, September 23, 1956.

HENZE'S second opera, *Il Re Cervo*, is an adaptation of one of
the fables of Carlo Gozzi, the Venetian contemporary and
rival of Goldoni and source of such twentieth-century operas as
Busoni's and Puccini's *Turandot*, Casella's *La Donna Serpente*
and Prokofiev's *The Love for Three Oranges*. The first version of
the opera would have run for more than five hours, and it was
heavily cut for the Berlin première in 1956, according to those
who already knew it, to its considerable detriment. By 1962, the
composer had decided on a revised version, half as long, and
this was first heard in Cassel. The full-length version was restored in Stuttgart in 1985.

King Leandro (*tenor*; Deramo in Gozzi's play) has grown up
in the forest among animals. He succeeds to the throne, returns
as an innocent to the complicated world of men, is crowned,
chooses a bride, only to abdicate when his Chancellor, Tartaglia (*bass-baritone*), has her arrested. Through magic the King
takes possession of the body of a dead stag, but the Chancellor
uses the same spell to assume the lifeless form of the King. He
reduces the country to ruins until the Stag King reappears to the
joy of the populace. The false king is killed and the true one re-
enters his body to general acclamation.

ACT I. The King's castle. Preparations are in hand for Leandro's coronation. A fearful storm rages (depicted in the *Vivace*
orchestral opening) and an early candidate for the role of
Queen – Scollatella (*coloratura soprano*) – emerges to complain

of the appalling effect the weather has had on her clothes. She is still confident that she will win the King's hand, but frightened at being alone. She looks into a mirror and summons up a double. Scollatella II (*soubrette*) comes out of the mirror, also complaining about the weather, and it is not long before Scollatella III (*mezzo-soprano*) and Scollatella IV (*alto*) are also involved in thinking up schemes to win the King's favour, although Scollatella I insists that, if their plans go right, she alone will be called Queen.

The Coronation Procession. Scollatella I hides as Tartaglia, the King's Chancellor, comes in and conceals himself. Celebratory choral music can be heard, and Tartaglia storms about the futility of it all. He will strike fear into all their hearts, and he even invokes the elements to put a stop to the farcical proceedings. Scollatella thinks Tartaglia must be King and makes herself known before disappearing into the background.

Costanza (*soprano*) is brought in by two guards. Tartaglia questions her and offers to release her, but she does not want to go. What is the King like? Obviously, judging from her arrest, less kind-hearted than the man she is now face to face with. Tartaglia assures her that the King is a monster and gives her a dagger with which he instructs her to murder him. He forces her to conceal the weapon and tells her to wait for him outside.

The animals, who have been the King's friends in the forest, form a semi-circle round him as in movingly direct vocal terms he bids them goodbye. The celesta introduces two statues (both *contraltos*) who warn him of the danger he faces amongst men. They assure the King that they will help him by laughing the moment anyone tells him an untruth.

Preceded by a fanfare, Tartaglia enters and announces to the King that the moment to choose the royal bride is at hand. Two more fanfares, Scollatella I comes in and makes her obeisance, followed by II, III and IV. The King asks which of them, if married to him, would be saddest if he died and the answer eludes them. The King is keen to get rid of Scollatella I and assures her that no one has given him more pleasure than she. The statues laugh and the King knows that none is worthy to be his bride.

Tartaglia introduces Costanza. She admits she is no longer afraid of him and he himself is reassured by the silence of the statues. They sing together in an *adagio* section, the first love duet in the opera, and at its end, Leandro, unable to bear the idea that he may lose Costanza, attacks the statues and breaks them. Immediately Tartaglia shows the King Costanza's concealed weapon. She is arrested by the guards and when the King, broken-hearted and without the statues to advise him, says he will exercise clemency, Tartaglia insists on death for a potential regicide. The King decides he will abdicate and leave for the forest, and Cigolotti (*spoken*; disguised as a parrot) leads him away.

Tartaglia rejoices. Spirits of the Wind dash across the stage, and Coltellino (*tenor buffo*), Tartaglia's hired assassin, and Checco (*tenor buffo*), a musician who follows Cigolotti and carries a guitar on his back, enter after them. Coltellino does not want Checco hanging around him. In the end Checco leaves, and Coltellino hastens to Tartaglia's summons. Doesn't he want to be an honest murderer like his father? Let him then follow the King into the forest and murder him! A group of six alchemists come in speaking happily and rhythmically to each other and announcing to the furious Tartaglia that they have come to give a party for King Leandro. They are too late, says Tartaglia.

ACT II takes place in the wood – a great breathing organism – and we hear the forest sounds as voices call to each other in alarm. There is a stranger present, a voice announces, and soon others proclaim that the wood is full of men. Leandro appears and it is not long before Scollatella's voice joins with his (she is being groomed by her mirror doubles who now act as maids). Scollatella is obsessed with the idea that she is in reality a Queen, and Leandro turns from her. The action is fast and furious but in a way simple. Animals flee from humans; the alchemists reappear disguised as animals and are themselves terrified of the huntsmen, who will try to kill them, and of the other animals, who may find them even easier prey. Tartaglia attempts to murder Leandro with his knife but fails, and both Checco and Coltellino complicate the action with their fears and failures.

Cigolotti plans that Checco alone shall know the secret of the transformation spell, which he shall give only to the King and thus save the King's life. Checco has a beautiful, enigmatic song, lightly accompanied on guitar. A stag appears and Tartaglia wounds it so that it escapes. Tartaglia's designs are murderous. He tries to get news of the King's whereabouts from Checco. By magical means, they see the stag die and Tartaglia hears the transformation spell from Checco, who intends only to give it to the King. Leandro by its aid changes into the stag and goes off, but Tartaglia in his own turn repeats the spell and assumes the King's body. Cigolotti laments a turn of events which has Tartaglia and his evil soul inhabiting the King's body. Tartaglia sets in motion a stag hunt which will eliminate Leandro for ever, but, as the act ends, the elements seem to be conspiring against him and a storm breaks over the wood.

ACT III. The deserted city, where Tartaglia has been exercising absolute rule. Decay has set in, the people are oppressed and their only hope comes from the legend that when a stag appears in the streets, the rule of peace will return. And this is in effect what happens. Quite quietly, Leandro as the Stag King walks through the streets, finding that no one answers his calls, although Coltellino melodiously laments his lack of prowess as a murderer.

Even the alchemists are persecuted under Tartaglia's rule, but gradually news of the King's return reaches the city, and Costanza comes to look for the man she was allowed to love for so short a time. The Stag King approaches her, and their second duet confirms their mutual love until her touch makes the stag flee, just as Tartaglia appears, in the guise of the King and armed to the teeth. He greets Costanza, as if he were the King she loves, but she detects the fraud straightaway and will have none of him. Tartaglia calls for his soldiers and defies his enemies.

People start to become conscious of the presence of the stag, against whom Tartaglia continues to rail, demanding that it be shot the moment it is sighted. Finally, Coltellino, taking straight aim with the assistance of Cigolotti but mistakenly thinking the King he sees is the King whom Tartaglia has retained him to murder, shoots his target – but it is of course Tartaglia who falls dead just as he is about to kill the stag.

Leandro works the transformation spell and is restored to his original shape, so that the opera may end with choral rejoicing, enclosing a short, simple duet for Leandro and Costanza, in which he claims her as his bride.

ELEGY FOR YOUNG LOVERS

OPERA in three acts by Hans Werner Henze; libretto by W. H. Auden and Chester Kallman. Première (in German), May 20, 1961, at Schwetzingen Festival (Munich Opera).

*E*LEGY FOR YOUNG LOVERS, like *The Bassarids*, was first performed in German translation. The librettists have told us that Henze asked them late in autumn 1958 for a libretto with 'a subject and situation which would call for tender, beautiful noises' and the composer planned a 'small, subtle orchestra' as the basis for his chamber opera.

'The artist as hero' is the great poet Gregor Mittenhofer (*baritone*), who goes every year to a mountain inn, the Schwarze Adler, in the Austrian Alps. This particular spring in 1910 he arrives with Carolina von Kirchstetten (*contralto*), his patroness and unpaid secretary, Elisabeth Zimmer (*soprano*), his young mistress, and Dr. Reischmann (*bass*), his doctor. He hopes that as in former years he will get inspiration from the crazy 'visions' of the widow Mack, who has lived at the inn for the past forty years, ever since her bridegroom was killed climbing the Hammerhorn on the first day of their honeymoon.

ACT I. *The emergence of the bridegroom* (each act and each scene has been given a title by the librettists).

I. FORTY YEARS PAST. Hilda Mack (*high soprano*) sings of the day her husband went to climb the Hammerhorn and of her determination to wait for his return.

II. THE ORDER OF THE DAY. The inside of the inn. Dr. Reischmann enters and watches Carolina sort press cuttings. Each is summoned in turn, the one to take the Master his second egg, the other to give him his morning injection. The fact that Carolina must finance the poet by hiding coins where he may expect to find them, elicits from Dr. Reischmann a 'What would poets do without their nannies?' and in duet they agree that they are essential to him.

III. A SCHEDULED ARRIVAL. The doctor is waiting for the arrival of his son Toni (*tenor*), who is going through a 'phase'. As soon as Toni comes in, his father starts to question him, every remark producing an exasperated comment from Toni.

IV. APPEARANCES AND VISIONS. Carolina entices Frau Mack inside just as Mittenhofer, his arm round Elisabeth Zimmer, makes his entrance. Mittenhofer is introducing the young people when Frau Mack starts on one of her coloratura visions, to the intense satisfaction of the poet, who starts to take notes. In her aria, Frau Mack seems to foretell what hindsight tells us is the death of the two young lovers.

V. WORLDLY BUSINESS. Mittenhofer, delighted at what he has got, starts to read yesterday's typing, interrupting it to yell at Carolina about a mistake she has made and taunting her until she falls in a faint at his feet. Dr. Reischmann runs in, and he and a maid carry Carolina to a chair.

VI. HELP. Mittenhofer disappears to his study, but reappears a moment later to search the room for his money, like a child looking for sweets. He finds what he is looking for and goes back to his room.

VII. UNWORLDLY WEAKNESS. Poor Carolina is in a state – 'death in fact looks dazzlingly attractive' is her comment.

VIII. BEAUTY IN DEATH. Josef Mauer (*spoken*), an Alpine guide, comes in to tell them that a body has been found on the Hammerhorn – fresh and young-looking, his skull cracked. It must be Frau Mack's husband!

IX. WHO IS TO TELL HER? Carolina says she is feeling too ill to break the news, and she and Dr. Reischmann agree that it must be Elisabeth.

X. TODAY'S WEATHER. Gently Elisabeth breaks the news to Frau Mack, who is full of foreboding for Elisabeth's own future. In the end she succeeds (in a beautiful canonic duet) in telling her the news, which Frau Mack appears to understand. Toni is moved by the unexpected warmth Elisabeth shows.

XI. A VISIONARY INTERLUDE. Toni sings a song in tender remembrance of his mother, who died long ago; then turns back to stare at the place where Elisabeth was standing.

XII. TOMORROW: TWO FOLLIES CROSS. Hilda, who has remained still throughout Toni's song, suddenly rises in a state bordering on ecstasy. To end the act, she joins in climactic duet with Toni, she because 'the crystal is broken', he because he realises he is falling in love with Elisabeth.

ACT II. *The emergence of the bride.*

I. A PASSION. A few days later: mid-afternoon. Elisabeth and Toni are now plainly in love, as witness their joyful duet; she must break with Mittenhofer. Carolina catches them in each other's arms and calls for the doctor to help her settle what she thinks of as nonsense.

II. SENSIBLE TALK. Dr. Reischmann tries to reason with Toni inside, Carolina with Elisabeth outside; 'what the world needs are warmer hearts, not older poets' is the gist of the discussion.

III. EACH IN HIS PLACE. In a duet which is composed of two separate monologues, the two young people express their outrage.

IV. THE MASTER'S TIME. Carolina's line, 'It's time for the Master's tea', precipitates a crisis: as Elisabeth in one room asks Toni to take her away, Mittenhofer in another is told by Carolina that there is a situation between Elisabeth and Toni, and asks Carolina to have Elisabeth join him at tea.

V. PERSONAL QUESTIONS. Mittenhofer's tack is to criticise himself and play on Elisabeth's guilt feelings. He is the best devil's advocate imaginable, and the scene is an *apologia pro vita sua*. At the monologue's end, Elisabeth leaves, without having told him anything.

VI. THE TROUBLES OF OTHERS. Elisabeth (and later the orchestra) is sad.

VII. WHAT MUST BE TOLD. Elisabeth admits to Toni that she has said nothing, partly because they know nothing about each other, partly because she did not dare. Toni says he will do the job.

VIII. THE WRONG TIME. The poet himself listens to Toni's protestations of love for Elisabeth. An ensemble builds up, involving all four characters, Mittenhofer, Elisabeth (Carolina taking her place at its end), Toni, the doctor.

IX. THE BRIDE. Elisabeth bursts into tears, a cow bell rings, and Frau Mack comes into sight, singing tipsily (and higher than ever) and rejoicing in the new situation. She demands 10% of Mittenhofer's future royalties, and starts to comfort Elisabeth.

'Frau Mack, do you think I'm a whore?' Mittenhofer resolves the situation by begging Dr. Reischmann to bless the lovers.

X. THE YOUNG LOVERS. In a grandiose ensemble, Mittenhofer explains his new poem, 'The Young Lovers'. The characters seem to breathe life from his words, which perfectly express their different situations for them.

XI. THE FLOWER. The doctor blesses the match and Mittenhofer begs the young couple to stay over and pick for him on the slopes of the Hammerhorn an Edelweiss, which he needs if he is to finish his poem. They agree; Frau Mack plans her departure.

XII. THE VISION OF TOMORROW. The young lovers will stay; Mittenhofer refuses his tonic – to watch young love is enough. Mauer comes in to tell Mittenhofer that tomorrow the weather on the slopes of the Hammerhorn will be propitious enough for them to find the Edelweiss he craves.

XIII. THE END OF THE DAY. The atmosphere changes to one of unbridled fury. In a furious monologue, Mittenhofer inveighs against all around him. Frau Mack comes back to confront him, so that he departs with a bellow of rage leaving her in uncontrollable laughter.

ACT III. *Man and wife.*

I. ECHOES. Hilda is ready to travel, Toni and Elisabeth to ascend the mountain, which they do singing a folk-song, while Hilda sings farewell. An ensemble mounts, during whose course Mittenhofer can be heard trying out rhymes and prepositions.

II. FAREWELLS. It remains for Frau Mack to bow tenderly out of the opera, giving Carolina the colossal scarf she has been knitting for the past forty years. Mittenhofer comes out to persuade Carolina to laugh, and Frau Mack has a good word even for him.

III. SCHEDULED DEPARTURES. 'The young in pairs, the old in two proceed'; the music is a quartet.

IV. TWO TO GO. Carolina makes some attempt to calm Mittenhofer, but to no great avail. Mauer hurries in to say that a threatening blizzard is blowing up and that in minutes the mountain will be blanketed in snow. Is anyone still up there? Mittenhofer, without looking at Carolina, denies knowledge of anyone.

V. MAD HAPPENINGS. Mittenhofer and Carolina confront each other and the Master slyly suggests that she go away 'for a change of scene'. If she was ever quite sane, she is no longer.

VI. A CHANGE OF SCENE. For the first time we are outside the inn, and the Hammerhorn is visible, in a blizzard. An extended orchestral interlude leads us to Toni and Elisabeth in the last stages of exhaustion on the mountain.

VII. MAN AND WIFE. Their duet takes the form of reminiscences of a long-married husband and wife.

VIII. TONI AND ELISABETH. They have discovered something beyond love: Truth. This will help them to die.

IX. ELEGY FOR YOUNG LOVERS. Mittenhofer is going on stage to read poetry in Vienna. He goes through a cheer sequence – 'One. Two. Three. Four. Whom do we adore?' – then dedicates the poem he is about to read to 'the memory of a brave and beautiful young couple, Toni Reischmann and Elisabeth Zimmer'. He mouths beneath an invisible ensemble of Hilda Mack, Elisabeth, Carolina, Toni and the doctor; the poem is, with the help of others, finished, and the opera therefore at an end.

THE BASSARIDS

O NE act (four movements), by Hans Werner Henze; première, Salzburg, 1966. In Thebes the tomb of Semele, lover of Zeus and mother of Dionysus (*tenor*), has become a shrine for the latter's cult. King Pentheus (*baritone*) cannot decide whether to recognise Dionysus's divinity. A voice proclaims Dionysus's arrival on Cythaeron and the people instantly take up his cult as Bassarids. The royal family assemble to hear that his worship is forbidden. But the people have all gone to Cythaeron. Pentheus in a fury orders his guards there. They return with various prisoners in a trance, Agave (*mezzo-soprano*), the King's mother, and Dionysus himself among them. Torture is ordered, but no one is able to describe the rites. An intermezzo follows, with an enactment of the Judgment of Calliope. Pentheus, determined, goes to Cythaeron. Dionysus exhorts his followers to hunt the trespasser and Pentheus is torn to pieces. Agave, at first not recognising it, carries his head back to the palace. Dionysus has achieved vengeance, and restores his dead mother to her eminent position.

DER JUNGE LORD
The Young Lord

T WO acts, by Hans Werner Henze; première, Berlin, 1965. A rich Englishman, Sir Edgar (*silent*), comes to live in a small German town. The townsfolk welcome him, although Luise (*soprano*) and Wilhelm (*tenor*) are more interested in each other. Sir Edgar refuses all invitations and thereby insults Baroness Grünwiesel (*mezzo-soprano*). A circus comes to town and Sir Edgar befriends the performers. Shrieks are heard from his house, but the people are told that it is Sir Edgar's nephew, Lord Barrat (*tenor*), learning German. At a party for the young

Lord he behaves eccentrically. Luise falls in love with him, to Wilhelm's dismay. Barrat dances Luise to exhaustion, swings from the chandeliers and finally reveals that he is – a monkey.

Giacomo Puccini
(1858–1924)

MANON LESCAUT

OPERA in four acts; text by Domenica Oliva and Luigi Illica, after the Abbé Prévost's novel. Première in Turin, February 1, 1893.

P UCCINI was thirty-four when his third opera, *Manon Lescaut*, was first heard in Turin, a week before the première of *Falstaff* in Milan. Seven different men, including the composer Leoncavallo, had worked on the libretto, but the result was a resounding success, the first of Puccini's career, and, though Verdi commented that Puccini seemed more a symphonist than an opera composer, the opera maintains a permanent place in the Italian repertory.

ACT I. In front of an inn at Amiens. A brilliant orchestral opening introduces Edmondo (*tenor*) and fellow students, who cavort in front of the townsfolk of Amiens. Des Grieux (*tenor*) is persuaded to sing a mocking serenade: 'Tra voi, belle, brune e bionde' (Among you, dark and fair beauties). The coach from Arras arrives to disgorge Lescaut (*baritone*), Geronte di Ravoir (*bass*) and Lescaut's sister Manon (*soprano*), the latter causing all hearts to flutter including that of des Grieux. He addresses her as 'Cortese damigella' (Gentle lady) to begin a duet which is starting to show the hallmarks of a full-blooded Puccinian love duet when Lescaut calls Manon inside.

Des Grieux muses rapturously in one of Puccini's most immediately attractive arias: 'Donna non vidi mai' (Never have I seen such a woman). Geronte has his eye on Manon and he and Lescaut seem about to reach an understanding. Geronte arranges for a carriage for two, but Edmondo overhears and warns des Grieux; the latter's duet with Manon ('Vedete? Io son' fedele': You see? I'm true to my word) suggests love returned. He quickly overcomes Manon's reservations, explains Geronte's plot, and together, applauded by the students, they elope in Geronte's carriage, leaving Lescaut and Geronte to plot the future, and Edmondo and the students to mock.

ACT II. An elegant room in Geronte's Paris house. Manon at her dressing-table is joined by Lescaut. He congratulates her on her present surroundings, splendid in comparison with the humble dwelling she once shared with des Grieux. It is obvious she still carries a torch for des Grieux, as she makes clear in an aria of genuine pathos: 'In quelle trine morbide' (Within these soft lace hangings). Lescaut, always the pimp, offers to bring des Grieux to her, and teach him moreover how to win at the tables so that she may continue to enjoy her accustomed comfort. Their voices join in anticipation of the future – Lescaut's finest musical moment.

Musicians come to sing a madrigal, but they bore Manon as much as the dancing master (*tenor*) who follows them. A lesson in the minuet begins, watched by Geronte and his friends. Manon sings a brilliant aria, 'L'ora o Tirsi, è vaga e bella', and says she will join Geronte and the others later on the promenade.

She has not long to wait before des Grieux precipitates himself into her room: 'Tu, tu, amore! Tu!' What starts with reproach rapidly becomes an impassioned love duet on a grand scale, but it ends when Geronte returns to surprise the lovers. Manon brazens it out: let Geronte look in the mirror if he wants to understand. He promises to return, and des Grieux urges instant flight, then berates her for the dance she leads him and for her incorrigible love of luxury: 'Ah, Manon, mi tradisce' (Ah, Manon, your foolish thoughts betray me). Lescaut rushes in to tell them Geronte has mobilised guards to arrest them, Manon lingers to collect her jewellery and the delay is fatal. They are arrested as thieves.

An intermezzo represents not only the journey to Le Havre but des Grieux's despairing determination to follow Manon to the ends of the earth.

ACT III. The harbour at Le Havre. The plan des Grieux and Lescaut have hatched to rescue Manon from imprisonment fails and the roll is called of the women who are to be transported. When it is Manon's turn, des Grieux stays at her side, defies anyone to take her away from him and sings frenziedly: 'Guardate! pazzo son'!' (Have a care! I'm driven to madness). The ship's captain (*bass*) makes a gesture and offers des Grieux passage to America.

ACT IV. A deserted plain. Manon and des Grieux, victims of intrigue and jealousy, have left New Orleans. Manon is exhausted with the journey. The music is a melancholy duet, and when des Grieux goes off to get help, Manon's despair is expressed in a grandiose aria, 'Sola, perduta, abbandonata' (Alone, lost, abandoned). Puccini at one point removed it from the score but later restored it, having slightly reworked it. When des Grieux returns, Manon is dying. He collapses by her side.

LA BOHÈME
The Bohemians

OPERA in four acts by Giacomo Puccini; text by Giacosa and Illica. Première Teatro Regio, Turin, February 1, 1896.

IN *La Bohème*, Puccini's melodic invention and its turn to expressive use is at fullest flood, and he combines it with an epigrammatic, conversational conciseness that is unique in his output, technically adroit though that always is. In the way it puts across conversation economically and with heightened expression, it is without question his highest achievement – something of an Italianate parallel to *Der Rosenkavalier* – but so attractive is the melodic flow, so memorable the lyrical invention that few of its vast army of fans bother to notice that points are made, contrary to the work's reputation for wearing its heart on its sleeve, almost too fast for any but connoisseurs to take in!

ACT I. A garret in the Latin Quarter of Paris where live the four students. Christmas Eve, about 1830. Rodolfo (*tenor*) is writing, Marcello (*baritone*) at work on a painting, 'The Passage of the Red Sea'. It is freezingly cold and Rodolfo sacrifices his manuscript to keep the stove going. Colline (*bass*) returns from unsuccessfully trying to pawn some books but relief comes with the entry of Schaunard (*baritone*) who has been engaged, and well paid, for music lessons by an eccentric Englishman. Nobody listens to his story, though they are quite ready to hear his invitation to supper at Café Momus. A knock at the door brings Benoit (*bass*), looking for the rent. They flatter him at first but pretend to be indignant when he boasts of an amorous conquest and chuck him out. The others go off to the café while Rodolfo stays to finish an article.

Again a knock at the door; this time a woman's voice. Mimì (*soprano*) asks Rodolfo to light her candle, which has gone out as she climbed the stairs. She collapses in a fit of coughing, but quickly revives and makes to leave. This time, she finds she has dropped her key and soon each is searching the by now darkened room for it. Rodolfo's hand meets hers and the flood of melody which has been threatening ever since Mimì's appearance bursts its banks: 'Che gelida manina' (Your tiny hand is frozen). There is perhaps no better known aria for tenor in all Italian opera. Mimì's own description of her work as an embroiderer is no less persuasive: 'Sì, mi chiamano Mimì' (I am called Mimì). The voices of Rodolfo's friends call from below, Rodolfo is overcome by the sight of Mimì standing in the moonlight, and the act ends with an impassioned avowal of love on both sides: 'O soave fanciulla' (Lovely maid in the moonlight).

ACT II. A square, with the Café Momus. In a mere eighteen minutes the Act introduces Mimì to the other students, and a vital new character, Musetta (*soprano*), Marcello's love, to the narrative. From the bustle of street-vendors and citizens in the last throes of Christmas shopping, tendrils of melody ascend to describe Colline's reaction to a second-hand coat, Schaunard's to a battered horn, Parpignol's (*tenor*) to the crying of his wares, and Mimì's to a pink bonnet she wants Rodolfo to buy her. In the end, Rodolfo in a few impassioned phrases introduces Mimì to his friends and all start to order dinner when a commotion precedes the entry of Musetta, attended by the ludicrous Alcindoro (*bass*). Musetta starts a slow waltz, famous as 'Musetta's waltz song', which she aims deliberately and with maximum effect at Marcello. She gets rid of Alcindoro on the pretext that her shoe pinches, and she and Marcello fall into each other's arms to watch a military procession which crosses the square. The sight of the bill causes general alarm, calmed by Musetta's insistence that it be lumped with hers and presented to Alcindoro.

ACT III. A toll-gate on the Orléans road into Paris. Open fifths in the orchestra suggest winter's cold, as customs-house men search scavengers and milk women on their way into town. Mimì comes looking for Rodolfo and Marcello comes out of the inn. He tells her he is painting signboards and Musetta giving music lessons. Won't Mimì join them? In a passage of real feeling, she tells him Rodolfo is so insanely jealous she fears they must part, and her story is fully borne out when Rodolfo emerges to give his side of the picture. 'Mimì è una civetta' (Mimì is a heartless creature), he claims, but goes on to admit that he fears she is dying. A paroxysm of coughing gives away her presence, and they agree the time has come to part, less in anger than regret. Tenderness runs through Mimì's farewell: 'Donde lieta uscì', with its closing line: 'Addio, senza rancor' (Farewell then, I wish you well). Marcello inside the pub has caught Musetta flirting and a row flares up to combine in a quartet with the much gentler farewell of Mimì and Rodolfo, whose duetting might be mistaken for an avowal of love.

ACT IV. The attic familiar from Act I. Rodolfo longs for Mimì, from whom he has not heard, Marcello for Musetta. Their duet, 'Ah, Mimì, tu più non torni', suggests the withdrawal pangs are anything but false. Schaunard returns and thrusts a bottle of water into Colline's hat as if it were a champagne cooler, the prelude to a riotous student frolic, which culminates in organised dancing and a mock duel between Colline and Schaunard. This is interrupted by the arrival of Musetta, frantic with worry about Mimì, whom she has found half dead of her tuberculosis at the foot of the stairs. Rodolfo carries her in and lays her on the bed the others have prepared. Rodolfo's presence restores her strength a little and for a moment she seems happy although it is plain that she is very weak. Her hands are cold, and Musetta gives Marcello her earrings to sell for medicine. Colline is not to be outdone and sings a sad little farewell to his coat ('Vecchia zimarra, senti') before taking it off to the pawn-shop.

When they are alone, Mimì and Rodolfo invoke past happiness and the music of earlier acts reflects their thoughts. Musetta and the others return, but Mimì is beyond help and she dies so quietly that Rodolfo does not at first notice what has happened, then explodes in grief.

TOSCA

OPERA in three acts by Giacomo Puccini; text by Giacosa and Illica after the play by Victorien Sardou. Première, Teatro Costanzi, Rome, January 14, 1900.

THE opera is set in 1800, when Napoleon invaded Italy. During the action, the Austrian General Melas is reported to have defeated Napoleon and the consequent celebrations are likely to be attended by Queen Marie Caroline, wife of the Neapolitan King Ferdinand IV, daughter of Empress Maria Theresa of Austria and sister to Queen Marie Antoinette of France. Baron Scarpia, the much-feared Chief of Police, is based on a real-life Sicilian figure, who incidentally affected old-fashioned dress; hence the white wig Scarpia wears.

ACT I. The Church of Sant'Andrea della Valle, Rome. Three chords, played *fff tutta forza* and attached to the sinister Baron Scarpia, introduce the opera before we meet Angelotti (*bass*), a fugitive from prison who must find the Attavanti chapel in which his sister has hidden a key and clothes. He disappears as the Sacristan (*baritone*) comes looking for the painter Mario Cavaradossi (*tenor*). He is not at his easel and the picnic in his basket has not been touched. The Sacristan kneels for the Angelus, and when Cavaradossi uncovers the picture he has been painting, recognises in the blonde Mary Magdalene a woman he has seen several times lately at prayer. Yes, he painted her, says Cavaradossi, then abandons his work as he dreams of his love, Floria Tosca (*soprano*): 'Recondita armonia di bellezze diverse' (Strange harmony of contrasts deliciously blending). It is one of the most convincing of all Puccini's tenor arias. The Sacristan grumbles, then to his delight hears that the painter plans to leave his picnic untouched.

315

Angelotti comes out of hiding and recognises in Cavaradossi a political sympathiser. Cavaradossi wants to help but, hearing Tosca's voice outside, urges Angelotti into the chapel.

Tosca's jealousy immediately suggests someone is with Cavaradossi but he reassures her and it is not long before she is making an assignation for later that night. Cavaradossi seems less than enthusiastic and it takes all Tosca's blandishments ('Non la sospiri la nostra casetta': Do you not long for our cottage secluded?) to bring his thoughts round to her. She recognises the Magdalene as a portrait of Marchesa Attavanti and suspicion becomes certainty. There is nothing to it, he says; he saw her yesterday, and painted her at prayer, demanding rhetorically what eyes could compare with Tosca's ('Qual'occhio al mondo'). From Tosca's entrance, the entire duet, with its contrasting episodes, constitutes one of Puccini's finest and most detailed.

Tosca leaves, Angelotti emerges from the chapel and he and Cavaradossi talk with hatred of the bigoted satyr Scarpia (*baritone*) who has kept Angelotti in prison (the chords of the opera's introduction). In case of necessity, Angelotti should hide in the well in Cavaradossi's garden ('al pozzo del giardino'). A cannon shot is heard and they make a hurried escape as the Sacristan returns. He summons the choristers who dance madly round him, only for the chords to announce the arrival of Scarpia in person. His orders are quickly given, and a fan is found in the chapel: Marchesa Attavanti's! An agent brings in the basket, now empty of the picnic the Sacristan tells him Cavaradossi planned not to eat. It is clear to Scarpia that Cavaradossi has been an accomplice in Angelotti's escape. When Tosca returns, Scarpia affects to contrast her seemly behaviour in church with that of others who come perhaps to meet their lovers, and points to the fan which was (he pretends) on the easel. Jealousy comes easily to Tosca, and when she leaves, Scarpia orders one of his men to follow her, then himself joins in the *Te Deum*, genuflecting to the Cardinal in procession but singing lustily of the satisfaction he will have in revenging himself on Cavaradossi and bending Tosca to his pleasure.

ACT II. Scarpia's apartment in the Palazzo Farnese, where he is at supper. His passions rise as he reflects that he infinitely prefers a forced conquest to a passive surrender ('Ha più forte sapore'), then Spoletta (*tenor*) brings the bad news that Angelotti was nowhere to be found when he tracked Tosca to Cavaradossi's villa, followed by the good – he arrested Cavaradossi. The cantata begins and Tosca's voice can be heard through the open window as Cavaradossi is brought in. Scarpia starts to interrogate his prisoner who denies all knowledge of Angelotti, and continues his questioning as Tosca comes in. Tosca has no idea that the torture chamber is next door, and she and Scarpia at first converse as if there were no external pressures; but not for long. Her heated denial of any knowledge of Angelotti's whereabouts prompts Scarpia to describe the torments Cavaradossi is undergoing. She says she will tell him the truth, and a scream of anguish from the inner room brings an admission: 'Nel pozzo nel giardino' (In the well in the garden).

Cavaradossi haltingly asks Tosca if he gave anything away. She reassures him just as Scarpia instructs Spoletta: 'In the well in the garden!', but the tables are turned when Sciarrone (*bass*) hurries in with the news that Melas was after all defeated, Napoleon victorious. Cavaradossi finds the strength to stand up and hurl defiance at Scarpia.

Scarpia holds the cards. Perhaps, he suggests, they may together concoct a plan to save Cavaradossi. 'Your price?' demands Tosca. Scarpia laughs at her naïveté. 'Già mi dicon venal' (Venal my enemies call me) he sings in a passage of great power: *she* is the price that must be paid for Cavaradossi's life. Distant drums suggest an escort about to conduct a prisoner to the scaffold. In the opera's most famous aria (one Puccini is said to have grudged its place as interrupting the flow of the action), Tosca prays movingly for strength ('Vissi d'arte, vissi d'amore'). Spoletta announces Angelotti took poison as he was arrested, then waits for instructions about the other prisoner. Tosca reluctantly nods to Scarpia, who tells Spoletta there has been a change of plan. For Cavaradossi there will be a mock execution, simulated only – 'just as we did in the case of Palmieri. You understand: *just* like Palmieri'. Spoletta seems to grasp the emphasis. Tosca demands safe conduct and, as Scarpia writes at his desk, sees a knife on the supper table, picks it up and stabs Scarpia to the heart. He falls dying and she searches for the paper, then, placing a candle on either side of the dead man's head, slowly leaves the room.

ACT III. A platform high on Castel Sant'Angelo; St. Peter's can be seen in the distance. A shepherd sings below (*contralto*), and as dawn approaches Cavaradossi is brought in. He bribes the gaoler (*bass*) to deliver a letter to Tosca, before losing himself in memories of her. 'E lucevan le stelle' (When the stars were brightly shining) is in great contrast to 'Recondita armonia', with which he began the opera, a moving farewell to life as opposed to a panegyric to a loved one. Tosca joins Cavaradossi, who listens to the story of Scarpia's killing, then lovingly takes her hands in his: 'O dolci mani mansuete e pure' (Oh, gentle hands, so pitiful and tender). They plot their departure and their voices join in a duet ('Amaro sol per te m'era il morire': The sting of death I only felt for thee, love) which ends on a note less of love than of defiance as the execution is prepared. When the firing squad leaves, Scarpia is found to have kept one last card, a joker, up his sleeve. The mock execution was real after all, and with a last cry, Tosca eludes Spoletta and plunges over the parapet.

MADAMA BUTTERFLY

OPERA in three acts by Giacomo Puccini; text by Giacosa and Illica. Première la Scala, Milan, February 17, 1904.

MADAMA BUTTERFLY's first performance in Milan was a fiasco. The public audibly objected to a resemblance it found between the theme of Butterfly's entry (heard again, notably in the love duet) and Mimì's first act aria in *La Bohème*, and to the fatiguing length of the second act, given without interval. It was heard only once in that form but a revised version (with a much heavier soprano than in Milan) triumphed in Brescia. Substantial revision brought a new theme for Butterfly's entrance and the love duet, the second act divided into two, and in the third an aria for Pinkerton.

But that was not the end of it. There were further revisions for Covent Garden in 1905, for America in 1906 and, at the behest of the experienced Albert Carré, for the Opéra-Comique at the end of the same year. That 1906 version was the composer's last word. 'Genre' scenes featuring Butterfly's relations were cut from the first act, and revision of the second went far beyond the cosmetic, mainly because the composer had effective second thoughts but also (modern speculation has it) because some of the first thoughts were too 'modern' for an audience of the early 1900's. That Puccini had seventeen years in which to revise the 1906 score but never did has not prevented attempts since the early 1980's to come up with a new 'version' for almost any new production.

ACT I. A house overlooking Nagasaki harbour. Goro (*tenor*) is showing Lieutenant Pinkerton (*tenor*) over the house the latter has leased for the Japanese bride he is to marry ('Tied for 999 years but with the option at every month to cancel the contract'). Goro introduces the servants and is describing the bridal party when the Consul (*baritone*) makes his entrance. Pinkerton delights in the elasticity of local law and, in spite of Sharpless's obvious disapproval of the step he is taking, a rampant sexuality pervades the music of his toast to the future ('Amore o grillo').

The arrival of the bride, Cio-Cio-San (Butterfly; *soprano*) is imminent and her voice soars over those of her relations as she makes her entrance. She discloses her age – fifteen; her mother's poverty, that her father committed *hari kiri*, and that she has abandoned her own religion to take up Pinkerton's. The Commissioner (*bass*) performs the ceremony, the Consul and other officials leave, and Pinkerton is proposing a toast which he hopes will get rid of the relations when there is an interruption. Butterfly's uncle the Bonze (*bass*) has got wind of her conversion and denounces her. The relations follow him out and Pinkerton is left to comfort his bride.

It is the moment for the most extended love duet Puccini ever wrote. It builds slowly while Butterfly rids her mind of the cries of the Bonze, turns to her confused thoughts when it was suggested she should marry an American, passes through an exquisite passage pleading for reassurance ('Vogliatemi bene': Ah, love me a little) until it reaches a climax with a reminiscence of the music of Butterfly's entrance.

ACT II. Inside Butterfly's house. Three years have passed since Pinkerton left, promising, according to Butterfly, to return 'when the robins nest in spring'. Perhaps they nest less often over there? To comfort herself as much as her servant Suzuki (*mezzo-soprano*), she sings 'Un bel dì vedremo' (One fine day), a description of his future homecoming which has become possibly the most popular aria of the twentieth century. Sharpless now comes on a mission which is little to his taste – to tell Butterfly he has heard from Pinkerton that he is returning, but does not intend to see her. He is constantly interrupted: by indignation at Goro's suggestion she should take a Japanese husband, by the appearance of her suitor Prince Yamadori (*baritone*), and finally, while reading the letter, by Butterfly's over-enthusiasm. He takes the bull by the horns: what would be her reaction if he were never to come back? She reacts as if struck in the face, then fetches her little boy, born since Pinkerton's departure, and releases her pent-up emotion in an aria ('Che tua madre'). The child's name is 'Dolore' (Trouble), she says, and Sharpless goes resignedly away, his message only partly delivered.

Goro is dragged in and castigated for spreading a false rumour about the baby's parentage, then a cannon shot diverts all attention to the harbour. Through the telescope, Butterfly makes out that it is the *Abraham Lincoln*, Pinkerton's ship, and apprehension turns to jubilation; flowers must be scattered to celebrate Pinkerton's return. She puts on her wedding garment, and she, Suzuki and Trouble will together watch until Pinkerton arrives, while a wordless chorus suggests the warm night outside.

ACT III. The curtain rises on the same scene, with dawn breaking, Butterfly still on watch. She sings a sad little lullaby as she carries the baby to bed. Suzuki has not long to wait. Pinkerton and Sharpless appear and a moment later Suzuki learns that the woman outside is Pinkerton's wife (*mezzo-soprano*). The strands of grief and consternation are gathered in a trio, after which Pinkerton, unable to face the situation, sings a tearful farewell to the house he once knew so well (the interpolated, often maligned but effective 'Addio, fiorito asil'), and leaves.

Butterfly is convinced Pinkerton is there and only gradually comes to terms with the reality. She sees Mrs. Pinkerton, comforts the weeping Suzuki, then contrives to wish her rival happiness for the future. To Pinkerton she sends a message that, if he will come for his son in half an hour, he may have him. In this last scene, Butterfly acquires tragic dignity, and it is on this level that she reads the words engraved on her father's sword, 'To die with honour when one can no longer live with honour', before embracing the child whom Suzuki, in one last effort to avert disaster, has brought in. She sings heartbreakingly to Trouble, then blindfolds him, retreats behind a screen and commits *hari kiri*. Pinkerton returns to find Butterfly dead on the floor and his son waving an American flag.

La Fanciulla del West
The Girl of the Golden West

OPERA in three acts by Giacomo Puccini; text by G. Civinini and C. Zangarini, from the play by David Belasco. Première at Metropolitan, New York, December 10, 1910.

ACT I. 1849. The inside of 'The Polka', the inn where the miners come to drink and gamble. It is presided over by Minnie (*soprano*), whom they respect, love and protect, and who in return has even ventured to set up a sort of elementary school for the roughest of the inhabitants. Miners greet each other, and a game of faro starts up. Larkens (*bass*) is observed to be melancholy – he has got gold fever, says Nick (*tenor*), the bartender. Jake (*baritone*) comes through singing a melancholy song, in whose refrain all join. Larkens breaks down, and Sonora (*baritone*) takes up a collection for him. Sid (*baritone*) is caught cheating and the miners are for meting out justice to him themselves, but Rance (*baritone*), the Sheriff, tells them rather to pin a card on Sid's chest as a token that he must not play; pass the word round the camp, and string him up if he takes off the mark of shame. Ashby (*bass*), the Wells Fargo agent, comes in and tells Rance that he is close on the heels of the notorious Ramerrez. Minnie sends in hot whisky and lemon, and they all drink to her, Rance taking the opportunity of mentioning that she is likely soon to become Mrs. Rance. Sonora mocks him, and they fight, but are separated by Minnie.

Rance and Ashby talk apart, as Minnie takes down the Bible and starts to teach from it.

The post arrives, and Ashby has a letter from Nina Michel-torena, a cast-off girlfriend of Ramerrez's, indicating where he is to be found that night.

A stranger is outside, Nick says, asking for whisky with water. They all laugh at the notion. Rance comes up to Minnie and starts to tell her how much he loves her, but she will have none of it. He goes sulkily away, and bursts out into an avowal of his passion: 'Minnie della mia casa son partito.' He left every-thing without regret when his gambler's heart impelled him to come out West, but now he would give a fortune for a kiss from her. Minnie says that love is not like that; she has happy memories of her parents and her home-life, and would not take a husband unless she loved him as they loved each other: 'Lag-giù nel Soledad.'

Nick brings in the stranger, Dick Johnson (*tenor*). Rance is rude to him, but Minnie recognises him and talks about the time they first met. Rance demands to know what is the stranger's business. The miners are about to take Rance's part when Minnie says she will vouch for him. Johnson takes Min-nie off to dance. While they are away, Castro (*bass*) is brought in; he is a member of Ramerrez's band and has been captured. He says he will lead them to the bandit's camp if they will spare him, then, seeing Johnson's saddle lying on the ground, thinks to himself they have already captured him. A moment later he notices his chief come from the other room. Asking for some-thing to drink, he tells Johnson that he has given nothing away, and that the gang is all round, only waiting until the Sheriff and his men are out of the way before they fall on the defenceless camp and pillage it.

Johnson remains behind with Minnie when the others ride off. He comments on her defenceless state and on the strange fact that she is guarding the miners' gold. She tells him that she loves the life she lives. They are interrupted by Nick who says that a bandit has been seen skulking round near the camp. Johnson comforts her, and agrees to her suggestion that he should come up later that evening to her cabin to continue the conversation and have a meal.

ACT II. Minnie's hut – a single room, above which is a loft. Wowkle (*mezzo-soprano*) is singing a lullaby to her papoose. Minnie tells Wowkle that there will be two for supper. She starts to dress up in what little finery she has. Johnson arrives and comments that the life up here must be lonely. 'Oh, you've no notion how exciting my life is,' says Minnie. The mountains and the wild flowers, and her school for the miners – these keep her very busy: 'O, se sapeste.'

They sing of their happiness, and Minnie makes up a bed for herself in front of the fire. She has persuaded Johnson to spend the night there, as he would inevitably get lost in the heavy snow. There is a noise from outside, and voices demand admittance. Minnie hides Johnson behind the curtains of the bed, and lets in Rance, Nick, Ashby, and Sonora. They were worried for her safety – Dick Johnson, they have discovered, is none other than the notorious Ramerrez. They were led by Castro to his hiding-place, where they found his girl, Nina Micheltorena, who showed them a photograph of him – Rance hands it to Minnie, who laughs loudly.

She says goodnight to them, then rounds furiously on Johnson. He admits he came to rob, but at sight of her, changed his purpose. In an aria he explains his upbringing: his father was a bandit, and when he died six months ago ('Or son sei mesi') left nothing for him, his mother and his brothers, but the gang of thieves he led. He was fated to take to the road, but from the moment he met Minnie he longed to lead an honest life. He does not expect forgiveness, only understanding.

Johnson rushes out, and a moment later there is the sound of a shot. A body falls against the door; Minnie opens it, and he staggers in. She cries that she loves him and will help him, and, putting the ladder in place, drags him up to the loft. No sooner is he in hiding than Rance is again at the door. He searches everywhere for his quarry, then, asking Minnie to swear that he is not hidden there, tries to embrace her. She backs away from him; he accuses her of loving the bandit. With a gesture of defiance, Rance swears to Minnie that she shall never be Johnson's. A drop of blood falls on his outstretched hand, then another. Rance calls to Johnson to come out of hiding; he descends the ladder, helped by Minnie, and collapses at the bottom. Minnie tries a last desperate expedient. She suggests to Rance that they should play a game of poker: if she wins, Johnson's life is hers, if she loses, Rance wins her love. He cannot resist the gamble. They play two hands, each winning one, but before the last Minnie shows signs of distress and asks Rance to get her a drink. She has previously secreted some cards in her stocking, and substitutes the cards for the hand she has been dealt. Rance returns, and against his three kings, Minnie is able to show three aces and a pair. He leaves the house, and Minnie is left alone with the lover whose life she has saved.

ACT III. A clearing in the forest. Nick, Rance, and Ashby are resting there round a fire. They reflect bitterly on the change that Johnson's arrival has brought into their lives. Ashby goes off, while Rance shouts triumphantly that Minnie will not see her lover again, except at the end of a rope. Sonora gallops in shouting that they have caught him at last. Ashby hands over

Johnson to the Sheriff, who suggests that they string him up forthwith. He asks for one thing only, that he be allowed to speak before he dies. He makes an impassioned plea that Minnie shall think he has gone free: 'Ch'ella mi creda libero e lontano' (Let her believe that I have gained my freedom). It is one of Puccini's most famous arias.

Almost before Johnson has finished speaking, Rance rushes up to him and hits him in the face, to sounds of disapproval from the bystanders. They are about to hang their prisoner when Minnie's voice is heard. In a moment she is among them, threatening the first man that takes a step towards Johnson, and defying them all to do their worst. For years she shared their troubles and their dangers – will they deny her the first thing she has ever asked of them? She and Johnson were planning to start a new life together, the bandit having died in her cabin a week before, when the honest man was born. Sonora goes to her side and takes her part; they agree that they owe her too much to deny her this. She and Johnson go off arm-in-arm, to seek a new existence together.

IL TABARRO
The Cloak

OPERA in one act by Giacomo Puccini; text by G. Adami, after the play by Didier Gold, *La Houppelande*. Première at Metropolitan, New York, on December 14, 1918, the first part of the *Trittico*

PUCCINI'S *Trittico* consists of an example of Grand Guignol, a piece which risks sentimentality, and a comedy. The action of *Il Tabarro* takes place on board a barge, whose master is Michele (*baritone*). It is moored in the Seine near Notre Dame. The curtain rises before the music begins. A swaying orchestral figure denotes the gentle movement of a boat tied up to the shore.

It is the end of the day, and workmen are finishing loading the barge. Giorgetta (*soprano*) suggests to her husband that they should be offered a drink before they go. Michele goes up to embrace her, but she only offers her cheek, and he goes discontentedly on shore. The workmen crowd round Giorgetta, and drink to her. Luigi (*tenor*) calls to a passing organ-grinder to play for them. Giorgetta says she only understands one kind of music, that which sets her feet dancing. Tinca (*tenor*) offers himself as a partner. His clumsiness becomes too much for her, and Luigi pushes him aside and takes his place, holding Giorgetta closer than is perhaps necessary. Talpa (*bass*) sees Michele coming and the dancing stops hurriedly, as the workmen disappear. Giorgetta asks Michele about arrangements for the morrow, when they are due to leave for Rouen; he will take the three – Tinca, Talpa, and Luigi – who have been helping him in Paris.

Frugola (*mezzo-soprano*), Talpa's wife, appears and talks of her occupation as a rag-picker. Talpa, Tinca and Luigi with other stevedores come up from the hold, and Tinca explains that he drinks to forget his sorrows. Luigi takes up the cue: he is right, their fate is a miserable one ('Hai ben ragione'). The solution, says Tinca, is to follow his example: drink!

Talpa and Frugola prepare to go wearily home, dreaming of the cottage in the country that they have always wanted but are never going to be able to afford. Giorgetta admits that her dream is for something quite different; she was born in the suburbs of Paris, and wishes that Michele might one day give up their nomadic existence and settle down: 'E ben altro il mio sogno.' This is one of the opera's purple passages, and Luigi joins his voice to hers as they agree that this former life was the happiest they have known. 'Ma chi lascia il sobborgo.'

Giorgetta and Luigi are alone. They listen to voices singing offstage; then Luigi moves quickly towards Giorgetta, who stops him with a gesture. They are lovers and Luigi complains of the barrier which prevents them being happy together. There is a short interruption as Michele comes up from down below. Luigi asks him to put him ashore next day at Rouen; he means to try his luck there as a labourer. Michele advises against this, and Luigi agrees to go on working for him. Michele says goodnight. Luigi's enthusiasm carries Giorgetta away, and the duet rises to a climax as Luigi agrees to come for her in an hour's time; they will use the same signal as last night, a lighted match will mean that all is safe.

Luigi departs and Giorgetta reflects sadly on the difficulties in the way of being happy in this life as Michele returns, wondering why she has not yet gone to bed. With an affectionate gesture, Michele asks why can they not renew their old love, which seems to have cooled since the death of their child: 'Perchè, perchè non m'ami più?' (Ah, why do you love me no more?) Why does she no longer come for warmth beneath his cloak?

She goes off to bed, and Michele stays on deck apparently reconciled to what she has told him. But the moment she has gone, he exclaims in fury: 'You whore!' He listens for a moment while two lovers on shore say goodnight then peers in at the window to see Giorgetta still dressed and apparently waiting: for what? What has changed her? Who is her lover? Would he could catch him and crush his life out between his hands.

He lights his pipe, unwittingly giving as he does so the signal agreed upon by Luigi and Giorgetta. Michele sees a movement.

It is Luigi. Michele's hands are round his throat as he demands an admission of guilt. He chokes Luigi, then, as Giorgetta, roused by the noise, appears, hides the body under his cloak and stands as if nothing has happened. Giorgetta comes up to him, and asks him to warm her under his cloak. With a terrible cry, he opens his cloak and reveals what is concealed beneath it.

SUOR ANGELICA
Sister Angelica

ONE act, by Giacomo Puccini; the second part of the *Trittico*. Première, New York, 1918. Suor Angelica (*soprano*) has taken the veil to expiate the scandal of her illegitimate child. Her aunt, the Princess (*contralto*), comes to the convent where Angelica has spent the last seven years alternating between re-pentance and longing for her child. The Princess tells her coldly that the child died two years ago. In a frenzy of despair Angelica prepares a poisonous draught and drinks it. She prays to the Virgin that she may not die in mortal sin, and in answer sees a vision of the Virgin leading a little child to her. A chorus sings of salvation as she dies.

GIANNI SCHICCHI

OPERA in one act by Giacomo Puccini, the third part of the *Trittico*; text by G. Forzano. Première at Metropolitan, New York, December 14, 1918.

GIANNI SCHICCHI, an historical character, has the honour of being mentioned by Dante in the Thirtieth Canto of *The Inferno*, where he appears in company with the incestuous Myrrha of Cyprus as a 'pallid, naked shape' (the connection between the two is that both counterfeited the shape of another for their own ends). The setting is Florence, 1299.

Before the curtain rises, there are a few bars of rapid music, whose impetus is however tempered to become a lament (in the minor) by the time the action begins. A chuckling figure is used to indicate that the shadow of Gianni Schicchi is already over them. The opera takes place in a bedroom in the house of Buoso Donati, who has recently died. The dead man is lying in bed, and his relations are kneeling round him. A whisper goes round; 'it is rumoured in Signa' that Buoso's wealth has been left to the monks. Simone (*bass*) tells them that if the will is already in the hands of lawyers, there is no hope for them, but if it is still in the room, something may yet be done about it.

An increasingly feverish search for the will begins. At last Rinuccio (*tenor*) holds it triumphantly aloft, but before giving it up asks for a reward for having found it, in the shape of permission to marry Lauretta (*soprano*), Gianni Schicchi's daughter (in the meanwhile, Rinuccio sends Gherardino (*alto*) off to fetch Gianni Schicchi and his daughter). They read the will in silence and, as they begin to understand its import, mounting horror; the rumour in Signa was by no means an exaggeration. Who would ever have thought, reflects Zita (*contralto*) broken-heartedly, that they would ever shed so many genuine tears when Buoso was taken from them?

A thought seems to strike them all at the same time; if only it were possible . . . They appeal to Simone but he can offer them no comfort. Rinuccio suggests that only one man can help them: Gianni Schicchi. There is furious opposition. Gherardino bursts into the room and says the man they are discussing is on his way. Rinuccio praises Schicchi's resourcefulness and cunning, and urges them to stop their spiteful gossip about his origins and lack of family tree. Has not majestic Florence herself got her roots in the countryside?

Gianni Schicchi (*baritone*) arrives with his daughter, and wonders if the long faces mean that Donati is better. He is told the sad facts of the will, and comments that this means they are disinherited. Zita repeats the word, and snaps out that he can take himself and his daughter back to where they came from; her nephew shall never marry a nobody. Schicchi denounces the snobbish money-grabbing old hag, who would sacrifice young people's happiness to her own greed. Rinuccio begs Schicchi at least to look at the will. Schicchi is reluctant, but Lauretta adds her plea to Rinuccio's and he gives way. 'O mio babbino caro' (O my beloved daddy) has become enormously popular over the years. Its lyrical charm must be taken in this context as a masterly piece of tongue-in-cheek writing.

Schicchi considers the will; 'it can't be done', he concludes, and immediately there is an outburst of sorrow from the lovers. Finally a ray of hope presents itself to Schicchi's agile mind. Lauretta is sent out on the balcony to feed the bird, and he asks if anyone apart from themselves yet knows of Buoso's death. No one, comes the answer: then there is hope, he concludes, and immediately gives orders that the funeral ornaments, etc., be removed from the room (to the sound of a muffled funeral march rhythm). Just then, a knock is heard, and in comes the doctor (*bass*), not however before Schicchi has had time to jump behind the curtains of the bed. Schicchi answers the doctor's queries in what he hopes is Donati's voice, and tells him he is feeling better. Schicchi outlines his plan: let them send for a lawyer, giving out that Buoso has had a relapse and wishes to make his will.

As Schicchi is helped into Buoso's night-clothes, each relative in turn offers him some reward if he will leave the particularly coveted things to him. He agrees to each.

When all is ready, he warns them of the danger they are collectively running. The law provides penalties for falsifying a will – exile, and the loss of the right hand for the malefactor and his accomplices. With due solemnity he bids a mock farewell to the city they all love, and the relations, seeing the force of his argument, sadly repeat the phrases after him: 'Farewell, dear Florence . . . I wave good-bye with this poor handless arm.'

A knock at the door. The lawyer (*baritone*) and the two witnesses are admitted. Schicchi answers their questions in a thin, assumed voice, and, with many comic touches, they go through the terms of the new will. The inexpensive funeral which Schicchi orders pleases the relations, and something is left in turn to each of them, until the moment arrives when there remain only the prizes . . . the villa in Florence, the sawmills at Signa, and the mule. Amidst protests he leaves each in turn to 'his devoted friend, Gianni Schicchi', and they understand only too well that they are caught in their own trap. As if to add insult to injury, he directs Zita to give twenty florins to each of the witnesses and a hundred to the lawyer.

As soon as the lawyer has gone, they all rush at Schicchi, who picks up Donati's stick and deals some shrewd blows with it as he chases them out of the house, which is now his. Lauretta and Rinuccio sing of the happiness they will know together, and Schicchi returns, saying to the audience: 'Could you imagine a better use for Buoso's money? . . . if you have enjoyed yourselves this evening, I trust you will applaud a verdict of "Extenuating Circumstances".'

TURANDOT

OPERA in three acts by Giacomo Puccini; text by Adami and Simoni, based on Gozzi's fable. Première at la Scala, Milan, on April 25, 1926.

*T*URANDOT is a version of the ancient fairy-tale of the cruel Eastern Princess who slays those who love her. The fame of Turandot's beauty has spread far and wide; her suitors come to Peking from distant lands, but before they can approach her they must submit to a trial. If they can answer three riddles they win the bride and, with her, the throne of China. But if they fail they must accept the penalty – death.

ACT I. Outside the Imperial Palace. A mandarin (*baritone*) tells the mob that the Prince of Persia has failed the trial and must lose his life. The crowd is overjoyed and looks eagerly for the moon whose rising is the signal for execution.

327

Among the crowd is Timur (*bass*), the blind banished King of Tartary, and his faithful slave girl, Liù (*soprano*). He is recognised by his son, Calaf (*tenor*), whom Timur thought dead. The joy of their reunion has its dark side: the usurpers would kill Calaf if they knew he was alone and defenceless; thus has his father kept his birth and name a secret. He tells his son of his flight, aided only by Liù. Why has she risked so much, asks the Prince; because, she says, he once smiled at her in the Palace.

The crowd urges on the executioner and his assistants to sharpen the ceremonial sword ('Gira la cote'). The moon rises, to music subtly suggestive of half-dark, half-light. As the execution procession appears, the crowd takes pity on the young Prince of Persia, calling for a reprieve. Turandot (*soprano*) herself appears and gestures that the execution shall proceed.

As the procession moves on, Calaf, struck by Turandot's beauty, declares himself a candidate for her love. In vain his father and Liù (who loves him) implore him to desist. In vain the three ministers of the Imperial Household, Ping (*baritone*), Pang (*tenor*) and Pong (*tenor*), attempt to dissuade him. Liù, in an exquisite passage, 'Signore, ascolta' (My Lord, hear me), begs him to relinquish his attempt. Calaf comforts her ('Non piangere, Liù'; Do not weep, Liù), but his determination is absolute. He strikes the gong three times to declare his suit.

ACT II. Scene i. A pavilion. Ping, Pang and Pong lament the state of China and what they see as the end of its kingly race of rulers. Heads fall like rotten apples and no one can bring peace. The music is remarkable for the consistent way in which Puccini suggests the kaleidoscopic nature of the three dignitaries.

Trumpets and the sounds of a majestic march lead to the throne room. High above all sits the old Emperor (*tenor*). Calaf is led to his presence. The Emperor addresses the unknown Prince and asks him to retire from the contest; Turandot has claimed too many victims already. He refuses. Turandot, in a celebrated aria 'In questa reggia' (Within this Palace), tells the story of her ancestress, betrayed by a foreign conqueror who sacked the city and carried her into exile, where she died of grief. It is to avenge her that Turandot has devised the trial. She, too, tells Calaf to desist and warns him that while the riddles are three, there is but one chance of escaping death. Calaf answers her somewhat rhetorically but with immense confidence, and their joint voices in their excitement soar thrillingly to a top C.

Turandot puts the riddles to Calaf: 'What is the phantom that is born every night and dies every day?' He replies, 'Hope'. 'What is it that at times is like a fever, yet grows cold when you die, that blazes up if you think of great deeds?' He answers, 'Blood'. 'What is the ice that sets you on fire?' After deliberation he guesses correctly: 'Turandot'.

Angry and fearful, Turandot begs the Emperor not to treat her like a slave given to the foreign Prince, for she would die of shame. The Emperor says his oath is sacred and the contest has been fairly won. Magnanimously the victor himself comes to the rescue: if by morning she can guess his name, he will die; otherwise, she will be his.

ACT III. Before the Palace. Turandot's orders are that no one shall sleep in Peking until the Prince's name is discovered. Calaf hears the proclamation, but is unmoved. In his celebrated aria, 'Nessun dorma' (None shall sleep), he expresses the conviction that he alone will reveal the secret; when the sun is high in the heavens Turandot will be his bride.

Ping, Pang and Pong interrupt, offering him slaves, riches, power, a safe way out of China, anything if he will but tell them his name. He refuses. Turandot's guards bring in Timur and Liù, who have been seen speaking to the young Prince. Turandot orders that Timur be tortured. Fearing for the old man's life, Liù steps forward and says that only she knows the stranger's name. But she refuses to divulge it, even under torture. She addresses Turandot: 'Tu, che di gel sei cinta' (Thou, who with ice art girdled), in an aria which is the emotional climax of the opera, Liù embodying the female virtues so conspicuously lacking in Turandot. Liù snatches a dagger from a soldier and stabs herself. There is an outburst of rage from Timur, then Liù's body is carried away followed by the crowd.[1]

Calaf upbraids Turandot with her cruelty, then he seizes her and kisses her on the mouth. Turandot's strength is gone and with it all thought of revenge, all her fierceness and courage. She weeps in the arms of Calaf: 'Del primo pianto' (The first tears). She begs Calaf to leave with his secret intact. Calaf, knowing he has won, reveals his name and offers his life.

Trumpets are heard and the scene changes to the throne room, where Turandot tells the Emperor and his courtiers that she knows the stranger's secret. 'His name is — Love'.

Of the concluding duet, only some twenty-three pages of music were found at Puccini's death. Alfano based his realisation of the final scenes on them and for a few years after the première, performances generally followed his reconstruction. In Italy however the opera was heard in a much shorter version which had the sanction of Toscanini and which was performed at la Scala after the first night, and it was not long before this was generally adopted. Curiously enough, mutterings about

---

[1] This funeral music for Liù, dying away as the crowd leaves, was the last Puccini completed. At the opera's première in Milan in 1926, as it ended Toscanini laid down his baton, turned to the audience and said: 'The opera ends here because at this point the maestro died.'

the inadequacy of Alfano's work were based on something he neither planned nor executed and it was not until a London concert performance in 1982 that Alfano's ending was restored in full and was heard as far as was known for the first time for well over half a century.

Francesco Cilea
(1866–1950)

ADRIANA LECOUVREUR

OPERA in four acts; text by Colautti, from the play by Scribe and Legouvé. Première on November 26, 1902, at the Teatro Lirico, Milan.

ACT I. Paris, 1730. The foyer of the Comédie-Française. Actors and actresses going on to the stage demand their swords, hats, coats from Michonnet (*baritone*), who complains that everyone expects him to do everything at the same time. The Prince de Bouillon (*bass*) comes in with the Abbé de Cha-zeuil (*tenor*) and greets the actors and actresses. The visitors look through at the stage, and comment on the fullness of the house; hardly surprising, says Michonnet, since both Duclos and Adriana Lecouvreur are playing tonight. Adriana (*soprano*) comes in trying over her speech. She acknowledges the cries of admiration modestly, and says that she is only the handmaid of the arts: 'Io son l'umile ancella' (I am but the humble hand-maid). The tune is heard frequently throughout the opera as a 'motto' theme for Adriana.

Michonnet is her best friend, she tells them all, and the faith-ful Michonnet bursts into tears of emotion; when all have left he admits the reason – he has been in love with Adriana ever since she joined the company. Dare he tell her now? He starts to, but she tells him that she is in love with an unknown cavalier, attached to the Count of Saxony. Michonnet leaves her alone, and in a moment her as yet unknown lover (*tenor*) is at her side. He addresses her in a passionate *arioso*: 'La dolcissima effigie' (The loveliest portrait). Adriana says she will play only for him tonight, and leaves him, giving him before she does so violets for his buttonhole.

The Prince and the Abbé come in, and the latter reads a letter which they have intercepted; it is from the Prince's wife, but because it makes an assignation for eleven o'clock in the villa of the Prince's mistress, the actress Duclos, they think it is from her. They plan to surprise the lovers.

ACT II. The Princesse de Bouillon (*mezzo-soprano*) – it is she who has arranged the assignation – is seated, listening to the voices of the night. She reflects agitatedly on the torments of love in a soliloquy: 'Acerba voluttà.' Maurizio arrives, and excuses his lateness; he was followed. She notices the violets and asks whether they had nothing to do with his lateness; he says it was for her he brought them: 'L'anima ho stanca' (My spirit is tired).

Their conversation is interrupted by the sound of a carriage outside. The Princess hides, and the Prince de Bouillon, accompanied by the Abbé, comes in to find Maurizio alone. They taunt him that he is caught, and are astonished when he threatens a duel. Why should he make so much fuss? The Prince is tired of la Duclos; why should not the Count of Saxony take her on as his mistress? Maurizio begins to understand, when, a moment later, Adriana is led in and introduced to him. This time, the astonishment is hers; the man she had thought a retainer turns out to be the Count of Saxony himself. The Prince and the Abbé go out to see that they are not kept waiting longer for supper, and Adriana and Maurizio are alone.

In a short duet they renew their passionate vows. Michonnet comes in, asking that he may speak to Duclos, as an important decision has to be made over a new role before morning. She is here, says the Abbé; Maurizio tries to silence him, but Michonnet takes the decision into his own hands and goes firmly into the room which Maurizio has tried to bar. Maurizio swears to Adriana that Duclos is not there; his appointment had to do with his political position, not with love. She believes him, and when Michonnet comes out saying it was not Duclos, and the Abbé wishes to discover the lady's identity, it is Adriana who prevents him. She says to Michonnet that she means to keep her word to Maurizio and help whoever it is.

Adriana knocks at the door and says she can save the lady inside with the aid of the key of the garden which she has in her hand. The Princess plies her with questions, and eventually admits that she loves Maurizio. Adriana proudly claims his love as her own, to the tune of her recent duet with him. The act ends as the Princess escapes just before the Prince and his followers return.

ACT III. A party is being prepared in the house of the Prince de Bouillon. The Princess wonders where she has heard the voice of her rival; she cannot place it. The guests arrive, among them Adriana, whom the Princess naturally recognises immediately, and who sings the tune originally heard to the words of 'Io son l'umile ancella'. Maurizio comes in, and is persuaded to talk about his battle experiences. A ballet entertainment has been arranged, and during its course the conversation continues, developing in the end into a battle of wits between the Princess and Adriana.

ACT IV. The scene is the same as that of Act I. Michonnet waits for Adriana who presently appears in a mood bordering on suicide. Various actors and actresses come in to congratulate her on her birthday, and presently a casket is brought in. Adriana opens it as the others leave, and sees in it violets, the very ones she had given Maurizio the previous evening, but by now shrivelled and old. She sings sadly to the violets, in whose shrivelled appearance she sees the dying of Maurizio's love for her: 'Poveri fiori'. Michonnet tries to comfort her, and smiles when he hears Maurizio's voice outside. Adriana cannot resist Maurizio's protestation of innocence, least of all when he proposes marriage to her. For a moment she tries to impress him by saying that the stage is the only throne she can ever mount, but her love is too much for her, and she and Maurizio rest happily in each other's arms.

Suddenly, she turns pale and would fall if Maurizio did not catch her. She thinks it may have something to do with the flowers which she gave Maurizio and which he returned to her, but he denies having ever done such a thing. Adriana is convulsed with pain, and for a moment does not recognise her lover. Maurizio sends for help, and Michonnet suggests the flowers may have been poisoned by a rival. After a further convulsion, Adriana dies in their arms. The Princess's revenge is complete.

Ferruccio Busoni
(1866–1924)

DOKTOR FAUST

OPERA in six tableaux; text (in German) by the composer. Première, Dresden, May 21, 1925.

B USONI drew his text from the old puppet-play of *Faust*, and he is indebted to Goethe only for the richness and nobility of the language in which he has expressed his conception.

The orchestral prelude is in the nature of an 'impressionistic study of distant bells'.[1] Towards the end of the prelude the chorus behind the scenes can be heard singing the single word

---

[1] E. J. Dent, *Ferruccio Busoni* (O.U.P.); translations also by Dent.

'Pax' (Edward Dent has aptly pointed out that this part of the work was written at Zürich in 1917). An actor steps out in front of a drop-curtain to recite the verse prologue, in which Busoni explains how the subject came to be chosen.

The sixteenth century. The scene is Faust's (*baritone*) study in Wittenberg. Wagner (*baritone*) tells him that three students are asking to see him, explaining that they have with them a re-markable book, called 'Clavis Astartis Magica'. Faust is excited; this is perhaps the book which will give him the magic power he has so long sought. The three young men, dressed in black, enter and announce themselves as students from Cracow. The students give him the book, a key with which to unlock it, and a letter which makes it his property. He offers them hospitality, but they take their leave. Wagner returns, and Faust wonders why he does not show the visitors out. He saw no one, says Wagner, and Faust begins to understand the identity of the strangers.

The second prologue. The scene is unchanged. It is night. With the key in hand which the students have given him, Faust loosens his girdle and with it draws a magic circle. Standing in-side it, he calls upon Lucifer to send down his servant. Six tongues of flame appear hovering in the air. Each of them repre-sents one of Lucifer's intimates. Faust questions the first five – how fast is each? – and dismisses each with contempt at the answer he gets. He steps out of the circle and seems reluctant to question the last spirit in case it too should disappoint him. A voice addresses him by name, and proclaims that it is as fast as human thought. 'The scene with six flames', says Edward Dent, 'is conceived musically as a set of variations on a theme; the first spirit is a deep bass, and the voices rise progressively, so that the last – Mephistopheles – is a high tenor'.[1]

Faust summons him to appear in physical shape. Of Mephis-topheles, Faust makes an unusual demand: 'Give me for the rest of my life the unconditional fulfilment of every wish; let me embrace the world, the East and the South that call me; let me understand the actions of mankind and extend them; give me Genius! give me its pain too, that I may be happy like no other – make me *free*.' But Faust has stepped outside the magic circle, and Mephistopheles will only agree to serve him at a price: after he has done Faust's bidding, Faust must agree to serve him for ever. Faust says he will serve no one, and is about to dismiss him when Mephistopheles reminds him that his creditors are at the door, that the brother of the girl he has seduced is searching for him to kill him, and that no help but the devil's will suffice

---

[1] *op. cit.*

to extricate him from his predicament. Faust with great reluctance signs the agreement.

Intermezzo. The Romanesque side-chapel of a great cathedral. The whole scene is dominated by the sound of the cathedral organ. A soldier (*baritone*), described as the 'girl's brother', is praying that he may be enabled to avenge her seduction. Mephistopheles, disguised as a monk, kneels beside the soldier, who does his best to get rid of him. Suddenly, soldiers appear in the doorway and point out the soldier as the man who killed their captain. They fall upon him and kill him, leaving Mephistopheles triumphant; sacrilege and murder – and both laid to Faust's account.

The main part of the action now begins. Scene i is the court of the Duke of Parma (*tenor*) who has just married a beautiful wife (*soprano*). The celebrations are suggested by the orchestral Cortège with which the scene starts. Having regard to the end of this scene, when Faust elopes with the Duchess, it is hardly surprising that the music for all its brilliance has a sinister tang to it and Busoni's diabolism seems to owe something to Berlioz's crackling essays in the same vein. The master of ceremonies proposes that the Duke and his Duchess shall receive Faust, by now famous for his learning, and reputedly a man of sinister reputation. Mephistopheles, on hand as Faust's herald, announces his master. The chorus expresses open admiration; the Duchess wholeheartedly concurs but the Duke has misgivings.

Faust proceeds to show his powers by turning light into darkness. He asks the Duchess what he shall do for her delectation. She would like to see Solomon, she declares; in a moment he appears before them, with the Queen of Sheba at his side. The Duke is quick to notice that the Queen has a look of the Duchess about her, and that Solomon closely resembles Faust. For her next wish, the Duchess insists that Faust shall not only perform it but divine beforehand what it is. Samson and Delilah appear. Once again the visions wear the features of the Duchess and Faust. The third apparition is conjured up by Faust of his own accord; Salome and John the Baptist, and near them the executioner. Again, the protagonists seem to have borrowed the masks of Faust and his noble hostess, and this time the executioner resembles the Duke. 'At a word from Salome, his head falls,' comments Faust. 'He must not die,' answers the Duchess eagerly. Faust is confident that the Duchess loves him.

The Duke ends the performance by inviting Faust to the ducal table, but Mephistopheles dissuades his master, warning him that the food is poisoned, and together they leave. The Duchess comes in, convinced that Faust is calling her. She sings rapturously of her love for him, then goes slowly out. Her voice can be heard calling offstage.

It is suddenly daylight. The Duke of Parma's Chaplain tells him that the Duchess has eloped with Faust on winged horses. It would be best to hush everything up and marry the sister of the Duke of Ferrara, who otherwise threatens war. The Duke accepts his Chaplain's counsel, and we see the hand raised in blessing turn to a claw.

The Sarabande, an extended and solemn orchestral piece described as a symphonic intermezzo, ushers in Scene ii: an inn at Wittenberg, where Faust sits drinking and discussing philosophy with his students. The discussion soon approaches a quarrel, and Faust does his best to calm things down. The company divides into Catholics and Protestants, and a Latin *Te Deum* is heard in violent opposition to 'Fin' feste Burg'.

Faust sits pensively aside until one of the students asks him to tell them of his amorous adventures. The orchestra *sotto voce* remembers the Cortège, and Faust starts to tell them of the most beautiful woman he ever loved, a Duchess, on her wedding day, only a year ago. Does she ever think of him now, he wonders. At that moment, in comes Mephistopheles. The Duchess of Parma, who has just died, sends something to Faust for a remembrance. At Faust's feet he places the corpse of a new-born baby, to the general horror of the company. He proceeds to tell Faust's story in unromantic terms, and sets fire to the bundle, which was only straw. From the smoke he summons Helen of Troy.

At this point Mephistopheles leaves Faust alone. Faust raves of his dream of beauty but, just as he seems about to grasp the vision, it disappears into nothing. He turns to see three dark figures demanding the return of the book, the key and the letter which went with them. Faust motions them away: he has destroyed what they are demanding from him. They tell him his hour has come.

Scene iii. A street in Wittenberg. It is winter, snow is on the ground, the Nightwatchman's voice informs the citizens that ten has struck (it is Mephistopheles in the last of his disguises). Students congratulate Wagner on his opening speech as Rector of the University, where he has succeeded Faust.

Faust comes in and sees a beggar woman, a child in her arms. As soon as he sees her, he recognises the Duchess. She gives him the child. It is dead. She disappears. Faust tries to get into the church to pray, but his way is barred by the soldier who was killed in the Romanesque chapel. Faust removes him – his power still extends to spirits – and tries to pray before a crucifix. But he cannot find words, and he sees the form of Helen of Troy upon the crucifix.

With a cry of horror he turns away, then masters himself for a supreme trial of strength. (At this point Busoni's score ends; the ending was supplied by the composer's pupil, Philipp Jarnach, working from Busoni's papers. Research some fifty years later by the English conductor Anthony Beaumont suggested that the composer had music in mind other than that selected by Jarnach and he reworked the ending of the opera with results that were first heard in Bologna in 1985 and which have been deemed an improvement on Jarnach's.) Faust lays the dead body of the child on the ground and covers it with his cloak. He throws his girdle on the ground, and steps within the circle. He exerts his will in a final effort to project his personality into the body of the child. He dies, and as the Watchman announces midnight, a naked youth with arms uplifted and bearing a green twig in his hand rises from Faust's body and walks unconcernedly through the snow. The Nightwatchman looks down at the dead body. Has this man had an accident, he asks?

Ermanno Wolf-Ferrari
(1876–1948)

I QUATTRO RUSTEGHI
The School for Fathers

THREE acts; première, Munich, 1906. Lunardo's wife Margarita (*mezzo-soprano*) and her step-daughter Lucieta (*soprano*) sadly reflect on the fun other people have. Lunardo (*bass*) and his friend Maurizio (*bass*) arrange to marry Lucieta to Maurizio's son Filipeto (*tenor*), though the two have never met. Filipeto's aunt, Marina (*soprano*), and her friend Felice (*soprano*) determine to help. While the men grumble, lamenting the good old days when women did as they were told, the women make a plan for the young couple to meet, but although they approve of each other it goes awry and Lunardo calls off the wedding. The men want to punish the women but realise they would themselves suffer. When Felice puts forward unanswerable arguments, they somewhat ungraciously concede that no harm was done, and the wedding goes ahead.

Luigi Dallapiccola
(1904–1975)

IL PRIGIONIERO
The Prisoner

OPERA in a prologue and one act; text by the composer from *La Torture par l'espérance* by Villiers de l'Isle-Adam and *La Légende d'Ulenspiegel et de Lamme Goedzak* by Charles de Coster. Première, 1949, Radio Italiana, Turin; first staged at Teatro Comunale, Florence, May 20, 1950.

IL PRIGIONIERO develops with intensity, even desperation, an aspect of the subject of liberty; the Prisoner 'goes to his death with the most atrocious doubt that can torment the human soul. and death then appears not as a supreme act of liberation but as the final annihilation of the existence and wholeness of the human personality. This doubt is at the bottom of the sense of man's tragedy; it is the most profound motivation known to man, and not even saints are immune from its temptation. Previously Dallapiccola had not experienced it, or at least had never expressed it; *Il Prigioniero* is his first tragic opera.'[1]

Dallapiccola has substituted the anonymous Prisoner for the named hero of Villiers de l'Isle-Adam's story and has added the figure of the Mother. The opera, in which sparing use is made of *Sprechstimme*, is in seven parts and lasts about fifty minutes.

Prologue. Late sixteenth century, Saragossa. The Mother (*dramatic soprano*) is waiting to visit her son in prison, and sings in a *Ballata* of the recurring dreams which haunt her sleep and in which she sees at the end of a dark cavern a figure, which terrifies her as it approaches and can be recognised as King Philip II until it changes imperceptibly into the image of Death. As the Mother's voice rises to a hysterical B flat, the offstage chorus cuts her short with 'Fiat misericordia tua, Domine, super nos' (Let thy mercy prevail, O Lord) in the first *Intermezzo Corale*.

Scene i. The curtain rises on a dark cell within the Inquisitor's Prison in Saragossa, where the Prisoner (*baritone*) is in process of telling his Mother of the torture he has suffered and of how the Gaoler (*tenor*), addressing him finally as 'Fratello' (Brother), has led him back to faith and hope and even to want to pray as in childhood.

Scene ii. The conversation is interrupted by the Gaoler who gently encourages the Prisoner to new hope with the news that

---

[1] Roman Vlad, *The Score*.

Flanders is in revolt and the great bell Roelandt, symbol of liberty, about to ring out again. In this section of the opera appear first two fundamental rows which Dallapiccola has described as 'rows of hope and liberty'. The Gaoler's description of events takes place in an *Aria in tre strofe*, and he leaves the Prisoner with the words 'There is one who watches over you . . . Have faith, brother. Sleep now . . . and hope.' The Prisoner repeats the words as if he cannot believe them, then notices that the Gaoler has left the cell door slightly ajar and rushes out.

Scene iii. A short orchestral interlude leads to the third scene, which shows the successive stages of the Prisoner's slow and agonised attempt to make his way through the underground passages of the prison to freedom. Musically the scene is divided into three *Ricercari*, and dramatically the path of the Prisoner's 'escape' is complicated by the sight of a torturer, who does not see him, the passage of a couple of monks (*tenor, baritone*) too engrossed in theological discussion to notice him, and finally by his perception of a draught of fresh air which encourages him to think he is nearing safety. He prays 'Signore, aiutami a salire!', and a moment later opens the door to hear as he thinks the great bell Roelandt.

A second *Intermezzo Corale*, sung as before by offstage chorus, provides a climax, and indeed in the score the composer instructs that its 'sonority . . . must be formidable; every spectator must feel literally swept away and drowned in the immensity of the sound. Mechanical means (loudspeakers etc.) should unhesitatingly be used if necessary to obtain this effect.'

Scene iv. The last scene finds the Prisoner in a spring garden, under a starry sky. 'Alleluja!' he sings at the prospect of freedom and moves towards a great cedar which dominates the foreground. In a kind of ecstasy, he spreads his arms towards the tree in a gesture of love towards all humanity – only for the choral background to his exuberant cries to shut off abruptly and to be succeeded by a soft 'Fratello', this time from the lips of the Grand Inquisitor (*tenor*), whose arms open as if part of the tree to embrace his captive: 'Why do you want to leave us now, on the very eve of your salvation?' As if to underline the thoughts of both protagonists, a brighter light is seen in the background, and the Prisoner comes to see that his ultimate fate is to gain salvation at the stake, just as certainly as he knows that the ultimate torture was hope. A small chorus intones, almost muffling the last whispered 'La libertà?' (Freedom?) of the Prisoner.

Gustave Charpentier
(1860–1956)

LOUISE

OPERA in four acts; text by the composer. Première, Opéra-Comique, Paris, February 2, 1900.

ACT I. After a short prelude, which reiterates a figure associated with freedom and used extensively in the course of the opera, the first scene is set in a room in the Paris tenement in which Louise and her parents live. Through the window can be seen the terrace of Julien's studio. Julien (*tenor*) is there, serenading Louise ('O coeur aimé! O coeur promis!': Oh heart I love! Oh heart so true![1]). Louise (*soprano*) comes in. It appears that she has suggested Julien should write formally to her parents asking for her hand in marriage; if they refuse, she will run away with him. But this, she insists, must be a last resort, as she hates the thought of parting with her parents on bad terms.

Louise asks Julien to tell her again how he first fell in love with her. He goes over it in detail from a description of his dreams (he is a poet) to the meeting of their realisation – herself – on the staircase: 'Depuis longtemps j'habitais cette chambre' (For quite a while I have lived as your neighbour). At the climax of his story, in comes Louise's Mother (*contralto*), who hides to listen to what is being said. The tender conversation is not without its disparaging reference to the Mother, who finally drags Louise away and shuts her in the kitchen.

Louise makes an effort to keep up appearances and arranges the supper, but her Mother mocks Louise's love for Julien. The Father (*bass*) comes in and opens the letter which Julien has left for him. Louise and her Father embrace – they are obviously very fond of one another – and the family sits down to table.

Louise takes the letter to her Father, who has left it by his plate, then goes to the kitchen to help wash up. The Father re-reads the letter, and appears to want to consider it. But the Mother is furious, and, when Louise contradicts a particularly vicious insinuation about Julien, she slaps her face, to the Father's obvious displeasure. Her Father asks Louise to read the paper to him. She starts, but dissolves in tears.

ACT II. The prelude is called 'Paris s'éveille' (Paris awakes). A street at the foot of the hill of Montmartre, outside the house where Louise works as a dressmaker. Five o'clock in the morning in April. Various derelict citizens of Paris go about their business. One of the figures in this scene is the Night-Prowler

---

[1] English translations by Edmund Tracey.

(*tenor*). He is represented as a late reveller returning home, but he is also intended to symbolise the 'Plaisirs de Paris' for which Louise and those like her long so ardently.

Julien, accompanied by some Bohemian friends, comes to wait for Louise. Street cries are heard. The girls who work at the dressmaker's begin to arrive, and they are soon followed by Louise and her Mother. Louise enters the house, but is soon dragged out of it by Julien, who questions her furiously about the answer to the letter. Will she go back on her promise to come away with him?

The dressmaker's work room. The girls are sitting round the tables, sewing and chattering. They notice that Louise has been crying, and suggest that she is in love. She denies it, but Irma (*soprano*) launches into a song on the subject of love, and soon the sound of a polka is heard from down below, immediately followed by the voice of Julien serenading Louise: 'Dans la cité lointaine' (Within the far-off city). Louise can bear the situation no longer, dashes out, and is later seen walking arm in arm with Julien down the street. Peals of laughter from the girls.

ACT III. A little garden on the side of Montmartre. Almost twilight. Louise sings her celebrated romance, 'Depuis le jour où je me suis donnée' (Oh day of joy when you became my lover). Life has changed for her since she came to live with Julien, and a new happiness has come into her existence: 'Ah, je suis heureuse!' (Ah, I am so happy!). 'Depuis le jour' with its soaring lyricism has sufficient fervour to enable it to make a considerable impression even when heard out of its context.

Louise explains that even her father, who loves her, always treated her as a little girl, and her mother beat and scolded her. Together she and Julien rejoice at the sight of the lights of Paris coming up one after another, together they sing rapturously of their freedom: 'Libres!'

There follows the curious episode of the 'Couronnement de la Muse'. Into the garden come Bohemians, followed by a crowd and a procession whose centrepiece turns out to be none other than the Night-Prowler of Act II, now dressed up as the King of the Fools. Louise is crowned Queen of Bohemia and Muse of Montmartre. But the jollity is interrupted when a sad figure is seen standing apart. It is Louise's Mother. Louise's Father is very ill and desperately anxious to see her again. Julien eventually agrees that Louise may go home, the Mother having promised that she shall return to him as soon as she wishes.

ACT IV. The scene is the same as Act I. Louise is still with her family. Her Father is just recovering from his illness, but he has become a grumbler: 'Les pauvres gens peuvent-ils être heureux?' (How can the poor know what happiness is?) He complains of the ingratitude of children, who would throw off the authority of those who are prepared to die for them.

The significance of what he says is not lost on Louise. But when her Mother says that they cannot think of letting her go back to Julien, in spite of their promise, she says wanly that he who laughs last laughs best. She says good night to her Father, who kisses her lovingly and long and takes her in his arms. She draws away unresponsively, but he calls her to him, puts her on his knee as if she were still a child, and sings a *berceuse* to her: 'Reste . . . repose-toi . . . comme jadis toute petite' (Stay here . . . stay here and rest . . . as once you did when you were little).

Louise's distress is too poignant to be ignored for long. She reminds them of their promise, and then quietly but feelingly asserts her right to be free: 'Tout être a le droit d'être libre' (All men have a right to their freedom). The sound of a waltz she heard during her brief period of freedom – the voice of Paris itself – calls to Louise. She responds passionately and invokes the name of the city to set her free. At last her Father loses his temper completely, orders her from the house, and even chases her round the room, until she runs out of the door. His anger spent, the Father calls pitiably for Louise. Then he shakes his fist at the city, and the curtain falls on his cry: 'O Paris!'

Claude Debussy
(1862–1918)

Pelléas et Mélisande

Opera in five acts; text from Maeterlinck's play of the same name. Première, Opéra-Comique, Paris, April 30, 1902.

Act i. Scene i. In a forest, Golaud (*baritone*), grandson of King Arkel, while hunting has lost his way following a wild boar and come to a place unknown to him. There he sees a girl sitting by a spring. She behaves like a person isolated from the world. Golaud succeeds in inducing Mélisande (*soprano*) – she at last tells him her name – to follow him.

Scene ii. A room in the castle. Geneviève (*alto*), mother of Golaud and Pelléas, is reading to the aged, almost blind King (*bass*) a letter which Golaud has written to his half-brother: 'Voici ce qu'il écrit à son frère Pelléas' (This is what he has written to his brother Pelléas[1]). From this letter we learn that

---

[1] English translations by Hugh Macdonald.

Golaud has already been married for six months to the mysterious Mélisande. He loves her, but knows no more about her today than he did at first in the woods. So he fears that his grandfather may not forgive him for this union and asks Pelléas (*tenor* or *high baritone*) to give him a sign that the King is ready 'to honour the stranger as his daughter'. Otherwise he will steer his ship to a remote land and never return home. King Arkel pardons Golaud and commissions his grandson Pelléas to give his brother the sign agreed upon. Pelléas has asked him if he may leave to say farewell to a dying friend; but Arkel reminds him that his duty is to await his brother's return, and tend his father who lies sick above them.

Scene iii. Before the castle. Geneviève seeks to calm Mélisande's distress at the gloominess of the world into which she has wandered. Pelléas too is there. Together they watch a ship sail away out to sea.

ACT II. Scene i. A fountain in the park. Pelléas and Mélisande go together to this thickly shaded spot in the heat of the day. Water attracts her wonderfully. Pelléas bids her take care: 'Prenez garde de glisser' (Take care not to slip). Because she cannot reach the water, she is tempted to play with the ring that Golaud sent her. It slips from her hand to the sound of a harp *glissando*, and sinks.

Scene ii. There must have been some peculiar condition attached to the ring. At the same hour that it fell in the fountain Golaud's horse shied so that he fell and now lies injured in bed. Mélisande is taking care of him. She tells Golaud that she is oppressed by foreboding, she does not know what it is. Golaud tries to comfort her; he seizes her hands and sees that the ring is missing. He drives her out into the night to look for it. Pelléas will help her find it.

Scene iii. Before a grotto in the rocks. Mélisande has deceived Golaud by telling him that the ring has slipped from her hand into the sea. So Pelléas must now lead her to this grotto in order that she may know at least the place in which she can claim that she lost the ring – a dreadful place in which the shadow of death stalks. There they see three mysterious bearded beggars.

ACT III. Scene i. A tower in the castle. At the window of the tower Mélisande is standing combing her hair that she has let down: 'Mes longs cheveux' (My hair's so long). Pelléas comes to say farewell; early the next morning he is going away. So Mélisande will at least once more reach out her hand to him that he may press it to his lips. Mélisande leans forward so far her long hair falls over Pelléas's head and fills him with passionate feelings. Their words become warmer – then Golaud comes near and reproves their 'childishness'. He goes off with Pelléas.

The whole scene, from the ravishing harp sound of the opening until the appearance of Golaud, is no more and no less than a passionate love scene (although no word of love is spoken) – but with what sensitivity has Debussy set it!

Scene ii. In the vault under the castle. Like a gloomy menace Golaud leads Pelléas into these underground rooms where the breeze of death blows. Seized with shuddering they leave.

Scene iii. On the terrace at the entrance to the vault. Golaud warns Pelléas to keep away from Mélisande.

Scene iv. Before the castle. Jealousy devours Golaud's heart. So now he lifts up his little son Yniold (*soprano*), offspring of his first marriage, to spy through a window on the intimacy of Pelléas and Mélisande. The child cannot tell him of anything improper, yet Golaud senses that there is something between the couple. Dramatically, this is one of the tensest scenes of the whole score, and Golaud's agony and impotence are made more apparent by the innocence and fright of Yniold as he reports what he sees.

ACT IV. Scene i. In a room in the castle Pelléas and Mélisande meet. This evening he must see her. She promises to go to the old fountain in the park where she lost the ring.

Scene ii. The old King Arkel enters the room. He has taken Mélisande to his heart. He feels that the young wife is unhappy. Golaud also enters. The sight of his wife, who appears the picture of innocence, irritates him so much ('Une grande innocence': Nothing but innocence in them) that finally in a mad rage he throws her on her knees and drags her across the room by her hair. Only Arkel understands and pities.

Scene iii. By the old spring in the park. There is a feeling of disaster in the air. Only little Yniold does not feel it. He has dropped something behind a stone and is looking for it. He catches sight of some sheep being driven past and listens to them as they go. (This scene is often omitted in performance.)

Scene iv. It is already growing dark when Mélisande goes to Pelléas. And yet in their farewell the couple clearly see what has caused their condition, and there comes over them something like the affirmation of death and the joy of dying. Fate shuts the gates of the castle upon them; like fate they see Golaud coming. They rejoice in the idea of death. Pelléas falls by Golaud's sword, Mélisande flees from her husband into the night.

ACT V. A room in the castle. Mélisande lies in bed. Arkel, Golaud and the physician (*bass*) are conversing softly in the room. Mélisande is not dying from the insignificant wound Golaud has given her. Perhaps her life will be saved. But Golaud's remorse cannot be calmed: 'J'ai tué sans raison! . . . Ils s'étaient embrassés comme des petits enfants . . . Je l'ai fait malgré moi' (I have killed without cause! . . . They were kissing like children, just playing games . . . An uncontrollable impulse).

Mélisande awakes as if from a dream. Desperately Golaud begs her pardon, and asks for the truth. He is willing to die too, but before his death he wants to know whether she has betrayed him with Pelléas. She denies it. Golaud presses her so forcibly and makes her suffer so that she is near death. It is not possible to bring her back now. Arkel brings her the child she has borne and offers the last services for the dying woman, to make the way free for her soul escaping from earthly pain and the burden of the tears of persons left behind.

Maurice Ravel
(1875–1937)

L'Heure Espagnole
The Spanish Hour

ONE act; première, Paris, 1911. On the clock-maker Torquemada's (*tenor*) regular day for attending to the clocks in Toledo, his wife Concepción (*soprano*) enjoys her love affairs in freedom. Ramiro (*baritone*) arrives to have his watch fixed, and to Concepción's annoyance is asked to wait. He offers to carry a heavy clock to her room. Her lover Gonzalve (*tenor*) appears and is hidden inside the clock which Ramiro then unwittingly takes upstairs. A similar performance takes place when Inigo (*bass*), another admirer, comes in; neither lover is satisfactory, and Concepción falls for Ramiro. Torquemada returns and, finding three lovers, reckons there is safety in numbers. The opera ends with a sparkling quintet.

L'Enfant et les Sortilèges
The Child and the Magic

OPERA in two parts by Maurice Ravel; text by Colette. Première, Monte Carlo, March 21, 1925.

COLETTE'S libretto originally began as a scenario for a ballet, which she sent to the director of the Opéra in Paris; he in turn sent it on to Ravel, who was then serving with the French Army at the front. He began work on it in the summer of 1920 and finished – with a few interruptions – in 1924.

Scene i. A room in an old Norman country house, giving on to a garden. Big armchairs, a grandfather clock, wallpaper with shepherds and shepherdesses on it. A round cage with a squirrel in it hangs near the window. Remains of a fire in the grate, kettle singing. The cat also singing. It is afternoon. The Child (*mezzo-soprano*), aged six or seven, is sitting at his lessons.

His mother (*contralto*) comes in and is vexed that he has done nothing but make a blot on the table-cloth. When she asks him to promise to work, the child puts out his tongue. She leaves him saying he will be left alone in the room until suppertime as a punishment. The Child suddenly loses control, and dashes about the room indulging in an orgy of destruction. He smashes the cup and teapot, pricks the pet squirrel with his pen, pulls the cat's tail, flourishes the poker, stirs up the fire, and upsets the kettle into it to produce clouds of steam and ashes. Then, brandishing the poker like a sword, he swoops on the wallpaper and pulls great strips of it off the wall. He opens the grandfather clock, swings on the pendulum, and finally makes a dash at his books and tears them up with a scream of delight. All this takes place in a few seconds.

From now until the end of the opera, the Child is going to realise the consequences of his destructive actions, and in a way that is likely to astonish him more than any other – from the objects of his temper themselves. He sinks into a chair (*basse chantante*), but, to his infinite surprise, it moves slowly away from him, to the creaking sound of a contra bassoon, and, bowing gravely to a Louis XV chair (*soprano*), leads her in a stately but grotesque dance. They say that they will never again have to put up with the weight and the pranks of the naughty child they have had to stand for so long. The Settle, Sofa, Ottoman, and Wicker Chair join in.

Next comes the mutilated clock (*baritone*), striking uncontrollably and complaining bitterly of the treatment which has deprived him, literally, of his balance. From the floor come the voices of the Chinese cup (*mezzo-contralto*) and teapot (*tenor*) ('Wedgwood noir' says the score): 'How's your mug? Rotten . . . better had . . . come on! . . . I punch, Sir, I punch your nose . . . I boxe you, I marm'lad you.' The words are nonsense, compounded from English and the more nebulous orientalisms such as 'Mah-jong', 'kong-kong', 'Harakiri' and even 'Caskara'; the music, a brilliant parody of the foxtrot of American jazz (1920's style), is justly one of the most famous moments of the score.

The Child goes towards the fire (*soprano léger*), which spits in his face and announces to coloratura music that warmth is only for those who are good; bad children will be burnt. The fire pursues the Child round the room until it succumbs quietly to the ashes, which dance with it for a moment and then extinguish it altogether. There is a procession, half comic, half pathetic, of the shepherds and shepherdesses from the torn wallpaper, after which the Fairy Princess (*soprano léger*) rises out of the torn picture book. The Child was half-way through her story, but now that the book is torn he will never know how it will all turn out.

There is just a chance that the end of the story may be amongst the pages which lie round his feet, and he looks for it, but in vain. All he can find are the torn sheets of an arithmetic book, from which emerges an old man (*tenor*) covered with arithmetical symbols and crowned with a Pi. He and his platoon of figures torment the Child with quick-fire arithmetical nonsense. The Child is whirled into the dance, and sinks down exhausted.

He does not notice the black cat (*baritone*) come out from under the armchair, yawn, and start to wash itself. The Child says wearily that he supposes it too has acquired the habit of speech. The cat signs that it has not, and spits at him, before going off to the window, where a white cat (*mezzo-soprano*) has appeared. Now comes the famous Cats' love duet, which caused such a storm at the first performance. The 'Mi-inhou' and 'Mornaou', which Colette has chosen to represent cat's speech, are set to exact notes and marked 'nasal'. The animals work themselves up to a frenzy of excitement before bounding out of the window into the garden, followed hesitatingly by the Child.

Scene ii. At this point the stage directions require that the room walls fall away, the ceiling disappear, and the Child with the two cats be transported into the garden. The short and very beautiful orchestral interlude is for strings; piccolo and Swanee whistle imitate bird noises and the whole atmosphere is one of pure moonlight and magic. A chorus of frogs can be heard from behind the scenes, and the Child is delighted to be out in the garden he loves so well.

But even here he is not to escape his accusers. The tree (*bass*) complains about the cuts made in his flanks the day before, and the Child leans his cheek against the tree in sympathy. A dragonfly (*mezzo-soprano*) flashes across the scene calling for a mate she has lost, and who is now pinned to the wall in the Child's room. A nightingale (*soprano léger*) is heard against the background of the frogs' chorus, and a bat complains that his mate was killed by the Child, leaving the family helpless. Frogs come out of the water and sit round the edge until the pool is ringed with them. One (*tenor*) lays its head on the Child's knee, and is immediately admonished by a squirrel, whose mate now languishes in a cage in the Child's room. The squirrel makes a moving plea for freedom.

The Child realises that the animals are happy all round him, and begins to feel lonely with no one paying any attention to him. Suddenly he cries out 'Maman'. Immediately the atmosphere of peace is broken. Some animals disappear, but those who stay behind form a menacing chorus. Each has a grudge to pay off, and together they rush at the Child, catch hold of him, buffet him, turn him round, shove him. In their excitement, they turn on each other, forgetting the Child.

He notices a little squirrel who has been wounded limping towards him. The Child takes a ribbon and binds up the squirrel's paw, watched by the other animals, who exclaim in amazement at the Child's kindly action. What can they do to help him, now that he looks so helpless and lonely? They try to call 'Maman', thinking that will help the Child, whom they now know to be good and kind. The animals help him up and lead him to the house whose windows have just been lit up. The opera ends as the Child calls simply and confidently 'Maman'.

Francis Poulenc
(1899–1963)

LES MAMELLES DE TIRÉSIAS
The Breasts of Tiresias

OPÉRA-BOUFFE in a prologue and two acts; text by Guillaume Apollinaire. Première, Opéra-Comique, Paris, June 3, 1947.

AFTER a quiet orchestral introduction the theatre director *(baritone)* appears in front of the curtain and appeals directly to the audience in calm, measured, serious tones. His description of what the audience is going to see touches frenzy before returning to the seriousness of the start and the work's motto: 'Et faîtes des enfants, vous qui n'en faisiez guère' (You must make babies now as you never have before).

ACT I. 1910. The main square of Zanzibar, on the Riviera, complete with houses, café, a view of the port. The charming and energetic Thérèse *(soprano)* announces herself feminist, refuses to submit to her husband's *(tenor)* desires, wants to be a soldier. His cries from the house – 'Donnez-moi du lard' (Let me have my meat) – only inspire her to a denunciation of love and further proclamations of ambition. At this moment her breasts seem anxious to escape from their owner, she opens her blouse (on a top C) and they escape, two children's balloons attached to her now only by the strings. After celebrating their loss and their beauty in a slow waltz, she reflects that they are a cause of sin and so – 'Débarrassons-nous de nos mamelles' (Now I shall get rid of my attractions). She feels her beard sprouting, and congratulates herself on the discovery in a brisk *paso doble*.

The husband emerges, a bouquet of flowers in his hands, assumes that what appears to be a stranger in Thérèse's clothing has murdered his wife, but is disillusioned by Thérèse's announcement that she has ceased to be his wife and will be in future known as Tirésias. Thérèse-Tirésias disappears into the house and drum rolls accompany the descent from the window of intimate household objects, explained deprecatingly by the husband as 'the piano', 'the violin'.

As the husband returns to his house, a polka starts up and a couple of drunks, Presto (*baritone*) the fat one and Lacouf (*tenor*) the thin one, come out of the café. They have been gambling and in the friendliest possible way they quarrel, arrange a duel and happily shoot each other. It is left to Thérèse, now dressed in the height of masculine fashion, and her husband, disguised as a rather untidy housewife, to mourn the loss of these worthy citizens.

Quick music and a drum roll precede the appearance of the husband and the gendarme (*baritone*), the latter of whom theoretically pursues crime but prefers paying court to the husband, whom he takes for a female, to the latter's undisguised mockery.

In an arietta, the husband explains to the gendarme that he feels it essential that Zanzibar should have children and, if women refuse to provide them, he will.

The first act ends with a scene of considerable vivacity, a newspaper-seller (*mezzo-soprano*) denouncing a hoax, the husband assuring the gendarme that he has managed, single-handed as it were, to produce children; even Lacouf and Presto reappear apparently full of life, the chorus meanwhile providing a solemn chorale against which the liveliness of the others produces a suitable contrast. For the rapid *stretta à la Rossini*, the stage direction has the curtain descend until only the singers' legs are visible.

The Ravel-like entr'acte has a solemn opening before six mixed couples from the chorus enter and dance a kind of farcical gavotte in front of the curtain, a manoeuvre interrupted only when strange noises are heard coming from the orchestral pit – the cries of infant children.

ACT II. The scene filled with cradles, and in front of them writing material and a gigantic pot of glue. The husband is delighted with his success – forty thousand new children in a single day! – and the voices of the children echo their father's self-satisfaction. In comes a journalist (*tenor*), demanding to know the husband's secret and presuming that he must be very rich to afford so large a family. Not at all, returns the husband, but they should be able to support him once they are grown up. He already has one called Joseph whose novel has to date sold 600,000 copies. A vast tome descends in front of the journalist who starts, with the greatest possible difficulty, to read it, then, impressed by the evidence of the husband's income, tries to touch him for a small loan.

The husband seems to read (unaccompanied) a moral from the whole affair: the more children you have, the richer you'll be. He will start by making a journalist, but the eighteen-year-old (*baritone*) who results from his curious activities starts to blackmail him, so that the boy's departure elicits no more comment than a quick 'That one worked out badly'. He is contemplating further creative activities when he bumps into the gendarme, who remonstrates about the addition of over 40,000 inhabitants to the population of Zanzibar.

The Cartomancienne (fortune-teller) offers to tell everyone's future. She counsels fecundity, severely condemning the gendarme, who appears to be sterile. His attempt to avenge his honour by attacking her ends in his strangling by the fortune-teller, who reveals herself, when the husband tries to restrain her, as none other than Thérèse. The husband is delighted and even the gendarme revives. The only trouble is that her figure seems, much to her husband's dismay, no more ample than it had in her recent masculine manifestation. She makes light of the problem and, as the sun sinks and the scene lights up for night, the husband joins her in a lazy, amorous waltz. The action ends with a *stretta* and then the moral: 'Ecoutez, O Français, les leçons de la guerre, et faîtes des enfants, vous qui n'en faisiez guère.'

DIALOGUES DES CARMÉLITES

OPERA in three acts by Francis Poulenc; libretto by Emmet Lavery from the drama by Georges Bernanos, itself inspired by a novel of Gertrude von Le Fort and a scenario of Rev. Fr. Bruckberger and Philippe Agostini. Première, January 26, 1957, at la Scala, Milan.

A CT I. Scene i. The Library in the Paris house of the Marquis de la Force, April 1789. The Marquis (*baritone*) is resting, but the Chevalier (*tenor*), his son, bursts in; rumour has it there is a mob about and his sister Blanche is out late in the carriage. The Marquis loses his calm as he remembers nearly twenty years before when his pregnant wife was jolted in her carriage by a mob and died in giving birth to Blanche (*soprano*). The

Chevalier is particularly worried because of Blanche's impressionable, not to say morbid, nature, but when she comes in it is to say that the long and exhausting service that morning has tired her and she will go to bed. A moment later her scream is heard from the passage – she has unexpectedly caught sight of a lamp carried by a servant. It is more than a momentary fear that the shock releases in Blanche, and she formally and with no sign of panic asks her father's permission to join a Carmelite convent; how else is someone as nervous as she is to find salvation?

Scene ii. The Parlour of the Carmelite Convent at Compiègne a few weeks later. The aged Prioress (*contralto*) on one side of a screen interviews Blanche who sits on the other. When Blanche professes to be attracted even by the privations of the Order, the Prioress emphasises that prayer is the sole reason for the Carmelites' existence. Under her questioning Blanche breaks down in tears, but the Prioress softens towards her and asks her whether she has already chosen her religious name in case she is admitted to the Order; Blanche answers 'Soeur Blanche de l'Agonie du Christ'.

Scene iii. In the Convent. Blanche and Constance (*soprano*), now novices, are busy with household work. Constance prattles away about her country upbringing, until Blanche snubs her levity with the reminder that the Prioress is gravely ill. Constance's reaction is to try to get Blanche to join her in offering their lives to God in place of that of the old Prioress, but Blanche rejects the idea in an agony of fear. Constance has dreamed that she and Blanche will die together.

Scene iv. The cell of the Prioress. The Prioress on her deathbed is obsessed with fear of death, and the Assistant Prioress, Mother Marie (*mezzo-soprano*), tries to give her strength. The Prioress entrusts to her the care of Blanche, for whom the Prioress feels a special responsibility. Sister Blanche comes in to say goodbye and is admonished to preserve her innocence of character through trust in God. The Prioress asks for more drugs, if only to be strong enough to bid a public farewell to her charges. She sees visions of an altar desecrated, the chapel laid waste, and nothing Mother Marie can do will restrain the flood of words that pours from her. Mother Marie sends a message that the Sisters cannot be allowed to see the Prioress, who is powerless any more to impose her will. Blanche returns, the Prioress tries to speak to her, but falls dead.

ACT II. Scene i. The Chapel of the Convent. The body of the old Prioress lies in state. Blanche makes a half-hearted attempt to pray and then rushes towards the door; here she is met by Mother Marie, who leads her towards her cell; let her not talk about her failure – tomorrow it will fill her with sorrow, at present it can only cause her shame.

Blanche and Constance are taking flowers to the grave of the old Prioress. They hope that Mother Marie will be chosen to succeed her and Constance wonders at the difficulty the old Prioress had found in dying; one would have said she had been given the wrong death by mistake. Perhaps someone when it comes to their turn to die will find a better death than they deserve.

Scene ii. The Hall of the Chapter House. It is not Mother Marie who is chosen Prioress but a certain Madame Lidoine (*soprano*), from outside. She speaks to the nuns in an aria. She leaves Mother Marie to finish the address, after which in a beautiful ensemble the nuns offer up an 'Ave Maria'.

The bell at the side door rings. It is the Chevalier de la Force asking to see his sister before he goes abroad.

Scene iii. The Parlour of the Convent. With a screen between them and with Mother Marie in the background, the Chevalier accuses Blanche of staying in the Convent because of her fear of fear; Blanche forbids him to leave on a note of anger.

Scene iv. The Sacristy of the Convent. The Father Confessor (*tenor*) has just finished saying what he tells the nuns is his last Mass. The priesthood has been proscribed and he must go into hiding. When Constance asks rhetorically if there are no men left in France, the Prioress says, 'When there are not priests enough, there will be plenty of martyrs, and the balance of grace will thus be restored.' Mother Marie seizes on her words: it is the duty of the daughters of Carmel to give their lives so that France may once again have priests. The Mother Superior firmly corrects her: it is not for them to decide if their names shall one day be inscribed amongst the martyrs.

The bell rings again violently, and a mob pours in. Two commissars announce the expulsion of the nuns from the Convent. The first Commissar takes Mother Marie aside and reveals he was once a Sacristan and is at heart a true servant of the Church. He leads the mob out.

ACT III. Scene i. The ruined Chapel of the Convent. As the Prioress is away, Mother Marie in the presence of the Father Confessor addresses the assembled nuns. She proposes that together they take a vow of martyrdom to save the Order from harm. They vote; there is one voice against. Immediately Constance, to save Blanche from embarrassment, says that the vote was hers: she will retract, and thus they will be unanimous. Blanche and Constance as the youngest go first to take the vow; no sooner has Blanche passed the Father Confessor than she takes advantage of the general confusion to escape.

Outside the Convent, an Officer congratulates the nuns, who

leave in civilian costume, on their discipline and public spirit, but advises them that they will be watched. The Prioress wants to warn the Father Confessor against coming to celebrate Mass; it would be too dangerous for them all. Mother Marie reacts with smouldering violence: how can they reconcile this caution with their vow? The Prioress says that each is responsible before God as an individual, but she herself must answer for them all and she is old enough to know how to keep her accounts.

Scene ii. The ruined library in the Paris house of the Marquis de la Force. Blanche in peasant costume is cooking when Mother Marie comes in to tell her that she has come to fetch her. Blanche tells Mother Marie that her father was guillotined and she is now alone. Mother Marie gives her an address, where she will be safe and where she (Mother Marie) will wait for her until the following night. Blanche says that she cannot go, but Mother Marie is quietly confident.

In a street near the Bastille, Blanche hears that they have arrested all the members of the Convent at Compiègne.

Scene iii. The prison of the Conciergerie. The Prioress tries to comfort the nuns, saying she will consider herself bound by their vow of martyrdom, though it was made in her absence. Constance is convinced that Blanche will return, because of a dream she has had. The Gaoler announces the findings of the Tribunal: it is death for each one of them. The Mother Superior places them once more under an oath of obedience and gives them her blessing.

In a dark corner of a street, Mother Marie hears of the death sentence from the Father Confessor. She must die with them, she says, but the Father Confessor suggests that this may not be the will of God.

Scene iv. In the Place de la Révolution the scaffold is prepared and the crowd watches as the Prioress leads in her little band of fourteen Carmelite followers. Singing the 'Salve Regina', one after another they mount the scaffold, and each time the guillotine drops there is one voice the fewer to sustain the singing. When Sister Constance is alone, she sees Blanche in the crowd, stops for an instant, then goes with renewed confidence to her death. Blanche takes up the chant, and with a new serenity follows her sisters to accomplish the vow they swore together.

LA VOIX HUMAINE
The Human Voice

ONE act, by Francis Poulenc; première, Paris, 1959. A woman is abandoned by her lover. She has tried to commit suicide after he has told her that he is getting married next day. This is the last time she will talk to him on the telephone. She veers from hysteria to calm, running through every emotion. Fear, incoherence, suffering, lies fill her conversation, but the essential truths are never spoken; finally the receiver drops lifelessly to the ground and the connection is broken.

Igor Fedorovich Stravinsky
(1882–1971)

LE ROSSIGNOL
The Nightingale

OPERA in three acts; text by the composer and S. Mitousoff after Hans Andersen's fairy-tale. Première, Paris, Opéra, May 26, 1914.

ACT I. A forest on the seashore at night. The Fisherman (*tenor*) on his boat is waiting to hear the Nightingale (*soprano*) which delights him every night. After a while the Nightingale begins to sing. Other interested spectators arrive – the Emperor's Chamberlain (*bass*), a Bonze (priest; *bass*) and the Emperor's Cook (*mezzo-soprano*), the latter bringing her confederates and other courtiers to give the Nightingale a formal invitation to court to sing before the Emperor of China. The Nightingale remarks that her voice is far sweeter in the forest than in the palace. Since, however, the Emperor wills it otherwise, the Emperor shall be obeyed. The bird alights on the hand of the Cook, who takes it to the palace while the Fisherman continues to sing the bird's praises.

ACT II. The act opens with an entr'acte (with chorus) during which the stage is hidden by veils. The chorus inquires of the cook (who has been appointed 'Grand Cordon Bleu') about the Nightingale. The Cook describes the little bird, whose songs fill the eye with tears. As the veils rise the Chamberlain announces the Emperor (*baritone*), who arrives in great state with the Nightingale. At a sign from the Emperor the Nightingale begins to sing and the Emperor is so charmed that he offers the Nightingale the order of the Golden Slipper. But the bird requires no other honour than that of having charmed the great monarch. Three envoys from the Emperor of Japan offer the Emperor a mechanical bird which also sings. As soon as the mechanical nightingale's song begins the real one flies away. The Emperor, affronted, condemns it to perpetual banishment. The voice of the Fisherman is heard again as the act ends.

ACT III. The Emperor is ill and Death (*alto*) sits at the foot of his bed wearing the imperial crown and grasping his standard. The ghosts of his good and his bad deeds crowd round the bed. The Emperor calls for his musicians. The Nightingale answers the call. It has come to banish ghosts and to sing of the coming dawn. Even Death is persuaded by the loveliness of the song to give back the crown and the standard. The Nightingale's charm has conquered disease, and as the courtiers arrive in solemn procession to salute the ruler whom they expect to find dead, the sun floods the room with light, Death disappears and the Emperor rises from his bed and wishes his courtiers a good morning. The Fisherman bids all acknowledge in the song of the Nightingale the voice of heaven.

Le Rossignol was begun in 1908 just before the death of Stravinsky's teacher, Rimsky-Korsakov, but interrupted after the completion of the first act by the commissioning by Diaghilev of *The Firebird*. A request from the newly founded Free Theatre of Moscow to complete the opera led, in 1913, to a resumption of work, but now, of course, by a much maturer composer than the comparative beginner of 1908. The styles of Act I and Acts II and III are, however, not so sharply contrasted that unity is ruled out, particularly taking into account the fact that Act I is little more than a lyrical prologue to the action of the two succeeding acts; but some critics have found a discrepancy.

Stravinsky made a symphonic poem out of material from the opera (*Le Chant du Rossignol*), using for the first part the prelude and Chinese March from Act II; for the second, the song of the real Nightingale and music associated with the clockwork model from Japan, followed by the Fisherman's song; and for the third, a reworking of music from Act III entitled 'Illness and Recovery of the Emperor of China'.

OEDIPUS REX

OPERA-ORATORIO in two acts by Igor Stravinsky; text by Jean Cocteau after Sophocles, translated into Latin by J. Daniélou. Première, Paris, May 30, 1927 (in concert); on stage, Vienna, 1928.

THE action is continuous, although divided into two acts. It is put forward in the shape of six tableaux, with a minimum of action (the characters are directed to give the impression of living statues), and that explained beforehand in the language of the audience by a narrator. The text is in Latin.

ACT I. i. The Narrator sets the scene for the audience; of Oedipus he says: 'At the moment of his birth a snare was laid for him – and you will see the snare closing'. In the opening chorus, 'Kaedit nos pestis',[1] the men of Thebes lament the plague which is destroying the inhabitants of the town. They beg their king, Oedipus (*tenor*), to help them in their affliction. This he promises to do.

ii. Creon (*bass-baritone*), Jocasta's brother, who has been sent to Delphi to consult the oracle, returns. In an aria, he reports that the god has revealed that Laius's murderer still lives on in Thebes, undetected and unpunished. He must be discovered. Oedipus answers that he himself, with his skill in solving riddles, will track down the murderer.

iii. The chorus prays to Minerva, Diana and Phoebus (or Athene, Artemis, and Apollo, as they would be in Greek), and welcomes Tiresias (*bass*), whom Oedipus has decided to consult. Tiresias is blind, and referred to by the Narrator as 'the fountain of truth', but at first he refuses to answer the King's questions. Oedipus taunts him, and he makes it clear that he will hold nothing more back; the King's assassin is a king! Oedipus is furious at the implication behind the words, and suggests that Creon and Tiresias are in league to oust him from the throne: 'Stipendarius es' he snarls at Tiresias. The aria dies away in silence, and is succeeded by a magnificent chorus of greeting and praise to Queen Jocasta (*mezzo-soprano*): 'Gloria!'

Act II begins with a reprise of the sonorous 'Gloria' chorus.

iv. Jocasta is now seen on the stage. She has come, says the Narrator, attracted by the dispute of her husband and her brother. How can they raise their voices thus in anger in the stricken city? Oracles, she says, are accustomed to deceive those who consult them ('Mentita sunt oracula'); did they not predict that her former husband, Laius, would be killed by his own son, and was he not in fact murdered by robbers at the cross-roads ('trivium') between Daulia and Delphi? The chorus takes up the word 'trivium', but its repetition has the effect of filling Oedipus with horror. In a duet with Jocasta he explains that on his way from Corinth to Thebes he himself killed a stranger at that very cross-roads. Jocasta makes an attempt to reassure him, but it is of little avail.

v. The messenger (*bass-baritone*) steps forward to inform Oedipus that King Polybus is dead, and that Oedipus, so far from being his son, was only adopted by him. The messenger

---

[1] The spelling used is often onomatopoeic, to ensure uniform pronunciation.

goes on to tell how Oedipus as a baby was rescued by a shepherd after he had been abandoned on the mountain side and then handed over to King Polybus. The shepherd (*tenor*) corroborates his evidence, and his words so overwhelm the Queen that she disappears from the scene, convinced and horrorstricken by what she has heard. Oedipus, however, thinks she is merely ashamed of his apparently lowly birth, and it is only after the messenger and the shepherd unite to accuse him of parricide and incest that he is conscious of his crime and its enormity. The chorus repeats the words of the King's accusers, after which shepherd and messenger withdraw. With a quiet dignity that has not been in evidence in his previous utterances, Oedipus resigns himself to acknowledging the truth. On the words 'Lux facta est', he disappears.

vi. The messenger reappears, and the Narrator explains that the audience is about to hear the monologue: 'The divine Jocasta is dead'; he describes how she has hanged herself and how Oedipus has pierced his eyeballs with the golden pin Jocasta wore. He bids farewell to Oedipus – Oedipus whom his people loved. The great scene in which the messenger and the chorus bewail Jocasta's suicide ('Divum Jocastae caput mortuum!') brings the work to its emotional climax. As the messenger disappears, and Oedipus is seen with his pierced eyes, the chorus comments gently on his broken condition and bids him a last farewell.

THE RAKE'S PROGRESS

OPERA in three acts and an epilogue by Igor Stravinsky; text by W. H. Auden and Chester Kallman. Première, Venice Festival, September 11, 1951.

A CT i. Scene i. After a short prelude, the scene opens to show the garden of Trulove's house in the country. It is spring. Anne (*soprano*) and her sweetheart Tom Rakewell (*tenor*) are rejoicing in the season which seems made for their love ('The woods are green'), and Trulove (*bass*) expresses the hope that his fears about Tom's future may prove unfounded. Anne goes indoors and Trulove tells Tom that he has secured for him the offer of a city position. When Tom declines, he comments that his daughter may choose a poor husband, but he will see to it she does not marry a lazy one.

Tom is scornful. He has other plans, and proposes to rely primarily on the goddess of fortune. 'Since it is not by merit we rise or we fall' is the burden of his aria, whose vigorous expression suggests that Tom underestimates his own energies.

He breaks off: 'I wish I had money.' Immediately a figure appears at the garden gate, and asks for Tom Rakewell. It is Nick Shadow (*baritone*), the bearer, so he says, of good tidings for Tom and anyone else who wishes him well. Tom calls into the house for Anne and Trulove, and Nick tells all three that Tom has been left a fortune by an unknown uncle.

Tom rejoices in his good luck ('I wished but once, I knew that surely my wish would come true'), and thanks Nick for his tidings. Nick in his turn thanks him that he has found a new master, and Anne and Trulove thank God for the turn in Tom's fortune. For a moment, Tom and Anne sing happily to one another ('O clement love'), but Nick interrupts to say that the inheritance of a fortune entails certain business transactions; they must go up to London immediately. Anne starts to say goodbye to Tom, Nick returns to say the carriage waits, and Tom agrees to reckon up what his services have been worth a year and a day after his engagement. A further farewell, a further warning on the part of Trulove that fortune so easily come by may prove an inducement to idleness, and the stage is clear. Nick turns to the audience: 'The Progress of a Rake begins.'

Scene ii. Mother Goose's brothel. It opens with a brilliant introduction and chorus for Whores and Roaring Boys. Nick asks Tom to recite to Mother Goose (*mezzo-soprano*) what he has been taught: 'One aim in all things to pursue: My duty to myself to do,' etc. Only when Nick mentions the word 'love' does Tom falter in his lesson: 'That precious word is like a fiery coal, it burns my lips.' Nick introduces Tom to the company as 'a stranger to our rites', and according to custom, Tom is asked to sing. 'Love, too frequently betrayed' is the theme of his beautiful cavatina, with its rippling clarinet accompaniment.

'How sad a song,' comment the habitués of the brothel; but sorrow is quickly forgotten in such surroundings. Mother Goose claims Tom as hers for the night, and they walk slowly off. The chorus sings away merrily and their refrain, 'Lanterloo', brings the scene to an end.

Scene iii. Trulove's house. Anne is sad that no word has come from Tom since he left for London. 'Quietly, Night, O find him and caress' she sings in a full-scale aria. There is an interruption as Trulove calls from the house, and Anne makes up her mind that Tom needs her more than her father does. This gives the cue for the cabaletta; it is a lively tune punctuated by a brilliant little orchestral *ritornello*: 'I go to him. Love cannot falter'.

ACT II. Scene i. The morning room of Tom's house in London. Tom is at breakfast. He has not found happiness in London, and he sings of the city's disillusion, which he contrasts with life as it would have been at the side of the one true person he knows and of whom now he dare not even think. The music is in the form of an extended, loosely knit *scena*: 'Vary the song, O London, change!'

At Tom's words 'I wish I were happy', Nick appears and shows his master an advertisement for a circus, in which is featured Baba the Turk (*mezzo-soprano*), the bearded lady. Let him advise his master: marry Baba! The music of Nick's aria, 'That man alone his fate fulfils', for the first time suggests the sinister purpose behind the façade of bonhomie. It is agreed that Tom shall marry Baba the Turk.

Scene ii. Outside Tom's house in London. Anne has arrived and is waiting apprehensively for him to return home. A sedan chair is borne in. Tom gets out of it and comes quickly up to Anne. She must leave London, where 'Virtue is a day coquette', and forget him; he is not worthy of her. At that moment a head is poked out of the sedan chair; it is Baba, heavily veiled, demanding to know how much longer she is to be kept waiting. Tom admits she is his wife. There is a trio in which Anne and Tom sing of their might-have-beens, and Baba expresses her extreme dislike of being kept waiting. Anne leaves, Tom helps Baba from the chair, and, to the acclamations of a crowd which has gathered to welcome her, she enters the house. As a climax to the scene, she unveils and reveals her beard.

Scene iii. The morning room now cluttered up with every conceivable kind of object: stuffed animals and birds, cases of minerals, china, glass, etc. Tom and Baba are at breakfast. Tom sulks, but Baba chatters on. After a bit she becomes conscious that Tom has not spoken, and turns lovingly to him. He repulses her, and, losing her temper, she paces furiously about the room, smashing the more fragile but less valuable parts of her collection, and proclaiming that Tom must be in love with the girl he met when they first came to the house. She embarks on a florid phrase, but Tom seizes his wig which is standing nearby, and shoves it over her face back to front so that she is cut off in mid-note.

His misery is complete, and there is only one remedy: sleep. While he is asleep, Nick comes in, wheeling an object covered with a dust sheet. He discloses a fantastic baroque machine, into which he puts first a loaf of bread, and then above it a piece of broken china. He turns the handle, out comes the loaf. Tom wakes up with the words 'I wish it were true', and explains to Nick that he has had a dream in which he invented a machine which turned stones to bread, and so relieved the sufferings of mankind. Nick asks him if it was anything like what he sees beside him, and Tom demonstrates it to his own complete satisfaction. Nick encourages Tom to think he may make his fortune with this invention, then suggests he ought to tell his wife.

'My wife?' says Tom with a gesture in her direction, 'I have no wife. I've buried her.'

ACT III. Scene i. Tom's room; everything is covered in dust and cobwebs. Baba is still sitting motionless at the table, the wig over her face. An auction is about to take place. Anne comes in, searching for Tom, but no one can give her any definite news of him. She decides to look for him in the house.

The door is flung open and in comes Sellem (*tenor*), the auctioneer, whose patter is as resourceful (and as meaningless) as one would expect. It is all carried off with great style. Finally he comes to Baba, whom he introduces in an awe-struck whisper. The bidding rises higher and higher, and Sellem, to calm the crowd, snatches off the wig. Baba finishes her phrase, and turns to strike consternation into the bystanders. Even the sound of the voices of Tom and Nick offstage (singing a ballad tune which resembles 'Lilliburlero') in no way disconcerts her: 'The pigs of plunder' is her only comment. She comforts Anne: 'You love him, seek to set him right: He's but a shuttle-headed lad'; then, with the greatest dignity, announces her intention of returning to the stage and her interrupted career.

Again, the voices of Tom and Nick are heard below, and Anne leads the *stretto-finale*: 'I go to him, I go, I go, I go, I go to him.' Baba tells Sellem to fetch her carriage, and orders the crowd out of her way.

Scene ii. A churchyard. The smell of death is in the music, with the harpsichord somehow providing a colour which is deeply sinister, and Tom's utterances have a new sense of seriousness. Nick reveals himself in his true colours (to the tune of the ballad): 'A year and a day have passed away, Since first to you I came . . . 'Tis not your money but your soul, Which I this night require.' The vocal writing for Tom, caught in the trap of his own devising, is Stravinsky at his most expressive and his most powerful; the crucial scene of the opera. Nick relents to the extent of inviting Tom to play cards in a last effort to save himself from hell. Tom wins the game, but in his rage Nick condemns him to insanity.

Nick sinks into a nearby grave and the stage remains dark for a moment. When the lights come up again, Tom is sitting on a green mound, putting grass in his hair and singing in a child-like voice: 'With roses crowned, I sit on ground, Adonis is my name' (the ballad-tune again).

Scene iii. Bedlam. Tom is surrounded by madmen. In his own mind he is still Adonis, and he exhorts the company to prepare for his wedding with Venus. The gaoler (*bass*) brings in Anne, who addresses Tom as Adonis, and in a moment he is happy not only that she has come, but that he is proved right in the sight of his fellow madmen, who predicted that no Venus would answer his call. There is a love duet, and at its end Anne helps the exhausted Tom on to the straw pallet, which lies in the middle of the room. She rocks him to sleep with a Lullaby. The gaoler brings in her father, who leads her gently away.

Tom wakes and raves of his Venus, who was with him and has disappeared. The others will not believe that she was ever there, and he sinks back dead on the mattress.

The curtain descends and in front of it step Anne, Baba, Tom, Nick and Trulove, to sing the epilogue.

Sergei Sergeyevich Prokofiev
(1891–1953)

THE GAMBLER
Igrok

FOUR acts, after Dostoevsky; première, Brussels, 1929. In a German spa town the General (*bass*) with his children, his stepdaughter Pauline (*soprano*) and the children's tutor Alexey (*tenor*), await news of the death of a rich old aunt. The General, who is smitten with Blanche (*contralto*), a *demi-mondaine*, has borrowed heavily from the Marquis (*tenor*), with whom Pauline once had an affair; Alexey loves Pauline. Alexey has lost the money Pauline gave him, but he refuses to give up gambling. Pauline asks him to prove his love by doing whatever she asks, and orders him to insult a German Baroness; consternation ensues. Alexey worries about his predicament. The aunt, Babulenka (*mezzo-soprano*), arrives, in better health and determined to try gambling. The old lady gambles away her fortune, to the General's dismay. The Marquis insults Pauline over money, but when Alexey suggests that she borrow from a rich Englishman the two quarrel. Alexey at the tables has an extraordinary run of luck and breaks the bank. He offers Pauline his winnings to throw in the Marquis's teeth, but when he hands her the money she hurls it back at him. He is left staring fixedly at an imaginary roulette wheel.

THE LOVE FOR THREE ORANGES
Lyubov k trem Apelsinam

OPERA in a prologue and four acts by Sergei Prokofiev; text by the composer after the comedy of Carlo Gozzi. Première, Chicago, December 30, 1921.

PROLOGUE. A dispute between the protagonists of the various forms of theatre is interrupted by ten masked announcers, who tell them they are going to see something quite different, *The Love for Three Oranges*. The curtain parts to allow a 'trumpeter' (playing a bass trombone) to announce a herald, who in his turn announces that the burden of the story is the apparently incurable hypochondria of the son of the King of Clubs.

ACT I. Scene i. The King's palace. The doctors inform the King (*bass*) that his son (*tenor*) cannot be cured. The King, fearful that his odious niece, Clarissa (*contralto*), will therefore succeed to the throne, decides that his son must be made to laugh – as the physicians say this might cure him. Pantaloon (*baritone*) suggests that the most likely way of doing it would be through feasts and theatrical performances. He shouts for Truffaldino (*tenor*), the jester, who undertakes to arrange everything, and disappears.

The King sends for the prime minister, Leandro (*baritone*), and orders that plans for feasts and spectacles be put in train. Leandro, not at all anxious for the Prince's recovery, tries to raise objections to the scheme, and the scene ends with Leandro and Pantaloon shouting abuse at each other.

Scene ii. The stage darkens, a curtain covered with cabalistic signs descends, and the magician Tchelio (*bass*) and the witch Fata Morgana (*soprano*), surrounded by a chorus of little devils, proceed to play against each other with gigantic cards. Behind their chairs, the representations of the King of Clubs and the King of Spades respectively show that the game is in effect that of the King's protector against Leandro's. Tchelio loses.

Scene iii. Back in the palace, Leandro and the wicked Clarissa have reached an understanding; the Princess undertakes to marry Leandro, who must encompass the Prince's death and so clear the way for her accession. She is not satisfied with progress, but Leandro is confident that his method – to fill the Prince full of tragic prose and boring verse – will yet prove lethal. Leandro discovers Smeraldina (*mezzo-soprano*) eavesdropping. Under threat, she reveals that Tchelio protects the Prince and may yet succeed in his stratagems to make him laugh. Only through the intervention of Fata Morgana, her mistress, can this be avoided. The three voices call for Fata Morgana.

ACT II. Scene i. The Prince's room. He is ill and bored, and none of Truffaldino's antics has made him laugh. Truffaldino persuades him to dress and watch the diversions planned for his benefit. The well-known march takes us to the second scene, the great hall of the palace. The King is there with

Clarissa, and also in evidence are Leandro and Pantaloon. The Prince is covered in furs lest he catch cold.

Scene ii. Truffaldino stages a comic battle between 'Monsters', and later turns loose a crowd of drunkards and gluttons to fight for food and drink; all to no avail – the Prince does not laugh. In despair, Truffaldino looks round and catches sight of the witch Fata Morgana. He is horrified that such an old hag should intrude and tries to eject her. In their struggle, she loses her balance, does an involuntary somersault, and achieves the apparently impossible: the Prince starts to laugh. The whole court, and even the spectators, join in, and everyone – apart from Leandro and Clarissa – starts to dance.

Fata Morgana, quickly recovered, curses the Prince and pronounces his fate: he will fall in love with three oranges, and will pursue them to the ends of the earth. Immediately, the Prince announces he will depart forthwith on his journey, accompanied by Truffaldino. Amidst general lamentation, the little devil Farfarello (*bass*) with a pair of bellows wafts the wanderers on their way.

ACT III. Scene i. The desert. Tchelio makes a vain attempt to restrain Farfarello from wafting the Prince and his companion to perdition, but Farfarello tells him that his loss at cards has rendered Tchelio's magic powers inoperative – and he proves as much by disobeying him. The Prince and Truffaldino appear, and the Magician, having discovered they are seeking the three oranges, advises them, if they ever find them, to cut them open only near water. He also warns them that they are in the keeping of the terrible Creonte (*bass*), who takes the form of a gigantic cook. In case it may help, he gives Truffaldino a magic ribbon, hoping it may distract the cook's attention while they filch the oranges.

Scene ii. The castle. While Truffaldino diverts the colossal cook with the ribbon, the Prince creeps silently into the kitchen and emerges with three oranges, which are of a calibre that befits their vast guardian. The cook is given the ribbon and capers with delight, while the Prince and Truffaldino, to the music of the *scherzo*, make their escape.

Scene iii. The desert. The oranges have grown to huge dimensions. The Prince falls asleep, but Truffaldino is so thirsty he cannot resist cutting open one of the oranges. Out steps Princess Linetta (*contralto*). She says she will die of thirst if she is not immediately given water; when none is forthcoming, she proves as good as her word. The same happens when Princess Nicoletta (*mezzo-soprano*) comes from the second orange. Truffaldino rushes despairingly off into the desert.

The Prince awakes and orders four soldiers who conveniently appear to bury the dead girls with all due honour. Then he cuts open the third orange with his sword, and a third girl (*soprano*) appears, more beautiful than the others; he immediately recognises her as the one being he has waited for since birth. She asks for water, and sinks into the Prince's arms. The spectators produce a bucket of water from one of the boxes and the Princess's life is saved. When the Prince tells his bride they must return to his father's palace, she demurs: he must fetch her a suitable dress.

Princess Ninetta is alone. Towards her glides the figure of Smeraldina, behind whom looms the shadow of Fata Morgana. Smeraldina sticks a long magical pin into Ninetta's head. She turns into a rat. Fata Morgana tells Smeraldina that she must take Ninetta's place when she meets the King.

A procession appears, with the King and Prince at its head. They come to Smeraldina, who proclaims herself the Princess, much to the Prince's dismay. He is forced to give her his arm and lead her back to the palace.

ACT IV. Scene i. The cabalistic curtain of Act I, Scene ii. Fata Morgana and Tchelio are having a furious argument. The spectators get out of their boxes, and lock Fata Morgana away. Smoke and fire can be seen, and for the moment Tchelio is triumphant.

Scene ii. The royal throne room. A large rat is seen sitting in the Princess's place; it is Ninetta in her metamorphosed state. Tchelio eventually transforms the rodent into the Princess he knows it to be. The Prince is beside himself with joy, and Smeraldina's discomfiture is complete. She is recognised as an accomplice of Leandro and is accused with him and Clarissa of treason. For a moment the court watches the King go through the agonising process of making up his mind; then he turns to them full of resolve: all the culprits shall be hanged.

As the guards move towards them, the guilty ones take flight. Suddenly Fata Morgana appears, a trapdoor opens, and her followers disappear down it to safety. The courtiers arrive too late, and there is nothing to do but cry 'God save the King!', which the King immediately amends to 'God save the Prince and Princess!'

THE FIERY ANGEL
L'Ange de Feu

OPERA in five acts and seven tableaux by Sergei Prokofiev. Libretto by the composer from a novel by Valery Briusoff. First complete performance (in concert) at the Théâtre des Champs Elysées, Paris, November 25, 1954.

Prokofiev worked on *The Fiery Angel* between 1920 and 1926, beginning it, that is to say, in America after the failure of *The Love for Three Oranges*. The work, set in sixteenth-century Germany, is allegorical on two simultaneous levels. On one plane, Renata symbolises the struggles between good and evil, and the capacity to believe that evil is good and to act on this belief. She is haunted by visions of an Angel, and her passion for him amounts to obsession; to her he is Good, and no one else she meets is of any significance, except as help in her search for the Angel, or his physical embodiment, Heinrich. On another level, this is the account of an all-absorbing but ultimately unsuccessful love affair, seen through the suffering eyes of the male, but more damaging in the final analysis for the female protagonist than for him.

ACT I. A room in a shabby inn. The hostess (*contralto*) conducts Ruprecht (*baritone*), a knight, to his room for the night. No sooner has she left him than he hears hysterical and terrified imprecations coming from behind an apparently disused door. He forces it, and Renata (*soprano*), distraught and dishevelled, throws herself into his arms for protection. The music vividly portrays her exhaustion as Ruprecht prays and her terror abates.

She tells her story in an extended narration of considerable musical splendour. It was when she was eight that an Angel first appeared to her, dressed in white with blue eyes and golden hair and surrounded by flames. His name was Madiel and he appeared to her day and night, eventually announcing to her that her destiny was to be a saint. When she was seventeen, her urgent desire for carnal love drove him away, to her utter despair, but eventually he told her in a dream that he would return in human form. As soon as she saw Count Heinrich she knew, in spite of his denial, that he was Madiel in human form. Her desires were fulfilled and there ensued with Heinrich a year of happiness. In the end he abandoned her, and now Ruprecht has saved her from the fiend who has pursued her with visions and nightmares ever since.

The noise attracts the attention of the hostess and her servant. Renata is a loose woman, the hostess explains to Ruprecht; she bewitched the Count and tormented the villagers, and now she must leave the inn. Ruprecht cannot understand what is going on, but he shrugs his shoulders and decides that, once the hostess goes, this attractive girl, witch or no witch, shall be his. As she looks out of the window yearning for Heinrich, Ruprecht tries to seduce her. He quickly abandons the attempt, but from that moment Ruprecht becomes involved in the search for Heinrich almost as much as Renata herself.

The hostess brings in a fortune-teller (*mezzo-soprano*), who, in an impressive musical scene, makes obscure references to Renata's guilt.

ACT II takes place in Cologne. Renata is alone reading a book of magic when Ruprecht comes in, complaining that the week they have been in the city has been spent only in feverish search for Heinrich. Without Heinrich she cannot live, is her answer. Jakob Glock (*tenor*) has been commissioned to bring more books of magic, and Renata fastens on them, telling Ruprecht that, despite his uncomplaining love, his declared lack of jealousy, beside Heinrich he is nothing; were she to be walking with Heinrich and to find Ruprecht's body self-slain in the gutter, she would take no more notice than to ask for the body's removal.

Renata burns the magic herbs acquired from the sorceress, and soon a knock is heard on the wall – it is a spirit, she says, announcing the arrival of Heinrich. With some remarkable *divisi* writing for the strings, Prokofiev expresses Renata's obsession. The door opens, but the music subsides to impotence and Ruprecht finds nothing. Glock reappears; he will take Ruprecht to speak with the philosopher-magician, Agrippa von Nettelsheim (*tenor*)

A fine symphonic interlude takes us to Agrippa's studio, where he sits surrounded by books, bottles of medicine, human skeletons, and three black dogs. In a scene whose impressive music caps even the feverish excitement of its predecessor, Agrippa reveals himself as a master of the diabolical arts. As a philosopher, however, he refuses to help Ruprecht.

ACT III. Renata is in despair outside the door of a house. It is Heinrich's; she has seen him and been rejected as a woman possessed by the devil. Ruprecht returns from his encounter with Agrippa and hears the story of Renata's *volte face* – she no longer loves Heinrich, who, she is convinced, was an impostor, not the embodiment of her Madiel. If Ruprecht will kill her seducer, she will be his! After a moment's hesitation, Ruprecht demands entrance to Heinrich's house, while Renata offers up a prayer to Madiel for forgiveness that she mistook Heinrich for him and for strength for the future.

Ruprecht can be seen at a window as he challenges Heinrich, who himself suddenly becomes visible; in appearance he is the very incarnation of all that Renata has ever ascribed to Madiel, a true angel of fire. Renata is overwhelmed at the sight of him, and when Ruprecht reappears, in another complete change of heart, she forbids him to shed a drop of Heinrich's blood, rather to allow himself to be killed.

An interlude depicts the duel. At its end, Ruprecht is discovered lying wounded on the banks of the Rhine, where Renata tends him, and in a lyrical aria sings of her love for him, swearing that if he dies she will enter a convent. After Renata's *berceuse*, delirium suddenly seizes both in music of uncanny intensity, a chorus of women behind the stage commenting ironically the while on the instability of love. A doctor (*tenor*) pronounces that Ruprecht will live.

ACT IV. A public garden. Renata tells Ruprecht, who has hardly recovered from his wound, that she must leave him; to accomplish the salvation of her soul, she must take the veil. When Ruprecht protests his love for her, she tries to commit suicide, turning the attack on him as he tries to prevent her. Mephistopheles (*tenor*) and Faust (*baritone*) have come into the garden and watch the scene. When the pot-boy, in response to their order, only brings wine, Mephistopheles threatens to swallow the child, and a little later at a single gulp makes good his boast, subsequently restoring him to life.

ACT V starts with beautiful slow music chanted by the nuns of the convent of which Renata has become a member. The music is the more welcome by its contrast with the frenzy which has preceded it. The same abstraction from the world is apparent when the Mother Superior (*mezzo-soprano*) asks Renata about her visions: has she seen evil spirits? No, says Renata, she always turned her back on them. The fact remains, the Mother Superior points out, that since she entered the convent, the place has been in an uproar, full of strange noises and the sisters attacked by devils.

The nuns in the meanwhile have filled one side of the crypt, and now the Inquisitor (*bass*) and his followers enter to examine Renata. He asks her to furnish him with proof that her visions have never been inspired by Hell. The spirit who visits her, she tells him, has always spoken of virtue, of the import- ance of the life to come – are these the words of the devil? Immediately two young sisters (*sopranos*) cry out in terror, knocks are heard on the wall, and the scene becomes one of pandemonium. The exorcism proceeds, but finally, as Mephis- topheles and Ruprecht appear, the nuns rush frenziedly at the Inquisitor and his supporters, and the opera ends as he pro- nounces Renata a heretic and sentences her to death. The final scene, with its intricate part-writing for the women against the *cantus firmus* of the Inquisitor, is masterly in its effect and brings the opera to an overwhelming conclusion.

WAR AND PEACE
Voina y Mir

OPERA in thirteen scenes by Sergei Prokofiev; libretto by the composer and Mira Mendelson, after Tolstoy. The original version (heavily cut) given in concert in Moscow, June 7, 1945.[1] Première of so-called 'Final' version (eleven scenes only, omitting scenes 7 and 11), Maly Theatre, Leningrad, April 1, 1955.

Aᴄᴄᴏʀᴅɪɴɢ to Mira Mendelson, for whom Prokofiev had left his Spanish-born wife, the composer was thinking of writing an opera on Tolstoy's *Resurrection* when she started to read *War and Peace* to him. He was immediately struck by its operatic possibilities, the scene of the meeting between Natasha and the wounded Prince Andrei particularly appealing to him. He worked at it on and off during the last eleven years of his life and the opera has gone through a number of different versions. The final version is in thirteen scenes, together with the Overture and choral Epigraph. It is long (more than four hours of music) and sections or occasionally whole scenes are sometimes cut in performance.

ᴘᴀʀᴛ ɪ. *Peace*

The granite-hard choral movement called Epigraph in the score, and often appropriately substituted at the start of the opera for the much less interesting Overture, is a massive piece of block harmony and with its emphasis on the primordial strength of Russia in the face of her enemies makes a most effective opening.

Scene i. The garden of Count Rostov's estate at Otradnoye. It is a moonlit night in May, 1806. The widower Prince Andrei Bolkonsky (*baritone*), who is visiting the estate on business, cannot sleep. His romantic idealism, full of thoughts of spring, gives way to disillusion. From an upstairs room, the Count's daughter Natasha (*soprano*) complains to her cousin, Sonya (*mezzo-soprano*), that she too cannot sleep. Andrei is moved by the romantic situation and the innocence and charm of the young girl. How could he have believed that his life was at an end? The lyrical and expressive mood of the scene exactly fits the Byronic romanticism of the characters.

Scene ii. New Year's Eve, 1810, a ball in a palace in St. Petersburg. Count Rostov (*bass*) enters with Natasha and Sonya, and they are followed by Count and Countess Bezukhov – Madame Akhrosimova (*contralto*) comments with asperity to a friend on the beauty of the celebrated Hélène Bezukhova (*mezzo-soprano*). The Tsar (a silent role) makes his entrance. As Polonaise is succeeded by Mazurka, Natasha wonders if anyone will ask her to dance. Pierre Bezukhov (*tenor*) suggests to his friend Prince Andrei that he ask Natasha to dance – which he does, to a waltz. But Andrei is not the only man taken with Natasha; the

---

[1] The same day as the première of *Peter Grimes* in London.

.glittering and dissolute Prince Anatol Kuragin (*tenor*) has earlier asked his sister, Hélène Bezukhova, to arrange an introduction to the new young beauty. The scene ends with an Écossaise.

Scene iii. February, 1812. Prince Andrei has proposed to Natasha, and her father brings her to meet old Prince Bolkonsky (*bass-baritone*), who has meanwhile insisted that Andrei should spend a year abroad. They are told the old man cannot see them, but his unmarried daughter Princess Marya (*mezzo-soprano*) comes in and Count Rostov makes his excuses and departs. The old Prince appears, in nightcap and dressing-gown. With boorish insincerity, he apologises for his attire to Natasha, mutters threateningly and leaves. Marya starts to excuse his behaviour, but Natasha understands all too well that he is the obstacle to her marriage. Count Rostov returns and goes to speak with Marya, leaving Natasha alone. She is outraged at the behaviour of the Bolkonskys but is still very much in love with Andrei. With some dignity, she puts off Marya's attempts at polite conversation.

Scene iv. The living room of Pierre Bezukhov's house, May 1812. Hélène lets slip to Natasha that Prince Anatol had admitted to them only the previous night that he pined for love of Natasha. Hélène laughs at her embarrassment. Natasha reflects that since neither Hélène nor Pierre seems at all shocked at Anatol having fallen in love with her, she will not be shocked either. The dancing resumes and Anatol proceeds to woo Natasha passionately, giving her a letter of assignation.

Scene v. Dolokhov's apartments, June 12, 1812. Dolokhov (*baritone*), who has arranged Anatol's elopement with Natasha, tries unsuccessfully to argue his old friend out of going through with so mad a project. Enter Balaga (*bass*), who has procured a carriage and fast horses, and the three drink to the adventure as Anatol says a musically nostalgic goodbye to Moscow and to his gipsy mistress Matriosha.

Scene vi. The same night: a room in the house of Maria Dmitrievna Akhrosimova, where Natasha is staying while her father is away. Natasha waits alone for Anatol. Her maid Dunyasha rushes in to say that Sonya has revealed the elopement plans. Anatol's way is barred by the butler and Akhrosimova berates Natasha, who begs to be left alone. Akhrosimova softens: can Natasha not think of her father and of Prince Andrei? Natasha runs off sobbing.

Pierre comes in and, as Natasha returns, consoles her and assures her that Anatol is already married. She begs him to explain to Andrei and ask him to forgive her. Pierre promises and, in an outburst of frankness, tells Natasha that were he free, he would be on his knees asking her hand in marriage.

He runs off, followed by Natasha, whose voice is heard calling for Sonya.

Scene vii. The same night. Hélène is entertaining guests, Anatol among them. Pierre attacks his brother-in-law, insisting he leave Moscow immediately. Anatol, taken aback by Pierre's vehemence, agrees, leaving Pierre to reflect on the pointlessness of his existence. Denisov (*baritone*) brings the news that Napoleon is about to cross the Russian frontier. It means war.

PART II. *War*

Scene viii. Near Borodino. Soldiers and peasants fill the scene with their fervent working and marching songs. Prince Andrei has trained his own regiment. By sheer coincidence he meets Lieutenant-Colonel Denisov, who was once engaged to Natasha, and takes him to Field-Marshal Kutuzov (*bass*). Andrei sees the highly unmilitary figure of Pierre Bezukhov, who explains he has come to Borodino as a mere observer. Andrei expresses his disillusion with a war which is devastating Russia and has already killed his father. But, as he tells Pierre, he is still patriotically convinced of ultimate victory. The two men embrace, both certain they have met for the last time. As Pierre departs, Kutuzov enters. He offers Andrei a position on his staff, which he declines. Kutuzov is half vexed that he is deprived of a valuable adviser, half delighted to find that the man he chose prefers to serve in the front line. The soldiers proclaim their patriotic fervour until the sound of a shot heralds the start of battle.

Scene ix. The Shevardino redoubt. The same day. Napoleon (*baritone*) directs the battle surrounded by his staff. The music is a sinister sort of *scherzo* in Prokofiev's most sardonic vein. The French commander-in-chief broods on the possible outcome of the battle. Moscow is at his mercy; he will earn history's gratitude by showing clemency. In spite of urgent requests from his Marshals, he refuses at first to commit his reserves, but eventually gives in. De Beausset (*tenor*) tries unsuccessfully to get the Emperor to eat luncheon, and the scene ends with a cannonball landing almost at their feet.

Scene x. Two days later. A peasant's hut in the village of Fili. Marshal Kutuzov is holding a Council of War, surrounded by his generals. They face a dilemma; defend Moscow and put the army at risk; or retreat and leave the capital at the enemy's mercy. After listening to his generals, Kutuzov orders a retreat, confident that only through the sacrifice of Moscow is there a hope of final victory. Kutuzov's faith is expressed in soliloquy to a broad tune of immediate appeal and memorability.

Scene xi. Moscow's inhabitants have set fire to the great city rather than surrender it to the invader. Pierre learns that the

Rostovs have left, taking with them the wounded from their house, Natasha still not knowing that Andrei is among them. Pierre is shoved in among a group of Muscovites accused of having started the fires. Most of the incendiaries, including Pierre and the veteran Karataev (*tenor*), are reprieved and marched off as prisoners. French actresses rush in, screaming that the theatre is on fire, and lunatics save themselves as the hospital burns. Surrounded by his staff, Napoleon makes his way through the thick smoke of burning Moscow, defeated by the city's resistance and mightily impressed by the courage of its inhabitants.

Scene xii shows Prokofiev at his most intense and dramatic. Andrei lies wounded in a peasant's hut at Mitishi. He is delirious and the chorus can be heard singing 'Piti-piti-piti' as the blood pounds in his ears. Natasha comes to his deathbed to beg forgiveness. Andrei tells her that he loves her more than ever before and their voices join to celebrate what he thinks of as new happiness. He falls asleep dreaming of their first dance together. As his last spasm comes, the sound of 'Piti-piti-piti' becomes ever more insistent until it suddenly stops.

Scene xiii. November 1812. On the road to Smolensk. A storm is raging. French troops are in retreat, escorting a group of Russian prisoners of war, amongst them Pierre and Karataev. Karataev can go no further and is shot as a straggler. Guerrillas attack the French and free the prisoners, and Pierre is recognised by Denisov, who assures him of victory and tells him that Andrei is dead but Natasha safe in Moscow. The Russian advance guard appears preceding Kutuzov himself. He is tired but he knows that the French are beaten and his work done. All join in a great peroration to the eternal Russian spirit.

Dmitri Dmitrevich Shostakovich
(1906–1975)

THE NOSE
Nos

THREE acts, after Gogol; première, Leningrad, 1930. Platon Kuzmich Kovalyov (*baritone*) is obsessed with his modest status as a civil servant and with his plans for advancement. At breakfast the barber Ivan Yakovlevich (*bass-baritone*) finds a nose in his roll. His wife orders him to get rid of it. Meanwhile Kovalyov awakes, realises his nose is missing and hastens to report this disaster to the police. On his way he stops at the cathedral, where to his astonishment he sees his Nose (*tenor*). It refuses all his cajoling to come back to him. He advertises for it in a newspaper but is overwhelmed by despair at the prospect of a noseless future. The Police Inspector (*high tenor*), hot on the trail of the Nose, arrests it, whereupon it returns to its normal size and shape. The Inspector triumphantly carries it to Kovalyov's house. But poor Kovalyov cannot stick it on again. Gossip about the Nose pervades the city and even a visiting prince pretends to identify it. At last Kovalyov awakes to find his nose fully restored. His recovery is signalled when he makes an assignation with a flower-girl.

KATERINA ISMAILOVA
Lady Macbeth of Mtsensk

OPERA in four acts by Dmitri Shostakovich; libretto, after N Leskov, by A. Preis and the composer. Première, Leningrad, January 22, 1934.

L ESKOV'S original story, a masterpiece in its way, is dated 1865. Shostakovich and his librettist decided to retain little of its ironical character, choosing instead to accentuate the dislikable qualities of the characters of the old regime to the point in some cases of caricature. The exception is Katerina herself, to whom the composer has given sympathetic characteristics and lyrical music.

ACT I. Scene i. Katerina's (*soprano*) room. She is lying on her bed, bored with the tedium of her life and the loveless marriage she contracted five years ago. Heralded by a bassoon tune, Boris Timofeevich (*high bass*), her disagreeable old father-in-law, comes upstairs to complain that she has not yet given his son an heir – no doubt she would like to take a lover, but his watchfulness will prevent any idea of that sort. As he goes out he tells Katerina to get ready the poison for the rats, and she mutters that nothing would please her better than to feed it to him. Boris returns with his son, Zinovy (*tenor*), and some servants. A dam has broken and must be mended and Zinovy prepares to set off to superintend the work. Zinovy introduces to his father Sergei (*tenor*), whom he has just engaged. Boris insists that Zinovy make his wife swear an oath to be faithful to him while he is away. They all go out and Aksinya comments on the saucy looks of Sergei who was dismissed from his last place because the mistress fell for him.

An orchestral interlude leads to Scene ii, the Ismailovs' yard. The servants, amongst them Sergei, have caught Aksinya (*soprano*) and are pinching and prodding her. Katerina appears and berates them for their unkindness and for wasting time. Sergei insists on shaking her by the hand, and in a moment Katerina is wrestling with him. He throws her just as Boris Timofeevich comes out of the house. He threatens to tell Zinovy about his wife's behaviour.

Scene iii. Another interlude takes us to Katerina's bedroom. The voice of her father-in-law is heard outside scolding her for wasting the candle. When he has gone, she looks out of the window and sings a beautiful song contrasting her lonely state with the freedom of the birds she sees outside her window. On the pretext of wanting to borrow a book, Sergei appears at the door. They embrace, make passionate love and are only momentarily disconcerted when Boris Timofeevich is heard outside the door asking if Katerina is safely in bed.

ACT II. Scene iv. The Yard. To the accompaniment of highly suggestive music, Boris Timofeevich prowls underneath Katerina's window, uttering lecherous thoughts about her. Sergei is seen at the window kissing Katerina goodbye. During the rapturous farewell, Boris recognises Sergei and when he climbs down the drainpipe catches him. Shouting for assistance, Boris has Sergei stripped and, after summoning Katerina to the window to watch, proceeds to flog him. Katerina screams to be let out of her room, and in the end she slides down the drainpipe and throws herself at her father-in-law. Sergei is carried away and Boris demands supper from his daughter-in-law.

With Sergei safely locked up in the store-room, Boris sends a message to his son to tell him there is trouble at home. But Katerina has poisoned the mushrooms. Boris begins to feel the effects. He cries for a priest, but Katerina takes the keys from his pockets and leaves him to die alone. Some workmen coming back from a drink cannot understand his babbling, but the priest (*bass*) arrives in time to hear him accuse his daughter-in-law of murder. She for her part mourns so eloquently that the priest is left to muse, in music of inanely popular style, on the mysteries of dying. As the scene ends, an extra battery of brass, not so far heard, lets loose with shattering effect a series of discords which lead into the entr'acte, itself the opera's biggest single movement, a massive *passacaglia* which powerfully sums up the overheated drama.

Scene v. Katerina's bedroom. The lovers are together. Katerina's passion is reflected in her music, but Sergei is already more disposed for sleep – an erotic predicament fully reflected in the music. Sergei is worried Zinovy's return will inevitably mean the end of their love. Her thoughts are interrupted by the appearance of the ghost of Boris Timofeevich (bass chorus offstage), at first unable to frighten her, but in the end causing her shrieks of terror to wake up Sergei, who cannot see the ghost.

They fall asleep again, until Katerina thinks she hears someone stealthily approaching the door. They realise it is Zinovy Borisovich, and Sergei hides.

Katerina lets her husband in. How has she spent her time? Father's death was very sudden. Why is the bed made up for two – and why is there a man's belt on it? He knows all about her scandalous behaviour, he says, and picking up the belt he starts to beat her with it. Sergei rushes out and he and Katerina overpower Zinovy and throttle him. To the tune of a grotesque march, they carry the body down to the cellar and bury it.

ACT III. Scene vi. Katerina and Sergei on their wedding day brood about the body in the cellar. As they leave to go to the party, a drunk (*tenor*) enters on the prowl for more liquor. In a brilliantly funny scene, he finally breaks down the cellar door, but emerges almost immediately holding his nose. Further investigation convinces him that he has found the decomposing corpse of Zinovy Borisovich.

Scene vii. The local police station, where the Sergeant (*baritone*) and his men are sitting, frantically doing nothing. They are annoyed at not having been invited to the Ismailov wedding feast. When the drunk bursts in with news that he has found a corpse in the Ismailovs' cellar, the Sergeant and his men hurry off to make their arrests.

A short and brisk entr'acte takes us to Scene viii, where, in the Ismailovs' garden, the wedding feast is in progress. Suddenly Katerina notices that the padlock of the cellar is broken. She tells Sergei the game is up and they must leave immediately. The Sergeant and his men enter the garden. Katerina quickly realises there is no point in pretence and holds out her wrists for the handcuffs. Sergei tries to escape but they catch him, beat him and secure him too. Completely happy, the police march their prisoners off to gaol.

ACT IV. Scene ix. It is evening and a large band of convicts, all of them shackled, has halted near a bridge. Men and women are in separate groups. In contrast to the grotesque and even farcical happenings of the previous act, this last scene is entirely tragic and mostly lyrical. An old convict (*bass*) sings movingly of the long unforgiving road they must travel to Siberia. A subdued Katerina bribes a guard to let her go through to the men and she makes her way to Sergei, who rejects her and blames her for their situation. She goes sadly back to the other women, lamenting (in a beautiful *arioso* with cor anglais obbligato) that Sergei hates her.

Meanwhile Sergei flirts with Sonyetka (*contralto*), who insists that her favours must be paid for – with stockings, to replace her torn ones. On the pretext that his legs hurt him, Sergei wheedles her only spare pair out of Katerina. Immediately he gives them to Sonyetka and carries her off triumphantly, leaving Katerina in an agony of jealousy. The women mock her. Katerina laments slowly and agonisingly, before the Sergeant in charge wakes everyone up and gets the column ready to move off. The stupefied Katerina gets slowly to her feet, goes up to Sonyetka who is standing on the bridge, seizes her and jumps with her into the river. The Sergeant looks after them, decides there is nothing to be done as the current is too strong, and orders everybody to move off. With the old convict trying to brace up their morale, they start on their way.

Katerina Ismailova is undeniably a mixture of styles, parody jostling lyricism, and farce elbowing tragedy. But, if it is the creation of a young opera composer, it is also a work of flair and brilliance and unfailing vitality. Its early success was very considerable, but in January, 1936, an article in *Pravda* denounced *Katerina Ismailova* as modernist and confused, its music 'leftist' and discordant. The once popular *Lady Macbeth of Mtsensk* (abroad, the opera usually carried the name of Leskov's story) became something of a legend, never performed in its native land and very seldom outside owing to the tight control kept on orchestral material. Rumours of work on a new version were current from about 1957. When it was finally heard (in 1963) the revision turned out to consist of no more than some smoothing out of the extremities of the vocal line, of some changes in the words and stage directions, and of the composition of new interludes between Scenes i and ii and Scenes vii and viii. Ten years later still, the original version again became available.

Frederick Delius
(1862–1934)

A VILLAGE ROMEO AND JULIET

Six scenes; première, Berlin, 1907. Manz and Marti (*baritones*), two farmers, are rivals for a piece of land. Sali and Vreli, their children, play together. The land rightfully belongs to the Dark Fiddler (*baritone*), but he has no legal claim. The two men quarrel and forbid their children to play together again. Six years later, Sali (*tenor*) and Vreli (*soprano*) are clearly drawn to each other. The Dark Fiddler appears and reminds them of their childhood. Marti tries to drag Vreli away, and Sali fells him with a blow. Marti has lost his mind as a result, and his house must be sold. The lovers want one day of happiness, and go to the fair; when they are recognised, they move on to the Paradise Garden. At an inn the Dark Fiddler is telling his vagabond friends the story when Sali and Vreli come in. They realise there is no way out for them but to 'drift down the river'. They climb into a barge; Sali removes the plug, and the boat moves slowly away as the lovers embrace.

Ralph Vaughan Williams
(1872–1958)

HUGH THE DROVER

TWO acts; première, London, 1924. The music makes extensive use of folk-song. At a country fair in about 1812, Mary (*soprano*) sings of her forthcoming wedding to John the Butcher (*bass baritone*), whom she does not love. When Hugh the Drover (*tenor*) comes by, he and Mary immediately fall in love. John and Hugh fight, and Hugh wins, but John accuses him of being a French spy and he is put into the stocks. John and his friends taunt him, but Mary manages to free him. They are about to escape when the alarm is given; the Constable (*bass*), her father, arrives to find Mary in the stocks beside Hugh. John rejects her while the crowd sympathises. The Sergeant (*baritone*) who comes to arrest Hugh recognises his old comrade and vouches for his loyalty; he takes John away instead. Hugh and Mary together set out on the open road.

RIDERS TO THE SEA

ONE act, by Ralph Vaughan Williams, text by Synge; première, London, 1937. In an Irish fishing community Maurya (*contralto*) and her daughters Cathleen and Nora (*sopranos*) mourn her son Michael who, like his father and four brothers, has been lost at sea. Nora brings in some clothes which turn out to be Michael's. The remaining son, Bartley (*baritone*), is to take the horses in the boat to the Galway Fair. Maurya has a vision of him riding to the sea with Michael; she knows this means that he too will drown. As she sings of the deaths of all her menfolk, the door opens and Bartley's body is brought in. Maurya sings of her resignation which is almost relief: the sea can take nothing more from her.

Gustav Holst
(1874–1934)

Sāvitri

O NE act, from the Mahā Bhārata; première, London, 1916. Death (*bass*) calls to Sāvitri (*soprano*) that he is coming for her husband Satyavān (*tenor*). He is young and strong; she cannot understand why he should be chosen. When Death comes she cradles her husband's body and bravely faces the 'Just One'. She asks that she may accompany Satyavān, but this cannot be; however, since she did not shrink from Death, he will grant her one boon. She asks for life; when he points out that she is alive, she explains that life for a woman means sons and daughters: life is eternal. True to his word, Death leaves and Satyavān comes to life again.

William Walton
(1902–1983)

Troilus and Cressida

Opera in three acts; text by Christopher Hassall. Première, Covent Garden, London, December 3, 1954.

A CT I. Before the Temple of Pallas in the citadel of Troy. Quiet timpani and a murmuring chorus of worshippers from within the temple set the scene, but soon the muttering becomes desperate, and it is apparent that the starving population of Troy is liable to riot against conditions. Calkas (*bass*), the High Priest, tries to quieten them and reminds them that the oracle at Delphi has already spoken. His unequivocal if defeatist interpretation is to advise them to parley with the Greeks while there is still time. Antenor (*baritone*), intent on a foray with his warrior companions, overhears him and challenges his right to utter such counsel of despair. He rouses the crowd, and Calkas is obviously in some danger until Prince Troilus (*tenor*) appears and restores order. His friend guesses that it is the presence of the beautiful Cressida (*soprano*), Calkas's daughter, which draws him to the temple.

In a gently lyrical aria Troilus admits to himself that he loves Cressida, and as the music reaches a climax the temple doors open and Cressida appears in the doorway. Troilus has never spoken to her before and her first musical utterance is subdued: 'Morning and evening I have felt your glance follow me out of sight.' She is a widow and is soon to take her vows as a priestess.

Troilus unavailingly protests his love, and as Cressida disappears her place is taken by her uncle Pandarus (*tenor buffo*), whose arrival produces a complete change of musical mood, from the lyrical to something much more volatile. He takes in the situation at a glance and proceeds to win Troilus's confidence, so that the Prince departs in high hopes. Pandarus is about to enter the temple in search of Cressida when the doors open and Calkas emerges, followed by Cressida and her servant Evadne (*mezzo-soprano*). Pandarus listens to Calkas admit to his daughter and her companions that he plans to quit the city and desert to the enemy. Cressida's pleas fail and he departs, leaving her to sing of an incident in childhood which she now recognises as representing presentiments of desertion, always connected with her father ('Slowly it all comes back'). The warrior in her dream of long ago is the Troilus of today – the Troilus they (and the gods who preside over our destinies at birth) will not allow her to love!

Calkas has deserted, and Pandarus prays to Aphrodite to ensure that his tongue has not lost its golden touch: only with its aid can he rescue the family from a crisis. In lively, flexible music, he starts to plead Troilus's cause with Cressida but is interrupted by the arrival of the Prince himself. Troilus is met by Antenor's soldiers with the news that their captain has been taken prisoner. Troilus swears that he will be rescued, either through an exchange of prisoners, or else by force of arms. Pandarus persuades Cressida to come next day to a supper party at his house, then, before she leaves, prevails upon her to leave her crimson scarf as a token of esteem for Troilus. Troilus for his part has discovered that Calkas, the father of his beloved, is a traitor, but the music returns, as he catches sight of Cressida's scarf, to the ecstatic lyricism of his aria earlier in the scene.

ACT II. A room in Pandarus's house the following evening. The music, with its syncopated rhythms, immediately recalls us to the mood induced by Pandarus's arrival in the previous act. Supper is over, a storm is blowing up and Pandarus, thinking this will suit his book, dispatches a messenger to fetch Troilus. At the first sign of rain, Pandarus urges Cressida and the other guests to stay the night. In gently decorative music, her ladies prepare Cressida for the night. She cannot sleep and in an aria admits to herself that she is in love – her basically cool music (the languor of the beauty long accustomed to admiration?) soon turns to passion as she proclaims 'friend and foe, Troilus my conqueror'.

377

Pandarus, who has a different story for each of them, comes in to say that Troilus is in the house, racked with jealousy and begging to see her. 'On jealousy's hot grid he roasts alive', begins the ensemble which becomes a trio when Troilus overhears Pandarus's barefaced fabrication – one of the liveliest and most successful moments of the score, cut by the composer at Covent Garden's 1963 revival. Troilus interrupts, denounces the trickster who admits he has made it all up, and starts to woo Cressida from her tears. A love duet develops, under the star, as it were, of Aphrodite. Pandarus looks in, is delighted at what he sees, and tiptoes away without interrupting the lovers.

The storm breaks in an orchestral interlude, which depicts the love-making within as well as the wind and rain outside. It ends with peaceful dawn and the opening of Scene ii as Troilus and Cressida together watch the sun rise over the roofs of Troy. They are disturbed to hear the sound of approaching drums, and Pandarus is particularly concerned for the good name of his family. Troilus must not be discovered; Pandarus will cope with the visitors.

It is Diomede (*baritone*), a young Greek commander, who explains that Calkas wishes to have his daughter restored to him and that the commanders of the army have agreed that Cressida shall go to the Greek camp in exchange for the Trojan warrior Antenor. When Pandarus claims that Cressida is not in his house, Diomede searches, discovers her and marvels at her beauty. Troilus emerges at Diomede's departure and says he will not rest until the agreement is revoked. He will send daily messages and will corrupt the sentries so that he may visit her in the Greek camp. There is a moving vocal postlude, as it were, to their grand duet, and Troilus gives her back the crimson scarf to keep as a token of their love.

ACT III. The Greek encampment. Early evening ten weeks later. Calkas's tent can be seen at the side. A sad cor anglais solo introduces the scene and the sound of nightwatchmen's voices can be heard. Cressida, whose distraught loneliness is all too apparent, implores Evadne to see if there is a message from Troilus. She has not heard from him since they parted and is beginning to despair. Evadne knows Cressida's coldness to Diomede jeopardises their safety, and her solo ('Night after night the same') offers her mistress no comfort. Cressida for her part is a prey to every kind of fear, and she prays movingly to the goddess either to allay or confirm her fears. Calkas protests that it is madness to continue to flout Diomede, whom Cressida admits to finding attractive. Diomede stands in front of her, demanding her final decision as to whether she will become his wife. Abandoning all hope of seeing Troilus again (return of cor anglais solo), Cressida yields to Diomede's demands, even ced-

ing him the scarf he begs from her as a favour. Evadne overhears and secretly destroys the last of the many messages
Troilus has sent Cressida, all of which at Calkas's behest she has
concealed from her mistress.

Troilus and Pandarus have gained admittance to the Greek
lines in an hour of truce, and they urge Evadne to fetch Cressida, whose ransom has at last been arranged. Cressida comes
from her tent, richly dressed to meet Diomede, but her music
speaks of heartbreak rather than rejoicing, and only the sound
of Troilus's voice brings a quickening of the musical pulse. His
pleading is full of tenderness, but the news of her ransom obviously perplexes her. Before she can convince Troilus that he is
too late, Greeks can be heard acclaiming her as the bride.

Diomede himself comes into view wearing the crimson
favour on his helmet and in time to hear Troilus claim Cressida
as his, body and spirit. Diomede orders Cressida to denounce
him, and when she hesitates, he is overcome by the public
humiliation and begins an embittered lament which develops
into a full-scale sextet eventually swelled by the chorus. It is
broken off by the infuriated Diomede, who stamps on Cressida's scarf. Troilus falls on him with his sword and is getting the
better of the fight when Calkas stabs him mortally in the back.
Diomede gives orders that the body of the gallant Trojan prince
be carried away with due honours, that Calkas be sent in fetters
back to Troy, and that Cressida shall stay in the camp of the
Greeks for the enjoyment of whoever chooses her. Left alone
for a moment, she utters a final lament to the gods, then, seeing
Greek soldiers approach, snatches up Troilus's sword and,
binding it with her scarf, kills herself.

Michael Tippett
(b. 1905)

THE MIDSUMMER MARRIAGE

OPERA in three acts; text by the composer. Première, Covent Garden,
January 27, 1955.

*T*HE MIDSUMMER MARRIAGE is of course a comedy, concerned,
as Tippett says,[1] 'with the unexpected hindrance to an eventual marriage', the hindrances basically 'our ignorance or illu-
sion about ourselves'. In it Tippett emphasises myth, investi-
gating the problems of carnal and spiritual union and the

---

[1] Michael Tippett, *Moving into Aquarius*, Routledge & Kegan Paul.

nature of self-knowledge. Mark and Jenifer are the young lovers, and we see their misunderstandings, clashes, adjustments of personality, reaction to opposition – the predicament of most young couples in love, though here made explicit and symbolical where usually implicit and matter-of-fact. The opera is essentially the story of their inner development.

ACT I (Morning). 'A clearing in a wood, perhaps at the top of a hill, against the sky. At the back of the stage is . . . a kind of sanctuary, whose centre appears to be an ancient Greek temple.' Steps to the right lead upwards and end abruptly in mid-air; to the left, steps lead down through gates into the hillside itself. It is half light before sunrise on a midsummer day, and the music is of the utmost vigour and brilliance. To keep an assignation with Mark and Jenifer, who plan to marry, come their friends. Caution and purpose are immediately apparent. They greet the rising sun on midsummer morning, then perceive the temple building and hear the music coming softly from it. The chorus hides as the dancers emerge, led by Strephon (*dancer*) and followed by the Ancients (*bass, mezzo-soprano*). The dance is formal and interrupted by the entrance of Mark (*tenor*), calling for a new dance for his wedding day. He is told to watch, with the admonition 'change the unchanging ritual, there'll be no point of rest', but the He-Ancient to Mark's indignation trips Strephon with his stick, eventually ordering the party back into the temple.

In an extended, florid aria, Mark exhorts them to celebrate his love with him. Jenifer (*soprano*) appears, dressed much to Mark's surprise for a journey and not a wedding; their duet (with six-part chorus beneath it) is rapturous enough, but all Mark's pleading makes little difference: 'It isn't love I want, but truth,' says Jenifer. Her feminine instinct for chastity and intellectual independence is affronted by Mark's masculine desire and assertion. They have to learn to accommodate each other's point of view – hence the events of the drama.

Jenifer starts to climb up the broken stairs, disappearing suddenly. Mark is half-laughingly consoled: 'She'll come back', but hearing the voice of Jenifer's businessman father, King Fisher (*baritone*), he decides complementarily to emulate Jenifer and go in search of that element in himself which corresponds with the feminine principles of instinct, fertility and love – the qualities for whose lack he appears temporarily to have lost Jenifer. He goes down through the gates and into the hillside.

King Fisher enters. He stands for all elements, parental and otherwise, which are hostile to Jenifer and Mark and obstructive to their development. Using his secretary Bella (*soprano*) as intermediary, he enlists the help of the Ancients in tracing his daughter who has, he assumes, eloped with Mark. When they refuse to open the gates, he sends Bella for her boyfriend Jack (*tenor*), a workman who will do the job for them, and himself turns on the men and women who crowd round. He suborns the men with money and drives them off, but has less luck with the women, who refuse to work for him.

Enter Jack, who with Bella represents the uncomplicated, Papageno-Papagena pair of lovers, able to live their lives by means of intuition. Jack agrees to do the job, but is confronted by a warning voice from behind the gates: the voice of Sosostris (*contralto*) is vehement in urging caution. The men cry forward, the women are for restraint, but King Fisher gets his way until at the decisive moment Jenifer reappears at the top of the steps.

She has hardly started to explain her experience when Mark too becomes visible, also transfigured. They postulate different points of view and the Ancients and the dancers come from the temple and demand that each shall put a case.

First Jenifer in a splendid statement, then Mark in a hardly less magnificent aria, 'As stallions stamping', refer in rather oblique terms to their experiences. The dancers and their friends meanwhile force King Fisher away from the protagonists, until Jenifer moves across the stage to confront Mark and show him the animal she feels he has become. The mirror she holds up to him falls from her hand and she starts to descend as he climbs the steps up which she had formerly sought enlightenment, each now attempting to recover the spiritual balance which is tottering with the symbolical reversal of roles. King Fisher rushes out, while the friends of Mark and Jenifer understand that 'Mark and Jenifer endure for us', proclaiming themselves 'the laughing children' as the act comes to an end in something close to ecstasy.

ACT II (Afternoon) shows the same physical scene from a rather different angle. Strephon starts to dance below the temple steps, then hides when the chorus is heard offstage, celebrating the longest day. Jack and Bella come on with a few friends, but are soon left alone. Bella brings up the subject of marriage.

They go into the wood, Strephon takes up a dancing position and there begins the central section of the act, an elaborate and closely worked out ballet sequence in which the unconscious conflict between the sexes is shown at its most savage, albeit in music of unusual and persuasive richness even for Tippett. The sequence is as follows:

    I   The Earth in Autumn: the Hound chases the Hare.
    II   The Waters in Winter: the Otter chases the Fish.
    III The Air in Spring: the Hawk chases the Bird.

Bella sings a charming arietta as she refurbishes her make-up

('They say a woman's glory is her hair'). The act ends with off-stage cries in praise of midsummer.

ACT III (Evening and Night). In the last act Tippett takes us nearer the magical and ritual forces which influence our actions. The scene is as at the opera's start; it is plain that a picnic has taken place and on one side of the stage is dancing. The action is languid until King Fisher announces that he has brought his own brand of magic to counteract that of the Ancients: Madame Sosostris, a clairvoyante. The crowd is to escort her to the spot, where he will have a confrontation with the Ancients, whom Bella now calls. In spite of the Ancients' attempt to dissuade him, King Fisher persists, and a procession comes up the hill bearing a litter, on which is a cloaked figure whom Bella recognises as Jack.

A contraption is seen, of vaguely human form and covered in veils, to which King Fisher explains the situation briefly, calling upon Madame Sosostris to locate his absent daughter. In music of impressive cast, at first slow and measured, Sosostris begins her invocation, gradually mounting in tempo and intensity and rising in *tessitura* as she follows it with a divination of the union of Jenifer and Mark, both physical in that they are in love and symbolical in that Jenifer is now ready to accept the masculine in Mark which she has come to understand (and vice versa).

King Fisher interrupts and dashes the bowl to the ground, demanding that Jack unmask Sosostris's imposture. At the end of an ensemble Jack throws down belt and holster, his symbols of office, and turns his back on King Fisher who reluctantly picks them up. He moves to unveil Sosostris. The last veil falls to disclose an incandescent bud, which falls open like huge lotus petals. Inside, transfigured, are Mark and Jenifer. They turn to King Fisher, who falls dead. Chorus and She-Ancient antiphonally sing his threnody over a Purcellian bass.

Strephon and a female dancer, with wooden stick and block, begin to make ritual fire. The chorus joins in, and Mark and Jenifer celebrate their vision: 'Sirius rising as the sun's wheel rolls over at the utter zenith', and all including He- and She-Ancient proclaim their belief in carnal love and fertility. As the fire dance proceeds, Mark, Jenifer and Strephon seem to be drawn inside the lotus bud, whose petals close upon them so that finally nothing but the torch lighted at the start of the dance can be seen. Eventually even this is drawn into the veils, which break into flame, glow, die out and leave the stage dark.

'Was it a vision? Was it a dream?' The light starts to return but the temple is shrouded in dawn mist as at the opening. As warmth pervades the music again, Mark and Jenifer can be heard, and soon they are visible too as their mortal selves, proclaiming that they have found truth, and that 'All things fall and are built again, and those that build them again are gay'.

KING PRIAM

OPERA in three acts; words and music by Michael Tippett. Première, May 29, 1962, at Coventry (and later at Covent Garden).

WITH the isolated orchestral features and stark musical lines of his second opera, *King Priam*, Tippett breaks to some extent with the luxuriant writing of *The Midsummer Marriage*, something which disturbed the nostalgic admiration of many lovers of the earlier work. The composer explained at the time of the first performance that the work was concerned with Choice – Priam's after the prophecy over the fate of Paris, Paris's after the hunting episode to go to Troy, Priam's to accept him, Helen's to leave Sparta with Paris, Paris's between the three Graces, and so on throughout. But, essentially, it is Tippett's reaction to the events and circumstances of one of the world's greatest myths, with its tensions and heroic loves, its themes of courage and suffering, and public and private trial.

ACT I. Troy. Heralds with trumpets in front of the curtain and a wordless chorus behind it (the latter much used throughout the opera to express stress and particularly battle, the former as 'links' between the episodes of the heroic drama) usher in the action, which starts with discussion of Hecuba's (*dramatic soprano*) dream – that her newly-born son Paris will cause his father's death. Hecuba's reaction to the Old Man's (*bass*) reading of the dream comes in an aria, 'Then am I no longer mother to this child', which quickly reveals her forthright, passionate nature. Priam's (*bass-baritone*) reaction is less positive and exposed in a ruminative soliloquy, whose first words, 'A father and a King', are used later to pinpoint the moment when choice was available to him and he allowed heart (typified in this phrase) to rule head (which insisted on the child's death), and more culpably, did not hide this reaction from the Young Guard (*tenor*), to whom he gave the job of killing the child and who knew Priam's feelings contradicted his words.

A vocal Interlude, involving the Nurse (*mezzo-soprano*), Old Man and Young Guard – the opera's 'Greek Chorus' – discusses choice in its relation to the particular situation.

Priam's son Hector (*baritone*), attempting to demonstrate his physical prowess by subduing and capturing a wild bull single-handed, is dismayed when a young lad (*boy soprano*) jumps on its back and rides it away. Eventually, the boy comes in, revealing that he loves the bull as his best friend but would like to join the young heroes of Troy. Hector offers to teach him the arts of war, a proposition Priam accepts provided the boy's father agrees and he makes a free choice. This the boy does, saying that his name is Paris, a revelation which startles Priam into a soliloquy. He cannot conceal his joy that the gods have reversed his 'Choice' of long ago, and his fear that Hecuba's dream may yet prove inspired; in effect, he accepts the new turn of fate.

Nurse, Old Man and Young Guard witness the decision and comment in a second Interlude on its importance. Guests come rejoicing from the wedding feast of Hector and Andromache (*soprano*), at the same time admitting that the mutual hostility of Hector and Paris has caused Paris to set sail from Troy to the court of Menelaus at Sparta.

We see Helen (*mezzo-soprano*) and Paris (now *tenor*), obviously already consumed with passion. Paris insists that Helen must choose between him and Menelaus and at the end of their duet exacts her promise to leave with him if he comes to fetch her. Paris in his soliloquy turns to wonder whether there is in fact any element of choice in human affairs – do he and Helen 'choose' when, having been apart, their bodies rush together as one? Hermes (*high tenor*), as if in answer to his question, comes to tell him he must choose between three Graces: Athene, Hera and Aphrodite (sung by Hecuba, Andromache, Helen). How in choosing one can he escape the wrath of the others? Hermes answers that he will not escape – but he must still choose. Athene offers him courage on the battlefield, Hera satisfaction in marriage, and each curses him when it is obvious he will choose Aphrodite and therefore elope with Helen and plunge Greece and Troy into war.

ACT II. Troy is besieged and Hector taunts Paris with having run away in battle from Menelaus. Priam tries to patch up their quarrel, and Paris eventually follows Hector to battle. The first Interlude has the Old Man asking Hermes to let him see the Greek hero Achilles sulking in his tent.

Except in one short crucial scene, it is the private Achilles (*heroic tenor*) whom we meet in the opera, and he is found in his tent with Patroclus (*light baritone*), singing sadly to the sound of guitar, 'O rich soiled land', a song of longing for peace and beauty quite at variance with the actions for which Achilles is renowned. Patroclus weeps that Achilles should have so taken to heart the loss of a girl, given as booty after the sack of Thebes and then taken away again, as to refuse to join the battle. Together they cook up the idea that Patroclus shall wear Achilles's armour against the Trojans, and Achilles pours a libation to the gods in order that Patroclus may return safely.

The act's second Interlude has the Old Man begging Hermes

to warn the Trojans of their peril at Patroclus's hands. Paris comes to tell Priam that Hector has killed Patroclus in single combat, and Hector to parade before his father in Achilles's armour. A fine trio celebrates the victory and the prospect the Trojans now have of destroying the Greek fleet, but it is interrupted at its climax by the blood-curdling sound of Achilles's war cry.

ACT III. Cellos alone introduce Andromache, waiting for her warrior to return from single combat. In her aria, she remembers her foreboding the day Achilles killed her father and brothers, but she refuses to go on the walls of Troy in order to call Hector back from the field of battle; why does King Priam not end the war by sending Helen back to Sparta? Hecuba retorts that it is not for Helen that the Greeks have gone to war, but to win Troy itself. When Helen appears, Andromache insults her. Helen's answer takes the form of a great aria, its burden: 'Women like you, wives and mothers, cannot know what men may feel with me'. The voices of the three women join in a fine trio in which each invokes the name and attributes of her mate and predicts death.

The others leave Andromache. In the Interlude, serving women pretend to go about their business in Hector's house, but they have already heard the rumour: ' . . . we could tell the story too, the pathetic story of our masters, viewed from the corridor' Priam feels alone, isolated by his subjects from some disaster. Only Paris has the courage to tell him that Hector is dead; he proclaims his intention of absenting himself until he has worked out his destiny by killing Achilles.

The last section of the opera begins as Paris leaves and Priam moans to himself: 'A father and a King.' Had the augurs predicted Hector's death and not his own, he would not only have ordered but also willed the killing of the infant Paris. His conscience speaks in the guise of the Young Guard, the Old Man and the Nurse who make him recite the dread chain of events, with vengeance inevitably following military murder, and he gradually accepts the inexorable laws by which mankind lives.

The second Interlude, purely orchestral, ushers in the scene in Achilles's tent, climactic if undemonstrative, in which King Priam begs the body of Hector from the Greek who slew him. Achilles seems to start to urge the law of retribution, but his mention of the name of Patroclus shows the full extent of the wound his friend's death caused him. Priam kisses his hands, 'The hands of him who killed my son', and Achilles grants him the body of Hector. Achilles and Priam discuss the destiny of each, Achilles's to die at the hands of Paris, Priam's to be killed by Achilles's son Neoptolemus.

The third Interlude has Hermes announcing the deaths of

the protagonists and hymning music's all-healing supremacy. Paris offers to fight to defend Priam, who has refused to leave Troy with him. Priam prays and fails to recognise Hecuba. Stress mounts in the chorus, Andromache spurns Paris and his defence of Priam, and Helen takes her place. 'They stand silent together, the beautiful ill-fated pair', and Priam sends Paris on his way to a hero's death, leaving Helen to make her peace with her lover's father. Priam comforts her – and himself – with the idea, which she enunciates, that neither he nor Hector ever reproached her for her part in events. Finally, as the offstage sound of the chorus dies away, Priam sinks inaudibly down before the altar where, as Hermes appears before him and departs, Neoptolemus runs his sword through him to kill him instantly. 'Choice' is at an end.

THE KNOT GARDEN

OPERA in three acts; words and music by Michael Tippett. First performed at Covent Garden, December 2, 1970.

IN a preface to the published score, the composer describes the dramatic action of *The Knot Garden* as 'discontinuous, more like the cutting of a film. The term used for these cuts is Dissolve, implying some deliberate break-up and reformation of the stage picture'.

As an introduction to Act I, which has the sub-title Confrontation, Tippett wrote in the original Covent Garden programme: '*The Knot Garden* is about the loves and hates of seven people in modern England. Mangus, a psychoanalyst, has been invited to stay in the house of Faber and his wife Thea. She hopes that Mangus can help with the problems of their young ward Flora, who is obsessed by the half-real, half-imagined sexual threat of Faber. Mangus discovers that it is not Flora that is sick but the marriage, and engineers a series of confrontations and "games" to resolve the difficulties. He sees himself as a modern Prospero, manipulating the characters. Dov, a musician, and his lover Mel, a young negro writer, are also staying in the house, but as Thea's guests rather than Faber's. The arrival of Thea's sister Denise, a revolutionary, changes all the relationships.'

ACT I. Uncompromising, strenuous, wide-striding music (the storm) introduces Mangus ('*high tenor baritone*'), who at his first appearance is described as 'a still point in a whirling storm'. Straightaway, he alludes to Prospero and seems full of self-confidence. Here occurs the first Dissolve, ten bars of loud *allegro molto* followed by five of *diminuendo* timpani roll and soft horn call (sometimes on cellos); it is the same each time it occurs in Acts I and II, but varies in Act III. Thea (*dramatic mezzo*) comes slowly from the inner garden. Mangus offers to help, but Thea's authority in the garden is absolute. Flora ('*light high soprano*') rushes screaming into Thea's arms. Faber ('*robust baritone*') follows her, but Thea sends Flora away with Mangus and turns harshly to Faber. Thea leaves, and Faber, who has been put in the wrong, wonders how this now happens so regularly, then goes off to work. Mangus is left to muse. Dissolve.

Thea recommends flower therapy to Flora – or, more prosaically, tells her to arrange some roses in a bowl – and Flora hums enigmatically to herself before saying that Thea's sister Denise has sent a message that she will be arriving later that day. Flora's desultory and now solitary humming turns more purposefully into 'eeny, meeny, miny, moe', but is interrupted by the rumbustious arrival of Dov (*lyric tenor*) and Mel (*lyric bass-baritone*) in fancy dress, the one tricked out as Ariel, the other as Caliban (jazz drummer's kit in the orchestra). They introduce themselves, Mel as a writer, Dov as a musician, then sing a nonsense rhyme together as Thea and Mangus come from the house.

Mangus is of course delighted at the augmentation of *The Tempest* cast, which now has Ariel, Caliban, Ferdinand and Miranda as well as his Prospero. He takes Flora off to look for costumes and each of the two men who are left takes a glass from Thea's tray until Mel seems hypnotically drawn to Thea, leaving Dov alone to smash his glass to smithereens and start to howl like Ariel's dog. Faber is amazed at what he sees on his return, but Dov's reprise of the ditty he and Mel have already sung leads to an explanation of identities, and Dov moves towards Faber at exactly the moment when Thea and Mel reappear on the opposite side of the stage.

Tension builds but is exploded by the sound of Flora's renewed screams as she starts half-hysterically to describe the disconcerting nature of Denise's arrival, explained the moment Denise (*dramatic soprano*) comes into view and it can be seen that she is disfigured by the torture she has endured in her one-woman efforts to set the world to rights. She starts in an extended and passionate aria to explain what she has been through. Mel attempts to relieve the tension by starting a blues, itself developed into a considerable ensemble which eventually includes even Mangus and finally Denise herself, just before the act comes to an end with Mel's softly spoken, 'Sure, baby'.

ACT II. Labyrinth. The composer's programme note tells us all the action of the opera takes place in Thea's garden, and especially in the Knot Garden of the title.

The music is violent from the outset and the first to be whirled in are Thea and Denise, aware of each other, not dissimilar in their sentiments but not properly conversing. Thea is whirled off and Faber makes some kind of contact with Denise, who ripostes that she is just as tough as Thea before being herself whirled off and replaced by Flora (her ditty again), who backs away from Faber with renewed screams. No amount of reasoning from Faber can change her attitude towards him, she drops the flowers she has been carrying and is whirled off as Thea reappears to strike Faber with a horse-whip. When Thea disappears, Dov, dressed now as himself, takes her place, still howling like a dog, but prepared to sympathise with Faber's predicament – each of them, he feels, humiliated by a woman. Faber is obviously attracted in spite of himself, but his 'Come, I never kissed a man before' only just precedes his disappearance, as Mel is whirled on. Mel's very effective scene with Dov has as its refrain 'One day we meet together, brother' and as its burden the discovery that two souls, who thought they were twin, need to discover their true natures. Dov is whirled off as the music calms and Denise appears to play on Mel's feelings for oppressed men anywhere. As Mel turns to Denise, Dov is thrown from the labyrinth, Thea returns and so does Faber until Flora and Dov, after the act's first Dissolve, are left together.

Dov comforts Flora with music, in an infinitely touching scene, first getting her to sing the opening phrases of Schubert's *Die liebe Farbe*, orchestrated with a magical touch. Dov ripostes with his own song, much less simple in outline. The magic of love is in the air but the spell is broken by Mel, who enters the garden.

ACT III. Charade. After some scene-setting, the first Charade. Mangus-Prospero explains the island and its inhabitants to Flora-Miranda, conjuring Mel-Caliban to stand upright, to his daughter's delight, and Dov-Ariel to leave the tree where Sycorax has imprisoned him. But Dov-Ariel flings himself on Mel-Caliban and belabours him, far beyond the calls of the script. Dissolve.

There is an exchange between Thea and Denise. Both agree that Mel could be Denise's salvation. Dissolve.

Flora-Miranda is asleep; Dov-Ariel is on guard; Mangus-Prospero watches through a telescope. Mel-Caliban creeps up on the sleeping girl, leaps on her and tries to tear her clothes off. Denise protests and Mel says he is only playing the role he was given and no more. Let Denise lay her head against his pounding heart (where, says Dov, *his* head often lay), and she will understand, but she will not – yet. There is a short duet for Dov and Mel, 'Black earth for white roses?', at the end of which Thea asks Mangus whether he is man of power or voyeur. Mangus's answer is to disclose Faber-Ferdinand and

and Flora-Miranda playing chess – but not for long, as Flora-Miranda upsets the board.

The board is set again, and Thea, left alone, expresses new-found confidence in an *arioso* full of melismas: 'I am no more afraid. So we swing full circle back towards the sanctity of marriage.' Dissolve.

A dénouement seems called for and Mangus-Prospero offers to provide it, at least for Dov and Mel. As judge, with Faber-Ferdinand as some sort of gaoler, he tries first Dov-Ariel and frees him, then Mel-Caliban. The Charades are at an end, and it is a time for quotation, musical and Shakespearean. Mel leaves with Denise, Flora goes off alone in spite of Dov's anxiety to follow her, so that in the end he follows Mel and Denise. Mangus can see only Thea and Faber alone in the garden (Dissolve: modified version of original), and they begin to speak, though not to each other. 'I put away the seed packets. I put away the factory papers . . . Our enmity's transcended in desire.'

That the problems of each couple, or of each individual, are resolved is evident; but their catalyst seems to have been musical rather than explicitly contained in the events of the drama.

Benjamin Britten
(1913–1976)

THE story of Benjamin Britten's sixteen operas can be told in terms of a search for twentieth-century operatic form. Essentially, he cut for himself four different paths. First, a traditional-force line, involving a big apparatus, designed by implication for nineteenth-century-style buildings and comprising *Peter Grimes*, *Billy Budd* and *Gloriana*. Next, a new form of chamber opera, with initially an orchestra of 13, no chorus, a small number of soloists, and intended for smaller theatres (*The Rape of Lucretia*, *Albert Herring*, *The Beggar's Opera* and *The Turn of the Screw*). Even more out of the ordinary, and also made for smaller forces and buildings, were the children's operas – *The Little Sweep*, *The Golden Vanity* and *Noye's Fludde*, the last designed for performance in church. A fourth and wholly original category was the church parable, of which there were three examples: *Curlew River*, *The Burning Fiery Furnace* and *The Prodigal Son*. There is contrast between the forms he evolved but flexibility within them, and *A Midsummer Night's Dream*, *Owen Wingrave*, and *Death in Venice* (which are neither traditional nor chamber in form, nor in the forces they require) have proved almost as viable in theatres as large as the San Francisco Opera, Covent Garden and the Metropolitan as in Aldeburgh's Jubilee Hall, on television, or at the Snape Maltings, for which they were first designed.

PETER GRIMES

OPERA in a prologue and three acts by Benjamin Britten; text by Montague Slater, after the poem by George Crabbe. Première, Sadler's Wells, London, June 7, 1945.

THE idea of *Peter Grimes* came to Britten in America in 1941 after he read an article by E. M. Forster on George Crabbe, the poet of East Anglia. Shortly afterwards, Koussevitzky, the conductor, commissioned Britten to write an opera. On the composer's return to Britain (in spring 1942), he set to work with Montague Slater to hammer out the libretto. It is freely adapted from Crabbe's story, which forms a part of his long poem, *The Borough*. The opera softens the character of Peter Grimes; he is not the uncomplicated sadist of Crabbe's poem, but a proud, self-willed misfit, whose independence and unwillingness to accept help ends in disaster.

PROLOGUE. The Moot Hall of the Borough, a fishing village on the East Coast; about 1830. An inquest is being held on Grimes's apprentice who died at sea. The people who crowd the hall suspect Grimes (*tenor*) of having caused the boy's death. Grimes tells Swallow (*bass*; the Borough lawyer and coroner) how he and the boy were driven off-course by a change of wind, how they were three days without water, when the boy died of exposure.

In confirming the details of what occurred when Grimes landed his boat, Swallow and Grimes refer in turn to Ned Keene (*baritone*), the Rector (*tenor*), Bob Boles (*tenor*), Auntie (*contralto*), Mrs. Sedley (*mezzo-soprano*), and Ellen Orford (*soprano*), who corroborate the evidence as their names are called. This device allows in the shortest possible time an expostion of the opera's main characters. The Coroner gives his verdict: '. . . your apprentice died in accidental circumstances. But that's the kind of thing people are apt to remember', and advises Grimes to get a grown-up, not a boy, to help him in future. Grimes vainly tries to make himself heard, but Hobson (*bass*) clears the court. Ellen, the schoolmistress, tries to comfort Grimes. Their duet begins with Ellen singing in E major, Peter in F minor, but as Peter warms to her quiet confidence in his future, he takes up her key and they finish together: 'Here is a friend'.

Britten begins each of his three acts with an Interlude, and also connects the two scenes of each of them with a similar orchestral piece. Prologue and Act I (which is set on the beach) are joined by the first Interlude, whose calm expresses the typical movement of waves and water, which so often heralds a new day for the fishermen.

ACT I. Scene i. The first part of the scene is in the form of an extended chorus with interruptions from various characters. Grimes is heard offstage calling for help with his boat. It is refused, until Captain Balstrode (*baritone*) and Keene decide to give him a hand. Keene tells Grimes he has found him another apprentice whom he has to fetch from the workhouse. Carter Hobson refuses to have anything to do with the transaction, and the chorus supports him. Finally, Ellen takes her stand against them: 'Let her among you without fault cast the first stone'. Her D minor *arioso* indicates Ellen's determination and tenderness. Hobson yields. Mrs. Sedley, a rentier widow, asks Keene, the apothecary, if he has her laudanum. He says she should meet him in the pub that night to collect it.

Balstrode spies the storm cone and leads a great fugal ensemble, in which join the voices of Keene, Auntie, the landlady of 'The Boar', and her two Nieces (*sopranos*), Bob Boles, the chorus and orchestra. The passage ends with a prayer: 'O tide that waits for no man, spare our coasts'. The storm music dominates the rest of the act.

Balstrode, commenting on Grimes's apparently convinced isolation, suggests he would be better off working on a merchantman, away from the gossip of the Borough. Grimes replies he is 'native, rooted here'; but, touched by Balstrode's kindness, he tells him in an *arioso* passage the story of his horrifying experience at sea with only the corpse of the dead boy as company. The duet grows in intensity as Grimes refuses to listen to Balstrode's advice. The interval of the ninth has been thought to characterise Grimes's maladjustment and we hear it in its minor form at the start of the scene, resolved into the major as he reflects passionately on the peace which could be his were Ellen to become his wife ('What harbour shelters peace?'). The following Interlude unleashes the full force of the storm.

Scene ii. The interior of the Boar. Warmth and calm contrast with the storm, which enters each time a character opens the door. Mrs. Sedley is waiting for her drugs; the Nieces are frightened by the storm; Bob Boles, who makes drunken advances to one of them, is overpowered by Balstrode, who leads the company in 'We live and let live, and look, we keep our hands to ourselves'.

Grimes bursts in. Mrs. Sedley faints. Grimes then sings introspectively of the mystery of the skies and human destiny ('Now the Great Bear and Pleiades') in a *scena* of haunting beauty. Consternation reigns but Ned Keene saves the situation by starting a round: 'Old Joe has gone fishing'. Three distinct tunes are combined in a 7/4 metre. Hobson, Ellen and the new apprentice arrive, chilled to the bone. Grimes makes off, taking the boy with him. 'Peter will take you home', Ellen sings. The chorus responds derisively, 'Home! Do you call that home?'

ACT II. Scene i. Sunday morning, peace after the storm, with the Prelude, a lively and brilliant *toccata*, depicting the sunlight reflected off the waves, and contrasting with a broad, lyrical tune. As the curtain rises, Ellen enters with John (*silent*), the new apprentice. The scene takes place within a frame provided by the music of the offstage church service. Ellen talks to the boy about his life at the workhouse and her own love of her teacher's life. She finds his coat torn and – worse – a bruise on his neck. Grimes enters and tells the boy they are off to work, answering Ellen roughly when she tells him it is a day of rest. She pleads with Peter, in music of great tenderness, and concludes, 'Peter! we've failed'. He cries out in agony, strikes her, and matches the chorus's 'Amen' with his own *fortissimo*, 'So be it, and God have mercy upon me!' Grimes drives the boy off in front of him, leaving Ellen to make her way home weeping.

The service ends, spilling its congregation on to the beach. Some have heard the quarrel, and the chorus murmurs in indignation at what it only half understands ('Grimes is at his exercise!'). Bob Boles calls on Ellen, who has come back to collect her things, to say what happened. She tries to explain, but the weight of opinion is too solidly against her. 'Murder!' cries the chorus. A party is organised to investigate what is going on at Grimes's hut. The men march off to the tune of a vindictive chorus, while Ellen, Auntie and the Nieces in a beautiful quartet reflect on their relationship with men.

The Interlude, a *Passacaglia*, is the centrepiece of the opera. Through it runs a desolate viola solo, a symbol of the fate of the apprentice caught up in Grimes's destiny.

Scene ii. Grimes's hut, an upturned, boarded-in boat on a clifftop. Grimes in an extended monologue seeks to contrast what he is in reality with what he has always dreamed and planned, with Ellen's help, to be. This gives way to a feverish description of his awful vigil with the dying apprentice in the boat. The sound of the investigatory procession can be heard. Grimes, believing the boy is the cause, warns him to be careful and hustles him down the cliff, turning as he senses the procession nearing his door to hear the boy scream as he falls down the cliff to his death. Grimes climbs quickly after him.

The Rector, Swallow, Keene and Balstrode enter. They find nothing but an open door on to the cliff. Swallow remarks that the whole episode seems to have ended by quieting village gossip once and for all.

ACT III. Scene i opens with a Moonlight prelude of great simplicity and beauty, whose rising theme is punctuated by a little figure for flute and harp. The Borough street and beach, night. A dance is in progress in the Moot Hall, to the sound of an offstage band, and there is a steady procession between there and The Boar. Swallow, all dignity discarded, makes a play for one of the Nieces who, with her sister, eludes him. Ned Keene, who has similar intentions to Swallow's, is waylaid by Mrs. Sedley, who, to an accompanying *Ländler*, tries to enlist Keene's interest in proving Grimes a murderer.

The older members of the community bid each other good-night (the Rector outdoing everyone in affability) while Mrs. Sedley broods in the darkness. She overhears Ellen and Balstrode say Grimes is nowhere to be seen; he has found the boy's jersey, which Ellen herself had made him, washed up by the tide. Ellen's extended aria, 'Embroidery in childhood was the luxury of idleness', is florid and exacting, yet with a tranquil, resigned effect. Balstrode says there may yet be something they can do for Grimes, in his hour of 'unearthly torment'.

Mrs Sedley goes officiously to the door of The Boar and calls for Mr. Swallow, who eventually materialises. He orders Hobson to take a posse of men and find Grimes. The atmosphere of hysteria and brutality is horrifyingly reflected in the big ensemble, 'him who despises us we'll destroy', and ends with *fortissimo* cries of 'Peter Grimes!'

The short sixth Interlude is described by Edward Sackville-West as music which 'transfers us from the one-track hysteria of the crowd to the echoing limbo of Grimes's mind . . . a single chord . . . held, *ppp*, throughout . . . by three muted horns. Figures of nightmare seabirds fly through the fog uttering fragments of themes which Grimes has sung earlier'.

Scene ii. As the curtain rises, the search-party can be heard crying 'Peter Grimes', while a fog-horn is heard. In a long mad soliloquy, Grimes babbles of home and sings snatches of music from the various stages of his tragic story. Ellen and Balstrode enter to tell him they have come to take him home. He is beyond help, and Balstrode, in ordinary speech, tells him to take his boat out to sea and sink her. He helps him with the boat, then leads Ellen away.

Three violins begin to play the prelude to Act I. It is morning and the chorus sings the same tune as the beginning of Act I. Swallow confirms the coastguard's report that a boat has been seen sinking out at sea, but no one is interested. The Borough has forgotten its manhunt and prepares to get on with another day.

THE RAPE OF LUCRETIA

OPERA in two acts by Benjamin Britten; text by Ronald Duncan, based on André Obey's play *Le Viol de Lucrèce*. Première at Glyndebourne, July 12, 1946.

ACT I. The Male and Female Choruses are sitting on thrones, on either side of the stage. They move about hardly at all during the course of the opera, and they are at times (e.g. during the interludes) cut off from the main part of the stage by a back-cloth.

We are *in medias res* straight away as the Male Chorus (*tenor*) announces *con forza* in the third bar: 'Rome is now ruled by the Etruscan upstart, Tarquinius Superbus.' In a nervous half *arioso*, half recitative style, he introduces the story by sketching in the historical background against which it is set (time: 500 B.C.). The particular situation – war against Greece – is specified by the Female Chorus (*soprano*) before the two voices join in a lyric statement.

The front-cloth rises, as the orchestra (muted strings and harp) suggests an atmosphere of oppressive heat, a night alive with the noise of crickets and bullfrogs. The scene is a camp outside Rome. The officers, who have been drinking, discuss the outcome of their bet the night before, when they rode home unannounced to see what their wives were doing in their absence. Only Lucretia (*contralto*), Collatinus's wife, was at home, and the others, not excluding Junius's Patricia, were all found in one compromising situation or another. 'And Collatinus has won the bet', shouts Tarquinius (*baritone*), 'And Junius is a cuckold . . .'

Tarquinius and Junius (*baritone*) quarrel and start to fight but are separated by Collatinus (*bass*), who suggests they drink a toast together. Tarquinius immediately proposes it and all join in. This becomes the Lucretia motif.

At its end, Junius rushes angrily from the tent. He is furiously jealous of Lucretia's chastity, and repeats her name again and again, easing his agony by abusing her. His aria is developed to a point at which the idea of revenge fills his mind, when for the second time the Male Chorus takes over from him. What Junius might not have said aloud, but what he would have admitted to feeling, is sung by him; the jealousy which causes his anger and the thoughts it suggests to him – things he would *not* have admitted to feeling – are described by the Male Chorus in music of insinuating character.

Junius ends his aria with a final explosive 'Lucretia!', and Collatinus walks out to reason with him and persuade him to take a less directly personal view of the situation. Collatinus goes off to bed, leaving Tarquinius and Junius to resolve their differences in a striking duet. Junius leaves Tarquinius alone, after suggesting that to prove Lucretia chaste is something even the Prince will not dare to attempt. The Male Chorus to the orchestral accompaniment of the opening of the scene comments on Tarquinius's indecision, until his cry of 'My horse! My horse!' reveals that his mind is now all too firmly made up.

The curtain falls rapidly and immediately the Male Chorus begins a graphic description of Tarquinius's Ride to Rome. The music's energy mounts until the Ride is brought to a temporary halt by the River Tiber. Tarquinius and his horse take to the water, and the Chorus describes their crossing. The Ride culminates in the Chorus's *ff* 'Lucretia' as the curtain goes up to reveal the hall of Lucretia's house.

All is apparently at peace. She and her two female companions are spinning, and the Female Chorus's beautiful spinning song, with its flute and harp accompaniment, not only sets the mood but also frames the three solo verses, each with its 'nostalgic ninth'. Lucretia thinks she hears a knock, but finding it is not Collatinus or his messenger, as she had hoped, sings an *arioso*, 'How cruel men are to teach us love'. The women prepare for bed, and a trio develops between Lucia (*soprano*) and Bianca (*contralto*), who vocalise while folding linen, and the Female Chorus who comments on this regular and calming feminine action.

'How quiet it is tonight', reflects Lucretia; '. . . it must be men who make the noise', retorts Bianca, and immediately we hear a suggestion of Tarquinius's Ride in the orchestra. Male and Female Choruses point to the contrast between the peace within and the man who is coming so fast to disturb it, and a loud knocking announces that Tarquinius has arrived. The rest of the scene is carried on in pantomime, to the expressive comment of the two Choruses, until Lucretia's two companions remark on the strangeness of a visit so late from the Prince whose palace lies only just across the city, but who is asking for Lucretia's hospitality. She cannot refuse it, and there starts a chain of 'Good nights', each one based on Tarquinius's motif.

ACT II. As before, the two Choruses introduce the act. The curtain rises to show Lucretia asleep in bed as the bass flute, muted horn, and bass clarinet introduce the Female Chorus's Lullaby, a tune of exquisite sensitivity. The hushed atmosphere is continued in the next section, in which the Male Chorus, accompanied only by percussion, describes Tarquinius's approach to Lucretia's room. In an extended and impressive aria, he sings of his feelings for Lucretia. He bends over her to wake her, as he has planned, with a kiss.

Lucretia wakes (to the sound of the 'whip' – a little used orchestral instrument) and immediately the character of the music changes. Lucretia pleads for mercy in music of rapidly rising tension, and Tarquinius does his best to establish that her resistance is diminishing: 'Can you deny your blood's dumb pleading?' The Choruses take Lucretia's part in the quartet which ensues, but it is too late, and Tarquinius pulls the cover from the bed and threatens Lucretia with his sword. The scene ends with a statement by the quartet *a cappella* of the music heard originally in Junius's soliloquy, and Tarquinius beats out the candle with his sword as the curtain falls rapidly.

The Interlude takes the form of a figured chorale sung by the two commentators, in which they interpret in Christian terms the scene they have just witnessed, while the orchestra depicts the physical events of the rape. The Interlude dies away and the front-drop goes up to show the hall of Lucretia's house as in the second scene of Act I. Everything is flooded with light, and Lucia and Bianca exult in the beauty of the day, then discuss whether it was Tarquinius they heard gallop out of the courtyard earlier in the morning.

Lucretia enters. She is obviously full of foreboding, and her initially quiet behaviour gives way to something like hysteria when she is offered the orchids to arrange: 'How hideous! Take them away!' She orders Lucia to send a messenger to Collatinus, telling him to come home. She laughs hysterically but calms sufficiently to arrange the rest of the flowers, which she does while she sings an aria, a miniature of beauty and pathos. She leaves. Collatinus and Junius come in, demanding to know where Lucretia is.

Lucretia herself comes in, dressed in purple mourning, and in eleven bars of orchestral music (cor anglais and strings) the essence of her tragedy is conveyed. Collatinus comforts her, affirming that they must never again be parted. Their voices blend before Lucretia makes her confession to Collatinus, the orchestra punctuating what she has to say with *sotto voce* memories of the music which went with what she is describing. Finally, she sings 'For me this shame, for you this sorrow'. Collatinus attempts to forgive her, but she is overcome by what has happened to her, and stabs herself, dying in Collatinus's arms.

Her funeral march takes the form of an extended *chaconne*, Collatinus and Junius first, then Bianca and Lucia, and finally the two commentators joining their voices in the magnificent ensemble. The Female Chorus cannot accept the finality with which the story has closed, and ends incredulously 'Is this it all?' to which she receives conclusive answer from her male companion: 'It is not all . . . For now He bears our sin, and does not fall . . . In His passion is our hope, Jesus Christ, Saviour, He is all, He is all.' The Christian ethic has been allowed – some commentators have said 'forced' – to draw a moral from the pagan story.

ALBERT HERRING

OPERA in three acts by Benjamin Britten; text by Eric Crozier, adapted from Maupassant's story *Le Rosier de Madame Husson*. Première, Glyndebourne, June 20, 1947.

ACT I. Suffolk, 1900. The curtain rises after two bars of the busy prelude to show the breakfast room of Lady Billows's (*soprano*) house, where Florence (*contralto*), her housekeeper, is tidying up the room. Lady Billows is half-heard calling instructions from her room (offstage). Florence admits Miss Wordsworth (*soprano*), the Vicar (*baritone*), the Mayor (*tenor*), and Mr. Budd (*bass*), the committee which is to decide between the rival candidates for the position of Queen of the May.

An *alla marcia* introduces her Ladyship, who seems at one point in danger of not noticing her visitors, except to complain that the room stinks of tobacco. But the situation is saved, and, while she greets the committee, the orchestra begins the fugal tune which develops after a bit into a full-blooded quintet: 'We've made our own investigations and bring you our nominees.'

They sit down. Lady Billows rhapsodises on the subject of the position of May Queen, and grows eloquent as she considers the 'state of complete moral chaos' from which it is expected to retrieve the town. The names are put forward *quasi ballata* by each member of the committee and vetoed with uncommon gusto by Florence. A short quartet leads to a furious aria for Lady Billows. She denounces the town as a 'spawning-ground of horror', and Florence takes particular pleasure in repeating her last words – 'sty the female sex has soiled'.

Superintendent Budd has a brainwave: why not a *King* of the May? He launches headlong into an aria: 'Albert Herring's clean as new-mown hay', but the other committee members hint delicately that he is perhaps an unusually backward boy, and Lady Billows snubs the suggestion as firmly as she can. The Vicar rises to the occasion with a string of persuasive platitudes. 'Right! We'll have him! May King! That'll teach the girls a lesson!' says Lady Billows and leads off the fugal finale. She leaves the room for a moment and returns to transform the finale into a florid, Purcell-like choral ode.

After an interlude, the scene is the interior of Mrs. Herring's grocer's shop, outside which can be seen playing Emmie, Cis, and Harry (*sopranos* and *treble*), village children: 'Bounce me high, bounce me low'. The ball bounces into the shop, and Harry goes in after it, taking the opportunity to pinch some apples for himself and the others. They are interrupted by Sid (*baritone*), who empties Harry's pockets, and, pausing to take an apple for himself, shouts for Albert (*tenor*).

The hero makes his entrance backwards through the door, and carrying a hundredweight of turnips (or so he tells us). The carefree Sid gives his order and offers to toss Albert for it, double or quits. Sid tempts him to break the apron strings with a recital of the pleasures of independence: 'Tickling a trout, poaching a hare.' Albert tries not to listen, and Sid is just off, when Nancy (*mezzo-soprano*), his girlfriend, the baker's daughter, comes in.

Sid buys Nancy a couple of peaches (from the firm's petty cash, he says), and tells her to bring them that night and meet him at quarter past eight for a walk together in the moonlight. Albert comments on the duet, which thus becomes a trio, moreover of true lyrical beauty. Sid and Nancy go off together, Sid of course forgetting to pay for his herbs. Alone, Albert, in an extended monologue, wonders if his mother's strictness really leads to anything valuable.

Florence comes into the shop and sends for Mrs. Herring (*mezzo-soprano*) to tell her that the Festival Committee is about to pay her a visit. There is no time for further explanation before Lady Billows is upon them, announcing 'great news', which in-cludes the information that the prize consists of twenty-five golden sovereigns.

The visitors leave. A jubilant Mrs. Herring is only momenta-rily put out when Albert says firmly that he intends to refuse the prize. She sends him upstairs to repent his abortive rebellion.

ACT II. The inside of a marquee in the vicarage garden. Sid tells Nancy what has been going on down at the church, in an aria that is richly ironical. What of Albert? 'The poor kid looks on tenterhooks. He's in the mood to escape if he could.' Sid takes Nancy outside to tell her his scheme. Miss Wordsworth brings in the children to rehearse the anthem they are going to sing in celebration of Albert's coronation as King of the May. They leave as Nancy and Sid return, the plot having been re-vealed. Sid pours rum into the lemonade glass in Albert's place (to the accompaniment of the *Tristan* chord) and all is ready for the reception of the official procession.

Miss Wordsworth hurries the children back, and Super-intendent Budd, Mrs. Herring, the Mayor, Florence, the Vicar, and Lady Billows come in successively, each singing charac-teristic music. The anthem goes off quite well, and all take their places to a confused burble of conversation (as highly organised as the rest of the music). The Vicar rises to introduce the first speaker.

This, of course, is Lady Billows, who begins with phrases of an ambitious range that rivals even Fiordiligi's. She loses her notes, but general applause covers the gap and she presents Albert with his prize of twenty-five sovereigns. In turn come speeches from the Mayor, Miss Wordsworth and Mr. Budd, and finally Albert is called on to make some sort of reply. He can get no further than 'Er . . . er . . . thank you . . . very much', but rejoicing is general, and the Vicar leads off a congratulatory ensemble, 'Albert the Good! Long may he reign!'

Albert drinks to the toast, enormously likes what he tastes, and comes round to Nancy for more, reaching her with a re-sounding hiccup (on a top C flat). He is cured, by drinking from the wrong side of a glass, and the curtain goes down as the feast gets under way.

After an interlude, Scene ii takes place inside Mrs. Herring's shop a little later that night. Albert sings exuberant remi-niscences of his triumph. Outside, Nancy comments sym-pathetically to Sid on Albert's plight and shyness, they sing a short but forceful duet, kiss, and are off, leaving behind a much shaken, even an excited Albert.

Gone are most of Albert's inhibitions, and for the first time he sees himself as others see him, a shy, gawky, mother-ridden boy. He decides to toss for it, whether he shall go off on the bust . . . or not. It comes down 'heads for yes'.

ACT III. The *prestissimo* prelude immediately suggests the atmosphere of the man-hunt which follows the discovery of Albert's disappearance. Nancy sings three verses of an aria before Sid comes wearily into the shop, complaining that one can hear nothing but Albert's name everywhere.

Superintendent Budd asks for Mrs. Herring, and observes to Sid that murder, arson, robbery, rape (*Lucretia* motif) he can deal with, but 'God preserve me from these disappearing cases'. Mrs. Herring comes down, a picture of inconsolable grief. She starts the quartet (*come un lamento*) which ensues.

Harry complicates matters with his shouted: 'There's a Big White Something in Mrs. Williams's well', and Mrs. Herring collapses, just as Lady Billows comes in. A procession appears escorting the Mayor, who carries a tray on which is Albert's orange-blossom wreath – 'Found on the road to Campsey Ash, crushed by a cart'.

There ensues the Threnody, a great ensemble for nine voices, on an *ostinato*. Each individual has a characteristic verse to him-self, the others meanwhile continuing the lament.

The shop bell rings, and Albert pokes his head round the door. 'What's going on?' he asks, and immediately a storm of recrimination and questioning breaks around his head. He must explain everything at once, and only Sid and Nancy take his part. Albert starts to tell them a story in which more is hinted at than actually described. All are horrified, and their horror is not diminished when Albert blames it all on the life of repression and mollycoddling he has been forced to lead. At the end of his recital of his doings, Albert sings a tune which is at the same time ridiculously mild and inoffensive, and also warm and curiously full of understanding, even wisdom. Its effect on everyone is electrical; they have met their match and can no longer patronise their innocent May King.

'I didn't lay it on *too* thick, did I?' Albert asks Sid and Nancy.

BILLY BUDD

OPERA in four acts by Benjamin Britten; words by E. M. Forster and Eric Crozier, based on the story by Herman Melville. Première, Covent Garden, December 1, 1951.

BRITTEN had already discussed the possibility of collaboration with the novelist E. M. Forster before deciding on a subject, and the story goes that writer and musician simultaneously and independently suggested Herman Melville's last story, *Billy Budd*, to each other.

In 1961 Britten condensed the opera to two acts. Act I's finale disappeared completely, with the consequence that Captain Vere is seen first in private and not until Act IV face to face with the ship's company; and that direct contact with Billy Budd is postponed to the second scene of that act. The original version has been followed in this synopsis.

ACT I. Prologue. The stage is in darkness. Captain Vere (*tenor*) is shown as an old man. He meditates on his career and what it has taught him, on the mystery of good and evil, and on the unfathomable ways of Providence which allows a flaw in every attempt at good. Vere's mind goes back to the year 1797:

The lights go up on the main deck and quarter-deck of HMS *Indomitable*. The men are working on the main deck, urged on by the first mate and supervised by Mr. Flint (*baritone*), the Sailing Master. A Novice (*tenor*) slips and the Bosun (*baritone*) turns savagely on him and has Squeak (*tenor*), the ship's corporal, list him for twenty strokes.

The deck empties, leaving Mr. Flint alone. A guard-boat returns from a press-ganging expedition, Mr. Redburn (*baritone*), the First Lieutenant, comes up on deck, Claggart (*bass*), the Master-at-Arms, is sent for, and preparations are made to receive the recruits. Mr. Ratcliffe (*bass*), who has led the party which boarded the merchantman *Rights o' Man*, has returned with three recruits. Claggart steps forward to question them. Red Whiskers (*tenor*) does his best to protest against his enforced enlistment, Arthur Jones (*baritone*) replies meekly enough, and finally Billy Budd (*baritone*) answers confidently that the sea is his life and his trade is 'Able Seaman'. When asked about his parents, he is undismayed: 'Haven't any. They say I was a . . . was a . . . ' – he stammers on the word 'foundling'. The officers are delighted with their new recruit and place him in the foretop. In an exhilarating passage, Billy rejoices in his new life: 'Billy Budd, king of the birds!' He ends with a farewell to what is past, and to the ship on which he served: 'Farewell to you, old comrades, farewell to you for ever . . . Farewell, *Rights o' Man*.' The officers jump to the conclusion that this has political significance.

As the decks are cleared, Mr. Redburn instructs Claggart to keep a watch on the new recruit. Claggart summons Squeak, and tells him to keep an eye on Billy Budd, and to provoke him by petty thefts from his kit-bag. The Novice's Friend reports that the flogging has taken place and that the offender has collapsed; he cannot walk. 'Let him crawl' is Claggart's cynical reaction. The Novice is half-carried in and, part of a subdued ensemble, expresses utter despair.

As they go out, Billy and Dansker (*bass*), followed by Donald (*baritone*) and Red Whiskers, emerge from the shadows where they have been watching, their *scherzando* quartet in contrast to what has gone before. Claggart appears, and Captain's Muster is heard. Donald has just time to refer to the captain as 'Starry Vere', before the ship's company falls in on deck.

As the music reaches a climax, Vere himself appears and informs the company they are nearing action and that victory must come from their combined efforts. Billy leads a chorus of praise for Vere as the act comes to an end (this is the section cut in the revised version).

ACT II. Scene i. Evening, a week later. Vere reads in his cabin and sends for his officers to take a glass of wine with him. Mr. Redburn and Mr. Flint are announced, and the three discuss the prospect of action, which they all think is imminent. Flint starts a *scherzando* duet, 'Don't like the French', in which Redburn joins with some relish. Vere admits he shares their sentiments. The word 'mutiny' creeps into the conversation, and immediately casts its shadow. 'We must be on guard' is Vere's conclusion. The others remember 'that young chap who shouted out "Rights o' Man"', but Vere says there is nothing to fear from that quarter. The sound of singing is heard from below as Mr. Redburn announces, 'Land on the port bow . . . Enemy waters.' Vere is left alone.

Scene ii. The berth-deck. After an orchestral interlude, making use of two shanties, the scene is animated and yet contented, as Donald starts another shanty, 'We're off to Samoa, by way of Genoa', and Red Whiskers and Billy, then full orchestra and chorus join in.

Billy goes to his kit-bag to find some tobacco for Dansker and the sound of his stammer is heard. He drags in Squeak, whom he accuses of pilfering. Squeak denies this, but draws a knife. Billy floors him in an instant. Suddenly Claggart appears and asks Dansker for an explanation. Squeak is arrested, clapped in irons and, when he threatens to blow the gaff on Claggart, gagged as well. Claggart turns to Billy and says, 'Handsomely done, my lad. And handsome is as handsome did it, too' (Melville's words).

Claggart, alone, sings a dark soliloquy, a musical denunciation of the power of good with which he finds his own evil face to face: 'I, John Claggart, Master-at-Arms upon the *Indomitable*, have you in my power, and I will destroy you.'

The Novice comes in. He has been summoned by Claggart and pressurised through fear of future punishment to obtain evidence against Billy by setting him up as a mutineer. He accepts the guineas which Claggart gives him to pass to Billy.

The Novice goes to wake up Billy, who does not at first understand what the Novice means. When he tumbles to it, the Novice scampers off as Billy is seized with another fit of stammering. Dansker appears, and Billy in agitated phrases tries to tell him what the fuss is about. Dansker understands all too well and, in a big-scale duet (*Passacaglia*), warns Billy about Claggart, 'Jemmy-legs is down on you'.

ACT III.[1] The main-space and quarter-decks. Some days later. Vere and Redburn are worried by the rapidly increasing mist. The Master-at-Arms appears and tells Vere that some sailor, as yet unnamed, is likely to endanger the safety of the ship. The interview is cut short by a yell from the main-top: 'Enemy sail on starboard bow!' At the same moment the mist lifts and the stage (like the music) hums with activity ('This is our moment').

All is ready and excitement reaches fever-pitch, but the enemy is still out of range. There is a general prayer for wind to fill the sails, the climax when a shot is fired, and then frustration which amounts almost to despair when the mist returns to render further pursuit impossible. Orders are given to dismiss.

The Master-at-Arms returns. This time Vere makes no attempt to hide his impatience at Claggart's evasive ways. Clag-

---

[1] Act II in the revised version.

gart names Billy Budd as the leader of the planned mutiny, and an incredulous Vere sends for him.

An Interlude summarises the conflicts going on in Vere's mind, but the curtain rises to show Vere's cabin with the Captain's mind made up: 'Claggart! John Claggart, beware! I'm not so easily deceived.'

Vere encourages Billy, who thinks he is going to be promoted, to talk. Claggart enters and, after Vere has cautioned both men to speak only the truth, charges Billy with mutiny. Billy is seized with stammering and hits out at Claggart, striking him in the middle of the forehead; he falls dead. Vere sends Billy into his stateroom, then orders his cabin boy to fetch the officers.

Vere has no doubt as to his predicament. Claggart's evil purpose was clear enough, and yet his innocent victim by his own action has doomed himself. The officers enter and Vere summons a drumhead court, which he will attend as witness. Billy is brought in and agrees that Vere's bare account of the facts is true. Billy is told to wait in the inner room. The three officers appeal for guidance to Vere, who refuses to intervene. The verdict is 'Guilty'. Vere orders that sentence be carried out next morning; the Master-at-Arms to be buried with full naval honours.

After an *arioso* for Vere, he goes to inform Billy of the verdict and the stage is left empty. In an extraordinary ending to the act, Britten writes a succession of thirty-five common chords, whose different dynamics and scoring convey the changes of emotion with which the message is given and received.

ACT IV. Scene i. A bay of the gun-deck, shortly before dawn. Billy, in irons, sings a slow, pathetic tune of resignation and farewell. The words are Melville's, taken from the poem which he describes as composed by a shipmate after the execution and put posthumously into the mouth of Billy himself ('Billy in the Darbies').

Dansker steals in and brings him a mug of grog, saying 'Some reckon to rescue you'. The notion that his death may precipitate a mutiny, the idea of which he abhors, fills Billy with new courage, which finds expression in an ecstatic ballad.

Scene ii. The main deck and quarter-deck. The ship's crew assembles to the sound of a funeral march. Vere takes his place and Billy is led in. Mr. Redburn reads the sentence, Billy turns to Vere and shouts to him, 'Starry Vere, God bless you', and his cry is taken up by the crew. Then he marches smartly out. Vere removes his hat and all eyes turn to follow Billy as he ascends the mast.

The men on the main deck suffer an immediate revulsion of feeling, and turn in revolt to the quarter-deck. Britten writes a *presto* fugue on a variation of the mutiny theme (to the sound of 'ur' in 'purple'), but this savage incoherence gradually changes to a passionate echo of the swelling music associated with the routine work in Act I. Such ending to the drama seems to indicate that this is no theme of disillusionment but rather carries a message of confidence, if not in Good itself, at least in Man's capacity to understand and be influenced by Good.

The light fades and Vere is seen standing alone, an old man as in the Prologue. 'I could have saved him . . . O what have I done?' he asks, but takes strength from Billy's ballad, as the epilogue comes quietly to an end.

GLORIANA

OPERA in three acts by Benjamin Britten; words by William Plomer. First performed Covent Garden at a Gala for the Coronation of Queen Elizabeth II, June 8, 1953.

ACT I. Scene i. Outside a tilting ground. A tournament is in progress inside. Cuffe (*baritone*) reports to the Earl of Essex (*tenor*) that Mountjoy has accepted a challenge and that the crowd acclaims its favourite. Essex is furiously jealous, when, to the evident delight of the crowd, Mountjoy (*baritone*) is victorious and receives his prize – a golden chessman – from Queen Elizabeth the First (*soprano*) herself. The crowd sings a hymn-like tune in praise of the Queen: the music symbolises the affectionate relationship between the Queen and her subjects, and is one of the opera's dominant themes.

Mountjoy bids his page bind his prize upon his arm. Essex accuses him of arrogance and provokes him to fight: Essex is slightly wounded. The Queen emerges from the tilting ground, and upbraids both lords for offending against the rule that no duel may be fought at court. She asks Sir Walter Raleigh (*bass*) for his view. In an aside, both Essex and Mountjoy make quite clear that they bitterly resent what they regard as Raleigh's insolence – he is older and more experienced than they are but of far less exalted rank. The Queen tells Essex and Mountjoy she has need of them both; let them come to court, but as friends, not as enemies, and they can count on her support and protection. After an ensemble, a trumpet march brings the scene to an end.

Scene ii. The Queen's ante-room in Nonesuch Palace. The Queen is alone with Cecil (*baritone*), the Secretary. She refers to the recent duel between the two young lords, and asks Cecil whether he has had news of the reaction of Lady Rich (*soprano*) to the fight – 'the dark Penelope' who is sister to Essex, mistress

to Mountjoy.[1] When she admits her liking for Essex, Cecil
warns her to be on her guard. The Queen reminds Cecil that
she has wedded herself to the realm; she seeks no husband and
is content if her people are happy. Cecil reminds her of his
father's ancient counsel to the sovereign whom he loved and
served so long.

The Queen and her counsellor turn to affairs of state. At
mention of the possibility of a new Armada from Spain, the
Queen laments the certain waste of life and money: 'We can but
watch and wait'. Essex is announced and Cecil withdraws.
Essex's greeting to his sovereign and his cousin[2] is exuberant
and the Queen asks her Robin – as she calls him – to soothe her
worries by singing and playing to her. Suiting the tune to the
words and accompanying himself on the lute, Essex sings
'Quick music's best when the heart is oppressed', a little lyric
whose enchanting, quicksilver grace is too remote from the
Queen's mood to afford her the comfort she seeks. Essex sings
again, this time quietly, slowly, and with a depth of feeling and
sensitivity that affords a complete musical recreation of that
quality which one may suppose caused the Queen to pin her
faith for the future to her brilliant but unpredictable cousin.

The music has a far-reaching significance in the opera and
epitomises their relationship. The words of the poem Britten
has set in one of his finest inspirations are by Essex himself.

An affectionate duet between the two is interrupted when
Elizabeth points to the silhouette of Raleigh, which can be seen
at the entrance. Essex refers to Raleigh as 'the jackal', and
denounces him as his enemy who is, with Cecil, determined to
prevent him going to Ireland, there to overthrow the Queen's
enemy, Tyrone. The Queen dismisses Essex and is alone.

Her thoughts run to duty and to love – the claims of one, the
solace of the other, and their mutual incompatibility. After a
triumphant resolution, 'I live and reign a virgin,/Will die in
honour,/Leave a refulgent crown', the Queen kneels and prays
to God for strength and grace.

ACT II. Scene i. The Guildhall at Norwich. It was Queen
Elizabeth's custom to make periodic tours of England – during
which time she was said to be 'On Progress' – and she is
attended by her court, Essex, Cecil, Raleigh, and Mountjoy
amongst them; the Recorder of the City of Norwich (*bass*) is
coming to the end of his address of welcome. The Queen
thanks him and the citizens for their greetings, is cheered by the
assembled populace, and, when the Recorder comes to kneel in

[1] Whom she married after the death of her husband, Lord Rich.
[2] His mother, Leicester's widow, was niece to Anne Boleyn, Queen
Elizabeth's mother.

homage and stumbles, helps him solicitously to his feet. The Queen consents to see a Masque, prepared in her honour. This provokes an impatient aside from Essex, chafing at the enforced inactivity. Ireland is again uppermost in his mind.

The Masque begins. The music is a set of six contrasted dances, introduced by the Spirit of the Masque (*tenor*) and set for unaccompanied voices. It ends in homage to Gloriana.

Scene ii. The garden of Essex's house. It is evening. Mountjoy sings of his love for Penelope Rich, who appears and greets him rapturously. Their duet is interrupted by Essex and Lady Essex (*mezzo-soprano*), who do not see them and are discussing the Queen's continued refusal to advance Essex to the position of Lord Deputy in Ireland, which he considers his due. Essex's anger mounts and his sister and his friend break off to warn him against talk which others might consider treasonable.

Scene iii. The great room in the Palace of Whitehall during the course of a Ball given by the Queen. The whole scene is built up on a series of dances in the Elizabethan style, which are played on the stage and used to frame a considerable development of the dramatic situation. The buzz of conversation quietens when the Queen's lady-in-waiting (*soprano*) comments admiringly on the splendour of Lady Essex's dress. 'Will the Queen approve?' is Frances's less confident reply.

The Queen enters, catches sight of Lady Essex, then orders that 'La Volta' be played. This is a brilliant, vigorous piece in 6/4 time; its salient feature was the tossing of the ladies in the air by their partners. The Queen commands that the ladies go to change their linen; a Morris dancer performs for the entertainment of those who remain. Lady Essex hurries in, breathlessly complaining that her new dress has disappeared while she was changing. The Queen suddenly returns, wearing the missing dress. It is much too short for her, and she looks grotesque. For a moment she stalks around, while the court looks on in amazement, then turns to Lady Essex:

> If being too short it becometh not me
> I have it in mind it can ne'er become thee.[1]

The Queen leaves, and in an ensemble Essex, Mountjoy, and Penelope attempt to comfort the stricken Frances Essex, who for her part is more concerned with the inflammatory effect the episode may have on her husband. As usual the Queen turns out to be unpredictable. She caps her insult to Essex's wife by returning to proclaim that Essex is appointed Lord Deputy in Ireland and charged to subdue the rebellious Tyrone. After an

---

[1] The episode may at first strike a modern audience as too grotesque to be credible, but it is based on an authenticated incident, when the Queen humiliated a lady of the court suspected of being Essex's mistress.

ensemble, the Queen commands a 'Coranto' which is danced by the entire court.

ACT III. The catastrophe which is to bring about the fall of Essex – the failure in Ireland – has already taken place when Act III begins; and it is the Queen we see take the 'tragic' decision, not Essex.

Scene i. The Queen's ante-room at Nonesuch. It is early morning and the maids of honour are talking of Ireland and Lord Essex. Soon Essex himself bursts in, demanding to see the Queen. When told she is not yet ready, he sweeps back the curtain behind which she can be seen without her wig at her dressing-table.

She dismisses her attendants, and turns to him. Their conversation is quiet, even tender, until Essex mentions the foes who 'beset me now here in England, at home'. The Queen rounds on him and puts her as yet unspoken accusations into words. He has failed in his trust; he is not only unfit but untrue. Essex pleads his devotion to her, and her anger quickly changes to sorrow, until he is reduced to memories: 'O put back the clock to the birth of our hope!' The scene grows in intensity as the music gets slower and softer, and anger is replaced by the agony of the might-have-been, until Essex and the Queen together recall the song which has symbolised their relationship.

The Queen is quickly joined by her ladies-in-waiting, who sing comfortingly to their mistress. When Cecil arrives, the Queen is majestically arrayed. He tells her that Tyrone is still unsubdued, and that Essex has not only failed in his mission but has brought with him a horde of his unruly followers. The Queen gives orders that Essex be kept under supervision.

Scene ii. The City of London. A blind Ballad-Singer (*bass*) sits outside a tavern and relays what he hears to his listeners. He recounts the progress of Essex's rebellion, from the moment when it is first discovered that the Earl is free until Essex is publicly proclaimed a traitor by the City Crier (*baritone*).

Scene iii. A room in the Palace of Whitehall. Cecil, Raleigh, and other members of the Council are unanimously agreed that Essex is guilty, but Cecil warns them that the Queen may yet hesitate to make up her mind, may even pardon him. When she enters they inform her of the verdict and, when Cecil tries to press her to make a quick decision lest the people should doubt Essex's guilt, she forbids him to prate to her of her duty.

She is alone and in a crucial scene her dilemma is forcefully portrayed until Raleigh steps in and announces that Lady Essex, Penelope Rich, and Mountjoy have come to intercede for the fallen Essex. After an ensemble, Lady Essex is promised that, whatever happens to her husband, her children will not suffer. Penelope asserts that it is not only Essex's service to his

Queen but his rank which entitles him to a pardon. The Queen is roused to fury by her words, and sends for the warrant to sign. Penelope shrieks with anguish.

The stage darkens and the action becomes unrealistic. Various episodes of the end of Queen Elizabeth's life are re-called – Cecil pleads to be allowed to approach James VI of Scotland about his succession, the Queen makes her so-called Golden Speech to the House of Commons ('I have ever used to set the last Judgment Day before mine eyes'), Cecil appears again in an effort to get the Queen to go to bed. As the Queen's life draws to its close, from behind the scenes can be heard the chorus singing softly.

Gloriana together with its composer was under considerable attack at the time of its Coronation première, some critics, amateur rather than professional, deciding that it was an insult to the young Queen Elizabeth to show her ageing predecessor partly in a human rather than an exclusively regal light. And yet the work is a product of the composer's early maturity, full of operatic insight, arguably the most relaxed he had yet written, and a vindication of his attempt to write at the same time a 'national' opera and for a specifically 'grand' occasion.

THE TURN OF THE SCREW

OPERA in a prologue and two acts by Benjamin Britten; libretto by Myfanwy Piper, after the story by Henry James. Première by the English Opera Group at the Venice Festival, September 14, 1954.

*T*HE TURN OF THE SCREW is an operatic adaptation of Henry James's story, preserving almost every detail intact; certain episodes have been run together, but almost nothing has been omitted. The composition of the orchestra is the same as in Britten's other chamber operas, except that a thirteenth player has been added to take care of piano and celesta.

With a view to musical unity in an opera which is continuous and has a prologue and sixteen scenes (with each of which is associated a dominant instrument), the work is based on a Theme. Each scene is connected to its successor by a musical variation on this Theme, which itself involves the twelve notes of the scale and is built up on alternately rising fourths and falling minor thirds. It first occurs after the Prologue and before the first scene of Act I, and employs the twelve semitones of the scale, but the music is so far from being dodecaphonic that each variation and its succeeding scene has a definite tonal centre. One of the features of James's story is a series of reflections on its implications, particularly on the exact states of tension and emotion in his central character, and the variations turn the screw and form musical counterparts to these literary soliloquies, increasing the tension little by little until the final catastrophe is reached.

The opera begins with an explanatory prologue, tenor accompanied by piano alone: 'It is a curious story. I have it written in faded ink – a woman's hand, governess to two children – long ago . . . ' The prologue sets out the visit to the children's handsome guardian, the conditions which should govern the engagement (that she must assume complete responsibility and make all decisions, referring nothing to him), her doubts, and her final acceptance. The setting is an English country house in the mid-nineteenth century.

ACT I. Scene i. The presentation of the Theme is followed without a break by music illustrating the Governess's journey to Bly. The Governess (*soprano*) voices her misgivings and wonders what her charges will be like. The variation takes us straight into the busy, everyday world of Bly.

Scene ii. The children, Miles (*treble*) and Flora (*soprano*), are agog to know what their future governess will be like, Mrs. Grose (*soprano*), the housekeeper, is more interested in getting them to practise their bows and curtseys, and before either enquiries or rehearsals are completed, the Governess is there to greet them. The children bow and curtsey and then, while Mrs. Grose chatters on, the Governess rhapsodises on the beauty of the children and the grandeur of Bly.

Scene iii. The second variation (theme in the bass, otherwise music associated with the children's everyday life) takes us to the porch at Bly. Mrs. Grose brings the Governess a letter: 'Mrs. Grose! He's dismissed his school.' (Here, for the first time, occurs the sound of the celesta, later associated with Quint.) The reason? 'An injury to his friends.' Has Mrs. Grose ever known Miles bad? Wild, she says, but not bad, and as if to reinforce her conviction the children are seen and heard in the background singing together the nursery rhyme 'Lavender's blue'; the grown-ups turn their duet into a quartet, and the scene ends with the Governess's determined answer to Mrs. Grose's anxious question: 'I shall do nothing'.

Scene iv. Variation III, an idyllic synthesis of bird-calls on the woodwind. The Governess's lyrical aria shows that the peaceful environment has quieted her initial fears, but it is just at the moment when she admits herself 'alone, tranquil, serene' that a chill comes over the evening and she turns to see an unknown male figure (*tenor*) high up on one of the towers of the house. The guardian? No! She knows everyone in the house; is it a stranger or some madman locked away?

Scene v. Variation IV, marked 'very quick and heavy', anti-

409

cipates the children's vigorous singing of 'Tom, Tom, the piper's son', which rapidly takes on the character of a sinister march. The Governess comes into the room, and, as the children's tune dies away, the enigmatic figure of the tower is visible outside the window. She runs to see who is there, finds nobody, and returns to describe to Mrs. Grose what she has seen. Mrs. Grose's reaction is instantaneous: 'Quint! Peter Quint!', and her grief and terror are made very evident as she tells the story of the manservant's domination of the household and of his eventual death. The way the colour drains from the orchestra, like blood from the face, as the Governess understands she saw a ghost, is one of Britten's most potent strokes. Her peace at Bly is at an end. Quint, in death as in life, returns to dominate the children, and her main charge must henceforth be their protection against influences which, if she cannot withstand their power, will ruin them. Mrs. Grose seems to understand nothing clearly, but promises her help.

Scene vi. A brisk double fugue introduces and rhythmically prepares the lesson scene. Miles recites the traditional Gender Rhymes to be found in every English schoolboy's Latin Grammar ('Many nouns in -is we find . . .') and Flora's enthusiasm for history is not allowed to divert him from repeating his lesson. What other tags does he know, asks the Governess; he answers in a curious, haunting melody, that seems to summarise everything mysterious that may lie behind his natural childlike gaiety, the only side we have seen of him so far:

> Malo: I would rather be
> Malo: in an apple tree
> Malo: than a naughty boy
> Malo: in adversity.

It disconcerts the Governess in its strangeness.

Scene vii. Flora and the Governess are by the lake at Bly, and Flora asks if it figures in her geography book. The Governess gets her to repeat the names of the seas she has learnt, and she announces dramatically that the lake they are standing beside is called the Dead Sea. She turns from geography to the task of singing her doll to sleep with a lullaby. The Governess looks up from her reading, sees the ghost of Miss Jessel (*soprano*), the former governess (to the sound of her characteristic gong and chords), and immediately deduces from Flora's unnatural silence that she has seen her too. She hurries Flora away.

Scene viii (Variation VII). It is night, and the sound of Quint's voice quietly breaks the silence with a long reiterated coloratura flourish on the word 'Miles!' It is a moment of chilling beauty, made more effective because it is the first time a man's voice has been heard since the Prologue. Quint is eventually made out, high in the tower as when the Governess first saw him, and Miles can be seen in the garden below him. 'I'm all things strange and bold . . .' he sings to Miles: 'In me secrets, half-formed desires meet.' Miles is fascinated and answers him, and soon Miss Jessel's voice can be heard calling Flora, who responds in her turn. A *pianissimo* duet in 3/8 time, marked 'quick and lightly', develops for Quint and Miss Jessel. It may be thought of as denoting contact between ghosts and children. At its end the voices of the Governess and Mrs. Grose can be heard calling for the children. The ghosts vanish, Mrs. Grose hustles Flora indoors, and the Governess is left to hear Miles's enigmatic answer to her question – one of Henry James's unforgettable strokes: 'You see, I am bad, aren't I?'

ACT II. Scene i. Variation VIII begins with the clarinet imitating Quint's opening flourish, and introduces a colloquy between Miss Jessel and Quint. The dramatic theme of their duet: 'Why did you call me from my schoolroom dreams? I call? not I! You heard the terrible sound of the wild swan's wings.' The duet mounts in urgency as each participant asserts that, with his or her peace of mind established, 'The ceremony of innocence is drowned' (the line is a quotation from Yeats). As the ghosts fade from sight, the Governess can be heard in an agony of meditation: 'Lost in my labyrinth, I see no truth'.

Scene ii. The churchyard scene is heralded with an orchestral invocation of church bells (Variation IX) and the lights fade in on the children as they sing a *Benedicite* which is half straight, half parody ('O amnis, axis, caulis, collis . . . bless ye the Lord'). Mrs. Grose does not realise the implications until her attempts at comfort elicit from the Governess all the horrors of the night before. Mrs. Grose bustles Flora into church, but Miles hangs back and asks when he is going back to school. His final remark before going inside – 'You trust me, my dear, but you think and think . . . of us, and of the others. Does my uncle think what you think?' – prompts the Governess to a horrified 'It was a challenge!' There is nothing for it but for her to leave Bly. She runs out, and Variation X (the theme in the bass) is a postlude to the scene of her flight.

Scene iii. The moment she is inside her room the Governess can feel Miss Jessel's presence and sees her sitting at the desk. In their duet, Miss Jessel exudes calm and inexorability, but the Governess's nerves are screwed almost to breaking pitch, and she now knows that she cannot abandon the children. When Miss Jessel has gone, she cries 'I must write to him now', then, in one of the most beautiful passages of the whole opera given at first to the orchestra without the voice, sits at her desk and writes to ask the children's guardian if he will see her.

Scene iv. At Variation XI's start, bass clarinet and bass flute have a canon on the Theme. Miles is humming 'Malo', whose music dominates the scene: a scene where taut nerves threaten at any moment to crack into the relief of tears. The Governess tries to get him to tell her what happened at school. Quint's voice is heard, Miles shrieks and the candle goes out leaving the question still unanswered, the tears unshed. The short Variation XII (Scene v) has Quint's voice singing and the theme in *pizzicato* strings. Quint tempts Miles to take the letter the Governess has written: 'Take it! Take it!' He does so. The scene ends with 'Malo' in the orchestra.

Scene vi. With Variation XIII the mood changes sharply, the solo piano imitates a late eighteenth-century sonata and nerves are seemingly under control again. Miles is seen playing to the Governess and Mrs. Grose while Flora, later joined by Mrs. Grose, plays at cat's cradle. Mrs. Grose nods off and Flora steals out. Miles's triumphant attack on the piano (it reaches into Variation XIV) leaves no room for doubt that he was acting as a decoy to distract the grown-ups' attention.

Scene vii. Variation XIV is built up on Quint's 'on the paths' with the orchestra varying the principal theme. Mrs. Grose and the Governess find Flora by the lake. The Governess is immediately aware of Miss Jessel's presence and tries to force Flora to acknowledge it, but her efforts are successful only in making Flora take refuge with Mrs. Grose, shrieking that she hates the Governess and won't have anything more to do with her: Flora's furious 'I can't see anybody' leads a quartet of female voices in which Miss Jessel rallies Flora to her side and Mrs. Grose affirms that she can see nothing.

Scene viii. Variation XV is concerned mostly with the music of 'I can't see anybody' (piccolo and timpani). The last scene takes place out of doors. Mrs. Grose takes Flora away and reveals to the Governess that her letter to the children's guardian must have been stolen. It remains for the Governess, almost as in ritual, to ask Miles to place his confidence in her and to tell her whether he stole her letter. His attempts at being straightforward are complicated by the admonitions of Quint, but, when the Governess presses him to tell her who it is that he can see, the struggle for his soul reaches a climax and he dies with a scream of 'Peter Quint! You devil!', aimed, equivocal to the last, at one – or other – of his tormentors. Quint's voice joins with the Governess's, and in the end is heard at a distance. The Governess is left with the body of the little boy, and it is with pathetic repetitions of his 'Malo' song that the opera comes to an end.

A MIDSUMMER NIGHT'S DREAM

OPERA in three acts by Benjamin Britten; text after Shakespeare by the composer and Peter Pears. Première, Aldeburgh Festival, June 11, 1960.

THE opera elevates the fairies, and particularly their king, Oberon, to a position of prime influence and also, to become the framework of the whole opera, places all except the final scene in the wood, and relegates the question of anachronistic Athenian ambience very much to the background. Britten's music moves on three sharply differentiated planes: fairies, mortals (lovers) and rustics.

ACT I. The wood is represented by a slow-breathing string texture which rises and falls as the curtain goes up, and is heard again frequently throughout the opera. The fairies in two groups make their entrance with 'Over hill, over dale, thorough bush, thorough briar'. They are Tytania's instruments but are soon interrupted by Puck (*acrobat*; trumpet and drum accompaniment throughout), of whom they are afraid. Puck announces Oberon (*counter-tenor* or *contralto*) and Tytania (*coloratura soprano*) who have quarrelled over an Indian page boy.

Tytania departs and Oberon alone plots vengeance, summons Puck and sends him to fetch that herb whose juice 'will make or man or woman madly dote Upon the next live creature that it sees'. Oberon, his plot in motion, disappears and the wood is left empty.

Of the lovers, we meet first Lysander (*tenor*) and Hermia (*mezzo-soprano*), eloping to avoid the forced betrothal of Hermia and Demetrius. They leave, the wood is empty again, Oberon returns with schemes in his heart and music, and the quarrelling Demetrius (*baritone*) and Helena (*soprano*) come in, the latter breathlessly pursuing the former, who for his part wants nothing more than to be re-united with his betrothed Hermia. Oberon decides to put right the destinies of these star-crossed lovers. He sends for Puck who gives him the flower he demanded and lies at his feet. 'I know a bank where the wild thyme blows' is, for all its sinister undertones, an aria of exquisite sensibility.

Into the silent wood cautiously come six rustics, heralded by trombone *pp*. Peter Quince (*bass*) calls the roll and, not without frequent interruption from Bottom (*bass-baritone*), the weaver, assigns to each a part in the play which they plan to rehearse. Each is neatly characterised, from the swaggering Bottom through the shy but tenacious Francis Flute (*tenor*) to Snug the joiner (*bass*), who is 'slow of study' and tends therefore to come in on the weak beat of the bar.

Hermia and Lysander are exhausted with their wanderings and they lie down together, only for Puck to discover them and mistakenly squeeze the juice of the magic flower on Lysander's eyes (*celesta*). Hermia sings in her sleep, and Helena and Demetrius, still quarrelling, enter in their turn. Helena perceives Lysander, he wakes and declares love for her and hatred for Demetrius, in either instance to her considerable discomfiture. What has she done to be thus mocked? She runs out, followed by Lysander; Hermia wakes and distractedly follows where Lysander led.

Tytania enters with her retinue whom she bids sing her to sleep before going to their respective nocturnal offices. They oblige, but Oberon moves invisibly past the single sentinel they have posted and squeezes the magic juice on to Tytania's eyes, bidding her 'Wake when some vile thing is near'.

ACT II is concerned with sleep. Tytania lies at the back. The six rustics enter for a rehearsal, which is, as ever, punctuated by Bottom's suggestions. Puck is watching, and he follows Bottom at his exit. When Flute has voiced his entire role without a pause, Puck brings Bottom back with an ass's head on his shoulders, to the disgruntlement of the cast which runs off at top speed.

Bottom sings – or bellows – to keep his spirits up and Tytania wakes to love him. A languorous tune on A flat clarinet and flute expresses Tytania's infatuation and eventually she sets the fairies to play and sing to him. Bottom announces 'I have an exposition of sleep come upon me', Tytania sings ecstatically and then in her turn falls asleep.

A short interlude brings Puck on the scene and after him Oberon, who expresses his delight at Tytania's predicament. But Puck has been mistaken over the Athenians, and Demetrius and Hermia are clearly at cross-purposes. Puck is dispatched to find Helena, and Oberon squeezes more juice on to Demetrius's eyes, before Puck returns with Helena and Lysander. Helena upbraids Lysander for his faithlessness to Hermia, but Demetrius wakes up, sees Helena, and provides her with a second adoring swain. Hermia's re-entry adds a further complication, as Helena decides she is at the bottom of a plot against her. All leave, the girls at odds, the men to fight a duel.

Oberon comes forward dragging Puck by the ear and instructs him so to order the comings and goings of Demetrius and Lysander that their efforts to confront each other in mortal combat shall end in exhaustion. Puck carries out his instructions, and the end of the act finds the four lovers correctly lined up so that awakening may provide appropriate reconciliation.

The fairies steal in to sing a benediction, 'Jack shall have Jill, Nought shall go ill' – their most involved musical intervention yet – and Puck squeezes the juice on Lysander's eyes.

ACT III. From the strings at the outset we sense reconciliation and resolution in the morning air. In the wood can be seen lying asleep Tytania with Bottom, and the four lovers slightly apart. Oberon likes what he sees and, having acquired the Indian boy who was the cause of the trouble, undoes the spell: 'Be as thou wast wont to be; See as thou wast wont to see'. Tytania awakes and is reconciled (very slow; *quasi saraband*) with Oberon, who himself proposes to unite the pairs of lovers in wedded bliss to coincide with the marriage of Duke Theseus (*bass*) with Hippolyta (*contralto*).

Oberon, Tytania and the fairies disappear as the lovers, to the sound of horns, awake and are in their turn reconciled: 'And I have found Demetrius like a jewel. Mine own, and not mine own', in a fine flowing ensemble.

They leave, and Bottom, alone on the stage, starts to wake. Snatches of what has passed before go through his mind and he is indignant that his fellow mummers have abandoned him. He has dreamt – mysteries. But a ballad shall be made of his dream, 'And I will sing it in the latter end of the play before the Duke'. As he walks away the others come in, still at a loss to explain Bottom's disappearance. But before long, the rustics too are reconciled. All questioning is halted at the news that 'The Duke hath dined and our play is preferred'. In a flurry of ensemble, they prepare to leave, to the Interlude of a quick march.

Theseus's palace. Theseus and Hippolyta enter with their court. The four lovers enter to beg successfully for the Duke's blessing, before Peter Quince comes in confidently with a playbill which he hands to Hippolyta: 'A tedious brief scene of young Pyramus, And his love Thisby.'

What follows is nothing less than a condensed comic opera. Its introduction has all six rustics singing together in block harmony and marked *pomposo*: 'If we offend, it is with our good will'. Prologue, in the person of Quince, introduces the characters, pushing them out while reiterating the word 'Remain'.

Wall, played by Snout (*tenor*), introduces himself, before Bottom launches himself, in the character of Pyramus, into a short if full-blooded apostrophe to Night and to the obstacle between him and his love, in the manner of a big Italianate aria – indeed the whole thing is a satire on nineteenth-century romantic opera, as is plain from the rather timid flute tune introducing Flute in the character of Thisby and the overwrought if insubstantial duet for Thisby and Pyramus which follows it. Wall prepares to leave, and is succeeded by Snug as Lion and eventually Starveling (*baritone*) as Moon. Thisby continues her *allegretto* flute-beset mood of before, but the music is quickly superseded by the roaring of Lion, who chases Thisby out. Pyramus enters, finds Thisby's mantle, assumes the worst and plunges a sword into his bosom. Thisby finds the body of Pyramus and, at the end of her wits, enters upon a mad scene to which the flute does full justice, before embarking on an *adagio lamentoso* with full orchestral postlude. Bottom offers the assembled worthies an epilogue or a Bergomask dance and it is the dance which is chosen. Midnight sounds, the rustics stop dancing and Theseus and Hippolyta, followed by the four lovers, adjure them and us 'Sweet friends, to bed'.

There is no change of scene but enter Cobweb, Mustardseed, Peaseblossom and Moth (*trebles*) to sing 'Now the hungry lion roars, And the wolf behowls the Moon'. Puck comes in with his broom, but the major musical statement is left to Oberon and the fairies with some help from Tytania. 'Now until the break of day', with its mesmeric Scotch snap, has an uncanny cathartic effect and confirms that a supreme musical magician has been at work. After this, who could gainsay Puck's valedictory 'Gentles, do not reprehend'?

Parables for Church Performance

BRITTEN's three Church Parables are medieval in setting, using plain-chant, but musically and dramatically also of Indonesian and Japanese inspiration. The accompaniment is not a full orchestra but a group of instruments carefully selected in each parable to suit the characters.

Curlew River

PARABLE for Church Performance by Benjamin Britten; première, Aldeburgh, 1964. The Abbot and the Monks enter and the characters of the parable robe on stage. The Ferryman (*baritone*) is told by the Traveller (*baritone*) that a Madwoman (*tenor*) is coming, looking for her lost child. As the Ferryman takes his passengers across the river he tells how, a year before, he ferried a little boy who had been held by robbers, but the child died. The mother starts to cry: it was her son. The Ferryman takes her to the child's grave. The spirit of the boy (*treble*) in a few phrases releases his mother from her torment, and she returns to sanity. The monks disrobe as the Abbot delivers an exhortation.

THE BURNING FIERY FURNACE

PARABLE for Church Performance by Benjamin Britten; première, Aldeburgh, 1966. The story is from the Old Testament. The Abbot and Monks again provide the cast of the parable. Shadrach (*baritone*), Meshach (*tenor*) and Abednego (*bass*), three young Israelites, have been captured and brought to Babylon. King Nebuchadnezzar (*tenor*) appoints them to rule three provinces. During a feast they refuse to betray their faith. At the instigation of the Astrologer (*baritone*) they are thrown into a furnace, but an Angel (*treble*) joins them and they emerge unscathed. The King repudiates the Astrologer and is converted to their faith.

THE PRODIGAL SON

PARABLE for Church Performance by Benjamin Britten; première, Aldeburgh, 1968. The story is from the New Testament. Again the cast is drawn from among the Abbot and Monks. The Father (*bass-baritone*), Elder Son (*baritone*) and Younger Son (*tenor*) toil on the land. The Younger Son is tempted by a Voice (*tenor*) to unknown delights; he asks for and obtains his inheritance, but in the city, Parasites remove it from him and he is left penniless and alone. He joins some Beggars, shares the food of swine, and determines to return home to ask his father's forgiveness. He is received with rejoicing, the fatted calf is killed, and even his envious Elder Brother is finally reconciled.

DEATH IN VENICE

OPERA in two acts by Benjamin Britten; libretto by Myfanwy Piper after the story by Thomas Mann. Première at the Maltings during Aldeburgh Festival, June 16, 1973.

ASCHENBACH is a solitary, and opposite him are ranged two groups of characters. The main function of one group is to propel Aschenbach towards his predestined end: Traveller, Elderly Fop, Old Gondolier, Hotel Manager, Hotel Barber, Leader of the Players, offstage voice of Dionysus. They are all played by the same baritone singer and they share the same musical material. The function of the other group is to lure him towards self-destruction, towards the Dionysian upsetting of his Apollonian (and therefore classical) balance. This group, headed by Tadzio and his mother but including also the other children who play on the beach, are represented by dancers. The music associated with Tadzio, his family and companions is generically different in that it is given to percussion. The percussion music in *Death in Venice* embodies and symbolises everything strange, everything alien to Aschenbach's well ordered, rational world.

ACT I. Scene i. Munich, 1911. Aschenbach (*tenor*) muses on his inability to work: 'My mind beats on . . .'; 'I . . . famous as a master-writer', at a loss – literally – for words. Near the entrance to a cemetery, he is confronted by a Traveller, whose presence as much as his words conjure up an image, so that Aschenbach obeys his injunction 'Go, travel to the South'.

Aschenbach embarks on the first of several monologues in which he comments on the course of events and the motives which have led him to his current position.

Scene ii. On the boat to Venice, youths shout to their girlfriends on shore (quiet chorus of 'Serenissima' underneath the banter), and are joined by an Elderly Fop, who has frequent recourse to a mincing falsetto and leads a vigorous song about the possibilities of life in Venice. He breaks off for an ironic greeting to Aschenbach ('Bound for Serenissima, I'm sure'), but Aschenbach finds him repulsive and starts to wonder why he ever decided to come to Venice.

Scene iii is preceded by an instrumental overture (Venice), marked *Lazily*, consisting of barcarolle-like gondola music of some tenderness. Aschenbach, by now looking forward to his stay, is rowed against his will by the Old Gondolier to his hotel on the Lido. There he is greeted by a Boatman and the Hotel Porter, but he finds when he turns to pay that the Old Gondolier has disappeared. He recognises the black gondola as a harbinger of death.

Scene iv. The first evening at the hotel. Aschenbach is welcomed by the Hotel Manager, then shown his room with a comment on the splendour of the view. Aschenbach soliloquises on the prospect before him in Venice, then watches the hotel guests assemble for dinner, discussing the day's experiences in a variety of languages. Aschenbach sees the Polish family enter – Governess, two girls and Tadzio – and comments on Tadzio: 'Surely the soul of Greece lies in that bright perfection.'

Scene v. On the beach. Aschenbach is not at his ease, but watches the children playing (rhythmical percussion). He buys fruit from a strawberry-seller, then decides that in spite of his misgivings he will stay by the sea. He watches Tadzio coming along the beach, approves as Tadzio mimes dislike of the Russian family, listens as voices apparently call 'Adziù' from the distance, but finally catches the boy's true name as he continues in monologue to admire his grace and beauty.

Scene vi. The foiled departure. On a visit to the city, importunate guides, street-vendors and beggars together with the discomfort he feels from the sirocco prompt Aschenbach to leave Venice. He returns to the hotel, where the Manager remains courteous and understanding, but the sight of Tadzio crossing the lobby impels second thoughts on the way to the station, which are confirmed when he discovers his luggage has been put by mistake on the train to Como. He will return to the Lido and his luggage must be sent to him there! He is greeted by the Hotel Manager with the news that the wind is now from a healthier quarter, from the east in fact, and when he looks out of his window he sees Tadzio and the others on the beach.

Scene vii. The games of Apollo. Aschenbach from his chair seems to hear the voice of Apollo, and in imagination turns the children's beach games into some sort of Olympiad with Tadzio crowned victor of the pentathlon. The music is a series of choral dances, percussion-accompanied, linked by the offstage counter-tenor Voice of Apollo. Aschenbach, after his impressive Hymn to Apollo, realises that through Tadzio he may find inspiration to write again. Tadzio smiles at him as he passes on his way to the hotel and Aschenbach falls helplessly back on what he thinks of later as the supreme cliché: 'I love you'.

ACT II sees an end of joy and the start of the process of destruction through corruption to which Aschenbach is inevitably committed. A slow orchestral introduction leads us to Aschenbach, who has been writing but is hardly less scornful of his inability to communicate with Tadzio than he is of his guilty feelings for the boy. Nevertheless, he must accept the situation.

Scene viii. The Hotel Barber's shop. From the professional patter of the Barber, Aschenbach picks up a reference to 'the sickness', which the Barber promptly plays down.

Scene ix. The pursuit. On his way to Venice, Aschenbach starts to worry and subsequent events tend to confirm his fears: the city is too quiet, people are reading notices advising against eating shellfish, the German newspapers talk of 'rumours of cholera in Venice officially denied'; and yet, when he sees the Polish family, his one thought is to keep the rumours from them in case they decide to leave Venice. Aschenbach follows the Poles, sits near them in a café, watches them pray in St. Mark's and comes to realise that Tadzio is conscious of his nearness. Suddenly he meets them face to face, raises his hat and turns away.

Scene x. The Strolling Players. Outside the hotel after dinner, a group of performers sing and dance, and their Leader sings a ditty before going round with his hat collecting from the guests. Aschenbach tries to pump him about the plague but he makes light of the whole affair.

Scene xi. The travel bureau. A young English clerk is attempting to cope with a crowd of hotel guests frantically seeking reservations to leave the city. To Aschenbach, when they have left, he admits that Asiatic cholera has spread from India and was diagnosed in Venice earlier that year. His advice is that Aschenbach should leave.

Scene xii. The Lady of the Pearls. Aschenbach decides he must warn Tadzio's mother, the Lady of the Pearls, but, when she appears, he goes towards her, then turns into his room.

Scene xiii. The dream. He hears the Voices of Dionysus and Apollo and finally in dream participates in a Dionysian orgy. Awake, he is resigned to his fall: 'Let the Gods do what they will with me'.

Scene xiv. The empty beach. Tadzio and a few friends are playing, watched by Aschenbach.

Scene xv. The Hotel Barber's shop. Aschenbach in a frenzied search for youth allows his grey hair to be tinted.

Scene xvi. The last visit to Venice. Aschenbach, in what the libretto describes as 'his new appearance', goes by gondola to Venice, follows the Polish family, sees Tadzio detach himself from his family and look full at him, then turns away. He buys some fruit from a strawberry-seller, finds it musty and over-ripe, and starts to take stock of his situation. In spite of illness, his mind is clarity itself, and, in the most sustained lyrical section of the opera, he recalls the Socratic dilemma of the poet who perceives beauty only through the senses: 'Does beauty lead to wisdom, Phaedrus?', an inspired passage.

Scene xvii. The departure. Hotel Manager and Porter discuss the weather and the departing guests. Aschenbach comes in wearily and goes to the beach. He watches Tadzio and his friends playing at first listlessly, then more roughly, until Tadzio's face is pressed into the sand. The children cry out and run off, Aschenbach starts to protest, but hears distant cries of 'Adziù' and is only able to answer them gently with 'Tadzio' before slumping dead in his chair as Tadzio walks slowly away. The final twenty-bar orchestral comment provides Aschenbach's threnody.

Harrison Birtwistle
(b. 1934)

PUNCH AND JUDY

A tragical comedy, or a comical tragedy, in one act; libretto by Stephen Pruslin. Première, Aldeburgh Festival, June 8, 1968.

Harrison birtwistle has said, 'When I embarked on *Punch and Judy* . . . I knew the kind of world I wanted to create long before I'd chosen the subject . . . I wanted a theatrical event that . . . was very formal, a myth and English. The subject . . . had the advantage of having a story everyone knew so that it wouldn't distract people from understanding what I was really trying to say.' He worked with the pianist Stephen Pruslin to produce what the librettist has described as 'a stylised and ritualistic drama for adults that used all of the imagery, the trappings and paraphernalia of the original as a departure-point'.

The scoring is for fifteen instrumentalists, including five wind players on a platform on stage, according to the composer's direction. It is to be played without interval (this instruction has not invariably been followed) and lasts just over 100 minutes. In organisation it is highly stylised, full of set-pieces – over 100 items altogether, some very brief.

The librettist invented the idea of Quest for Pretty Polly as a 'positive analogue' (as he calls it) to Punch's 'apparently motiveless acts of violence'. It is a very successful device and Pruslin emphasises that there is 'no *necessary* connection between the two sides of Punch's schizoid nature' – though there may be. In other words, that Punch murders in order to win Pretty Polly is plausible rather than an essential aspect of the plan.

Choregos (*lower baritone*) sings the prologue. Melodrama I. Punch (*higher baritone*) titters, sings to the baby a lullaby, described in the libretto as a serenade, emits his so-called war-cry, then throws the baby into the fire. Judy (*mezzo-soprano*) too has a lullaby, discovers the baby burned to death, confronts Punch as a murderer and plays with him a word-game in which Choregos joins in comment. Murder is in the air and while Doctor (*basso profondo*) and Lawyer (*high tenor*) sing the first Passion Aria, Judy prepares for death. After again venting his war-cry, Punch stabs her, celebrating in a catchy little gavotte of self-satisfaction (Resolve: it will recur at the other murders).

A very short toccata precedes and succeeds Passion Chorale I, for mezzo-soprano, tenor, baritone and bass, one of three very impressive ensembles described by this title.

421

The Quest for Pretty Polly I. In six short numbers – Travel Music, Weather Report, Prayer, Serenade, Pretty Polly's Rhapsody, Moral – Punch searches for Pretty Polly (*high soprano*), woos her only to lose her, and leaves Choregos to mourn his failure and attempt consolation. There are four such Quests in the opera, and in each Punch travels on a hobby-horse, a Prayer is made for clement weather, and Pretty Polly is unsuccessfully wooed, in the first instance being offered a vast flower which she rejects with an oblique reference to the murder of the baby.

A short sinfonia leads to the action's next movement, Melodrama II. Punch is accused, answers in riddles and paradox, until we reach the second Murder Ensemble, Punch's war-cry, and Punch's successful murder of the Doctor and the Lawyer.

A short Toccata before and after Passion Chorale II, another condemnation of Punch's murderous propensities. This leads us to the second Quest for Pretty Polly. We go through the same six sections as before, the Prayer being a particularly attractive example of vocal writing for quartet.

'Lights up, action frozen' during A Little Canonic Prelude to Disaster before we move on to the next dramatic phase, Melodrama III, a battle of wits between Choregos and Punch. At its height comes a fine tune for Punch to the words 'Let the Winds be gentle' but, in spite of Judy's intervention (called Recitative and Passion Aria II), Punch shoves Choregos into a bass viol case, bows vigorously on the viol, and opens the case to reveal Choregos dead. His war-cry is deliberately muted this time, unlike the splendid aria for Judy which came before it, but the chorus mourns Choregos effectively enough and a Transition (in darkness) moves us on to Travel Music III, Weather Report III, and Nightmare. The symptoms of a man in nightmare's grip are recited by Choregos (miraculously indestructible) and Chorus, and Fortune-Telling has Tarot Games until Judy is unmasked and leaves the Fortune-Teller's booth. There is a Black Wedding procession and Pretty Polly's Black Rhapsody (she is disguised as a witch) turns into a quartet. Punch is taunted in an adding song (very fast, detailing the horrors he has inflicted) and the movement ends with the rather surprising direction 'Punch faints and the Nightmare dissolves'.

The Quest for Pretty Polly III, this time with only four sections, goes through the hoops but Pretty Polly's place is now empty and Choregos sings Moral III without any need for her to reject Punch. Toccatas introduce and follow Passion Chorale III, which foresees the possibility of redemption through love.

Melodrama IV. Punch is in prison, but, even though condemned to death, his Resolve seems to indicate a certain confidence. Choregos enters disguised as Jack Ketch, the Public Hangman, and in the course of the action Ketch is tricked by

Punch into putting his own head, by way of demonstration, into the Hangman's noose, with the result that, after Punch's war-cry, he is hanged. 'Huzzah, Huzzah! the Devil's dead!' is Punch's victorious cry, and, with Pretty Polly again on the scene, it is logical that the last movement should be called Punch Triumphant. Pretty Polly sings exultantly of spring. The love duet for her and Punch signals release – Punch has turned the tables with his one good deed, the murder of the Hangman! – and the Apostrophe, for all except Choregos, marches us off into real life again, leaving Choregos with the Epilogue.

Oliver Knussen
(b. 1952)

WHERE THE WILD THINGS ARE

FANTASY opera in one act; libretto by Maurice Sendak from his children's book of the same name. Première Brussels, November 28, 1980.

LET the very articulate composer speak for himself:[1]
'Conceived for the resources of an opera house – six singers, dancers, an orchestra of 47 players, and extensive scenic requirements – Where the Wild Things Are is an attempt to revive and develop the too long neglected genre of fantasy opera, in the traditions of, among others, Hänsel und Gretel, Le Rossignol, and L'Enfant et les Sortilèges (whose final 'Maman' was in a sense the sound from which our ideas grew) . . . What resulted, to me at least, is a very big work articulated in miniature . . The score is headed by quotations from Moussorgsky (Boris Godounov) and Debussy (La boîte à joujoux). These references are symbolic: Moussorgsky is the supreme composer of music about children (The Nursery and Act II of Boris), and Debussy's music for his daughter Chouchou is the perfect example of how a composer can make children's music not by "writing down" to them, but by illuminating his harmonic language in particularly gentle and subtle ways. Both quotations can be heard in the music of Wild Things, overtly and covertly – which is a polite way of saying that virtually every note of the opera grows from one or the other.'

It is none the less Knussen's music and his response to the book (one cannot say 'response to the text' when most of Sendak's story is told in his marvellous pictures) which made the opera (perhaps because of, rather than in spite of, its short

---

[1] In the sleeve note for the first recording of the opera (by Unicorn Records), which he conducted himself.

duration) something of an instant classic for children, one of the few operas which seems aimed at them rather than at the grown-ups who go to the opera with them.

The story is simple. Max (*soprano*), like the child in Ravel's *L'Enfant et les Sortilèges*, is wilful, and after being cheeky to his mother (*mezzo-soprano*), is sent to bed without any supper. His confrontation with the Wild Things parallels that of the child in *L'Enfant* with his toys and characters from his books, but once he has learned to dominate the Wild Things, he puts his room in order and is ready for the food – *hot* food! – he can smell cooking.

The overture is short, quiet, even menacing. During its course, in less time than it takes to tell, a curtain with the face of a Wild Thing on it becomes visible, and soon, through it, the hall of the house where Max lives. A *scherzino* develops as Max cavorts into view, threatening his toy soldiers, and hanging a bear melodramatically from a coat hanger. He turns confidently to humming – there is no need to ask who is king of the castle. But his mother's shadow comes into view, and to her, particularly when he jumps out from ambush, he is a naughty rascal, and fit to be sent to bed without any supper. There is the noise of the vacuum cleaner as she comes into sight, an angry mother–son dialogue (Max: 'And I'll tell Papa *you* were bad'), and, as Max jumps down at her, a reprise of the *scherzo* music to which she made her entrance, and during whose course she shouts 'Wild Thing' at him.

They freeze, his mother leaves and the vacuum cleaner pursues Max round the hall and into his own room. He is alone and out of humour and sings Arietta 1, whose angular vocal writing does not conceal its innate lyricism. The atmosphere is that of *L'Enfant*, most of all when Max's room is transformed into a forest, round which he dances ecstatically (Arietta 2 to a quicker 'Rag' music). Water invades the scene and Max gets into a boat, which moves off.

Interlude 1, with its horn solo and jabbering flutes, is mysteriously atmospheric. It is black night, but the sun rises and proceeds to play Box and Cox with the moon. At dawn, the sea becomes turbulent and a great Sea Monster – the first of the Wild Things – appears, only to subside at a gesture from Max. He moors the boat to an island – we are now far from the world of Ravel – and quite soon the sound of the Wild Things, still off-stage, begins to make itself heard. They are pretty threatening, even though sleep sounds mingle with something more startling, and their noise rises to a great *crescendo* before they hurtle on to the stage, baiting Max and doing their best to scare the pants off him. It is a simple musical moment of inspired complication.

The row continues for a bit, the monsters using what Sendak has called 'a childish, naughty, upside-down pidgin Yiddish', sometimes yelled, sometimes whispered, until Max loses patience, stamps his foot and quells the din. He stares into the eyes of the Wild Things and they cower before him, and in turn sing quietly and gently, taking the opportunity to creep up on him threateningly when his back is turned, only to freeze when they think he can see them.

It is the beginning of the Coronation scene, which starts with the Goat-Dance. One by one, they prepare the accoutrements of the Coronation – velvet cushion, sceptre, casket, crown – and form a procession. The throne lights up and, after a chant of something like adoration on the part of the Wild Things, Max reaches it, sits and is crowned, at which point the opera's climax starts to build: a brilliantly direct, if highly compact, paraphrase of the Coronation scene from *Boris Godounov*, with the Goat (*tenor*) as Shouisky and the other Wild Things, *andantino alla marcia*, standing in for the Russian crowd.

Max announces *fortissimo* 'And now let the WILD RUMPUS start!!' The music begins *molto vivace*, moves into a *Valse-Mazurka* and, with Max on the Bull's (*bass*) back and the other Wild Things stamping round him, there is general jubilation, the music perhaps remotely indebted to Ravel, but to the Ravel of *La Valse*, not of *L'Enfant*. This is the opera's centrepiece.

Abruptly, Max stops the riot, dominating and controlling the Wild Things just as surely as his mother had him, and orders them too off to bed without supper. Max is alone and sings a tender aria about his dream of flying so high he was scared, his music for the first time a slow cantilena, marked at one point 'like an incantation, *calmissimo*'. He gets into his boat and suddenly there is a recrudescence of suppressed violence as the monsters whisper furiously, nightmarishly ('like an unbelievable rage when heard through ear-plugs'). Max turns round and the music changes instantly, first into a sanctimonious Barbershop quintet and then into nothing less than passionate fury again. The island recedes until, with the voices of the Wild Things still audible, the music becomes gently consolatory and in the Second Interlude a point of reconciliation seems achieved. After the Rumpus, we rejoin the world of *L'Enfant*, Max's vocal line takes on a note of ecstasy, and it is not long before Mama is heard singing reassuringly offstage, a palpable rather than a visible comfort. We are back in Max's room – and he can smell hot soup.

Leoš Janáček
(1854–1928)

In the canon of Janáček's operas, *Jenůfa* (1904) is preceded by *Šárka* and the one-act *The Beginning of a Romance*. Between *Jenůfa* and the four great works of his maturity are two operas which have not achieved universal fame: *Osud* (Fate), 1903/4, a highly unconventional conversational piece, and the fantastic burlesque *The Adventures of Mr. Brouček* (written between 1908 and 1917). *Osud* is usually thought of as representing a transition between Janáček's early style, which reached its height in *Jenůfa*, and his later and more mature work.

Janáček admired Dvořák rather than Smetana (compare *Káta*'s prelude with that of *Rusalka*), was a close student of folk music (though in his mature operas he composes rather than quotes it), and he recommended the operatic composer to study the natural rhythms (particularly those of speech) around him.

JEJÍ PASTORKYŇA (JENŮFA)
Her Stepdaughter

Opera in three acts by Leoš Janáček; text by the composer founded on a story by Gabriella Preissová. Première, Brno, January 21, 1904.

Long before the opera begins, Grandmother Buryjovka has had two sons, each of them dead before the action starts. The elder, who owned the family mill, married the widow Klemeň, who already had a son Laca. Together she and the Miller had another son Števa, who is of course heir to his father and grandmother. The second son, Tomas, had by his first wife a daughter named Jenůfa; after the death of Jenůfa's mother, he married Kostelnička (as she was later known because of her work as sacristan of the village chapel).

ACT I. A lonely mill in the Moravian mountains; nineteenth century. Jenůfa (*soprano*) stands by the stream looking into the distance. The old grandmother (*contralto*) sits in front of the mill peeling potatoes. Laca (*tenor*) is near her, shaping a whip-handle with his knife. It is late afternoon. The prelude (in 6/4 time) has running through it the tinkling sound of the mill at work (xylophone). Jenůfa laments that Števa has not yet returned. She is in love with him – in fact, carries his child within her – and her heart will break if he leaves her.

Laca makes sarcastic reference to his lowly place in the household; Števa has always been the idol of old Grandmother Buryjovka. Jenůfa reproaches him for the way in which he speaks to the old woman. Laca wonders aloud what would be

Jenůfa's reaction if Števa were taken for the army. She is dismayed at how he seems able to read her feelings.

Jano (*soprano*), the shepherd boy, is heard calling happily from the mill; Jenůfa seems as pleased as he. The foreman of the mill (*baritone*) comes in and asks Laca what he is working at. A whip-handle – but his knife is blunt, says Laca, and gives it to be ground (the xylophone is heard again in the orchestra). Laca and Jenůfa quarrel for a moment, and Laca taunts her with her love for Števa. She goes off, and Laca remarks bitterly to the foreman that she will make a splendid sister-in-law with those sweet ways of hers. The foreman warns him about his attitude towards Jenůfa. What if Števa be taken for a soldier, says Laca, but the foreman has heard that he has been passed over and is free. Jenůfa and Grandmother Buryjovka are delighted, but Laca cannot conceal his jealousy. Kostelnička (*soprano*) appears and goes into the mill, and Grandmother Buryjovka suggests they follow her. Jenůfa, however begs to be left alone to meet Števa when he returns.

The jaunty song of the approaching recruits can be heard in the distance, and they are followed by Števa (*tenor*), who is extremely drunk. With an almost hysterical cry, Jenůfa tries to bring Števa to his senses, but he answers crossly, boasting of his prowess with the girls. They start up a song, in which Števa joins, and in between the verses the orchestra plays for the dance, into which Števa drags the unwilling Jenůfa.

Kostelnička interrupts the festive scene imperiously. She is a formidable and authoritative – almost authoritarian – character, and she reads the company a lecture, making it apply particularly and unmistakably to her rich nephew Števa. Until he can prove that he has stopped drinking by a year of sobriety, there is to be no more talk of a wedding with Jenůfa. Grandmother Buryjovka sends the musicians packing, and tells Števa to go and sleep off his drunken condition.

Jenůfa and Števa are left alone, and Jenůfa pleads her love for him and her fear that her secret should be found out. Jenůfa's confession of love and anxiety is dragged out of her, almost in spite of herself, with long pauses between phrases, yet the music never fails to convey the warmth of her nature. Števa answers crossly, and practically accuses Jenůfa and her stepmother of nagging at him, so that Jenůfa loses her patience and shakes him vigorously. Even when he partially pulls himself together, his answers have a conventional gallantry which in no way reassures Jenůfa. When Laca returns Jenůfa is alone in her misery; he makes derisive reference to Števa, but this only provokes Jenůfa to take Števa's side even more firmly than before. Laca attempts to insult Jenůfa, then comments that Števa only looks at her because of her rosy-apple cheeks. He makes as if to embrace Jenůfa and slashes her across the cheek with the knife. She runs into the house screaming, while Laca laments the horrible thing he has done.

ACT II. The living-room of Kostelnička's house. A tense atmosphere is established in the music straightaway. Kostelnička and Jenůfa are sewing, the latter's wound still visible. The baby has been born, but Jenůfa has not seen his father for weeks now. Every utterance of Jenůfa's shows her joy in her child, every one of Kostelnička's, the pride which has been so cruelly hurt by the shame which has come to her beloved stepchild and which has become an obsession with her. Kostelnička gives Jenůfa a drink with a narcotic in it to make her sleep, and Jenůfa goes into the bedroom.

Kostelnička has sent for Števa. She reproaches him for not having been to see them. He shrinks from going in to see Jenůfa and his son, and seems half remorseful for what he has done to her, half resentful that her beauty has been spoilt – it means the end of his love for her. He will not grudge the child money – but no one must know that it is his.

Kostelnička pleads with him; at least he must see his child. As Števa says, her pleas would melt the heart of a stone. They grow in intensity when Števa breaks down, but he refuses to marry Jenůfa, and eventually admits that he is contracted to marry Karolka, the mayor's daughter. Števa runs out and, as Kostelnička screams in horror, Jenůfa's voice is heard coming from the inner room, calling in her sleep.

Laca comes in. He asks Kostelnička if Jenůfa is yet back from Vienna – it was given out that she went away – and is delighted to hear that she has returned. But Kostelnička has not the heart to hide the truth from him any longer, and she tells him about the child. He is horrified at the idea that marriage with Jenůfa involves taking Števa's baby, and Kostelnička, who sees Jenůfa's last chance slipping away from her, tells him that the baby is dead. Alone, Kostelnička decides that the baby must die. The music represents her agony and indecision, and the scene is one of terrible power, particularly towards its end, when Kostelnička yells her own name in horrible reproach at her shadow. She goes into the bedroom and brings the child out, wrapped in her shawl.

Jenůfa, half-drugged, comes in to find no one there; Kostelnička must have taken the baby to the mill to show Števa. In music suffused with sadness and tenderness, she prays for her child's future. Kostelnička returns in extreme agitation and tells Jenůfa that she has been unconscious and delirious for two days, during which time the baby's death and burial occurred.

Kostelnička tells Jenůfa that Števa has refused to marry her, even admitting that he was engaged to Karolka. When Laca comes in, his joy at seeing Jenůfa again is touching in its sincerity. He asks Jenůfa if they cannot finish their lives together. Jenůfa is at first dignified and reserved, but she cannot hide her tender feelings for Laca, and Kostelnička exclaims to herself that her action has put everything right. Just then, the window blows open, and the icy blast brings a horrible sense of foreboding and disaster to Kostelnička who cries out in alarm, and clings desperately to Jenůfa and Laca.

ACT III. The scene is the same as in Act II. Jenůfa is preparing for the wedding, and Laca sits by her side. Near them is old Grandmother Buryjovka. Kostelnička, looking haggard and worn, paces up and down the room. Even the mayor (*bass*), who arrives to offer congratulations, cannot restore Kostelnička to calm. Eventually, she takes them all in to see the trousseau she has made for Jenůfa. Laca cannot stop reproaching himself for what he has done to her; all his life must be spent making her amends. It transpires that it is at Jenůfa's insistence that Laca has been reconciled to Števa, even to the extent of asking him to the wedding, with his bride-to-be.

Karolka (*mezzo-soprano*) comes in with Števa to congratulate the happy couple. Laca asks him whether his own wedding-day is yet fixed. In two weeks' time, says Števa; but Karolka is determined to play the minx, and says she may yet change her mind. Števa is indignant at the idea that he might be jilted, but relapses into silence when Jenůfa expresses the hope that true love will never hurt him. Outside gathers a group of girls, headed by Barena (*soprano*) and bringing flowers to offer to Jenůfa. They sing a little wedding song, and then bride and bridegroom are blessed by Grandmother Buryjovka.

Suddenly, cries are heard outside. The body of the murdered baby has been discovered in the millstream now that the ice has melted. Jano rushes in screaming out the news and goes out, taking the mayor with him, followed by the others except Števa, Kostelnička and Grandmother Buryjovka. Kostelnička becomes hysterical, but attention shifts from her when the voice of Jenůfa can be heard from outside crying that she recognises the baby as hers. Feeling against her rises until the mob is ready to stone her. Silence falls on them all when Kostelnička raises her arms and tells them quite quietly that the guilt is hers. She tells the story, and for a moment Jenůfa turns from her in revulsion. But it is only too clear that her crime has been committed in an effort to do good, and Jenůfa's great act of forgiveness towards Kostelnička somehow redeems the crime. For a moment it looks as though Kostelnička will kill herself, then she remembers she will be needed as a witness if Jenůfa is not to suffer for something of which she is guiltless, and she goes quietly away with the mayor.

The others go, but Jenůfa and Laca remain behind. Sadly Jenůfa tells him to follow them. Laca begs to be allowed to remain at her side, and his reward is Jenůfa's great cry of exultation as she understands that their sufferings have brought them a greater love than she has ever known.

OSUD
Fate

THREE acts, by Leoš Janáček; radio première, 1934; stage, Brno, 1958. Míla (*soprano*) and the composer Živný (*tenor*) had an affair; Míla's mother (*soprano*) prevented their marriage, but Míla had a son. Živný expressed his bitterness in the opera he was writing. Now, on a beautiful day, with everyone cheerful in the sun, Míla and Živný meet again, and it is clear that their feelings have not changed. Míla tells Živný how she was forced into a false position by her mother. Four years later the two are married but the mother creates an uneasy atmosphere. The child innocently triggers off her rage, and she rushes at Živný. In the struggle Míla and her mother fall to their deaths. Eleven years later, Živný's opera is finished except for the finale. In a great scene Živný tells his students of the background to the opera and of his own life and creed, but as he collapses, insists that the end is still 'in God's hands'.

THE ADVENTURES OF MR. BROUČEK
Výlety Pàně Broučkovy

TWO parts, by Leoš Janáček; première, Prague, 1920. In Part I (The Adventures of Mr. Brouček on the Moon), Málinka (*soprano*) and her lover Mazal (*tenor*) are quarrelling. Mr. Brouček (*tenor*), tipsy, interrupts, insisting that there is life on the Moon. He is transported there, and meets Blankytný and Etherea, who resemble the two lovers. Etherea takes Brouček on horseback to the Temple of Arts, where he is an object of wonder to all the lunar dwellers. But they smell their food instead of eating it, and Brouček upsets them by consuming a sausage. Back on earth, he has to be carried home from the inn.

PART II. The Excursion of Mr. Brouček into the Fifteenth Century. At the inn, Brouček suddenly finds himself in the year 1420. He is enrolled with the Hussites as they prepare to march to war. They return victorious, but Brouček has been spotted in an act of cowardice and the people demand his death. As he laments, the scene returns to the inn, where he has been in a drunken sleep.

KATYA KABANOVÁ

OPERA in three acts by Leoš Janáček; text by Cervinka, founded on Ostrovsky's *The Storm*. Première, Brno, October 23, 1921.

IN 1917, on holiday in Luhačovice, Janáček met Kamila Stöss-lová, and at the age of sixty-three fell in love with this twenty-five-year-old married woman in such a way as to revolutionise the remainder of his life. Two-thirds of his greatest music was written in his last dozen years, much of it explicitly inspired by Kamila, and nowhere else in musical history is there an instance of such late flowering on so prolific a scale, and for so romantic a reason. Its first musical fruit is *Katya*.

The prelude, with its *pp* B flat chords and its fateful drum figure against muted trombones, sets the atmosphere which is to prevail throughout the opera, but at the same time it serves as an exposition of leading motifs. The time is about 1860.

ACT I. Scene i. Outside the Kabanovs' house, which stands on the banks of the Volga. Vanya Kudrjash (*tenor*), Dikoy's clerk, exclaims at the beauty of the river. Dikoy (*bass*) comes in, complaining at his nephew Boris's laziness. Dikoy makes no secret of his impatience with Boris (*tenor*), but he goes away when he has learned from Glasha (*mezzo-soprano*), the servant, that Kabanicha is still in church.

Kudrjash listens sympathetically while Boris explains that he only stays with his tyrannical relation because of the terms of his grandmother's will; the money is to go to him and his sister when they come of age, provided they do what their uncle tells them. If it were not for his sister, Boris himself would long ago have left Dikoy and given up his inheritance.

At that moment, churchgoers are seen coming back from the service, and Kudrjash has to be restrained from leaving by the overwrought Boris, who laments his rapidly-departing youth. Katya's theme is stated *dolce* and for the first time by the oboe.

Boris gazes into the distance and his rapturous phrases tell the listener as plainly as his words that he is in love.

Kabanicha (*contralto*) leads her little family party back from church. She urges her son Tikhon (*tenor*) to go that very day to the market at Kazan. He immediately agrees, but Kabanicha makes a sneering reference to his wife Katya (*soprano*), and suggests that since his marriage he has paid his mother less than the respect and deference due to her. Tikhon hotly protests that he loves both, but when Katya also gently claims to love her mother-in-law, Kabanicha turns on her. Katya goes into the house, and Kabanicha continues her abuse; Tikhon is too soft with Katya, and would make no protest even if she were to take a lover. Kabanicha goes, and Varvara (*mezzo-soprano*), her foster-daughter, abuses Tikhon for not taking Katya's part more firmly; she knows exactly what he will do now – drink to forget the scene.

Scene ii. Inside the Kabanovs' house. Katya pours out her heart to Varvara. She is unhappy in her present surroundings. When she was young and unmarried, she was as free as the birds. The music grows in intensity as she describes going to church alone; she saw visions of angels and felt as if she were flying over the mountains and forests.

Varvara encourages her to describe her dreams. Katya says she feels that someone is embracing her and urging her to go with him – and she yields to his persuasion. Katya says that no sin can be worse than that of loving some other man than one's husband, but Varvara asks why that should seem so dreadful.

Katya protests vehemently, and at this moment, Tikhon appears saying that he must leave immediately for Kazan. Katya asks him to make her swear a dreadful oath not to see or speak to a stranger while he is away, but he flatly refuses to do any such thing. Kabanicha bids her son prepare for the journey. Before he leaves, he must give his orders to his wife – and in the presence of his mother, so that she may hear exactly what he says. He repeats in a milder form the injunctions of Kabanicha; they include a prohibition against seeing other men.

ACT II. Scene i. Living-room of the Kabanovs' house, later the same day. Kabanicha is nagging at Katya. Why can't she be like other wives and stay weeping in her room when her husband goes away? Kabanicha leaves the room.

Varvara says the room is stuffy; she will go into the garden, using the key which Kabanicha *thinks* she has hidden, but for which Varvara has substituted another. If she should see 'him', says Varvara cryptically, she will tell him that Katya is waiting by the gate of the garden. Varvara goes out leaving the key. For a while Katya wrestles with temptation; she has the key to hand, should she use it? Suddenly, she can hear the voice of Kabanicha, but the danger passes, and the flood of relief which succeeds it tells her more certainly than could anything else that her love for Boris is too strong for her.

As Katya leaves, Kabanicha comes in, followed by Dikoy. He admits that he is a bit drunk but protests that he does not want to go home. 'Speak to me harshly' is the request he has come to make of Kabanicha – she alone dares to do such a thing.

Scene ii. The garden below the house. The summer night is hot. Vanya sings a carefree peasant song to balalaika accompaniment. He is waiting for Varvara, and is surprised to see Boris, who explains that someone he passed in the dark told him to come there. Varvara sings another snatch of folk-like melody, to which Vanya makes appropriate answer. As she passes Boris, she tells him that Katya will not be long. He waits with growing excitement as Katya comes in, admits her love for him and falls into his arms. The whole scene is saturated with the magic of the summer night, and a unique effect is produced by the blend and contrast of the characteristics of the two pairs of lovers, the one passionate and carefree, the other rapturous but guilty. The singing ends with a little folk-like duet for Varvara and Vanya, but the shattering emotional climax comes in the orchestra, when Katya and Boris return to the stage and their pent-up feelings are expressed in three highly charged orchestral phrases.

ACT III. Scene i. Ten days later. A tumbledown summer house on a terrace by the Volga. Kudrjash and Kuligin, his friend, take shelter from the storm which bursts upon them with considerable violence. Dikoy blunders in. Kudrjash suggests that the frequent storms indicate the village should have lightning-conductors; he meets short shrift from the superstitious Dikoy, who takes each storm to be a warning from God to sinful mankind.

The rain stops and all leave the shelter, except Boris and Kudrjash. Varvara appears, and whispers to Boris that Tikhon is back, and his return has driven Katya quite out of her senses. Boris hides as Katya comes in, supported by her husband and preceded by Kabanicha. The storm returns at just the moment when Katya catches sight of Boris. She calls to Tikhon and Kabanicha at the top of her voice, and confesses not only to her adultery but names the man with whom she has sinned. The scene has an added horror in that it builds up incredibly rapidly from comparative calm to climax and catastrophe. Tikhon is beside himself with unhappiness, but Kabanicha's comment is one of self-justification: 'Son, your mother warned you!'

Scene ii. The banks of the Volga. Katya has fled and her family are looking for her. It is night, and Tikhon's remarks to Glasha reveal that his mind is a turmoil of doubt; women like that should not just be killed, he says, but buried alive – and yet he still loves Katya, and how could he harm her? Varvara and Vanya run in. They agree that there is nothing for it but to run away together.

Tikhon and Glasha can be heard calling in the distance. Katya comes slowly in, hoping sadly to see Boris once again. Her experience has obviously affected her very strongly, and she cannot think coherently. The thought of the night overwhelms her with horror. Suddenly, remembrance of her love fills her heart with longing; she calls for Boris, and, as if in answer, he appears. He tries to comfort her, but her mind wanders. Sadly they say goodbye.

Katya goes towards the bank of the river and throws herself in. Voices are heard of one or two men who have seen her fall; Tikhon and Kabanicha rush to the spot, the latter restraining her son, Tikhon protesting that it is Kabanicha who has killed Katya. Her body is carried up on to the bank by Dikoy, and the last words of the opera are sardonically given to Kabanicha: 'Let me thank you, friends and neighbours, for your kindness.'

THE CUNNING LITTLE VIXEN
Příhody Lišky Bystroušky

OPERA in three acts by Leoš Janáček; text by the composer from R. Tešnohlídek's stories. Première, Brno, November 6, 1924.

FEW operas, even by Slavs, have an odder genesis than Janáček's *The Cunning Little Vixen*. The composer had read with growing pleasure a series of newspaper articles by the journalist Tešnohlídek, based on a Czech rural community and featuring a half-tame, half-wild vixen. He was particularly enthusiastic about the way the writer could jump naturally from the human to the animal worlds and, to the astonishment of Tešnohlídek himself, asked if he might make an operatic text from the newspaper strips.

ACT I. Scene i. A shady spot in the woods; the early afternoon sunlight plays through the leaves of the trees. Animals and insects dance in the heat, a badger (*bass*) smoking a pipe pokes his head out of his earth, a blue dragonfly hovers in a dance. The Forester (*bass-baritone*) comes from the wood looking for a place for a nap.

He goes to sleep; the insect noises begin again, there is an enchanting waltz, as the flies dance round the Forester, and the tempo (now in duple time) quickens as a frog chases a mosquito. A vixen cub (*soprano*) looks in amazement at the frog; can one eat it, she wonders. She pounces, the frog jumps quickly and lands cold and slippery on the Forester's nose. His eyes meet the vixen's, and after a couple of feints he catches her. The dragonfly darts towards the place where the vixen cub was playing, looks for her, and dances a touching little dirge for his lost friend.

The interweaving forest motifs, the contrasting dance rhythms, the varying and unfailingly apt orchestral invention, above all the homogeneity of the themes and Janáček's skill and lightness of touch in putting the whole thing together contribute to a musical scene in its way unparalleled in operatic literature.

Scene ii. Outside the Forester's house on an autumn afternoon. The Forester's Wife (*contralto*) pours some milk into a saucer for the dachshund (*mezzo-soprano*) and the fox cub, which she and her husband are bringing up as a pet for their child. The vixen is miserable and the dog tries to preach resignation as a desirable state of mind – is he not head-over-heels in love at the appropriate time of year? The vixen counters with chatter about the scandalous carrying-on of the starlings who nested over her home, but is quick to reject a rather half-hearted amorous approach on the part of the dachshund. When the Forester's son appears with a friend and teases the fox, he is rewarded with a sharp nip. The Forester quickly ties her up.

As it gets dark, there begins an extraordinary musical episode. The vixen seems almost to change into a girl and provokes passionate orchestral love music.

With the dawn, the Forester's Wife throws out food for the chickens, who cluck and strut around the yard until the vixen starts a revolutionary harangue. But the hens are unresponsive and in disgust the vixen digs herself a grave, lies down and shams dead. There is a headlong orchestral *stretta* to the scene as the vixen suddenly springs up and bites off the heads of one chicken after another. The Forester's Wife runs out in alarm; the vixen snaps her leash, trips up the Forester and escapes.

ACT II. Scene i. The wood. The vixen teases the badger, enlists the sympathy of the other animals, and when the badger goes off in a huff, moves as intended into his vacated sett.

Scene ii. The village inn. The Forester and the Schoolmaster (*tenor*) are playing cards, watched by the Parson (*bass*). In a song, the Forester mocks the Schoolmaster for his backwardness in courting his sweetheart, but the ribaldry is general. The Innkeeper (*tenor*) is worried at the amount of noise coming from the back room and warns the Parson to leave if his drinking is not to become a scandal with his new parishioners. The Forester orders another beer, the Innkeeper says he will one of these days get him to tell the details of his adventures with the vixen, but the Forester reacts crossly and leaves.

Scene iii. The wood at night. The moonlight shows a bridge. The Schoolmaster comes a little shakily down the road. The vixen peeps out from behind a sunflower, to the joy of the Schoolmaster, who takes her for the gipsy Terinka, a past love, and in his ardour topples over the fence and lies prone. The Parson comes down the road trying to remember the source of a classical tag. He catches sight of the vixen and confuses her in his mind with Terinka, whom he also loved in student days.

The appearance of the Forester puts an end to his moralising, and Parson and Schoolmaster fall into each other's arms in their fear of where the Forester may shoot.

Scene iv. The vixen's earth. Moonlight. Behind the scene the voices of the forest sing a wordless chant. The vixen meets a fox (*soprano*) and tells him a romanticised story of her life. When the fox refers to her as beautiful, she starts to wonder about the significance of his remark; is she *really* beautiful? He brings her a rabbit he has killed, kisses her, and asks her if she has ever been in love. There is a full-scale love duet, at the end of which they go off together into the vixen's earth, leaving the dragonfly – her guardian angel, surely – to rejoice. The owl (suitably, the same singer as the Forester's Wife) bubbles with joy at such a juicy bit of gossip. When the foxes emerge, the vixen whispers to the fox that she is now an expectant mother, and his reaction is to send for a priest, the woodpecker (*soprano*), who marries them as the wood voices celebrate the wedding in a paean of wordless joy.

ACT III. Scene i. It is midday under a clear autumn sky. The quiet is disturbed by the singing of Harašta (*bass*), out on a poaching foray. He comes on a dead hare lying where it had been killed by a fox, is about to pick it up when he catches sight of the Forester, who greets him sarcastically. Does he enjoy his lonely life? 'Lonely? I'm going to marry Terinka', is Harašta's answer. To cover his chagrin, the Forester sets a trap for the foxes.

The vixen's family of cubs rush out and dance, watched by their parents, round the clumsily set trap. The dog fox asks his vixen how many children they have had already and how many they will have in the future, but Harašta's song is heard in the distance and all hide except for the cunning little vixen herself. She attracts Harašta's attention as she limps away from him, and leads him a dance, which finishes with him flat on the ground as he trips over a tree root. He gets up to see the fox cubs pulling the poultry out of his basket, shoots into the middle of them and by pure chance hits the vixen, who falls dead.

Scene ii. The garden of the inn. The Innkeeper's Wife (*soprano*) brings the Forester his beer. He is out of humour and tells the Schoolmaster that every time recently he has been to the fox's earth he has found it deserted; he will never get the muff he has promised his wife. Terinka gets married today, says the Schoolmaster; *and* gets a new muff, sniffs the Innkeeper's Wife. They miss the Parson with his ready Latin tag: he writes sometimes, says the Innkeeper's Wife, and sounds homesick. The Forester pays and goes, as he tells them, off to the wood.

Scene iii. The clearing where the Forester caught the little vixen. Again he muses in music of movingly human character on the forest, where life provides never an ending, only a new beginning, and where men if they know how to look may find the happiness of eternal things. As he starts to fall asleep, he sees a fox cub playing on the edge of the clearing. He makes a move towards the cub, and finds a frog in his hand!

THE MAKROPULOS AFFAIR
Věc Makropulos

OPERA in three acts by Leoš Janáček; libretto by the composer, founded on Karel Čapek's play of the same name. Première, Brno, December 18, 1926.

FOR his penultimate opera, Janáček himself adapted Karel Čapek's *The Makropulos Secret*, using the play in spite of Čapek's offer to write him something round the figure of the 300-year-old woman, but more suitable for opera. The background to the story emerges gradually during the opera's action. Hieronymus Makropulos, court physician to the sixteenth-century Habsburg Emperor Rudolph II, succeeded in finding an elixir of life. The Emperor refused to believe him and compelled his daughter Elina (born in 1585) to drink it first. Makropulos died years later in prison, but Elina's life was prolonged through the potion. Every 60 or 70 years, she changes her identity to avoid suspicion, but throughout her 300 years and more of existence (it is now the 1920's) she has retained the initials 'E. M.'

As the Scottish singer Ellen MacGregor (in the opera, *Ellian*), early in the nineteenth century, she had a love affair in Prague with Baron 'Peppi' Prus, by whom she had a son, Ferdinand MacGregor, whom she entered under the name Makropulos in the parish register of the village in which he was born. In 1827, Baron Prus died intestate, and the estate went to a cousin. It was not long before a new claimant appeared, one Ferdinand MacGregor, whose case was circumstantially plausible in spite of there being no written proof. All the same, Baron Prus conceded that there was reasonable evidence to suggest that a certain Gregor Mack should be a major beneficiary. Since no one could claim this identity, the case between the families of Prus and Gregor has continued for nearly a century. The prelude contrasts lyrical themes with orchestral ejaculations, including brilliant fanfares for brass and kettledrums symbolising the Rudolphian period of Elina Makropulos's birth.

ACT I. The office of the lawyer Dr. Kolenatý (*bass-baritone*), where the chief clerk Vítek (*tenor*) is tidying away papers for the night. He is concerned with the case of Gregor v. Prus, which has been going on for as long as anyone can remember, and which Albert Gregor (*tenor*) now comes in to discuss. They are interrupted by the arrival of Vítek's daughter Kristina (*mezzo-soprano*), who is studying singing and is full of enthusiasm for the famous prima donna Emilia Marty (*dramatic soprano*). Kolenatý's voice is heard and he introduces none other than the great Marty herself. She explains that she is interested in the Gregor-Prus case, and proceeds to show extraordinary knowledge of its details. Kolenatý, with frequent comments from Emilia Marty, goes through the case. Marty states categorically that the son of the Baron Prus in question was Ferdinand Mac-Gregor, his mother a singer at the Hofoper, Ellian MacGregor.

Questioned further, she reveals the probable hiding place of the paper which could furnish proof, and Gregor excitedly insists that Kolenatý examine this crucial evidence, even though it appears to be amongst some love letters in the archives of his adversary in the case, the present Baron Prus (*baritone*). (Ellian MacGregor had left the paper containing the elixir's secret in Prus's hands, perhaps as a kind of pledge that she would return, and Emilia badly wants it back.)

Kolenatý goes off on what he is sure will prove a wild-goose chase, and Gregor is left alone with Emilia Marty. But Emilia will have none of him, and he is shocked to see her take on the look of an old woman. As she insists, apparently on the spur of the moment, that he give her some old Greek papers he will on inheriting find amongst his great-great-grandfather's effects, the scene is interrupted by the return of Kolenatý, who has found all exactly as Emilia Marty had described. Prus follows him and congratulates Gregor on having collected almost – but not quite – all the evidence he needs. Emilia offers to furnish written proof that the Ferdinand of the will and Ferdinand Gregor are the same person, but the curtain comes down with Kolenatý refusing to be persuaded to accept her assistance again.

ACT II. The empty stage of the opera house. A stage-hand and a dresser are gossiping. Prus arrives looking for Emilia Marty. He is followed by his son, Janek (*tenor*), and Kristina, who is mesmerised by Marty and tells Janek that their romance must take second place to her career. La Marty makes an entrance and Prus introduces to her Janek, who makes a poor showing. She is not in the mood for compliments, reimbursing Gregor for the jewellery hidden in a bunch of flowers which he brings her, and asking Kristina if she has yet slept with Janek.

Enter a stammering old roué, Count Hauk-Sendorf ('*operetta tenor*'), with flowers for the diva in whom he finds an uncanny resemblance to his one-time Spanish mistress, Eugenia Montez. In the course of a short but sharply-etched scene, it

transpires to Hauk's amazement that Marty is in fact the Andalusian singer to whom his heart was given fifty years ago.

An autograph for Vítek, a wave of dismissal for Janek and
Kristina, an evasion of Gregor's attempt to stay with her, and
Emilia Marty is alone with Prus. Immediately he questions her
about her special interest in Gregor, and goes on to ask about
the mysterious Ellian MacGregor, from whose illegitimate child
by the Baron Prus of more than a hundred years ago stems the
present litigation. Prus is fascinated by the mystery surrounding her; what was her real name? In her letters to his ancestor,
she signs only 'E. M.', and this could equally stand for Ellian
MacGregor, Eugenia Montez, Emilia Marty – or even Elina
Makropulos. He has discovered that it was in the last name that
the birth of a child, Ferdinand, was registered on the appropriate day, which seems to dispose of Gregor's claim to the
estate. His archives contain one further packet, still unopened;
with the announcement of this new mystery, Prus withdraws.

Marty is sitting exhausted when Gregor returns and renews
his protestations of love. When she asks him to get back from
Dr. Kolenatý the document he found in the Prus archives, he
threatens to kill her, at which she shows him a scar on her neck
where such an attempt has been made in the past. When he
renews his pleas, he is astonished to find her fast asleep in her
chair. When she wakes, it is to find the tongue-tied Janek gazing at her. Will he help her? His father has an old letter
addressed 'To my son Ferdinand' in a sealed packet; will he
steal it for her? He is about to agree when he is shamed and put
to flight by the appearance of his father. Prus and Emilia Marty
now face each other as adversaries but, like the others, he succumbs to her beauty and agrees in return for her favours to give
her the unopened packet.

ACT III. Marty's hotel bedroom. Emilia emerges and demands
the promised letter, which Prus silently gives her – due to her
coldness, it seems that the night together amounted to fraud.
She breaks the seal and agrees it is what she wanted. To Prus,
already depressed and disillusioned, is brought a message – his
only son Janek has committed suicide for love of Emilia. Emilia
continues to arrange her hair and refuses to accept any responsibility for his death. Hauk reappears to invite Emilia to come to
Spain with him, and in a short while Gregor, Dr. Kolenatý,
Vítek, Kristina, Prus and a doctor are announced. The doctor
removes the senile old man and Kolenatý says he has some
questions he must ask Emilia Marty. To begin with, the autograph she gave Kristina and the writing on the sealed packet
found in Prus's house are the same, indicating presumably that
the old letter was forged by her. She answers wearily that Ellian
MacGregor wrote the letter and goes off into the bedroom,

while Kolenatý and the others start to search her luggage. Finally, she starts to answer Kolenatý's questions.

She tells the extraordinary story of her long life, from her birth in Crete in 1585 through her various identities – Ekaterina Myshkin, Elsa Müller, Elina Makropulos – and Elina's stage name, Ellian MacGregor. To her son by Baron Prus she left the most precious thing she owned, the prescription for the elixir of life which her father made for the Emperor and which was tried out on her, causing her for more than 300 years to vindicate his alchemical skill. Now she must renew life with the elixir, or shrivel into old age and die.

In the course of the scene, Emilia Marty ages until at its end she can hardly stand up. Her sceptical listeners begin to wonder whether she has not been speaking the truth after all, and carry her to bed. When she reappears, she looks like a ghost. The former hardness of manner has disappeared and she has come to understand how desperately she has wanted to die. She gives the Makropulos 'secret' to Kristina, the youngest, who throws it into the fire as Marty sinks gratefully into death. With the understanding that Elina Makropulos can – must – die, comes the end of a splendid final scene, in which the music transcends the details and carries the burden of Čapek's drama – that length of life is far less important than man's fulfilment within it, that mankind's fear of death must be replaced by an awareness of what life would be without death.

FROM THE HOUSE OF THE DEAD
Z Mrtvé ho Domu

THREE acts, by Leoš Janáček, based on Dostoevsky; première, Brno, 1930. A penal settlement in Siberia, winter. A new prisoner, Alexander Petrovich Goryanshikov (*bass*), is brought in. The Commandant (*baritone*) orders him to be flogged. Alyeya (*soprano*), a young Tartar, is sympathetic but the other prisoners occupy themselves with a caged eagle which has a broken wing. Goryanshikov offers to teach Alyeya to read and write. Skuratov (*tenor*) describes his crime, a jealous murder. The prisoners put on a play on the story of Don Juan. Alyeya is attacked and wounded. In the hospital, Shishkov (*baritone*) relates his story, interrupted by the death of Luka (*tenor*), who turns out to be the villain of the piece. The Commandant drunkenly apologises to Goryanshikov and frees him. As he leaves, the prisoners release the eagle. There are alternative endings: in one the prisoners are herded back inside; in the other, the optimism of the final chorus is maintained.

Bohuslav Martinů
(1890–1959)

Julietta

OPERA in three acts, based on the play *Juliette ou La Clé des Songes* by Georges Neveux. Première at National Theatre, Prague, March 16, 1938.

THE spectator must make of *Julietta* what he chooses. It is a philosophical poem on the nature of man and experience; it is a dream, in which inevitably all situations, all persons, however sharply defined, are projections of the dreamer's subconscious; it shows the lurching of a mind between sanity and madness; it is pure schizophrenia.

ACT I. Michel (*tenor*), the travelling bookseller from Paris – the only 'real' man in the story, through whose eyes we view it all – once paid a visit to a village with a harbour, and ever since has been haunted by the memory of a song he heard a beautiful girl singing through an open window He wants to find her again and returns to the town. It seems the same, but something crucial has changed: none of the people he meets has any memory of the past. A little Arab boy (*mezzo-soprano*) has never heard of the Sailors' Inn and can't carry Michel's bag because he has no legs. Michel starts to give him some money but the boy demands more, and then calls his father, who behaves in a threatening manner and shoves Michel through the hotel door. The argument becomes general until the little Arab calls for someone to play the accordion, which has the effect of calming people down. But the sound is too much for the man in a helmet (*baritone*), who has more authority than the others and is captain of a ship.

Michel seems to be fighting his way out of the Inn and the Policeman (*tenor*) is quickly on the scene. The bystanders are less than helpful and when Michel complains about the Sailors' Inn, no one seems to know of it or indeed any other hotel. Michel maintains that the old Arab (*bass*) threatened him with a knife until he told the story of his life. The trouble, explains the Policeman, is that all in the town have lost their memories. Suddenly the man at the window (*bass*) asks if he has ever been to Warsaw, and the Policeman is happy that someone will vouch for Michel. The Policeman asks him about his earliest memories and Michel dredges up something about a little duckling he used to play with.

The Policeman remembers that the village statutes lay down that anyone who can precisely recall any subject from his childhood by sunset will be chosen Mayor. Michel is therefore now Mayor! He is invested with chain and top hat, a parakeet, and a pistol, which he must not use.

Michel starts to talk about going home and of having come by train, but nobody remembers either train or station. He starts to recall his election as Mayor, only to have everyone tell him he is dreaming. At last he gets a chance of telling the man with a helmet about his shop in Paris, his earlier visit to the village and the beautiful girl he saw there. But the man maintains they were interrupted in the middle of a game of dominoes; Michel says he does not even know how to play!

Just then, the sound of Julietta's (*soprano*) voice can be heard and with it lyricism returns to the music, as for a moment she and Michel seem to recognise each other. She is perhaps an idealised fantasy and represents for him security.

Michel sees the Policeman coming by but he claims he is the village postman and they play cards for a moment until Julietta returns. Michel and Julietta come very close to declaring their mutual love and she makes a date to meet him at the crossroads in the forest.

ACT II. The Forest. Michel goes off to keep his assignation with Julietta as three gentlemen who have lost their way appear. They call for Julietta and are confident they will find her. Michel is offered a glass of wine by Grandfather 'Youth' (*bass*), who makes no more sense than anyone else. He gossips with an old couple and then a Fortune-Teller (*mezzo-soprano*) offers to read his hand – foretelling the past, naturally, not the future.

When Julietta appears, she seems to exhibit true affection and they embark on a love scene, of deep seriousness on Michel's side but mostly of fantasy on Julietta's. They are interrupted for a moment by the Seller of Memories (*baritone*) and Michel tries to tell Julietta what really happened when he saw her first three years ago; she starts to tease him and they quarrel. As Julietta leaves, Michel draws the pistol and shoots in her direction. A scream comes from the woods. He cannot believe that he really fired but the inhabitants of the village descend on him. The Fortune-Teller intervenes and suggests he tell them some story of his past – that way they will forget why he is there.

A Gamekeeper (*tenor*) turns up and agrees he heard a shot; he himself fired it. On his way back to Julietta's house Michel meets some sailors and asks them the way, then begs them to go back and see if Julietta is in the wood. They find nothing but her scarf. The man with a helmet asks Michel if he is not the passenger who booked on his ship. In desperation, Michel bangs on a door but an old woman complains that he has just woken her up. The man with a helmet shouts 'all aboard!', as Julietta's melody can be heard from the distance. There seems no escape for Michel.

ACT III. The Central Office of Dreams, where everyone, on payment of a small fee, may choose his dream. Tension mounts as the official in charge (*tenor*) says that Michel, a regular, has already been to visit him a few hours ago, before his journey. Now it is time to wake up and go home. 'I am the only one not dreaming. I have no time to dream!' says the official. In succession come a bell-boy (*mezzo-soprano*), to dream about Westerns; a beggar (*baritone*) to dream of a stay at the seaside; a convict (*bass*) to dream about rooms whose vastness will contrast with the tiny size of his cell; and an engine driver (*tenor*) to look at photographs of his dead daughter in the blank pages of an album – deeply-etched musical portraits, all of them.

Michel meets them all and tries, as each leaves the inside room – a cinema, as it might be – to get in to look for Julietta, whose image somehow seems to dominate every customer's conversation. The official warns Michel that his dream is ending and, if he stays there when it is finished, he will become like the men in grey, who are wandering about and who failed to wake from their dream and had to stay for ever.

Suddenly Julietta's voice can be heard; but he cannot open the door. The Nightwatchman (*bass*) announces closing time and when Michel demands to go in, flashes his torch round the empty space and shows that there is no one there. Michel's obsession is now total and, in the words of the composer (written in New York in April 1947) 'rejecting sanity and reality, he settles for the half life of dreams'.

The Arab boy reappears and the action ends, or starts again.

THE GREEK PASSION
Řecke Pasije

FOUR acts, by Bohuslav Martinů, text after Kazantzakis; première, Zurich, 1961. At Easter the Priest (*bass-baritone*) appoints various villagers to the roles they will fill at next year's Passion play. Yannakos (*tenor*) will be Peter, Katerina (*soprano*) Mary Magdalene, Panait (*tenor*) Judas, and Manolios (*tenor*), a shepherd, will play Jesus. Manolios's fiancée Lenio (*soprano*) cannot understand his coldness. A band of refugees arrives and begs for land. Ladas (*spoken*) proposes to Yannakos that he offer the refugees the necessities of life in return for their jewellery. Katerina is drawn to Manolios, who manages to resist her. Yannakos goes to the refugees' settlement and is shamed into giving up his mission. Manolios has vivid dreams. He allows Lenio to marry the shepherd Nikolio (*soprano*). The village Elders are infuriated with Manolios's tendency to live his role. At Lenio's wedding the priest anathematises Manolios, who confesses that thoughts of Lenio and Katerina made him unworthy. He pleads for the refugees. The villagers react violently and Panait strikes him dead. The refugees sorrowfully depart.

Karol Szymanowski
(1882–1937)

KING ROGER
Król Roger

OPERA in three acts; libretto by J. Iwaszkiewicz. Première, Warsaw, June 19, 1926.

*K*ING ROGER is Szymanowski's second opera; the first, *Hagith* (1912–13; performed 1922) is a one-acter with a lurid plot, modelled according to his biographer B. M. Maciejewski on *Salome*. Before 1914, Szymanowski travelled rather extensively in Russia and Europe and even ventured as far as Algiers, developing a strong taste for the Orient.

Intellectually, the opera represents conflict between Christian and pagan ideals, or between the pulls of the Dionysian and the Apollonian within each of us. The music has something of the opulence and texture of Szymanowski's contemporaries Strauss and Scriabin, with occasionally the sharp insight of Debussy.

ACT I. The interior of a Byzantine cathedral in Sicily, rich with characteristics of East and West; twelfth century. It is filled with worshippers and the Archbishop (*bass*) stands in front of the altar as the sound is heard of a great psalm of praise to God. King Roger II (*baritone*) and his court enter ceremonially, and Archbishop and Abbess (*contralto*) abjure him to protect the Church from her enemies and in particular from a new voice who corrupts men and women alike. Edrisi (*tenor*), an Arab scholar, explains that they are speaking of a young shepherd boy, and the Queen, Roxana (*soprano*), raises her voice to beg the King at least to hear the boy in his own defence. The King commands that he be brought before him as the throng calls for his destruction.

The Shepherd (*tenor*) answers the King's questions elliptically in a long, ecstatic utterance of considerable lyrical impact

– his god is young, beautiful and full of life. Roxana's reaction to his words is favourable, to the King's obvious discomfiture, and for a moment he is disposed to order the Shepherd's instant death but relents and agrees to let him go free. Finally, to the fury of the worshippers, he orders his appearance that very night at the palace gate. The Shepherd leaves on the same note of ecstasy as had characterised the explanation of his philosophy.

ACT II. The inner courtyard of the King's Palace, where that night the King awaits his visitor. The gorgeous texture of the music perfectly conveys the hot Mediterranean night, as well as the tension in the King's mind, much of it, as Edrisi finds when he tries unavailingly to comfort him, on account of the sympathy he senses between his beloved Roxana and the Shepherd. In the distance they hear the sound of tambourines and zithers and immediately, on high A flat, Roxana starts to sing, wordlessly at first, but with rapt concentration and in a highly evocative manner.

The King is enraptured by the song but knows it is sung in honour of the Shepherd. Watchmen announce the Shepherd's appearance and, with a group of four followers carrying musical instruments, he advances towards the King's throne. He greets the King in the name of eternal love and tells him he comes from Benares on the banks of the Ganges in India. He proclaims that it is God who has sent him, from God that he derives his powers, and in another extended lyrical passage sings the praises of his faith, until the King stops him, horror-stricken at what he does not hesitate to brand as blasphemy. Immediately, Roxana's song starts again, rousing the Shepherd's delight and the King's jealousy.

Eventually, the Shepherd's followers start an Arabic dance, and gradually all join in, until Roxana herself becomes visible in the gallery above the courtyard and in her turn starts to sing with the Shepherd and the others. Beside himself with rage, King Roger orders the guards to bind the Shepherd with chains, so that he stands fettered by Roxana's side. Angrily, the Shepherd breaks the bonds and casts them at the King's feet, then calls to Roxana and the people and leads them slowly from the King's presence into what he describes as the Kingdom of Light. The King is left alone in his grief with Edrisi, then suddenly announces that he too will follow the Shepherd, as a pilgrim, no longer as King.

ACT III. Among the ruins of a Greek Temple appear King Roger and the faithful Edrisi, the former still lamenting his powerless state in the face of his lost love. At last his cry of 'Roxana!' gets from the distance an immediate answer in the unmistakable voice of Roxana, only for his second attempt to receive a

similar answer in the Shepherd's voice. The King's consternation is only partly assuaged by the Shepherd's admonition to
leave his fear where he left his sword, and when a moment later
Roxana reaches her hand towards him, he still cannot believe
that the Shepherd is not playing a cruel joke. Roxana tries to
persuade him that the Shepherd is in fact all round him, in
every natural thing, and it is not long before Roxana and the
King begin to throw great heaps of flowers on the fire which
burns on the altar. The Shepherd has by now turned into the
Greek god Dionysus and the members of his train into bac-
chants and maenads, and they whirl into a mad dance, in which
Roxana joins, until gradually all disappear, leaving Roger alone
with Edrisi. But through his trials the King has grown and it is
with confidence, indeed rapture, that he greets the rising of the
sun in a splendid paean of thanksgiving.

Béla Bartók
(1881–1945)

DUKE BLUEBEARD'S CASTLE
A kékszakállú Herceg Vára

OPERA in one act; text by B. Balázs. Première, Budapest, May 24, 1918.

BARTÓK'S short opera (it lasts less than an hour) is one of the
most impressive of his early works. Whatever it may owe in
conception to Debussy and to Maeterlinck, the music is characteristic of its composer. Wrote Desmond Shawe-Taylor in 1972
in *The Sunday Times*: 'The fable can be understood on many
levels: as a foreshortened process of mutual discovery between
two persons such as in real life would take many years; as a conflict between rational, creative Man and emotional, inspiring,
never fully comprehending Woman; more deeply still, as an
allegory of the loneliness and solitude of all human creatures.'

A bard appears before the curtain to establish in spoken
word that the action of the opera is legendary. (This scene is
sometimes omitted.) When the curtain rises, it reveals a large
room, gothic in style, with seven doors.

Bluebeard (*bass*) enters with Judith (*mezzo-soprano*). She
sees the doors and wants to open them to let light and air into
the castle. She knocks at the first door, and hears a long sigh
like that of the wind. With the key that Bluebeard gives her, she
opens the door, from which immediately streams red light (vio-

lins *tremolo*, flutes *arpeggio*). It is the Torture Chamber, and Judith exclaims that the walls are wet with blood; but she is not afraid.

In succession she opens four more doors. A shaft of bronze-coloured light (solo trumpet, woodwind trills) comes from the Armoury; golden light (violin solo, three trumpets) pours from the Treasury, from which she takes a jewelled cloak and a crown; bluish light (harp *glissando*, strings *tremolo*, solo horn) comes from behind the door which conceals the Garden; and a dazzling white light (full orchestra, organ) blinds her as she opens the door which gives on to Bluebeard's Kingdom. Not even perhaps in *Fidelio* or *Die Meistersinger* has C major been more grandly confident than in the magnificent outburst which accompanies the opening of the fifth door. At each door Judith sees signs of blood: on the weapons in the Armoury, on the jewels and robes in the Treasury, on the flowers in the Garden, even in the colour of the cloud over the Kingdom itself.

Judith will not heed Bluebeard's warning, but opens the sixth door (harp, clarinet *arpeggios*). When she asks Bluebeard what is the significance of the water behind it, he answers 'Tears'. He tries to turn her from completing her purpose and takes her lovingly in his arms. She asks him if he has loved other women, and, when he tries to evade the question, demands that he give her the seventh key so that she may find out what the door conceals. As he gives it her, he tells her that it will show her all his former wives.

She opens the seventh door and immediately the sixth and fifth doors close; at the same time the light in the hall begins to grow dimmer. Three beautiful women emerge. Bluebeard kneels before them and assures them that they are not forgotten, and even Judith is filled with awe at their beauty. In his first wife Bluebeard sees the embodiment of the morning of his existence, in the second of his noonday, in the third of evening. One by one they disappear through the door, and the fourth door closes. Then he addresses Judith. She is the most beautiful of all, and her he met in the night; after her is eternal darkness. He goes slowly to fetch the crown and robe from the third door, which closes after him, and adorns Judith with them. For a moment she pleads with him, then turns and goes through the seventh door which shuts after her. Bluebeard is alone once more.

Manuel de Falla
(1876–1946)

LA VIDA BREVE
The Short Life

OPERA in two acts, text by C. Fernandez Shaw; French version by P. Milliet. Première, Nice, April 1, 1913.

ACT I. The curtain rises after a dozen bars of introduction. Courtyard of a gipsy habitation. On one side of the stage, the house where the gipsies live, on the other the entrance to a smithy, from which can be heard singing. Salud's old grandmother (*mezzo-soprano*) is feeding some birds in a cage. One is going to die, she thinks – perhaps of love, like Salud. The voices of street-sellers (offstage, like that of the tenor soloist in the smithy) can be heard.

Salud (*soprano*) comes in, looking unhappy. Her grandmother tries to reassure her; of course Paco (*tenor*) will come. Salud is fearful that she may lose one of the two things she most values: the loves of Paco and of her grandmother. Alone she sings a song with a sad philosophy – long live those who laugh, short life to those who cry: 'Vivan los que rien!' The poignant beauty of the music is like that of a folk-song, and indeed it is founded on the Andalusian style.

Her grandmother comes to tell Salud that Paco is on his way. Her joy is complete, and in their duet her sincerity and innocence contrast with his more conventional utterances. Salud's grandmother and her uncle (*bass*) observe the scene, and he mutters that he would gladly take revenge on Paco, who he knows is going to marry another girl the very next day. He is only playing with Salud.

Intermezzo: a view of Granada from Sacro Monte.

ACT II. A small street in Granada. Through the open railings can be seen the courtyard in which is being celebrated the betrothal of Paco and Carmela (*mezzo-soprano*). A professional singer (*baritone*) sings an Andalusian song, which is followed by a dance, made famous all over the world by generations of fiddlers.

Just before the dance finishes, Salud appears and rushes to see what is going on. She finds her worst fears realised, and Paco laughing and talking with the girl who is separating him from her for ever. Her grief spills over in a terrible lament. Her grandmother and uncle arrive, and the latter tries to relieve the situation by cursing Paco. Salud hears Paco's voice and makes up her mind to speak to him once again. She repeats the sad song of the forge: 'The man that's born of a woman, is born in an evil day.'

During an interlude the scene changes to the courtyard of the house. There is more dancing. Paco has heard the voice of Salud and is uneasy. Manuel (*baritone*) makes a speech to congratulate the happy pair, but Paco becomes more and more uncomfortable as Uncle Sarvaor comes into the patio, followed by Salud. She denounces Paco's treachery towards her in tones that would almost appear calm did they not so obviously conceal deep feeling. She falls dead of shock at Paco's feet, and her grandmother and Uncle Sarvaor curse Paco as the opera ends.

El Retablo de Maese Pedro
Master Peter's Puppet Show

ONE act, by Manuel de Falla, after Cervantes; première, Paris, 1923. In the stable of an inn at La Mancha, Master Peter (*tenor*) has set up his puppet show. Among the guests who come to watch are Don Quixote (*bass* or *baritone*) and Sancho Panza. The show is to be The Deliverance of the fair Melisendra by her husband Don Gayferos from the Moors. Charlemagne, Melisendra's father, is angry that Gayferos prefers to play chess with Roland rather than rescue his wife. A Moor steals a kiss from her, and is sentenced to 200 strokes. Don Gayferos crosses the Pyrenees on horseback and rescues his wife. The Moors ride in pursuit. At this Don Quixote, who has interrupted throughout with corrections to the story, leaps up sword in hand and attacks the Moorish puppets, triumphant; Master Peter sadly contemplates the ruins of his show.

Carl August Nielsen
(1865–1931)

Saul and David
Saul og David

FOUR acts; première, Copenhagen, 1902. King Saul (*baritone*) anxiously awaits Samuel (*bass*), who alone may sacrifice to the Lord, so that the Israelites will have God's blessing in their coming battle with the Philistines. Impatient, Saul himself performs the priestly office. Samuel upbraids him, proclaiming him an outcast. Saul's son Jonathan (*tenor*) brings in his friend David (*tenor*), a shepherd. News comes of Goliath's challenge, to which David responds. With his sling David kills Goliath and is rewarded with the hand of Saul's daughter Michal (*soprano*), but Saul in a jealous rage banishes him. David's loyalty is strikingly proved when he refrains from harming Saul. Samuel anoints David the new King; Saul bids his men seize David and Michal but is disobeyed. Saul consults the Witch of Endor (*mezzo-soprano*), who conjures Samuel's spirit; he foretells the deaths of Saul and Jonathan. A battle leads to the last scene, in which Jonathan is dying. Saul, wounded, curses God and turns his sword on himself. David and Michal mourn them both as David is proclaimed King.

MASQUERADE
Maskarade

THREE acts, by Carl Nielsen; première, Copenhagen, 1906. Leander (*tenor*), son of Jeronimus (*bass*), and his valet Henrik (*bass-baritone*) have been to a masquerade. Leander fell in love with an unknown girl, but Henrik reminds him that his father has promised him to Mr. Leonard's daughter, whom he has not met. Jeronimus's wife, Magdelone (*mezzo-soprano*), would clearly like to visit the masquerade but her husband disapproves. Leander and Henrik are thoroughly ticked off and Leander refuses point-blank to marry Leonard's daughter. Everyone sets off for the masquerade, even Jeronimus, who is sure Leander has gone there. At the festivities Leander and his Leonora (*soprano*) dance and sing happily, while Henrik discovers that Jeronimus is there and contrives to get him drunk. The moment arrives when all must unmask, and Leander and Leonora realise that they are the intended wedding pair.

George Gershwin
(1898–1937)

PORGY AND BESS

OPERA in three acts; text by Du Bose Heyward and Ira Gershwin. Première, Boston, September 30, 1935.

THE scene is laid in Catfish Row, which is, according to the synopsis in the published score, 'a former mansion of the aristocracy, but now a negro tenement on the waterfront of Charleston, South Carolina'.

ACT I. Scene i. Inside the tenement. After a short *allegro con brio* introduction, we are introduced to the variegated night life of the building. There is singing and dancing and presently a lazy Lullaby can be heard, sung by Clara (*soprano*), who nurses her baby. It is 'Summertime', and the song's lyric beauty has made it the most famous in the opera, and one of the best known in the entire song literature. A crap game is going on. Jake (*baritone*) says he will take it on himself to send his and Clara's baby to sleep, and he sings 'A woman is a sometime thing'.

The honeyman's (*tenor*) call is heard before Porgy (*bass-baritone*) is spied coming towards the tenement. He is a cripple who gets about in a little goat-cart. 'I think he's soft on Crown's Bess,' says Jake. Porgy defends Bess's reputation and blames her present low ebb on 'the Gawd fearin' ladies an' the Gawd damnin' men'. Crown (*baritone*), a stevedore, comes in with Bess (*soprano*), calling loudly for drink and going unsteadily to join the crap school. Crown objects to losing his money when Robbins (*tenor*) beats him. He attacks Robbins with a cotton hook and kills him. Bess gives Crown money and urges him to escape. He says firmly that he will be back; any arrangement she may care to make in the meanwhile with another man will be with his permission – but strictly temporary.

Sportin' Life (*tenor*), a dope peddler, approaches Bess and offers to take her to New York, but she spurns his offer, and tries to find shelter from someone in the tenement – un-successfully, until Porgy lets her in, just as the police whistles can be heard outside.

Scene ii. Serena's (*soprano*) room, where Robbins's body lies on the bed, a saucer on its chest to receive contributions against the expense of his burial. Porgy and Bess enter and Porgy leads a rhythmic spiritual before a detective comes in. By accusing Peter of the murder he gets the others to say that Crown did it – but he hauls off the protesting and inoffensive Peter (who is half deaf) as a 'material witness'.

Porgy reflects on this injustice. The wake goes on, and Serena, swaying to her words, begins a grandiose lament, 'My man's gone now', supported by the chorus. The undertaker agrees to bury Robbins for the $15 in the saucer. Bess leads the last of the spirituals, 'Oh, we're leavin' for the Promise' Land'.

ACT II. Scene i. A month later. Jake and the fishermen are re-pairing their nets and preparing to put to sea, singing as they do so, 'It take a long pull to get there'. In spite of the warning of September storms, Jake and his friends are determined to set out. Porgy appears at his window, singing his Banjo song, 'Oh, I got plenty o' nuttin',' a brilliant piece with an infectious lilt which causes the chorus to comment on the improvement since Bess has been living with him.

Sportin' Life is sauntering around the court when Maria the cook (*contralto*) sees that he has dope on him. She grabs him and gives him a piece of her mind. Lawyer Frazier (*baritone*) comes in, looking for Porgy, to whom he sells a 'divorce' for Bess.

A Mr. Archdale (*spoken*), a white man, appears, also asking for Porgy. At first everybody is too suspicious to tell him, but he wins them over, and informs Porgy that he will go bond for his friend Peter now in gaol. Sportin' Life sidles up to Bess and again suggests they should team up and go off to New York, but she tells him she hates the sight of him – and she will have nothing more to do with the 'happy dust' he offers her.

It is the day of the organised picnic, and everybody disappears to get ready, leaving Porgy alone with Bess, who tells him she does not want to go since he cannot. There is an extended love duet for the two of them, 'Bess, you is my woman now', at whose end the stage fills with life, a military band strikes up a *Tempo di Marcia giocoso,* and the picnickers start on their way. Maria persuades Bess that she must come along after all, and she takes a fond farewell of Porgy.

Scene ii. Kittiwah Island, that evening. The picnickers dance riotously and Sportin' Life treats them to a sermon, 'It ain't necessarily so', in praise of the virtues of scepticism. Serena denounces the whole pack of them for sinners, also reminding them, more prosaically, that the boat is leaving soon. Bess dawdles and Crown appears in front of her. She pleads to be allowed to stay in peace with Porgy, who has taught her to live decently. Crown laughs, and says he regards her living with Porgy as a temporary arrangement. Bess suggests he find some other woman ('Oh, what you want wid Bess?'), but she cannot resist Crown's old fascination, and when he takes her in his arms, she is too weak to deny him anything. She stays behind with him and the boat goes without her.

Scene iii. Jake and the fishermen prepare to go fishing. Peter is back from prison, and the sound of Bess's voice coming in a delirium from Porgy's room indicates that she too has returned from Kittiwah Island. She was lost for two days and was incoherent when she finally got home. Serena prays for her to get well. The cries of respectively the strawberry woman, the honeyman, and the crab man are heard, before Bess calls from offstage, evidently well on the way to recovery. She talks to Porgy, who says that he knows she has been with Crown, but that it makes no difference to his love for her. She admits that she told Crown she would go with him when he came for her, but pleads with Porgy to keep her for himself; she wants to stay but is afraid of the effect Crown's presence may have on her: 'I loves you, Porgy.' Porgy tells her he will take good care of

Crown if he returns. The scene ends with the sound of the hurricane bell.

Scene iv. Serena's room. Everyone is huddled together praying, while the storm rages. 'I hear death knockin' at de do',' sings Peter – and almost immediately a real knock comes. It turns out to be Crown. He orders Bess to him, throwing down Porgy who makes a move to come between them. Crown stops the keening with his violent opposition, and in his turn he strikes up a cheerful jazz number. Suddenly, Clara sees Jake's boat floating upside down in the river. She deposits the baby in Bess's arms while she goes off to learn the worst. Bess urges some man to follow her, but only Crown will venture out. The act ends with a renewal of the prayer for mercy.

ACT III. Scene i. Inside the courtyard. The inhabitants are mourning Clara, Jake, and Crown, all of whom they think lost in the storm. Sportin' Life hints that he knows Crown is not dead, and he slyly wonders what will be the upshot of the rivalry between Crown and Porgy over Bess. Bess is heard singing Clara's Lullaby to the baby she left behind her when she rushed off into the storm, and the inhabitants drift off to bed.

Crown is at the gate. As he passes Porgy's window, an arm is extended, grasping a long knife, which it plunges into Crown's back. Crown is seized round the neck in Porgy's iron grip and slowly throttled.

Scene ii. Next afternoon. The police come to clear up the mystery of Crown's death. They question Serena, who it appears has been ill and knows nothing of the death of the man who – every inhabitant of Catfish Row is prepared to swear – was responsible for killing her husband, Robbins. Porgy is roped in to identify Crown's body, and is dragged away protesting that he won't have anything to do with Crown.

Bess is left alone, and Sportin' Life offers her some 'happy dust' to tide over her nerves. She cannot resist it, and Sportin' Life sings a persuasive *Blues*, 'There's a boat dat's leavin' soon for New York', with the object of tempting her to come away with him. He goes out, leaving a second packet of dope. Bess sneaks out of her room, and takes it inside with her.

Scene iii. Catfish Row, a week later. Normal life is going on, and Porgy is welcomed home after his week away – he would not look at Crown and was gaoled for contempt of court. Everyone is disconcerted by Porgy's arrival, but he distributes the presents he has brought them all (as a result of some successful crap-shooting in prison), and does not notice anything is wrong until he looks for Bess, whose present is the last and best. She is nowhere to be found, and he sees Serena looking after Clara's baby, which had been left in Bess's charge. 'Oh, Bess, oh where's my Bess?' he sings; Serena and Maria join in. Porgy's longing is admirably expressed in this trio, and in the final 'Oh, Lord, I'm on my way', a spiritual with chorus. He drives out of Catfish Row in his goat-cart with his mind made up that, wherever she is, he will find Bess and bring her back.

Gian Carlo Menotti
(b. 1911)

THE MEDIUM

OPERA in two acts; text by the composer. Première, Brander Matthews Theatre, Columbia University, May 8, 1946.

OF *The Medium*, the composer himself has written (in notes to a complete recording): 'Despite its eerie setting and gruesome conclusions, *The Medium* is actually a play of ideas. It describes the tragedy of a woman caught between two worlds, a world of reality which she cannot wholly comprehend, and a supernatural world in which she cannot believe. Baba, the medium, has no scruples in cheating her clients . . . until something happens which she herself has not prepared. This insignificant incident . . . shatters her self-assurance, and drives her almost insane with rage.' He goes on to explain that the idea for the opera came to him in 1936 when, staying near Salzburg, he was asked to go to a séance by some friends. It was not so much his own scepticism that struck him as the way his friends were pathetically anxious to believe that the spirit of their dead daughter was talking to them through the medium.

ACT I. Madame Flora's parlour. A puppet-theatre in one corner of the room. Toby (*dancer*), a mute, is kneeling near a trunk from which he takes out bits of stuff and improvises a costume. Monica (*soprano*), Baba's daughter, combs her hair and sings to herself. The sound of the door slamming down below frightens them, and they stand rigidly still. Madame Flora (Baba; *contralto*) enters: 'How many times I've told you not to touch my things . . . Is anything ready? Of course not.' They prepare for the séance, Monica putting on a white dress and veil, and Toby testing the various devices.

The clients arrive. One of them has not been before, but the others tell her how wonderful Madame Flora is. Mrs. Gobineau (*soprano*) talks about her little child who was drowned. The séance begins. All the lights, except the candle in front of the Madonna, are put out, and they sit round the table, their hands touching. Baba moans, and Monica slowly appears in a faint blue light, singing 'Mother, mother, are you there?' Mrs. Nolan (*mezzo-soprano*) is convinced it is her daughter, and she asks her various simple questions, which are answered to her satisfaction. Monica asks her about a gold locket, but it appears she has never had one, and immediately the apparition starts to disappear; Mrs. Nolan dashes towards the place where the figure appeared, but is restrained by Mr. Gobineau (*baritone*) and his wife.

Monica next imitates the sound of a child laughing, for the benefit of the Gobineaus. Suddenly, Baba shouts hysterically, and turns on the light. 'Who touched me?' They try to reassure her, but she sends them away. As they go they sing a trio: 'But why be afraid of our dead?'

Baba is in a paroxysm of fear, and she seizes Toby and tries to blame the whole phenomenon on him. Monica soothes her with an extended melody, which Toby accompanies on a tambourine: 'O black swan, where, oh where, is my lover gone?' Baba suddenly thinks she can hear voices; she falls on her knees and prays.

ACT II. A few days later. Monica sits in front of the puppet-theatre watching a performance which Toby is giving. She sings while he dances barefoot round the room. The dance becomes a sort of love duet, in which Monica sings for both.

Baba drags herself up the stairs, and Toby retreats into a corner, Monica having already left to go to her own room. Baba questions Toby about the incident of a few days back; did he touch her throat? Was he the one? She cannot get him to admit it, tries to keep her temper, then seizes a whip and beats Toby. The doorbell rings, and the Gobineaus and Mrs. Nolan enter. Is it not the night of the séance? Yes, she says; but there will be no more – they were all frauds. She wants to give them their money back, but they will not admit they have been cheated. Even the sight of the stage props and the sound of Monica imitating the children's voices does not convince them; those were not the voices they heard. Nothing will convince them, but Madame Flora yells to them to get out. She tries to send Toby away too, but Monica pleads for him. Baba however is insistent, and Monica has only just time to say goodbye to Toby before he has run out into the street.

The voices come back to Baba. In desperation she pours herself several drinks. 'Afraid? Am I afraid?' she asks herself. She passes her life in review, then tries to comfort herself with the song of the black swan.

Toby comes up the stairwell, tiptoes across to Monica's room, finds the door locked, and hides behind the sofa when Baba stirring in her sleep knocks the bottle over. He starts to look in the trunk, but the lid falls with a bang, Baba wakes up with a start, and Toby hides behind the puppet-theatre. She yells 'Who's there?' but gets no answer, and taking out a revolver from a drawer shoots hysterically at the curtain. There is a moment of stillness, then a spot of blood appears on the white curtain. Toby's hands clutch the side of the screen, which collapses with his weight, and he falls dead into the room. 'I've killed the ghost,' says Baba, as Monica pounds on the door and asks to be let in: 'I've killed the ghost.'

THE TELEPHONE

ONE act, by Gian Carlo Menotti; première, New York, 1947. In her apartment Lucy (*soprano*) is opening a present from Ben (*baritone*), who has something to tell her. At the crucial moment the telephone rings, and she answers at length. A wrong number interrupts next, then Lucy has to dial to check the time. Another call and Lucy seems to quarrel with a boyfriend. She leaves for a moment and Ben is about to cut the cord of this impossible rival when it rings loudly and Lucy takes it up protectively. Ben goes out, to her surprise. He can be seen dialling from a telephone box, and when she answers he quickly proposes and is accepted. Lucy demands only one thing – that he not forget . . . her number.

THE CONSUL

OPERA in three acts by Gian Carlo Menotti; text by the composer. Première, Philadelphia, March 1, 1950.

ACT I. Scene i. The home of John Sorel, somewhere in Europe; just after World War II. It is early morning, and the room is empty and dark. The sound of a gramophone record is heard coming from a café across the street. Suddenly the door is flung open and Sorel (*baritone*) staggers into the room and throws himself into a chair. Magda (*soprano*), his wife, hears the noise and runs to him, and immediately starts to bandage the wound which she sees in his leg. He tells her and the Mother (*contralto*) the usual story: there was a secret meeting, the police had been tipped off about it and shot at them as they made their escape across the roofs. Magda looks out of the window and sees the police. John goes to what is obviously an agreed hiding-place.

As the secret police agents enter, the Mother is rocking the cradle, in which lies the little child of Magda and John. She sings a lament for the peace which has vanished from their lives. The agent (*bass*) starts to question Magda, who answers non-committally. His threats carry potential danger.

The agents leave, and Magda and the Mother watch as they arrest somebody opposite. John. comes down from his hiding place; he must get away. He tells them that the signal that there is a message from him will be the breaking of their window by a stone. When this happens, they are to send for Assan (*baritone*), the glass-cutter, who will bring them news. Magda and John bid each other farewell, and their duet becomes a trio when the Mother joins her voice with theirs.

Scene ii. The cheerless waiting-room of the Consulate; the Secretary's (*mezzo-soprano*) desk, and behind it a door leading to the Consul's room. Mr. Kofner (*bass-baritone*) comes forward to renew his application for a visa; the photographs turn out to be the wrong size. A 6/8 *allegretto* movement suggests the automatic nature of the dealings between applicant and Secretary. As he moves away, the Foreign Woman (*soprano*) starts to make an enquiry. She does not know the Secretary's language, and another complication seems to have been introduced, but Mr. Kofner volunteers to act as interpreter. Her daughter ran away with a soldier, who has now left her with a three-months-old baby. The daughter is ill and needs her mother's help; can she have a visa to visit her? Yes, if she fills out the forms.

More people come into the waiting-room, and Magda advances to the desk. The surreal dialogue between her and the Secretary is typical of Menotti's style: 'Explain to the Consul, explain . . . that the web of my life has worn down to one single thread . . . ' But it is still a question of filling in forms and making applications and Magda is handed a batch of forms as Nika Magadoff (*tenor*) comes forward. He starts to do some simple conjuring tricks in an effort to impress the Secretary with his *bona fides*, but a slow ensemble begins ('In endless waiting-rooms'), and he joins in. It becomes a quintet in which Magda, Anna Gomez (*soprano*), Vera Boronel (*contralto*), the Magician and Mr. Kofner express the agony of frustration which their daily attendance at the Consulate entails.

ACT II. Scene i. Sorel's house, a month later. Magda and her Mother are discussing the possibility of getting a visa. When Magda goes out, her Mother sings the baby a lullaby, and, after Magda has returned to the room and fallen asleep in a chair, goes out in her turn. Magda in her nightmare sees John and the Secretary, whom he introduces to her as his sister. The nightmare comes to an end with a horrible vision of a dead child.

Magda wakes up with a scream, and is comforted by her mother. Suddenly, a stone shatters the glass of the window, and Magda rushes to the telephone to carry out John's instructions. She has no sooner finished talking to Assan than the Secret

Police Agent is admitted. He starts to insinuate that there would be no obstacle to her joining her husband if she would only give him a little information about her husband's friends. She yells at him to get out, and threatens to kill him if he returns. He is by the door when Assan arrives to mend the window.

Assan tells Magda that John is still hiding and will not leave the country until he knows that his wife has a visa and can follow him. She says to tell him that arrangements are complete.

Meanwhile, the Mother suddenly realises that the baby has died quietly in his sleep. As soon as she looks at her, Magda knows what has happened. She stops her mother weeping, but the Mother says she is thinking of John.

Scene ii. After an interlude, we are again at the Consulate, a few days later. Anna Gomez, the Magician and others are waiting. Magda comes in and asks to jump the queue, but the Magician explains in a kindly but firm way that he has been several times to the Consulate, and always when his turn came it was time to close; he *must* take his turn now. He again demonstrates his powers of conjuring and hypnotism. He puts all the occupants of the waiting-room in a trance, and makes them dance happily together, until the Secretary becomes quite desperate over the unaccustomed turn events have taken. She begs Magadoff to return everyone to normal.

The others allow Magda to go ahead of them. The Secretary does not remember her until she has looked her up in the card-index, and Magda is frantic. She demands to see the Consul but is again refused. Finally she throws self-control to the winds, denouncing bureaucracy and the injustice it leads to. The rest of the act is given up to a *scena* for Magda, with interruptions from the Secretary and the others waiting at the Consulate: 'To this we've come: that men withhold the world from men.' Her passionate indignation is summed up in a brave phrase: 'Oh, the day will come, I know, when our hearts aflame will burn your paper chains. Warn the Consul, Secretary . . .'

The Secretary cannot conceal her own feelings, although she does her best. She goes into the Consul's office, saying that she will ask if he can see her just a minute. The improbable happens when she comes out and informs Magda that she may go in when the important visitor who is with him has left. Anticipation rises as two shadows are seen on the glass panel of the door. The visitor shakes hands, but, when he turns into the room, he is seen to be the Secret Police Agent. Magda faints.

ACT III. Scene i. The Consulate. Magda is waiting to see the Consul, in spite of the Secretary's warning that the place will be closed in ten minutes' time. Vera Boronel comes in, states her name, and is greeted with something like pleasure by the Secretary; at last there is somebody to whom she can give good news – her papers are through!

Assan hurries in, looking for Magda. He tells her that John has heard that his child and his mother are dead, and intends to come back to fetch his wife. Magda writes a note which she confides to Assan, refusing however to tell him what is in it.

Everyone leaves, and presently the Secretary too is ready to go. John rushes into the room. He asks if Magda has been there, and is told he may still catch up with her if he hurries after her. But that he cannot do, he protests, since he was followed to the Consulate by the police, who will not allow him to leave. At that moment, a confused noise is heard outside, and as John pulls out his gun, the Secret Police Agent comes in, followed by two plain-clothes men. The Secretary protests that no arrest can be made in the Consulate, and the Secret Agent says that Sorel will be coming with him of his own free will.

As they leave, the Secretary dials furiously, and when the curtain goes up again on Scene ii, the telephone can be heard ringing in Magda's room, which she presently enters, though only after the bell is silent. She makes preparations to commit suicide, and turns on the gas.

As she bends over towards the stove with a shawl over her head, the walls dissolve and figures from the Consulate appear. Behind them are John and the Mother. Magda talks to them, and the ghostly chorus sings the march tune of the interlude. Gradually the figures disappear, and all that can be heard is the sound of Magda's deep breathing. Suddenly the telephone begins to ring. Magda stretches out her hand as if to answer it, but her reaction is feeble, and she falls inert over the chair, while the telephone bell continues to ring.

AMAHL AND THE NIGHT VISITORS

OPERA in one act by Gian Carlo Menotti; libretto by the composer. Première, NBC studios, New York, December 24, 1951. First stage performance, Indiana University, Bloomington, February 21, 1952.

AFTER a few introductory bars the scene is the outside of a little shepherd's hut, where Amahl (*treble*), a crippled boy of about twelve, sits playing his pipe. Beside him on the ground is his home-made crutch. Inside the hut his mother (*soprano*) listens to him for a bit, then calls him in. He makes one excuse after another to stay outside and tries to persuade her to go out to look at the brilliant new star – 'as large as a window and with a glorious tail'. She thinks it is another of his stories and scolds him for lying, but eventually breaks down in tears at the prospect of going out begging next day.

In the distance can be heard the voices of the three Kings. As they draw near, their way is lit by their black Page (*baritone*), bowed under the weight of rich-looking bundles, everything from a jewel box to a parrot in a cage. They stop at Amahl's home and King Melchior (*baritone*) knocks. Amahl goes to the door and scurries back to his mother. Three times she thinks he is lying, but eventually she follows him to the door, the Kings bid her a grave good evening, and she offers her meagre hospitality to the splendid visitors. They accept with gratitude, especially Kaspar (*tenor*) who is inclined to get carried away and has to be restrained by his companions.

To a jaunty march, the Kings make their way into the hut. As the Page spreads out the treasures on a rug, the woman goes off to look for firewood, telling Amahl not to pester their visitors in her absence. As soon as she is out of the way, Amahl goes straight to the Nubian King Balthazar (*bass*) and bombards him with questions, meanwhile looking out of the corner of his eye at Kaspar, who is feeding his parrot with bits of food from his pocket. Amahl cannot resist Kaspar's eccentricity and soon it is his turn for cross-questioning. Kaspar however is deaf and things do not warm up until Amahl asks what is in the box whereupon Kaspar becomes enthusiastic and shows Amahl the precious stone he keeps against all kinds of misfortune.

Amahl goes off to fetch the other shepherds and the Kings tell his mother that they are looking for the Child, and in an *andante* describe their vision. In her mind the mother identifies the Child with her own son.

They fall silent, and the sound of the shepherds' calling is heard. When they reach the door of the hut with their baskets of fruit and vegetables they are struck dumb by the splendour of the Kings, but the mother urges them to come in and shyly they present their humble gifts. The Kings thank them, and the mother asks the young people to dance for her guests. They do so, at first slowly and formally but gradually accelerating into a kind of *tarantella*.

Balthazar thanks the dancers and they file out. As their song grows fainter, Amahl wistfully asks Kaspar if he has perhaps a magic stone to cure a crippled boy. But Kaspar, as usual, does not hear properly and Amahl goes sadly to his straw bed.

They all settle down for the night, the Kings sitting side by side on the bench and the Page lying at their feet, his arms round the precious gifts. The lights are lowered to indicate the passage of time and when they come up again, dawn is breaking. Everyone is asleep except the mother, who sings of the unfairness of all this wealth going to an unknown child while her own is starving. She takes hold of one of the bundles and the Page wakes up. The noise of their struggle disturbs Amahl who flings himself at the Page, beating him and pulling his hair in a desperate attempt to rescue his mother. Kaspar orders the Page to release the woman, and King Melchior says she may keep the gold as the Child they seek has no need of it.

The mother is enthralled with Melchior's glowing description and begs him to take back the gold – were she not so poor she would herself send a gift to the Child. Amahl wants to send his crutch. He lifts it and then, to everyone's amazement, takes a step without it. For a moment no one believes the miracle, then the Kings give thanks to God, as Amahl dances and leaps about the room until at last he falls down. One at a time the Kings ask Amahl to let them touch him. Amahl begs to be allowed to go with the Kings to give the crutch to the Child and the mother gives her permission. With a wealth of maternal advice to sustain him, Amahl sets off with the Kings and, as the procession moves away, he plays on his pipe the tune which began the opera.

Philip Glass
(b. 1937)

AKHNATEN

OPERA in three acts; libretto by the composer in association with Shalom Goldman, Robert Israel and Richard Riddell (vocal text derived from original sources by Shalom Goldman). Première, Stuttgart, March 24, 1984.

PHILIP GLASS'S third opera follows the style of the previous two, about Einstein and Gandhi, in taking a central figure in world thinking and mythology and portraying him on the operatic stage. Narrative is at a discount and the libretto of *Akhnaten* draws on ancient texts mostly sung in the original languages. If there is a similarity here with Stravinsky's use of sung Latin in *Oedipus Rex*, it might be argued that Glass's music has something in common with the neo-classical outlook of its great predecessor. Infinite repetitions of cell-like musical statements; often triads, arpeggios; patterns derived perhaps from Monteverdi's procedures, ostinati, bounding rhythms – this is the stuff of the 'minimalist' school, as it has been called. The sophistication and fastidious sense of instrumental colouring in Glass's music (no violins in the orchestra of *Akhnaten*) belong however to the techniques of the 'learned' composer (as have been most other members of the school!), and words like 'serene', 'incantatory', expressions such as 'elegantly mechanised simplicities', 'gently atmospheric', 'trance-like' have been used to describe the music. More important, Glass has certainly demonstrated an ability with his operas to touch the public's sensibility as have few of his contemporaries.

Amenhotep IV changed his name to Akhnaten and after five or six years on the throne of Egypt abandoned its capital Thebes for a site to the north. There he took up a position of hostility to Amon, the God of Thebes, and not only built a new capital but developed a monotheistic and exclusive worship of the sun under the name of the Aten (or solar disc). Twenty-five years later, he was dead and his capital abandoned. His mummy was never found, but his capital, Akhetaten, has been excavated to reveal a ground plan which suggests a city of great splendour. He and his wife, Queen Nefertiti, were constantly depicted by artists, and the effigy of Nefertiti, now in Berlin, suggests a classical beauty of the Middle East.

ACT I. Thebes, 1370 B.C. Prelude. The funeral of King Amenhotep III is being prepared by the priests of Amon. Amenhotep's son, together with his widow, Queen Tye (who ruled as Regent until her son came of age) and other members of the Royal entourage join the procession – Aye, Queen Tye's brother and the late King's counsellor; Horemhab, Commander of the Army; and Nefertiti, Aye's daughter and wife to the new Pharaoh.

The funeral of Amenhotep III. With beating of drums and chanting, eight Priests of Amon, together with Aye, celebrate the rites of Isis, Osiris and Horus, and the King's body is carried in procession through the temple.

The Coronation. A gentler mood prevails as the new King undergoes a purification ceremony before he is crowned. Then the double crown of Egypt is placed on his head and he is greeted by the High Priest of Amon (*tenor*), Horemhab (*baritone*) and Aye (*bass*) in trio as the incarnation of Horus, son of Isis and Osiris.

The Window of Appearances. The new Pharaoh, who has the otherworldly voice of a counter-tenor, is a reformer with religious ideas quite different from those of his predecessor. He draws the symbol of the Aten, with the rays of the sun containing each an Ankh, the symbol of life. The High Priest of Amon, who does not yet know that the King will change his name to Akhnaten, is bewildered and affronted by the rejection of the old God and he departs, leaving the voices of Akhnaten, Nefertiti (*alto*) and Queen Tye (*soprano*) – that powerful figure, the Queen Mother – to combine almost ritualistically before they dance blasphemously through the Temple of Amon.

ACT II. The Temple. Amon's Priests, led by the High Priest, chant ritually, surrounded as they are by the images and totems of the many gods amongst whom Amon was supreme. It is not long before, almost gently, they are overthrown by the King, his mother and their followers. Everything – temple, the images of the gods, even the priests – is destroyed, and Queen Tye's re-iterated top A's, B's, and A flats provide a trumpet-like top line to the implacable chant.

Akhnaten and Nefertiti. Queen Tye is the leader of the new thinking and she teaches Akhnaten a poem to the Aten, which he in duet (slow, as has been all the vocal music, even when at its most urgent) teaches to Nefertiti. The Queen Mother gives over to Akhnaten the maiden Bekhetaten, whom many believe to have been their daughter.

The City. The plan for the city is ready and celebrated in a solemn dance.

Hymn. Akhetaten is built and Akhnaten sings a hymn to the Sun, one of the score's most appreciable and extended vocal movements. The words are by Akhnaten himself. Psalm 104 is intoned by the chorus and Aye is rewarded for the part he has played in bringing the new city to reality. Akhnaten in his delight and ecstasy attempts to touch the sun.

ACT III. Akhetaten, 1358 B.C. Portrayals of Akhnaten and his family are well known, he slouching, with spindly legs and slanting eyes, pot-bellied and full-hipped, Nefertiti beautiful and long-necked, and the pair surrounded by their nude daughters with shaven heads. The opening of the act shows them living inside the city which the King has built.

The Family. The six daughters sing in block harmony, Nefer-titi and Akhnaten join them, and the gentle, almost idyllic mood of togetherness is inescapable. But in this case, con-tentment goes before a fall. Letters to the King from princes in outlying provinces are read to him by Aye and Horemhab, all calling for help against the hostile powers which threaten to in-vade Egypt. The King will not listen and finally even the faithful Aye in despair deserts him. In the unkindest cut, he takes with him his daughter Nefertiti.

Attack and Fall. The High Priest of Amon is now in a position to ally with Aye and Horemhab to overthrow the King. The new triumvirate in music of energy and resolve, soon joined by the chorus, destroys the city. Akhnaten disappears – perhaps, if theories connecting him with Oedipus are to be believed, he blinds himself.

The Ruins. A prologue celebrates the eclipse of Akhnaten and reinstatement of Amon as Egypt's God.

Akhetaten; the present. Tourists are guided round the ruins.

Epilogue. The spirits of its founder, his mother and his wife, still hover ghost-like over the ruins of the city, and theirs is, vocally speaking, the last word.

John Adams
(b. 1947)

NIXON IN CHINA

OPERA in three acts; libretto by Alice Goodman. Première, Houston, October 22, 1987.

BORN ten years after Philip Glass and described by Alice Goodman as 'a minimalist bored with minimalism', John Adams is nonetheless regularly grouped with Steve Reich and Philip Glass. It was Peter Sellars, because he prefers to work on a new opera rather than one that already exists, who came up with *Nixon in China* as an operatic subject. The three collaborators agreed from the start that this was to be a heroic opera and in no sense a satire. Its strength they believed would come from the extreme familiarity all over the world of characters such as the Nixons and Henry Kissinger, and the fame of Mao Tse-Tung, his wife and Chou En-Lai. The time is February 1972.

ACT I. Beijing. Rising scales open the opera and continue as Chinese soldiers, waiting for the arrival of the American President (*baritone*), engage in slow, repetitive patriotic singing. Tension grows to the moment when the Presidential 'plane (*The Spirit of '76*) comes to a stop. Nixon's aria, 'News has a kind of mystery' (the word 'news' reiterated twelve times), is neo-classical in style, and during its course Chou (*baritone*) attempts to introduce various civic worthies while Nixon goes into ecstasy over the idea that the 'eyes and ears of Hissstory' are taking note of their actions.

Scene ii. Chairman Mao's (*tenor*) study, where he receives President Nixon. His three secretaries (*sopranos* and *contralto*) echo Mao's words and the ensemble bubbles along, with Mao dispensing 'philosophical apophthegms, and gnomic jokes'. Nixon falls back on diplomatic fencing, and Kissinger (*bass-baritone*), cast throughout as a kind of villain, is constantly, as he himself admits, out of his depth. Suddenly Mao has a brain-wave: 'Founders come first, then profiteers', and this will return to him every now and then until the end of the scene. Nixon finally attempts to seize the initiative. Mao is left to his books and his dictation: 'Founders come first . . .'

Scene iii. A banquet is being held in the Great Hall of the People. The atmosphere is more relaxed and Nixon and Pat (*soprano*) exchange a few words at the start. Gentle verbal fencing between the principals precedes a toast – 'Gambei' – before Premier Chou's speech, which is assured and yet subtle. Nixon seems at first nervous but confidence grows as he speaks, until he reaches a purple climax and enthusiasm takes over. Nixon plays a trump card:

> Nixon: . . . *Everyone*
> *Listen, just let me say one thing*
> *I opposed China. I was wrong.*

The act ends in an orgy of toasts.

ACT II. Scene i. It is the morning of the second day – Mrs. Nixon's turn to meet China. She is taken to a glass factory, a clinic and a pig farm, she meets crowds of children and finishes with a visit to the Ming Tombs. The action occurs in the interludes of an extended *scena* and aria.

Scene ii. Together with Madam Mao (Chiang Ch'ing; *high soprano*) and Premier Chou, the Nixons are to see a ballet performance, 'The Red Detachment of Women', a revolutionary farrago devised in real life (for the cultural revolution in 1966) by Chiang Ch'ing. Her aim was to remove western cultural influences and to replace them with scenarios of political significance. The trouble is that the music written specially for them (probably, as John Adams once suggested, by a committee) had distinct overtones of the nineteenth-century Russian ballets they so despised.

From the outset the atmosphere for the ballet is one of expectancy. It is a bizarre affair. Young women are chained to posts on an estate and Lao Szu, the landlord's factotum (played by the singer of Kissinger), has one of them, Ching Hua, beaten into insensibility. Pat Nixon cannot bear the stage action and intervenes. The People's Army takes over and Ching Hua is presented with a rifle. Ching Hua attempts rebellion. This is the cue for Chiang Ch'ing to start an aria and somehow bring the action to an end.

The music is ostinato-based and frequently builds a considerable head of rhythmic steam. Chiang Ch'ing's aria 'I am the wife of Mao Tse-Tung' is an extended solo, studded with top B flats, C's and the occasional D, and the music's relentless nature mirrors that of the character.

ACT III. It is the last night in Beijing and the elegiac music suggests we are in another world, contemplative and almost devoid of action, with the protagonists reduced to musing on present, past and future. Only Mao appears to retain a

semblance of vitality, and he dances with his wife and reminisces of their first meeting and campaigning together.
Chiang Ch'ing takes to wordless coloratura, Chou is the most
cogently philosophical, Mao content to babble, Nixon to talk
aimlessly of the war and risks perceived but not quite confronted, Pat to react to what her husband says. Often the composer, while writing lyrical music of considerable beauty,
seems unconcerned to make the words audible, but we hear
clearly Nixon's claim to have won at poker and what he says became his political motto, 'Speak softly and don't show your
hand'. Whatever we miss, we hear Chou's summing up of his
own outlook and of the memorable five days:

> *I'm old and I cannot sleep*
> *For ever, like the young . . .*
> *How much of what we did was good?*

INDEX

INDEX

INDEX